Dear West Customer:

West Academic Publishing has changed the look of its American Casebook Series®.

In keeping with our efforts to promote sustainability, we have replaced our former covers with book covers that are more environmentally friendly. Our casebooks will now be covered in a 100% renewable natural fiber. In addition, we have migrated to an ink supplier that favors vegetable-based materials, such as soy.

Using soy inks and natural fibers to print our textbooks reduces VOC emissions. Moreover, our primary paper supplier is certified by the Forest Stewardship Council, which is testament to our commitment to conservation and responsible business management.

The new cover design has migrated from the long-standing brown cover to a contemporary charcoal fabric cover with silver-stamped lettering and black accents. Please know that inside the cover, our books continue to provide the same trusted content that you've come to expect from West.

We've retained the ample margins that you have told us you appreciate in our texts while moving to a new, larger font, improving readability. We hope that you will find these books a pleasing addition to your bookshelf.

Another visible change is that you will no longer see the brand name Thomson West on our print products. With the recent merger of Thomson and Reuters, I am pleased to announce that books published under the West Academic Publishing imprint will once again display the West brand.

It will likely be several years before all of our casebooks are published with the new cover and interior design. We ask for your patience as the new covers are rolled out on new and revised books knowing that behind both the new and old covers, you will find the finest in legal education materials for teaching and learning.

Thank you for your continued patronage of the West brand, which is both rooted in history and forward looking towards future innovations in legal education. We invite you to be a part of our next evolution.

Best regards,

Heidi M. Hellekson
Publisher, West Academic Publishing

SALES AND LEASES
A PROBLEM–SOLVING APPROACH

■ ■ ■

By

Linda J. Rusch

Frederick N. and Barbara T. Curley Professor in Commercial Law
Co-director, Commercial Law Center
Gonzaga University School of Law

Stephen L. Sepinuck

Professor of Law
Co-director, Commercial Law Center
Gonzaga University School of Law

AMERICAN CASEBOOK SERIES®

WEST®
A Thomson Reuters business

Mat #40741230

American Casebook Series is a trademark registered in the U.S. Patent and Trademark Office.

© 2009 Thomson Reuters
  610 Opperman Drive
  St. Paul, MN 55123
  1–800–313–9378
Printed in the United States of America

ISBN: 978–0–314–19203–5

 TEXT IS PRINTED ON 10% POST CONSUMER RECYCLED PAPER

To Dick Speidel, a mentor and friend to us, a scholar and role model for us all.

LJR & SLS

PREFACE

This book is designed for a three-credit course on sales and leases. Our goals are: (i) to assist students in becoming adept at statutory interpretation; (ii) to give them the context needed to understand both the policies underlying the legal rules governing sales and leases and the practical significance of those rules; and (iii) to help prepare students for both transactional and litigation practice. The book contains excerpts of several cases, a lot of explanatory text, and a great number of problems. Many of the problems ask students to analyze how the law applies to the facts presented. Several problems ask students to draft one or more provisions of an agreement. We believe that the problem-based approach to teaching this material serves all of our goals.

This book is organized somewhat differently from other books on the subject, particularly when covering performance, breach, and remedies. Our guiding philosophy was to present the material in the order that would be most accessible to someone trying to learn it, rather than in the order it appears in the Uniform Commercial Code or in the order that would appeal most to those already knowledgeable about the subject. We hope we have been successful in this regard.

We invite all who use this book, both students and teachers, to send us their comments about it. Only with input from the users can we hope to improve it.

WEB SITE FOR UPDATES & TEACHER RESOURCES

Periodic updates and supplements will be posted in electronic form on the web site for this book.

The teacher's manual and other resources for instructors are also available on a teachers-only portion of the web site.

http://www.ruschsales.com

Summary of Contents

* *See* http://www.ruschsales.com

TABLE OF CONTENTS

* *See* http://www.ruschsales.com

TABLE OF CASES

TABLE OF STATUTES

Uniform Commercial Code

SALES AND LEASES
A PROBLEM–SOLVING APPROACH

*

CHAPTER ONE

INTRODUCTION TO COMMERCIAL TRANSACTIONS

SECTION 1.   THE STUDY OF COMMERCIAL LAW

A.   TRANSACTIONAL LAW AND THE COMMERCIAL LAWYER

Millions of "deals" occur each day in the United States and around the world. Many are between businesses, many are between consumers, and many are between a business and a consumer. These deals range in value and complexity from the purchase of a candy bar at the local market to the leveraged buyout of a multi-national business empire. They include purchases and leases of goods, licenses of intellectual property, sales of receivables, service contracts, and all manner of loans.

These deals are conducted with a varying degree of negotiation about terms. Sometimes lawyers are involved in negotiating and documenting the deal, but often the negotiation (if any) occurs without involvement of legal counsel. Particularly in the business-to-consumer context, it is customary for the business to conduct business through the use of standard written forms or dialog boxes on web pages. Standard forms and dialog boxes are also used in varying degrees in business-to-business transactions. However, even when they are not involved in negotiating or documenting a particular transaction, lawyers are often involved in drafting standard forms and advising their clients on how to use them.

To grossly oversimplify, transactions typically have at least two distinct phases: the pre-transaction stage and the performance stage. In the pre-transaction stage, the parties contemplate entering into the deal, may negotiate terms, and may prepare and execute the documentation for the deal. In the performance stage, the parties either perform their contractual obligations or fail to perform in some way or another. In some circumstances, a party may be excused from performing its contractual obligation.

The role of lawyers in the pre-transaction phase differs depending on whether they are negotiating and documenting a particular deal or drafting a standard form for repeated use in multiple transactions. In a negotiated deal, the lawyers try to document the deal that has been negotiated – often by the parties themselves – and to allocate the risks associated with that transaction. In other words, they try to faithfully put on paper the parties' basic understanding of the deal, imagine everything that might go wrong, and consider which of those contingencies to provide for in the transaction documents. In these negotiated transactions, the lawyers and client will usually discuss the various risks and determine which risks the document terms should address. In such situations, both the parties and their lawyers have an incentive to try and make the deal happen in accord with the parties' objectives. In drafting standard forms for use in multiple transactions, lawyers try to construct a form that will allocate risks in transactions with as yet unknown parties based not only on the legal issues that might arise but also taking into account the client's perspective on what will work in the market place.

Some transactions have a third phase: dispute resolution. This occurs when one of the parties fails – or is claimed by the other party to have failed – to adequately perform one or more contractual obligations to which it has agreed. The parties in this stage of a transaction may disagree about what their respective obligations were, which (if any) of those obligations were not fulfilled, or what remedy for the aggrieved party is appropriate. Fortunately, the number of transactions that enter this third stage is quite small compared to the numerous deals agreed to.

Many courses in law school – including most courses on sales of goods – are taught in the context of this third stage, when something goes wrong. The question usually posed to a student is "what are the rights and liabilities" of the parties in the transaction gone wrong? To answer that question, students are often referred to the applicable statute, as interpreted by judicial decisions. While ascertaining how disputes may be resolved is important, for two main reasons it is not the principal focus of this book. First, as just noted, the portion of deals that enter the dispute phase is small. The percentage that are litigated is significantly smaller. The portion that yield a published opinion is even tinier. As a result, even though those decisions may be relevant in analyzing the parties' legal rights and responsibilities, it is far from clear that those decisions play a major role in dispute resolution. Indeed, there is a substantial body of scholarship that suggests that the law itself may have little relevance to how parties resolve their disputes.[1] Second, particularly if you consider the role of the lawyer in drafting standardized forms and procedures, lawyers are far more likely to be involved in a deal at the pre-transaction phase than in the dispute resolution phase. Moreover, even if we are wrong in this assessment,

---

[1]   *See, e.g.,* Lisa Bernstein, *Merchant Law in A Merchant Court: Rethinking the Code's Search for Immanent Business Norms,* 144 U. PA. L. REV. 1765 (1996); Lisa Bernstein, *Opting Out of the Legal System: Extralegal Contractual Relations in the Diamond Industry,* 21 J. LEGAL. STUD. 115 (1992); Stewart Macaulay, *An Empirical View of Contract,* 1985 WIS. L. REV. 465, 476–68.

we strongly believe that law schools need to do more to provide their students with the skills necessary to be transactional lawyers. Learning how to anticipate and resolve issues before they become the subject of a dispute is significantly better for the client than having deals go sour and spending client's resources on resolving the situation.

A transactional lawyer's responsibility is to consider how to accomplish creatively the contracting parties' objectives within the boundaries of the applicable legal rules. This perspective requires the lawyer to imagine all the possible risks to the client and advise the client on how to manage those risks prospectively. To pick a common example in the sale of goods context, consider a client who sells small kitchen appliances and who wants the lawyer to draft a standard sales agreement that will work for all types of those appliances. The client wants to give a warranty on the products it sells as a way of enhancing sales. One of the things the lawyer will need to do is to determine what specifically the client wants to warrant about the goods. Is it that the goods will be free from defects in material and workmanship at the time of sale, that the goods will function properly at the time of sale, or that the goods will function properly for a certain period of time? Each of these promises about the quality of the goods exposes the seller to a different type of risk under the law governing remedies for breach. In connection with this, the lawyer will need to consider the potential problems that may arise. For example, if one of the small appliances is a toaster, in all likelihood, the client expects that the toasters it sells will be fit for their ordinary purpose, will readily acknowledge that a toaster that does not make toast is not fulfilling its ordinary purpose, and would be happy to repair or replace such a malfunctioning toaster. But suppose a toaster lacks a temperature control shut off mechanism or has one that fails to work. As a result, the toaster overheats and causes a fire. If the client warranted that the toaster was "fit for its ordinary purpose," would the warranty be breached? Is toasting bread without roasting the house the ordinary purpose of the toaster? If so, does the client really want liability for the full value of the house and its contents? If not, the lawyer should find a different way to phrase the warranty or some other way to limit the client's liability.

Restricting potential liability for malfunctioning products sold is just one of the many clauses the transactional lawyer must consider. Should the documentation contain clauses governing how disputes are handled, such as an arbitration clause, a choice-of-law clause, a choice-of-forum clause, or an attorney's fees clause? If so, how should those clauses be drafted? Are they enforceable? If the law of a particular jurisdiction is chosen, what legal rules are being chosen? Are all the legal rules of that jurisdiction appropriate for the particular type of transaction?

The issue underlying all these questions is risk allocation. To identify and appreciate the relevant risks, a transactional lawyer must have intimate knowledge of the underlying legal principles, the client's business, and the activities of the client's counter-parties as they relate to your client's interaction with them. The transactional lawyer must also have the ability to imagine or anticipate problems that have, as yet, not arisen. The transactional lawyer must then be able to clearly articulate the issues to the client, generate options for dealing with the identified issues and risks, help the client decide among the various options, and at least in some situations, negotiate the deal points and documentation with the client's counter-party. In doing this, the transactional lawyer also has to pay meticulous attention to the language used in any agreement to ensure that it means what the parties intend. A transactional lawyer thus must have many skills in addition to the knowledge of legal rules and principles applicable to a particular transaction.[2]

This book is designed to assist students of the law in several ways. First, it will help students learn the legal rules and principles applicable to transactions in goods. Second, it will help students acquire the skills essential to a transactional practice, including the skill of statutory construction. Third, it will help students learn how to deal with disputes that often arise in goods transactions. These three goals are not mutually exclusive. Certainly, knowledge of the operative legal principles is critical to practice from both a transactional and a dispute resolution perspective. Understanding how the dispute is likely to be resolved helps a transactional lawyer determine how to structure the transaction to avoid the dispute or to minimize a potential dispute's negative impact. Understanding how the transaction arises and is structured, including the documentation that is part of the transaction, helps the lawyer in the dispute resolution phase to craft the arguments and strategy to help the client resolve the dispute. In much of the material that follows, we will ask the student to try out both roles, how they would approach an issue as a transactional lawyer and how they would approach the issue if there was a dispute in a transaction. Keeping these two roles in mind will, we hope, result in an in-depth understanding of the legal principles and policies that operate in this area of law, as well as the development of the essential skills needed to represent clients effectively in transactional and dispute resolution work.

---

[2]   *See generally*, Tina L. Stark, *Thinking Like a Deal Lawyer*, 54 J. LEGAL EDUC. 223 (2004).

B. THE UNIFORM COMMERCIAL CODE: STRUCTURE & SCOPE

1. *A Very Short History*

The principal source of commercial law in this country – at least the principal source applicable to sales of goods – is the Uniform Commercial Code. The UCC is the joint product of two organizations: the National Conference of Commissioners on Uniform State Laws (NCCUSL)[3] and the American Law Institute (ALI). In reality, however, the UCC is not law; it is merely a model for state legislatures to enact. Originally drafted in the early 1950s,[4] by 1968, the UCC had been enacted in every state except Louisiana.[5] A "Permanent Editorial Board" (PEB) was established by the sponsoring organizations to comment on problems that arise and consider the wisdom of proposed amendments to the UCC.[6]

Over the years, NCCUSL and the ALI have modified the UCC to adjust it to changes in commercial practices. The most recent round of revisions started in the late 1980s. They added Articles 2A and 4A and made major revisions to all the other Articles. Most of the revisions have been widely adopted. However, some of the substantive changes have generated significant opposition. Even the revision process itself has not been without controversy,[7] with concerns expressed that this unique "private" law making process may not always produce rules that are "consonant with democratic values."[8] In particular, the 2003 amendments to Article

---

[3]   In 2008, NCCUSL officially changed its name to the Uniform Law Commission.

[4]   The drafting process is discussed extensively in a symposium to which five drafters contributed. *See* Symposium, *Origins and Evolution: Drafters Reflect Upon the Uniform Commercial Code,* 43 OHIO ST. L.J. 535–84 (1982).

[5]   Louisiana has now adopted most of the Articles of the UCC, except for Articles 2 and 2A.

[6]   *See PEB Commentaries on the Uniform Commercial Code*, some of which are reprinted in THOMSON/WEST, SELECTED COMMERCIAL STATUTES issued every year for classroom use.

[7]   *See* Robert E. Scott, *The Rise and Fall of Article 2*, 62 LA. L. REV. 1009 (2002); Symposium, *Perspectives on the Uniform Laws Revision Process*, 52 HASTINGS L.J. 603–701 (2001).

[8]   *See* David V. Snyder, *Private Lawmaking*, 64 OHIO ST. L.J. 371, 448 (2003). *See also* Amelia H. Boss, *The Future of the Uniform Commercial Code Process in an Increasingly*

2 (Sales of Goods) and Article 2A (Leases of Goods) (finished in 2003) were subject to extensive lobbying and political compromise, and no state has yet adopted them.

2. *The Structure of the UCC*

The Code is now divided into eleven substantive articles. The first is a general article bearing on various aspects of the entire Code. The remaining ten articles each address a somewhat unique part of commercial law. What follows is a brief description of each article of the UCC and the fate of the most recent round of proposed revisions to each article.

Article 1: General Provisions. Article 1 contains definitions and general rules applicable to transactions governed by other articles of the UCC. UCC § 1-102. Article 1, therefore, is not a free-standing Article; if a substantive transaction is not governed by the Code, Article 1 does not apply. In 2001, NCCUSL and the ALI approved a revised Article 1, which 34 states have enacted to date.[9] The remaining states have former Article 1. Except where otherwise indicated, the references in these materials to Article 1 are to revised Article 1.

Article 2: Sales. Article 2 applies to "transactions in goods," UCC § 2-102, but deals almost exclusively with the formation, adjustment, construction, performance, and enforcement of contracts for the sale of goods. Every state but Louisiana has enacted Article 2. The major innovations of Article 2 were the de-emphasis of title in deciding issues regarding performance and enforcement of sales contracts and several novel provisions on the formation of sales agreements. It has also proven to be a major force in moving contract law from a subjective theory of contract to a more objective one. In 2002, NCCUSL approved a set of amendments to Article 2 and in 2003, the ALI approved those same amendments. However, to date no state has enacted those amendments. Because it appears unlikely that a significant number of states will enact the amendments in the near future, these materials focus on pre-amended Article 2, which remains the law of the land. The Appendix to this book (which is available on line) contains a

---

International World, 68 OHIO ST. L.J. 349 (2007).

[9]   NCCUSL maintains a website where the current enactments are tracked: www.nccusl.org. In addition, the UNIFORM LAWS ANNOTATED series also tracks the enactments.

discussion of the major differences between the unamended and amended versions of Article 2.

Article 2A: Leases. Article 2A was originally promulgated in 1987 to deal with leases of goods, a type of business transaction that has existed for a long time but which was increasing almost exponentially (largely for tax reasons) both in numbers and in dollar amounts. Article 2A's rules and principles are drawn from Article 2, but with variations to accommodate the fact that the transactions it governs involve the transfer of a property interest for a limited period of time (a lease) as opposed to the transfer of complete ownership (a sale). Every state but Louisiana has enacted Article 2A. Article 2A amendments were also approved in 2002 by NCCUSL and in 2003 by the ALI.[10] To date no state has enacted the 2003 amendments to Article 2A. Because it appears that few or no states will enact the 2003 amendments any time soon, these materials deal with Article 2A prior to its amendment in 2003. The Appendix to this book contains a discussion of the major differences between the pre-amended and amended versions of Article 2A.

Article 3: Negotiable Instruments. Article 3 deals with checks, drafts, promissory notes, certificates of deposit, and other types of commercial paper. It provides rules on negotiability, the rights of holders, and the liabilities of issuers and endorsers. Article 3 governs these types of items only if they are "in writing" and thus does not apply to the electronic equivalent of these items.[11] NCCUSL and the ALI revised Article 3 in 1990 and every state except New York has adopted those revisions. Another minor set of amendments to Article 3 was promulgated in 2002. To date, six states have enacted the 2002 amendments. Because those amendments are not particularly controversial and are likely to be uniformly adopted, the references to Article 3 in this book are to Article 3 as amended in 2002.

Article 4: Bank Deposits and Collections. Article 4 deals with checks and other demand instruments that are drawn on a bank and collected through the banking system. Article 4 covers the contractual relationship between the drawer and the payor bank, the relationship between the payee and the depositary bank, and the relationship among the banks in the collection process, including the

---

[10]   In 1994, the Article 2A Drafting Committee was appointed and charged with considering the Article 2 revision to the extent those revisions made sense for leasing transactions.

[11]   In states that have enacted the Uniform Electronic Transactions Act (UETA), promissory notes, if created electronically, are governed by UCC Article 3 to the extent of rights of holders of these electronic notes. UETA § 16.

responsibilities of the payor bank when a check is presented for payment.[12] Article 4 also applies only to items that are "written" and generally does not apply to electronic collection of payments that started out as a written item.[13] Every state except New York has enacted Article 4 as revised in 1990. A small set of amendments to Article 4 were adopted in 2002. To date, six states have enacted the 2002 amendments. These materials refer to Article 4 as amended in 2002.

Article 4A: Funds Transfers. Article 4A was promulgated in 1989 and governs the transfer of funds from one bank account to another bank account as long as the bank accounts are not consumer bank accounts covered by federal regulation.[14] Such a transfer is initiated by a customer's payment order (given in any manner, orally, in writing, or electronically) to its bank and concluded when the beneficiary's bank accepts the payment order for the benefit of the beneficiary. The payment orders are communications that are followed in very short order by the transfer of credits from the originator to the beneficiary in settlement of the payment order. Article 4A has been enacted in every state.[15]

Article 5: Letters of Credit. A letter of credit is a written promise by the issuer – typically a bank – to pay a specified sum of money to the beneficiary upon a presentation of specified documents. The bank's letter of credit is issued at the request of an applicant, usually in furtherance of some business relationship between the applicant and the beneficiary. The bank's obligation to pay on the letter of credit is conditioned on the beneficiary presenting the documents required

---

[12]   Article 4's provisions are supplemented and in some cases superseded by federal regulations. For example, Federal Reserve Regulation J, 12 C.F.R. Part 210, governs check collection through use of the federal reserve banks. Similarly, the Federal Expedited Funds Availability Act, 12 U.S.C. § 4001 *et seq.*, and its accompanying Regulation CC, 12 C.F.R. Part 229, preempts Article 4 on questions of when deposited funds are available for withdrawal as a matter of right and some of Article 4 on the check return process after a check presented for payment has been dishonored.

[13]   Article 4 does apply if a payor bank agrees to accept electronic presentments. UCC § 4-110.

[14]   If any part of the funds transfer is governed by the federal Electronic Fund Transfer Act, 15 U.S.C. § 1693 *et seq.* and its implementing Regulation E, 12 C.F.R. Part 205, Article 4A does not apply. UCC § 4A-108. The federal act and regulation, not Article 4A, govern electronic funds transfers to or from a consumer's bank account.

[15]   Federal Reserve Regulation J, 12 C.F.R. Part 210, governs payment orders transmitted through the federal reserve banks, and it adopts many parts of Article 4A.

and those documents "strictly complying" with the terms of the letter of credit. The issuing bank's obligation on the letter of credit is independent of the applicant's obligation to the beneficiary on the underlying business transaction. Letters of credit are designed to substitute the creditworthiness of the issuer for that of the applicant and are commonly used in international sales of goods when the seller wants assurance that the goods will be paid for. Article 5 was revised in 1995 and every state has enacted those revisions.[16]

Article 6: Bulk Sales. Article 6 deals with bulk transfers by a seller. It is designed to protect the creditors of a business that sells in bulk all or virtually all of its inventory by requiring advance notice to the creditors of the sale. NCCUSL and the ALI have recommended repeal of Article 6, largely because the modern Bankruptcy Code and various laws governing fraudulent transfers have made the Article – and its rather cumbersome rules – unnecessary. To date, 45 states have repealed Article 6 and two other states have enacted a revised version.

Article 7: Documents of Title. Article 7 applies to documents of title, which are documents issued by a bailee of goods by which the bailee promises to deliver the goods to the holder of the document.[17] To qualify as a document of title, it must be issued by or to a bailee and be recognized in the commercial world as a document that entitles the holder to possession of the goods covered by the document. Documents of title include warehouse receipts, which are issued by warehouses, and bills of lading, which are issued by carriers. A document of title should not be confused with "certificates of title" that are issued by state licensing authorities and cover motorized vehicles of various sorts. Article 7 was revised in 2003 and to date 31 states have enacted those revisions. References in these materials to Article 7 are to the revised version.[18]

---

[16]   In many instances, the parties agree that the letter of credit will be governed by the Uniform Customs and Practices (UCP) 600 or International Standby Practices (ISP) 98, both promulgated by the International Chamber of Commerce. Article 5 allows the parties to choose non-Article 5 principles.

[17]   Federal law also plays a role in governing documents of title through the United States Warehouse Act (codified at 7 U.S.C. § 241 *et seq.*) and the Carriage of Goods by Sea Act, *see* 46 U.S.C. § 30701 *et seq.*, among others.

[18]   As part of the Article 7 revision process, conforming amendments to other articles of the UCC were promulgated. As states enact the Article 7 revision, they also amend the other UCC articles with those conforming amendments. References in these materials to the other UCC articles are to the versions as amended by the Article 7 conforming amendments.

Article 8: Investment Securities. Article 8, often called the "negotiable instruments" law for investment securities, defines the rights and liabilities of issuers, transferors, and transferees of securities and securities entitlements. Article 8, however, does not supersede state or federal regulatory laws governing the issuance of securities. Article 8 was last revised in 1994. The 1994 revision has been enacted in all states.

Article 9: Secured Transactions. Article 9 deals with the creation, perfection, priority, and enforcement of security interests in personal property. In 1999, NCCUSL and the ALI completed a major revision of Article 9, which every state has adopted.

3. The UCC in Context

As you can see by the brief descriptions of each UCC article, the scope of the UCC is broad, applying to a wide range of transactions. There is not, in the UCC, a single "scope" provision which defines the *subject matter* to which the *entire* UCC applies. Instead, the UCC is divided into several articles as described above. The precise scope of each article must usually be determined by examining not merely a specific "scope" provision within the article (if there is one) but other provisions as well, some of which are definitions. While many of the articles of the UCC can, in relation to some kinds of transactions, apply separately and alone, frequently provisions from more than one article will be applicable to the transaction at hand. The UCC recognizes the possibilities of conflict between Articles, and includes provisions governing such possibilities. *See, e.g.,* UCC §§ 2-102, 3-102, 4-102(a), 8-103(d), 9-109, 9-110.

Despite its seemingly wide sweep, the UCC is far from comprehensive. There are some transactions it does not govern at all. There are also many aspects of covered transactions which, for the reasons noted below, the UCC instead defers to some other source of law.

First, the parties can generally make their own "law." They do so expressly through agreement, implicitly through their actions and course of dealing, and collectively through custom and resultant usage of trade.[19] By their own agreement,

---

[19]   Commercial law, by definition, concerns commercial enterprise where customs and modes of interaction between business people evolve over time. This history has an effect on how people understand the agreements they have made and also influences the development of the commercial law itself.

then, the parties to a commercial deal can vary the effect of many of the provisions of the UCC. *See* UCC §§ 1-302, 1-303.

Second, the UCC by its own terms does not purport to control many types of transactions that can fairly be called commercial. For example, it does not apply to sales of commercial realty or to security interests therein. It does not apply to the formation, performance, and enforcement of insurance contracts. It does not apply to suretyship transactions (except where a surety is a party to a negotiable instrument or involved in a secured transaction). It does not encompass the law of bankruptcy. It does not govern legal tender.

Third, there are state statutes, most of which are regulatory in nature, which either supplement or supersede UCC provisions altogether. *See* UCC §§ 2-102, 9-201(b), (c) (referencing the possible existence of such statutes). Usury laws and so-called "Lemon Laws" are common examples.[20]

Fourth, the Uniform Commercial Code is *state* law. There is a large body of *federal* law that supplements state commercial law in general and the UCC in particular.[21] More important, several federal statutes and treaties supercede or preempt portions of the UCC.[22] Of particular note to the sale of goods is the United Nations Convention on the International Sale of Goods (CISG), which has been ratified by the United States and over 70 other countries, including Canada and Mexico. Unless otherwise agreed, the CISG applies to contracts for sale of goods between private commercial parties (not consumers) whose places of business are

---

[20] Lemon laws are discussed in Chapter Eight. Another fairly common example is the right of consumers to rescind certain transactions for a brief period of time. *E.g.*, Va. Code Ann. § 59.1-21.3 (involving in-home sales); *see also* 16 C.F.R. § 429.1 (providing a similar rule for door-to-door sales of consumer goods and services). Others are less common state and local rules, for which careful lawyers must always be on the lookout. *See, e.g.*, *Consolidated Aluminum Corp. v. Krieger*, 710 S.W.2d 869 (Ky. Ct. App. 1986) (in an Article 2 transaction, applied a statute that invalidates contract clauses printed below the signature line unless referenced above the signature line).

[21] For example, the federal Food, Drug, and Cosmetic Act (codified at 21 U.S.C. § 301 *et seq.*) imposes controls on the quality of goods sold and on the ways they are marketed. The Robinson-Patman Act (codified at 15 U.S.C. §§ 13a, 13b and 21a) operates to regulate the price of some goods.

[22] Thus, for example, the federal Consumer Credit Protection Act (codified at 15 U.S.C. §§ 1601–1693r), the Magnuson-Moss Warranty Act (codified at 15 U.S.C. §§ 2301–2312), and the federal Insecticide, Fungicide, and Rodenticide Act (codified at 7 U.S.C. §§ 136–136v) all preempt parts of Article 2.

in different nations, if both nations have ratified the convention. *See* CISG Art. 1(a). Thus, the CISG, and not the UCC, would apply when an Illinois corporation buys goods from a Canadian supplier or sells goods to a Mexican buyer, unless the parties opt out of application of the CISG. CISG Art. 6. The CISG, however, does not purport to be a complete statement of international law principles that govern an international sale of goods.[23] CISG Art. 7(2). Thus, some domestic principles of law may apply even in a transaction otherwise governed by the CISG.[24]

Other international conventions or model laws may have an effect on commercial transactions.[25] Of particular note for the subject of international sales contracts is the UNIDROIT Principles of International Commercial Contracts, a statement of international contract law principles. These principles were originally promulgated in 1994 and updated and reissued in 2004. These principles are not a treaty but represent a body of rules that parties can choose by agreement to apply to their transaction. A working group is currently considering additional provisions.

Fifth, the UCC does not even purport to govern exhaustively all aspects of the transactions to which its provisions do apply. Resort to supplemental common-law doctrines and equitable principles outside the UCC is often necessary and is expressly authorized. *See generally* UCC § 1-103. The importance of this cannot be overstated.[26] Dozens of doctrines and centuries of jurisprudence remain relevant.

---

[23]   *See* Franco Ferrari, *What Sources of Law for Contracts for the International Sale of Goods? Why One has to Look Beyond the CISG*, 25 INT'L REV. L. & ECON. 314 (2005); Filip De Ly, *Sources of International Sales Law: An Eclectic Model*, 25 J. L. & COM. 1 (2005).

[24]   For an example of a court considering whether certain legal or equitable principles are preempted by the CISG, *see Geneva Pharms. Tech. Corp. v. Barr Labs., Inc.*, 201 F. Supp. 2d 236, 286–87 (S.D.N.Y. 2002) (promissory estoppel as alleged in case not preempted by the CISG even though the CISG was governing law), *rev'd in part on other grounds*, 386 F.3d 485 (2d Cir. 2004).

[25]   Four ready examples are: (i) the Convention on the Limitation Period in the International Sale of Goods (1974) as amended by the Protocol of April 11, 1980 (ratified by 20 countries, including the United States); (ii) the Convention on International Financial Leasing (ratified by ten countries, signed but not yet ratified by ten more, including the United States); (iii) the Convention on the Use of Electronic Communications in International Contracts (signed by 18 countries but not yet ratified by any); and (iv) the UNIDROIT Draft Model Law on Leasing, finalized in November, 2008. To view these and other international conventions and to determine what countries are bound by them, *see* http://www.uncitral.org and http://www.unidroit.org.

[26]   The authors of the main hornbook on the UCC have stated, in an earlier edition, that

In some places the UCC text or comments expressly note this.[27] In others, the point is implicit though the UCC's adoption of a common-law term.[28] Nevertheless, even when there is no explicit or implicit reference to other legal concepts in the UCC, supplemental rules of law may apply.[29]

Finally, and most important, is a point that relates to all the others. Commercial transactions do not fall neatly under one legal regime. In the real world, even simple transactions do not necessarily fall within the scope of a single law school course. Commercial law may be based upon contract law and principles, but it is far broader. It encompasses property-law concepts, tort rules, and agency principles. It also includes a whole host of national and international regulations.

To illustrate the breadth of legal principles that a simple commercial transaction may implicate, assume a manufacturer agreed to sell a warehouse full of toasters to a retailer. What legal issues may arise in this very simple transaction? At what point does the retailer acquire property rights in the toasters? This point might be particularly important if the retailer purported to sell the toasters before paying the

---

"[s]ection 1-103 is probably the most important single provision in the Code." JAMES J. WHITE & ROBERT S. SUMMERS, UNIFORM COMMERCIAL CODE § 2, at p. 6 & § 5, at p. 19 (3d ed. 1988). In addition to substantive legal principles outside of the UCC, the procedural law relevant to resolving disputes is an important part of the practice of commercial law. In the event there is a dispute in a transaction, the resolution of that dispute may be as much a matter of having the relevant evidence and the allocation of the burden of proof as it is of determining and applying the legal principles. Knowledge of the rules of evidence and civil procedure thus will also influence the transactional lawyer as well as the lawyer involved in dispute resolution. For the most part, the UCC does not deal with such evidentiary and procedural issues.

[27] *See, e.g.*, UCC § 1-204 (defining "value" to include "any consideration sufficient to support a simple contract"), § 1-308(b) & cmt. 3 (referencing the doctrine of accord and satisfaction); § 2-318 cmt. 3 (referring to the common-law rules on privity of contract).

[28] *See, e.g., D.O.M. Farms v. Nakamoto*, 718 P.2d 262 (Colo. Ct. App. 1986) (concerning "breach"); *Neptune Research & Development, Inc. v. Teknics Indus. Systems, Inc.*, 563 A.2d 465 (N.J. Super. Ct. App. Div. 1989) ("substantial impairment" means the same as "material breach" in the RESTATEMENT (SECOND) OF CONTRACTS, and thus can include delay if time is of the essence, even though the contract did not say it was); *Mullan v. Quickie Aircraft Corp.*, 797 F.2d 845 (10th Cir. 1986) (because "unconscionable" is undefined in the UCC, courts must look to the common law).

[29] *See, e.g., Hopper Dev., Inc. v. John T. Arnold & Assocs., Inc.*, 163 P.3d 385 (Kan. Ct. App. 2007) (promissory estoppel principles may provide an exception to the writing requirement of the statute of frauds).

manufacturer for them. Does the manufacturer incur tort liability to persons other than the retailer, such as buyers and users of the toasters, when the retailer further distributes the toasters and those persons are injured when the toasters malfunction? Under what circumstances would the retailer's agent or employee incur liability to the manufacturer if the retailer fails to pay? What if the manufacturer or retailer wants to sell the toasters outside the country in which the toasters are manufactured? Are there export restrictions in the country of manufacture? Are there import restrictions in the country to which the toasters will be sent? A transactional lawyer must be able to think beyond one area of law and see how issues may arise under a multitude of areas of law that are separately studied in law school.

C. STATUTORY INTERPRETATION

Using a statute such as the UCC to help structure a transaction or to anticipate issues that may arise in litigation can be a challenging endeavor. The methodology of statutory interpretation is both similar to and different from the process you have used in reading cases to understand common-law principles. It is similar in that it requires attention to detail and nuances of language. But it is different in that there is often a lot less explanation of what the text means. Most judicial opinions, no matter how complex the issues, have three main components: a brief story, after which the court says what it is doing and identifies the reasons for its actions. In other words, most judicial opinions provide context, apply a rule to that context, and explain why. Statutes, on the other hand, give you only one-third of this: they tell you merely the rule. They typically provide no obvious context for their application. They also usually provide no rationale for their rules or guidance on how to apply them. Yet without those additional things, you cannot truly understand the statute. You need to understand the context and appreciate the purpose of each rule, yet you have to supply those things for yourself.

So how do you begin? Not surprisingly, you should start with the text of the statute. The paramount rule of statutory interpretation is read it all, then read it again. Pay attention to each word. Parse out each provision, so that you understand it grammatically. Understand the syntax (to which clause, phrase, or word does each modifier relate). Sometimes the cadence (where to pause) of a clause is not clear, so try different possibilities. As you do so, the meaning may become more clear.

Once you have a linguistic understanding of a clause or phrase, try to provide the relevant context. Hypothesize. Imagine a situation to which the provision at issue might apply. Then test that paradigm against the language of the statute. Then pause to make sure the result makes sense. If not, there is a strong possibility – although by no means a certainty – that you are misreading the provision.

Now discard your initial paradigm. Imagine other situations to which the provision might also apply. This helps to make sure that your initial paradigm is not too limited. Then imagine similar or related situations to which the provision does not apply. Test these against the language of the statute and question whether it makes sense for the small differences in facts to yield a different result. This helps ensure that your initial paradigm is not too broad.

To take an example that seems simple on its face, but is more complex the deeper you go, read UCC § 2-102 up to the semicolon. What is a "transaction in goods"? In thinking about those three words, what questions do you need to ask and answer? Perhaps, what is a "transaction"?, what are "goods"?, and what is a "transaction *in* goods?" How do you begin to track down more information that would help you answer those questions? The temptation to think that you know what a word means and that this meaning applies to the word when used in the statute should be resisted.

This leads directly to the second rule of statutory interpretation: find the definitions. Beginners to the UCC (or to statutory construction in general) sometimes overlook the possibility that terminology in a particular section may be defined elsewhere in that section, in another section, or even in another Article. In fact, the UCC includes more than the usual quota of definitions and even a relatively mundane word may be statutorily defined, occasionally in a surprising way. For example, in the UCC "purchase" includes a gift, *see* UCC § 1-201(b)(29), and "goods" can include the unborn offspring of animals, *see* UCC § 2-105(1). Thus, the first step in interpreting or construing a statutory provision is to define the key terms.

There are a number of places in the UCC to check for such definitions. Section 1-201 contains 43 definitions, and is applicable to every article of the Code. Additionally, each article contains definitions of terms for purposes of that article; such definitions usually are near the beginning of the article. *E.g.,* UCC §§ 2-103, 2-104, 2-105, 2-106. *See also* UCC §§ 2A-103, 3-103, 4-104, 4-105, 9-102, 9-103, 9-104, 9-105, 9-106 & 9-107. Finally, in Articles 2 and 2A, there are cross references at the end of the "Official Comment" to each section. However, you should not depend on these references to be exhaustive. For example, section

2-316(2) details when the implied warranty of merchantability may be disclaimed and requires that written exclusions or modifications of the warranty be "conspicuous." The definitional cross references neglect to indicate that "conspicuous" is defined in section 1-201(b)(10). Do not assume that a word is undefined. Reach that conclusion reluctantly, only after you look in all the places the word may be defined and find nothing.

This process of determining the meaning of statutory language must be done in reference to the purposes of the entire statute or the particular statutory provision. Overall, the UCC "must be liberally construed and applied to promote its underlying purposes and policies which are: (1) to simplify, clarify, and modernize the law governing commercial transactions; (2) to permit the continued expansion of commercial practices through custom, usage, and agreement of the parties; and (3) to make uniform the law among the various jurisdictions." UCC § 1-103. Thus, if you reach an interpretation that would seem to run contrary to these stated objectives, you should reconsider it. Similarly, if your interpretation would frustrate the parties' reasonable expectations or put a loss on the party least able to avoid it, there may be a better interpretation.

Next, you should consider how the section you are analyzing fits in with the other sections in the same statute. A statutory scheme such as the UCC is an interrelated set of rules. Each section has a relationship to the other sections of the same statutory scheme. The job of a careful lawyer is to figure out how each section relates to all of the other sections in that enactment. The lawyer must build a blueprint of how the entire statutory structure fits together. This is important in order to come to a complete understanding of even the seemingly most simple section that may apply to a particular set of facts.

Finally – after your own textual analysis, not before – you should look for interpretations of the relevant statutory language in court or administrative decisions, legislative history, and legal scholarship. This inquiry may provide information about how the language has been perceived by those who wrote it, enacted it, applied it, or thought about it. Language has inherent ambiguity of varying degrees and this research may help you identify those ambiguities. It may confirm your initial understanding or lead to a change in your thinking. However, no matter what those sources say or fail to say, they do not excuse you from considering problems the statutory text may pose in light of the fact situation you are concerned about, whether that fact situation be litigation you are involved in or a transaction that you are attempting to structure.

A word of caution. Study of the UCC in law school is of the uniform version. However, the UCC is merely a model designed for enactment at the state level. Each state legislature, as it considers an article of the UCC for enactment, decides whether to adopt the uniform version or whether it should enact a modified version of the uniform text. As you study the UCC in its uniform version, remember that the law in any particular state may be different. When you give advice to a client, you should never rely on the uniform version, but always look at the version as enacted by the applicable state. Given that the UCC has a uniform version and slightly non-uniform versions that are enacted by each state, it is somewhat unique in that there are several kinds of "legislative history" relevant to interpreting it, each posing its own special problems. The four types of such history are: (1) Official Comments, (2) prior versions of the UCC, (3) legislative hearings and reports made prior to enactment in specific states, and (4) books and articles by the UCC drafters.

Official Comments. As promulgated by the ALI and NCCUSL, the Official Text of the UCC appears with comments on each section. These comments often provide valuable information about the purpose or scope of a particular provision. Bear in mind, however, that state legislators enact only the statutory text (with whatever amendments they choose to make to the Official Text), not the Official Comments. Indeed, some of the comments were not yet written when the sections to which they relate were enacted. Similarly, the Permanent Editorial Board occasionally modifies a comment long after the statutory text has been enacted. Accordingly, the Official Comments do not have the force of law and, in the event of a conflict between the Official Text and the comments, the Official Text controls. In a conflict between the Official Text and the state-enacted statutory text, the state-enacted text controls.

Even when there is no conflict, the comments should not be blindly accepted at face value. For some important portions of the UCC, the person who drafted the comments was not the person who drafted the statutory text to which they relate. Perhaps most telling, the reporter and chair of the drafting committee have control over the comments but the drafting committee has control over the statutory text. Thus, on occasion, the reporter may put into a comment a point that the drafting committee expressly rejected from the text.[30]

---

[30]   Karl N. Llewellyn, *Why A Commercial Code?*, 22 TENN. L. REV. 779, 782, 784 (1953) ([W]hen we weren't allowed to put in where we wanted to go . . . , we at least got the thing set up so that we are allowed to state in accompanying comments where the particular

Still, the Comments have influenced many judicial decisions and will continue to do so.[31] That they are not entitled to exactly the same weight as true legislative history may, therefore, be unimportant.

Earlier Versions of the UCC. Earlier versions of the UCC may serve as a source of guidance in resolving problems of interpretation and construction. However, inferences based on changes in the language of successive revisions of UCC sections are inherently unreliable; the change in language may or may not indicate a change in meaning. Indeed, a comment to a section in the 1952 text expressly noted that "[p]rior drafts of text and comments may not be used to ascertain legislative intent" because "frequently matters have been omitted as being implicit without statement and language has been changed or added solely for clarity." Ironically, this section itself was eventually deleted from the Official Text of the UCC. It should have been left in.[32]

Despite this admonition, lawyers should be aware of the existence and content of earlier drafts. In particular, it is worth noting that shortly after the UCC was proposed, between 1953 and 1955, the New York Law Revision Commission made a thorough study of the UCC and recommended many changes in the official text. In 1956, the Editorial Board of the UCC revised the earlier Official Text, drawing largely from the criticisms made at the New York Law Revision Commission Hearings. This history, in particular, can be a useful interpretive tool.[33]

---

sections are trying to go. . . . I am ashamed of it in some ways; there are so many pieces that I could make a little better, there are so many beautiful ideas I tried to get in that would have been good for the law, but I was voted down"). *See generally* Robert H. Skilton, *Some Comments on the Comments to the Uniform Commercial Code,* 1966 WIS. L. REV. 597; Grant Gilmore, *On the Difficulties of Codifying Commercial Law,* 57 YALE L. J. 1341 (1948).

[31]   *See* Sean M. Hannaway, Note, *The Jurisprudence and Judicial Treatment of the Comments to the Uniform Commercial Code,* 75 CORNELL L. REV. 962 (1990).

[32]   For a view that the legislative history is critical to interpretation of the UCC, *see* John M. Breen, *Statutory Interpretation and the Lessons of Llewellyn,* 33 LOY. L.A. L. REV. 263 (2000). Access to prior versions of uniform acts as they go through a revision process is now facilitated by the internet. For example, earlier drafts of Article 2 as it went through the decades-long revision provision can be accessed through http://www.law.upenn.edu/bll/ulc/ulc_frame.htm. Final versions of the revised UCC articles may be obtained from the ALI or are available in commercially printed statutory compilations.

[33]   *See generally* Robert Braucher, *The Legislative History of the Uniform Commercial Code,* 58 COLUM. L. REV. 798 (1958). An extensive treatment of the major research sources

Legislative History of Enactment in Particular State. Another relevant resource in resolving problems of UCC interpretation are the records of legislative hearings, committee reports, and state bar association reports. These do not exist in each state, but where they do, they form the more immediate background of UCC enactment in the state in which they arose. They can be particularly valuable in ascertaining the purpose of any nonuniform amendments.

Books and Other Commentary. As is true for any legal issue, books and articles authored by experts – those who teach the subject and those who practice in the area – can be useful in resolving interpretive problems. For the UCC, this type of scholarship is accompanied by books and articles written by those involved in the drafting. Almost every dispute that reaches an appellate court is accompanied by citations to treatises or law review articles expressing opinions on the issue.[34]

Once you have completed your own textual analysis and exhausted your research, there may still be interpretive questions that remain. Sometimes none of the sources you have found addresses the problem you have identified. Other times the authorities disagree or do not provide a convincing analysis. In these cases, you should look for a tie-breaker, a structuring policy that you can resort to solve the issue. This policy might be found in the policies stated in UCC § 1-103 or those immanent in contemporary views of social welfare or justice.

SECTION 2.   TRANSACTION TYPES

One of the first tasks for a lawyer involved in a commercial transaction – whether in the pre-transaction phase or the dispute resolution phase – is to ascertain what law or laws govern. This is critical because it can affect almost every aspect of the transaction and significantly impact the parties' rights and responsibilities. If the lawyer reaches a wrong conclusion about the law that applies, almost every decision the lawyer makes will be wrong or at least questionable.

---

on the UCC is Igor I. Kavass, *Uniform Commercial Code Research: A Brief Guide to the Sources*, 88 COM. L.J. 547 (1983). *See also* ELIZABETH SLUSSER KELLY, UNIFORM COMMERCIAL CODE DRAFTS (1984).

[34] *See* JAMES J. WHITE AND ROBERT S. SUMMERS, THE UNIFORM COMMERCIAL CODE (5th ed. 2006 & Supp. 2008); WILLIAM D. HAWKLAND, UNIFORM COMMERCIAL CODE SERIES (2008).

As you can see from the description of the various UCC articles, there are often several possibilities just within the UCC itself, let alone all the other possible sources of law. So what should a lawyer consider in deciding what law governs? Four principal factors:

(i) The type of property or other subject matter of the transaction (*e.g.,* goods, real estate, services, intellectual property, accounts receivable);

(ii) The nature or extent of the rights being transferred (*e.g.,* a sale, lease, license, lien, bailment, gift);

(iii) The location of the parties to the transaction; and

(iv) What, if anything, the parties' agreement says about governing law.

The following chart summarizes *some* of the possibilities based on the first two factors.

THE LAW GOVERNING VOLUNTARY TRANSFERS OF PROPERTY RIGHTS

Type of Transfer	Type of Property				
	Real Estate	Goods	Securities (stocks & bonds)	Commercial Paper	Intellectual Property
Sale	real estate law	UCC Art. 2 or CISG	UCC Art. 8 or securities laws	UCC Arts. 3 & 4	UCC Art. 2, state common law, or federal law
Gift	real estate law	common law	UCC Art. 8	UCC Arts. 3 & 4	state common law or federal law
Lease or License	real estate law	UCC Art. 2A	UCC Art. 8 or federal law	N/A	state common law or federal law
Security Interest or Mortgage	real estate law	UCC Art. 9	UCC Art. 9	UCC Arts. 3, 4 & 9	UCC Art. 9 or federal law
Bequest or Devise	real estate law or law of wills	law of wills	UCC Art. 8 or law of wills	law of wills	law of wills or federal law

In analyzing a transaction or proposed transaction, we suggest that you examine these factors in the order presented. And for the moment, let us focus on the first factor: the nature of what is being transferred. Most of the time, this will be easy to ascertain. On occasion, however, it can be exceptionally difficult and even controversial. Consider the following example.

Example

You are the lawyer for Steadman Appliances, Inc., which is located in Dearborn, Michigan. You have been asked to draft a standard form purchase agreement for your client's use in its business. Steadman wants to use the form for a typical transaction such as selling and installing new gas stoves and refrigerators in individual customers' houses. Most of the customers are located in Michigan, but some are in nearby Ohio or Indiana, and some are located in Ontario, Canada. The stoves and refrigerators have software as part of the control circuitry. They also come with a one-year, in-home service warranty. Steadman typically supplies the new stove and refrigerator selected by the customer and delivers it to the house, placing it in the location the customer designates. Sometimes Steadman will have to run a gas line to the stove location or run a water pipe to the refrigerator location in order to supply water for the automatic ice maker.

In order to draft the standard form, you need to determine the governing law so that you have the right set of rules to guide the risk allocation you need to think about. The possibilities include UCC Article 2, UCC Article 2A, non-UCC domestic law (such as real estate law or the common law of contracts), the CISG, and Canadian law (at least as to Canadian customers). Is the subject matter of the transaction goods, software, or services? The first step is to read the scope provisions of the possibly applicable statutes and treaties to determine if the transaction falls within any of them. If none of the statutes or treaties applies, then you must consider what other law will govern, such as some state's common law or Canadian law.

Let's start with Article 2. Read section 2-102 which states that Article 2 applies to "transactions in goods." What do you need to think about to determine if Article 2 will govern this type of contract? First consider "goods." Is there any doubt that stoves and refrigerators in Steadman's inventory are goods? There should be. After all, in many cases the appliances will become fixtures of the customer's real estate upon installation. When you deal with a statute, such as the UCC, you must be careful and look for definitions. Read section 2-105(1), which defines "goods." Note how opaque the definition is. Among other things, it refers to things that are movable "at the time of identification to the contract for sale." What does this mean? When is property "identified to the contract"? That question is answered in section 2-501. Statutes often have many interrelated provisions, and you need to review all of them to reach reliable conclusions. You might ask, "but how was I supposed to know to look to at section 2-501?" See the cross-references after the comments to section 2-105. Section 2-501 is listed there in reference to "point 1."

But even after all this, you should not be done. Consider how the client may conduct its business. Perhaps on occasion Steadman will purport to sell an appliance that has been backordered and has not yet been manufactured. Would Article 2 apply to such a transaction? Read sections 2-105(2) and 2-106(1). Collectively, they refer to four concepts: a present sale, a future sale, existing goods, and future goods. The intersection of those four concepts creates at least four possible transactions: (i) a present sale of existing goods; (ii) a purported present sale of future goods, (iii) a future sale of existing goods, and (iv) a future sale of future goods. Are all of these transactions within the scope of Article 2?

Okay, now it is time for a few problems.

Problem 1-1

A. Adroit Industries Inc. sells medical supplies to hospitals and recently converted to a totally green environment by installing solar panels for its power needs. To which of the transactions, if any, does Article 2 apply?
   1. Selling radioactive isotopes suspended in solution for the purpose of nuclear imaging.
   2. Selling oxygen to fill the hospital's oxygen tanks.
   3. Selling to the local utility the excess electricity generated from Adroit's solar panels.
B. Benjamin recently purchased the following four items in four separate transactions. To which of the transactions, if any, does Article 2 apply?
   1. A 1908 Indian Eagle $2.5 gold coin for $2,500.00.
   2. 500 euros (ten 50-euro notes) from Bank for use on an upcoming vacation in Florence, Italy.

3. 100,000 Japanese yen through his investment broker. The yen are credited to Benjamin's brokerage account.

4. 1,000 shares of Microsoft stock, in certificated form. Benjamin has possession of the certificate.

C. Cheyenne Industries, Inc. recently purchased the following four items in four separate transactions. To which of the transactions, if any, does Article 2 apply?

1. A building from Lumber Yard. Lumber Yard is responsible for removing the building from its concrete foundation and putting it on skids. Cheyenne Industries is responsible for hauling the building away. *See* UCC § 2-107(1).

2. All the timber standing on Forester's land. Cheyenne Industries is responsible for cutting and removing the timber. *See* UCC § 2-107(2).

3. All the oil and natural gas that Cheyenne can find and remove underneath Jed Clampett's property.

4. 20 gallons of gasoline from Service Station for one of Cheyenne's trucks.

Let us return to the example of Steadman Appliances. Even if you conclude that the stoves and refrigerators it sells are normally "goods" within the meaning of Article 2, does it matter that Steadman is not merely selling the items but also providing the service of installing them and promising to repair them if necessary? If the transaction were for services, only – such as if Steadman were hired to install appliances that its customers acquired from someone else or to fix appliances the customer already owned – then Article 2 would not apply.[35] In that circumstance, the common law of contracts would apply to the services.

This difference in applicable law would not matter except for the fact that the rules in Article 2 and the rules at common law are likely to differ in some significant respects. These differences may include the rules on whether and when a contract is formed, the standard for measuring the quality of the promised performance, and what the applicable remedies are for non-performance or

---

[35]   If you question this statement by noting that Article 2 applies to "transactions in goods," *see* UCC § 2-102, and posit that installation or repair services might well be a "transaction in goods," then you are on the right track. In fact, though, while Article 2 does apply to transactions in goods, most of its provisions apply only to sales of goods. *See* UCC § 2-106(1).

substandard performance. So, how then are we to deal with mixed transactions involving both a sale of goods and the provision of services? Does Article 2 apply to the whole transaction, part of the transaction, or not at all?

This is one issue on which the Code itself is silent. Most courts apply what is known as the "predominant purpose test." Under this test, courts ask whether the predominant purpose of the transaction was the provision of goods, in which case Article 2 applies, or the provision of services, in which event Article 2 does not apply. Factors that courts tend to recite as relevant to that inquiry include: (i) the contract language; (ii) the nature of the supplier's business; and (iii) the value of the materials and services provided under the contract. For the most part, courts state the facts and then declare an answer, without providing an analysis that is useful to other fact patterns. Perhaps because of this, they have reached conflicting results.[36]

Another type of mixed transaction is one involving both the provision of goods and software. Some courts have held that software is a "good" and thus a transfer of software is covered by Article 2. Others have disagreed.[37] This problem is also complicated by the increase in so called "smart goods": goods with one or more computer chips and integrated software. Many cars now come equipped with a computer to monitor and run various systems of the car. Smaller smart goods have become ubiquitous. Virtually all hand-held data organizers, cell phones, digital cameras, and microwave ovens have built-in software. Should the predominate purpose test be used to determine whether Article 2 governs a transaction in which both goods and software are provided?[38] Even if Article 2 would apply to the

---

[36]   *See* WILLIAM D. HAWKLAND, UNIFORM COMMERCIAL CODE SERIES § 2-102:4 (2008).

[37]   On the side of applying Article 2, *see, e.g.*, *Olcott Intern. & Co. v. Micro Data Base Sys., Inc.*, 793 N.E.2d 1063 (Ind. Ct. App. 2003); *Sagent Tech., Inc. v. Micros Sys., Inc.*, 276 F. Supp. 2d 464 (D. Md. 2003); *Micro Data Base Sys., Inc. v. Dharma Sys., Inc.*, 148 F.3d 649 (7th Cir. 1998); *Advent Sys., Ltd. v. Unisys Corp.*, 925 F.2d 670 (3d Cir. 1991). On the side of not applying Article 2, *see, e.g.*, *Specht v. Netscape Communic'ns Corp.*, 306 F.3d 17 (2d Cir. 2002) (doubting whether Article 2 applied to downloaded software); *Pearl Inv. LLC v. Standard I/O, Inc.*, 257 F. Supp. 2d 326 (D. Me. 2003); *Multi-Tech Sys., Inc. v. Floreat, Inc.*, 2002 WL 432016 (D. Minn. 2002).

[38]   *See* PRINCIPLES OF THE LAW OF SOFTWARE CONTRACTING § 1.07 (Tentative Draft No. 1, March 24, 2008). The American Law Institute has sponsored production of the "Principles of the Law of Software Contracting" which addresses contract principles in the context of software licensing. As a "principles" project, it does not have the force of law and instead is primarily a statement of principles that courts can consider when confronted with legal issues germane to software contracting. For a discussion of that project see Maureen A.

software, federal intellectual property law will also apply to any license of software that is the subject of a patent or a copyright.

Problem 1-2

Danielle recently purchased the following four items in four separate transactions. To which of the transactions, if any, does Article 2 apply?

A. New book from Bookstore.
B. A new music CD from Music Retailer.
C. A song downloaded onto her MP3 player from Internet Company.
D. New word processing software (to replace the software she currently uses but hates) from Software Retailer. The software comes on three CDs in a box with a manual.

Not every jurisdiction has adopted the "predominant purpose" test to deal with transactions involving both goods and services. The most notable alternative —sometimes called the "gravamen of the claim test" – was formulated in *Anthony Pools v. Sheehan*, 455 A.2d 434, 441 (Md. 1983).[39] In essence, that test asks whether the claim relates to the goods or to the services. If it relates to the goods, Article 2 applies; if it relates to the services, Article 2 does not apply. More specifically, the court ruled that even when services predominate, if the goods supplied (a diving board) were unmerchantable and caused loss (personal injuries), Article 2 could be applied both to impose an implied warranty of merchantability and to determine whether a clause purporting to disclaim the implied warranty of merchantability was enforceable. The court stressed that the goods had to be supplied under a commercial transaction, rather than a contract for professional services, and must "retain their character . . . after completion of the performance promised." *Id.*

While the gravamen of the claim test has some appeal, it is subject to the same major criticism frequently leveled on the predominant purpose test: it is difficult

---

O'Rourke, *An Essay on the Challenges of Drafting a Uniform Law of Software Contracting*, 10 LEWIS & CLARK L. REV. 925 (2006).

[39]   *See also J.O. Hooker & Sons, Inc. v. Roberts Cabinet Co.*, 683 So.2d 396, 400 (Miss. 1996) (stating that the test in a mixed transaction – a construction contract – turned on the nature of the contract and "upon whether the *dispute* in question primarily concerns the goods furnished or the services rendered under the contract").

to apply. Specifically, how are courts and parties to determine if the claim relates to the goods or to the services? For example, if your new contact lenses irritate your eyes, is it because the lenses are defective or the optometrist erred in measuring your eyes? Moreover, what if the dispute does not involve damages from an allegedly nonconforming tender, but something entirely different, such as contract formation, parol evidence, or the Statute of Frauds? Should Article 2 apply then or not? Perhaps for these reasons, the gravamen of the claim test has not had much traction; the predominant purpose test remains the prevailing approach in most states.

Problem 1-3

A. Are Steadman Appliance's contracts with its U.S. customers governed by Article 2? Which of the facts provided are the most significant to the analysis of this question? What facts that you do not know would also be significant?

B. Superior Robotics, Inc. has agreed to design, build, and install a robotic welder in Bonneville Motors' assembly plant. The robot will be equipped with and controlled by custom software that Superior Robotics must write. Is this agreement governed by Article 2? Why or why not?

Now consider the phrase "unless the context otherwise requires" which is at the beginning of section 2-102. What does that phrase mean? Does it mean that even if the transaction is a "transaction in goods," there are contexts in which the court should not apply Article 2? As you study Article 2's substantive provisions, consider when it might be inappropriate to apply Article 2 to a transaction that otherwise concerns goods. For example, should Article 2 apply to a bailment of goods (where goods are deposited with a bailee for storage, transport, or other specified purpose) or to a lease of goods?

To continue our painstaking look at the language of section 2-102, consider the language after the semicolon. Article 2 does not apply to a transaction in goods "intended to operate only as a security transaction." Does the Official Comment explain what that phrase means?

Other law. The entire discussion so far on the scope of Article 2 has focused on section 2-102 and its reference to "transactions in goods." However, sometimes other law – outside the UCC – can affect or limit the coverage of Article 2. We have already seen that various state and federal laws supplement Article 2, often in important ways.[40] Indeed, section 2-102 recognizes this possibility in its last clause, which expressly provides that Article 2 does not "impair or repeal any statute regulating sales to consumers, farmers or other specified classes of buyers." More significantly, sometimes other laws render Article 2 wholly inapplicable. Consider the following problem, consulting the statutes that follow it as necessary.

Problem 1-4

A. Blood Bank, located in Washington, enters into an agreement with Hospital, located in Alaska, to supply Hospital with all the whole blood, plasma, and similar blood products it needs to perform surgeries and other medical procedures for the next three years.   Is that agreement governed by Article 2?

B. Shylock, a resident of Kentucky, offers to sell one of her kidneys to the highest bidder, advertising that offer through an online auction website. The terms of the offer provide that the location of the surgery will be determined by mutual agreement, but that the high bidder must pay all of Shylock's expenses of traveling to that location.   Is this transaction governed by Article 2?   Does it matter if the high bidder is located in a different state, such as California?

Alaska Statutes
§ 45.02.316 Exclusion or modification of warranties.
* * *

(e) Implied warranties of merchantability and fitness are not applicable to a contract for the sale of human blood, blood plasma or other human tissue or organs from a blood bank or reservoir of tissue or organs. The blood, blood plasma, tissue, or organs may not, for the purposes of this chapter, be considered commodities subject to sale or barter, but shall be considered medical services.

Revised Code of Washington
§ 70.54.120. Immunity from implied warranties and civil liability relating to blood, blood products, tissues, organs, or bones – Scope – Effective date.
The procurement, processing, storage, distribution, administration, or use of whole blood, plasma, blood products and blood derivatives for the purpose of injecting or transfusing the same, or any of them, or of tissues, organs, or bones for

---

40   *See supra* notes 20–25 and accompanying text.

the purpose of transplanting them, or any of them, into the human body is declared to be, for all purposes whatsoever, the rendition of a service by each and every person, firm, or corporation participating therein, and is declared not to be covered by any implied warranty under the Uniform Commercial Code, Title 62A RCW, or otherwise, and no civil liability shall be incurred as a result of any of such acts, except in the case of wilful or negligent conduct: *Provided, however,* That this section shall apply only to liability alleged in the contraction of hepatitis, malaria, and acquired immune deficiency disease and shall not apply to any transaction in which the donor receives compensation: *Provided further,* That this section shall only apply where the person, firm or corporation rendering the above service shall have maintained records of donor suitability and donor identification: *Provided further,* That nothing in this section shall be considered by the courts in determining or applying the law to any blood transfusion occurring before June 10, 1971 and the court shall decide such case as though this section had not been passed.

Kentucky Revised Statutes
§ 311.171 Prohibitions and restrictions relating to transplantable organs.

(1) No person shall sell or make a charge for any transplantable organ.

(2) No person shall offer remuneration for a transplantable organ.

(3) No person shall broker for the sale or transfer of a transplantable organ.

(4) No person shall charge a fee associated with the transplantation of a transplantable organ in excess of the direct and indirect costs of procuring, preserving, distributing, or transplanting the transplantable organ.

(5) Nothing in this section shall be construed in any way to relate to the use, sale, distribution, procurement, preservation, distribution, experimentation, research, drug manufacture, or other treatment of any human or nonhuman part other than transplantable organs.

California Penal Code
§ 367f. Sale of human organ for transplantation; removal or transplant of organ with knowledge of sale; definitions; application; exceptions; punishment.

(a) Except as provided in subdivisions (d) and (e), it shall be unlawful for any person to knowingly acquire, receive, sell, promote the transfer of, or otherwise transfer any human organ, for purposes of transplantation, for valuable consideration.

(b) Except as provided in subdivisions (d), (e), and (f), it shall be unlawful to remove or transplant any human organ with the knowledge that the organ has been acquired or will be transferred or sold for valuable consideration in violation of subdivision (a).

(c) For purposes of this section, the following definitions apply:

(1) "Human organ" includes, but is not limited to, a human kidney, liver, heart, lung, pancreas, or any other human organ or nonrenewable or nonregenerative tissue except plasma and sperm.

(2) "Valuable consideration" means financial gain or advantage, but does not include the reasonable costs associated with the removal, storage, transportation, and transplantation of a human organ, or reimbursement for those services, or the expenses of travel, housing, and lost wages incurred by the donor of a human organ in connection with the donation of the organ.

* * *

(e) This section shall not apply to the person from whom the organ is removed, nor to the person who receives the transplant, or those persons' next-of-kin who assisted in obtaining the organ for purposes of transplantations.

* * *

(g) Any person who violates subdivision (a) or (b) shall be punished by a fine not to exceed fifty thousand dollars ($50,000), or by imprisonment in the state prison for three, four, or five years, or both.

CISG. In addition to preemptive state laws, there may be federal law that preempts Article 2. Recall the discussion of the CISG.[41] To what transactions involving goods does the CISG apply? Read Articles 1 through 6, and Article 10 of the CISG. Does Steadman Appliances have to worry about the CISG?

Problem 1-5

In each of these transactions, determine whether Article 2, the CISG, or some other law applies to the transaction. Detail all of your analytical steps.

A. Ahmad, a United States resident, placed a telephone order for a new computer from a Canadian manufacturer. The manufacturer agreed to ship the computer to Ahmad's home in Lansing, Michigan.

B. Bethlehem Steel, located in Pennsylvania, agreed to sell 500 steel frames to a Canadian building contractor. The goods are to be shipped by rail within ten days.

C. Controlled Heating Corp., a New York company, agreed to manufacture and install new heating units for Northern Lights, Inc., a Canadian company, at Northern Lights' office in Detroit, Michigan.

---

[41] *See supra* notes 23–24 and accompanying text.

D. What difference, if any, would it make to the analysis of Part B if the parties had expressly provided that the law of Pennsylvania would govern the transaction? *See* UCC § 1-301.[42]

SECTION 3.   STRUCTURING TRANSACTIONS

As mentioned above, transactional lawyers are often involved in preparing documentation to reflect the deal the parties have made. While the lawyer may inform the client of the applicable legal rules and advise the client how to comply with them, the lawyer must be prepared and have the drafting skills necessary to accurately and clearly reflect the deal the parties wish to make and to make sure that the documentation complies with applicable legal rules.

What are the hallmarks of good drafting? First and foremost, you must understand the deal. That means you must understand the client's business, what the client hopes to achieve, and any relevant usage of trade. You must know the difference between representations, warranties, covenants, and conditions, and be able to determine which of those should be used for each term of the deal.

Second, you must know the legal rules and the options that are available for allocating the risks of the transaction in accordance with the legal rules.

But this is merely the beginning. It relates only to the substance of the transaction. Good drafting is a skill that requires close attention to every word used, to make sure that the point expressed is the point intended. This, in turn, requires compliance with several important principles.

- Avoid ambiguity. Clauses should not be subject to multiple and different meanings. To help ensure this, observe the rules of grammar and punctuation. Tabulation and other formatting conventions can also help avoid confusion and make the meaning clear.
- Use consistent language. Always use the same words when you mean the same thing and never say the same thing if you mean something different.

---

[42] *See Travelers Prop. Cas. Co. of Am. v. Saint-Gobain Technical Fabrics Canada Ltd.*, 474 F. Supp. 2d 1075 (D. Minn. 2007) (selecting Minnesota law did not exclude application of CISG as part of the law of Minnesota).

- Provide a logical structure for the document; its provisions should relate to each other in a logical and cohesive manner. This helps avoid contradiction, which should never exist.
- Clearly identify and distinguish general rules from exceptions.
- Avoid legalese and convoluted language. Use short sentences with simple sentence structure.
- Use the active voice.

This book will provide you with several opportunities to draft contract clauses and to practice applying these seemingly simple principles. Here is the first such opportunity.

Problem 1-6

Return to the example with Steadman Appliances. Draft a choice-of-law clause for inclusion in the form agreement that will make Washington's UCC Article 2 apply to the transaction in its entirety, no matter who the customers are and no matter how the transaction is structured.

CHAPTER TWO

CONTRACT FORMATION AND BASIC TERMS

Once you determine what law governs a particular transaction (such as the common law of contracts, UCC Article 2, or the CISG), the next step is to determine whether an agreement was formed, if the parties have already dealt with one another, or how to form one, if you are planning a future transaction. If an agreement was or will be formed, the next issue is to determine if that agreement is in fact enforceable. That is, does the agreement form the basis of an enforceable contract? In connection with this, you need to ascertain what the terms of the agreement are.

Lawyers, particularly transactional lawyers, need to be aware of the rules and principles that govern these three issues – formation, enforceability, and terms – bearing in mind that the different potentially applicable bodies of law are likely to have different rules on these subjects. From a transactional perspective, the lawyer wants to be able to advise his or her client what is required to have an enforceable agreement and, just as important, how to avoid entering into an enforceable agreement.

This Chapter considers formation, enforceability and some very basic terms issues under both UCC Article 2 and the CISG. With this basic understanding, Chapters Three through Five then examine additional rules on contract terms in UCC Article 2 and the CISG. Later in this book, in Chapter Eleven, we investigate how UCC Article 2A deals with these issues in the context of leases.

SECTION 1.   CONTRACT FORMATION PRINCIPLES

A. CONTRACT FORMATION UNDER UCC ARTICLE 2

1. *Basic Concepts*

The place to begin any study of the principles of contract formation under the UCC is the definitions of "agreement" and "contract" in section 1-201. The two terms are related, but are different in several important respects. An *agreement* is the "bargain of the parties in fact." That bargain is typically evidenced by the parties' communications with each other. However, as suggested by the reference to course of performance, course of dealing, and usage of trade, their bargain may also be evidenced by the parties' conduct (either in the transaction at issue or in prior transactions between them) or from their participation in a common trade. *See* UCC § 1-303.

The *contract* consists of the parties' legal obligations resulting from their agreement. This can be both less and more than their agreement. A contract encompasses more than the agreement from which it arises whenever the law adds a term to the parties' bargain. For example, the warranty of merchantability may arise as a matter of law if the seller is a merchant with respect to the kind of goods sold in the transaction. *See* UCC §§ 2-314, 2-316. Article 2 has a variety of other "gap filler" rules designed to add detail to the parties' agreement. *See, e.g.,* UCC §§ 2-307, 2-308, 2-309, 2-310, 2-312, 2-315.

The contract is less than the agreement whenever all or part of the agreement is unenforceable. Thus, for example, an agreement for the sale of contraband is not a contract because it is not enforceable. Neither is an agreement that fails to satisfy the statute of frauds. *See* UCC § 2-201. An agreement with an unconscionable term may not be enforceable at all or may be enforceable without the offending term. *See* UCC § 2-302(1). In either case, the parties' contract is something less than their agreement.

It is worth noting that both "agreement" and "contract," because they are based on the parties' bargain, are broader than what the common law would traditionally regard as a contract. For example, the Restatement (Second) of Contracts defines a contract as a "promise or a set of promises for the breach of which the law gives a remedy." RESTATEMENT (SECOND) OF CONTRACTS § 1 (1981). Certainly the parties' bargain may consist of an exchange of explicit or implied promises. However, a bargain may also include the parties' consummated transaction. Consider the following.

Illustration

You go to a supermarket, select the items you want, proceed to the checkout counter, and pay for them. Arguably, at no time did either you or the store promise anything to the other. You tendered payment and completed a transaction, but arguably there were no promises. Thus, the common law would not regard this as a contract. The UCC does. There may not have been a promise, but there was a "bargain." Hence there was an "agreement." As long as there was no bar to enforceability – such as might be true if you were a minor purchasing cigarettes or alcohol – there would also be a "contract" within the meaning of the UCC.

At what point in time will the parties have engaged in enough discussion or conduct to create a "bargain in fact" which may be enforceable as a contract? The common-law construct with which you are familiar is that a contract is formed when there is an offer that is accepted, provided the promise is supported by consideration.[1] The rules regarding offer, acceptance, and consideration can be somewhat technical. They were no doubt explored in your contracts course, and that coverage will not be repeated here.

Article 2 begins with this common-law foundation to determine when a contract is formed. This reliance on the common law is evidenced by Article 2's failure to provide a complete set of rules on contract formation. Therefore, the common-law principles of offer and acceptance remain important for transactions governed by Article 2. Article 2 then builds upon this common-law foundation. The common law provides general principles governing contract formation, with several provisions of Article 2 providing different rules on a few points. These different rules are needed, at least in part, to account for the fact that Article 2's notion of a contract is based on the broader concept of a "bargain," rather than the more narrow concept of a "promise."

Article 2's rules on contract formation are contained in sections 2-204 *through* 2-207, and the starting point for examining them is section 2-204. Subsection (1) provides that a contract can be formed in any manner sufficient to show agreement.[2] Thus, while the parties may engage in offer and acceptance, as under the common law, there is no need for the parties to follow the formalities of an offer and acceptance to form an agreement, the bargain in fact of the parties. Subsection (2) then adds that we need not be able to point to the precise moment of formation, as long as we have agreement. This accounts for the fact that when parties have actually engaged in offer and acceptance, it is usually fairly easy to identify those communications, but when their bargain is evidenced in some other manner, such as by performance, it may be difficult to identify the precise moment when they reached agreement. Subsection (3) then adds an extremely important rule. It allows for a contract to be formed even though one or more terms of the transaction are left open, as long as there is a reasonable basis for providing a remedy in the event of breach. This represents a substantial deviation from the common law, which

---

[1]   *See* RESTATEMENT (SECOND) OF CONTRACTS §§ 3, 17, 22.

[2]   For an example of the factual nature of this inquiry, *see E.C. Styberg Eng'g Co. v. Eaton Corp.*, 492 F.3d 912 (7th Cir. 2007).

typically conditions formation of a contract on the parties having reached agreement on all the material terms.[3] In Chapters Three through Five we will examine the "gap filler" rules that UCC Article 2 uses to supplement an incomplete agreement.

These gap filler provisions are often critical to the requirement in section 2-204(3) that there be a "reasonably certain basis for giving an appropriate remedy" in order to create an enforceable agreement. Keep in mind that the need to resort to gap filler provisions arises only if the parties' bargain, as supplemented by applicable usage of trade, course of dealing, and course of performance, does not deal with a particular term. At common law, which lacks gap filler provisions, enforceable contracts require agreement on all the material terms.

Now read section 2-205. Under the common law, the offeror may generally revoke an offer any time before the offeree has accepted. A promise to keep an offer open is normally enforceable only if supported by consideration (so that there is, in essence, an option contract).[4] Section 2-205 provides an additional basis for making enforceable the promise to keep the offer open. Notice, this section does not purport to define what an offer is, and therefore implicitly relies on the common law to determine what qualifies as an offer.

Now read section 2-206. It too implicitly relies on the common-law rules regarding what constitutes an offer but contradicts old common-law rules on what qualifies as an acceptance. Specifically, paragraph (1)(a) abrogates the rules that presumed that an acceptance has to be sent in the same manner and medium as the offer.[5] An offeror may still specify the manner and medium of an acceptance. Paragraph (a) does not abrogate the common-law rule that the offeror is "master of its offer," it merely does away with the presumption that the acceptance must be transmitted in the same manner and medium as the offer. Paragraph (1)(b) does something more significant. It allows an offer to buy to be accepted either by a return promise or by performance: the shipment of goods. Even shipment of nonconforming goods can constitute an acceptance. By allowing the shipment of nonconforming goods to qualify as an acceptance, section 2-206 slightly modifies the common-law distinction between a counter-offer and an acceptance.[6] Finally,

---

[3]   *See* RESTATEMENT (SECOND) OF CONTRACTS § 33.

[4]   *See* RESTATEMENT (SECOND) OF CONTRACTS § 17(1). *Cf.* § 87.

[5]   *Compare* RESTATEMENT (SECOND) OF CONTRACTS §§ 30, 60, 65.

[6]   *Compare* RESTATEMENT (SECOND) OF CONTRACTS §§ 39, 59, 61.

subsection (2) gives the offeror the ability to treat the offer as lapsed if not notified of the acceptance within a reasonable time.[7]

Even though sections 2-204 through 2-206 provide rules regarding how a contract is formed, the parties are free to specify the circumstances that must exist in order to have an enforceable contract. *See* UCC § 1-302. For example, the parties may agree that they will not have a contract until both parties execute a writing containing all of the final terms.[8] Thus, Article 2 does not alter the fundamental contract principle that the parties may expressly determine the manner in which they will form an enforceable contract. Remember that we are addressing contract formation assuming the transaction is covered by Article 2. Later on we will consider contract formation using CISG principles. Now it is time for a few problems.

Problem 2-1

A. After reading Seller's catalogue of hi-fi equipment, Buyer orders a $470 amplifier by completing the order form included in the catalogue and faxing it to Seller. Upon Seller's receipt of the fax but prior to acknowledgment or shipment, is there an agreement?

B. Buyer faxes Seller an order for "1,000 lbs. of Grade A bananas at 25¢/lb., delivery by November 15, payment within 30 days after delivery."

1. Seller faxes back a response that says, "Received your order. Expect to ship for delivery on November 10." Is there an agreement? If so, when is payment due?

2. Instead of sending the response, Seller shipped Buyer 1,000 lbs. of Grade A bananas for delivery on November 10. Prior to delivery, is there an agreement? If so, what are the payment terms? What if Seller shipped apples instead of bananas?

---

[7]   *Compare* RESTATEMENT (SECOND) OF CONTRACTS § 56. *See also Scoular Co. v. Denney*, 151 P.3d 615 (Colo. Ct. App. 2006) (buyer's actions in reselling the goods was not the beginning of performance of the contract with the seller).

[8]   *See, e.g., Flanagan v. Consolidated Nutrition, L.C.*, 627 N.W.2d 573 (Iowa Ct. App. 2001).

C. Seller faxes Buyer the following:

> Pleased to offer you 1,000 lbs. of Grade A cherries at 43¢/lb., delivery by November 15, payment within 30 days after delivery. E-mail or call me by end of the day if that's okay.

Buyer responds two days later with the following e-mail message:

> That sounds great. Look forward to delivery.

Is there an agreement? What if, after receiving Buyer's response, Seller ships the cherries?

D. Seller faxes Buyer the following:

> Pleased to offer you 500 lbs. of dates at 94¢/lb., delivery by November 15, payment within 30 days after delivery.

Buyer responds with the following message, also sent by fax:

> Price too high. Can't buy for more than 68¢/lb.

Is there an agreement? What if, after receiving Buyer's response, Seller ships the dates?

Problem 2-2

Sedgwick manufactures and sells bolts for use in airplane manufacture. The bolts are customarily sold by "lot," a term based on total weight.

A. On March 1, after some negotiations with Butler, but before Sedgwick had manufactured any bolts for Butler, Sedgwick sent Butler the following form in the mail:

> Will sell you ten (10) lots of No. 6 bolts for $2,000 per lot. This offer will be held open until March 15.

On March 14, Butler telephoned Sedgwick to accept the offer, but before Butler could say anything, Sedgwick said, "That offer I sent you is off the table. I can't sell you the bolts for that price." Butler protested that Sedgwick had promised to keep the offer open. Butler then stated she accepted the offer. Has a contract been formed?

B. On April 1, after some negotiations with Barker but before Sedgwick had manufactured any bolts for Barker, Sedgwick sent Barker a signed letter that stated:

> Will sell you ten (10) lots of No. 8 bolts for $2,000 per lot. This offer will be held open until April 15.

At the bottom of the letter was a line for the buyer to signify acceptance by affixing a signature. Barker signed the form on that line and mailed the form back to Sedgwick on April 6. On April 10, Barker bought bolts from another supplier and called Sedgwick, leaving a message on the answering machine that he would not be buying any bolts from Sedgwick. Is there a contract between Sedgwick and Barker?

C. On May 1, after some negotiations with Baxter but before Sedgwick had manufactured any bolts for Baxter, Sedgwick sent Baxter a preprinted form in the mail. The form had several paragraphs of standard sales terms. In the middle of the form was the following handwritten sentence:

> Baxter will buy ten (10) lots of No. 7 bolts for $2,000 per lot.
> This offer will be held open until May 15.

At the bottom of the form was a line for the buyer's signature. Baxter signed the form on that line and sent the form back to Sedgwick by mail on May 6. On May 10, Baxter bought bolts from another supplier and called Sedgwick, leaving a message on the answering machine that he would not be buying any bolts from Sedgwick. On May 11, Sedgwick called Baxter and purported to accept Baxter's offer to buy the bolts. Is there a contract between Sedgwick and Baxter?

D. After negotiation with Baker regarding the bolts that Baker needed for the type of plane that Baker makes, Sedgwick started to retool her manufacturing process to produce those bolts. About a week after that retooling process was started, Baker called Sedgwick to tell her that he was buying the bolts from someone else. Sedgwick sued Baker for breach of contract, arguing that by starting the retooling process, she had begun the requested performance and thereby accepted the offer to buy that Baker had made during the course of their negotiations. Assume that Baker indeed made an offer to buy. Is Sedgwick correct?

Problem 2-3

Stable Earth, Inc., a manufacturer of fertilizer, and Brittany, a farmer, had done business with each other for five years. When fertilizer was needed, Brittany would call the Stable Earth order desk and order a specific quantity and quality of fertilizer. Stable Earth's order desk would send that order to the warehouse, where personnel would ship the goods to Brittany by carrier, accompanied by a bill based on Stable Earth's current wholesale price. Frequently, Stable Earth would ship less or more than the amount Brittany ordered, depending upon what Stable Earth had on hand in the warehouse, but the deviation never exceeded 15%. The bill reflected the quantity actually shipped and Brittany invariably accepted and paid for what was actually shipped without objection. On July 10, during a time of price instability in the fertilizer market, Brittany used the website to order 500 bags of a specified fertilizer "for prompt shipment." The wholesale price on that date was $18 per bag. On July 12, Stable Earth shipped 400 bags of fertilizer to Brittany and mailed an invoice for the wholesale price on that date, $20 per bag. On July 15, while the goods were still in transit and the wholesale price was $25 per bag, Stable Earth notified Brittany that the order had been rejected and diverted the shipment to Carl, who agreed to pay $26 per bag. Brittany sued Stable Earth for breach of contract. Is there a contract between Brittany and Stable Earth? If so, what is the price per bag under the contract?

Problem 2-4

After reading Seller's catalogue of unique and expensive items, Buyer telephones Seller to order a brass eagle designed for mounting at the top of Buyer's flagpole. The price is $675, which Buyer pays by giving Seller Buyer's credit card number. Seller's catalogue contains the following in fairly large print on the order form, just below Seller's phone number:

> Seller warrants all its products will be as described in this catalogue. In the event of any problem with a shipment, customer must notify Seller in writing of such problem within 20 days of receipt or be barred from any remedy.

Prior to shipment, is there an agreement? If so, are the terms in the catalogue part of the agreement?

2. Battle of the Forms

The rules of sections 2-204 though 2-206 were arguably only minor variations from the prevailing common law when Article 2 was adopted in the 1950s and 1960s. The common-law rules today are generally in accord with these provisions of Article 2.[9] In contrast, section 2-207 was and remains a far more significant deviation of the common law. Consider this following typical scenario:

Illustration

> Buyer sends Seller an order form which is an offer to buy. The form has on it numerous terms, including the description, quantity, and price of the desired goods. Seller responds by sending an order acknowledgment form which contains numerous terms, some different from those on the Buyer's form and some additional terms. The two forms match on the major transaction-specific terms: the description of the goods, quantity, and price.

At common law, Seller's responsive form was a counter-offer, not an acceptance. Thus, even though the parties may have thought they had an agreement – a likely situation given that neither party was apt to scrutinize and compare the terms on the two standardized forms – they did not. Accordingly, if at this point either reneged on their apparent deal, the other would have no legal recourse. On the other hand, if Buyer, thinking they had a deal, followed their communications by sending payment, Buyer would be deemed to have accepted Seller's counter-offer and a contract would be formed based on the terms in Seller's acknowledgment form. Alternatively, and probably more likely, if Seller (also thinking they had a deal) shipped the goods and Buyer accepted them, Buyer's conduct would again be an acceptance of the terms of Seller's counter-offer. Thus, in either case, the terms on Seller's form would control. Note, this result was not based on Seller's role in the transaction, but on the sequence of their communications. If Seller had sent the first offer and Buyer had responded with a form that included slightly different or additional terms, then subsequent performance by the parties would generate a contract based on the terms in Buyer's form. In short, the terms of the last communication before performance would be the ones that controlled. This was called the "last shot" rule, and most legal scholars thought it was arbitrary and produced a result that frequently bore no relationship to what the parties expected.

Section 2-207 tries to deal with this "battle of the forms" scenario. It does so by addressing two different but related issues: (1) when and how an agreement is formed; and (2) what the terms of the resulting agreement are. Unfortunately,

---

[9]   *See* RESTATEMENT (SECOND) OF CONTRACTS §§ 39, 58, 59, 61.

section 2-207 is a bit confusing and has generated a significant amount of litigation. To understand the issues that the section raises, you must understand how the section works. Read Section 2-207.

The most important thing to understand about section 2-207 is that each of its three subsections deals with something different. Subsection (1) deals with when the parties' communications form an agreement. It abrogates the common-law mirror image rule by allowing a response that contains different or additional terms to nevertheless function as an acceptance. Subsection (2) provides guidance on the terms of an agreement formed under subsection (1). Thus, subsection (2) applies only if there is an agreement formed under subsection (1). Notice, subsection (2) provides two different rules for dealing with additional terms in an acceptance, one rule for communications "between merchants" and another rule for all other situations. As to who is a merchant, *see* UCC § 2-104. Subsection (3) then deals with situations in which no agreement is formed under subsection (1). It provides rules for: (i) when agreements are created not through the parties' "writings" but through their conduct; and (ii) what the terms for such agreements are.

The flow chart on the next page is one way to diagram the basic steps in the analysis. Although not reflected in the flow chart, notice that subsection (1) applies to "confirmations" as well as acceptances. A confirmation differs from an acceptance in that it confirms a pre-existing agreement. In other words, whereas an acceptance might begin "I agree," a confirmation might begin, "as we have already agreed" or "this note is to memorialize our agreement that." *See* UCC § 2-207 cmt. 1. When you think about it in those terms, subsection (1) seems to be written in Orwellian doublespeak: "a written confirmation . . . operates as an acceptance." This bit of alchemy treats a confirmation – which under the common law would have little or no relevance to whether an agreement exists or what the terms of any agreement are – as if it were part of the offer and acceptance process.

Notice also that the flow chart does not cover most of subsection (2). That is partly to keep it simple and partly because there is disagreement over how subsection (2) applies to different terms. That disagreement is a function of some rather unfortunate drafting. Reread subsections (1) and (2) and comments 3 and 6. Then consider the case that follows. It is a classic.

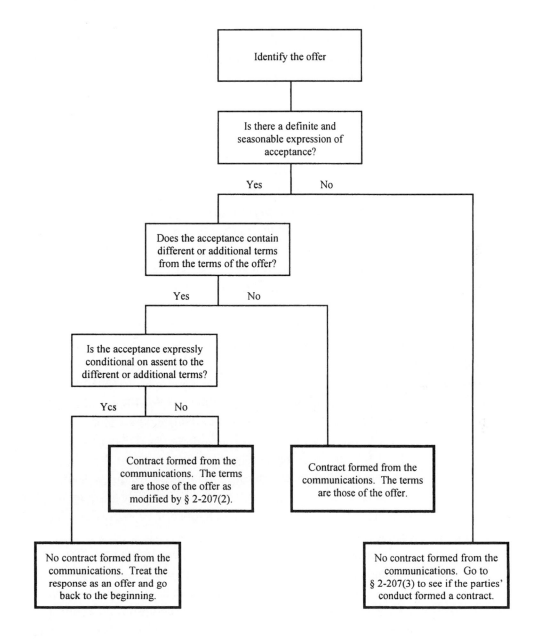

DAITOM, INC. V. PENNWALT CORP.
741 F.2d 1569 (10th Cir. 1984)

William E. Doyle, Circuit Judge

[On September 7, 1976, the seller (Pennwalt), after negotiations with the buyer (Daitom), submitted a proposal for the sale of two rotary vacuum dryers with dust filters. The proposal was made in a typewritten writing to which pre-printed form conditions were attached and explicitly made part of the proposal. One term in the form conditions imposed a one year period after delivery within which Daitom could bring a law suit. On October 5, 1976, Daitom issued a purchase order, which consisted of a pre-printed form and 17 standard terms and conditions on the back. One of the terms of the "boilerplate" reserved to Daitom "all of its rights and remedies available at law." Pennwalt delivered the goods in May, 1977 but, because the plant in which they were to be installed was under construction, left the crates outside. On June 15, 1978, the goods were finally installed and operated. Serious defects were discovered, of which Pennwalt was notified on June 17, 1978. When Pennwalt was unable to repair the defects, Daitom brought suit for breach of warranty on March 7, 1980. The trial court held, *inter alia*, that the one year limitation became part of the contract and, since the law suit was brought more than one year after delivery, granted a summary judgment against Daitom. On appeal, the judgment was reversed and the case remanded to the trial court.] . . .

C. The Writings and the Contract

The trial court concluded that the parties' exchanged writings formed a contract. Thus, there was not a formal single document. Pennwalt's September 7, 1976 proposal constituted the offer and Daitom's October 5, 1976 purchase order constituted the acceptance.

It is essentially uncontested that Pennwalt's proposal constituted an offer. The proposal set forth in some detail the equipment to be sold to Daitom, the price, the terms of shipment, and specifically stated that the attached terms and conditions were an integral part of the proposal. One of those attached terms and conditions of sale limited the warranties to repair and replacement of defective parts and limited the period of one year from the date of delivery for any action for breach of warranty.[10]

---

[10]   Paragraph 5 of the terms and conditions of sale stated in full (emphasis added):
6. WARRANTIES:

The proposal was sent to Kintech and forwarded to Daitom with a recommendation to accept the proposal. Daitom sent the October 5, 1976 purchase order to Pennwalt. This purchase order constituted an acceptance of Pennwalt's offer and formed a binding contract for the sale only pursuant to 2-207(1), despite the statement of terms additional to or different from those in the offer.[11] But these terms were not without meaning or consequence. However, the acceptance was not expressly conditioned on Pennwalt accepting these additional or different terms.

There is a provision which Daitom contends made the acceptance expressly conditional on Pennwalt's accepting the additional or different terms which

---

a. Seller warrants that at the time of delivery of the property to the carrier, it will be, unless otherwise specified, new, free and clear of all lawful liens and security interests or other encumbrances unknown to Buyer. If, within a period of one year from the date of *such delivery* any parts of the property (except property specified to be used property or normal wear parts) fail because of material or workmanship which was defective at the time of such delivery, Seller will repair such parts, or furnish parts to replace them f.o.b. Seller's or its supplier's plant, provided such failure is due solely to such defective material or workmanship and is not contributed to by any other cause, such as improper care or unreasonable use, and provided such defects are brought to Seller's attention for verification when first discovered, and the parts alleged to be so defective are returned, if requested, to Seller's or its supplier's plant. *No action for breach of warranty shall be brought more than one year after the cause of action has accrued*

SELLER MAKES NO OTHER WARRANTY OF ANY KIND, EXPRESS OR IMPLIED, INCLUDING ANY WARRANTY OF FITNESS OF THE PROPERTY FOR ANY PARTICULAR PURPOSE EVEN IF THAT PURPOSE IS KNOWN TO SELLER.

In no event shall Seller be liable for consequential damage.

b. Because of varied interpretations of standards at the local level, Seller cannot warrant that the property meets the requirements of the Occupational Safety and Health Act.

[11]   The principal additional or different terms referred to the reservation of warranties. Specifically:

(8) WARRANTY. The Seller warrants that the supplies covered by this purchase order will conform to the specifications, drawings, samples, or other descriptions furnished or specified by buyer, and will be fit and sufficient for the purpose intended, merchantable, of good material and workmanship, and free from defect. The warranties and remedies provided for in this paragraph . . . shall be in addition to those implied by or available at law and shall exist not withstanding [sic] the acceptance by Buyer of all or a part of this applies with respect to which such warranties and remedies are applicable.

appeared in the pre-printed, standard "boilerplate" provisions on the back of the purchase order. It stated:

Acceptance. Immediate acceptance is required unless otherwise provided herein. It is understood and agreed that the written acceptance by Seller of this purchase order or the commencement of any work performance of any services hereunder by the Seller, (including the commencement of any work or the performance of any service with respect to samples), shall constitute acceptance by Seller of this purchase order and of all the terms and conditions of such acceptance is *expressly limited to such terms and conditions, unless each deviation is mutually recognized therefore in writing.* (Emphasis added.)

This language does not preclude the formation of a contract by the exchanged writings pursuant to § 2-207(1). Nor does it dictate the adoption of a conclusion holding that as a result the acceptance provided the applicable terms of the resulting contract. First, it is well established that a contract for the sale of goods may be made in any manner to show agreement, requiring merely that there be some objective manifestation of mutual assent, but that there must be. There is not a contract until it takes place. *See* U.C.C. § 2-204; . . . Here there is such an objective manifestation of agreement on essential terms of equipment specifications, price, and the terms of shipment and payment, all of which took place before the machinery was put to any test. The purchase order explicitly referred to and incorporated on its front Kintech's equipment specifications and Pennwalt's proposal. But we are unwilling to hold such a typewritten reference and incorporation by Daitom brings the matter to a close. The acceptance and warranty terms as provided for by the above excerpted acceptance clause, does manifest a willingness on all essential terms to accept the offer and form a contract. . . . This was, of course, before an attempt was made to use the equipment.

Second, the boilerplate provision does not directly address the instant case. The purchase order is drafted principally as an *offer* inviting acceptance. Although this court recognizes that the form may serve a dual condition depending on the circumstances, the imprecision of language that permits such service detracts from Daitom's argument of conditional acceptance.

Third, the courts are split on the application of § 2-207(1) and the meaning of "expressly made conditional on assent to the additional or different terms.". . . . *Roto-Lith Ltd. v. F.P. Bartlett & Co., Inc.,* 297 F.2d 497 (1st Cir. 1962) represents one extreme of the spectrum, that the offeree's response stating a term materially altering the contractual obligations solely to the disadvantage of the offeror constitutes a conditional acceptance. The other extreme of the spectrum is represented by *Dorton v. Collins & Aikman Corporation*, 453 F.2d 1161 (6th Cir. 1972), in which case the court held that the conditional nature of the acceptance should be so clearly expressed in a manner sufficient to notify the offeror that the offeree is unwilling to proceed with the transaction unless the additional or different terms are included in the contract. The middle of the spectrum providing that a response merely "predicating" acceptance on clarification, addition or modification is a conditional acceptance is represented by *Construction Aggregates Corp. v. Hewitt-Robins, Inc.*, 404 F.2d 505 (7th Cir. 1968), *cert. denied*, 395 U.S. 921 (1969).

The facts of this case, Daitom asserts, are not of a character that would suggest that there had been an unequivocal acceptance. The defendant-appellee was aware that the machinery had not even been tried. Once it was tried, it broke down in a very short time. It is hard to see a justifiable acceptance, Daitom asserts, when the buyer does not even know whether it works, and, in fact, learns after the fact, that it does not work. This fact alone renders the "contract" to be questionable.

The better view as to the meaning and application of "conditional acceptance," and the view most likely to be adopted by Pennsylvania, is the view in *Dorton* that the offeree must explicitly communicate his or her unwillingness to proceed with the transaction unless the additional or different terms in its response are accepted by the offeror. . . .

Having found an offer and an acceptance which was not made expressly conditional on assent to additional or different terms, we must now decide the effect of those additional or different terms on the resulting contract and what terms became part of it. The district court simply resolved this dispute by focusing solely on the period of limitations specified in Pennwalt's offer of September 7, 1976. Thus, the court held that while the offer explicitly specified a one-year period of limitations in accordance with § 2-725(1) allowing such a reduction, Daitom's acceptance of October 5, 1976 was silent as to the limitations period. Consequently, the court held that § 2-207(2) was inapplicable and the one-year limitations period controlled, effectively barring Daitom's action for breach of warranties.

While the district court's analysis undertook to resolve the issue without considering the question of the application of § 2-207(2) to additional or different terms, we cannot accept its approach or its conclusion. We are unable to ignore the plain implication of Daitom's reservation in its boilerplate warranties provision of all its rights and remedies available at law. Such an explicit reservation impliedly reserves the statutory period of limitations; without such a reservation, all other reservations of actions and remedies are without effect.

The statutory period of limitations under the U.C.C. is four years after the cause of action has accrued. UCC § 2-725(1). Were we to determine that this four-year period became a part of the contract rather than the shorter one-year period, Daitom's actions on breach of warranties were timely brought and summary judgment against Daitom was error.

We realize that our conclusion requires an inference to be drawn from a construction of Daitom's terms; however, such an inference and construction are consistent with the judicial reluctance to grant summary judgment where there is some reasonable doubt over the existence of a genuine material fact. . . . When taking into account the circumstances surrounding the application of the one-year limitations period, we have little hesitation in adopting the U.C.C.'s four-year limitations reservation, the application of which permits a trial on the merits. Thus, this court must recognize that certain terms in Daitom's acceptance differed from terms in Pennwalt's offer and decide which become part of the contract. The district court certainly erred in refusing to recognize such a conflict.

The difficulty in determining the effect of different terms in the acceptance is the imprecision of drafting evident in § 2-207. The language of the provision is silent on how different terms in the acceptance are to be treated once a contract is formed pursuant to § 2-207(1). That section provides that a contract may be formed by exchanged writings despite the existence of additional or different terms in the acceptance. Therefore, an offeree's response is treated as an acceptance while it may differ substantially from the offer. This section of the provision, then, reformed the mirror-image rule; that common law legal formality that prohibited the formation of a contract if the exchanged writings of offer and acceptance differed in any term.

Once a contract is recognized pursuant to § 2-207(1), § 2-207(2) provides the standard for determining if the additional terms stated in the acceptance become a part of the contract. Between merchants, such *additional* terms become part of the resulting contract *unless* 1) the offer expressly limited acceptance to its terms, 2) the additional terms materially alter the contract obligations, or 3) the offeror gives notice of his or her objection to the additional terms within a reasonable time. Should any one of these three possibilities occur, the *additional* terms are treated merely as proposals for incorporation in the contract and absent assent by the offeror the terms of the offer control. In any event, the existence of the additional terms does not prevent a contract from being formed.

Section 2-207(2) is silent on the treatment of terms stated in the acceptance that are *different,* rather than merely additional, from those stated in the offer. It is unclear whether "different" terms in the acceptance are intended to be included under the aegis of "additional" terms in § 2-207(2) and, therefore, fail to become part of the agreement if they materially alter the contract. Comment 3 suggests just such an inclusion.[12] However, Comment 6 suggests that different terms in exchanged writings must be assumed to constitute mutual objections by each party to the other's conflicting terms and result in a mutual "knockout" of both parties' conflicting terms; the missing terms to be supplied by the U.C.C.'s "gap-filler" provisions.[13] At least one commentator, in support of this view, has suggested that the drafting history of the provision indicates that the word "different" was intentionally deleted from the final draft of § 2-207(2) to preclude its treatment under that subsection.[14] The plain language, comments, and drafting history of the provision, therefore, provide little helpful guidance in resolving the disagreement over the treatment of different terms pursuant to § 2-207.

Despite all this, the cases and commentators have suggested three possible approaches. The first of these is to treat "different" terms as included under the aegis of "additional" terms in § 2-207(2). Consequently, different terms in the acceptance would never become part of the contract, because, by definition, they would materially alter the contract (*i.e.*, the offeror's terms). Several courts have adopted this approach. . . .

---

[12] Comment 3 states (emphasis added):
Whether or not *additional or different* terms will become part of the agreement depends upon the provision of subsection (2).
It must be remembered that even official comments to enacted statutory text do not have the force of law and are only guidance in the interpretation of that text. *In re Bristol Associates, Inc.,* 505 F.2d 1056 (3d Cir. 1974) (while the comments to the Pennsylvania U.C.C. are not binding, the Pennsylvania Supreme Court gives substantial weight to the comments as evidencing application of the Code).

[13] Comment 6 states, in part:
Where clauses on confirming forms sent by both parties conflict each party must be assumed to object to a clause of the other conflicting with one on the confirmation sent by himself . . . . The contract then consists of the terms expressly agreed to, terms on which the confirmations agree, and terms supplied by the Act, including subsection (2).

[14] *See* D.G. Baird & R. Weisberg, *Rules, Standards, and the Battle of the Forms: A Reassessment of § 2-207,* 68 VA. L. REV. 1217, 1240, n.61.

The second approach, which leads to the same result as the first, is that the offeror's terms control because the offeree's different terms merely fall out; § 2-207(2) cannot rescue the different terms since that subsection applies only to *additional* terms. Under this approach, Comment 6 (apparently supporting a mutual rather than a single term knockout) is not applicable because it refers only to conflicting terms in confirmation forms following *oral* agreement, not conflicting terms in the *writings* that form the agreement. This approach is supported by Professor Summers. J.J. WHITE & R.S. SUMMERS, UNIFORM COMMERCIAL CODE, § 1-2, at 29 (2d ed. 1980).

The third, and preferable approach, which is commonly called the "knock-out" rule, is that the conflicting terms cancel one another. Under this view the offeree's form is treated only as an acceptance of the terms in the offeror's form which did not conflict. The ultimate contract, then, includes those non-conflicting terms and any other terms supplied by the U.C.C., including terms incorporated by course of performance (§ 2-208), course of dealing (§ 1-205), usage of trade (§ 1-205), and other "gap fillers" or "off-the-rack" terms (*e.g.*, implied warranty of fitness for particular purpose, § 2-315). As stated previously, this approach finds some support in Comment 6. Professor White supports this approach as the most fair and consistent with the purposes of § 2-207. WHITE & SUMMERS, *supra*, at 29. Further, several courts have adopted or recognized the approach. . . .

We are of the opinion that this is the more reasonable approach, particularly when dealing with a case such as this where from the beginning the offeror's specified period of limitations would expire before the equipment was even installed. The approaches other than the "knock-out" approach would be inequitable and unjust because they invited the very kind of treatment which the defendant attempted to provide.

Thus, we are of the conclusion that if faced with this issue the Pennsylvania Supreme Court would adopt the "knock-out" rule and hold here that the conflicting terms in Pennwalt's offer and Daitom's acceptance regarding the period of limitations and applicable warranties cancel one another out. Consequently, the other provisions of the U.C.C. must be used to provide the missing terms.

This particular approach and result are supported persuasively by the underlying rationale and purpose behind the adoption of § 2-207. As stated previously, that provision was drafted to reform the infamous common law mirror-image rule and associated last-shot doctrine that enshrined the fortuitous positions of senders of forms and accorded undue advantages based on such fortuitous positions. WHITE & SUMMERS, *supra* at 25. To refuse to adopt the "knock-out" rule and instead adopt one of the remaining two approaches would serve to re-enshrine the undue advantages derived solely from the fortuitous positions of when a party sent a form. *Cf.*, 3 DUESENBERG & KING at 93 (1983 Supp.). This is because either approach other than the knock-out rule for different terms results in the offeror and his or her terms always prevailing solely because he or she sent the first form. Professor Summers argues that this advantage is not wholly unearned, because the offeree has an opportunity to review the offer, identify the conflicting terms and make his or her acceptance conditional. But this joinder misses the fundamental purpose of the U.C.C. in general and § 2-207 in particular, which is to preserve a contract and fill in any gaps if the parties intended to make a contract and there is a reasonable basis for giving an appropriate remedy. UCC §§ 2-204(3); 2-207(1); 2-207(3). Thus, this approach gives the offeree some protection. While it is laudible [sic] for business persons to read the fine print and boilerplate provisions in exchanged forms, there is nothing in § 2-207 mandating such careful consideration. The provision seems drafted with a recognition of the reality that merchants seldom review exchanged forms with the scrutiny of lawyers. The "knock-out" rule is therefore the best approach. Even if a term eliminated by operation of the "knock-out" rule is reintroduced by operation of the U.C.C.'s gap-filler provisions, such a result does not indicate a weakness of the approach. On the contrary, at least the reintroduced term has the merit of being a term that the U.C.C. draftpersons regarded as fair.

We now address the question of reverse and remand regarding Counts I and II. The result of this court's holding is that the district court erred in granting summary judgment against Daitom on Counts I and II of its complaint. Operation of the "knock-out" rule to conflicting terms results in the instant case in the conflicting terms in the offer and acceptance regarding the period of limitations and applicable warranties cancelling. In the absence of any evidence of course of performance, course of dealing, or usage of trade providing the missing terms, §§ 2-725(1), 2-313, 2-314, 2-315 may operate to supply a four-year period of limitations, an express warranty, an implied warranty of merchantability, and an implied warranty of fitness for a particular purpose, respectively. The ruling of the district court on Counts I and II does not invite this kind of a broad inquiry, and thus, we must recognize the superiority in terms of justice of the "knock-out" rule. Consequently, the ruling of the district court on Counts I and II must be reversed and the matter remanded for trial consistent with this court's ruling. . . .

BARRETT, CIRCUIT JUDGE, dissenting:

I respectfully dissent. Insofar as the issue of contract formation is concerned in this case, we are confronted with a "battle of the forms" case involving the interpretation and application of U.C.C. 2-207. I would affirm.

Pennwalt's proposal of September 7, 1976, was an "offer." It was submitted to Daitom in response to solicitations initiated by Daitom and it contained specific terms relating to price, delivery dates, etc., and its terms were held "open" for Daitom's acceptance within 30 days. In my view, Daitom accepted the offer with its purchase order. That order repeated the quantity, model number, and price for the items as those terms appeared in the Pennwalt proposal and, by reference, it incorporated four pages of specifications attached to Pennwalt's proposal or "offer." The purchase order did contain some different and additional language from that contained in Pennwalt's proposal. However, the Code has rejected the old mirror image rule. Thus, I agree with the district court's finding/ruling that a contract was formed in the circumstances described.

I also agree with the district court's conclusion that the terms of Pennwalt's proposal constituted the "terms of the contract." I do not agree, as Daitom argues, that its "acceptance" was made "conditional" upon Pennwalt's assent to the additional/different terms set forth in Daitom's purchase order. The court correctly found no such *express* condition in Daitom's acceptance.

The "knock-out" rule should not, in my view, be reached in this case. It can be applied only if, as Daitom argues and the majority agrees, the "conflicting terms" cancel each other out. The "knock-out" rule does have substantial support in the law, but I do not believe it is relevant in this case because the *only* conflicting terms relate to the *scope* of the warranty. In this case, it is not an important consideration because, pursuant to the express time limitations contained in Pennwalt's "offer," Daitom lost its right to assert any warranty claim. There was no term in Daitom's purchase order in conflict with the express one-year limitation within which to bring warranty actions. . . .

Questions

1. One source of the "knock-out rule" is section 2-207(3). Another is comment 6 to that section. Which of these did the court in *Diatom* rely upon? Does either apply according to its terms?

2.   Do you agree with the *Diatom* court's decision to adopt the "knock-out rule"?

3.   The other issue that the *Diatom* court addressed was when is a response that *purports* to be an acceptance "expressly made conditional on assent to the additional or different terms," so that it fails to qualify as an acceptance under section 2-207(1). Do you agree with the court's analysis of Diatom's responsive form language?

4.   The two issues directly confronted by the court in *Diatom* are merely two of several that frequently arise in connection with section 2-207. Other recurring issues include: (i) how to distinguish additional terms from different terms; and (ii) if one or more of the parties is not a merchant, and thus additional terms in the acceptance are merely "proposals for addition to the contract," whether assent to the proposals can be manifested by the failure to object. The *Diatom* court implicitly dealt with the first of these two issues as it concluded that it was dealing with different terms. Do you agree with the court's conclusion on this point? What is the dissent's point regarding that issue? For a different view of the effect of a reservation of rights clause, *see Robert Bosch Corp. v. ASC Inc.*, 195 Fed. Appx. 503 (6th Cir. 2006).

The effect of the knock-out rule is often to leave the parties with whatever default term would exist under Article 2's gap filler rules. In other words, the parties' conflicting terms cancel each other out, and the contract is formed using whatever term Article 2 would supply when the parties' communications are silent on the subject involved. If one assumes that Article 2's gap fillers are fair terms, then perhaps the knock-out rule makes sense. However, consider the following scenario:

Illustration

Salvage Company acquires goods from Insurer. The goods had been stored in a warehouse that was flooded during a storm. Insurer had paid its client the replacement value of the goods and then sold the goods to Salvage Company for a small fraction of their original value. Salvage Company examined the goods and discarded the ones that were obviously defective but is unable to readily determine which of the remaining goods are merchantable and which are not. Salvage Company then sends an e-mail message to Wholesaler, offering to sell the goods without any warranty of merchantability or other warranty of quality. Wholesaler responds by sending Salvage Company a purchase order for the goods on Wholesaler's standard form. The form includes a provision that the seller warrants that the goods are merchantable. If the knock-out rule applies, Salvage Company will likely be making a warranty. *See* UCC § 2-314(1). Indeed, even if Salvage Company immediately reads Wholesaler's form, sees the problem, and calls Wholesaler to object, it is too late to change the terms of the contract (at least without Wholesaler's consent). The knock-out rule would have already bound Salvage Company to a term it expressly did not want.

Problem 2-5

A. Buyer, a consumer, telephones Seller to get a price quote and delivery date for organic apples for Buyer to use in making homemade applesauce. Buyer makes clear to Seller that Buyer is in the process of shopping for a supplier and will get back to the Seller if the Buyer is interested. After the telephone call, Seller faxes to Buyer an offer to sell 10 bushels of Crispy Pink apples for $10 per bushel, offer open until 5:00 p.m. that same day. Seller's fax contained an arbitration clause requiring binding arbitration of all disputes arising out of the agreement. Buyer sent Seller an e-mail message at 4:00 p.m. that same day stating that he would buy 10 bushels of Crispy Pink apples for $10 per bushel, delivery by Nov. 15. Is there an agreement? If so, on what terms?

B. After reading an advertisement, Buyer in Indiana telephones Seller in Illinois to order a sub-zero freezer designed for commercial use. The price is $9,200, which Buyer pays using a major credit card. Prior to shipment, Seller mails Buyer an acknowledgment of the transaction that properly describes the item and price. It also indicates that the transaction is subject to all of the terms printed on the back of the form. These terms include:

   (i) In the event of any problem with a shipment, customer must notify Seller in writing of such problem within 20 days of receipt or be barred from any remedy.

   (ii) The contract is to be governed by the law of the State of Illinois.

(iii) Any dispute arising out of this transaction shall be subject to binding arbitration.

(iv) All goods will be shipped using Careful Carriers, Inc.

Prior to shipment, is there an agreement? If so, on what terms?

C. Buyer mails Seller a purchase order for 1,000 lbs. of green beans at $78¢/lb., delivery by November 15, payment within 30 days after delivery. The purchase order indicates that the transaction is subject to all of the terms printed on the back of the form. One of these terms says: "Buyer objects in advance to any additional or different terms on Seller's acknowledgment or confirmation." Seller responds with an acknowledgment of the order which correctly restates the quantity, price, and delivery terms but indicates that, on the date of delivery, interest will start accruing on the outstanding balance due. Prior to shipment, is there an agreement? If so, on what terms?

D. Buyer mails Seller a purchase order for 1,000 lbs. of honeydew melons at $1.28¢/lb., delivery by November 15, payment within 30 days after delivery. Seller responds with an acknowledgment of the order which correctly restates the quantity, price, and delivery terms, but indicates that all disputes arising out of the transaction will be subject to binding arbitration. In addition, the acknowledgment states the following: "This acknowledgment is expressly conditional on Buyer's assent to the terms hereof." Prior to shipment, is there an agreement? If so on what terms? If not, and an agreement is created by performance, is the arbitration clause part of the agreement?

E. Buyer mails Seller a purchase order for 1,000 gallons of vanilla ice cream at $1.85/gal., delivery by November 15, payment within 30 days after delivery. The purchase order contains the following: "This purchase order is expressly conditional on assent to the terms hereof. Buyer objects in advance to any different or additional terms in any acceptance." Seller responds with an acknowledgment of the order which correctly restates the quantity, price, and delivery terms, but indicates that all disputes arising out of the transaction will be subject to binding arbitration. One week later, Seller ships the goods and Buyer accepts them shortly after delivery. Is the arbitration clause part of the agreement?

F. Buyer telephones Seller to order 1,000 lbs. of jelly beans. During the conversation, which is very brief, they agree on a price and a delivery date. Later that day, Seller mails Buyer a written acknowledgment that states, among other things, that:

(i) In the event of any problem with the shipment, customer must notify Seller in writing of such problem within 20 days of receipt or be barred from any remedy.

(ii) The contract is to be governed by the law of the State of Illinois.

(iii) Any dispute arising out of this transaction shall be subject to binding arbitration.

The next day, before receiving Seller's acknowledgment, Buyer sends Seller its own acknowledgment of the transaction. Among other things, Buyer's acknowledgment states that:

(i) Seller will correct any problem with the shipment within 3 days of receiving notice thereof from Buyer, which notice may come within any reasonable time, regardless of whether Buyer still has possession of the goods.

(ii) Any dispute arising out of this transaction shall be subject to binding arbitration.

Prior to shipment, is there a contract? If so on what terms?

G. Buyer, who operates a small business, sees an advertisement for personal computers made by Seller. Buyer writes to Seller stating the type of computer needed and the requisite components. Seller telephones Buyer and they agree on the computer and the price. Buyer gives Seller a credit card number and Seller charges that card for the price of the computer. Seller then ships the computer. In the box are two pages of standard terms, one of which commits the parties to arbitrate all disputes under ICC Rules in New York. The terms state in bold type: "Use of the computer will constitute an acceptance of these terms." Buyer uses the computer, which turns out to be unmerchantable. Buyer concedes that a contract was formed but argues that the arbitration clause was not part of the contract. What result?[15]

---

[15]   *See Stenzel v. Dell, Inc.*, 870 A.2d 133 (Me. 2005). Judge Easterbrook, concluded that even though the buyer paid for and the seller shipped the goods before the terms were disclosed, there was a "rolling contract" that was not concluded until the buyer used the goods and section 2-207 did not apply if only one party used a standard form. *ProCD, Inc. v. Zeidenberg*, 86 F.3d 1447 (7th Cir. 1996); *Hill v. Gateway 2000, Inc.*, 105 F.3d 1147 (7th Cir. 1997), *cert. denied*, 522 U.S. 808 (1997); *accord, Westendorf v. Gateway 2000, Inc.*,

Problem 2-6

A. You represent Savanna Industries, a wholesaler of fine, colonial-style furniture to retailers throughout the country. Most of Savanna's customers telephone or fax in orders from Savanna's catalogue. Some of the faxed orders arrive on the customer's own purchase order form. Others are on the form that is included in Savanna's catalogue. Savanna is very proud of the quality of its furniture but over the years there have been a few, isolated problems. For these reasons, Savanna wants to be sure that all of its sales contracts: (i) include an agreement to arbitrate all disputes relating to the transaction; (ii) provide that the buyer must notify Savanna in writing of any problem with the goods sold within four months of delivery or be barred from any remedy; and (iii) limit Savanna's liability for defective goods to refund of the purchase price (*i.e.*, disclaim responsibility for consequential damages). Draft Savanna's acknowledgment form so that these terms will be part of Savanna's sales contracts.

B. You represent Bountiful Merchandise, Corp., which owns department stores in several states. Bountiful purchases goods from many different suppliers. Most of Bountiful's purchases are made by completing one of Bountiful's own order forms and faxing the completed form to the

---

2000 WL 307369 (Del. Ch. 2000), *aff'd*, 763 A.2d 92 (Del. 2000) (table). This analysis was rejected in *Klocek v. Gateway, Inc.*, 104 F. Supp. 2d 1332 (D. Kan. 2000), *dismissed for lack of subject matter jurisdiction*, 2000 WL 1372886 (D. Kan. 2000), *refusing to vacate first order*, 2001 WL 1568346 (D. Kan. 2001), in which the court held that the terms that came with the product were proposals for addition to the contract under section 2-207 and that the buyer did not expressly agree to that proposal. *But see Brower v. Gateway 2000, Inc.*, 676 N.Y.S.2d 569 (N.Y. Sup. Ct. App. Div. 1998), where the court refused to apply section 2-207 to a transaction where the contract was not formed until the 30-day period had expired but held that the arbitration clause, because of the prohibitive cost involved in the arbitration, was substantively unconscionable.

Of course, there are a legion of law review articles on this issue. *See, e.g.,* Ronald J. Mann & Travis Siebeneicher, *Just One Click, The Reality of Internet Retail Contracting*, 108 COLUM. L. REV. 984 (2008); Wayne R. Barnes, *Toward a Fairer Model of Consumer Assent to Standard Form Contracts: In Defense of Restatement Subsection 211(3)*, 82 WASH. L. REV. 227 (2007); Peter A. Alces, *Guerilla Terms*, 56 EMORY L.J. 1511 (2007); Robert A. Hillman, *Online Boilerplate: Would Mandatory Web Disclosure of E-Standard Terms Backfire?*, 104 MICH. L. REV. 837 (2006); Stephen E. Friedman, *Improving the Rolling Contract*, 56 AM. U. L. REV. 1 (2006).

seller.   Bountiful insists that all its suppliers: (i) warrant the merchantability of their goods and be responsible for all consequential damages; (ii) agree that payment will be due, without interest, 90 days after delivery; and (iii) agree that if they sell the same goods to anyone else at a lower price within six months after the sale to Bountiful, they will retroactively lower the price charged to Bountiful to the lowest price charged to anyone else, and promptly rebate the difference. Draft Bountiful's order form so that these terms will be part of Bountiful's sales contracts.

C. Assume that Bountiful ordered goods from Savanna using the form you drafted in Part B. Savanna responded on the acknowledgment form you drafted in Part A.

   1. Before shipment, is there a contract? If so, what are its terms?

   2. How, if at all, would the analysis of Subpart 1 change if Savanna shipped the goods and Bountiful accepted and paid for them?

D. Based upon the above exercise, what methodology would you recommend to Bountiful to ensure that the terms it wanted were always a part of a contract, no matter how the contract was formed? Would you have a different methodology to recommend to Savanna to ensure that it would have the terms it wanted, no matter how the contract was formed?

The Article 2 revision struggled with the question of how to deal with the battle of the forms problem. Discussion of amended section 2-207 is in the Appendix. In essence, the issue is how to deal with the fact that businesses use standard forms to try to set terms of their contracts, in case something goes awry in a transaction. That being said, however, the vast majority of transactions are performed properly and nothing goes wrong. Thus, business people involved in the exchange of standard forms routinely pay no attention to the terms in the forms they give and receive. The only time the terms matter is if a dispute arises.[16] Given that

---

[16]   Section 2-207 results in significant amounts of litigation. *See, e.g., Foamade Indus. v. Visteon Corp.*, 2008 WL 582566 (Mich. Ct. App. 2008); *Tacoma Fixture Co. v. Rudd Co.*, 174 P.3d 721 (Wash. Ct. App.), *review denied*, 190 P.3d 55 (Wash. 2008); *Coosemans Specialties, Inc. v. Gargiulo*, 485 F.3d 701 (2d Cir. 2007); *E.C. Styberg Eng'g Co. v. Eaton Corp.*, 492 F.3d 912 (7th Cir. 2007); *Robert Bosch Corp. v. ASC Inc.*, 195 Fed. Appx. 503 (6th Cir. 2006); *Roanoke Cement Co., L.L.C. v. Falk Corp.*, 413 F.3d 431 (4th Cir. 2005); *Marvin Lumber and Cedar Co. v. PPG Industries, Inc.*, 401 F.3d 901 (8th Cir. 2005);

operational construct, what legal principles should be used to determine whether a contract was formed from an exchange of forms? What legal principles should apply to determine the terms of such contracts?[17]

3.   *Electronic Contracting and Assent*

An increasing percentage of sales contracting is conducted through electronic means. We do not mean merely through electronically transmitted communications, such as e-mail and fax. We mean also through computer-assisted technologies that obviate the need for a human representative of one or both of the parties involved. For example, one common practice with which you are no doubt familiar is for a customer to visit the website of the seller and order goods or services on line. In such situations, no human representative of the seller participates in the contract-formation process

Typically, two different methods are used to manifest assent in such transactions. In so-called "click-wrap" agreements, the person using a computer to conduct a transaction (typically the buyer) uses a mouse to click an "I agree" button after the terms of the agreement are displayed. This form of agreement is commonly used in the downloading or installation of software but it could just as easily be used in a sale of goods or a lease of goods.[18] Another practice in the

---

Standard Bent Glass Corp. v. Glassrobots Oy, 333 F.3d 440 (3d Cir. 2003); *Polytop Corp. v. Chipsco, Inc.*, 826 A.2d 945 (R.I. 2003) (per curium); *Southern Illinois Riverboat Casino Cruises, Inc. v. Triangle Insulation and Sheet Metal Co.*, 302 F.3d 667 (7th Cir. 2002).

[17]   Lawyers (and law professors) love this issue and have produce extensive law review articles on it. *See, e.g.,* Stephen W. Ranere, Note, *Charting a Course: How Courts Should Interpret Course of Dealing in a Battle-of-Forms Dispute*, 41 SUFFOLK U. L. REV. 671 (2008); Corneill A. Stephens, *Escape From the Battle of the Forms: Keep It Simple, Stupid*, 11 LEWIS & CLARK L. REV. 233 (2007); Colin P. Marks, *The Limits of Limiting Liability in the Battle of the Forms: U.C.C. Section 2-207 and the "Material Alteration" Inquiry*, 33 PEPPERDINE L. REV. 501 (2006); Omri Ben-Shahar, *An Ex-Ante View of the Battle of the Forms: Inducing Parties to Draft Reasonable Terms*, 25 INT'L REV. L. & ECON. 350 (2005).

[18]   *See* Robert Lee Dickens, *Finding Common Ground in the World of Electronic Contracts: The Consistency of Legal Reasoning in Clickwrap Cases*, 11 MARQ. INTELL. PROP. L. REV. 379 (2007); Nancy S. Kim, *Clicking and Cringing*, 86 OR. L. REV. 797 (2007); Christina L. Kunz, *et al.*, *Click-Through Agreements: Strategies for Avoiding Disputes on Validity of Assent*, 57 BUS. LAW. 401 (2001). *See, e.g., Hotels.com, L.P. v. Canales*, 195

electronic environment is the use of so-called "browse-wrap" agreements. In this type of transaction, the user of the electronic interface may click on a button that says "place order," "confirm order," or "I agree," but the only terms of the agreement that are displayed are the description of the goods, the price, the quantity, and perhaps the shipping terms. The other terms are not displayed, but the website may provide a link to them or may simply display a notice that the transaction is governed by a set of terms and that using the website or engaging in some defined conduct will bind the user to the terms.[19]

At this point we are examining electronic contracting as it impacts the issue of assent to a bargain. We will consider some of the other issues in electronic contracting later in this Chapter.

Problem 2-7

Abel visits Retailer's website and decides to order a new toaster advertised for sale on the website. Abel clicks on the picture of the toaster and adds the toaster to his electronic shopping cart.

A. A screen pops up with the various terms including the following: "Any disputes concerning any product provided through this website must be resolved in binding arbitration." Two buttons are under the pop up screen one of which states "I agree" and the other of which states "I disagree." To actually complete the purchase, Abel must click on the "I agree" button. Clicking on the "I disagree" button removes the item from the electronic shopping cart. Abel clicks on "I agree" and completes ordering of the toaster. When the toaster arrives, it is a miserable failure at toasting anything. Is Abel bound by the arbitration clause?

S.W.3d 147 (Tex. Ct. App. 2006).

[19]   *See* Ian Rambarran & Robert Hunt, *Are Browse-Wrap Agreements All They Are Wrapped Up to Be?*, 9 TUL. J. TECH. & INTELL. PROP. 173 (2007); Mark A. Lemley, *Terms of Use*, 91 MINN. L. REV. 459 (2006); Christina L. Kunz, *et al.*, *Browse-Wrap Agreements: Validity of Implied Assent in Electronic Form Agreements*, 59 BUS. LAW. 279 (2003). *See, e.g.*, *Southwest Airlines Co. v. BoardFirst, L.L.C.*, 2007 WL 4823761 (N.D. Tex. 2007).

For a discussion of other perspectives on electronic contracting, see Sylvia Mercado Kierkegaard, *E-contract Formation: U.S. and EU Perspectives*, 3 SHIDLER J. L. COM. & TECH. 12 (2007); Jane K. Winn & Brian H. Bix, *Diverging Perspectives on Electronic Contracting in the U.S. and EU*, 54 CLEV. ST. L. REV. 175 (2006).

B. Assume instead of the pop up screen as described above, when Abel clicks on the picture of the toaster to place the toaster in his electronic shopping cart, the screen changes to provide a hyperlink which states, "click here for terms of sale." Abel does not click on the hyperlink but rather completes his purchase of the toaster. If Abel had clicked on the hyperlink, Abel would have seen the same arbitration clause as stated above. When the toaster arrives, it is a miserable failure at toasting anything. Is Abel bound by the arbitration clause?

C. You have been asked to advise a retailer who is in the process of establishing a website on which customers may place their orders. What reasons, if any, are there for recommending a browse-wrap agreement rather than click-wrap agreement?

B. CONTRACT FORMATION IN INTERNATIONAL TRANSACTIONS

1. CISG

The provisions for forming a contract governed by the CISG are found in Articles 14 through 24. These rules resemble the offer and acceptance rules of the common law more closely than they do the contract formation rules of Article 2. Article 14 defines an offer and requires that it be definite about the description of the goods, the quantity, and the price. Articles 15, 16, and 17 govern the effectiveness and revocation of offers. Articles 18, 20, 21, and 22 govern the manner and timing of acceptances.

Most notable is Article 19, which presents another approach to the battle of the forms.[20] To understand it, it is advisable to read its three sub-articles in order. Sub-article (1) adopts something very much like the common-law mirror image rule. A reply which purports to be an acceptance but which contains different or additional terms is really a rejection and counter-offer. Sub-article (2) cuts back on

---

[20]   *See* Henry D. Gabriel, *The Battle of the Forms: A Comparison of the United Nations Convention for the International Sale of Goods and the Uniform Commercial Code*, 49 BUS. LAW. 1053 (1994). For a survey of different countries' approaches to the battle of the forms issues concerning standard terms, *see* Kevin C. Stemp, *A Comparative Analysis of the "Battle of the Forms,"* 15 TRANSNATIONAL L. & CONTEMP. PROB. 243 (2005); James R. Maxeiner, *Standard-Terms Contracting in the Global Electronic Age: European Alternatives*, 28 YALE J. INT'L L. 109 (2003).

sub-article (1) by indicating that if the additional or different terms do not materially alter the terms of the offer, then the reply is an acceptance. The additional or different terms will become part of the contract unless the offeror promptly objects to them. Sub-article (3) significantly minimizes the scope of sub-article (2), however, by providing that virtually every conceivable term is in fact material.

To illustrate, assume that a buyer in California sends an offer in a record to a seller in Mexico City.[21] The seller responds with a record that purports to accept the offer but also contains a clause changing the delivery date. The seller ships later than the buyer expected but in accord with the seller's delivery date. The buyer accepts the goods and then uses them, even though it is very unhappy about the timing of the delivery. Under CISG Article 19, the seller's reply is a counter-offer because it contains an additional term (the delivery clause) that materially alters the offer. Buyer's conduct in accepting the goods indicates assent to the counter-offer, including the delivery clause. CISG Art. 18(3). In essence, the CISG adopts something like the last-shot rule that UCC section 2-207(1) sought to avoid. Under this construct, commercial parties under the CISG must read and object to terms in the forms or risk agreeing to them.

Problem 2-8

Revisit Problem 2-5. What would be the result in Parts B, C, and D if the transaction were governed by the CISG? What would be the result in each of those Parts if the transaction were governed by the CISG and the parties went ahead and performed (shipped and accepted the goods).[22]

---

[21]   Both the United States and Mexico have ratified the CISG.

[22]   *See Chateau des Charmes Wines Ltd. v. Sabate USA Inc.*, 328 F.3d 528 (9th Cir. 2003) (party who did not object to forum selection clause in other side's invoice sent after agreement formed did not agree to clause as the CISG requires agreement to terms and does not enforce unilateral attempts to modify terms).

Even if an arbitration clause is part of the parties' agreement under the CISG analysis, it still might not be enforceable. The United Nations Convention on the Recognition and Enforcement of Foreign Arbitral Awards (the New York Convention) requires an "agreement in writing" to arbitrate and then defines "agreement in writing" to "include an arbitral clause in a contract or an arbitration agreement, signed by the parties, or contained in an exchange of letters or telegrams." Art. II(2).

2.   *UNIDROIT Principles*

The UNIDROIT Principles of International Commercial Contracts are for international contracts what the Restatement (Second) of Contracts is for domestic transactions. They are not law, but they may provide persuasive guidance to courts and to parties. The UNIDROIT Principles on contract formation are closely analogous to the UCC Article 2 rules on contract formation. Offer and acceptance as well as the conduct of the parties may be sufficient to show agreement. UNIDROIT Art. 2.1.1. In addition, if the parties intend to agree, they may leave terms open yet still have a valid agreement. UNIDROIT Art. 2.1.14. The Principles contain a number of familiar offer and acceptance rules. UNIDROIT Arts. 2.1.2 through 2.1.13.

In a battle of the forms, a response that purports to be an acceptance but which contains non-material additional or different terms is treated as an acceptance. UNIDROIT Art. 2.1.11. The non-material terms become part of the agreement unless the offerer objects to the terms. *Id.* If the term is a standard term (whether material or non- material), the term is not effective if it is "not reasonably expected" by the other party or the other party has not "expressly accepted" it. UNIDROIT Art. 2.1.20. If the parties agree to terms and they also have standard terms that are "common in substance" the parties have a contract on those terms unless the other party indicates in advance or without undue delay that it does not intend to be bound to the contract. UNIDROIT Art. 2.1.22. Standard terms are "provisions which are prepared in advance for general and repeated use by one party and which are actually used without negotiation with the other party." UNIDROIT Art. 2.1.19.

SECTION 2.   BARRIERS TO ENFORCEABILITY

A. STATUTE OF FRAUDS

1.   *In General*

Some oral agreements are not enforceable because a statute of frauds requires that the agreement be evidenced by a signed writing to become a valid contract. Historically, the types of agreements covered by a statute of frauds include agreements to buy and sell real estate and agreements that cannot be performed within one year.[23] The Uniform Commercial Code has several provisions that could fairly be regarded as a statute of frauds,[24] including one applicable to the sale of goods. Read section 2-201.

The statute of frauds functions as a barrier to enforcement of an alleged agreement. If the plaintiff cannot prove compliance with the statute of frauds, the plaintiff's claim will fail. The typical lawsuit follows either of two patterns. After the plaintiff sues the defendant for breach of contract, the defendant either:

(i)   submits a motion to dismiss, alleging that the plaintiff has not pled satisfaction of the statute of frauds; or

(ii) pleads the statute of frauds as an affirmative defense in its answer, and later moves for summary judgment on the basis that the plaintiff has not been able to produce a writing or other sufficient evidence to satisfy the statute of frauds.

Bear in mind that even if the plaintiff submits evidence that satisfies the statute of frauds, that does not mean that the plaintiff has proven that a contract exists. Satisfying the statute of frauds merely unlocks the door to the courthouse and allows the plaintiff the opportunity to prove the rest of its case. The plaintiff still has the burden of proving that the contract existed, what its terms were, and that the defendant breached it.

Two principal justifications have been asserted for the statute of frauds. First, the statute of frauds avoids fraudulent or perjured claims that an agreement was made. Second, the statute encourages the useful business habit of making a writing.[25] You should question these assertions. With respect to the first, it is worth noting that the CISG does not have a statute of frauds, *see* CISG Art. 11, and the UNIDROIT Principles do not require a writing of any sort, *see* UNIDROIT Art. 1.2. Indeed, England, which is where the statute of frauds originated, abandoned it more than a half-century ago. Moreover, while the statute of frauds may prevent one type of fraud – seeking judicial enforcement of an agreement that never existed

---

[23]   *See* RESTATEMENT (SECOND) OF CONTRACTS § 110(1)(d), (e).

[24]   *See* UCC §§ 5-104, 9-203(b)(3). Article 8 used to have a statute of frauds, *see* former § 8-319, but it was repealed as part of the 1994 revisions. *See* Art. 8 Prefatory Note IV.B.7. The pre-revision version of Article 1 also had a general statue of frauds for transactions in excess of $5,000, *see* former § 1-206, but that too was repealed in the revision process.

[25]   *See* Lawrence Vold, *The Application of the Statute of Frauds Under the Uniform Sales Act,* 15 MINN. L. REV. 391, 393–94 (1931); Jason S. Johnston, *The Statute of Frauds and Business Norms: A Testable Game-Theoretic Model,* 144 U. PA. L. REV. 1859 (1996).

– it would seem to increase the likelihood of another: denial of the existence of an agreement that was reached. The second justification presumes that encouraging individuals and businesses to memorialize their agreements is worth the added cost and that individuals and businesses will in fact modify their behavior because of the law. Both of these require some empirical research to confirm.

Problem 2-9

What does a plaintiff have to plead and prove to demonstrate compliance with section 2-201(1)? Based upon these requirements, what would you advise a client who is entering into transactions to do to ensure there is sufficient evidence to satisfy the statute of frauds?

2. The Exceptions

The general rule in section 2-201(1) is subject to four exceptions: one in subsection (2) and three in subsection (3). Subsection (2) is known as the "merchants must read their mail rule."[26] It provides that a merchant's receipt of a confirmation may be sufficient to satisfy the statute of frauds if the merchant fails to object in writing within ten days. Is it a good idea to limit this exception to communications "between merchants?"[27] Who qualifies as a merchant for the purposes of this rule? *See* UCC § 2-104 & cmt. 2.

Problem 2-10

A. The exception in section 2-201(2) applies only if the confirmation is "sufficient against the sender." What does that phrase mean and how does it limit the scope of subsection (2)? Construct a scenario in which the confirmation is sufficient against the sender and another in which the confirmation is not.

B. Silas runs a hardware store as a sole proprietor. Brittany is starting a landscaping business and needs to buy a large riding mower. On April

---

[26] A point that is also borne out by UCC § 2-207(2).

[27] *See* Larry T. Garvin, *Small Business and the False Dichotomies of Contract Law*, 40 WAKE FOREST L. REV. 295 (2005).

1, Brittany visited Silas's store and discussed purchasing a Jack Stallion 3000 riding mower for $3,700. The following day, Brittany sent an e-mail message to Silas, stating the following:

> Thanks for talking with me yesterday. This message is to confirm our agreement that I will be buying a Jack Stallion 3000 for $3,700, payment to be 90 days after delivery. I will come by on April 15 to pick up the mower. Thanks. – Brittany

Silas responded with the following message:

> I never agreed to payment in 90 days. I cannot possibly do business on such terms. I am happy to try to work something out with you or to arrange for alternative financing, but you'll have to come in to discuss it. – Silas.

If Brittany and Silas have no further discussions, and Brittany sues Silas for breach of contract, can Silas successfully raise the statute of frauds defense? If not, do they have a contract? What should Silas have done to preserve the statute of frauds defense?

CASAZZA V. KISER
313 F.3d 414 (8th Cir. 2002)

Bowman, Circuit Judge

This appeal arises from James Casazza's ill-fated effort to purchase a fifty-two-foot sailboat named the *"Andante"* from Joseph C. Kiser. Casazza sued Kiser seeking damages under the legal theories of breach of contract and promissory estoppel for Kiser's failure to sell him this boat. The District Court granted Kiser's motion to dismiss. We affirm.

I. Background

In late May 2001, Casazza read Kiser's listing of the *Andante* on an internet sales site. Shortly thereafter, Casazza contacted Kiser and expressed an interest in purchasing the boat. They agreed to meet during the weekend of June 2, 2001, in Ft. Lauderdale, Florida, where the *Andante* was located. Casazza first viewed the boat on June 2 and looked at it again with Kiser the following day. Casazza and Kiser met again on June 4, 2001, and, according to Casazza, negotiated an agreement for Casazza's purchase of the *Andante*. The details of this agreement were handwritten by each party on separate sheets of paper and at some point converted, presumably by Casazza, into a typewritten agreement (collectively, the "purchase terms"). That agreement provided for a sales price of $200,000 for the boat. The agreement further stated the sale was contingent on a marine survey, including a sea trial, satisfactory to Casazza. Among other provisions, the agreement also required payment by wire transfer and replacement of the mast step, and it detailed the logistics of transferring the boat from Florida to Virginia. Kiser never signed the agreement and the marine survey and sea trial did not take place.

During their meeting on June 4, Kiser gave Casazza a blank Coast Guard bill of sale to complete. The next day, Kiser and Casazza executed a software license transfer agreement for the boat's navigational software. This license agreement is the only document in the dispute signed by both parties and it does not refer to the *Andante*. Following these events, Casazza arranged for a marine survey, obtained an estimate for repair of the mast step, visited marinas, and tentatively reserved slip space for the *Andante* at a marina in Virginia. Things apparently went awry a week later, however, when Kiser informed Casazza that he would not sell him the boat. In response, Casazza initiated this suit and sought a temporary restraining order (TRO) to prevent Kiser from selling the *Andante* to someone else. While the application for the TRO was pending, but before Kiser had notice of it, Kiser sold the boat. Casazza amended his complaint and Kiser moved to dismiss the case on the basis of the statute of frauds. Casazza responded to Kiser's motion to dismiss and filed a Federal Rule of Civil Procedure 56(f) motion and affidavit requesting that the District Court's consideration of the motion to dismiss be delayed pending additional discovery.

On January 15, 2002, the District Court dismissed the action, concluding that additional discovery would not assist the court in the resolution of whether the statute of frauds applies to the dispute and that the defense barred Casazza's breach of contract and promissory estoppel claims. The District Court denied Casazza's motion for reconsideration. On appeal, Casazza argues the District Court erred in dismissing his claims.

II. Discussion

. . . We review de novo a district court's order granting a motion to dismiss, viewing the allegations in the complaint in the light most favorable to the plaintiff. . . . Like the District Court, we must accept the allegations of the complaint as true and dismiss the case only when "it appears beyond doubt that the plaintiff can prove no set of facts in support of his claim which would entitle him to relief." *Conley v. Gibson,* 355 U.S. 41, 45-46 (1957).

A. *The Statute of Frauds Defense*

Casazza contends the District Court erred when it dismissed his breach of contract claim, holding it was barred by the statute of frauds. Subject to certain limited exceptions, the statute of frauds renders unenforceable any unwritten contract for the sale of goods with a value over $500.... [Court applied Minnesota law – Eds.] Because Kiser raised the statute of frauds defense in his motion to dismiss, Casazza was required to affirmatively show the existence of an appropriate writing or an exception to this defense in order to avoid dismissal by the District Court. In this appeal, Casazza argues that the alleged contract was taken out of the statute of frauds by (1) the doctrine of part performance, (2) the existence of a sufficient writing, and (3) the possibility that Kiser may have a sufficient writing or that Kiser might admit a contract was formed between the parties had the District Court granted Casazza's request for additional time for discovery. All these arguments are without merit.

(1) *Part Performance*

Under the part-performance exception to the statute of frauds, a writing is not required "with respect to goods for which payment has been made and accepted or which have been received and accepted." [§ 2-201(3)(c)]. Here, Casazza contends that his acceptance of the navigational software constitutes part performance of the parties' alleged agreement concerning the sale of the *Andante*. In support of this claim, Casazza relies on section [2-606(2)], which provides that "[a]cceptance of a part of any commercial unit is acceptance of that entire unit." According to Casazza, the navigational software is part of the *Andante*. Thus, Casazza argues, when he accepted this software, he accepted the *Andante*.

First, we question the applicability of section [2-606(2)] to the present dispute. The drafters of the commercial code designed this provision to limit a buyer's right of revocation of acceptance to whole units. As the Ninth Circuit observed of the uniform provision at issue here, "The commercial unit provision is included to protect *a seller* from having a buyer return *less* than a commercial unit. Return of less than a commercial unit would leave the seller with only components of a commercial unit, which would have severely reduced market value." *S & R Metals, Inc. v. C. Itoh & Co. (America),* 859 F.2d 814, 817 (9th Cir.1988) (first emphasis added) (citing *Abbett v. Thompson,* 263 N.E.2d 733, 735–36 (Inc. Ct. App. 1970) (holding buyer could not keep some parts of a car wash machine and revoke acceptance of the rest because the entire machine was a commercial unit and would have little value to the seller if incomplete)).

Second, even assuming section [2-606(2)] applies to the instant dispute, we conclude that under no circumstances could the software and the *Andante* be considered a single "commercial unit." Minnesota's Uniform Commercial Code states that:

> "Commercial unit" means such a unit of goods as by commercial usage is a single whole for purposes of sale and division of which materially impairs its character or value on the market or in use. A commercial unit may be a single article (as a machine) or a set of articles (as a suite of furniture or an assortment of sizes) or a quantity (as a bale, gross, or carload) or any other unit treated in use or in the relevant market as a single whole.

Minn.Stat. § 336.2-105(6) (2000). Viewing Casazza's allegations in the light most favorable to him, we are hard-pressed to see how the navigational software and the *Andante* are a "single whole." Notably, Casazza concedes that the navigational software was purchased years after the *Andante* was built and that Kiser sold the boat to another party without it. Though Casazza distinguishes some cases cited in Kiser's brief, Casazza fails to cite a single case in support of his position that this Court should treat the *Andante* and the navigational software as a commercial unit, and our own research has not revealed any authority supporting this position. In short, we agree with the District Court that the doctrine of part performance cannot transmute Kiser's gift of the navigational software into a contract for the sale of the *Andante*.

(2) *Sufficient Writing*

Casazza also argues that the statute of frauds is inapplicable to this dispute because there is a sufficient writing showing the existence of a contract between the parties. The primary purpose of the writing requirement in the statute of frauds is to demonstrate that a contract for sale has indeed been made. *See* 1, JAMES J. WHITE & ROBERT S. SUMMERS, UNIFORM COMMERCIAL CODE § 2-4, at 63 (4th ed.1995). But the statute does not require one writing containing all the terms. *See Simplex Supplies, Inc. v. Abhe & Svoboda, Inc.,* 586 N.W.2d 797, 801 (Minn. Ct. App. 1998). Rather, "[s]everal papers may be taken together to make up the memorandum, providing they refer to one another, or are so connected together, by reference or by internal evidence, that parol testimony is not necessary to establish their connection with the contract." *Id.* (quoting *Olson v. Sharpless,* 55 N.W. 125, 126 (Minn. 1893)). In addition, "[t]he signature can be found on any document and may consist of 'any symbol executed or adopted by a party with present intention to authenticate a writing.'" *Id.* (quoting [§ 1-201(39)]). Casazza argues that the purchase terms, in particular the notes allegedly made by Kiser, and the executed software license transfer agreement constitute a sufficient writing. We disagree.

Casazza admits that he does not have a copy of a document that satisfies the statute of frauds. Casazza attempts to overcome this obstacle by arguing his pleadings reference the existence of a handwritten document allegedly prepared by Kiser, which – along with the executed software transfer agreement – constitute a sufficient writing. The typewritten agreement attached to Casazza's amended complaint is not signed by Kiser and there is no allegation that Kiser participated in its preparation. While Kiser did sign the software license transfer agreement, that document does not refer to any contemplated, proposed, or agreed contract for the sale of the *Andante*. We refuse to allow Casazza to proceed with his breach of contract claim on this basis because to do so would eviscerate the statute of frauds. Casazza has failed to produce any document, or combination of documents, that satisfy the statute of frauds' writing requirement. Casazza's statements that a writing sufficient to satisfy the statute of frauds *may* exist is not enough to defeat Kiser's motion to dismiss.

(3) *Admissions Exception*

In a related argument, Casazza argues that the admissions exception to the statute of frauds applies to this dispute. *See* [§ 2-201(3)(b)]. That subsection provides that even when there is no signed writing sufficient to satisfy the writing requirement, the proponent of the exception can escape the requirements of the statute of frauds "if the party against whom enforcement is sought admits in pleading, testimony or otherwise in court that a contract for sale was made." *Id.* Here, Kiser has made no such admission. Nonetheless, Casazza argues that had the District Court granted his request for additional time for discovery pursuant to Fed. R. Civ. P. 56(f), Kiser might have made such an admission. Specifically, Casazza claims that Kiser may have a sufficient writing or that Kiser might admit a contract was formed between the parties if he were deposed. The District Court denied the request and found that resolution of whether the statute of frauds applies to the dispute did not require further factual development.

In light of our decision affirming the District Court's decision to dismiss Casazza's breach of contract claim, we need not reach the discovery issues raised in Casazza's Rule 56(f) petition. . . . The District Court held a hearing on the motion to dismiss on January 14, 2002. By that time – six months after the suit was filed – Casazza still had not produced any writing sufficient to satisfy the statute of frauds nor had he obtained an admission from Kiser that a contract existed. Given the period of time that elapsed and the conclusory nature of Casazza's request for a continuance, we find the District Court did not abuse its discretion by denying further discovery and ruling on the motion to dismiss. . . .

B. *Promissory Estoppel*

Casazza alternatively argues that even if the alleged contract fails to satisfy the statute of frauds, his case should be permitted to proceed because a statute of frauds defense is inapplicable to his promissory estoppel claim. The District Court rejected this argument, holding that Casazza's promissory estoppel claim rests on the same purported promise that forms the basis of his breach of contract claim and that to allow Casazza to pursue the promissory estoppel claim, despite the lack of a sufficient writing, "would negate the purpose of the statute of frauds." Memorandum and Order, January 15, 2002, at 5 n.1.

Promissory estoppel implies "a contract in law where none exists in fact." *Grouse v. Group Health Plan, Inc.,* 306 N.W.2d 114, 116 (Minn. 1981). "Under promissory estoppel, a promise which is expected to induce definite action by the promisee, and does induce the action, is binding if injustice can be avoided only by enforcing the promise." *Cohen v. Cowles Media Co.,* 479 N.W.2d 387, 391 (Minn. 1992).

In *Del Hayes & Sons, Inc. v. Mitchell,* 230 N.W.2d 588, 593-94 (Minn. 1975), the Minnesota Supreme Court identified three approaches courts have taken concerning the applicability of the statute of frauds defense to promissory estoppel claims. Under the first (or "RESTATEMENT") approach, "promissory estoppel will defeat the statute of frauds only when the promise relied upon is a promise to reduce the contract to writing." *Id.* The second approach described by the court, and adopted in numerous jurisdictions, rejects "the view that promissory estoppel can remove an oral contract from the statute of frauds." *Id.* at 594; *see also Lige Dickson Co. v. Union Oil Co.,* 635 P.2d 103, 107 (Wash. 1981) (holding "promissory estoppel cannot be used to overcome the statute of frauds in a case which involves the sale of goods"). According to the court, jurisdictions that have adopted this approach "do so because a promissory estoppel exception would likely render the statute of frauds nugatory." *Del Hayes,* 230 N.W.2d at 594; *see also McDabco, Inc. v. Chet Adams Co.,* 548 F. Supp. 456, 461 (D.S.C.1982) ("The [South Carolina] legislature has provided that the only exceptions to the requirements of a written contract of sale are provided in [section 2-201(2) and (3)]. Promissory estoppel is not included within these subsections."). The third and least restrictive approach described by the court states that an oral promise can satisfy the statute of frauds only "where the detrimental reliance is of such a character and magnitude that refusal to enforce the contract would permit one party to perpetrate a fraud." *Del Hayes,* 230 N.W.2d at 594. The court went on to note that "[a] mere refusal to perform an oral agreement, unaccompanied by unconscionable conduct, however, is not such a fraud as will justify disregarding the statute." *Id.; see also Resolution Trust Corp. v. Flanagan,* 821 F. Supp. 572, 574 (D. Minn.1993) ("under the doctrine of promissory estoppel, a party seeking to take an agreement out of the 'statute of frauds must demonstrate that application of the statute of frauds would protect, rather than prevent, the perpetration of a fraud' "). The *Del Hayes* court did not endorse any particular view and held that, under any approach, promissory estoppel was not available so as to remove the oral contract at issue in that case from the statute of frauds. *Del Hayes,* 230 N.W.2d at 594.

In this case, the District Court apparently adopted the second or "restrictive" approach, which prohibits Casazza from doing an end-run around the statute of frauds because his promissory estoppel claim is based on the very promise that the statute otherwise bars. We might be inclined to agree with Casazza that Minnesota does not endorse such a hard-nosed view. . . . Nonetheless, we affirm the District Court's dismissal of Casazza's promissory estoppel claim. Even if we assume Casazza is correct that Minnesota does not endorse the view that promissory estoppel can never overcome the statute of frauds defense in a case such as this, he fails to convince us that his claim could proceed under either of the remaining approaches discussed by the Minnesota Supreme Court in *Del Hayes.*

Casazza's promissory estoppel claim fails under the RESTATEMENT approach because he did not sufficiently allege that Kiser promised to reduce their oral agreement to writing. Casazza argues he made a sufficient allegation in his amended complaint, where he alleged that Kiser asked him to complete a blank Coast Guard bill of sale. In ruling on Casazza's motion for reconsideration, the District Court rejected this argument and held that "[e]ven a liberal reading of the Complaint . . . does not support the inclusion of such a claim." Order, February 7, 2002, at 2. Based on our own review of the amended complaint, we agree. The bill of sale is mentioned in only one line of Casazza's five-page amended complaint. Nowhere in this complaint does Casazza specifically allege that Kiser promised to reduce their oral agreement to writing. . . .

Casazza's promissory estoppel claim also fails under the so-called least restrictive approach. Under this approach, Casazza's promissory estoppel claim can only proceed "where the detrimental reliance is of such a character and magnitude that refusal to enforce the contract would permit one party to perpetrate a fraud."

Del Hayes, 230 N.W.2d at 594. . . . Here, Casazza alleges that he and Kiser reached an agreement on the sale of the *Andante* and that he subsequently arranged for a survey, obtained an estimate for some repairs, visited marinas, and tentatively arranged slip space for the boat. Casazza also alleges that a week later, Kiser told him he was not going to sell him the boat. Nowhere in Casazza's amended complaint does he allege that Kiser did anything that would constitute a fraud. At most, Casazza alleges that Kiser broke their oral agreement after Casazza had expended some money and time in anticipation of buying the boat.

Casazza's allegations simply do not amount to detrimental reliance of the sort required to take this agreement out of the statute of frauds. *See Del Hayes,* 230 N.W.2d at 594 n.11 ("The fraud most commonly treated as taking an agreement out of the Statute of Frauds" occurs where "the other party has been induced to make expenditures or a change of situation . . . , *so that the refusal to complete the execution of the agreement is not merely a denial of rights which it was intended to confer, but the infliction of an unjust and unconscionable injury and loss.*" (quoting 3 WILLISTON, CONTRACTS (3d ed.) § 533A, p. 798) (emphasis added by *Del Hayes*)). Whatever we might think of Kiser's behavior, we find nothing in the pleadings to suggest that judicial refusal to enforce the oral agreement "would permit one party to perpetrate a fraud." *Id.* "[A] mere refusal to perform an oral agreement unaccompanied by unconscionable conduct . . . is not such a fraud as will justify disregarding the statute." *Id.* Casazza's promissory estoppel claim therefore must fail.

III. Conclusion

For the reasons stated, we affirm the order of the District Court dismissing Casazza's suit.

Notes

1. For a slightly different view on the amount of discovery a plaintiff may conduct before dismissing the complaint, see *DF Activities Corp. v. Brown,* 851 F.2d 920 (7th Cir 1988) (once defendant denies under oath the existence of the agreement, case should be dismissed).

2. For a different take on the use of promissory estoppel to circumvent the statute of frauds, see *B & W Glass, Inc. v. Weather Shield Mfg., Inc.,*

829 P.2d 809 (Wy. 1992) (promissory estoppel may justify enforcement of oral promise otherwise within the scope of UCC § 2-201).

Problem 2-11

What should Casazza have done in the interaction with Kiser to make sure that he would have been able to satisfy the statute of frauds? Would a confirming memorandum under section 2-201(2) have worked in this situation? Are Casazza and Kiser merchants? *See* UCC § 2-104.

Assume both parties are merchants and you are advising Casazza during the course of this interaction. What should Casazza have done? Now change sides and consider how Kiser should respond to the advice you gave Casazza.

Modifications to an existing agreement also may have to be in writing, either because the initial agreement requires modifications to be in writing or because the statute of frauds applies to the agreement as modified. *See* UCC § 2-209(2), (3). We will consider modifications further in Chapter Three.

Problem 2-12

BIM and Silicon Solutions allegedly entered an oral agreement for Silicon Solutions to produce and sell to BIM 50,000 integrated circuits for use in computers. The circuits were to conform to particular specifications furnished by BIM. BIM then issued purchase orders for 7,000 circuits. After manufacture and delivery, BIM accepted and paid for 4,000 circuits but rejected the remaining 3,000 on the basis of alleged quality problems. Silicon Solutions sued for damages caused by BIM's "wrongful" rejection of 3,000 circuits and for breach of contract for BIM's failure to order the remaining 43,000 circuits. BIM moved for a summary judgment on the basis of section 2-201. Silicon Solutions argued that the summary judgment should be denied because the statute of frauds was satisfied under section 2-201(3)(a) and (c). *See* UCC § 2-606 as to goods accepted.

Silicon Solutions cited *Impossible Electronic Techniques, Inc. v. Wackenhut Protective Systems, Inc.*, 669 F.2d 1026, 1036–37 (5th Cir. 1982), in which the court stated that the "statute exempts contracts involving 'specially manufactured' goods from the writing requirement because in these cases the very nature of the goods serves as a reliable indication that a contract was indeed formed." Further:

> Where the seller has commenced or completed the manufacture of goods that conform to the special needs of a particular buyer and thereby are not suitable for sale to others, not only is the likelihood of a perjured claim of a contract diminished, but denying enforcement to such a contract would impose substantial hardship on the aggrieved party. . . . The unfairness is especially acute where . . . the seller has incurred substantial, unrecoverable expense in reliance on the oral promise of the buyer. . . . The crucial inquiry is whether the manufacturer could sell the goods in the ordinary course of his business to someone other than the original buyer. If with slight alterations the goods could be so sold, then they are not specially manufactured; if, however, essential changes are necessary to render the goods marketable by the seller to others, then the exception does apply.

How should the court rule?

3. More on Electronic Contracting

Both the federal Electronic Signatures in Global and National Commerce Act ("E-Sign")[28] and the Uniform Electronic Transactions Act ("UETA")[29] potentially apply to transactions under Article 2. E-Sign's operative section, codified at 15 U.S.C. § 7001, does not apply if a state has enacted UETA.[30] Both E-Sign and UETA provide that signatures, contracts, or other records shall not be denied validity "solely" because they are in electronic form or that an electronic record was used in contract formation. Similarly, electronic records can satisfy the requirement

---

[28]   E-Sign is codified at 15 U.S.C. § 7001 *et seq.* Section 7003(a) does not exempt Article 2 transactions from its scope.

[29]   UETA is in effect in 46 states and the District of Columbia. UETA section 3 does not exempt Article 2 transactions from its scope. In order for UETA to govern an Article 2 transaction, however, the parties have to agree to conduct the transaction electronically. UETA §§ 3 and 5(b).

[30]   15 U.S.C. § 7002.

of a writing that may be imposed under other law, such as by a statute of frauds. E-Sign § 7001(a); UETA § 7. No party is required to use electronic communications, and E-Sign incorporates some disclosure rules to use regarding electronic communications in transactions with consumers. E-Sign § 7001(b); UETA § 5. The United Nations Convention on the Use of Electronic Communications in International Contracts has provisions of similar import. Arts. 8 through 14. The United States has not yet ratified this Convention.[31]

The theory of these various promulgations is that electronic communication is a medium that may require some additional rules but does not require any change in the basic underlying legal principles of contract law. Hence their provisions are minimal and encourage electronic commerce, rather than impose an elaborate scheme of rules or directive.[32]

B. UNCONSCIONABILITY

Courts have always had the discretion to refuse to enforce an agreement. Sometimes they would declare an agreement void as against public policy.[33] Other times they would invalidate an agreement because it was unconscionable. That is, the agreement shocked the conscience of the court.[34] Article 2 codifies this rule in section 2-302. It authorizes a court to refuse to enforce an unconscionable

---

[31] For a comparison, *see* Charles H. Martin, *The Electronic Contracts Convention, the CISG, and New Sources of E-commerce Law*, 16 TUL. J. INT'L & COMP. L. 467 (2008); Jennifer A. Puplava, *Use and Enforceability of Electronic Contracting: The State of Uniform Legislation Attempting to Regulate E-commerce Transactions*, 16 MICH. ST. J. INT'L L. 153 (2007); Henry D. Gabriel, *United Nations Convention on the Use of Electronic Communications in International Contracts and Compatibility with the American Domestic Law of Electronic Commerce*, 7 LOY L. & TECH. ANN. 1 (2006–07); Charles H. Martin, *The UNCITRAL Electronic Contracts Convention: Will it Be Used or Avoided?*, 17 PACE INT'L L. REV. 261 (2005).

[32] *See* Ronald J. Mann & Travis Siebeneicher, *Just One Click, The Reality of Internet Retail Contracting*, 108 COLUM. L. REV. 984 (2008); John M. Norwood, *A Summary of Statutory and Case Law Associated with Contracting in the Electronic Universe*, 4 DEPAUL BUS. & COM. L.J. 415 (2006).

[33] *See* RESTATEMENT (SECOND) OF CONTRACTS §§ 178–96.

[34] *Compare* RESTATEMENT (SECOND) OF CONTRACTS § 208.

agreement entirely or to excise the unconscionable provisions and enforce the remainder.

Unfortunately, nothing in the UCC purports to define the meaning and scope of the term "unconscionable." Still, there is some guidance. The UCC tells us that unconscionability is to be determined at the time of contracting, not at some later point when circumstances have changed. UCC § 2-302(1). In addition, it is a legal issue for the court, and thus not a factual one for the jury. *Id.* The comments then supply more help by identifying the underlying principle as "the prevention of oppression and unfair surprise." UCC § 2-302 cmt. 1.

This comment has prompted courts and commentators[35] to suggest that there are two aspects to unconscionability: substantive unconscionability and procedural unconscionability. Substantive unconscionability (*i.e.,* "oppression") deals with the substantive terms of the contract, such as price, warranties, and limitations on remedy. Procedural unconscionability (*i.e.,* "unfair surprise") deals with the bargaining process and covers such things as lack of meaningful choice, deception, small print, and language barriers. Many courts require some aspect of both substantive and procedural unconscionability before they will give relief. Others are more lenient, and will permit an abundance of one to make up for a lack or minimal amount of the other.

Most of the successful claims of unconscionability arise in the consumer context. The early cases under Article 2 tended to involve sales of furniture or appliances at inflated prices to poorly educated or non-English speaking customers.[36] More recently, the cases tend to involve the enforceability of an arbitration clause in a consumer contract. The consumer's first attack on such a clause is usually to argue that the clause is not part of the agreement at all, relying

---

[35]   Unconscionability is another area that is a favorite for law professors to write about. *See, e.g.,* Edith R. Warkentine, *Beyond Unconscionability: The Case for Using "Knowing Assent" as the Basis for Analyzing Unbargained-For Terms in Standard Form Contracts,* 31 SEATTLE UNIV. L. REV. 469 (2008); Wayne R. Barnes, *Toward a Fairer Model of Consumer Assent to Standard Form Contracts: In Defense of Restatement Subsection 211(3),* 82 WASH. L. REV. 227 (2007).

[36]   *See, e.g., Morris v. Capitol Furniture & Appliance Co.,* 280 A.2d 775 (D.C. 1971); *Toker v. Westerman,* 274 A.2d 78 (N.J. Dist. Ct. 1970); *Toker v. Perl,* 247 A.2d 701 (N.J. Sup. Ct. 1968), *aff'd,* 260 A.2d 244 (N.J. Super. Ct. App. Div. 1970); *Frostifresh Corp. v. Reynoso,* 274 N.Y.S.2d 757 (N.Y. Dist. Ct. 1966), *rev'd only as to remedy,* 281 N.Y.S.2d 964 (N.Y. Sup. Ct. 1967); *Williams v. Walker-Thomas Furniture Co.,* 350 F.2d 445 (D.C. Cir. 1965).

on the contract formation rules of section 2-207. With some minor exceptions,[37] those arguments have not fared well.[38]

The consumer's second attack is to argue that the arbitration clause is unconscionable. All claims of unconscionability face an uphill battle. Courts generally are loathe to interfere with freedom of contract. Unconscionability claims against an arbitration clause face an even steeper incline, because the Federal Arbitration Act , 9 U.S.C. § 1, *et seq.*, codifies a strong national policy in favor of arbitrating private disputes. Nevertheless, there is a growing body of law that recognizes that – at least in consumer transactions – arbitration agreements can be unconscionable, particularly if they require arbitration in a remote location or require payment of a fee in excess of the amount of the underlying transaction.[39] While few of these cases have arisen under Article 2, some have.[40] Consider this recent example.

---

[37]   *E.g., Klocek v. Gateway, Inc.*, 104 F. Supp. 2d 1332 (D. Kan.), *dismissed for lack of subject matter jurisdiction,* 2000 WL 1372886 (D. Kan. 2000), *refusing to vacate first order,* 2001 WL 1568346 (D. Kan. 2001). *See also Rogers v. Dell Computer Corp.*, 138 P.3d 826 (Okla. 2005) (laying out the analysis but concluding that the record was not sufficiently complete to reach a determination).

[38]   *E.g., Fiser v. Dell Computer Corp.*, 165 P.3d 328 (N.M. Ct. App. 2007), *rev'd on other grounds*, 188 P.3d 1215 (N.M. 2008); *M.A. Mortenson Co. v. Timberline Software Corp.*, 998 P.2d 305 (Wash. 2000); *Hill v. Gateway 2000, Inc.*, 105 F.3d 1147 (7th Cir.), *cert. denied*, 522 U.S. 808 (1997).

[39]   *See Ingle v. Circuit City Stores, Inc.*, 328 F.3d 1165 (9th Cir. 2003), *cert. denied*, 540 U.S. 1160 (2004) (arbitration clause in employment agreement unconscionable because of its one-way application, one-year limitations period, bar on class actions, and cost splitting provisions). *See also Ting v. AT&T*, 319 F.3d 1126 (9th Cir.(, *cert. denied*, 540 U.S. 811 (2003) (arbitration clause was unconscionable because it barred class actions, split costs inappropriately, and mandated that results be kept confidential); *Szetela v. Discover Bank*, 118 Cal. Rptr. 2d 862 (Cal. Ct. App. 2002), *cert. denied*, 537 U.S. 1226 (2003) (striking a ban on class actions from an arbitration clause). *But see Anders v. Hometown Mortgage Services, Inc.*, 346 F.3d 1024 (11th Cir. 2003) (limitations on remedies do not affect the enforceability of an arbitration agreement); *Rosen v. SCIL, LLC*, 799 N.E.2d 488 (Ill. Ct. App. 2003) (credit card arbitration agreement not unconscionable because it prohibited class actions).

[40]   *See Brower v. Gateway 2000, Inc.*, 676 N.Y.S.2d 569 (N.Y. Sup. Ct. App. Div. 1998) (arbitration clause unconscionable because it made arbitration prohibitively expensive).

FISER V. DELL COMPUTER CORP.
188 P.3d 1215 (N.M. 2008)

Serna, Justice

We granted certiorari to review whether Defendant Dell Computer Corporation's Motion to Stay and Compel Arbitration pursuant to the Federal Arbitration Act was properly granted. We hold that, in the context of small consumer claims that would be prohibitively costly to bring on an individual basis, contractual prohibitions on class relief are contrary to New Mexico's fundamental public policy of encouraging the resolution of small consumer claims and are therefore unenforceable in this state. We reverse.

I. FACTUAL BACKGROUND AND PROCEEDINGS BELOW

Plaintiff Robert Fiser purchased a computer from Defendant via the company's website. He subsequently filed a putative class action lawsuit contending that Defendant systematically misrepresents the memory size of its computers. He alleges violations of the New Mexico Unfair Practices Act (UPA), the New Mexico False Advertising Act, the New Mexico Uniform Commercial Code (UCC), and common law concepts of breach of contract, breach of warranty, misrepresentation, violations of the covenants of good faith and fair dealing, bad faith, and unjust enrichment.

Central to the issue presented is the scant amount of damages alleged: Plaintiff estimates that Defendant's alleged misrepresentation results in a monetary loss to its customers of just ten to twenty dollars per computer.

Defendant filed a Motion to Stay and Compel Arbitration pursuant to the Federal Arbitration Act (FAA). *See* 9 U.S.C. §§ 3, 4 (2000). Defendant argued that, pursuant to the "terms and conditions" on its website at the time of the purchase, Plaintiff is required to individually arbitrate his claims and is precluded from proceeding on a classwide basis either in litigation or arbitration. The "terms and conditions" included an arbitration clause mandating that "any claim, dispute, or controversy . . . against Dell . . . [was subject to] binding arbitration administered by the National Arbitration Forum (NAF)." The terms also included a clause (hereinafter referred to as the class action ban) which directed that the arbitration was "limited solely to the dispute or controversy between [Plaintiff] and Dell."[41]

---

[41]   Although, in the past, the procedural rules of the NAF also did not allow for classwide arbitration, the rules have apparently been amended to provide for such a procedure since

Finally, the "terms and conditions" contained a choice-of-law provision declaring Texas law to be controlling. Although the parties disagree over whether Plaintiff assented to Defendant's "terms and conditions," we do not reach that issue. We assume without deciding, for the purpose of our analysis, that he assented to the terms.

The district court agreed with Defendant that Plaintiff was bound by the arbitration provision and thus granted Defendant's motion. The Court of Appeals affirmed. Plaintiff petitioned for a writ of certiorari; both the New Mexico Attorney General and Public Justice filed amicus briefs in support of Plaintiff. Because we conclude that the class action ban is contrary to fundamental New Mexico public policy, we reverse.

II. DISCUSSION

A. Application of Texas Law Would Violate New Mexico Public Policy

1. New Mexico Respects Choice-of-Law Provisions Unless Application of the Chosen Law Would Contravene New Mexico Public Policy

The threshold question in determining the validity of the class action ban is which state's law must be applied to this potentially multi-state class action that was filed in New Mexico by a New Mexico resident against a defendant that maintains its principal place of business in Texas for damages relating to a contract that contains a choice-of-law clause directing that Texas law be applied.

New Mexico respects party autonomy; the law to be applied to a particular dispute may be chosen by the parties through a contractual choice-of-law provision. However, when application of the law chosen by the parties offends New Mexico public policy, our courts may decline to enforce the choice-of-law provision and apply New Mexico law instead. New Mexico courts will not give effect to another state's laws where those laws would "violate some fundamental principle of justice." *Reagan v. McGee Drilling Corp.,* 933 P.2d 867 (N.M. 1997).

Application of Texas law to the instant matter would likely require enforcing the class action ban. Unless enforcement of the class action ban would run afoul of fundamental New Mexico public policy, our conflict of law rules counsel respecting the choice-of-law provision and applying Texas law.

---

briefing was completed. *See* http:// www. arb- forum. com/ default. aspx and proceed through the links as follows: "programs and rules," "arbitration," "the code of procedure," "arbitration class procedures."

2. It is Fundamental New Mexico Policy that Consumers Have a Viable Mechanism for Dispute Resolution, No Matter the Size of the Claim

New Mexico policy strongly supports the resolution of consumer claims, regardless of the amount of damages alleged. That policy is demonstrated by several of our statutes. For example, the New Mexico legislature enacted the UPA, which is unequivocal: "[u]nfair or deceptive trade practices and unconscionable trade practices in the conduct of any trade or commerce are unlawful." Section 57-12-3. The UPA was clearly drafted to include a remedy for small claims: a party need not show any monetary damage to be entitled to an injunction, § 57-12-10(A), and "[a]ny person who suffers *any* loss of money . . . [may] recover actual damages or the sum of one hundred dollars ($100), whichever is greater." § 57-12-10(B) (emphasis added).

The fundamental New Mexico policy of providing consumers a mechanism for resolution is also seen in the False Advertising Act, which specifically empowers private individuals to bring rights of action in the name of the state and for "all others similarly situated." § 57-15-5.

Yet another example of New Mexico's fundamental public policy in ensuring that consumers have an opportunity to redress their harm is the Consumer Protection Division of the Attorney General's Office, which is charged with protecting New Mexico citizens from unfair and deceptive trade practices. In this effort, the Consumer Protection Division is authorized and funded to investigate suspicious business activities, informally resolve the complaints of dissatisfied consumers, educate citizens about their consumer rights, and file lawsuits on behalf of the public.

3. The Class Action Device is Critical to Enforcement of Consumer Rights in New Mexico

The opportunity to seek class relief is of particular importance to the enforcement of consumer rights because it provides a mechanism for the spreading of costs. The class action device allows claimants with individually small claims the opportunity for relief that would otherwise be economically infeasible because they may collectively share the otherwise prohibitive costs of bringing and maintaining the claim.

The opportunity for class relief and its importance to consumer rights is enshrined in the fundamental policy of New Mexico and evidenced by our statutory scheme. *See, e.g.,* Rule 1-023 NMRA (setting forth the rules of civil procedure governing class actions). Notably, the UPA specifically references class actions as a private remedy available under the act. § 57-12-10(E). Further, the New Mexico

Uniform Arbitration Act declares that arbitration clauses that require consumers to decline participation in class actions are unenforceable and voidable. *See* NMSA 1978, §§ 44-7A-1(b)(4)(f), 44-7A-5 (2001). While this provision may be preempted by the FAA, *see Perry v. Thomas,* 482 U.S. 483, 492 n.9 (1987) ("A state-law principle that takes its meaning precisely from the fact that a contract to arbitrate is at issue does not comport with [the FAA]."), it is clear evidence of the fundamental New Mexico policy of allowing consumers a means to redress their injuries via the class action device.

In New Mexico, we recognize that the class action was devised for "vindication of the rights of groups of people who individually would be without effective strength to bring their opponents into court at all." *Romero v. Philip Morris, Inc.,* 109 P.3d 768 (N.M. 2005). A purpose of the class action is to conserve party resources. As the United States Supreme Court recognized,

> [t]he policy at the very core of the class action mechanism is to overcome the problem that small recoveries do not provide the incentive for any individual to bring a solo action prosecuting his or her rights. A class action solves this problem by aggregating the relatively paltry potential recoveries into something worth someone's (usually an attorney's) labor.

Amchem Prods., Inc. v. Windsor, 521 U.S. 591, 617 (1997). "Where it is not economically feasible to obtain relief within the traditional framework of a multiplicity of small individual suits for damages, aggrieved persons may be without any effective redress unless they may employ the class-action device." *Deposit Guar. Nat'l Bank, Jackson, Miss. v. Roper,* 445 U.S. 326, 339 (1980). The Federal Rules Advisory Committee recognized the critical nature of the class action to individuals with small claims when it directed that one of the grounds on which class certification may be appropriate is where "the amounts at stake for individuals [are] so small that separate suits would be impracticable." Fed. R. Civ. P. 23(b)(3), advisory committee note (1966 amendment).

Thus, beyond merely a procedural tool, the class action functions as a gatekeeper to relief when the cost of bringing a single claim is greater than the damages alleged. When viewed in this light, a contractual provision that purports to ban class actions for small claims implicates not just the opportunity for a class action but the more fundamental right to a meaningful remedy for one's claims. This Court has recognized that the right of access to the courts is part of the right to petition for redress of grievances guaranteed by both the United States and New Mexico constitutions. While the class action ban may or may not rise to the level of a constitutional violation, a prohibition on class relief where there is no meaningful alternative for redress of injury certainly does not provide for effective vindication of rights.

In view of the fact that Plaintiff's alleged damages are just ten to twenty dollars, by attempting to prevent him from seeking class relief, Defendant has essentially foreclosed the possibility that Plaintiff may obtain *any* relief. Thus, we conclude that Defendant's prohibition on class action relief, when applied to small claims plaintiffs, is contrary to New Mexico's fundamental public policy to provide a forum for relief for small consumer claims. The words of the California Supreme Court are apropos:

> By imposing this clause on its customers, [Defendant] has essentially granted itself a license to push the boundaries of good business practices to their furthest limits, fully aware that relatively few, if any, customers will seek legal remedies, and that any remedies obtained will only pertain to that single customer without collateral estoppel effect. The potential for millions of customers to be . . . without an effective method of redress cannot be ignored.

Discover Bank v. Super. Ct., 113 P.3d 1100, 1108 (Cal. 2005).

Defendant contends that Plaintiff has not met the evidentiary burden of proving that his damages are outweighed by the cost of bringing an individual claim. While we recognize that, in some cases, more extensive factfinding will be required, we emphasize that Plaintiff only alleges his damages to be between *ten and twenty dollars.* We do not find it necessary to engage in an exhaustive analysis regarding whether the economic and opportunity costs of bringing a ten to twenty dollar claim are prohibitive. In light of attorney's fees, the costs of gathering evidence and preparing the case, and the time spent educating himself on the issues and organizing and presenting the claim, the likelihood that Plaintiff's actual costs will exceed ten to twenty dollars is certain. The economic realities of the present case are clearly more tangible than the mere "risk" that Plaintiff will be faced with prohibitive costs. *Cf. Green Tree Fin. Corp.-Ala. v. Randolph,* 531 U.S. 79, 90–91 (2000) (holding that arbitration agreement's failure to address how parties would allocate arbitration costs does not render it per se unenforceable on the grounds that the claimant may be subjected to steep costs where claimant did not present evidence that she would be subjected to such high costs). Suffice it to say that "only a lunatic or a fanatic sues for [ten to twenty dollars.]" *Carnegie v. Household Int'l, Inc.,* 376 F.3d 656, 661 (7th Cir. 2004).

For all of the foregoing reasons, New Mexico's fundamental public policy requires that consumers with small claims have a mechanism for dispute resolution via the class action. Therefore, application of Texas law, that would allow the class action ban, is contrary to New Mexico public policy. Accordingly, we invoke the public policy exception and apply New Mexico law rather than Texas law to analyze the validity of the class action ban.

　　B.　Under New Mexico Law, the Class Action Ban is Invalid Because It is Contrary to Public Policy and Therefore Unconscionable

Plaintiff contends that the class action ban is unconscionable. This determination is a matter of law and is reviewed de novo. We agree.

The classic articulation of unconscionability is that it is comprised of two prongs: substantive unconscionability and procedural unconscionability. Substantive unconscionability relates to the content of the contract terms and whether they are illegal, contrary to public policy, or grossly unfair. *Padilla v. State Farm Mut. Auto. Ins. Co.,* 68 P.3d 901 (N.M. 2003); *Guthmann v. La Vida Llena,* 709 P.2d 675, 679 (N.M. 1985). Procedural unconscionability is determined by analyzing the circumstances surrounding the contract's formation, such as whether it was an adhesive contract and the relative bargaining power of the parties. *Guthmann,* 709 P.2d at 679. "The weight given to procedural and substantive considerations varies with the circumstances of each case." *Id.*

As set forth above, we concluded in the course of our conflict analysis that the class action ban violates New Mexico public policy. By preventing customers with small claims from attempting class relief and thereby circumscribing their only economically efficient means for redress, Defendant's class action ban exculpates the company from wrongdoing. "Denial of a class action in cases where it is appropriate may have the effect of allowing an unscrupulous wrongdoer to retain the benefits of its wrongful conduct." *Discover Bank,* 113 P.3d at 1106. On these facts, enforcing the class action ban would be tantamount to allowing Defendant to unilaterally exempt itself from New Mexico consumer protection laws. It is not hyperbole or exaggeration to say that it is a fundamental principle of justice in New Mexico that corporations may not tailor the laws that our legislature has enacted in order to shield themselves from the potential claims of consumers. Because it violates public policy by depriving small claims consumers of a meaningful remedy and exculpating Defendant from potential wrongdoing, the class action ban meets the test for substantive unconscionability.

In the instant case, the nature of the "terms and conditions" may or may not rise to the level of an adhesive or procedurally unconscionable contract. When a court makes an analysis into whether a particular contract is adhesive, it typically inquires into three factors: (1) whether it was prepared entirely by one party for the acceptance of the other; (2) whether the party proffering the contract enjoyed superior bargaining power because the weaker party could not avoid doing business under the particular terms; and [(3)] whether the contract was offered to the weaker party without an opportunity for bargaining on a take-it-or-leave-it basis. *Guthmann,* 709 P.2d at 678. The Court of Appeals held that the terms did not constitute a contract of adhesion because there was no evidence that Plaintiff could not avoid doing business under the particular terms mandated by Defendant. While we agree that Defendant's "terms and conditions" may not rise to the level of an adhesive contract, we nevertheless conclude that the terms are unenforceable because there has been such an overwhelming showing of substantive unconscionability. For these reasons, the agreement is unconscionable under New Mexico law and will not be enforced in this state.[42]

C. Invalidation of the Arbitration Agreement and Embedded Exculpatory Class Action Ban is Not Preempted by the FAA

Having held that the class action ban is unenforceable in New Mexico, we turn to an examination of whether the FAA preempts our ruling. Congress enacted the FAA to counteract judicial hostility to arbitration. The Act provides that arbitration agreements "shall be valid, irrevocable, and enforceable, save upon such grounds that exist at law or in equity for the revocation of any contract." Section 2. While the FAA prevents "[s]tates from singling out arbitration provisions for suspect status," *Doctor's Assocs., Inc. v. Casarotto,* 517 U.S. 681, 687 (1996), it does not give arbitration provisions special protection either. It only requires that they be placed "upon the same footing as other contracts." *Scherk v. Alberto-Culver Co.,* 417 U.S. 506, 511 (1974). "Thus, generally applicable contract defenses, such as fraud, duress, or unconscionability, may be applied to invalidate arbitration agreements without contravening § 2." *Doctor's Assocs.,* 517 U.S. at 687. Because our invalidation of the ban on class relief rests on the doctrine of unconscionability, a doctrine that exists for the revocation of any contract, the FAA does not preempt our holding. Class action bans that effectively deny consumer plaintiffs relief are invalid in New Mexico, regardless of the contracts in which they are found.

---

[42]   We note that numerous other jurisdictions have also concluded that class action bans are unconscionable. *See, e.g., Shroyer v. New Cingular Wireless Servs., Inc.,* 498 F.3d 976, 984 (9th Cir. 2007); *Skirchak v. Dynamics Research Corp.,* 432 F. Supp. 2d 175, 180–81 (D. Mass. 2006); *Szetela v. Discover Bank,* 118 Cal. Rptr. 2d 862, 867 (Cal. Ct. App. 2002); *Kinkel v. Cingular Wireless, LLC,* 857 N.E.2d 250, 274–75 (Ill. 2006).

D. The Class Action Ban is Not Severable

When a provision of a contract is determined to be unconscionable, we "may refuse to enforce the contract, or [we] may enforce the remainder of the contract without the unconscionable clause, or [we] may so limit the application of any unconscionable clause as to avoid any unconscionable result." [§ 2-302]. Here, the class action ban is part of the arbitration provision and is central to the mechanism for resolving the dispute between the parties; therefore, it cannot be severed. We decline to enforce the arbitration provision.

III. CONCLUSION

Contractual prohibition of class relief, as applied to claims that would be economically inefficient to bring on an individual basis, is contrary to the fundamental public policy of New Mexico to provide a forum for the resolution of all consumer claims and is therefore unenforceable in this state. The arbitration provision is invalid and the Court of Appeals reversed. We remand for proceedings consistent with this opinion.

The CISG does not have any provisions that address the concept of unconscionability, perhaps because it does not apply to consumer transactions. *Cf.* CISG Art. 4 (disclaiming any concern with the "validity" of the contract or any of its provisions). The UNIDROIT Principles do not deal with invalidity arising from "immorality or illegality," UNIDROIT Art. 3.1, but do deal with issues of "gross disparity." UNIDROIT Art. 3.10.

Problem 2-13

In a contract for sale of a car from a car dealer, the document signed by the buyer provided that all disputes arising under the contract must be resolved in arbitration, with the arbitrator chosen by the seller. The clause also provided that the buyer would be responsible for half of the arbitrator's fee unless the seller won the dispute in which case, the buyer would be responsible for all fees. The buyer is college educated and read the document prior to signing it. The buyer did not like the clause and objected to it but the seller refused to sell the car to the buyer unless the buyer signed the document. The buyer really wanted the car and grudgingly signed the document. Predictably the car was a lemon and the buyer is consulting you regarding what to do now. In your research, you find that all car dealers in the area have the same clause in their sales contracts. Is the buyer stuck with the arbitration clause?

Problem 2-14

You represent an office supply store that purchased a high end printer for use in the store. The office supply store placed the order for the printer by telephone and the seller responded by promptly sending the office supply store an acknowledgment form. That form included a choice-of-forum clause that requires all litigation against the seller to be commenced in Illinois, where the seller's chief executive office is located. The office supply store is located in Florida and has never done business in Illinois. The printer broke down a few months after it was delivered and the seller refused to replace it. The office supply store, which had paid no attention to the acknowledgment form, then sued the seller in the state court in Florida. The seller moved to dismiss the case based upon the choice-of-forum clause. Is the choice-of-forum clause enforceable? What are the best arguments that it is not?

Problem 2-15

Sly Electronics's sales force consists largely of college students who sell stereo components out of their vans. The sales force is trained to make people believe – but without actually saying – that the goods are stolen. The gimmick is that customers (*i.e.,* "marks") will think they are getting a really good deal (a steal, so to speak), because they are buying stolen goods. In fact, the goods are not stolen and the sales force is properly licensed to sell goods on the street. Moreover, the deal is not very good at all. The typical markup is quite high. A component that Sly Electronics sells for $600 will typically cost it only $200 and retail for about $300. If a customer learns the truth after a purchase and sues to rescind the transaction, will the customer have a good claim of unconscionability? Why or why not? In analyzing this question, which comparison is the more appropriate consideration and why: (i) price to cost; or (ii) price to value?

CHAPTER THREE

TERMS OF THE CONTRACT – PART I

SECTION 1.   TERMS OF THE AGREEMENT

A. USAGE OF TRADE, COURSE OF DEALING, AND COURSE OF PERFORMANCE

By now you know that there is a difference between the terms "agreement" and "contract." Review the definitions of those terms in section 1-201. Any analysis of the terms of a *contract* must begin with the terms of the parties' *agreement.*

The bargain that comprises the parties' agreement is based not merely on their exchange of promises or other communications. The agreement encompasses a much broader scope of relevant behavior. In addition to any statements made, the bargain can be derived from the particular parties' past, present, and future conduct, as well as the practices and usages of others engaging in the same trade or market. Read section 1-303.

In the UCC, course of performance, course of dealing, and usage of trade are concepts that encompass both the parties' behavior and the practices in a trade or market. Each of these concepts, which are defined in section 1-303(a)–(c), can be used to explain or cast meaning on the parties' express terms, or to otherwise supplement the parties' express terms. *See* UCC § 1-303(d).

A course of performance concerns how the parties to a particular transaction exercise the rights created or perform the duties imposed by their contract. It is a sequence of conduct by the parties to a particular transaction and can arise when the contract calls for the same act to be repeated multiple times. A course of performance often arises in an installment contract, but it is not limited to such transactions. *See* UCC § 2-612(1). A course of dealing is the conduct of these parties in prior dealings or transactions with one another. Usage of trade is how the members of the relevant industry or trade behave and informs the meaning they ascribe to particular terms. It is their set of standard practices and their lexicon for communicating with one another. And they follow these practices and use this lingo with such regularity that, unless expressly disclaimed, agreements among them can fairly be said to be based on the expectation such practices and meanings are part of their agreement.

There are three primary questions in thinking about course of performance, course of dealing, and usage of trade as part of the agreement and thus ultimately part of the contract of the parties. First, is there sufficient evidence to establish that a course of performance, course of dealing, or usage of trade exists? A party seeking to rely on such evidence generally has the burden to demonstrate the existence of the course of performance, course of dealing, or usage of trade.

Second, is evidence of a course of performance, course of dealing, or usage of trade admissible in a court proceeding concerning the transaction? This depends on two things. First, the party seeking to demonstrate the course of performance, course of dealing, or usage of trade must give advance notice to prevent unfair surprise. UCC § 1-303(g). In addition, the parol evidence rule in section 2-202 may, on some occasions, bar admission of the evidence. The parol evidence rule is discussed later in Chapter Five.

Third, whenever reasonably possible, evidence of course of performance, course of dealing, and usage of trade is to be construed as consistent with each other and with the parties' express terms. If it is not reasonable to construe them consistently,[1] the hierarchy set forth in section 1-303(e) controls: express terms govern, then course of performance, then course of dealing, and last, usage of trade.

Problem 3-1

You are a partner at a large law firm. One of the firm's clients is Orion Technologies, a company that manufactures and sells custom-designed robotics for use in extreme environments: space vehicles, deepwater research facilities, and subterranean excavations. Because its products are used in locations where they cannot readily be repaired, Orion has to be sure that its products will function properly.

Orion's long-time supplier of titanium rods has recently gone out of business. Its long-time supplier of resins and plastics has indicated that it will be raising prices by 20%. In response to these developments, Orion is negotiating with other companies to provide the needed materials. You will be asked to draft the supply contracts. Might there be any usages of trade that could be relevant to your task? If so, what might they be and how will you go about ascertaining what they are?

---

[1]   *See Archer Daniels Midland Co. v. Brunswick County*, 129 Fed. Appx. 16 (4th Cir. 2005) (considering whether course of performance was consistent with or contradictory to the express terms of the agreement).

CISG and UNIDROIT Principles. The CISG also recognizes that agreements are made within the context of the parties' practices and usages in international trade, and that those practices and usages are part of the parties' agreement. CISG Art. 9. Interpreting the intent of the parties to an agreement also requires taking into account the parties' practices and usages in the trade. CISG Art. 8(3). The UNIDROIT Principles are similar. UNIDROIT Art. 1.9, Art. 4.3.

B. GOOD FAITH

The UCC imposes a duty of good faith in the performance and enforcement of every transaction to which it applies. Read section 1-304. A similar duty exists in every contract. *See* RESTATEMENT (SECOND) OF CONTRACTS § 205. What does the obligation to act in good faith add to a party's contractual obligations? The answer to that requires a brief exploration of two things: (i) the scope of the good faith obligation; and (ii) the standard by which good faith is measured.

As to the scope of the good faith obligation, notice the language of section 1-304. It requires good faith in the "performance and enforcement" of a contract. The implications of this language are twofold. First, the duty of good faith does not arise until there is an underlying contract. That is, there must be a binding agreement between the parties. A corollary to this is that the obligation of good faith does not apply to pre-contract negotiations.[2] Second, the obligation of good faith is something that colors and illuminates contractual duties and rights, but it does not create an independent cause of action for breach. *See* UCC § 1-304 cmt.1. In this sense, the obligation is something like course of performance, course of dealing, and usage of trade. It is a lens through which to view and interpret the parties' agreement, but it does not and should not be used to contradict express terms.[3]

As to the standard for measuring good faith, that depends on two things: (i) whether the state has adopted the uniform version of revised Article 1; and (ii) whether the party is a merchant. Begin with Article 1. Under old Article 1, good faith meant merely "honesty in fact in the conduct or transaction concerned."

---

[2]   *But see* UCC § 2-314 cmt. 3 (suggesting that the obligation of good faith requires a non-merchant to disclose – presumably before contracting – known but hidden defects in the goods).

[3]   *See* PEB Commentary No. 10 (Feb. 10, 1994).

Former UCC § 1-201(19). This was a purely subjective standard. Revised Article 1 expands upon this standard by requiring "honesty in fact and the observance of reasonable commercial standards of fair dealing." UCC § 1-201(b)(20). This definition, which adds an objective element to good faith, was chosen in part because Article 2 had already had a similar definition of good faith for merchants. Read section 2-103(1)(b), which requires "honesty in fact and the observance of reasonable commercial standards of fair dealing in the trade." Note, the limitation to fair dealing "in the trade" was not incorporated in revised Article 1. Thus, the applicable standard depends on whether the state whose law governs has enacted revised Article 1 and, if so, whether the legislature adopted the heightened standard of good faith.[4]

	Standard from Old Article 1 Applies	**Standard from Revised Article 1 Applies**
Merchant	Honesty in fact and the observance of reasonable commercial standards of fair dealing in the trade.	Honesty in fact and the observance of reasonable commercial standards of fair dealing.
Non-merchant	Honesty in fact.	

As the comment to the revised definition in Article 1 makes clear, the requirement of "reasonable commercial standards of fair dealing" is not about commercial reasonableness, it is about "fair dealing." In other words, the duty of good faith is not a requirement to act non-negligently, it is a directive to act "fairly" in the transaction. *See* UCC § 1-201 cmt. 20.

So, what does good faith mean in the context of a particular transaction? In other words, how can one identify, based upon the standards noted above, whether a person has acted in good faith or bad faith? Does the concept merely limit the discretion that the contract purports to grant to one party, such as when a party has the discretion to fix the price in good faith under section 2-305? Consider the following case which arose in a context outside the UCC. To what extent do these

---

[4]   Several states that have enacted revised Article 1 have not adopted the heightened standard of good faith.

ideas have force in the context of an Article 2 transaction?[5] Is Judge Posner talking about "honesty in fact" or the "observance of reasonable commercial standards of fair dealing" or about a different concept altogether?

MARKET STREET ASSOCIATES LTD. PARTNERSHIP V. FREY
941 F.2d 588 (7th Cir. 1991)

Posner, Circuit Judge

Market Street Associates Limited Partnership and its general partner appeal from a judgment for the defendants, General Electric Pension Trust and its trustees, entered upon cross-motions for summary judgment in a diversity suit that pivots on the doctrine of "good faith" performance of a contract. *Cf.* Robert Summers, *"Good Faith" in General Contract Law and the Sales Provisions of the Uniform Commercial Code,* 54 VA. L. REV. 195, 232–43 (1968). Wisconsin law applies – common law rather than Uniform Commercial Code, because the contract is for land rather than for goods, UCC § 2-102, and because it is a lease rather than a sale and Wisconsin has not adopted UCC art. 2A, which governs leases. . . .

In 1968, J.C. Penney Company, the retail chain, entered into a sale and leaseback arrangement with General Electric Pension Trust in order to finance Penney's growth. Under the arrangement Penney sold properties to the pension trust which the trust then leased back to Penney for a term of 25 years. Paragraph 34 of the lease entitles the lessee to "request Lessor [the pension trust] to finance the costs and expenses of construction of additional Improvements upon the Premises," provided the amount of the costs and expenses is at least $250,000. Upon receiving the request, the pension trust "agrees to give reasonable consideration to providing the financing of such additional Improvements and Lessor and Lessee shall negotiate in good faith concerning the construction of such Improvements and the financing by Lessor of such costs and expenses." Paragraph 34 goes on to provide that, should the negotiations fail, the lessee shall be entitled to repurchase the property at a price roughly equal to the price at which Penney sold it to the pension trust in the first place, plus 6 percent a year for each year since the original purchase. So if the average annual appreciation in the property exceeded

---

[5]   *See, e.g.,* Harold Dubroff, *The Implied Covenant of Good Faith in Contract Interpretation and Gap-Filling: Reviling a Revered Relic,* 80 ST. JOHN'S L. REV. 559 (2006); Terri J. Dobbins, *Losing Faith: Extracting the Implied Covenant of Good Faith From (Some) Contracts,* 84 OR. L. REV. 227 (2005); James J. White, *Good Faith and the Cooperative Antagonist,* 54 SMU L. REV. 679 (2001).

6 percent, a breakdown in negotiations over the financing of improvements would entitle Penney to buy back the property for less than its market value (assuming it had sold the property to the pension trust in the first place at its then market value).

One of these leases was for a shopping center in Milwaukee. In 1987 Penney assigned this lease to Market Street Associates, which the following year received an inquiry from a drugstore chain that wanted to open a store in the shopping center, provided (as is customary) that Market Street Associates built the store for it. Whether Market Street Associates was pessimistic about obtaining financing from the pension trust, still the lessor of the shopping center, or for other reasons, it initially sought financing for the project from other sources. But they were unwilling to lend the necessary funds without a mortgage on the shopping center, which Market Street Associates could not give because it was not the owner but only the lessee. It decided therefore to try to buy the property back from the pension trust. Market Street Associates' general partner, Orenstein, tried to call David Erb of the pension trust, who was responsible for the property in question. Erb did not return his calls, so Orenstein wrote him, expressing an interest in buying the property and asking him to "review your file on this matter and call me so that we can discuss it further." At first, Erb did not reply. Eventually Orenstein did reach Erb, who promised to review the file and get back to him. A few days later an associate of Erb called Orenstein and indicated an interest in selling the property for $3 million, which Orenstein considered much too high.

That was in June of 1988. On July 28, Market Street Associates wrote a letter to the pension trust formally requesting funding for $2 million in improvements to the shopping center. The letter made no reference to paragraph 34 of the lease; indeed, it did not mention the lease. The letter asked Erb to call Orenstein to discuss the matter. Erb, in what was becoming a habit of unresponsiveness, did not call. On August 16, Orenstein sent a second letter-certified mail, return receipt requested-again requesting financing and this time referring to the lease, though not expressly to paragraph 34. The heart of the letter is the following two sentences: "The purpose of this letter is to ask again that you advise us immediately if you are willing to provide the financing pursuant to the lease. If you are willing, we propose to enter into negotiation to amend the ground lease appropriately." The very next day, Market Street Associates received from Erb a letter, dated August 10, turning down the original request for financing on the ground that it did not "meet our current investment criteria": the pension trust was not interested in making loans for less than $7 million. On August 22, Orenstein replied to Erb by letter, noting that his letter of August 10 and Erb's letter of August 16 had evidently crossed in the mails, expressing disappointment at the turn-down, and stating that Market Street Associates would seek financing elsewhere. That was the last contact between the parties until September 27, when Orenstein sent Erb a letter stating that Market Street Associates was exercising the option granted it by paragraph 34 to purchase the property upon the terms specified in that paragraph in the event that negotiations over financing broke down.

The pension trust refused to sell, and this suit to compel specific performance followed. Apparently the price computed by the formula in paragraph 34 is only $1 million. The market value must be higher, or Market Street Associates wouldn't be trying to coerce conveyance at the paragraph 34 price; whether it is as high as $3 million, however, the record does not reveal.

The district judge granted summary judgment for the pension trust on two grounds that he believed to be separate although closely related. The first was that, by failing in its correspondence with the pension trust to mention paragraph 34 of the lease, Market Street Associates had prevented the negotiations over financing that are a condition precedent to the lessee's exercise of the purchase option from taking place. Second, this same failure violated the duty of good faith, which the common law of Wisconsin, as of other states, reads into every contract. . . . In support of both grounds the judge emphasized a statement by Orenstein in his deposition that it had occurred to him that Erb mightn't know about paragraph 34, though this was unlikely (Orenstein testified) because Erb or someone else at the pension trust would probably check the file and discover the paragraph and realize that if the trust refused to negotiate over the request for financing, Market Street Associates, as Penney's assignee, would be entitled to walk off with the property for (perhaps) a song. The judge inferred that Market Street Associates didn't want financing from the pension trust – that it just wanted an opportunity to buy the property at a bargain price and hoped that the pension trust wouldn't realize the implications of turning down the request for financing. Market Street Associates should, the judge opined, have advised the pension trust that it was requesting financing pursuant to paragraph 34, so that the trust would understand the penalty for refusing to negotiate.

We begin our analysis by setting to one side two extreme contentions by the parties. The pension trust argues that the option to purchase created by paragraph 34 cannot be exercised until negotiations over financing break down; there were no negotiations; therefore they did not break down; therefore Market Street Associates had no right to exercise the option. This argument misreads the contract. Although the option to purchase is indeed contingent, paragraph 34 requires the pension trust, upon demand by the lessee for the financing of improvements worth at least $250,000, "to give reasonable consideration to providing the financing." The lessor who fails to give reasonable consideration and thereby prevents the negotiations from taking place is breaking the contract; and a contracting party cannot be allowed to use his own breach to gain an advantage by impairing the rights that the contract confers on the other party. . . . Often, it is true, if one party breaks the contract, the other can walk away from it without liability, can in other words exercise self-help. . . . But he is not required to follow that course. He can stand on his contract rights.

But what exactly are those rights in this case? The contract entitles the lessee to reasonable consideration of its request for financing, and only if negotiations over the request fail is the lessee entitled to purchase the property at the price computed in accordance with paragraph 34. It might seem therefore that the proper legal remedy for a lessor's breach that consists of failure to give the lessee's request for financing reasonable consideration would not be an order that the lessor sell the property to the lessee at the paragraph 34 price, but an order that the lessor bargain with the lessee in good faith. But we do not understand the pension trust to be arguing that Market Street Associates is seeking the wrong remedy. We understand it to be arguing that Market Street Associates has no possible remedy. That is an untenable position.

Market Street Associates argues, with equal unreason as it seems to us, that it could not have broken the contract because paragraph 34 contains no express requirement that in requesting financing the lessee mention the lease or paragraph 34 or otherwise alert the lessor to the consequences of his failing to give reasonable consideration to granting the request. There is indeed no such requirement (all that the contract requires is a demand). But no one says there is. The pension trust's argument, which the district judge bought, is that either as a matter of simple contract interpretation or under the compulsion of the doctrine of good faith, a provision requiring Market Street Associates to remind the pension trust of paragraph 34 should be read into the lease.

It seems to us that these are one ground rather than two. A court has to have a reason to interpolate a clause into a contract. The only reason that has been suggested here is that it is necessary to prevent Market Street Associates from reaping a reward for what the pension trust believes to have been Market Street's bad faith. So we must consider the meaning of the contract duty of "good faith." The Wisconsin cases are cryptic as to its meaning though emphatic about its existence, so we must cast our net wider. We do so mindful of Learned Hand's warning, that "such words as 'fraud,' 'good faith,' 'whim,' 'caprice,' 'arbitrary action,' and 'legal fraud' . . . obscure the issue." *Thompson-Starrett Co. v. La Belle Iron Works,* 17 F.2d 536, 541 (2d Cir.1927). Indeed they do. . . . The particular confusion to which the vaguely moralistic overtones of "good faith" give rise is the belief that every contract establishes a fiduciary relationship. A fiduciary is required to treat his principal as if the principal were he, and therefore he may not take advantage of the principal's incapacity, ignorance, inexperience, or even naïveté. . . . If Market Street Associates were the fiduciary of General Electric Pension Trust, then (we may assume) it could not take advantage of Mr. Erb's apparent ignorance of paragraph 34, however exasperating Erb's failure to return Orenstein's phone calls was and however negligent Erb or his associates were in failing to read the lease before turning down Orenstein's request for financing.

But it is unlikely that Wisconsin wishes, in the name of good faith, to make every contract signatory his brother's keeper, especially when the brother is the immense and sophisticated General Electric Pension Trust, whose lofty indifference to small (= < \$7 million) transactions is the signifier of its grandeur. In fact the law contemplates that people frequently will take advantage of the ignorance of those with whom they contract, without thereby incurring liability. . . . The duty of honesty, of good faith even expansively conceived, is not a duty of candor. You can make a binding contract to purchase something you know your seller undervalues. . . . That of course is a question about formation, not performance, and the particular duty of good faith under examination here relates to the latter rather than to the former. But even after you have signed a contract, you are not obliged to become an altruist toward the other party and relax the terms if he gets into trouble in performing his side of the bargain. . . . Otherwise mere difficulty of performance would excuse a contracting party-which it does not. . . .

But it is one thing to say that you can exploit your superior knowledge of the market – for if you cannot, you will not be able to recoup the investment you made in obtaining that knowledge – or that you are not required to spend money bailing out a contract partner who has gotten into trouble. It is another thing to say that you can take deliberate advantage of an oversight by your contract partner concerning his rights under the contract. Such taking advantage is not the exploitation of superior knowledge or the avoidance of unbargained-for expense; it is sharp dealing. Like theft, it has no social product, and also like theft it induces costly defensive expenditures, in the form of overelaborate disclaimers or investigations into the trustworthiness of a prospective contract partner, just as the prospect of theft induces expenditures on locks.

The form of sharp dealing that we are discussing might or might not be actionable as fraud or deceit. That is a question of tort law and there the rule is that if the information is readily available to both parties the failure of one to disclose it to the other, even if done in the knowledge that the other party is acting on mistaken premises, is not actionable. . . . Before the contract is signed, the parties confront each other with a natural wariness. Neither expects the other to be particularly forthcoming, and therefore there is no deception when one is not. Afterwards the situation is different. The parties are now in a cooperative relationship the costs of which will be considerably reduced by a measure of trust. So each lowers his guard a bit, and now silence is more apt to be deceptive.

Moreover, this is a contract case rather than a tort case, and conduct that might not rise to the level of fraud may nonetheless violate the duty of good faith in dealing with one's contractual partners and thereby give rise to a remedy under contract law. This duty is, as it were, halfway between a fiduciary duty (the duty of *utmost* good faith) and the duty merely to refrain from active fraud. Despite its moralistic overtones it is no more the injection of moral principles into contract law than the fiduciary concept itself is. . . . Summers, *supra,* at 204–07, 265–66. It would be quixotic as well as presumptuous for judges to undertake through contract law to raise the ethical standards of the nation's business people. The concept of the duty of good faith like the concept of fiduciary duty is a stab at approximating the terms the parties would have negotiated had they foreseen the circumstances that have given rise to their dispute. The parties want to minimize the costs of performance. To the extent that a doctrine of good faith designed to do this by reducing defensive expenditures is a reasonable measure to this end, interpolating it into the contract advances the parties' joint goal.

It is true that an essential function of contracts is to allocate risk, and would be defeated if courts treated the materializing of a bargained-over, allocated risk as a misfortune the burden of which is required to be shared between the parties (as it might be within a family, for example) rather than borne entirely by the party to whom the risk had been allocated by mutual agreement. But contracts do not just allocate risk. They also (or some of them) set in motion a cooperative enterprise, which may to some extent place one party at the other's mercy. "The parties to a contract are embarked on a cooperative venture, and a minimum of cooperativeness in the event unforeseen problems arise at the performance stage is required even if not an explicit duty of the contract." *AMPAT/Midwest, Inc. v. Illinois Tool Works, Inc.,* 896 F.2d 1035, 1041 (7th Cir. 1990). The office of the doctrine of good faith is to forbid the kinds of opportunistic behavior that a mutually dependent, cooperative relationship might enable in the absence of rule. " 'Good faith' is a compact reference to an implied undertaking not to take opportunistic advantage in a way that could not have been contemplated at the time of drafting, and which therefore was not resolved explicitly by the parties." *Kham & Nate's Shoes No. 2, Inc. v. First Bank,* 908 F.2d 1351, 1357 (7th Cir. 1990). The contractual duty of good faith is thus not some newfangled bit of welfare-state paternalism or the sediment of an altruistic strain in contract law, and we are therefore not surprised to find the essentials of the modern doctrine well established in nineteenth-century cases. . . .

The emphasis we are placing on postcontractual versus precontractual conduct helps explain the pattern that is observed when the duty of contractual good faith is considered in all its variety, encompassing not only good faith in the *performance* of a contract but also good faith in its *formation,* Summers, *supra,* at 220–32, and in its *enforcement. Harbor Ins. Co. v. Continental Bank Corp.,* 922 F.2d 357, 363 (7th Cir. 1990). The formation or negotiation stage is precontractual, and here the duty is minimized. It is greater not only at the performance but also at the enforcement stage, which is also postcontractual. "A party who hokes up a phony defense to the performance of his contractual duties and then when that defense fails (at some expense to the other party) tries on another defense for size can properly be said to be acting in bad faith." *Id.* . . . At the formation of the contract the parties are dealing in present realities; performance still lies in the future. As performance unfolds, circumstances change, often unforeseeably; the explicit terms of the contract become progressively less apt to the governance of the parties' relationship; and the role of implied conditions-and with it the scope and bite of the good-faith doctrine-grows.

We could of course do without the term "good faith," and maybe even without the doctrine. We could, as just suggested, speak instead of implied conditions necessitated by the unpredictability of the future at the time the contract was made. Suppose a party has promised work to the promisee's "satisfaction." As Learned Hand explained, "he may refuse to look at the work, or to exercise any real judgment on it, in which case he has prevented performance and excused the condition." *Thompson-Starrett Co. v. La Belle Iron Works*, 17 F.2d at 541. . . . That is, it was an implicit condition that the promisee examine the work to the extent necessary to determine whether it was satisfactory; otherwise the performing party would have been placing himself at the complete mercy of the promisee. The parties didn't write this condition into the contract either because they thought such behavior unlikely or failed to foresee it altogether. In just the same way – to switch to another familiar example of the operation of the duty of good faith – parties to a requirements contract surely do not intend that if the price of the product covered by the contract rises, the buyer shall be free to increase his "requirements" so that he can take advantage of the rise in the market price over the contract price to resell the product on the open market at a guaranteed profit. *Empire Gas Corp. v. American Bakeries Co.,* 840 F.2d 1333 (7th Cir. 1988). If they fail to insert an express condition to this effect, the court will read it in, confident that the parties would have inserted the condition if they had known what the future held. Of similar character is the implied condition that an exclusive dealer will use his best efforts to promote the supplier's goods, since otherwise the exclusive feature of the dealership contract would place the supplier at the dealer's mercy. *Wood v. Duff-Gordon,* 118 N.E. 214 (N.Y. 1917) (Cardozo, J.).

But whether we say that a contract shall be deemed to contain such implied conditions as are necessary to make sense of the contract, or that a contract obligates the parties to cooperate in its performance in "good faith" to the extent necessary to carry out the purposes of the contract, comes to much the same thing. They are different ways of formulating the overriding purpose of contract law, which is to give the parties what they would have stipulated for expressly if at the time of making the contract they had had complete knowledge of the future and the costs of negotiating and adding provisions to the contract had been zero.

The two formulations would have different meanings only if "good faith" were thought limited to "honesty in fact," an interpretation perhaps permitted but certainly not compelled by the Uniform Commercial Code, and anyway this is not a case governed by the UCC. We need not pursue this issue. The dispositive question in the present case is simply whether Market Street Associates tried to trick the pension trust and succeeded in doing so. If it did, this would be the type of opportunistic behavior in an ongoing contractual relationship that would violate the duty of good faith performance however the duty is formulated. There is much common sense in Judge Reynolds' conclusion that Market Street Associates did just that. The situation as he saw it was as follows. Market Street Associates didn't want financing from the pension trust (initially it had looked elsewhere, remember), and when it learned it couldn't get the financing without owning the property, it decided to try to buy the property. But the pension trust set a stiff price, so Orenstein decided to trick the pension trust into selling at the bargain price fixed in paragraph 34 by requesting financing and hoping that the pension trust would turn the request down without noticing the paragraph. His preliminary dealings with the pension trust made this hope a realistic one by revealing a sluggish and hidebound bureaucracy unlikely to have retained in its brontosaurus's memory, or to be able at short notice to retrieve, the details of a small lease made twenty years earlier. So by requesting financing without mentioning the lease Market Street Associates might well precipitate a refusal before the pension trust woke up to paragraph 34. It is true that Orenstein's second letter requested financing "pursuant to the lease." But when the next day he received a reply to his first letter indicating that the pension trust was indeed oblivious to paragraph 34, his response was to send a lulling letter designed to convince the pension trust that the matter was closed and could be forgotten. The stage was set for his thunderbolt: the notification the next month that Market Street Associates was taking up the option in paragraph 34. Only then did the pension trust look up the lease and discover that it had been had.

The only problem with this recital is that it construes the facts as favorably to the pension trust as the record will permit, and that of course is not the right standard for summary judgment. The facts must be construed as favorably to the nonmoving party, to Market Street Associates, as the record permits (that Market Street Associates filed its own motion for summary judgment is irrelevant, as we have seen). When that is done, a different picture emerges. On Market Street Associates' construal of the record, $3 million was a grossly excessive price for the property, and while $1 million might be a bargain it would not confer so great a windfall as to warrant an inference that if the pension trust had known about paragraph 34 it never would have turned down Market Street Associates' request for financing cold. And in fact the pension trust may have known about paragraph 34, and either it didn't care or it believed that unless the request mentioned that paragraph the pension trust would incur no liability by turning it down. Market Street Associates may have assumed and have been entitled to assume that in reviewing a request for financing from one of its lessees the pension trust would take the time to read the lease to see whether it bore on the request. Market Street Associates did not desire financing from the pension trust initially – that is undeniable – yet when it discovered that it could not get financing elsewhere unless it had the title to the property it may have realized that it would have to negotiate with the pension trust over financing before it could hope to buy the property at the price specified in the lease.

On this interpretation of the facts there was no bad faith on the part of Market Street Associates. It acted honestly, reasonably, without ulterior motive, in the face of circumstances as they actually and reasonably appeared to it. The fault was the pension trust's incredible inattention, which misled Market Street Associates into believing that the pension trust had no interest in financing the improvements regardless of the purchase option. We do not usually excuse contracting parties from failing to read and understand the contents of their contract; and in the end what this case comes down to – or so at least it can be strongly argued – is that an immensely sophisticated enterprise simply failed to read the contract. On the other hand, such enterprises make mistakes just like the rest of us, and deliberately to take advantage of your contracting partner's mistake during the performance stage (for we are not talking about taking advantage of superior knowledge at the formation stage) is a breach of good faith. To be able to correct your contract partner's mistake at zero cost to yourself, and decide not to do so, is a species of opportunistic behavior that the parties would have expressly forbidden in the contract had they foreseen it. The immensely long term of the lease amplified the possibility of errors but did not license either party to take advantage of them.

The district judge jumped the gun in choosing between these alternative characterizations. The essential issue bearing on Market Street Associates' good faith was Orenstein's state of mind, a type of inquiry that ordinarily cannot be concluded on summary judgment, and could not be here. If Orenstein believed that Erb knew or would surely find out about paragraph 34, it was not dishonest or opportunistic to fail to flag that paragraph, or even to fail to mention the lease, in his correspondence and (rare) conversations with Erb, especially given the uninterest in dealing with Market Street Associates that Erb fairly radiated. To decide what Orenstein believed, a trial is necessary. As for the pension trust's intimation that a bench trial (for remember that this is an equity case, since the only relief sought by the plaintiff is specific performance) will add no illumination beyond what the summary judgment proceeding has done, this overlooks the fact that at trial the judge will for the first time have a chance to see the witnesses whose depositions he has read, to hear their testimony elaborated, and to assess their believability.

The judgment is reversed and the case is remanded for further proceedings consistent with this opinion.

Problem 3-2

Strawberry Computer Co. manufactures and sells consumer electronic equipment. One of its biggest distributors is Better Buy, which sells the products of several manufacturers. Pursuant to a master agreement between the parties, Better Buy places orders on the 1st and 15th of each month, for delivery within 20 days. The contract calls for payment at "80% of Strawberry's suggested retail price on the day the order is accepted."

In July, Strawberry brought a new hand-held computer to the market with great fanfare. Customers lined up all night to buy them the next morning from the retailers who stocked them. Since then, sales have been brisk, but some consumers have complained that the device has inadequate memory. On October 12, Strawberry decided to lower the price of the new hand-held computer by 30% and to enhance its memory. Knowing of the contract with Better Buy, however, Strawberry made no announcement about these decisions. Instead, it waited until the 15th, when Better Buy placed an order for a large number of the hand-held computers. Strawberry immediately accepted the order and one hour later publicly announced the price decrease and memory enhancement. As a result, the computers that Better Buy agreed to purchase will be unmarketable except at a huge discount. Has Strawberry breached the duty of good faith?

C. MODIFICATION

1. *Modification by Agreement*

Contracting parties are, of course, free to modify their agreements or to waive their contractual rights. Indeed, course of performance itself can be viewed as a kind of implicit modification or waiver. Review UCC § 1-303(f). But course of performance is not the only source of modifications. The parties may expressly agree to modify the terms of their pre-existing agreement.

Traditionally, under the common law of contracts, agreements to modify a pre-existing contract were not enforceable unless supported by consideration. More modern authorities dispense with the requirement of consideration, and use some other principle to ensure a modicum of fairness. For example, under section 89 of the Restatement (Second) of Contracts, an agreement to modify is enforceable if "the modification is fair and equitable in view of circumstances not anticipated by the parties when the contract was made."

Article 2 is even more lenient. Read section 2-209(1) and comment 2. It uses "good faith," not consideration, as a policing mechanism to determine whether an agreement to modify should be enforced. Is that an adequate safeguard against extortion or economic duress? Consider the following case on whether a modification was sought and made in good faith.

ROTH STEEL PRODUCTS V. SHARON STEEL CORP.
705 F.2d 134 (6th Cir. 1983)

[In November, 1972, Sharon contracted to sell 200 tons of "hot rolled" steel per month to Roth through December, 1973. The price was $148 per ton. Sharon also "indicated" that it could sell "hot rolled" steel on an "open schedule" basis for $140 and discussed the "probability" that Sharon could sell 500 tons of "cold rolled" steel at prices varying with the type ordered. At that time, the steel industry was operating at 70% of capacity, steel prices were "highly competitive" and Sharon's quoted prices to Roth were "substantially lower" than Sharon's book price for steel. In early 1973, market conditions changed dramatically due to the development of an attractive export market and an increased domestic demand for steel. During 1973 and 1974, the steel industry operated at full capacity, steel prices rose and nearly every producer experienced substantial delays in filling orders. In March, 1973, Sharon notified all purchasers, including Roth, that it was discontinuing price concessions given in 1972.

After negotiations, the parties agreed that Roth would pay the agreed price until June 30, 1973 and a price somewhere between the agreed price and Sharon's published prices for the balance of 1973. Roth was initially reluctant to agree to this modification, but ultimately agreed "primarily because they were unable to purchase sufficient steel elsewhere to meet their production requirements." Sharon was supplying one-third of Roth's requirements and all other possible suppliers were "operating at full capacity and . . . were fully booked." The parties proceeded under this modification during the balance of 1973, although Sharon experienced difficulties in filling orders on time.

During 1974, the parties did business on an entirely different basis. Roth would order steel, Sharon would accept the order at the price "prevailing at the time of shipment." During 1974 and 1975, Sharon's deliveries were chronically late, thereby increasing the price to Roth in a rising market. Roth, however, acquiesced in this pattern because it believed Sharon's assurances that late deliveries resulted from shortages of raw materials and the need for equitable allocation among customers and because there was "no practical alternative source of supply." This acquiescence was jolted in May, 1974 when Roth learned that Sharon was allocating substantial quantities of rolled steel to one of Sharon's own subsidiaries for sale at premium prices. After several more months of desultory performance on both sides, Roth sued Sharon for breach of contract, with special emphasis upon the modified contract for 1973. Sharon raised several defenses, including impracticability and, in the alternative, the agreed modification. The district court, after a long trial, held, *inter alia,* that Sharon was not excused from the 1973 contract on the grounds of impracticability and that the modification was unenforceable. A judgment for $555,968.46 was entered for Roth.

On appeal, the court of appeals affirmed the district court's decision on the impracticability, modification and other issues, but remanded the case for factual findings on whether Roth gave Sharon timely notice of breach. On the impracticability defense under section 2-615(a), the court held that "Sharon's inability to perform was a result of its policy of accepting far more orders than it was capable of fulfilling, rather than a result of the existing shortage of raw materials." In refusing to enforce the modification of the 1973 contract, the court had this to say. – Eds.]

Celebrezze, Senior Circuit Judge

. . . C. In March, 1973, Sharon notified its customers that it intended to charge the maximum permissible price for all of its products; accordingly, all price concessions, including those made to the plaintiffs, were to be rescinded effective April 1, 1973. On March 23, 1973, Guerin [Roth's vice pres.] indicated to Metzger [Sharon's sales manager] that the plaintiffs considered the proposed price increase to be a breach of the November, 1972 contract. In an effort to resolve the dispute, Guerin met with representatives of Sharon on March 28, 1973 and asked Sharon to postpone any price increases until June or July, 1973. Several days later, Richard Mecaskey, Guerin's replacement, sent a letter to Sharon which indicated that the plaintiffs believed that the November, 1972 agreement was enforceable and that the plaintiffs were willing to negotiate a price modification if Sharon's cost increases warranted such an action. As a result of this letter, another meeting was held between Sharon and the plaintiffs. At this meeting, Walter Gregg, Sharon's vice-president and chairman of the board, agreed to continue charging the November, 1972 prices until June 30, 1973 and offered, for the remainder of 1973, to charge prices that were lower than Sharon's published prices but higher than the 1972 prices. Although the plaintiffs initially rejected the terms offered by Sharon for the second half of 1973, Mecaskey reluctantly agreed to Sharon's terms on June 29, 1973.

Before the district court, Sharon asserted that it properly increased prices because the parties had modified the November, 1973 contract to reflect changed market conditions. The district court, however, made several findings which, it believed, indicated that Sharon did not seek a modification to avoid a loss on the contract. The district court also found that the plaintiffs' inventories of rolled steel were "alarmingly deficient" at the time modification was sought and that Sharon had threatened to cease selling steel to the plaintiffs in the second-half of 1973 unless the plaintiffs agreed to the modification. Because Sharon had used its position as the plaintiffs' chief supplier to extract the price modification, the district court concluded that Sharon had acted in bad faith by seeking to modify the contract. In the alternative, the court concluded that the modification agreement was voidable because it was extracted by means of economic duress; the tight steel market prevented the plaintiffs from obtaining steel elsewhere at an affordable price and, consequently, the plaintiffs were forced to agree to the modification in order to assure a continued supply of steel. . . . Sharon challenges these conclusions on appeal.

The ability of a party to modify a contract which is subject to Article Two of the Uniform Commercial Code is broader than common law, primarily because the modification needs no consideration to be binding. [UCC § 2-209(1)]. A party's ability to modify an agreement is limited only by Article Two's general obligation of good faith. . . . In determining whether a particular modification was obtained in good faith, a court must make two distinct inquiries: whether the party's conduct is consistent with "reasonable commercial standards of fair dealing in the trade," . . . and whether the parties were in fact motivated to seek modification by an honest desire to compensate for commercial exigencies . . . [UCC § 2-103]. The first inquiry is relatively straightforward; the party asserting the modification must demonstrate that his decision to seek modification was the result of a factor, such as increased costs, which would cause an ordinary merchant to seek a modification of the contract. *See* Official Comment 2, [UCC § 2-209)] (reasonable commercial standards may require objective reason). The second inquiry, regarding the subjective honesty of the parties, is less clearly defined. Essentially, this inquiry requires the party asserting the modification to demonstrate that he was, in fact, motivated by a legitimate commercial reason and that such a reason is not offered merely as a pretext. . . . Moreover, the trier of fact must determine whether the means used to obtain the modification are an impermissible attempt to obtain a modification by extortion or overreaching. . . .

Sharon argues that its decision to seek a modification was consistent with reasonable commercial standards of fair dealing because market exigencies made further performance entail a substantial loss. The district court, however, made three findings which caused it to conclude that economic circumstances were not the reason that Sharon sought a modification: it found that Sharon was partially insulated from raw material price increases, that Sharon bargained for a contract with a slim profit margin and thus implicitly assumed the risk that performance might come to involve a loss, and that Sharon's overall profit in 1973 and its profit on the contract in the first quarter of 1973 were inconsistent with Sharon's position that the modification was sought to avoid a loss. Although all of these findings are marginally related to the question whether Sharon's conduct was consistent with reasonable commercial standards of fair dealing, we do not believe that they are sufficient to support a finding that Sharon did not observe reasonable commercial standards by seeking a modification. In our view, these findings do not support a conclusion that a reasonable merchant, in light of the circumstances, would not have sought a modification in order to avoid a loss. . . .

In the final analysis, the single most important consideration in determining whether the decision to seek a modification is justified in this context is whether, because of changes in the market or other unforeseeable conditions, performance of the contract has come to involve a loss. In this case, the district court found that Sharon suffered substantial losses by performing the contract *as modified.* . . . We are convinced that unforeseen economic exigencies existed which would prompt an ordinary merchant to seek a modification to avoid a loss on the contract; thus, we believe that the district court's findings to the contrary are clearly erroneous. . . .

The second part of the analysis, honesty in fact, is pivotal. The district court found that Sharon "threatened not to sell Roth and Toledo any steel if they refused to pay increased prices after July 1, 1973" and, consequently, that Sharon acted wrongfully. Sharon does not dispute the finding that it threatened to stop selling steel to the plaintiffs. Instead, it asserts that such a finding is merely evidence of bad faith and that it has rebutted any inference of bad faith based on that finding. We agree with this analysis; although coercive conduct is evidence that a modification of a contract is sought in bad faith, that prima facie showing may be effectively rebutted by the party seeking to enforce the modification. . . . Although we agree with Sharon's statement of principles, we do not agree that Sharon has rebutted the inference of bad faith that rises from its coercive conduct. Sharon asserts that its decision to unilaterally raise prices was based on language in the November 17, 1972 letter which allowed it to raise prices to the extent of any general industry-wide price increase. Because prices in the steel industry had increased, Sharon concludes that it was justified in raising its prices. Because it was justified in raising the contract price, the plaintiffs were bound by the terms of the contract to pay the increased prices. Consequently, any refusal by the plaintiffs to pay the price increase sought by Sharon must be viewed as a material breach of the November, 1972 contract which would excuse Sharon from any further performance. Thus, Sharon reasons that its refusal to perform absent a price increase was justified under the contract and consistent with good faith.

This argument fails in two respects. First, the contractual language on which Sharon relies only permits, at most, a price increase for cold rolled steel; thus, even if Sharon's position were supported by the evidence, Sharon would not have been justified in refusing to sell the plaintiff's hot rolled steel because of the plaintiffs' refusal to pay higher prices for the product. More importantly, however, the evidence does not indicate that Sharon ever offered this theory as a justification until this matter was tried. Sharon's representatives, in their testimony, did not attempt to justify Sharon's refusal to ship steel at 1972 prices in this fashion. Furthermore, none of the contemporaneous communications contain this justification for Sharon's action. In short, we can find no evidence in the record which indicates that Sharon offered this theory as a justification at the time the modification was sought. Consequently, we believe that the district court's conclusion that Sharon acted in bad faith by using coercive conduct to extract the price modification is not clearly erroneous. Therefore, we hold that Sharon's attempt to modify the November, 1972 contract, in order to compensate for increased costs which made performance come to involve a loss, is ineffective because Sharon did not act in a manner consistent with Article Two's requirement of honesty in fact when it refused to perform its remaining obligations under the contract at 1972 prices.[6] . . .

---

[6]   The district court also found, as an alternative ground, that the modification was voidable because the plaintiffs agreed to the modification due to economic duress. *See, e.g., Oskey Gasoline & Oil Co. v. Continental Oil*, 534 F.2d 1281 (8th Cir.1976). Because we conclude that the modification was ineffective as a result of Sharon's bad faith, we do not reach the issue whether the contract modification was also voidable because of economic duress. We note, however, that proof that coercive means were used is necessary to establish that a contract is voidable because of economic duress. Normally, it cannot be used to void a contract modification which has been sought in good faith; if a contract modification has been found to be in good faith, then presumably no wrongful coercive means have been used to extract the modification.

2. Statute of Frauds

Even if the parties have agreed, in good faith, to modify their contract, in some circumstances that modification may not be enforceable due to the application of the statute of frauds. In fact, there are in essence two different statutes of fraud that can apply in such circumstances. First read section 2-209(3), review section 2-201 and the material in Chapter Two on the statute of frauds, and consider the following problem.

Problem 3-3

A. S and B enter into an oral agreement to sell 100 widgets for the total price of $400. Before any performance has occurred, the parties modify their agreement to double the quantity and the total price. Does the agreement have to meet the requirements of section 2-201 to be enforceable?

B. S and B enter into an agreement to sell 100 widgets for the total price of $1,000. There is a writing sufficient to satisfy section 2-201. Before performance, the parties agree to increase the quantity to 110 widgets, but with no change in price. Must the modification satisfy section 2-201 to be enforceable?

C. S and B enter into an agreement to sell 100 widgets for the total price of $1,000. There is a writing sufficient to satisfy section 2-201. Subsequently the parties agree to reduce the quantity to 90 widgets and to decrease the sale price to $900. Must the modification satisfy section 2-201 to be enforceable? *Compare Costco Wholesale Corp. v. World Wide Licensing Corp.*, 898 P.2d 347 (Wash. Ct. App. 1995) *with Zemco Manufacturing Inc. v. Navistar Int'l Transportation Corp.*, 186 F.3d 815 (7th Cir. 1999).

D. S and B enter into an agreement to sell 100 widgets for the total price of $1,000, delivery on June 1. There is a writing sufficient to satisfy section 2-201. Subsequently, the parties agree to change the delivery date to July 1. Must the modification satisfy section 2-201 to be enforceable?

Even if the agreement as modified satisfies the statute of frauds in section 2-201, perhaps because it is for a price of less that $500, it may still run afoul of a second sort of statute of fraud: one created by the initial agreement of the parties.

Read section 2-209(2). This provision authorizes parties to a contract for sale to require that any modification to the agreement be in writing. This type of clause, which some refer to as a private statute of frauds, is more commonly known as a "no-oral modification" (NOM) clause. What is the purpose of the NOM clause? Why is there a "separate signing" requirement if a NOM clause is in a form supplied by a merchant to a non-merchant? Are there good reasons for not having a NOM clause in an agreement?

What happens if the parties' initial agreement has a NOM clause, the parties then orally agree to a modification, but the requirements of section 2-209(2) are not met? Does the agreed modification have any effect on the parties' rights and obligations? Unfortunately, the answer to this is complicated and involves the interaction of several related concepts: modification, waiver, and estoppel. Read section 2-209(4) and (5) and then consider the following illustration.

Illustration

S and B enter into a signed, written agreement for S to sell to B 1,000 widgets for $10,000, with delivery in four equal installments on four consecutive Mondays, beginning in one week. The agreement contains a clause providing that "no modification to this agreement will be binding unless made in writing and signed by both parties." Before the first delivery was due, S telephoned B and asked if the deliveries could be on Tuesday. B agreed. S delivered the first installment on the first Tuesday.

The agreement to modify the day for delivery was not in writing and, under the NOM clause and section 2-209(2), would be unenforceable. However, even though the modification is unenforceable, B may have waived the right to insist on delivery on Monday. To determine whether B has in fact made such a waiver, and if so, whether that waiver can be retracted, we need to analyze section 2-209(4) and (5).

Even a quick reading of section 2-209(4) should be enough to tell you that it does not actually say what qualifies as a waiver, merely that a failed modification can operate as one. Thus, we presumably need to consult the common law to determine whether B has made a waiver. The traditional definition of "waiver" is "the voluntary relinquishment of a known right." *See* RESTATEMENT (SECOND) OF CONTRACTS § 84 cmt. b. B's actions appear to be voluntary and knowing, so in all likelihood B has waived the right to delivery on Monday.[7] In other words, B's agreement to modify, which may not be enforceable as a modification due to the no oral modification clause, nevertheless may act as a waiver of the right to claim that S has breached by the Tuesday delivery. However, absent either an enforceable agreement to modify or an express waiver, the mere act of accepting the one late delivery will not normally operate as a waiver of the right to complain about (or sue for breach because of) the late delivery. *See* UCC § 2-607(2), (3).

If B has waived its right to insist on Monday delivery, can B retract the waiver? Yes, but only by giving reasonable notification and only if S has not relied to its detriment so that such a retraction would be unjust. The application of this standard will likely produce a different result for the past delivery than for the future deliveries. B probably cannot retract the waiver for the first delivery for two reasons: (i) notification after the fact would probably not be reasonable; and (ii) S has relied on the waiver in such a way that retraction now would be unjust. However, B can probably retract the waiver with respect to future deliveries.[8]

Can S successfully argue that B's agreement to the first late delivery was not only an agreement to modify the delivery date for all four deliveries but in addition a waiver of the enforcement of the NOM clause? If S wins that argument, then B's agreement to modify the delivery dates for the future would be enforceable and B could not insist on the old delivery schedule absent S's agreement.[9]

Now try your hand at the following problem, which adds course of performance to the analysis.

---

[7]   *See BMC Industries, Inc. v. Barth Indus., Inc.,*160 F.3d 1322 (11th Cir. 1998), *cert. denied*, 526 U.S. 1132 (1999). Another circuit insists that to have an enforceable waiver, there must be detrimental reliance on that waiver. *Wisconsin Knife Works v. National Metal Crafters*, 781 F.2d 1280 (7th Cir. 1986).

[8]   B might not be able to retract the waiver even as to the future deliveries if S – after getting B's initial agreement to Tuesday delivery and before learning of the retraction – made arrangements for deliveries on Tuesdays and those arrangements would be difficult or expensive to change.

[9]   *See Royster-Clark, Inc. v. Olsen's Mill, Inc.*, 714 N.W.2d 530 (Wis. 2006); *Honeywell Intern. Inc. v. Air Products & Chemical Co.*, 872 A.2d 944 (Del. 2005).

Problem 3-4

On March 15, S and B enter into a signed, written agreement for S to sell to B 10,000 widgets each month for the next twelve months. The agreement calls for delivery to B's premises by the 5th of each month, beginning in April. In April, S delivers the goods to a carrier on April 4, and the carrier delivers the widgets to B on April 7. B accepted the delivery without complaint.

A. Have the parties modified their agreement by their course of performance? *See* UCC § 2-208 cmt. 4. Has B waived its right to complain about the late delivery?

B. Subsequently, in both May and June, S delivered the widgets to the carrier before the 5th but the goods were not delivered to B until after the 5th. B did not complain about either delivery. Have the parties modified their agreement by their course of performance? May B notify S that all deliveries have to be at B's premises on time and that B will no longer accept late deliveries?

C. How, if at all, would your analysis change if the initial agreement provided that "no modification to this agreement will be binding unless made in writing and signed by both parties"?

CISG and UNIDROIT Principles. CISG Article 29 addresses modifications. Agreements to modify are enforceable. Although no general statute of frauds applies to modifications, CISG Art. 11, the parties may have a "no oral modification" clause. CISG Art. 29(2). The UNIDROIT Principles are similar, UNIDROIT Art. 2.1.18. Both the CISG and UNIDROIT Principles recognize the possibility of a party waiving the application of the NOM clause.

SECTION 2. ADDING TO THE AGREEMENT: EXPRESS WARRANTIES

When the seller agrees to sell goods to the buyer, the parties' agreement will usually include terms – either expressly or implicitly through course of performance, course of dealing, or usage of trade – relevant to the nature and quality of the goods that the seller is to provide. These terms are called warranties. Most consumer think warranties are promises about how long the goods will last or will continue to function. While such promises are indeed warranties, the Article 2 concept of warranty is much broader and encompasses far more. Read section

2-313. Notice that each subsection and paragraph of this section contains both words of inclusion and words of exclusion or limitation. Let's parse it out. An express warranty can be created by any statement of fact or promise made by the seller to the buyer that relates to the good, UCC § 2-313(1)(a), or any description of the goods, UCC § 2-313(1)(b). Use of the words "warranty" or "guaranty" is not required. UCC § 2-313(2). Furnishing a sample or model also gives rise to an express warranty. UCC § 2-313(1)(c).

Let's pause for a moment, before looking at the limitations, to consider what this means. Consider a Seller who agrees to sell a "new brown horse" to Buyer for $3,000. That is a warranty. If, at the appointed place and time where the exchange is to occur, Seller tenders a child's 2-inch plastic horse, Seller will be in breach. The parties are free to make their own agreement, but "the probability is small that a real price is intended to be exchanged for a pseudo-obligation." UCC § 2-313 cmt. 4. Thus, Article 2 rejects, at least in part, the idea of "caveat emptor."

However, not every statement made during the contract formation process qualifies as a warranty. A statement purporting to be merely "the seller's opinion or commendation" does not create an express warranty. UCC § 2-313(2). Moreover, no express warranty is ever created unless the statement, promise, description, sample, or model is part of the "basis of the bargain." UCC § 2-313(1)(a), (b), (c). Accordingly, the first step in analyzing whether an express warranty claim has been created is to determine whether the language or actions of the seller is such as to rise to the level of a warranty. In other words, has the seller made an affirmation of fact or promise regarding the goods, supplied a description of the goods, or provided a sample or model of the goods, and is whatever the seller provided more than mere opinion or commendation? The second step is to determine whether the affirmation of fact, promise regarding the goods, description, sample or model is part of the "basis of the bargain."

Affirmation of fact or opinion. By far, most of the litigation regarding whether the seller has made an express warranty involves the distinction between an "affirmation of fact" and an "opinion." How do we know whether a statement is an affirmation of fact? One court described the distinction as follows:

> The decisive test for whether a given representation is a warranty or merely an expression of the seller's opinion is whether the seller asserts a fact of which the buyer is ignorant or merely states an opinion or judgment on a

matter of which the seller has no special knowledge and on which the buyer may be expected also to have an opinion and to exercise his judgment.[10]

Do you agree? Try the following problem. As you do so, identify the factors that are relevant in distinguishing fact from opinion.

Problem 3-5

In which, if any, of the following situations, has the seller made a statement that would qualify as an express warranty if the statement were part of the basis of the bargain?

A. A seller of women's clothing tells a customer that the dress the customer is trying on "looks good on you."

B. A seller of artwork tells a buyer that "it's a beautiful painting by a talented artist."

C. A seller of antiques describes a desk as a "Queen Anne," a vase as a "Ming," and a table as "antique."

D. A seller of sports memorabilia says that "this is the ball that Mike Lowell caught to win game four of the 2007 World Series."

E. A dealer in new cars stated to a buyer that a new car model was "the safest car in its class." *Cf. Gallagher v. WMK Inc.*, 2007 WL 4322531 (Ohio Ct. App. 2007).

F. A manufacturer of roofing shingles stated that the shingles had "improved waterproofing" and "longer life." *See Viking Yacht Co. v. Composites One LLC*, 496 F. Supp. 2d 462 (D. N.J. 2007).

G. A camera manufacturer advertised its new camera as providing "superior performance" and "professional quality" digital images. *See National Mulch and Seed, Inc. v. Rexius Forest By-Products, Inc.*, 2007 WL 894833 (S.D. Ohio 2007).

H. A dealer in yachts stated to a buyer that a used boat was "seaworthy." *See Keith v. Buchanan*, 220 Cal. Rptr. 392 (Cal. Ct. App. 1985).

I. A dealer of thoroughbred race horses stated in negotiations with a potential buyer that a particular horse was "sound." *See Sessa v. Riegle*, 427 F. Supp. 760 (E.D. Pa. 1977), *aff'd* 568 F.2d 770 (3d Cir. 1978); *see also Simpson v. Widger*, 709 A.2d 1366, 1371 (N.J. Super. A.D. 1998) (discussing the meaning of the phrase "sound horse").

---

[10]   *Royal Business Machines, Inc. v. Lorraine Corp.*, 633 F.2d 34, 41 (7th Cir. 1980).

Now that you have worked on Problem 3-5, do you think the distinction between fact and opinion is a sound basis for drawing a line between what qualifies as an express warranty and what does not? Is it easy for buyers to distinguish between them?[11]

Basis of the bargain. We now turn to the second limitation on what qualifies as an express warranty: the requirement that the affirmation of fact, promise, description, sample or model must be part of the "basis of the bargain." At first blush, this may seem like an innocuous or even obvious requirement. Yet bear in mind that no other express terms must meet this test to become part of the parties' agreement. For example, if the seller stated during negotiations it would deliver the goods at a specified time and place, we would not inquire whether the statement is a "basis of the bargain" to determine if it was an enforceable promise. So why should affirmations of fact, promises related to the goods, descriptions of the goods, or a sample or model of the goods, be subject to this test? Does this test make any sense if the seller's representation regarding the quality of the goods is contained in the purchase agreement documentation? For example, if the seller states in the purchase agreement document that the good has a precise capability (such as 100 RPM, or a top speed of 50 MPH), should the buyer have to engage in further proof to demonstrate that this representation was part of the basis of the bargain?

What does the phrase "basis of the bargain" mean? Must the buyer demonstrate reliance on the seller's representation in order to prove the seller made an express warranty? Comment 3 to section 2-313 suggests not but courts do not all agree.

> There is a clear split of authority among the jurisdictions as to whether a buyer must show reliance on a statement or representation for it to be considered part of the "basis of the bargain." Some jurisdictions require a strict showing of reliance. Other jurisdictions have no reliance requirement. And still other jurisdictions have applied a rebuttable presumption of reliance.[12]

---

[11]   *See* David A. Hoffman, *The Best Puffery Article Ever*, 91 IOWA L. REV 1395, 1435 (2006) ("Jurists and regulatory authorities routinely assume that buyers of goods, services and securities ignore puffing statements. This . . . is simply untrue. Marketing scholars have demonstrated that puffing statements are believed on their own terms, and lead some individuals to further imply facts about the puffed speech that are untrue.").

[12]   *Cole v. General Motors Corp.*, 484 F.3d 717, 726 (5th Cir. 2007).

Related to this is whether statements made or received after the offer and acceptance process – or even after the parties have tendered their performance – can be part of the "basis of the bargain." Given that no consideration is needed to modify a sale-of-goods contract, *see* UCC § 2-209, do the assertions made on documents inside the package of prepackaged products constitute express warranties? It is hard to deny that such statements could and should give rise to liability; indeed, cases hold that assertions in operating manuals for automobiles and the like that are never read by the buyer prior to the purchase may constitute express warranties.[13]

If the bargain can include things seen or heard after the agreement is formed, then what about advertisements published by the seller but never seen by the buyer? Perhaps never seen by any resident of the particular buyer's state? For example, would an assertion by a manufacturer about product quality made in the interior of China, only in Chinese, and seen only by Chinese citizens constitute an express warranty that is part of the basis of the bargain for a buyer in New Jersey? If reliance means anything, that case is hard to swallow, but where then does one draw the line between the case of the manual or package insert and the case of the advertising published in a distant land and never seen? Of course, one can say that the purchaser of a product expects to get some instructions and statements within the box and that the buyer of a GM pickup truck expects the same. In that sense there might possibly be "reliance." Is that a satisfactory distinction?

Now consider the following case. Should it matter that the buyer knew that the seller's representation was unlikely to be true? What does this case add to your understanding of the requirements for an express warranty, more specifically, the requirement that the seller's representation be part of the basis of the bargain?

ROGATH V. SIEBENMANN
129 F.3d 261 (2d Cir. 1997)

McLaughlin, Circuit Judge

BACKGROUND

This case revolves around a painting, entitled "Self Portrait," supposedly painted in 1972 by a well-known English artist, Francis Bacon.

---

[13] *See, e.g., Forbes v. General Motors Corp.*, 935 So.2d 869 (Miss. 2006) (statement in owner's manual); *Rite Aid Corp. v. Levy-Gray*, 894 A.2d 563 (Md. 2006) (pharmacy package insert). *Compare Jarrett v. Duro-Med Indus.*, 2008 WL 89932 (E.D. Ky. 2008).

In July 1993, defendant Werner Siebenmann sold the Painting to plaintiff David Rogath for $570,000. In the Bill of Sale, Siebenmann described the provenance of the Painting and warranted that he was the sole owner of the Painting, that it was authentic, and that he was not aware of any challenge to its authenticity.

Problems arose three months later when Rogath sold the Painting to Acquavella Contemporary Art, Inc., in New York, for $950,000. Acquavella learned of a challenge to the Painting's authenticity and, on November 1, 1993, requested that Rogath refund the $950,000 and take back the Painting. Rogath did so, and then sued Siebenmann in the Southern District of New York (Batts, J.) for breach of contract, breach of warranty and fraud.

Rogath moved for partial summary judgment on the breach of warranty claims, and the district court granted his motion. *See Rogath v. Siebenmann*, 941 F. Supp. 416, 422-24 (S.D.N.Y. 1996). The court concluded that (1) Siebenmann was unsure of the provenance of the Painting when he sold it to Rogath; (2) he was not the sole owner of the Painting; and (3) when he sold the Painting to Rogath he already knew of a challenge to the Painting's authenticity by the Marlborough Fine Art Gallery in London. *See id.* The court awarded Rogath $950,000 in damages, the price at which he had sold it to Acquavella. *See id.* at 424-25. The court dismissed, *sua sponte*, Rogath's remaining claims for fraud and breach of contract "in light of the full recovery on the warranties granted herein." *Id.* at 425. Finally, a few days later, the court denied Rogath's motion to attach the money that Siebenmann had remaining from the proceeds of the initial sale to Rogath.

Siebenmann appeals the grant of partial summary judgment. Rogath cross-appeals the denial of his motion for attachment and the dismissal of his fraud and breach of contract claims.

DISCUSSION

Siebenmann concedes that his promises and representations set forth in the Bill of Sale constitute warranties under New York law. He claims, however, that Rogath was fully aware when he bought the Painting that questions of authenticity and provenance had already been raised regarding the Painting. He maintains that, under New York law, Rogath therefore cannot rest claims for breach of warranty on the representations made in the Bill of Sale.

We review *de novo* the district court's disposition of Rogath's motion for partial summary judgment. . . . The parties agree that New York law applies.

A. Breach of Warranty under New York Law

The Bill of Sale provides:

> In order to induce David Rogath to make the purchase, Seller . . . make[s] the following warranties, representations and covenants to and with the Buyer.
>
> 1. That the Seller is the sole and absolute owner of the painting and has full right and authority to sell and transfer same; having acquired title as described in a copy of the Statement of Provenance signed by Seller annexed hereto and incorporated herein; [and] that the Seller has no knowledge of any challenge to Seller's title and authenticity of the Painting. . . .

Because the Bill of Sale was a contract for the sale of goods, Rogath's breach of warranty claims are governed by Article Two of the Uniform Commercial Code ("UCC"). . . . Section 2-313 of the UCC provides that "[a]ny description of the goods which is made part of the basis of the bargain creates an express warranty that the goods shall conform to the description." N.Y.U.C.C. § 2-313(1)(b) (McKinney 1993).

Whether the "basis of the bargain" requirement implies that the buyer must rely on the seller's statements to recover and what the nature of that reliance requirement is are unsettled questions. . . . Not surprisingly, this same confusion haunted the New York courts for a time. . . .

Some courts reasoned that the buyer must have relied upon the accuracy of the seller's affirmations or promises in order to recover . . . .

Other courts paid lip service to a "reliance" requirement, but found that the requirement was met if the buyer relied on the seller's promise as part of "the basis of the bargain" in entering into the contract; the buyer need not show that he relied on the truthfulness of the warranties. . . .

Finally, some courts reasoned that there is a "reliance" requirement only when there is a dispute as to whether a warranty was in fact given by the seller. These courts concluded that no reliance of any kind is required "where the existence of an express warranty in a contract is conceded by both parties." . . . In these cases, the buyer need establish only a breach of the warranty.

In 1990 New York's Court of Appeals dispelled much of the confusion when it squarely adopted the "basis of the bargain" description of the reliance required to recover for breach of an express warranty. In *CBS Inc. v. Ziff-Davis Publishing Co.*, 553 N.E.2d 997 (N.Y. 1990), the court concluded that "[t]his view of 'reliance' – i.e., as requiring no more than reliance on the express warranty as being a part of the bargain between the parties – reflects the prevailing perception of an action for breach of express warranty as one that is no longer grounded in tort, but essentially in contract." *Id.* at 1001. The court reasoned that "[t]he critical question is not whether the buyer believed in the truth of the warranted information . . . but whether [he] believed [he] was purchasing the [seller's] promise [as to its truth]." *Id.* at 1000–01 (quotations omitted and some insertions altered).

CBS was not decided on the basis of the UCC, probably because the sale of the magazine business at issue did not constitute the sale of goods. . . . Nevertheless, the court relied heavily on UCC authorities, *see CBS*, 553 N.E.2d at 1000–01, expressly noting that "analogy to the Uniform Commercial Code is 'instructive'." *Id.* at 1002 n.4.

In 1992, in a case also involving the sale of a business, we followed the New York Court of Appeals and delineated fine factual distinctions in the law of warranties: a court must evaluate both the extent and the source of the buyer's knowledge about the truth of what the seller is warranting. "Where a buyer closes on a contract in the full knowledge and acceptance of facts *disclosed by the seller* which would constitute a breach of warranty under the terms of the contract, the buyer should be foreclosed from later asserting the breach. In that situation, unless the buyer expressly preserves his rights under the warranties . . ., we think the buyer has waived the breach." *Galli v. Metz*, 973 F.2d 145, 151 (2d Cir. 1992) (emphasis added) . . . . The buyer may preserve his rights by expressly stating that disputes regarding the accuracy of the seller's warranties are unresolved, and that by signing the agreement the buyer does not waive any rights to enforce the terms of the agreement. *See Galli*, 973 F.2d at 150.

On the other hand, if the seller is not the source of the buyer's knowledge, *e.g.*, if it is merely "common knowledge" that the facts warranted are false, or the buyer has been informed of the falsity of the facts by some third party, the buyer may prevail in his claim for breach of warranty. In these cases, it is not unrealistic to assume that the buyer purchased the seller's warranty "as insurance against any future claims," and that is why he insisted on the inclusion of the warranties in the bill of sale. *Galli*, 973 F.2d at 151 . . . .

In short, where the seller discloses up front the inaccuracy of certain of his warranties, it cannot be said that the buyer – absent the express preservation of his rights – believed he was purchasing the seller's promise as to the truth of the warranties. Accordingly, what the buyer knew and, most importantly, whether he got that knowledge from the seller are the critical questions. *See Galli*, 973 F.2d at 151; *Chateaugay*, 155 B.R. at 650–51.

1. What Siebenmann Knew

Here, as the district court pointed out, Siebenmann, the seller, produced no evidence to contradict Rogath's evidence that Siebenmann knew of the cloud that hung over the Painting's authenticity before he sold it to Rogath. Siebenmann admits that he was told that the Marlborough Gallery was troubled by certain peculiarities of the Painting – including shiny black paint (as opposed to the matte black that Bacon apparently preferred) and the use of pink paint (which Bacon evidently did not use) – that suggested that Bacon was not the painter.

Siebenmann also admits that Julian Barran, a London art dealer, had earlier refused to buy the Painting because of doubts harbored by the Marlborough Gallery. Moreover, there was uncontroverted evidence that, on a prior occasion, Siebenmann's attempted sale of the Painting to a client of Robert Peter Miller, the owner of an art gallery in New York, was aborted when (1) Miller learned that the Marlborough had concerns about the Painting's authenticity, and (2) David Sylvester, a British art critic, advised Miller not to proceed with the purchase because of the Marlborough objection and because Sylvester himself was not sure of the authenticity of the Painting.

Finally, Siebenmann does not deny that in June 1993 he received a fax from Anita Goldstein, an art dealer in Zurich, Switzerland, stating that "everybody is afraid of the authenticity" of the Painting.

2. What Siebenmann Told Rogath: Reasonable Inferences

In an affidavit in opposition to Rogath's motion for partial summary judgment, Siebenmann stated that "I spoke directly with David Rogath about the controversy created by the Marlborough Gallery towards this painting." He also said that, in a phone conversation with Rogath on July 13, 1993, "I specifically mentioned Marlborough Gallery and the 'problems' or the 'controversy' that it had produced for this painting. . . . Mr. Rogath brushed aside the Marlborough Gallery controversy. He told me he had experienced difficulties with this particular gallery in the past and did not consider them to be especially reputable." In his deposition, Siebenmann added that he told Rogath on the phone "that I had problems with the Marlborough Gallery."

Siebenmann also filed an affidavit from Ronald Alley, the curator of the Tate Gallery in London, England, and the author of a survey of Bacon's work as well as several other writings about Bacon. Alley stated:

> I was phoned by Mr David Rogath, hitherto unknown to me, who said that
> he was thinking of buying the painting and asked whether it was correct

that I had seen it and thought it to be authentic. My reply, to the best of my recollection, can be summarized as follows: "It is a picture which did not pass through Marlborough Fine Art and is said to have a provenance which sounds quite plausible but is more or less impossible to check. Both Ms Beston of Marlborough Fine Art and David Sylvester say they don't think it is by Bacon, but Sylvester knows it only from a photograph. I flew to Geneva for the day to look at it in a warehouse and felt convinced it was genuine."

For his part, Rogath denied that he was aware of any challenges to the authenticity or provenance of the Painting before entering into the Bill of Sale. He stated in his affidavit:

> During our telephone conversation, Mr. Siebenmann did not tell me that the Marlborough Gallery had "questioned" or "reserved judgment" about the Painting, or had caused any "problems" or "controversy" concerning the Painting. He said nothing at all like that during the conversation. Neither did Mr. Alley, in our subsequent conversation, refer to any such matters. He certainly did not tell me that Ms. Beston and Mr. Sylvester "don't think it is by Bacon." In fact, I spoke with Mr. Alley after the inauthenticity of the Painting had become known to me. . . . Had either Mr. Siebenmann or Mr. Alley hinted to me that the Painting was of questioned authenticity, it would have been a "red flag" for me, as I had no desire to spend some $600,000 dollars to purchase a painting the authenticity of which was in dispute. . . .

Here, the Bill of Sale states that the warranties induced Rogath to buy the Painting, but Rogath did not "expressly preserve his rights" under the Bill of Sale, as required by *Galli.* . . . Accordingly, exactly what Siebenmann told Rogath is clearly crucial. . . . On the other hand, what Alley may have told Rogath about the authenticity and provenance of the Painting is immaterial. . . . Only if the seller, Siebenmann himself, informed Rogath of doubts about the provenance or challenges to authenticity will Rogath be deemed to have waived any claims for breach of warranty arising from the written representations appearing in the Bill of Sale. . . .

As Rogath emphasizes, Siebenmann nowhere specifically alleges that he informed Rogath of his doubts about the authenticity and provenance of the Painting. He merely alluded to the "controversy" or "problems" with the Marlborough Gallery. Still, Siebenmann's testimony, however ambiguous, may justify the inference that Rogath knew more than he now claims to have known when he entered into the Bill of Sale.

At the very least, there is indisputable ambiguity in the affidavits about the pivotal exchange between Rogath and Siebenmann. We are satisfied that genuine issues of fact persist. In this posture, we must draw all reasonable inferences in Siebenmann's favor. . . . Accordingly, as regards the Marlborough challenge, summary judgment on Rogath's claims for breach of the warranties of provenance and no challenges to authenticity is inappropriate. . . .

3. What Sylvester Said

Sylvester's doubts about the Painting also cannot justify summary judgment for Rogath, but for different reasons. Siebenmann was aware that "Sylvester advised Miller not to proceed with the purchase of the Painting because of the 'Marlborough objection and that he wasn't sure himself of the authenticity of the painting.' " Siebenmann did not claim to have disclosed to Rogath Sylvester's statement. Indeed, in his affidavit opposing Rogath's summary judgment motion, Siebenmann stated that he did not consider Sylvester's doubts to be a challenge. Siebenmann's nondisclosure could constitute a breach of warranty-but only if Sylvester's statement was a "challenge" to authenticity. We conclude that the question of whether Sylvester's statement constituted a challenge poses factual issues for trial.

A contractual term is ambiguous where it may be ascribed "conflicting reasonable interpretations." *Mellon Bank, N.A. v. United Bank Corp. of N.Y.*, 31 F.3d 113, 116 (2d Cir. 1994). "As a general matter, we have held that when a contract is ambiguous, its interpretation becomes a question of fact and summary judgment is inappropriate." *Id.*

Although the parties apparently agree as to what Sylvester said, reasonable minds could differ as to whether what he said constituted a challenge apart from the Marlborough challenge. Sylvester's recommendation that the buyer not proceed "because of the Marlborough objection" could reasonably be interpreted as merely advice to heed the Marlborough challenge. Further, a rational juror could interpret the statement that "[Sylvester] wasn't sure" as evincing an ambivalence on the part of Sylvester that did not rise to the level of a challenge, especially given that Sylvester himself had not seen the Painting, but only photographs of it.

In this context, moreover, the term may well be a specialized one. It is hardly clear as a matter of law that "challenge" includes every mention by one person of the fact that a challenge has been made by another person (or, for example, that it would include Anita Goldstein's statement that "everybody is afraid of the authenticity" of the Painting). Nor is it clear as a matter of law whether the term "challenge" would include an expression of uncertainty by someone who had never seen the painting in question. If Siebenmann proffers art-industry or other evidence as to the meaning of this ambiguous contract term, its meaning will be a question for the jury at trial. . . .

CONCLUSION

The order granting Rogath's motion for partial summary judgment is vacated, and the case is remanded to the district court for disposition not inconsistent with this opinion.

Problem 3-6

Buyer needed a high-speed printer for use in Buyer's offices. In discussions with Seller's sales representative, Buyer received assurances that its X3000 printer could print 35 black-and-white pages per minute and 20 color pages per minute. The sales representative also assured Buyer that Buyer would be very happy with the printer. Buyer also picked up the sales brochure for the X3000, which stated that the X3000 had a "60,000 pages per month duty cycle." Buyer purchased the printer. Inside the box containing the printer was an owner's manual which contained the following language: "Seller warrants that the printer will be free of defects in material and workmanship for one year from date of delivery." Which, if any, of the statements made by the sales representative, in the brochure, and in the owner's manual constitute an express warranty?

Privity. Many courts have held that a lack of privity is not a bar to recovery on an express warranty.[14] In other words, if a manufacturer or other remote seller makes a representation that otherwise meets the test of section 2-313, the fact that the buyer suing on the express warranty was not in privity with (did not buy the

---

[14]   *See e.g., Tex Enterprises, Inc. v. Brockway Standard, Inc.*, 66 P.3d 625 (Wash. 2003) (distinguishing express warranty from implied warranty regarding relaxation of privity requirement). *See* Harry M. Flechtner, *Enforcing Manufacturers' Warranties, "Pass Through" Warranties, and the Like: Can the Buyer Get a Refund?* 50 RUTGERS L. REV. 397 (1998); Curtis R. Reitz, *Manufacturers' Warranties of Consumer Goods*, 75 WASH. U. L.Q. 357 (1997); Donald F. Clifford, *Express Warranty Liability of Remote Sellers: One Purchase, Two Relationships*, 75 WASH. U. L.Q. 413 (1997).

goods from) the remote seller did not preclude the suit. The rationale for this is very simple:

> To hold otherwise could allow unscrupulous manufacturers who make public representations about their product's performance to remain insulated from express-warranty liability if consumers did not purchase the product directly from them.[15]

See also UCC § 2-318. We will return to the question of privity in Chapter Seven, when we discuss buyer's remedies, and in Chapter Eight, when we discuss the relationship of Article 2 to other law.

CISG. Article 30 of CISG states that the seller "must deliver the goods . . . as required by the contract and this Convention." Article 35(1) then provides that the seller "must deliver goods which are the . . . quality and description required by the contract and which are contained or packaged in the manner required by the contract." Unless the parties have agreed otherwise, the goods do not conform to the contract unless they "possess the qualities of goods which the seller has held out to the buyer as a sample or model" and "are contained or packaged in the manner usual for such goods or, where there is not such manner, in a manner adequate to preserve and protect the goods." CISG Art. 35(2)(c)-(d). Note that neither the phrase "express warranty" nor "basis of the bargain" is used and the "sample or model" issue is treated as a "gap filler."

The key question is what does the contract require. The answer is easy when the description of the goods and representations and promises dealing with the quality of the goods are contained in a writing assented to by both parties. But suppose that the core description or that representations about the goods made to the buyer during negotiations or after the contract is formed do not appear in the written contract. Presumably, the buyer must prove that the description or affirmations are part of the contract and that the goods failed to conform. In this process, there is considerable latitude for extrinsic evidence to be admitted. *See* CISG Art. 8, 9, 11, and 12.[16]

---

[15]   *U.S. Tire-Tech, Inc. v. Boeran, B.V.*, 110 S.W.3d 194, 198 (Tex. Ct. App. 2003).

[16]   *See also* Andrew J. Kennedy, *Recent Developments: Nonconforming Goods Under the CISG–What's A Buyer to Do?*, 16 DICK. J. INT'L L. 319 (1998).

UNIDROIT Principles. Because the Principles are not directed solely to the provision of goods, its default rules on the quality of performance are somewhat difficult to apply. A party may have an obligation to achieve a particular result (as opposed to a "best efforts" standard. To determine if a party has that obligation, the contract must be interpreted. Factors in that interpretation include the way the obligation is expressed, the price or other terms, the degree of risk involved in achieving that result, and the ability of the other party to influence that performance. UNIDROIT Arts. 5.1.4, 5.1.5. If the quality of performance is not fixed or determined by the contract terms, a party is bound to render a performance "of a quality that is reasonable and not less than average in the circumstances." UNIDROIT Art. 5.1.6.

SECTION 3.   ADDING TO THE AGREEMENT: GAP FILLERS

A. OVERVIEW

When most sales agreements are made, the parties have not discussed all of the terms of their deal. This is certainly true for most informal transactions but it is also true for some formal, negotiated deals. Think about the last time you ordered goods over the phone or on the internet. In all likelihood, you and the seller agreed on the nature and quantity of the goods involved, the price, and the method of payment. But did you discuss who would bear the risk of loss if the goods were damaged or destroyed en route? Did you detail what your rights would be if the goods were not delivered on time or were defective?

Because it would be too burdensome for the parties – and to commerce generally – to require contracting parties to reach express agreement on all the terms that could be relevant to a transaction, the law allows them to omit some or even many terms from their *agreement* (which includes usage of trade, course of performance, and course of dealing). The law then supplies the missing terms into their *contract*. These supplied terms – known as gap fillers – can include such minor matters as risk of loss and method of payment, but can also include more significant terms, such as the price and warranties. Even most remedies for breach can be thought of as gap fillers because the parties are free by agreement to change them.

Before exploring the gap fillers in detail and considering whether there is a common policy underlying them, it is necessary to understand that there are two conditions to having an enforceable contract. Read section 2-204(3). It allows the parties to make an enforceable agreement – *i.e.,* a contract – if they have "intended to make a contract" and there is a "reasonably certain basis for giving an appropriate remedy." Gap fillers can play a role in the analysis of both of these conditions.

If there are unresolved material terms, and one of the parties is resisting enforcement of the bargain, the court must decide whether the parties intended to make a bargain that the legal system should enforce. In line with basic contract principles, the parties' intent to enter into an enforceable agreement must be manifested objectively in some manner. What factors are relevant to this determination of intent? Section 2-204(1) indicates that the parties' conduct can be relevant. Presumably, the relative completeness of the agreement is also relevant. In other words, the more terms they have discussed and agreed to – or which can be implied into their agreement by applicable course of performance, course of dealing, or usage of trade – the more likely it is that they intend to be bound. After all, parties often intend to be bound by their agreements even though they still need and expect to work out a few details later. If the parties have left matters to be specified later, those specifications must generally be made in good faith. UCC § 2-311(1). Conversely, the fewer terms they have resolved, the more likely it is that they are still in the midst of negotiations and do not yet intend to have a contract. That said, sometimes the parties may have omitted a single term because they have not yet been able to agree on it and they expect not to be bound until they do. Similarly, sometimes when parties have resolved only a few terms they nevertheless expect to be bound and expect the unresolved matters will be resolved later or supplied by gap fillers. Even a sketchy agreement can be filled in and made complete. Thus, the parties' intent to be bound will often have to be judged from something other the presence or absence of some terms.

If the parties did intend to enter into an enforceable bargain, the next question is whether there is a "reasonably certain basis for giving an appropriate remedy." Because we have not yet studied the remedies built into Article 2, consider the following very brief summary of the remedies for breach.

In a sale of goods contract, the basic obligation of the seller is to deliver goods that conform to the contract requirements and the basic obligation of the buyer is to accept those goods and pay for them. UCC § 2-301. If the buyer breaches the contract by failing to pay as agreed when goods are delivered to and accepted by the buyer, the seller's damage remedy is to recover the price of the goods. UCC § 2-709. If the buyer breaches the contract by refusing conforming goods, the seller is damaged if the price of the goods in the marketplace is less than the contract price that the buyer agreed to pay. UCC § 2-708. Conversely, if the seller breaches the contract by tendering nonconforming goods and the buyer rejects those goods, the buyer is damaged if the market price for conforming goods is higher than the price that the buyer agreed to pay for the goods. UCC § 2-713. If the seller breaches by tendering nonconforming goods and the buyer accepts those goods, the buyer is damaged by the difference in value of the goods which the buyer got and the goods the buyer contracted for. UCC § 2-714.

From this very brief summary, it is clear that to have a "reasonable basis" for determining a remedy, the terms addressing price, quantity, quality, and delivery are very important. The gap fillers in Article 2 address all of these issues. They can be, and often are, used to help determine what the duties of each party are, whether there is a breach, and if there is a breach, how to measure damages. Thus the Article 2 gap fillers permit parties who intend to contract to leave terms open or indefinite with the security that some standard will be available to create an enforceable contract because there is a "reasonably certain basis for giving an appropriate remedy." *See* UCC § 2-204(3).

As we study the gap fillers in this Chapter and the next, consider how the ability to have an enforceable agreement prior to nailing down every term, and the presence of the Article 2 gap fillers, effects the negotiation of the sales contract.[17] Does the policy choice to have statutory gap fillers influence what clauses are drafted as part of the written documentation of the contract? Does it influence the scope of the negotiations? Does it foster an undue amount of disputes as courts wrestle with "incomplete" agreements? If you were revising the law, would you make different choices about how to deal with the problem of incomplete agreements? What are the gap fillers? Here is an incomplete list.

---

[17]   *See, e.g.*, Scott Baker & Kimberly D. Krawiec, *Incomplete Contracts in a Complete Contract World*, 33 FLA. ST. U. L. REV. 725 (2006).

Warranties	§ 2-312 (warranty of title) § 2-313 (express warranties)[18] § 2-314 (implied warranty of merchantability) § 2-315 (implied warranty of fitness)
Quantity and price of the goods	§ 2-305 (open price term) § 2-306 (output and requirements contracts)
Payment	§ 2-304 (price payable in money) § 2-310 (time for payment) § 2-507(1) (condition to duty to tender payment) § 2-511(2), (3) (manner of tendering payment) § 2-512 (payment before inspection)
Manner and time of the seller's duty to tender the goods	§ 2-307 (delivery in a single lot) § 2-308 (place of delivery) § 2-309 (time of delivery) § 2-503 (manner of delivery) § 2-504 (duties in a shipment contract) § 2-511(1) (condition to duty to tender)
Buyer's inspection, acceptance, and rejection of the goods	§ 2-513 (buyer's right to inspect goods) § 2-601 (buyer's rights on improper tender) § 2-602 (manner and effect of rejection) § 2-606 (acceptance of goods) § 2-607 (effect of acceptance of goods) § 2-612(2) (rejection in installment contracts)
Risk of loss	§ 2-509 (risk of loss generally) § 2-510 (risk of loss after breach)
Other	§ 2-311 (obligations in making specifications) § 2-508 (seller's right to cure) § 2-603 (buyer's duties as to rejected goods) § 2-604 (buyer's rights to rejected goods) § 2-608 (revocation of acceptance)

Based upon what we have looked at so far, the sequence of analytical steps in determining the terms of a sale of goods transaction should be as follows. First, determine whether the parties have reached an agreement. To do this, consult the rules on contract formation discussed in Chapter Two. Then identify the express terms of their agreement and ask whether the parties have intended to contract. *See*

---

[18]   Express warranties themselves are not gap fillers, but the rules in section 2-313 on how express warranties are formed could, presumably, be changed by agreement. Thus, the rule on how express warranties are created are themselves a sort of gap filler.

UCC § 2-204. In looking at that question, the completeness of the agreement is relevant but not determinative. Next, identify the remaining terms of the parties' agreement by considering any applicable course of dealing, course of performance, or usage of trade. Then, consider whether there are any gaps. If there are, and if filling in those gaps is not precluded by the parties' agreement as previously determined, look to the provisions of Article 2 to fill them. Finally, determine if there is an appropriate basis for providing an appropriate remedy for breach of contract. Test your understanding of these analytical steps by considering the following problem.

Problem 3-7

A. Seller agreed in a record signed by both parties to sell one skid loader to Buyer for $20,000. Nothing was stated in the record concerning delivery of the skid loader. Buyer insisted Seller deliver the skid loader to Buyer's place of business and Seller insisted that Buyer come pick it up. Buyer refused to pick up the skid loader or to pay any amount of the purchase price until Seller delivered the skid loader. Seller sued Buyer for breach of contract.
   1. Is this an enforceable contract?
   2. If so, has anyone breached the contract?
B. Brad and Stephanie, who are both merchants, agree during a telephone conversation to buy and sell, respectively, $1,000 worth of widgets. Brad sends a written confirmation stating, "Enjoyed doing business with you. Look forward to receiving 50 widgets for a price of $1,000." On the same day, Stephanie sends Brad a written confirmation stating, "Thanks for the order. Will promptly ship 40 widgets for total price of $1,000." The confirmations cross in the mail. Prior to any further action by either party, do the parties have a contract?
C. Would it make a difference in Part A above, if Buyer had purchased several pieces of construction equipment in the past year from Seller and in each of those previous purchases, Seller had delivered the equipment to Buyer?

The policies underlying gap fillers. Once the UCC drafters made the policy decision that agreements with open terms could be treated as enforceable contracts, and that missing terms could be supplied by law, the drafters had to determine the content of the gap fillers. Should the gap fillers be the terms that are the most fair?

The most economically efficient? The most common? The ones most consistent with the parties' likely expectations? Should the rules strive for neutrality between sellers and buyers or favor one over the other? Should the rules be the same for both consumer and commercial transactions? Should agreements for long-term relationships be treated the same as single, isolated transactions? Perhaps the rules should be ones that the parties would not likely agree to, so as to encourage them to reach an express agreement, or designed to force one party to reveal critical information to the other. Consider these different objectives as we study the gap fillers in more detail. Do you see a common underlying policy? If so, do you agree with it?

CISG and UNIDROIT Principles. The CISG contains several provisions detailing the obligations of the seller and the buyer in a contract for a sale of goods, and which can be thought of as gap fillers. In terms of the seller's delivery obligation, Article 31 states where the seller must deliver, Article 33 provides when the seller must deliver, and Article 35 addresses the quality of the goods the seller must deliver. In terms of the buyer's obligation to take the goods and pay the price, Article 55 addresses open price contracts, Article 57 states the place of payment, Articles 58 and 59 address when the buyer must pay, and Article 60 addresses the obligation to take delivery of the goods.

The UNIDROIT Principles also contain several general statements regarding the obligations of the contracting parties. The Principles recognize the ability to contract with open terms. Art. 4.8. The Principles address the price term in Article 5.1.7 and the payment obligation in Article 6.1.7. The Principles also address performance obligations in Articles 6.1.1 through 6.1.6.

B. EXAMINING PARTICULAR GAP FILLER PROVISIONS: WARRANTIES

1. *Implied Warranty of Merchantability*

Article 2 provides that, unless properly disclaimed,[19] some sellers make an "implied" warranty that goods are merchantable. Read section 2-314. Understanding this section requires analysis of two basic issues. First, which sellers make the implied warranty of merchantability? In other words, under what

---

[19]   *See* UCC § 2-316. Disclaimers of implied warranties are considered in Chapter Five.

circumstances does the warranty arise? Second, what does it mean to promise that the goods are "merchantable"?

As to the first issue, note that only sellers who are merchants make the implied warranty of merchantability. Although a non-merchant seller can, of course, expressly warrant that the goods are merchantable, *see* UCC § 2-314 cmt. 4, only merchant sellers make the warranty as an implied warranty. However, not even all merchants make the implied warranty of merchantability; the warranty arises only if the seller is a "merchant with respect to goods of that kind." As to what this limitation means, see UCC §§ 2-104 cmt. 2; 2-314 cmt. 3.

Problem 3-8

Which, if any, of the following sellers make the implied warranty of merchantability?

A. Artisan makes stained glass baubles to be hung in windows and sells the baubles at the local, semi-annual crafts fair. If Artisan has a full-time job as an accountant, is that relevant to the analysis?

B. Best Car Rental, which is in the business of renting cars on a daily and weekly basis, sells the oldest cars in its rental fleet every four months.

C. Caterer, who regularly provides and cooks food for, and serves the food at, wedding receptions.

D. Directed Decorating, Inc. is in the business of finding antiques for decorating expensive hotel lobbies. When it locates items that it thinks are suitable for a client, it puts the client in touch with the seller and receives a finding fee from the client.

As to the second issue – what does "merchantable" mean? – see UCC § 2-314(2). The most important paragraph is (2)(c), which requires the goods be fit for their ordinary purpose. In other words, a washing machine must wash clothes, presumably without tearing them to shreds. A clothes dryer must dry without incinerating the clothes or setting the buyer's house on fire. If this seems obvious, bear in mind that it represents a huge change from old common law, under which the buyer received no more than what the seller expressly promised. Courts examine the "fit for the ordinary purpose" aspect of merchantability from the perspective of the reasonable expectation of the average purchaser or user as to how the good will perform when put to its ordinary use.[20]

The remaining standards in subsection (2), while perhaps less important, can still be significant. Consider section 2-314(2)(f), which requires that the goods conform to promises and affirmations of fact on the container or label. How does that comport with the requirement for express warranties that they be part of the basis of the bargain? Consider also the requirement in section 2-314(2)(b) that fungible goods be of "fair average quality." Does that mean that half of all fungible goods – all of them below average quality – breach the warranty of merchantability? Note that section 2-314(2)(b) – along with paragraph (a) – is keyed to the contract description of the goods. Thus, analysis of what this warranty covers must begin with an identification of the contract description of the goods.

Now consider the requirement in section 2-314(2)(a) that the goods pass without objection in the trade. Without any proof of what the relevant trade standards are, a claim for breach under this provision may fail. Similarly, if a product is new and no average or usual standards have arisen for assessing performance or quality, this aspect of merchantability may not help the buyer.

Nothing in the text of section 2-314 limits the warranty of merchantability to new goods. Accordingly, the warranty is made even for used goods, as long as the seller is a merchant with respect to goods of that kind and the seller has not successfully disclaimed the warranty. However, the scope and meaning of the warranty is significantly reduced for used goods. Read comment 3 to section 2-314. As one court stated:

> [The] ordinary buyer in a normal commercial transaction has a right to expect that the goods . . . will not turn out to be completely worthless. The purchaser cannot be expected to purchase goods offered by a merchant for sale and use and then find the goods are suitable only for the junk pile. On the other hand, a buyer who has purchased goods without obtaining an express warranty as to their quality and condition cannot reasonably expect that those goods will be the finest of all possible goods of that kind.

---

[20]   *See Moss v. Batesville Casket Co.*, 935 So.2d 393, 401–02 (Miss. 2006) (plaintiffs failed to establish how long they would expect wooden casket to preserve remains, breach of implied warranty of merchantability claim fails). *See also Koken v. Black & Veatch Const., Inc.*, 426 F.3d 39, 51–52 (1st Cir. 2005); *Mitchell v. BBB Services Co.*, 582 S.E.2d 470 (Ga. Ct. App. 2003); *Castro v. QVC Network, Inc.*, 139 F.3d 114 (2d Cir. 1998); *Jackson v. Nestle-Beich, Inc.*, 589 N.E.2d 547 (Ill. 1992).

Protection of the buyer under the uniform commercial code lies between these two extremes. If an item is used or is second hand, surely less can be expected in the way of quality than if the item is purchased new. . . . The buyer's knowledge that the goods are used, the extent of their prior use, and whether the goods are significantly discounted may help determine what standards of quality should apply to the transaction.[21]

To what extent should the buyer's misuse of the good impact the analysis of whether the good is merchantable? Given the focus on the buyer's expectations regarding the goods in defining merchantability, what uses should the seller reasonably expect the buyer to have for the goods? For example, should the seller of a hair dryer anticipate that buyers may use the hair dryer in a high humidity environment (*i.e.*, the bathroom after a shower)? Would a hair dryer that shorts out in that circumstance be merchantable? In many states, the buyer's misuse of the product will mean that the product did not breach the implied warranty of merchantability or may reduce the damages that the buyer may recover if part of the damages are attributable to the misuse of the product.[22]

Problem 3-9

In which, if any, of the following scenarios has the implied warranty of merchantability been breached?

A. Aparicio purchased a new lawn mower from Dealer on May 1. On each of the next three weekends, Aparicio successfully used the mower to cut the grass at Aparicio's home. The fourth time Aparicio attempted to use the mower, the ignition malfunctioned so the motor would not start. *See* UCC § 2-725(2). *See also Gillespie v. Sears, Roebuck & Co.*, 386 F.3d 21 (1st Cir. 2004).

B. Boggs was served a salmon fillet at the local restaurant, Fish 'N Chips. While eating the salmon, Boggs choked on a bone and had to have the bone surgically extracted from Bogg's throat at the local hospital. *See Webster v. Blue Ship Tea Room, Inc.*, 198 N.E.2d 309 (Mass. 1964).

---

[21] *International Petroleum Services, Inc. v. S & N Well Service, Inc.*, 639 P.2d 29, 32, 34 (Kan. 1982).

[22] *See Gillespie v. Sears, Roebuck & Co.*, 386 F.3d 21 (1st Cir. 2004) (seller was entitled to an unreasonable use instruction when buyer operated table saw without the safety guards).

Compare Mexicali Rose v. Superior Ct., 822 P.2d 1292 (Cal. 1992); *Schafer v. JLC Food Systems, Inc.*, 695 N.W.2d 570 (Minn. 2005).

C. Conigliaro, a professional weaver, purchased five lots of yarn from Stannick Looms, Inc. The yarn was all supposed to be Magenta No. 02. When it was delivered, there were noticeable variations in color although each was labeled Magenta No. 02. Conigliaro objected and Stannick stated that the difference in color was due to natural differences in the yarn composition and how each lot of yarn had taken the dye. Stannick maintains that the color variations are permissible variations that are normal for each dye lot.

D. DiMaggio purchased a new car from Dealer for $30,000. The car complied with all government required product safety equipment but was rated low by national consumer reporting firms for front impact safety due to compartment invasion at high speed impact. DiMaggio was severely injured in a high velocity, head-on collision because the engine was pushed 12 inches into the passenger compartment.

E. Eckersley, a photographer, purchased an expensive new digital camera on line from 34th Street Camera, a retailer. When the camera arrived, Eckersley removed the camera from its box and noticed that the serial number on the camera was preceded by the letters "UK." Eckersley telephoned the manufacturer and learned that: (i) the camera was intended for distribution in Europe; (ii) although the manufacturer expressly warranted all cameras of the same model that were intended for distribution in the U.S., the manufacturer made no warranty for the camera Eckersley had purchased; and (iii) the manufacturer would not permit any of its authorized repair facilities to fix the camera if indeed it ever did malfunction.

F. Foxx purchased a used six-year-old pickup truck from Dealer for $5,000. The truck had been driven 80,000 "tough" miles without any serious mechanical problems. The day after the sale, the engine failed. Assume that the $5,000 purchase price was at the low end of the "blue book" range for this model truck but that such a truck with this kind of engine problem has a fair market value of $750.

G. Garciaparra purchased a two-year old used car from Dealer. A few weeks later, the car's entire electrical system shorted out, requiring extensive and expensive repair efforts. During the repairs, Garciaparra's mechanic discovered and informed Garciaparra that the car has extensive water damage that must have resulted from a flood or hurricane. Does it matter to the analysis if Dealer was aware at the time of sale that the car had been salvaged from a storm?

H. Hoyt purchased a box of gloves from Home Improvement Supplier that indicated that the gloves were "latex free." The box was mislabeled and the gloves contained latex. Hoyt suffered a severe allergic reaction. Does Hoyt have a cause of action against Supplier?

What is the rationale for imposing this implied warranty on some merchant sellers but not others? Does that rationale help determine the meaning of "merchantable" goods? In an influential article,[23] William L. Prosser, suggested three overlapping justifications for the implied warranty of merchantability. The first was that the seller had made a "misrepresentation of fact" upon which the buyer had relied. For Prosser, this was "obviously" a tort theory. The second was that the warranty "has in fact been agreed upon by the parties as an unexpressed term of the contract for sale." The warranty was inferred from language, conduct, circumstances and was "pure" contract. The third was that the warranty was "imposed by law" as a matter of policy. The loss from "defective" goods should be placed upon the seller "because he is best able to bear it and distribute it to the public, and because it is considered that the buyer is entitled to protection at the seller's expense." For the third justification, Prosser had in mind cases where defective food caused personal injuries to buyers and consumers.

Privity. Whether a person not in privity with the seller may recover for breach of the implied warranty of merchantability is a hotly debated issue as to which the states have varying answers.[24] *See* UCC § 2-318. We will return to the question of

---

[23] *See* William L. Prosser, *The Implied Warranty of Merchantable Quality*, 27 MINN. L. REV. 117, 122 (1943). There is close relationship between the idea of unmerchantable and the concept of product defect in tort law for purposes of strict liability under RESTATEMENT (SECOND) OF TORTS § 402A. *See Castro v. QVC Network, Inc.*, 139 F.3d 114 (2d Cir. 1998). We will consider the relationship between products liability as a matter of tort law and implied warranty of merchantability liability in Chapter Eight.

[24] *Compare Blanco v. Baxter Healthcare Corp.*, 70 Cal. Rptr. 3d 566 (Cal. Ct. App. 2008) (privity required) *with Gonzalez v. Pepsico, Inc.*, 489 F. Supp. 2d 1233 (D. Kan. 2007) (privity not required in consumer transaction based upon interpretation of state statute other than the UCC as overriding the UCC requirement of privity).

privity in Chapter Seven, when we discuss buyer's remedies, and in Chapter Eight, when we discuss the relationship of Article 2 to other law.

CISG. Article 35(2)(a), (c), and (d) are the counterparts to UCC § 2-314.

2. *Implied Warranty of Fitness for Particular Purpose*

Read section 2-315. Packed in only a few lines of text are four requirements for this implied warranty to arise:

1. The seller must have reason to know of the buyer's particular purpose;
2. The buyer must have a particular purpose;[25]
3. The seller must have reason to know that the buyer is relying on the seller's skill or judgment to select or supply suitable goods; and
4. The buyer must in fact rely on the seller's skill or judgment.[26]

Notice what is not a requirement. The seller need not be a merchant with respect to the goods of that kind, or even a merchant at all. That said, the third and fourth requirements are unlikely to be satisfied if the seller is not a merchant. Notice what else is not required. Nothing in the statute indicates that the buyer's reliance has to be reasonable. Of course, in situations in which it would be wholly unreasonable for the buyer to rely on the seller, the seller may have no reason to know that the buyer is in fact relying, and the warranty will still not arise.

The warranty of fitness arises only if the buyer has a particular purpose. What distinguishes a "particular purpose" from an ordinary purpose? Consider the following case excerpt.

> Ingram's purpose for the goods it purchased from Pott was to use them to carry heavy petroleum products on the Mississippi and its tributaries and to heat those products to facilitate their discharge in cold climates. Pott characterizes the goods at issue as heating-coil-equipped tank barges, and argues that carrying and heating heavy petroleum products is the customary

---

[25] Section 2-315 does not actually say this, but it can be inferred from the first clause.

[26] Section 2-315 does not actually say this either, but again it can be inferred from what is said. The point is also made in the last sentence of comment 1 and by numerous courts. *E.g., Leal v. Holtvogt*, 702 N.E.2d 1246, 1256 (Ohio Ct. App. 1998)

use of such products. Pott maintains that Ingram's use of the barges and the heating coils is not unique or peculiar to Ingram's business, since others use heating-coil-equipped tank barges in precisely the same manner; Pott itself had constructed over thirty such barges for use in the same manner before it built these four for Ingram.

Ingram, however, rejoins that Pott errs in suggesting that its use of the goods must be unique to fall within the fitness-for-a-particular-purpose warranty, arguing instead that the question is one of degree. According to Ingram, the proper characterization of the goods here is tank barges, rather than heating-coil-equipped tank barges. Tank barges, Ingram continues, are used to carry a multitude of cargoes, including a variety of chemicals, molasses, and oils and fuel oils of many kinds. The barges here were equipped with steam coils to enable Ingram to carry a particular kind of cargo – cargo that sometimes requires heating to aid discharge. Further, neither Pott nor Ingram deals solely or predominantly in barges that have steam coils; Pott builds and Ingram operates all sorts of barges. In these circumstances, Ingram concludes, the particular-purpose requirement is met.

We agree with Ingram that its use of the goods need not be one-of-a-kind to meet the requirements of [§ 2-315]. It is doubtful that even the Comment's example of using a shoe to climb mountains would qualify as a unique use of the shoe. Instead, as we read Comment 2, the key inquiry is not whether anyone else can be found who puts the goods to the same use, but whether the buyer's use is sufficiently different from the customary use of the goods to make it not an ordinary use of the goods; that a buyer's use is not entirely idiosyncratic does not mean that it is ordinary. . . . Therefore, that others put tank barges to the same use as Ingram does not preclude finding that a warranty of fitness exists.

Whether Ingram's purpose diverges sufficiently from the customary purposes of other buyers to be considered particular turns to a great extent on whether one accepts Pott's characterization of the goods as heating-coil-equipped tank barges, or instead accepts Ingram's portrayal of them as tank barges, which have been equipped with heating coils to serve a particular purpose. And this in turn hinges upon how the factual context in which Ingram and Pott struck their bargain is interpreted. To return to the Comment's shoe illustration, is this case more like one in which a buyer goes to a general shoe store and buys a pair of shoes for mountain climbing, or one in which a buyer goes to a mountain-climbing gear store to buy shoes for this purpose? This is, ultimately, a question of fact. . . . Here, since Ingram operates and Pott builds barges for a variety of uses, we are unable to conclude that the District Court was clearly erroneous in finding that an implied warranty of fitness for a particular purpose arose.[27]

What other issues do you see in applying the implied warranty of fitness for a particular purpose? Is it good policy to make the seller liable for this implied warranty? What is the difference between this warranty and the implied warranty of merchantability or an express warranty?

Privity. Because of the reliance requirement that is part of the implied warranty of fitness for particular purpose, liability under this warranty is usually restricted to the seller from whom the buyer purchased the goods. There may be some circumstances, however, where the buyer can demonstrate reliance on a manufacturer's specific assurances to the buyer regarding a product. Should the buyer be able to recover from the manufacturer based upon this implied warranty?[28] We will return to the question of privity in Chapter Seven, when we discuss buyer's remedies, and in Chapter Eight, when we discuss the relationship of Article 2 to other law.

CISG. Article 35(2)(b) is the counterpart to UCC § 2-315.

Problem 3-10

A. Construct a scenario in which the seller would be making an implied warranty of fitness for particular purpose. If it helps, think of a situation that might arise in a hardware or auto parts store.

B. Buyer purchased a new car from Dealer for $30,000. The car complied with all government required product safety equipment but was rated low by national consumer reporting firms for front impact safety due to compartment invasion at high speed impact. When Buyer visited with the Dealer's sales person regarding the Buyer's need for a car,

---

[27] *Ingram River Equip., Inc. v. Pott Indus., Inc.*, 816 F.2d 1231, 1233–35 (8th Cir. 1987).

[28] *See Duall Bldg. Restoration, Inc. v. 1143 East Jersey Ave., Associates, Inc.*, 652 A.2d 1225 (N.J. Super. Ct. A.D. 1995).

Buyer told the sales person that Buyer needed a car that was very safe. Buyer explained that she would be commuting on two-lane, winding mountain roads, and needed something that Buyer could rely on to keep her safe in the event of a serious collision. Dealer's sales person recommended the car that Buyer purchased. Buyer was severely injured in a high velocity, head-on collision because the engine was pushed 12 inches into the passenger compartment. Buyer sued Dealer for breach of the implied warranty of fitness for particular purpose. What result?

3. *Warranties of Title and Noninfringement*

The previous three warranties have all been concerned with the quality of the goods that are the subject of the sales contract. The warranties of title and noninfringement, on the other hand, are concerned with whether someone – other than the buyer or seller – will be able to interfere with the buyer's use or possession of the goods, or will put the buyer to the time and trouble of defending the buyer's right to use and possess the goods. Read section 2-312. Subsection (1) provides for the warranty of title; subsection (3) provides for the warranty of noninfringement.[29]

As you dissect these statutory provisions, consider the following basic questions about these two warranties. First, what kind of sellers make these warranties? Second, under what circumstances is the warranty made? Third, what is the content of the warranty? More specifically, what is "good title"? What is the difference between "good title" and "rightful transfer"? Consideration of these questions requires an excursion into the concept of title, both under Article 2 and the common law.

Title. Title can be defined as the right of ownership, or at least as evidence of the right of ownership (nominal ownership). Article 2 has relatively few provisions on "title" to goods. Indeed, the drafters consciously chose to de-emphasize the role of title in sales-of-goods transactions. This point is made expressly in section 2-401, which states that "[e]ach provision of this Article with regard to the rights, obligations and remedies of the seller, the buyer, purchasers or other third parties

---

[29] Section 2-312(2) governs the ability to disclaim the warranty of title and is discussed in Chapter Five.

applies irrespective of title to the goods except where the provision refers to such title." In spite of this attempt to de-emphasize title as a concept to be used to resolve disputes between the seller and the buyer, the definition of a "sale" under Article 2 is the "passing of title from the seller to the buyer for a price." *See* UCC § 2-106(1). And, we have seen, many of the provisions of Article 2 depend upon there being a "sale" transaction.

The rules about title in section 2-401 may be relevant in resolving a wide variety of controversies that are beyond the scope of Article 2, *e.g.*, the right of the buyer's creditors to levy on goods still in the seller's possession, the coverage of an insurance policy, the applicability of a state sales tax, the criminal responsibility of a person accused of larceny, or whether property becomes part of the buyer's estate in a bankruptcy.[30] However, for issues within the scope of Article 2, title is relevant only if the applicable provisions expressly refer to title. The most important of these are sections 2-403 and 2-312.

Rights of a transferee. Read section 2-403. The first sentence of subsection (1) specifies the basic rule applicable to almost any transfer of property: a purchaser takes the rights that the transferor had or had power to transfer. The second and third sentences expand on that general rule by indicating when a transferor has the power to transfer more rights than the transferor owns. In other words, in the circumstances described in the statute, a purchaser is able to obtain greater rights than its transferor had. These circumstances all involve situations when the transferor has "voidable title" (as opposed to void title or no title). A transferor with voidable title can transfer good title to a good faith purchaser for value. Read the definitions of "purchase," "purchaser," and "good faith" in UCC § 1-201. Notice that a good faith purchaser for value acquires good title from a transferor with voidable title only if the purchaser takes delivery of the goods under a "transaction of purchase."

A classic example of "voidable" title at common law arises when a seller of goods, induced by a fraudulent representation by the buyer, delivers the goods to the buyer under a contract for sale. In that case, the buyer's title to the goods is "voidable" in the sense that the seller can go to court to rescind the transaction and get the goods back. However, the buyer is nevertheless able to transfer good title

---

[30]   *See Iker v. Estate of Jones*, 863 N.E.2d 666 (Ohio Ct. App. 2006); *Concord General Mut Ins. Co. v. Sumner*, 762 A.2d 849 (Vt. 2000). We will consider property issues in Chapter Ten.

to a good faith purchaser for value. After such a transfer, the original seller no longer can reclaim the goods.

The case of *Johnson & Johnson Products, Inc. v. Dal International Trading Co.,*[31] illustrates these principles. In that case, the seller misrepresented to its supplier that the goods supplied would be distributed only in Poland. In fact, the seller distributed the goods through various intermediaries in the so-called "gray market" to buyers in the United States. When the supplier sought an injunction against further sales in the United States, one of the buyers claimed the seller had had voidable title and that the buyer was a "good faith purchaser for value" under section 2-403(1). The court agreed, holding that the buyer had no reason to suspect that there was fraud (even though it had reason to believe it had purchased "gray" goods) and, therefore, there was no duty to investigate or inquire as to whether there might have been a misrepresentation. In short, the buyer was "honest in fact" because it did not "subjectively" suspect that the title was flawed and proceeded with the purchase "despite his or her suspicions."

The classic instance of "void" title occurs when a thief steals goods from the rightful owner. This act involves no voluntary transfer of possession. A buyer of the goods from the thief – or any person to whom the thief has delivered the goods – gets no protection under section 2-403.

Entrustment. Section 2-403 has another provision that expands on the general rule that a transferee receives only those rights that the transferor has or has power to convey. Read sections 2-403(2), (3), and 1-201(b)(9) on the definition of "buyer in ordinary course of business."[32] These provisions allow a merchant to whom goods have been entrusted to transfer good title to a buyer in ordinary course of business. A classic example of the entrustment provisions occurs when the owner of a piece of jewelry in need of repair delivers it to jeweler who both repairs and sells goods of that kind. If the jeweler sells and delivers the item to a buyer in ordinary course of business, that buyer will acquire all the owner's rights in the item. As one court put it:

---

[31]   798 F.2d 100 (3d Cir. 1986).

[32]   For an example of an analysis of the requirements of entrustment, merchant status, and qualification as a buyer in ordinary course of business, *see Lindholm v. Brant*, 925 A.2d 1048 (Conn. 2007).

The entrustment provision of the UCC is designed to enhance the reliability of commercial sales by merchants who deal in the kind of goods sold. . . . It shifts the risk of resale to the one who leaves his property with the merchant. . . . When a person knowingly delivers his property into the possession of a merchant dealing in goods of that kind, that person assumes the risk of the merchant's acting unscrupulously by selling the property to an innocent purchaser. The entrustment provision places the loss upon the party who vested the merchant with the ability to transfer the property with apparent good title.[33]

Colorable claims against the title. Return now to the text of section 2-312(1). The seller warrants that the title the buyer is receiving is "good." What if the title is "good" but the circumstances are such that there are colorable claims regarding whether the title is good? Consider the words of the South Dakota Supreme Court:

Comment 1 to UCC § 2-312 states a buyer is entitled to "receive a good, clear title transferred . . . in a rightful manner so [the buyer] will not be exposed to a lawsuit in order to protect it." A split of authority persists on the scope of § 2-312. Decker relies on those cases which hold that a breach of warranty of title occurs only when an outstanding superior title exists.[34] Other courts hold that under § 2-312 mere initiation of a colorable challenge, one which is not spurious, regardless of the outcome, is sufficient to violate the warranty of title. . . . We find the latter to be the better rule. . . . Purchasers should not be required to enter into a contest on the validity of ownership over [the goods they purchased].[35]

---

[33]   *DeWeldon, Ltd. v. McKean*, 125 F.3d 24, 27–28 (1st Cir. 1997).

[34]   Indeed, the UCC drafters flatly stated "The warranty of quiet possession is abolished." UCC § 2-312 cmt. 1. Yet the same comment states, "Disturbance of quiet possession, although not mentioned specifically, is one way, among many, in which the breach of the warranty of title may be established."

[35]   *Colton v. Decker*, 540 N.W.2d 172, 175–76 (S.D. 1995). This case involved a car which was also subject to a certificate of title. In many states, a certificate of title will not be conclusive proof of ownership. The precise effect of certificate of title laws on the question of ownership of motor vehicles is beyond the scope of these materials.

Cases on the warranty of noninfringement are of similar import. They typically arise when some third party claims that the goods sold to the buyer infringe on the third party's copyright, patent or trademark. However, the third party need not have a valid claim of infringement for the seller to have breached the warranty. As one court put it recently:

> A third party's claim of infringement . . . must cast a "substantial shadow" on the buyer's ability to make use of the goods in question, in order to constitute a breach of the warranty against infringement. . . . [T]his does not mean that [the buyer] would have to actually prove the validity of the infringement claim to succeed on this warranty argument, only that . . . the infringement claim is of a substantial nature that is reasonably likely to subject the buyer to litigation, and has a significant and adverse effect on the buyer's ability to make use of the goods in question.[36]

More recently, another court stated an even more lenient test:

> [T]he section 2-312(3) warranty covers a broad scope of infringement claims and is not limited to claims that ultimately will prove successful in litigation. . . . [It] applies to all claims of infringement that have any significant and adverse effect on the buyer's ability to make use of the purchased goods, excepting only frivolous claims that are completely devoid of merit.[37]

Problem 3-11

What factors might be relevant to whether a purchaser is acting in good faith for the purposes of section 2-403? *See Tempur-Pedic International, Inc. v. Waste to Charity, Inc.*, 483 F. Supp. 2d 766 (W.D. Ark. 2007).

---

[36] *Sun Coast Merchandise Corp. v. Myron Corp.*, 922 A.2d 782, 796–97 (N.J. Super. Ct. App. Div. 2007).

[37] *Pacific Sunwear of Cal., Inc. v. Olaes Enters., Inc.*, 84 Cal. Rptr. 3d 182, 193 (Cal. Ct. App. 2008).

Problem 3-12

In which, if any, of the following scenarios has the seller breached the warranty of title?

A. Seller, who had stolen a diamond necklace, sold it to Buyer who knew nothing of the theft. Does it matter whether Seller is a merchant? What if Seller is homeless person in tattered clothing?

B. Seller purchased a used diamond necklace from Thackery, and a few days later sold and delivered the necklace to Buyer. Shortly thereafter, Seller and Buyer learn that Thackery had stolen the necklace from Owner.

C. Seller, who had acquired a diamond necklace by paying for it with a check that was later dishonored, sold and delivered the necklace to Buyer.

D. Seller, who had borrowed a diamond necklace from Friend to wear at a party, sold and delivered the necklace to Buyer.

E. Seller, a jeweler who had received a diamond necklace from Owner to repair and clean it, sold and delivered the necklace to Buyer.

F. Seller, a jeweler, contracted to sell a diamond necklace to Buyer, who made a down payment and promised to pay the remainder of the purchase price rest the following day. Buyer agreed to allow Seller to retain possession until Buyer paid the price in full. Later that day, Seller sold and delivered the same necklace to Purchaser. If Seller has breached the warranty of title, in which of the two transactions did that breach occur?

Privity. Generally, the buyer's remedy for breach of the warranty of title and the warranty of noninfringement is against the seller in privity of contract with the buyer. We will return to the question of privity in Chapter Seven, when we discuss buyer's remedies, and in Chapter Eight, when we discuss the relationship of Article 2 to other law.

CISG. Article 4(b) of the CISG provides that, except as otherwise expressly provided, the Convention, "is not concerned with . . . the effect which the contract may have on the property in the goods sold." In other words, the CISG says nothing about how a stranger to the contract may enforce its claim to the goods, whether by recovery of the goods or conversion. Similarly, it says nothing about whether or how the sales contract affects the third party's rights. In short, the CISG has no analog to the rules in section 2-401 on when good title can be transferred by a seller who does not have good title. For this reason, the provisions of the UCC may govern claims to the goods located in a U.S. jurisdiction.[38]

However, the CISG does have rules similar to the warranties of title and noninfringement. Specifically, Article 41, which deals with title or a security interest, is the counterpart to section 2-312(1) and Article 42, which deals with intellectual property, is the counterpart to section 2-312(3). Collectively, they provide that the seller, with certain limitations, must deliver goods which are free from third-party claims. Failure to do so is a breach of contract for which the buyer may pursue appropriate remedies. CISG Art. 45.

UNIDROIT Principles. The Principles do not specifically address title or infringement issues. However, to the extent the seller has promised to "sell" goods to the buyer, the provisions regarding the parties' performance obligations could perhaps be interpreted to provide for some type of warranty for the buyer. *See* UNIDROIT Arts. 5.1.1 through 5.1.6.

---

[38]   *See Usinor Industeel v. Leeco Steel Products Inc.*, 209 F. Supp. 2d 880 (N.D. Ill. 2002) (because the CISG does not cover the property rights aspects of the contract for sale, the provisions of the Illinois Commercial Code governed the seller's property claim to the goods located in Illinois).

CHAPTER FOUR

TERMS OF THE CONTRACT – PART II

This Chapter continues the discussion of gap fillers that began in Chapter Three, Section 3. It focuses on the gap filler rules regarding quantity, price, delivery, and payment. Remember, to the extent the parties' agreement already addresses these items, the gap fillers in Article 2 do not override that agreement.

SECTION 1.   QUANTITY

Quantity is the single term least susceptible to being supplied by a gap filler. Virtually no principle that the drafters might have chosen to base the gap filler rules on would yield an obvious answer. Beyond that, if the statute of frauds applies to a sale-of-goods transaction, quantity is the one essential term that the writing must contain. *See* UCC § 2-201. However, there are two situations in which a quantity term can be implied: (i) when the parties agree to buy and sell all or some fixed percentage of the seller's output; and (2) when the parties agree to buy and sell all or a fixed percentage of the buyer's requirements. Read section 2-306(1).[1]

There are several things worth noting about this provision. First, it is more a rule on how to interpret an output or requirements term that the parties have agreed to than a true gap filler. It never implies an output or requirements term when the parties have not agreed to one.

Second, some courts have been concerned with whether an output or requirements term is enforceable if it is not an "exclusive" arrangement to get "all" output or requirements from the counter party. The concern is that if the buyer does not commit to buy "all" its requirements from the seller, or the seller does not commit to sell "all" of its output to the buyer, there may really be no enforceable commitment (mutuality of obligation), and the agreement may amount to little more than the option of one party. However, as long as the agreement calls for a quantity measured by output or requirements, the lack of exclusivity should not matter.

---

[1]   A commitment to supply output or to buy requirements is a quantity term which, because it can be interpreted and limited under section 2-306(1), satisfies the statute of frauds. *See PMC Corp. v. Houston Wire & Cable Co.*, 797 A.2d 125, 128–31 (N.H. 2002).

Third, when do the requirements or output "occur in good faith"? Does that allow the buyer to have no requirements or the seller to have no output? As one court put it, the

> seller assumes the risk of all good faith variations in the buyer's requirements even to the extent of a determination to liquidate or discontinue the business. . . . The rule is based on a reliance on the self-interest of the buyer, who ordinarily will seek to have the largest possible requirements. Protection against abuse is afforded by penetrating through any device by which the requirement is siphoned off in some other form to the detriment of the seller. The requirement of good faith is the means by which this is enforced and self-interest in its undistorted form is maintained as the standard.[2]

What, then, is bad faith in this setting? What if the decision is simply to make more profit on an alternative segment of its business and thus limit losses on the line subject to the output or requirements term? The comments suggest that a buyer's decision to shut down based on a lack of orders is fine, but a similar decision made to "curtail losses" would not be. Can such a line really be drawn? Would not the amount of the projected loss from continued performance be relevant to the good faith question?

Fourth, does the "unreasonably disproportionate" language mean that a buyer or seller who goes out of business and thus ceases to have requirements or output will be in breach? Several courts have held that the answer is no, but that is not a universal approach.[3]

Fifth, how is the "unreasonably disproportionate" standard to be applied when there is no shut down? Consider one court's view:

---

[2] *HML Corp. v. General Foods Corp.*, 365 F.2d 77, 81 (3d Cir. 1966) (burden on seller to prove bad faith in the buyer's requirements).

[3] *See Empire Gas Corp. v. American Bakeries Co.*, 840 F.2d 1333 (7th Cir. 1988); *Brewster of Lynchburg, Inc. v. Dial Corp.*, 33 F.3d 355 (4th Cir. 1994); *Wiseco, Inc. v. Johnson Controls, Inc.*, 155 Fed. Appx. 815 (6th Cir. 2005). *But see Simcala, Inc. v. American Coal Trade, Inc.*, 821 So. 2d 197 (Ala. 2001) (holding both tests apply so that a buyer may be in breach if the requirements are unreasonably disproportionate to stated estimates even if the decrease is in good faith). For an example of a court holding that a decrease in seller's output is governed only by the good faith test and not by the unreasonably disproportionate test, *see Waste Stream Environmental, Inc. v. Lynn Water and Sewer Commission*, 2003 WL 917086 (Super. Ct. Mass. 2003).

Obviously this language [unreasonably disproportionate – ed.] is not the equivalent of "lack of good faith"– it is an elementary rule of construction that effect must be given, if possible, to every word, clause and sentence of a statute. . . . The phrase is keyed to stated estimates or, if there be none, to "normal or otherwise comparable prior" requirements. While "reasonable elasticity" is contemplated by the section (*see* Official Comment, par. 2 to UCC § 2-306), an agreed estimate shows a clear limit on the intended elasticity, similar to that found in a contract containing minimum and maximum requirements (*see* Official Comment, par. 2 to UCC § 2-306). The estimate "is to be regarded as a center around which the parties intend the variation to occur" (*supra*).

The limitation imposed by the term "unreasonably disproportionate" represents a departure from prior case law, wherein estimates were generally treated as having been made simply for the convenience of the parties and of no operative significance. . . . It is salutary in that it insures that the expectations of the parties will be more fully realized in spite of unexpected and fortuitous market conditions. . . . Thus, even where one party acts with complete good faith, the section limits the other party's risk in accordance with the reasonable expectations of the parties.

It would be unwise to attempt to define the phrase "unreasonably disproportionate" in terms of rigid quantities. In order that the limitation contemplated by the section take effect, it is not enough that a demand for requirements be disproportionate to the stated estimate; it must be *unreasonably* so in view of the expectation of the parties. A number of factors should be taken into account in the event a buyer's requirements greatly exceed the contract estimate. These include the following: (1) the amount by which the requirements exceed the contract estimate; (2) whether the seller had any reasonable basis on which to forecast or anticipate the requested increase . . . ; (3) the amount, if any, by which the market price of the goods in question exceeded the contract price; (4) whether such an increase in market price was itself fortuitous; and (5) the reason for the increase in requirements.[4]

---

[4]   *Orange & Rockland Utilities, Inc. v. Amerada Hess Corp.*, 397 N.Y.S.2d 814, 818–19 (N.Y. App. Div. 1977).

In that case, the court held that the buyer's doubling of its requirements was unreasonably disproportionate to stated estimates. Of particular relevance to that conclusion was that the buyer was demanding more oil in order to sell the increased quantity in the market for the increased price, whereas the buyer's estimates had been based upon its plans to burn oil to produce electricity for its customer base.

Problem 4-1

Seller, a wholesale dealer in plywood, and Buyer, a producer of pine veneer, entered into a five-year, written agreement under which Buyer agreed to purchase 50,000 square feet of plywood per year at $1.00 per square foot. The agreement, dated July 1, 2005, included terms on the time and method of shipment and payment.

A. On July 1, 2008, the market price of plywood had climbed to $4.00 per square foot. The increase was due, primarily, to sharpened demand for forest products. Seller wants to get out of the contract with Buyer in order to resell all of its plywood in the market at the higher price. Buyer has purchased the entire 50,000 square feet of plywood each year at the price of $1.00 per square foot. Does Seller have any argument?

B. Assume the same facts except that Buyer agreed to purchase its annual "requirements" of plywood from Seller at $1.00 per square foot. The contract did not explicitly say "all of our requirements exclusively from Seller." Furthermore, the contract did not provide for estimates of quantity or maximum-minimum quantities which Buyer could not exceed. Buyer's annual requirements for the first three years were 25,000, 32,500 and 35,000 square feet. During the fourth year, with the market price at $4.50 per square foot, Buyer requested a total of 60,000 square feet, the capacity of its production facility. Seller objected. Does Seller have any basis for resisting Buyer's demand?

C. Assume the same facts as B above except that in the fourth year, Buyer requested a total of 5,000 square feet of plywood due to an economic depression in the local building market, which dropped the demand for pine veneer. Seller objected. What arguments do you make on behalf of Seller?

SECTION 2.   PRICE

What if the parties do not have an express term setting the price of the goods and the relevant usage of trade, course of performance, or course of dealing do not help determine the price? In many cases, the absence of an agreed-upon price would suggest that the parties did not yet finish making their bargain. However, if the parties so intend, they may form a contract with an open or indefinite price, provided "there is a reasonably certain basis for giving an appropriate remedy." *See* UCC §§ 2-204(3), 2-305(1). If, on the other hand, the parties did not intend to be bound in the absence of fixing a price, there is no contract and each party is entitled to restitution to the extent it has performed. UCC § 2-305(4).

Section 2-305 addresses, and thereby implicitly authorizes, four different types of agreement on price:

  (i)   the agreement is silent on price;
  (ii) the price is to be agreed upon later by the parties;
  (iii) the price is to be fixed in reference to some market or other standard set by a third party; and
  (iv) the price is to be set by one of the parties.

The first three of these are covered by subsection (1). If the agreement is silent, the price is to be agreed upon later but if the parties fail to agree, or the mechanism for setting the price fails for a reason not the fault of either party, then the contract price is a "reasonable price at the time for delivery."

The third method is also governed, in part, by section 2-305(3). If the mechanism for setting the price fails through the fault of one of the parties, then the other party may either set a reasonable price or cancel the contract.

The final method – one party may set the price – is governed by section 2-305(2). That subsection uses the good faith concept to limit the price fixer's discretion. How much discretion does a party have to fix a price that is not a reasonable market price?[5] Consider the following case.

---

[5]   *See TCP Indus., Inc. v. Uniroyal, Inc.*, 661 F.2d 542 (6th Cir. 1981) (setting prices for a chemical within a range of market prices on both the spot and long term market was good faith); *Au Rustproofing Center, Inc. v. Gulf Oil Corp.*, 755 F.2d 1231 (6th Cir. 1985) (need not be the market price to be setting the price in good faith); *Havird Oil Co. v. Marathon Oil Co.*, 149 F.3d 283 (4th Cir. 1998) (good faith price fixed where seller charged all its customers a non-discriminatory wholesale price which was competitive with other wholesalers and conduct followed "reasonable commercial standards of fair dealing in the trade").

MATHIS V. EXXON CORP.
302 F.3d 448 (5th Cir. 2002)

Jerry E. Smith, Circuit Judge

This is a breach of contract suit brought by fifty-four gasoline station franchisees against Exxon Corporation ("Exxon") for violating the Texas analogue of the Uniform Commercial Code's open price provision. We affirm.

I.

Exxon markets its commercial gas bound for retailers primarily through three arrangements: franchisee contracts, jobber contracts, and company operated retail stores ("CORS"). A franchisee rents Exxon-branded gas stations and enters into a sales contract for the purchase of Exxon-brand gas. The contract sets the monthly quantity of gas the franchisee must purchase and allows Exxon to set the price he must pay. The franchisee pays the dealer tank wagon price ("DTW") and takes delivery of the gas at his station.

A jobber contract requires the purchaser to pay the "rack price," which usually is lower than the price charged to franchisees. There is no sale of gas to CORS by Exxon, because the stores are owned by Exxon and staffed by its employees. Instead, an intra-company accounting is recorded that is equivalent to the price charged franchisees in the same price zone.

All the plaintiff franchisees operate stations in the greater Houston, Texas, and Corpus Christi, Texas, areas. The genesis of the dispute is the allegation that Exxon has violated the law and its contracts with these franchisees for the purpose of converting their stores to CORS by driving the franchisees out of business.

Since 1994, franchisees have been barred from purchasing their gas from jobbers, so all their purchases have been governed by the terms of the Retail Motor Fuel Store Sales Agreement, under which the "DEALER agrees to buy and receive directly from EXXON all of the EXXON-branded gasoline bought by DEALER, and at least seventy-five percent (75%) of the volume shown in [a specified schedule]. . . . DEALER will pay EXXON for delivered products at EXXON's price in effect at the time of the loading of the delivery vehicle."

This "price in effect," also known as the dealer tank wagon price ("DTW"), forms the heart of the present dispute. Exxon claims this arrangement is the industry standard and that almost all franchisor-franchisee sales of gasoline are governed by a similar price term. Plaintiffs respond that the DTW price charged under this clause is "consistently higher" than the rack price paid by jobbers plus transportation costs.

The franchisees originally filed Sherman Act, Clayton, Act, and Petroleum Marketing Practices Act ("PMPA") claims against Exxon in addition to the breach of contract claim. The antitrust claims were abandoned, and the district court granted Exxon a judgment as a matter of law ("j.m.l.") on the PMPA claims. The court retained jurisdiction over the purely state law causes of action that had been supplemental to the federal claims.

Trial proceeded solely on the Texas breach of contract action, with only six plaintiffs testifying. The thrust of their testimony was that Exxon had set the DTW price at an uncompetitive level to drive them out of business (so as to replace their stores with CORS). Some of the plaintiffs testified that their franchises were unprofitable; they presented documents and witnesses to show that Exxon intended that result to drive them out of business.

The franchisees also submitted a market study showing that 62% of the franchisees in Corpus Christi were selling gas below the DTW price. The franchisees supported their theory of the case by calling Barry Pulliam as an expert witness on the economics of the gasoline market in Houston and Corpus Christi. Pulliam concluded that Exxon's DTW price was not commercially reasonable from an economic perspective because it was a price that, over time, put the purchaser at a competitive disadvantage. Pulliam noted that "commercial reasonableness" is a legal term, and he was not there to define it for the jury.

Pulliam's conclusion rested on two main facts. First, he showed that 75% of the franchisee's competitors were able to purchase gasoline at a lower price. Second, he calculated a commercially reasonable DTW price by adding normal distribution charges to the average rack price of gasoline charged by Exxon and its competitors. He concluded that Exxon's DTW price exceeded the sum of these other prices by four or more cents per gallon.

Exxon countered with Michael Keeley, who testified that Exxon's DTW price was commercially reasonable because it reflected the company's investment in land, the store, transportation, and managers. Keeley explained that Exxon recovers these costs through rent and the sale of gas.

The jury awarded $5,723,657 – exactly 60% of the overcharge calculated by Pulliam. . . . [Exxon appealed on three grounds, only one of which is reproduced here. – Eds.]

II.

Exxon contends that because it charged its franchisees a DTW price comparable to that charged by its competitors, the breach of contract claim is precluded as a matter of law. . . . The question is whether there was evidence permitting the jury to conclude that Exxon breached a term of the franchise agreement.

III.

Texas law, which tracks the Uniform Commercial Code, implies a good faith component in any contract with an open price term. Specifically,

> [t]he parties if they so intend can conclude a contract for sale even though the price is not settled. In such a case the price is a reasonable price at the time of delivery . . . A price to be fixed by the seller or by the buyer means a price for him to fix in good faith.

[§ 3-305]. The parties agree that the franchise agreement term governing the purchase of gasoline is an open price term.

The meaning of "good faith" is further defined in several other sections of the code. The definitions section explains good faith as "honesty in fact in the conduct or transaction concerned." [§ 1-201(19)]. Wherever the term "good faith" is used throughout the code, it means "as least what is here stated." [§ 1-201(19) cmt. 19].

Additional meaning to the term may be added within a given article. *Id.* Section [2-103], regarding merchants, further explains the term: " 'Good faith' in the case of a merchant means honesty in fact and the observance of reasonable commercial standards of fair dealing in the trade." Finally, "[g]ood faith includes the observance of reasonable commercial standards of fair dealing in the trade if the party is a merchant. [§ 2-103]. But, in the normal case a 'posted price,' 'price in effect,' 'market price,' or the like satisfies the good faith requirement." [§ 2-305] cmt. 3].

The key disagreement is over what constitutes a breach of the duty of good faith. Exxon contends it has satisfied that duty because it has charged the plaintiffs a DTW price within the range of its competitors' DTW prices, thereby satisfying the "commercial reasonableness" meaning of good faith. Plaintiffs respond that good faith encompasses both objective and subjective duties. Even if Exxon is right, and its prices are within the range of its competitors', the argument runs, a subjective intent to drive the franchisees out of business would abridge the good faith duty of the open price term.

The pivotal provision is comment 3 to [§ 2-305]. Some of the language of comment 3 and [§ 2-103] leaves the meaning of good faith for open price terms in doubt. Comment 3 mentions that good faith "includes" commercial reasonableness, but notes that certain established prices satisfy the good faith requirement. Section [2-103] defines good faith with the subjective "honesty in fact" test. Thus, plaintiffs argue that an open price set according to a fixed schedule is set in good faith only if there is no improper motive animating the price-setter. Exxon replies that comment 3 speaks directly to prices set by a fixed schedule and consecrates them as in good faith per se.

In the absence of comment 3, there is no doubt Exxon would be subject to both the subjective "honesty in fact" good faith of [§ 1-201(19)] and the objective "commercial reasonableness" good faith of [§ 2-103]. The difficult question is whether comment 3 creates an exception to the normal principles of good faith governing the sale of goods.

No court in this circuit, and no Texas state court, has squarely addressed this question. Fortunately, because the Texas open price provision replicates that of the UCC, we can seek guidance from other courts.

To decide whether comment 3 creates an exception, we turn first to the text of the comment and the related sections of the Texas version of the UCC. In full, comment 3 reads,

> Subsection (2), dealing with the situation where the price is to be fixed by one party rejects the uncommercial idea that an agreement that the seller may fix the price means that he may fix any price he may wish by the express qualification that the price so fixed must be fixed in good faith. Good faith includes observance of reasonable commercial standards of fair dealing in the trade if the party is a merchant. (Section 2-103). But in the normal case a "posted price" or a future seller's or buyer's "given price," "price in effect," "market price," or the like satisfies the good faith requirement.

[§ 2-305 cmt. 3].

The bare text offers little to resolve the question. First, the comment notes that good faith "includes" reasonable commercial standards. This implies that the good faith required of a merchant setting an open price term encompasses both objective and subjective elements. The comment also creates a good faith safe harbor for such merchants when they use various sorts of fixed prices. But this safe harbor is applicable only in the "normal case." This suggests the safe harbor is not absolute, but it does nothing to define what takes a case out of the safe harbor.

As we will explain, we conclude that the "normal case" of comment 3 is coextensive with a merchant's residual "honesty in fact" duty embodied in [§§ 1-201(19) and 2-103]. Thus, the comment embraces both the objective (commercial reasonableness) and subjective (honesty in fact) senses of good faith;

objective good faith is satisfied by a "price in effect" as long as there is honesty in fact (a "normal case"). This conclusion finds support in three sources: the structure of the UCC, its legislative history, and the caselaw.

Reading comment 3 to embody two different meanings of "good faith" tracks the general structure of the UCC. Courts and commentators have recognized that the meaning of "good faith" is not uniform throughout the code. The cases and commentary treat the "good faith" found in article 1 as subjective and the good faith found only in article 2 as objective. Thus, there is nothing inconsistent in comment 3's using "good faith" in both the objective and the subjective senses.

The history of comment 3 bolsters this conclusion. Some drafters of the UCC worried that for the "great many industries where sales are not made at fixed prices," such as the steel industry, where "practically every contract" is made at "the seller's price in effect," if § 2-305 "is to apply . . . it means that in every case the seller is going to be in a lawsuit . . . or he could be, because there isn't any outside standard at all." *Proceedings of Enlarged Editorial Bd. Of Am. Law Inst.* (Sunday Morning Session, Jan. 28, 1951) (statement of Bernard Broeker). The drafters considered wholly exempting such contracts from § 2-305, or stating that for a price in effect, the only test is whether the merchant engaged in price discrimination. One drafter explained that the steel industry wanted to make "clear that we do not have to establish that we are fixing reasonable prices, because that gets you into the rate of return of profit, whether you are using borrowed money, and all those questions." *Id.*

The committee responded to these worries with the current comment 3: "[I]n the normal case a 'posted price' or a future seller's or buyer's 'given price,' 'price in effect,' 'market price,' or the like satisfies the good faith requirement." The drafter's solution was to avoid objective good faith challenges to prices set by reference to some "price in effect," while preserving challenges to discriminatory pricing. *See Hearing Before the Enlarged Editorial Board January* 27–29, 1951, VI BUSINESS LAWYER 164, 186 (1951) (explaining this intent). Nothing in the proceedings leading to the addition of comment 3 suggests that the overall subjective good faith duty of §§ 1-201 and 2-103 was to be supplanted; the evidence is quite to the contrary.

The drafters ultimately rejected two suggested addendums to § 2-305:

An agreement to the effect that the price shall be or be adjusted to, or be based upon, or determined by reference to the seller's going price, price in effect, regular price, market price, established price, or the like, at the time of the agreement or at any earlier or later time, is not an agreement to which this subsection is applicable. . . .   An agreement such as this is an agreement under which the seller or the buyer does not have any burden of showing anything other than that he has not singled out the particular other party for discrimination.

Proceedings of Enlarged Editorial Bd. (statement of Bernard Broeker). Both of these recommendations are more sweeping than is the language ultimately adopted. The first would have omitted any mention of the good faith duty for open price provisions; the second would have limited the duty of the price-setter to that of avoiding discrimination.

The existing comment, however, avoids challenges to prices set according to an open price term unless that challenge is outside the normal type of case. Although price discrimination was the type of aberrant case on the minds of the drafters, price discrimination is merely a subset of what constitutes such an aberrant case. Any lack of subjective, honesty-in-fact good faith is abnormal; price discrimination is only the most obvious way a price-setter acts in bad faith – by treating similarly-situated buyers differently.

The caselaw supports this interpretation of comment 3. Courts that have addressed the normalcy question have consistently held that a lack of subjective good faith takes a challenge outside the bounds of what is normal.[6]

Like the plaintiffs in *Nanakuli, Allapattah,* and *Wayman,* the franchisees here are alleging a breach of good faith grounded not in Exxon's failure to price in accord with an established schedule, but in its failure to set the price in good faith. Suits recognizing such a cause of action are rare, and with good reason: We would be ill-advised to consider a case to be outside the norm based only on an allegation of improper motive by the party setting the price.

Plaintiffs produced enough evidence to escape comment 3's "normal case" limitation. They showed, for example, that Exxon planned to replace a number of its franchises with CORS, that the DTW price was higher than the sum of the rack

---

[6]   *See, e.g., Nanakuli Paving & Rock Co. v. Shell Oil Co.*, 664 F.2d 772, 806 (9th Cir.1981) (stating that "the dispute here was not over the amount of the increase – that is, the price that the seller fixed – but over the manner in which that increase was put into effect"); *Allapattah v. Exxon Corp.*, 61 F. Supp. 2d 1308, 1322 (S.D. Fla.1999) ("Because the parties' dispute is not over the actual amount of the purchase price Exxon charged for its wholesale gasoline to its dealers, but rather over the manner in which the wholesale price was calculated without considering the double charge for credit card processing, the instant action is not the 'normal' case."); *cf. Wayman v. Amoco Oil Co.*, 923 F. Supp. 1322, 1349 (D. Kan.1996), *aff'd*, 145 F.3d 1347 (10th Cir.1998) ("[T]his court believes the present case is a normal case. If there was evidence that Amoco had, for example, engaged in discriminatory pricing or tried to run plaintiffs out of business, then the court's decision might be different.").

price and transportation, that Exxon prevented the franchisees from purchasing gas from jobbers after 1994, and that a number of franchisees were unprofitable or non-competitive.[7]

For example, one Exxon document stated that the company's "Marketing Strategy for 1992-1997 is to reduce Dealer stores (est. 30%)." Another document set forth Exxon's plans to reduce dealer stations in Houston from 95 to 45, and to increase CORS from 83 to 150, between 1997 and 2003. James Carter, the Regional Director of the Exxon/Mobil Fuels Marketing Company, testified that Exxon made more of a profit from a CORS than from an independent lessee store. These plans and observations were validated by the fact that the number of dealer stations steadily declined.

An exhibit called the "Houston Screening Study" evaluated the strategy of "surplusing" (i.e., eliminating) 21 of 37 locations inside the Highway 610 loop. Of the 93 lessee-dealer stations, 69 would be done away with, but 73 of the 91 CORS would be kept.

Further indication of plans to shift from dealer-lessees to CORS is shown by Exxon's dissatisfaction with outlets featuring service bays. Exxon documents showed that service bays – generally associated with lessee-dealer locations – were becoming less profitable, while stations with convenience stores – generally associated with CORS – were the wave of the future. A document entitled "Retail Store Chain Outlook" revealed Exxon's plan to reduce stations with service bays from 2,506 to 190 from 1991 to 2005. That document included a plan to "[e]xpand CORS to improve profitability and to compete efficiently with private brands/distributors" and "[e]mphasize CORS operations in markets with high level of rack to retail competition."

Exxon's answer on appeal is that these documents "say nothing about using pricing to accomplish a 'plan' to eliminate dealers." Although that is so, there was sufficient evidence on this issue to go to the jury, which was free to, and apparently did, draw the inference connecting pricing to the elimination of dealer-lessees. The consequence of the jury's decision is that this case exceeds the "normal case" limit of [§ 2-305 comment 3].

---

[7]   This case is distinguishable from *Meyer v. Amerada Hess*, 541 F. Supp. 321 (D.N.J.1982), in which the court found "no evidence" of dishonesty in the setting of a DTW price. In Meyer, though, the only evidence tending to show bad faith was the retailer's unprofitability. *Id.* at 331. Significantly, other retailers were profiting, and the plaintiff retailer was being charged rent below the economic value of the property. *Id.* at 332.

We still, however, must examine the content of the duty of subjective good faith. Although no Texas or Fifth Circuit case has squarely addressed the meaning of the good faith clause of [§ 2-305], Texas courts repeatedly have held that the "honesty in fact" definition of good faith found in [§ 1-201(19)] is tied to the actual belief of the participant in the transaction. Thus, the same version of the facts accepted by the jury – that Exxon intended to drive the franchisees out of business – that takes this case out of the "normal" set of cases for purposes of comment 3 also satisfies the criteria for bad faith.[8]

Exxon's bad faith, in this regard, is shown by the record. Facing the competition of self-service stations that were either selling food and other goods or had bare pumps with no overhead costs incurred in servicing vehicles, Exxon decided years ago that retail marketing through franchise dealers was becoming economically unsound. Although Exxon decided to move to CORS in Houston and jobbers in Corpus Christi, this decision was not communicated to its franchisees. Because of profit from their other sales, CORS could, and did, sell gas for less than the franchise dealers paid to Exxon for their gas. And the jobbers delivered Exxon gas to their dealers for less than Exxon franchisees were required to pay for their delivered gas, but Exxon prohibited its franchisees from buying at this lower price from the jobbers.

The loss of competitive position and profit to plaintiff franchisees was inevitable and foreseeable to Exxon. Although Exxon witnesses denied receiving complaints, its dealers testified that they had complained often and for years, without success, until the very eve of trial.

Accordingly, the jury's finding that Exxon breached its duty of good faith in setting the DTW price it charged the plaintiffs is not without foundation in the law or the evidence. As we have recounted, plaintiffs offered ample evidence tending to prove their version of price-setting. Accordingly, there is no error in the refusal to grant Exxon j.m.l. on the breach of contract claim. . . . Affirmed.

---

[8]   See also *Allapattah*, 61 F. Supp. 2d at 1322 (explaining that "a merchant [who] acts in a manner intended to drive a franchisee out of business" violates the duty of good faith found in the UCC). Similarly, one court has recognized that a "predatory intent" to "set the prices with the intent to drive [franchisees] out of business and take over the stations" is a claim cognizable under the good faith provisions of the UCC. *E.S. Bills, Inc. v. Tzucanow*, 700 P.2d 1280, 1283–84 (Cal. Ct. App. 1985).

The *Mathis* reasoning was rejected in a remarkably similar case in Texas state court.[9] In that case, the court ruled that the wholesaler's price, which was on the high end – but nevertheless within – the range of prices charged by other wholesalers and which was applied on a non-discriminatory basis was fixed in good faith. The franchisees claimed that the wholesaler was trying to put them out of business, but there was no evidence on that point comparable to the evidence presented in *Mathis*. The *Mathis* interpretation of good faith was also rejected by the Sixth Circuit, which ruled that both prongs of good faith – "honesty in fact" and "reasonable commercial standards of fair dealing" have an objective meaning.[10] More recently, the First Circuit approved of the approach in *Mathis*.[11] In doings so, the court noted if the seller's obligation in fixing the contract price was merely to set a nondiscriminatory price, then section 2-305(2) would have been phrased in those terms, rather than in reference to good faith.

Problem 4-2

A. On February 1, Seller agreed in a writing signed by both Seller and Buyer to sell 1,000 sacks of Delaware Cobbler potatoes to Buyer, delivery at Buyer's plant by March 15, at a price "to be agreed at delivery." The market price on February 1 was $7 per sack. On March 15, Seller tendered delivery of the goods and requested the Buyer agree to a price of $15 per sack. The market price on March 15 was $12 and rising. Buyer rejected the tender and proposed price and obtained other potatoes for $13 per sack. In subsequent litigation, Buyer claimed that Seller breached the contract. Seller argued that there was no contract. Who should prevail?

B. On February 1, Seller agreed in a writing signed by both Seller and Buyer to sell 1,000 sacks of Delaware Cobbler potatoes to Buyer, delivery at Buyer's plant by March 15, at "the price on the Chicago commodities board of trade on March 15." The market price on February 1 was $7 per sack. On March 15, Seller tendered delivery of

---

[9]   *Shell Oil Co. v. HRN, Inc.*, 144 S.W.3d 429 (Tex. 2004).

[10]   *Tom-Lin Enterprises, Inc. v. Sunoco, Inc.*, 349 F.3d 277 (6th Cir. 2003)

[11]   *Marcoux v. Shell Oil Products Co.*, 524 F.3d 33 (1st Cir. 2008), *petition for cert. filed*, 77 U.S.L.W. 3106, 3209 (Aug. 21 & Sept. 19, 2008).

the goods. On March 14, the Chicago commodities board of trade had been shut down by the government agency regulating the board due to widespread fraud in trading on the board. On March 13, this type of potato was trading for $12 per sack. Seller demanded that price. Buyer rejected the tender and proposed price and obtained other potatoes for $11 per sack. In subsequent litigation, Seller claimed that Buyer breached the contract. Buyer argued that there was no contract. Who should prevail?

C. On February 1, Seller agreed in a writing signed by both Seller and Buyer to sell 1,000 sacks of Delaware Cobbler potatoes to Buyer, delivery at Buyer's plant by March 15, at a price "to be set by an independent third party agreed to by Buyer and Seller." The market price on February 1 was $7 per sack. On March 15, Seller tendered delivery of the goods. Buyer refused to agree to any third party that Seller suggested and refused to designate any third party. On March 15, the market price of potatoes was $13 per sack. Buyer refused the potatoes. Seller sued Buyer for breach of contract. What result?

SECTION 3.   DELIVERY AND PAYMENT

Article 2 contains several gap filler rules concerning the timing and manner of delivery of the goods and the timing and manner of payment. These terms often will be supplanted by the express or implied terms of the parties' agreement. However, in many transactions, some or all of these gap fillers will apply because the agreement is silent on these points.

Let's start by reviewing section 2-301. That section tells us that the seller's general obligation is to deliver goods that conform to the contract and that the buyer's general obligation is to accept and pay for those goods. What it does not tell us is how those obligations are to be fulfilled or who is to tender first.

Read sections 2-507(1) and 2-511(1). The first of these provisions makes the seller's tender of the goods a condition to the buyer's obligation to accept and pay for them. The second makes the buyer's tender of payment a condition to the seller's obligation to tender the goods. Does this make sense? Yes. These are concurrent conditions. Collectively they mean that, in the absence of agreement to the contrary, the parties are to tender simultaneously. If either fails to tender at the appropriate time and place, the other party is excused from further performance.

In the unlikely event that both parties fail to tender, then neither condition is met, with the result that neither party has breached the contract. In essence, by their mutual lack of performance, the parties have implicitly agreed to terminate their contract.

In most situations, however, either the parties expressly agree that one of them will tender performance first or such agreement is implicit in their course of performance, course of dealing, or in usage of trade. Although a dispute about tender can arise if the buyer is to perform first, most disputes about tender arise in the context of agreements when the seller is to tender before the buyer. In any event, the sequence does not significantly alter the parties' rights and responsibilities, so for purposes of continuing discussion, we will assume that the parties have agreed that seller is to tender the goods before the buyer is obligated to tender payment.

The three preliminary questions regarding the seller's tender are what, where, and when. As to what, read sections 2-106(2), 2-601, and 2-307. The first two of these provisions require the seller to tender conforming goods. In other words, the goods must conform to the contract description. The third of these provisions requires the seller to tender goods in one lot. *Cf.* UCC § 2-612(1).

As to where must the seller tender, read, section 2-308. In general, it requires the seller to tender at the seller's place of business or, if the seller has none, at the seller's residence. Why do you think the drafters chose to make tender presumptively due at the seller's place of business or residence rather than at the buyer's place of business or residence? As to when, read section 2-309(1). It requires tender within a reasonable time. That is, of course, an extremely fact-specific determination.[12]

The remaining aspects of the seller's duty to tender the goods vary depending on how the seller is to fulfill that obligation. Specifically, Article 2 has rules for three different scenarios: (i) the seller is to tender the goods directly to the buyer; (ii) the seller is authorized or has agreed to ship the goods to the buyer using a carrier; and (iii) the goods are in the possession of a bailee and are be tendered without being moved.

---

[12]   *See Marjam Supply Co. v. BCT Walls & Ceilings, Inc.*, 2003 WL 21497515 (E.D. Pa. 2003) (factors that determine reasonable time for delivery include the nature of the goods, the purpose that the goods will be used for, the extent of the seller's knowledge of the buyer's intentions, transportation conditions, and the nature of the market).

In each of these three scenarios, the primary questions are as follows. First, what must the seller do to fulfill the duty to tender the goods? Second, to what extent may the buyer inspect the goods prior to deciding whether to accept or reject them? Third, when is the buyer's obligation to tender the price due? Intertwined with these issues is the question of when the risk of loss passes. That is, at what point does the responsibility for any casualty to the goods pass from the seller to the buyer? We now explore these questions for each of the three scenarios in turn.

A. SELLER'S DIRECT TENDER OF THE GOODS

1. *Tender of Delivery*

Assume that the seller is to directly tender the goods to the buyer, rather than through an intermediary such as a carrier or a bailee of the goods. Read section 2-503(1), which sets forth the seller's basic tender obligations (for the present ignore subsections (2) through (5) of section 2-503). This provision uses quite a few vague and undefined terms, with the result that numerous issues can arise regarding the propriety of any particular tender of delivery. What does it mean to "put and hold" the goods? What notification is "reasonably necessary" to enable the buyer to take delivery? What is a "reasonable hour" and how long is "reasonably necessary to enable the buyer to take possession"? Consider also section 2-311 as it relates to the seller's tender obligation. Given all these vague standards, does section 2-503(1) accomplish anything? Does it help parties identify what their obligations are in advance or, if the parties cannot work out their differences, does it merely give a jury the license to find either party in breach? Consider the next problem. As you do so, remember that all of these provisions are subject to variation if the parties have otherwise agreed through express terms, course of performance, course of dealing or usage of trade.

Problem 4-3

A. Seller agreed to tender 100 bushels of wheat to Buyer for $4 per bushel. In each scenario described below, determine whether Seller has complied with its tender obligation. If you are unsure, identify what you need to know to be able to come to a conclusion on that issue.
   1. Seller called Buyer and told it the wheat was ready to be picked up. When Buyer arrived that afternoon, Seller only had 95 bushels

available and the auger usually used to load the wheat into trucks was broken down.

2. Seller called Buyer and told it the wheat was ready to be picked up. When Buyer arrived that afternoon, Buyer tested the wheat Seller had available and it was clearly moldy.

3. Seller called Buyer and told it the wheat was ready to be picked up, and told Buyer that someone better get there in 2 hours or Seller was going to sell the wheat to someone else.

4. Seller called Buyer and told it the wheat was ready to be picked up and Buyer protested that this delivery time was not convenient for Buyer and that Buyer could not take delivery for two months.

5. Seller called Buyer and told it the wheat was ready to be picked up at Seller's warehouse 300 miles away from both Buyer's and Seller's location.

6. Seller called Buyer and told it the wheat was ready to be picked up. When Buyer arrived that afternoon, Buyer did not have a truck capable of holding 100 bushels of wheat and wanted to take half that afternoon and half the next afternoon.

7. Buyer and Seller had agreed that Seller would deliver the wheat to Buyer's farm on April 3. On April 3, Seller drove onto Buyer's farm with the truckload of wheat in one of Seller's own trucks. Buyer did not have its storage facility cleaned out and asked Seller to come back the next day. *See* UCC § 2-311(3).

B. Go back in time and draft a term that would define the seller's tender of delivery obligation in the above scenario variations. What difficulties do you have in drafting that tender of delivery term?

2. *Buyer's Inspection*

Once the seller tenders goods, the buyer must either accept or reject the goods. Before deciding whether to accept or reject the goods, the buyer will often want to inspect them to determine if they in fact conform to the contract's requirements. Read section 2-513(1). It gives the buyer the right to inspect the goods at a reasonable time and place and in a reasonable manner,[13] unless the parties have

---

[13]   *See HCI Chemicals (USA), Inc. v. Henkel KGaA*, 966 F.2d 1018 (5th Cir. 1992) (holding

specified the timing, place, and method of inspection. This right to inspect precedes the buyer's obligation to accept and pay for conforming goods, and therefore protects the buyer from accepting or paying for nonconforming goods.

Two words of caution here. First do not confuse acceptance and rejection of *the goods* with acceptance and rejection of *an offer*. Acceptance and rejection of an offer relates to contract formation and was discussed in Chapter Two. Acceptance and rejection of the goods relates to contract performance and is discussed here.   Second, do not equate taking *possession* of the goods with *acceptance* of the goods.   One of the ways a buyer may inspect goods is to take possession and test the goods for a reasonable period of time to determine if they conform to the contract.   Indeed, if the goods are supposed to meet specified performance or purity standards, there may be no ready means to inspect without first taking possession. In such situations, taking possession of the goods is not, by itself, sufficient to constitute acceptance of them.

Either before or upon expiration of the buyer's inspection rights, the buyer must either accept or reject the goods. The buyer cannot do both,[14] and because failure to seasonably reject constitutes acceptance,[15] the buyer cannot do neither. However, the buyer may be permitted to accept some goods and reject others.[16] If the buyer accepts the goods, three principal consequences ensue. First, the buyer is precluded from rejecting the goods. UCC. § 2-607(2). Second, the buyer becomes obligated to pay the contract price. UCC § 2-607(1). Third, if there is a problem with the goods, the buyer will have the burden of proving that the goods fail to conform to the contract in order to be entitled to any remedy. UCC § 2-607(4). Even if the goods or tender fail to conform to the contract requirements, the buyer has only a small window of opportunity to revoke that acceptance and force the goods back on the seller. UCC § 2-608.

If the buyer rejects the goods, the buyer may not exercise ownership over them and, if the buyer has possession of them, the buyer must hold them for the seller. UCC § 2-602(2).

---

that the place for inspection specified in UCC § 2-513(1) was not displaced by agreement).

[14]   *See* UCC §§ 2-602(2)(a) (rejection makes any exercise of ownership of the goods by the buyer wrongful against the seller); 2-607(2) (acceptance precludes rejection).

[15]   *See* UCC § 2-606(1)(b) (failure to reject constitutes acceptance).

[16]   *See* UCC § 2-601(c).

The buyer's *decision* to accept or reject the goods is separate and distinct from the buyer's *right* to accept or reject the goods. If the goods conform to the contract, the buyer has no right to reject the goods. If the buyer nevertheless does reject them, the buyer will be in breach and the seller will have a cause of action. UCC § 2-703. However, if the goods fail in any respect to conform to the contract requirements, the seller will have breached the contract. *See* UCC §§ 2-301, 2-711. The buyer in that circumstance generally has the right to either accept or reject the goods. *See* UCC § 2-601.[17] If the buyer accepts, the buyer will become obligated to pay the contract price but may be entitled to recover damages caused by the nonconformity. UCC §§ 2-607(1), (2), (3), 2-714. If the buyer rejects the goods in a timely manner, the buyer may recover other damages for the seller's breach. UCC § 2-711.

In Chapter Seven, we will explore in more detail the interplay among rejection, acceptance, and revocation of acceptance. For now, focus on the interplay between the buyer's right to inspect the goods and the choice to accept or reject the goods. The buyer has an incentive to inspect the goods to avoid accepting goods that do not conform to the contract requirements. Remember, once the buyer accepts the goods, the buyer is obligated to pay the contract price even if the goods do not conform to the contract. In addition to not wanting to pay for non-conforming goods, the buyer may wish to avoid costly unloading and storage of the goods. Remember also that the length of the inspection period is not limitless. This point is contained both in section 2-513 itself and in section 2-606(1)(b), which provides that the buyer is deemed to have accepted the goods if the buyer fails to reject them after having had a reasonable opportunity to inspect. Thus, the buyer can effectively lose the right to inspect by waiting too long to exercise that right.

What if the buyer has agreed to pay the contract price before the goods are available for inspection? The buyer has a right to inspect before payment *or* acceptance. UCC § 2-513(1). Thus, even if the buyer has agreed to pay prior to *inspection*, the buyer still has the right to inspect the goods prior to *acceptance* of the goods. UCC § 2-512(2). Occasionally, the buyer will argue that even though it has agreed to pay before inspection, the nonconformity of the goods should excuse the buyer from paying before inspection. Section 2-512(1) addresses that circumstance.

---

[17]   The rules are slightly different in installment contracts. *See* UCC § 2-612(2).

3. Buyer's Payment

If the parties have so agreed, the seller may extend credit to the buyer to allow the buyer to pay later. However, a credit sale is not presumed. Therefore, the buyer generally is obligated to pay in full upon acceptance of the goods. UCC §§ 2-607(1), 2-310(a) cmt. 1. If either party has the right to have delivery occur in lots, then the seller may demand payment for each lot delivered if the price can be properly apportioned. UCC § 2-307.

The buyer may pay in money or by any other manner, UCC §§ 2-511(2), 2-304, unless the parties have agreed to a particular payment mechanism.

Problem 4-4

Seller agreed to tender 100 bushels of wheat to Buyer for $4 per bushel. Seller informed Buyer that the wheat was ready for delivery. Seller loaded the wheat in Seller's own truck and drove the load to Buyer's facility.

A. Seller insisted Buyer hand over the contract price before it would unload the wheat. Buyer protested that it had a right to inspect the wheat before having to give Seller the $400. What would you advise Seller to do?

B. Buyer insisted that Seller should unload the wheat and Buyer would send a sample of the load to a testing facility to test for contamination. If the test came back clean, Buyer would pay the $400 contract price. Seller protested when it found out the testing process takes two weeks. What would you advise Buyer to do?

C. You represent Buyer at the inception of the relationship between Buyer and Seller. Draft an inspection term to propose to Seller. If you represented Seller, would you agree to the term as drafted? What modifications would you make? What inspection term would you suggest that Seller include in the standard sales agreement that it proposes to all of its buyers?

Problem 4-5

A. In a writing signed by both parties, John has agreed to sell his entire collection of novels to Alice for $5,000. His entire basement is filled with these books, enough books to fill three medium size rental trucks. John is insisting that Alice come get all the books at one time, but has not agreed to any particular date when Alice is available. Alice wants John to deliver the books to her house on two different Saturdays and wants to pay for the books only after John has delivered them all and she has determined that all of them are in satisfactory condition. She wants to give him $4,000 of the purchase price in cash and the other $1,000 in the form of a used computer and printer. John does not want the computer, but wants $5,000 in cash. The signed writing did not contain any terms that addressed the time or manner of delivery or the time or manner of payment. Both parties are contending that the other has breached the contract. What result?

B. You represent one of the parties. Redraft the writing between the parties to avoid the problems you encountered in Part A.

4. Risk of Loss

Risk of loss refers to which party will suffer the loss of any casualty to the goods. In other words, assume that at some point after the contract is formed but before performance is completed, the goods are damaged or destroyed. That casualty may be the result of weather, vandalism, theft, fire, or any other similar event. Regardless of the nature of the event, the fact remains that the parties were – collectively – wealthier before the casualty than after. One of them (or their insurers) will have to suffer the loss. Put another way, before the transaction they – collectively – had both the goods and the contract price for them. After the casualty, they had only the contract price. The one who does not get the money will have the risk of loss.

Risk of loss is related to contract performance and breach. If the seller has the risk of loss and the goods are damaged or destroyed, the seller has to bear the financial loss. In addition, if the seller fails to tender conforming goods to the buyer, the seller may also be liable for breach.[18] Similarly, if the buyer bears the risk of loss and the goods are lost or damaged, the buyer will often be liable for the price of the goods, UCC § 2-709(1), and will not be able to recover against the seller because of the casualty to the goods.

---

[18]   Cf. UCC §§ 2-613, 2-615 (which occasionally excuse the seller from further performance if the goods or the seller's ability to provide them is damaged or destroyed).

So at what point in a sale-of-goods transaction does the risk of loss pass from the seller to the buyer? First, remember that the parties are free to reach agreement on this point; the rules in Article 2 are merely gap fillers in the event the parties' agreement is silent on risk of loss. *See* UCC § 2-509(4). Second, under Article 2, the passage of the risk of loss from the seller to the buyer does not depend upon passage of title to the goods.[19] Instead, allocation of the risk of loss depends on the manner in which the seller is to tender delivery and whether the seller has made a conforming tender.[20] There are three principles underlying the rules on risk of loss. First, the party who controls the goods, and is thus in the best position to avoid the loss, should bear the risk. *See* UCC § 2-509 cmt. 3. Second, the party most likely to have insurance protection under the circumstances should bear the risk. *Id.* Third, the party in breach should bear the risk of loss. *Compare* UCC § 2-509 *with* § 2-510.

Read sections 2-509 and 2-510. Absent an agreement otherwise and absent breach, if the tender of delivery is not being made through an intermediary such as a carrier or bailee, the relevant rule is in UCC § 2-509(3). That section provides two different rules based upon whether the seller is a merchant. If the seller is not a merchant, the risk of loss will pass to the buyer upon tender of delivery of conforming goods. If the seller is a merchant, the risk of loss will pass to the buyer upon the buyer's receipt of conforming goods. Section 2-103 contains a definition of receipt. *See* UCC §§ 2-104 (defining "merchant"), 2-106 (regarding the meaning of conformity).

Problem 4-6

Seller agreed to tender 100 bushels of wheat to Buyer for $4 per bushel. Seller informed Buyer that the wheat was ready for delivery.

---

[19]   *See* UCC § 2-401. There is more than a passing similarity among sections 2-503, 2-509, and 2-401. Title may be relevant to other issues, such as liability for taxes or for criminal acts regarding property. It may also determine who has rights under insurance policies. *See* Jeanne L. Schroeder, *Death and Transfiguration: The Myth that the U.C.C. Killed "Property,"* 69 TEMP. L. REV. 1281 (1996); *P & O Nedlloyd, Ltd. v. Sanderson Farms, Inc.*, 462 F.3d 1015 (8th Cir. 2006).

[20]   *See* Robert L. Flores, *Risk of Loss in Sales: A Missing Chapter in the History of the U.C.C.:   Through Llewellyn to Williston and A Bit Beyond*, 27 PAC. L.J. 161 (1996); Margaret Howard, *Allocation of Risk of Loss Under the UCC: A Transactional Evaluation of Sections 2-509 and 2-510*, 15 UCC L.J. 334 (1983); Note, *Risk of Loss in Commercial Transactions: Efficiency Thrown Into the Breach*, 65 VA. L. REV. 557 (1979).

A. Seller loaded the wheat in Seller's own truck. During the drive to Buyer's facility, the truck caught fire and all the wheat was destroyed. Who had the risk of loss? Does it matter whether Seller is a merchant?

B. After Seller informed Buyer that the wheat was ready to be picked up but before Buyer could arrive to get the wheat, Seller's storage facility burned to the ground, destroying the wheat that Seller intended for Buyer. Who had the risk of loss? Does it matter whether Seller is a merchant?

C. After Seller informed Buyer that the wheat was ready to be picked up, Buyer asked Seller to leave the wheat in big bins on Seller's dock and Buyer would pick up the wheat after hours. Seller did so, leaving the wheat in unlocked bins on Seller's loading dock. Before Buyer arrived, vandals poured paint on the wheat contained in the bins. Who had the risk of loss? *See McKenzie v. Olmstead*, 587 N.W.2d 863 (Minn. Ct. App. 1999).

D. Seller loaded the wheat in Seller's own truck and dropped the wheat at Buyer's storage facility after hours. The wheat was in unlocked bins. Buyer did not know that the wheat had been delivered. During the night, vandals poured paint over the wheat in the bins. Who had the risk of loss? *See In re Thomas*, 182 B.R. 347 (Bankr. S.D. Fla. 1995).

E. Buyer tendered a personal check to Seller. Seller is still in possession of the wheat in unlocked bins on Seller's property. Before the check cleared, vandals poured paint on the wheat. Who had the risk of loss? *See Capshaw v. Hickman*, 880 N.E.2d 118 (Ohio Ct. App. 2007).

B. SELLER'S TENDER OF THE GOODS THROUGH SHIPPING THE GOODS

Now consider a situation in which the seller has agreed to tender the goods before buyer must tender payment and has agreed to ship the goods to the buyer. If the seller uses its own vehicles or transportation device to deliver the goods to the buyer, the tender of delivery rules and risk of loss rules we have discussed above will control. However, if a seller ships goods to the buyer using a carrier, such as a railroad or trucking company, different tender of delivery rules apply.

When the seller uses a carrier to ship the goods to the buyer, the seller will agree with the carrier to a contract that instructs the carrier to deliver the goods to the buyer at a designated address. That contract with the carrier will also set the price of shipment and contain any special instructions needed to safely transport the goods. However, this contract between the seller and the carrier is separate and distinct from the contract between the seller and the buyer for the sale of the goods. Moreover, it is the seller's contract with the buyer that determines what responsibilities the seller has with respect to tender. For this purpose, sales contracts that call for shipping the goods using a carrier come in two varieties: "shipment" contracts and "destination" contracts.

1. *Tender of Delivery and Risk of Loss in a Shipment Contract*

Read comment 5 to section 2-503. The presumption is that when the seller agrees to deliver goods by shipping them using a carrier, the seller is agreeing to a "shipment contract." In a shipment contract, the seller's tender obligation is governed by sections 2-503(2) and 2-504. *See also* UCC § 2-311. Under those provisions, tender of the goods occurs when the seller delivers the goods to the carrier, makes a reasonable contract with the carrier to transport the goods, and informs the buyer of the shipment. As a result, the seller has no responsibility for the condition of the goods after that point. If the goods are damaged or destroyed during transit, the seller will have already fully performed. Section 2-509(1)(a) makes that clear by putting on the buyer the risk of loss of or damage to the goods during transit. The effect of this is that the buyer will be liable to the seller for the buyer's performance under the sales contract if the goods are lost or damaged during transit. This liability will either be for the price of the goods, UCC § 2-709(1)(a), or damages for breach of contract, UCC § 2-703. Of course, if the goods are lost or damaged in transit in a shipment contract, the buyer may have claims for the loss or damage to the goods against the carrier, or as against the parties that caused the loss or damage to the goods under other law.[21] *See* UCC § 2-722.

---

[21]   The carrier generally has the obligation to take reasonable care of the goods. UCC § 7-309. The liability of carriers is determined under federal and state legislation and international treaties that, in turn, depend upon the type of carrier and the scope of its operation. The liability of domestic overland carriers in interstate commerce, *i.e.*, railroads and truckers, is regulated by federal law and the liability of intrastate domestic carriers is regulated by state law, including section 7-309. *See* James C. Hardman, *Legal, Practical, and Economic Aspects of Third Party Motor Carrier Services: An Overview*, 34 TRANS. L.J. 237 (2007); Michael E. Crowley, *The Limited Scope of the Cargo Liability Regime Covering Carriage of Goods by Sea: The Multimodal Problem*, 79 TUL. L. REV. 1461 (2005); Paul Stephen Dempsey, *Transportation: A Legal History*, 30 TRANS. L.J. 235 (2003).

If the buyer has insured the goods, the insurance company will indemnify the buyer to the extent obligated under the policy and, through equitable or contractual subrogation, assert any claims that the buyer might have against persons who caused the loss, or any claims against the carrier. Notice however, that section 2-504 does not require that the seller insure the goods. The buyer is the one that must either insure against or personally suffer any loss of the goods in a shipment contract.[22] One of the functions of the notice requirement in section 2-504 is to allow the buyer to obtain insurance for the goods if the buyer does not already have insurance that covers the goods while in transit.

2.   *Tender of Delivery and Risk of Loss in a Destination Contract*

If the contract is a destination contract, the seller's obligation is to tender conforming goods to the buyer (not merely to the carrier). In other words, tender occurs after transportation of the goods, not before. UCC § 2-503(3). Section 2-509(1)(b) then governs the risk of loss in a destination contract. Under that provision, the seller has the risk of loss during transit and the risk of loss passes to the buyer only upon the tender of goods by the carrier to the buyer. Thus, as between the seller and the buyer, the seller has taken the responsibility for the condition of the goods in transit. *See* UCC § 2-311(3). If goods are lost or damaged in transit, the seller will have breached the sales contract because conforming goods were not tendered at the conclusion of the transit. UCC § 2-711. The seller will have the right to pursue the carrier or third parties for the loss or damage to the goods under other principles of law. *See* UCC § 2-722. If the seller insured the goods, the insurance company will indemnify the seller and, in all probability, assert any claims the seller may have against third parties through subrogation.

---

[22]   The buyer may have an insurable interest in the goods even though the buyer is not the owner of the goods, or in possession of the goods. UCC § 2-501. For the scope of insurable interest in property insurance cases, *see* John M. Stockton, *An Analysis of Insurable Interest Under Article Two of the Uniform Commercial Code,* 17 VAND. L. REV. 815 (1964). *See also* Robert S. Pinzur, *Insurable Interest: A Search for Consistency,* 46 INS. COUNSEL J. 109 (1979). For an example of a court using Article 2 to determine if a seller retained an insurable interest after tender of the goods to a buyer who had prepaid in full, *see Spirit of Excellence, Ltd. v. Intercargo Ins. Co.,* 777 N.E.2d 660 (Ill. Ct. App. 2002).

3.   *Shipment or Destination Contract*

How do you distinguish a shipment contract from a destination contract? Both are likely to specify the location to which the goods must be shipped. Thus, specifying a destination for the goods does not mean the seller has agreed to a destination contract. The key inquiry is whether the seller agreed to take responsibility for the goods during shipment. If not, then the contract is a shipment contract. If the seller has agreed to take that responsibility for the goods during shipment, then the contract is a destination contract.

One of the primary mechanisms for deciding to what the buyer and seller have agreed is the use of customary shipping terms, such as "F.O.B." (free on board) or "C.I.F." (cost, insurance and freight). *See* UCC §§ 2-319 through 2-324. In the absence of such terms, the assumption is that the sales contract is a "shipment" contract. Accordingly, clear evidence will be needed to show that the buyer and seller have agreed to a "destination" contract. Thus, whether the parties have agreed to a shipment or a destination contract is primarily a matter of interpreting the sales agreement, including the meaning of any shipping terms the parties have used.[23]

Problem 4-7

Seller in South Dakota contracted to manufacture and sell to Buyer in New York custom window wall panels to be used in a building that Buyer was constructing. The agreement provided that "all windows are to be shipped properly crated/packaged/boxed for cross-country motor freight transit and delivered to" the construction site in New York. Seller delivered the windows to Carrier, made a contract with Carrier to deliver the goods to Buyer at the construction site, and notified Buyer of the shipment. The goods were severely damaged during transit.

A. If the windows were properly packaged, who bears the risk of loss?

---

[23]   *See Wilson v. Brawn of California, Inc.*, 33 Cal. Rptr. 3d 769 (Cal. Ct. App. 2005) (consumer mail order was a shipment contract); Ademuni-Odeke, *Insurance of F.O.B. Contracts in Anglo-American and Common Law Jurisdictions Revisited: The Wider Picture*, 31 TUL. MAR. L.J. 425 (2007); Daniel E. Murray, *Risk of Loss of Goods in Transit: A Comparison of the 1990 Incoterms with Terms from Other Voices*, 23 U. MIAMI INTER-AM. L. REV. 93 (1991).

B. How, if at all, would the analysis change if the agreement had provided that "all windows are to be shipped properly crated/packaged/boxed for cross-country motor freight transit and delivered at" the construction site in New York? *See Windows, Inc. v. Jordan Panel Systems Corp.,* 177 F.3d 114 (2d Cir. 1999).
C. Assume the windows were improperly packaged.
 1. Who would bear the risk of loss if the damage was caused by the improper packaging?
 2. Who would bear the risk of loss if the damage was fully attributable to Carrier's negligence?

4. Buyer's Right to Inspect

How does shipment of the goods affect the buyer's right to inspect? Reread section 2-513. Unless the buyer and seller have agreed to alter the buyer's inspection rights, the buyer has the right to inspect goods before the buyer is obligated to pay for the goods or accept them. In both shipment contracts and destination contracts, such inspection may be at any reasonable time and place, and thus can occur at the beginning of shipment (before or when the seller delivers the goods to the carrier) or the place of delivery. The buyer may hire a third party to accomplish that inspection.

However, the timing of inspection does not affect the buyer's right to reject. If the goods in a shipment contract are not conforming when they arrive, the buyer will have a right to reject (and the seller will have the risk of loss) only if the goods also were not conforming at the time they were delivered to the carrier or if the tender to the carrier was otherwise defective. If the nonconformity is something that might have occurred in transit, it may be difficult for the buyer to prove that the goods were nonconforming before the carrier started to transport them. Thus, the buyer has some incentive to inspect the goods at the starting point to determine if the goods conform to the contract when tendered to the carrier. Of course, inspection at that point is often not practical.

The same point applies to the risk of loss. The timing of the inspection does not affect when the risk of loss passes. In a shipment contact, the risk of loss will have passed to the buyer if the goods conformed to the contract when the goods were placed in the possession of the carrier. If the goods were not conforming when tendered to the carrier, the risk of loss will not have passed. UCC § 2-510.

However, if the goods were completely destroyed during transit, the buyer may not be able to show that the tender was nonconforming, and thus may end up bearing the risk of loss.

Because the risk of loss in a destination contract passes upon tender of conforming goods at the destination, the buyer usually has little incentive to inspect the goods when they are delivered to the carrier and will usually wait to inspect them at the destination.

5. Payment Against Documents of Title and the Effect on Buyer's Right to Inspect

In both shipment and destination contracts, when goods are shipped by carrier, the carrier will usually issue a form of a document of title known as a bill of lading.[24] Read the definition of document of title and bill of lading in section 1-201. A carrier is a type of bailee, someone who takes possession, but not ownership, of the goods in order to do something with the goods that the bailor wants done with them, in this case transport the goods. A bill of lading issued by the carrier functions both as a receipt for the goods and as the contract for carriage of the goods. The carrier will then insist that the bill of lading be presented to it wherever the goods are to be offloaded in order to make sure that the carrier is releasing the goods to the right person.

In either a shipment or destination contract, the seller's tender obligation therefore includes tendering to the buyer all documents of title that are either required under the sales contact or are otherwise necessary for the buyer to obtain possession of the goods. UCC §§ 2-503(3), (5), 2-504(b). Thus, in shipment and destinations contracts, the seller must tender both the *conforming goods to the carrier* and the *required document of title to the buyer.*

If the buyer has not agreed with the seller to pay upon presentation of the documents to the buyer, the seller may simply send the bill of lading to the buyer

---

[24]   Rights and obligations arising out of a document of title and the bailment relationship are governed, in part, by UCC Article 7. Documents of title come in two flavors, negotiable and non-negotiable. UCC § 7-104. If the bill of lading is negotiable, it also serves as evidence of good title to the goods. UCC § 7-502. The carrier's responsibility during transit is governed by Article 7 (*see* UCC § 7-309 prescribing the duty of care) and applicable federal law. *See Paper Magic Group, Inc. v. J.B. Hunt Transport, Inc.*, 318 F.3d 458 (3d Cir. 2003).

or if an electronic bill of lading is used, enable the buyer to obtain control of the bill of lading. UCC § 7-106. The buyer will then be able to use the bill of lading to obtain the goods from the carrier. Once the buyer obtains access to the goods, the buyer will be able to inspect the goods and decide whether to accept and pay for them.

If the buyer has agreed with the seller to pay upon presentation of documents of title, the buyer has waived its right to inspect the goods prior to payment and must pay upon presentation of the documents. UCC §§ 2-310(b), (c), 2-513(3). The buyer may inspect the *documents* and reject the documents if the *documents* do not comply with the sales contract terms. If the buyer does pay upon tender of the documents, the buyer will no longer have a right to assert defects in the documents that are apparent on the face of the *documents*. UCC § 2-605(2). However, the buyer still retains its right to inspect the *goods* prior to acceptance, UCC § 2-513(1), and payment for the goods is not acceptance of the goods. UCC § 2-512(2). In other words, payment by the buyer upon tender of the documents of title does not waive any nonconformity with respect to the goods or impair the buyer's right to reject the goods. UCC §§ 2-601, 2-612.

Thus, if the buyer has agreed to pay upon tender of documents, the seller will typically place the goods with the carrier, obtain the necessary documents from the carrier, and then send the documents to the seller's agent at the location where the carrier is to release the goods to the buyer. The seller's agent will present the documents to the buyer and obtain the buyer's payment. The buyer will then take the documents to the carrier, obtain the goods, inspect them, and decide whether to accept or reject the goods.

How can you tell if the buyer has agreed to pay upon tender of the document of title? Merely because a document of title is used to facilitate transportation does not mean that the buyer has agreed with the seller to pay against documents. Rather, such agreement is generally reflected in the meaning of the shipping term it has agreed to with the seller. For example, if the buyer and seller have agreed to a "C.I.F." or "C & F" shipment term, the presumption is that the buyer has agreed to pay upon tender of the required documents of title. UCC § 2-320(4).[25]

---

[25]   If the buyer has agreed to pay only after the goods have arrived, inspection is allowed prior to the buyer being obligated to pay. UCC §§ 2-321(3), 2-513(3), 2-310.

6. Shipment under Reservation

One more Code section needs to be considered before trying your hand at some problems. When the seller is authorized to ship goods to the buyer, the seller may ship the goods under reservation. UCC § 2-310(b). Shipment under reservation is a method for the seller to reserve a security interest in the goods in order to make sure the goods are not released to the buyer until the buyer has paid for the goods. To ship the goods under reservation, the seller will obtain the documents of title from the carrier as set forth in section 2-505(1). Mere shipment under reservation does not undermine the buyer's right to inspect the goods before payment. UCC § 2-310(b). Rather, the buyer will often be able to have access to the goods to inspect them, although the carrier is not authorized to release the goods to the buyer until the buyer pays for the goods.

The seller's shipment under reservation, which serves to ensure the buyer pays upon receipt of the goods, is compatible with the default rule in Article 2 that payment is due upon the buyer's receipt of the goods. UCC § 2-310. A corollary to this is that if the seller has agreed to sell the goods on credit to the buyer, that is, if the buyer is obligated to pay sometime after receipt of the goods, the seller would be in breach of the sales contract if the seller shipped the goods under reservation.[26]

Problem 4-8

Seller contracted with Buyer to ship a carload of factory equipment from Chicago to Phoenix, F.O.B. Chicago. The contract price was $10,000, to be paid by a cashier's check. Nothing was said about when payment was to be made. Seller shipped the goods on October 1, with delivery expected on October 5. Carrier issued a negotiable bill of lading "to the order of Seller" and delivered it to Seller. That afternoon Seller sent the bill of lading to an agent in Phoenix. The bill of lading arrived on October 2 and on October 3, while the goods where still en route from Chicago, the agent tendered the bill of lading to Buyer and demanded payment. Buyer refused

---

[26] Even if the seller breaches the contract for sale with the buyer by shipping under reservation when it had no right to do so, the buyer's rights in regard to the goods or the rights under a negotiable document of title are not impaired. UCC § 2-505(2). In addition, if the seller was not entitled to ship under reservation because it had agreed that the buyer could pay after receipt of the goods, the seller would have made an improper contract for transportation under section 2-504.

to pay, arguing there was no duty to pay until the goods were tendered. Is Buyer correct?

Problem 4-9

Seller and Buyer agreed to a shipment contract. Seller then contracted with B & O Railroad to ship the goods to Buyer. Seller neglected to inform B & O that the goods needed to be securely tied down to avoid any shifting in transit. Even minor shifting had the potential to damage sensitive components installed inside the goods. B & O secured the goods in the usual manner which allowed some shifting of contents during shipment. When the goods arrived, the Buyer inspected them and determined that some of them were not functioning properly.

A. Assuming that Buyer could prove the failure to function properly was caused by the load shifts during transit, does Buyer have a good argument that Seller breached its tender obligation?

B. Who had the risk of loss for the damage during shipment?

Problem 4-10

Seller, in California, received a written order for lumber sent by Buyer from its place of business in Portland, Oregon. The order provided in part:

> To Seller:
> Ship to Buyer, Council Bluffs, Iowa Rate 1.20 (show on bill of lading) Routing SP UP (via Colby, Kansas) Shipment One week Terms: Regular 2% ADF 10 days Please Show Buyer as Shipper * * * Thoroughly Air Dried White Fir–WCLA Rules No. 15 Constr. & Btr., Allow. 25% standard ALS S4S EE DET–Clean Bright Stock one (1) Carload.

Two days later, Seller loaded a railroad car provided by the carrier with conforming lumber and sealed the door. Later that day, Seller prepared an invoice for Buyer as follows:

> Shipped to Buyer Council Bluffs, Iowa * * * F.O.B. delivered $1.20 rate. * * * 31,152' White Fir, A.D. 2 × 4 STD. & BTR. S4S at $84.00 Per M–$2,616.77.

Seller also prepared a non-negotiable bill of lading naming Buyer as both Consignor and Consignee and presented it to an agent of the railroad. The agent signed the bill of lading and Seller immediately mailed the bill and the invoice to Buyer.

Before the bill and invoice were received and before Carrier picked up the loaded car, fire broke out without the fault of Seller and the goods were destroyed. Buyer argued that the risk of loss had not passed before the fire. More specifically, Buyer argued that the term "F.O.B. delivered" in context meant that Seller had agreed to deliver the goods "at a particular destination" and that risk of loss would not pass until the goods were "duly tendered" at that destination. *See* UCC § 2-509(1)(b). Is that argument correct?

7. *Documentary Draft Transactions*

In any transaction in which the seller has procured documents of title from the carrier, the seller must somehow get the documents to the buyer to enable the buyer to retrieve the goods from the carrier. One way to do this is simply to send the documents to the buyer or the buyer's agent. However, if the buyer has agreed to pay against the documents, the seller will not want to release the documents to the buyer without getting the payment.

Instead of sending the documents to an agent located in the buyer's area, the seller may use the banking system as a method of getting the documents of title to the buyer when the buyer has agreed to pay against documents. When using the banking system to present the documents to the buyer, the seller will often use a draft payable to the order of the seller, drawn on the buyer, and signed by the seller. UCC § 3-104. Thus the seller is the payee, the buyer is the drawee, and the seller is the drawer. The seller will give that draft and accompanying documents of title to the seller's bank. The seller's bank will forward the draft and documents through the banking system to the buyer's bank. UCC § 4-501. When the draft and the documents arrive at the buyer's bank, the buyer's bank will present the draft and the documents to the buyer. UCC § 4-503.

Upon release of the documents of title to the buyer,[27] the buyer may obtain the goods from the carrier. If the buyer fails to pay or accept the draft as required, the buyer's bank (known as the 'presenting bank') has some ability to deal with the goods because the bank is not supposed to release the goods to the buyer. UCC §§ 4-503, 4-504. The presenting bank will seek instructions from its transferor, which request will be communicated back to the seller. UCC § 4-501. The seller will send instructions as to what it wants the presenting bank to do with the goods.

If the seller uses the documentary draft mechanism and the buyer has not agreed to pay against documents, the seller has breached its contract with the buyer by impairing the buyer's right to inspect the goods prior to payment.[28]

C. Seller's Tender of Goods in Possession of a Bailee When the Goods are to Be Delivered Without Being Moved

1. Tender of Delivery

Let us assume that the goods that are the subject of the contract for sale are stored in a warehouse operated by someone other than the seller. This may occur, for example, when a farmer wishes to sell grain stored in a silo operated by a cooperative. The seller and buyer agree that the seller will give the buyer access to the goods which will remain in the warehouse until the buyer needs them. A

---

[27] If the draft is payable within the three days after presentment, the bank will release the documents to the buyer only upon payment. UCC §§ 4-503, 2-514. If the draft is payable more than three days after presentment to the buyer, the bank will insist on the buyer's "acceptance" of the draft in order to release the documents to the buyer. UCC §§ 4-503, 2-514. Acceptance of a draft is the drawee's (in this case the buyer's) signed engagement to pay that the buyer/drawee writes on the draft when the draft is presented to the buyer/drawee. UCC § 3-409. The buyer's "acceptance" of the draft obligates the buyer to pay according to the terms of the draft as accepted when the draft is later presented for payment. UCC § 3-413.

[28] A variation on this basic transaction is the seller's sale of the draft and the documents to a bank for a discounted amount. The bank would have a security interest in the draft and the documents. UCC § 4-210. In addition, the bank is an Article 2 financing agency, section 2-104(2), and has rights as to the goods as specified in sections 2-506 and 2-707. For an excellent discussion of the documentary draft transaction in greater detail, *see* E. Allan Farnsworth, *Documentary Drafts Under the Uniform Commercial Code*, 22 BUS. LAW. 479 (1967).

warehouse is a type of bailee. A warehouse, when it takes goods for storage, may issue a warehouse receipt for the goods. A warehouse receipt, like a bill of lading, is a type of document of title. Read the definition of warehouse receipt in section 1-201.[29]

The seller's obligation to tender delivery may be satisfied in several ways, if the parties have not otherwise agreed. If the warehouse has issued a negotiable warehouse receipt, the seller's tender is complete upon the tender of that document to the buyer. UCC § 2-503(4)(a). That is because any warehouse that has issued a negotiable warehouse receipt covering goods will not release the goods to anyone other than the person presenting the warehouse receipt. UCC §§ 7-403(c), 7-502. Alternatively, if the warehouse has not issued a negotiable document of title, the seller may fulfill its tender obligation by obtaining an acknowledgment from the warehouse that the buyer has the right to possess the goods. UCC § 2-503(4)(a).

There are two other ways in which a seller may be able to tender the goods: (i) delivering to the buyer a nonnegotiable warehouse receipt issued by the warehouse; or (ii) giving the buyer a written direction to the warehouse to deliver the goods to the buyer (this document is known as a delivery order). UCC § 2-503(4)(b). However, both of these methods of tender fail if the buyer seasonably objects (unless the buyer has agreed otherwise). Moreover, if the bailee docs not honor the nonnegotiable warehouse receipt or the delivery order, the seller's tender is similarly defeated.

2. Buyer's Inspection Right

Unless agreed otherwise, the buyer has the right to inspect the goods prior to payment or acceptance. UCC § 2-513(1). Thus, upon the seller's tender as described above, the buyer has a reasonable opportunity to inspect the goods stored in the warehouse and decide whether to accept or reject the goods. After that inspection, if the buyer does not reject the goods, the buyer will have to pay for them.

As with sales contracts involving shipment of the goods, the buyer may have agreed in this situation to pay upon tender of the documents of title. If so, the consequences are the same as those discussed previously with respect to inspection

---

[29] Just as we saw with bills of lading, a warehouse receipt may be either negotiable or non-negotiable. UCC § 7-104.

after payment. However, just as when goods are shipped, merely because a document of title, such as a warehouse receipt, is issued does not mean that the buyer has agreed to pay upon tender of that document.

3. Risk of Loss

Under section 2-509(2), the risk of loss will pass to the buyer if the goods are in the hands of a bailee and the parties agree the goods are to be delivered without being moved.[30] There is a symmetry between sections 2-509(2) and 2-503(4). Thus if tender of delivery takes place through tender of a negotiable document of title, the risk of loss moves from the seller to the buyer at that time. UCC § 2-509(2)(a). If the tender of delivery is made by the bailee acknowledging that the buyer is entitled to possession of the goods, risk of loss passes to the buyer at that point. UCC § 2-509(2)(b).[31] If the seller tenders a nonnegotiable document or a delivery order, the risk of loss passes to the buyer after the buyer has had a reasonable time to present the document or delivery order to the bailee. UCC §§ 2-509(2)(c), 2-503(4)(b).

Even though the goods are in the possession of a bailee at the time of contracting, the parties may agree that the bailee is to ship or deliver the goods to the buyer (thus moving the goods in the delivery process) rather than simply acknowledge that the buyer is entitled to possession. If so, risk of loss is governed by the normal rules applicable to shipment or delivery contracts, rather than under section 2-509(2).[32]

Problem 4-11

Seller, an appliance manufacturer, contracted to sell 200 ovens to Buyer, an appliance retailer. Buyer did not have sufficient capacity to store the ovens at Buyer's premises, so Seller and Buyer agreed that the ovens would remain in the warehouse run by Bonded Storage, Inc. Delivery was

---

[30]   The warehouse has the obligation to take reasonable care of the goods. UCC § 7-204.

[31]   *See Jason's Foods, Inc. v. Peter Eckrich & Sons, Inc.*, 774 F.2d 214 (7th Cir. 1985) (the bailee's acknowledgment must be to the buyer).

[32]   *Commonwealth Petroleum Co. v. Petrosol Int'l, Inc.*, 901 F.2d 1314 (6th Cir. 1990).

due on April 5 and on that day Seller offered to indorse a negotiable warehouse receipt covering 200 ovens to Buyer if Buyer would pay the purchase price in full. Buyer refused because it wanted to pay for the ovens as it took each one out of storage after it was sold to a customer. Has Seller complied with its tender obligations? Does Buyer have a right to pay as it has asserted?

Problem 4-12

Red Feather, a fine filly, won her first race. Owner shipped her back to the stable by common carrier, taking a non-negotiable bill of lading naming Owner as the consignee. While the horse was in transit, Owner sold Red Feather to Buyer for $10,000. Owner accepted a check for $10,000, handed Buyer the non-negotiable bill of lading and stated "she's all yours." Two hours later, Red Feather was killed in an accident while still in the carrier's possession. Who had the risk of loss?

D. DELIVERY, INSPECTION, AND PAYMENT UNDER INTERNATIONAL LAW

1. CISG

The seller's general duties to deliver the goods and hand over the documents are particularized in Articles 31through 34 and are largely similar to the rules under the UCC. Article 31 deals with the place of delivery in cases where the seller is not "bound to deliver the goods at any other particular place." If the contract does not involve carriage of the goods, the place of delivery is the seller's place of business or the more specific location where the parties knew the goods were or would be manufactured. Art.31(b), (c). *Compare* UCC § 2-308. Article 34 governs the seller's obligation to deliver documents. The time for delivery is the time specified in or implied by the contract, if any, otherwise within a reasonable time. Art. 33.

If the contract involves carriage of the goods, the seller must hand over the goods "to the first carrier for transmission to the buyer." Art. 31(a). For example, if a seller in Chicago has agreed to transport the goods to a buyer in Paris (and there is no other delivery term), the first carrier might be a train from Chicago to New York, even though the goods will then be delivered to a vessel for shipment. Article 32 states what the seller's other obligations are when goods are handed over to the first carrier. Note that the seller has a limited duty to notify the buyer, Art. 32(1), and has no duty to arrange for the carriage of the goods or to obtain insurance on their carriage unless required by the contract. Art. 32(2)-(3). Please read these sections and compare them to UCC § 2-504.

Under Article 53, the "buyer must pay the price for the goods and take delivery of them as required by the contract and this Convention." In the absence of contrary agreement, the place for payment is the seller's place of business or where the documents are handed over. Art. 57. The time for payment is the time of the seller's tender. *See* Art. 58. The buyer has a right to inspect the goods "within as short a period as is practicable under the circumstances," Art. 38(a), and is not bound to pay until he has had an opportunity to examine the goods, unless the procedures for payment in the agreement are inconsistent with the right to examine. Art. 58(3).

If the contract involves "carriage of the goods, the seller may dispatch the goods on terms whereby the goods, or documents controlling their disposition, will not be handed over to the buyer except against payment of the price." Art. 58(2). *Compare* UCC § 2-310(b) (regarding the seller's shipment under reservation). No agreement by the buyer is required. The usual practice is that, unless otherwise agreed, the buyer must pay against documents of title even though the goods are still in the middle of the ocean. While the buyer must wait until the goods arrive to inspect, the buyer can discount the documents of title or use them as collateral to obtain a loan if the delay puts the buyer under a financial strain.

2. UNIDROIT *Principles*

Because the Principles are not focused solely on the sale of goods but instead may be used in a wide variety of contract types, the provisions do not directly address delivery and inspection of the goods. Rather the Principles focus on a more generalized statement of performance obligations in Articles 6.1.1 (time for performance), 6.1.2 (performance at one time or in installments), 6.1.3 (partial performance), 6.1.4 (order of performance), 6.1.5 (early performance), and 6.1.6 (place of performance). The Principles address payment in Articles 6.1.7 (payment by check or other instrument), 6.1.8 (payment by funds transfer), and 6.1.9 and 6.1.10 (payment by currency).

CHAPTER FIVE

TERMS OF THE CONTRACT – PART III

SECTION 1.   AGREEMENT TO OVERRIDE GAP FILLER PROVISIONS

A. PRINCIPLES OF UCC ARTICLE 1

As we learned in Chapters Three and Four, Article 2 contains a large number of gap fillers. If the parties' agreement – that is, their bargain in fact as supplemented by usage of trade, course of performance, and course of dealing – covers a particular term, there is no "gap" to fill. It is only when those sources of "agreement" do not address a particular term that resort to the Code's gap fillers is necessary to flush out the parties' contract. This point, which to some extent is implicit in the distinction between the defined terms "agreement" and "contract," is also borne out by section 1-302. Read section 1-302.

In general, parties are free to vary the effect of the Article 2 rules that apply to their contract. However, as section 1-302 indicates, there are two limitations on this freedom. First, the obligations of good faith, diligence, and reasonableness cannot be disclaimed, although the parties may determine standards for the fulfillment of those obligations, as long as those standards are not manifestly unreasonable. UCC § 1-302(b). Second, some provisions of Article 2 cannot be varied by agreement. The language of section 1-302(a) suggests that all such exceptions are expressly identified in the Code. However, this point is belied by comment 1, which indicates that the exceptions "vary in explicitness" and suggests that the statute of frauds in section 2-201 is not variable even though nothing in that provision so states. No doubt there are other provisions that are also not variable. As to what they are, that is an open question. One thing we do know is that, pursuant to section 1-302(c), we cannot infer that a provision is invariable merely because it fails to state that it can be varied.[1]

This discussion raises a related question. Can parties to a contract for the sale of goods opt out of application of usage of trade, course of dealing, and course of performance as part of their agreement? Why might parties want to do so?

---

[1]   For a humorous dissertation on this issue, *see* Scott J. Burnham, *Is Article 2 Regulatory or Facilitatory? A Socratic Dialogue*, 68 OHIO ST. L.J. 57 (2007). *See also* Sarah Howard Jenkins, *Contracting Out of Article 2: Minimizing the Obligation of Performance & Liability for Breach*, 40 LOY. L.A. L. REV. 401 (2006).

Problem 5-1

A. Review the gap filler provisions studied in Chapters Three and Four and identify the rules that impose an obligation of good faith, diligence, reasonableness or care.

    1. If your last name begins with a letter from A to M, identify for each of those rules what standard a buyer would want to specify to measure the performance of that duty. Be prepared to explain why the standard you have identified is not "manifestly unreasonable."

    2. If your last name begins with a letter from N to Z, identify for each of those rules what standard a seller would want to specify to measure the performance of that duty. Be prepared to explain why the standard you have identified is not "manifestly unreasonable."

B. Identify each Article 2 provision studied so far (other than section 2-201) that you think is not variable by agreement of the parties and explain why you think the provision is not variable by agreement.

B. WARRANTY DISCLAIMERS

In Chapter Three we explored express warranties, the warranty of merchantability, the warranty of fitness for particular purpose, and the warranty of title. Often, sellers wish to escape liability for breach of these warranties. One way to do that is to limit the seller's responsibility for damages (*i.e.*, to reduce the seller's exposure for breach). Remedy limitations are addressed in subsection C below. Another way for a seller to limit its exposure is to entirely disclaim one or all of the warranties (*i.e.*, to prevent certain problems with the goods from being a breach at all). Read section 2-316, which applies to express warranties, the implied warranty of merchantability, and the implied warranty of fitness for particular purpose. Now read section 2-312(2), which applies to the warranty of title. No explicit provision governs disclaimers of the warranty of noninfringement.

Express warranties. First consider section 2-316(1). It provides that words or conduct relevant to the creation of express warranty are, to the extent possible, to be read consistently with words purporting to negate or limit express warranties. Often, however, it is not possible to read the terms consistently. For example, suppose that Seller sends Buyer a sample of the goods along with a proposed written agreement that expressly states: "Seller makes no express warranties."

Buyer signs the written agreement after inspecting the sample. If the sample truly is part of the basis of the bargain – and it might not be given the language in the written agreement – then it would be virtually impossible to harmonize the conduct relevant to the creation of the warranty with the words purporting to negate it. In such a case, section 2-316(1) provides that the attempted disclaimer fails. The reason for this is expressed in comment 1 to section 2-313: " 'Express' warranties rest on 'dickered' aspects of the individual bargain, and go so clearly to the essence of that bargain that words of disclaimer in a form are repugnant to the basic dickered terms."

Because of this, it is almost a contradiction in terms for the seller to disclaim an express warranty. The seller can avoid an express warranty by not making it, but it is virtually impossible to disclaim one that has been made. Virtually impossible, but not completely impossible. The seller may be able to use the parol evidence rule to exclude evidence of an alleged express warranty. The parol evidence rule is discussed below in Section 2 of this Chapter.

Implied warranty of merchantability and implied warranty of fitness for particular purpose. One of the rationales underlying the implied warranty of merchantability as a gap filler is to give effect to the likely and reasonable expectations of the parties. Buyers of new goods from a merchant generally expect that the goods are fit for their ordinary purpose, that is, that the goods work. Admittedly, expectations might be different if the law were different. However, even if the legal rule were *caveat emptor*, it is likely that most buyers would expect merchant sellers to repair or replace defective goods or refund the price paid. Given that the implied warranty of fitness for particular purpose arises only when the buyer relies on the seller's skills or judgment, it is likely that giving efficacy to the parties' reasonable expectations is one of the rationales underlying this implied warranty too.

Nevertheless, because these warranties are merely gap fillers, not mandatory contract terms, it is possible for the parties by their agreement to exclude or disclaim them. That then raises the question of what the law should require for a disclaimer to be effective. Must the effort to disclaim be something that is likely to change the buyer's expectations? If a disclaimer is buried in fine print and expressed in dense legalese will it nevertheless be effective? Should it be? Read section 2-316(2) and (3). *See also* UCC § 1-201(b)(10) (defining "conspicuous"). Now try the following problems.

Problem 5-2

A. Identify all the methods for disclaiming the implied warranty of merchantability.

B. Silicon Solutions, Inc. manufactures and sells HDTVs. Last month, some of its televisions were damaged when the warehouse in which they had been stored was flooded during a storm. Silicon Solutions unpacked and examined the televisions and discarded those that were obviously damaged. However, it was unable to rule out the possibility that the remainder might have less visible damage. Silicon Solutions repackaged the remaining televisions and then offered to sell them to Retailer. In which, if any, of the following scenarios will the implied warranty of merchantability be disclaimed?

   1. The purchase agreement that both Retailer and Silicon Solutions signed contained the following language just above the signature lines in bold type: "There are no warranties, express or implied, included as a part of this transaction."

   2. The purchase agreement that both Retailer and Silicon Solutions signed contained the following language just above the signature lines in the same font as the remainder of the document: "The goods are sold as is."

C. Construct a scenario in which the implied warranty of merchantability would be disclaimed under section 2-316(3)(b).

Problem 5-3

Identify all the methods for disclaiming the implied warranty of fitness for particular purpose.

Compliance with the rules of section 2-316 is always necessary – but not always sufficient – to disclaim the implied warranties of merchantability and fitness for particular purpose. Even if a disclaimer complies with section 2-316, the disclaimer may still be unconscionable under section 2-302, and therefore unenforceable.[2] In addition, sometimes law outside Article 2 may invalidate an attempted disclaimer.[3]

Problem 5-4

Butler, an experienced commercial fisherman, purchased from Dealer a new diesel engine for Butler's fishing boat. In the discussions prior to the sale, Dealer and Butler discussed the power that Butler needed for the fishing boat. Based on Dealer's recommendation, Butler purchased the Powertrane 1000, which Dealer then installed on Butler's boat. Over the next four months, a number of mechanical problems arose, including the emission of excessive quantities of heavy black smoke. Dealer was unable to correct the problems and the engine was removed from the boat. Butler thinks that the engine did not function properly because it lacked the power to propel the fishing boat. Butler's expert will testify that the engine was unmerchantable due to the recurring mechanical problems.

When Butler took delivery of the engine, Butler signed Dealer's standard form purchase order. The front of the purchase order contained a number of terms and conditions. In the center of the front, this statement appeared:

> BOTH THIS ORDER AND ITS ACCEPTANCE ARE SUBJECT TO TERMS AND CONDITIONS STATED IN THIS ORDER.

On the reverse side of the order at the top of the page, the following words appeared: TERMS AND CONDITIONS. Under that caption were eleven numbered paragraphs, one of which contained a disclaimer in the following form:

> THE SELLER HEREBY DISCLAIMS AND EXCLUDES ALL IMPLIED WARRANTIES, INCLUDING THE IMPLIED WARRANTY OF MERCHANTABILITY.

Butler did not read and was not asked to read anything on the back of the purchase order.

---

[2] *See Hutton v. Deere & Co.*, 210 F.3d 389 (10th Cir. 2000) (concluding on facts that disclaimer of implied warranties was not unconscionable).

[3] *See* Donald F. Clifford, Jr., *Non-UCC Statutory Provisions Affecting Warranty Disclaimers and Remedies in Sales of Goods*, 71 N.C. L. REV. 1011 (1993).

A. Butler sued Dealer for damages resulting from breach of an implied warranty of merchantability and breach of the implied warranty of fitness for particular purpose. Dealer defended on the ground that it did not make or had successfully disclaimed both warranties under section 2-316(2). What result?

B. How, if at all, would the analysis change if Butler were not a commercial fisherman but instead purchased the engine for use on Butler's pleasure boat?

C. How, if at all, would the analysis change if Dealer were not a merchant?

Warranty of title. The warranty of title is not designated as an "implied" warranty, and thus cannot be disclaimed pursuant to the rules of § 2-316(3). *See* UCC § 2-312 cmt. 6. However, it is possible to disclaim the warranty of title. Read section 2-312(2).

Problem 5-5

A. Under what circumstances, if any, would a buyer be likely to agree to a disclaimer of the warranty of title?

B. Section 2-312 indicates that the warranty of title can be disclaimed by language or circumstances. Construct a scenario in which the parties say nothing about the warranty of title but, because of the specific circumstances, the warranty would nevertheless be disclaimed.

CISG and UNIDROIT Principles. The CISG does not have a comparable section on disclaiming warranties. Rather, Article 35(3) limits the seller's liability under that Article if the buyer "knew or could not have been unaware" of the nonconformity at the time of contract formation. The UNIDROIT Principles do not have any specific provisions on disclaimers of warranty.

C. REMEDY LIMITATIONS

Most merchant sellers are willing to stand behind the quality of the goods they sell. For many of them, market pressures and concern for business reputation almost require that they agree either to replace defective goods or refund the purchase price. Merchants who refuse to do so might benefit in the short run, but over time are apt to find themselves with few customers. Thus, few merchant sellers of new goods try to disclaim the warranty of merchantability.

What merchants as a rule do not want, however, is unlimited damages for any defective goods they sell. A seller of stereo components may be quite willing to replace a receiver that short circuits the day after the sale, but will not want to pay for the house that burned to the ground because of that defect. A seller of lawnmowers might be willing to replace a mower if the blades fly off during first use, but would rather not pay damages for the buyer's arm that got severed in the process. In short, most sellers are willing to accept some responsibility for their wares, but not unlimited responsibility. They do not want to be on the hook for damages that exceed – by several orders of magnitude – the price of or profit margin on the goods they sell.

Article 2 allows the parties to limit or alter the remedies that would normally be applicable for breach. In other words, the normal rules on remedy are a bit like gap-filler rules, which the parties are free to alter by agreement. However, just as there are hurdles a seller must jump over to disclaim the implied warranty of merchantability, the implied warranty of fitness, or the warranty of title, there are restrictions on the parties' ability to limit remedies. Before we turn our attention to these limitations, it is important to have a basic understanding of the remedies that Article 2 provides. We will explore remedies more in depth in Chapters Seven (buyer's remedies) and Nine (seller's remedies), so the following explanation is merely a synopsis of the basic remedy rules and is intended to provide a context for the rules on how parties may limit their remedies.

Traditional remedies. The buyer's and seller's remedies in Article 2 are consistent with the approach typically available for breach of contract in that they attempt to protect the aggrieved party's expectation interest.[4] Keep in mind that there are two things always in play when a seller or buyer breaches the sales contract: (1) what happens to the goods; and (2) how should the aggrieved party's damages be calculated.

Seller's breach and buyer's remedies. The buyer's remedies depend on the nature of the seller's breach and who has the goods. If the seller breaches by repudiating its obligations or by simply failing to tender the goods, the buyer has

---

[4]   We will consider remedies under the CISG and the UNIDROIT Principles in Chapter Seven on buyer's remedies and in Chapter Nine on seller's remedies.

the right to cancel the deal, recover the price that has been paid, and recover damages. Those damages will be based on either the difference between the contract price and the market price of the goods or, if the buyer purchases substitute goods from another source, the difference between the contract price and the price of the substitute goods. In addition, the buyer is entitled to consequential and incidental damages. *See* UCC §§ 2-711, 2-712, 2-713, 2-715. Alternatively, in some limited circumstances the buyer has the right to ask a court to require the seller to tender the goods. If the buyer is successful in that effort, the buyer will be liable for the price of the goods. *See* UCC §§ 2-502, 2-716, 2-709.

If the seller makes a nonconforming tender – such as if the goods themselves are nonconforming or tender is untimely – the buyer must decide whether to accept or reject the goods. If the buyer properly rejects the goods, the buyer may cancel the deal, recover the price that has been paid, and recover damages in the same manner as if the seller had repudiated or otherwise failed to make a tender of the goods. *See* UCC §§ 2-711, 2-601, 2-612. If the buyer accepts the goods, the buyer will be obligated to pay the contract price. However, the buyer will be entitled to damages arising from the nonconformity. Most commonly, these damages are the difference between the value of the goods accepted and the value of the conforming goods, plus consequential and incidental damages. *See* UCC §§ 2-607, 2-709, 2-714, 2-715.

In some limited circumstances, a buyer who has accepted nonconforming goods may revoke its acceptance. Such a revocation of acceptance is generally treated like a rejection of the goods. As a result, the buyer may cancel the deal, recover the price that has been paid, and recover damages based upon the difference between the contract price and the price of replacement goods or the market price of the goods, plus consequential and incidental damages. *See* UCC §§ 2-608, 2-711, 2-712, 2-713, 2-715.

Buyer's breach and seller's remedies. The seller's remedies for the buyer's breach also depend on who has the goods. If the buyer repudiates its obligations under the contract before the seller has delivered the goods, the seller may stop or withhold delivery of the goods, cancel the deal, and recover damages. Those damages will be measured in one of three ways: (i) the difference between the resale price and the contract price; (ii) the difference between the market price and the contract price; or (iii) the lost profit on the transaction. *See* UCC § 2-702(1), 2-703, 2-705, 2-706, 2-708. The seller is also entitled to incidental damages. UCC § 2-710. If the buyer has prepaid some or all of the price, the buyer has the right to restitution of that amount, subject to an offset of the seller's damages. UCC § 2-718(2).

In some cases, the buyer may make an effective rejection of the goods even though the seller's tender conformed to the contract requirements. In other words, the buyer's rejection is wrongful but effective, with the result that the seller gets the goods back. In such a case, the seller will have the same three possible damage remedies identified above.

If the buyer has accepted the goods, the buyer is obligated for the contract price of the goods plus any incidental damages the seller has suffered. UCC §§ 2-709, 2-710. In other words, a buyer who breaches by failing to pay is obligated for the price. However, in some limited circumstances, as an alternative to seeking a judgment for the price, the seller may be able to reclaim the goods from the buyer. UCC §§ 2-507, 2-712(2).

Rules on limiting remedies. We now examine the rules on how parties may limit the remedies that would otherwise be available. Read sections 2-718(1) and 2-719. These provisions provide two different methods for a party to limit liability for breach: (i) to liquidate damages; and (ii) to limit the type of remedies available. Before proceeding to analyze each of these rules, bear in mind that both types of limitations come into play only if a party is in breach. A warranty disclaimer, on the other hand, changes the seller's duty as to the goods so that a defect in quality or title might not become a breach at all. Thus, do not confuse the rules discussed above on disclaimer of warranty with the rules discussed below on limiting remedies.

1. Liquidated Damages

A liquidated damages clause is a term in the parties' agreement that mandates that damages for breach be computed in a manner different from the normal measures of damages that would otherwise apply. As a term of the parties' agreement, a liquidated damages clause is subject to the restrictions on enforceability that apply to all aspects of the agreement. Thus, for example, it must not be unconscionable. In addition, section 2-718(1) lists several other factors that affect the validity of a liquidated damages clause. Why are these factors important? What is the purpose of subjecting these terms to judicial scrutiny? Read section 1-305. Does that help provide an answer to these questions?

Problem 5-6

Butterfield Co., a baker, planned to expand its capacity by 30%. Accordingly, on March 1, it ordered a custom-made oven from Sure Fire, a manufacturer, to be delivered not later than September 1. Butterfield informed Sure Fire of its planned expansion and stated that "time was of the essence." Butterfield had developed a new bread for hotels and restaurants and wanted to be in production for the fall convention season. Sure Fire and Butterfield negotiated over how to deal with the risk of delay in delivery.

After discussing Butterfield's current profit margin and the probabilities that an expansion would be profitable, Sure Fire agreed, in a clause labeled "Liquidated Damages," to pay Butterfield $1,000 for every day of a non-excusable delay in delivery. Sure Fire did not deliver the oven until October 1. Butterfield claimed liquidated damages in the amount of $30,000. Sure Fire, however, can establish that the convention business during September was very slow and that, at best, Butterfield would have made only $2,500 in net profits if the oven had been delivered on time. Is the agreed damage clause enforceable under section 2-718?

2. *Limited Remedies*

In contrast to liquidated damage clauses, which tend to specify a dollar amount of damages or a formula for computing them, limitations on remedy tend to eliminate an entire category of damages or other type of remedy that would otherwise be available. For example, the agreement may specify that neither party will be entitled to consequential damages or that the buyer's only remedy for nonconforming goods will be repair or replacement of the goods. Because such a clause is a term of the parties' agreement, it is subject to all the normal tests of enforceability. In addition, Article 2 contains further qualifications on the enforceability of remedy limitations. Read section 2-719. Subsection (1) allows parties to agree to add to or reduce the types of remedies normally available. It also allows them to change the way in which damages are to be computed. Such contractual rules are presumed to be optional unless the agreement expressly makes them exclusive. UCC § 2-719(1)(b).

Subsections (2) and (3) then contain two important limitations on the freedom granted in subsection (1). Subsection (2) provides that if a limited remedy "fails of its essential purpose," then the normal statutory remedies become available. When does a limited remedy fail of its essential purpose? The classic case is when a seller limits remedy for breach to repair or replacement of defective parts and the entire good is destroyed because of a single defective part. At that point, replacing the one defective part would not be of much use to the buyer.

Problem 5-7

Construct another scenario in which a limited remedy fails of its essential purpose.

Subsection (3) allows the parties to limit or exclude consequential damages. However, a limitation on consequential damages is prima facie unconscionable with respect to personal injury resulting from defective consumer goods. Of course, the "prima facie" language merely creates a presumption of unconscionability, one that the seller can rebut.[5]

Problem 5-8

Construct a scenario in which an exclusion of consequential damages, including damages for personal injury, from defective consumer goods would not be unconscionable.

It is not uncommon for sellers to incorporate into their standard agreements two different remedy limitations: one that limits remedy to repair or replacement of defective goods and another that disclaims responsibility for consequential damages (other than damages for personal injury). In such situations, what happens if the limitation of remedy to repair or replacement fails of its essential purpose? Does the exclusion of consequential damages also fail? Consider the following case.

---

[5]   Remember from our study of unconscionability in Chapter Two that a court can refuse to enforce any particular term based upon that principle, even if it does not refuse to enforce the entire agreement. Section 2-719(3) merely provides a presumption of unconscionability for a particular term.

RAZOR V. HYUNDAI MOTOR AMERICA
854 N.E.2d 607 (Ill. 2006), *cert. denied*, 549 U.S. 1181 (2007)

Justice Freeman delivered the judgment of the court, with opinion:

[Plaintiff purchased a new Hyundai Sonata . In connection with the purchase, the manufacturer provided a written promise to "[r]epair or replace[] any component originally manufactured or installed by Hyundai Motor Company or Hyundai Motor America (HMA) that is found to be defective in material or workmanship under normal use and maintenance, except any item specifically referred to in the section 'What is Not Covered.' " However, the manufacturer also disclaimed responsibility for incidental and consequential damages. The car malfunctioned and, despite numerous repair efforts, could not be fixed. Plaintiff sued and the jury awarded her $5,000 for the diminished value of the car and $3,500 for aggravation, inconvenience, and lost use. – Eds.]

ANALYSIS
. . .

I. Enforceability of Hyundai's Disclaimer of Incidental/Consequential Damages

The main issue before this court is the enforceability of Hyundai's disclaimer of incidental and consequential damages. Hyundai argues that the disclaimer is independent of the limited remedy, and the disclaimer may stand even if its limited remedy failed of its essential purpose. Hyundai contends that the disclaimer may be overridden only if it is itself unconscionable, a standard which Hyundai argues has not been met in the instant case. Plaintiff responds that the disclaimer should fall with the limited warranty, and contends that even if this court finds them to be severable, the disclaimer in this case was unconscionable.

A. *"Independent" vs. "Dependent" Approach to*
Provisions Limiting Remedy and Excluding Consequential Damages

. . . . [T]o determine the enforceability of a consequential damages disclaimer in a limited warranty, we look to state law. In Illinois, the sale of goods is governed by article 2 of the Uniform Commercial Code (UCC). Central to this case is section 2-719 of the UCC. . . .

In this case, Hyundai's limited warranty contained both a limitation of remedy and an exclusion of consequential damages. The warranty expressly limited the buyer's remedies to repair and replacement of nonconforming parts, as permitted under section 2-719(1)(a). However, the warranty additionally provided that incidental or consequential damages were "not covered," as permitted under section 2-719(3).

Plaintiff claimed-and the jury found-that the Hyundai limited remedy had failed of its essential purpose because of the persistence of the no-start problem with plaintiff's car. Hyundai does not question this factual determination in this appeal. Thus, according to section 2-719(2) of the UCC, plaintiff was entitled to remedy "as provided in this Act.". . . This does not end the inquiry insofar as consequential damages are concerned, however. Subsection (3) of section 2-719 is part of "this Act" – *i.e.*, the UCC-and subsection (3) permits a seller to limit or exclude consequential damages unless to do so would be unconscionable. It still must be determined, therefore, whether a limited remedy failing of its essential purpose defeats a disclaimer of consequential damages.

There are two main schools of thought on the issue. Some courts and commentators conclude that a limited remedy failing of its essential purpose operates to destroy any limitation or exclusion of consequential damages in the same contract. This approach is known as the "dependent" approach, because the enforceability of the consequential damages exclusion depends on the survival of the limitation of remedy.

Our appellate court issued one of the seminal cases for the dependent approach, *Adams v. J.I. Case Co.*, 261 N.E.2d 1 (Ill. Ct. App. 1970). There, the plaintiff purchased a tractor, pursuant to a purchase agreement which limited his remedy to repair and replacement and also disclaimed consequential damages. The tractor had severe mechanical problems and was in a repair shop for over a year. Plaintiff filed suit, seeking consequential damages for the business he claimed to have lost because defendants were "wilfully dilatory or careless and negligent in making good their warranty." The court concluded:

> The limitations of remedy and of liability are not separable from the obligations of the warranty. Repudiation of the obligations of the warranty destroys its benefits. The complaint alleges facts that would constitute a repudiation by the defendants of their obligations under the warranty, that repudiation consisting of their wilful failure or their careless and negligent compliance. It should be obvious that they cannot at once repudiate their obligation under their warranty and assert its provisions beneficial to them.

Adams, 261 N.E.2d 1.

In defense of the dependent approach, the United States District Court for the Northern District of Illinois has reasoned:

> [P]laintiff also was entitled to assume that defendants would not be unreasonable or wilfully dilatory in making good their warranty in the event

of defects in the machinery and equipment. It is the specific breach of the warranty to repair that plaintiff alleges caused the bulk of its damages. This Court would be in an untenable position if it allowed the defendant to shelter itself behind one segment of the warranty when it has allegedly repudiated and ignored its very limited obligations under another segment of the same warranty, which alleged repudiation has caused the very need for relief which the defendant is attempting to avoid.

Jones & McKnight Corp. v. Birdsboro Corp., 320 F. Supp. 39, 43–44 (N.D. Ill. 1970) (applying Illinois law). . . .

Plaintiff suggests that the dependent approach is followed by a majority of jurisdictions to consider the issue. While this may have been true 15 to 20 years ago[6] (see D. Goetz, *Special Project: Article Two Warranties in Commercial Transactions: An Update,* 72 CORNELL L. REV. 1159, 1307 (1987) ("A majority of cases have answered correctly that the failure of an exclusive remedy voids the consequential damages exclusion clause")), it is no longer the case. Rather, the majority of jurisdictions now follow the other of the two main approaches, the "independent" approach. 1 E. FARNSWORTH, FARNSWORTH ON CONTRACTS § 4.28(a), at 605–06 (3d ed. 2004) ("some courts have gone so far as to hold that if UCC 2-719(2) applies, related limitations on remedies should all fall like a house of cards, so that a provision barring recovery of consequential damages would also be invalidated. However, most courts have rejected this view"). This school of thought holds that a limitation of consequential damages must be judged on its own merits and enforced unless unconscionable, regardless of whether the contract also contains a limitation of remedy which has failed of its essential purpose.

A representative case adopting the independent approach is *Chatlos Systems v. National Cash Register Corp.,* 635 F.2d 1081 (3d Cir. 1980) (applying New Jersey law). There, the court rejected the dependent approach, holding:

[T]he better reasoned approach is to treat the consequential damage disclaimer as an independent provision, valid unless unconscionable. This poses no logical difficulties. A contract may well contain no limitation on breach of warranty damages but specifically exclude consequential damages. Conversely, it is quite conceivable that some limitation might be

---

[6]   We note that all of the law review articles and all but one of the non-Illinois court decisions plaintiff cites were decided in 1990 or before. The sole post-1990 foreign authority plaintiff cites, *Bishop Logging Co. v. John Deere Industrial Equipment Co.,* 455 S.E.2d 183 (S.C. 1995), did not follow the dependent approach, but rather the "case-by-case" approach. *Bishop Logging,* 455 S.E.2d at 191-93.

placed on a breach of warranty award, but consequential damages would expressly be permitted.

The limited remedy of repair and a consequential damages exclusion are two discrete ways of attempting to limit recovery for breach of warranty. The [UCC], moreover, tests each by a different standard. The former survives unless it fails of its essential purpose, while the latter is valid unless it is unconscionable. We therefore see no reason to hold, as a general proposition, that the failure of the limited remedy provided in the contract, without more, invalidates a wholly distinct term in the agreement excluding consequential damages. The two are not mutually exclusive.
Chatlos Systems, 635 F.2d at 1086. . . .

A third approach, "applied relatively infrequently," is the "case by case" approach. D. Hagen, Note, *Sections 2-719(2) & 2-719(3) of the Uniform Commercial Code: The Limited Warranty Package & Consequential Damages,* 31 VAL. U. L. REV. 111, 131 (1996). Under this approach, "[a]n analysis to determine whether consequential damages are warranted must carefully examine the individual factual situation including the type of goods involved, the parties and the precise nature and purpose of the contract." *AES Technology Systems, Inc. v. Coherent Radiation,* 583 F.2d 933, 941 (7th Cir. 1978).

Neither of the parties to this appeal argues in favor of the case-by-case approach, which has been criticized as "not supported by the [UCC] or its official comments." 31 VAL. U.L. REV. at 132. The authorities espousing it have sometimes confused it with the "independent" approach (see, *e.g., Smith v. Navistar International Transportation Corp.,* 957 F.2d 1439, 1443–44 (7th Cir. 1992)) (erroneously stating that *Chatlos Systems* had adopted the case-by-case approach). Moreover, although one of the factors cited in favor of the case-by-case approach is that it "allows some measure of certainty" (*Smith,* 957 F.2d at 1444), it has been observed that it in fact "provides *less* predictability than the dependent or independent approaches." (Emphasis added.) 31 VAL. U.L. REV. at 131.

Additionally, notwithstanding that the case-by-case approach might appear to tread a middle ground between the dependent approach (which is generally more favorable for buyers) and the independent approach (which is generally more favorable for sellers), this is not necessarily so. In *AES Technology,* where the case-by-case approach originated, the contract at issue contained no disclaimer or limitation of consequential damages, only a limitation of remedy. The court affirmed the trial court's conclusion that the limited remedy had failed of its essential purpose. *AES Technology,* 583 F.2d at 940. However, the court inferred a consequential damage disclaimer from the limitation of remedy (*AES Technology,*

583 F.2d at 941 n. 9) and proceeded to enforce that inferred disclaimer against the buyer even though the limited remedy had failed of its essential purpose, because "the express provisions of the contract and the factual background" indicated that the parties intended for the buyer to "bear the risk of the project"(*AES Technology,* 583 F.2d at 941). The court inferred a consequential damages disclaimer where none existed, struck the language from which the disclaimer was inferred, then enforced the disclaimer against the buyer anyway, based on the court's understanding of "the factual background." This result could not have been reached under either the dependent or independent approach, and we find the analysis difficult to reconcile with the UCC itself.

We find the case-by-case approach injects uncertainty into the UCC, an area of the law in which uniformity and certainty are highly valued. [Citing former UCC § 1-102(2)(c)] . . . It leads to results which are difficult to reconcile with the provisions of the UCC, and has been criticized as having no basis in the UCC or its comments. 31 VAL. U.L. REV. at 132. We decline to adopt it.

Rather, we agree with the reasoning in *Chatlos Systems,* and adopt the independent approach. The independent approach is more in line with the UCC and with contract law in general. Nothing in the text or the official comments to section 2-719 indicates that where a contract contains both a limitation of remedy and an exclusion of consequential damages, the latter shares the fate of the former. To the contrary, as noted in *Chatlos Systems,* the different standards for evaluating the two provisions-"failure of essential purpose" versus "unconscionability"-strongly suggest their independence. *See also* 1 WHITE AND SUMMERS' UNIFORM COMMERCIAL CODE § 12-10(c), at 668 (4th ed. 1995) (endorsing the independent approach as most in accord with considerations of freedom of contract).

When a contract contains a limitation of remedy but that remedy fails of its essential purpose, it is as if that limitation of remedy does not exist for purposes of the damages to which a plaintiff is entitled for breach of warranty. . . . When a contract contains a consequential damages exclusion but no limitation of remedy, it is incontrovertible that the exclusion is to be enforced unless unconscionable. . . . Why, then, would a limitation of remedy failing of its essential purpose destroy a consequential damages exclusion in the same contract? We see no valid reason to so hold.

Indeed, the dependent approach operates to nullify all consequential damage exclusions in contracts which also contain limitations of remedy. For if the limited remedy fails of its essential purpose, the consequential damages exclusion would also automatically fall − regardless of whether it is unconscionable − and if the limitation of remedy does not fail of its essential purpose, the buyer would not be entitled to consequential damages in any event; he would be entitled only to the specified limited remedy.

The two provisions – limitation of remedy and exclusion of consequential damages – can be visualized as two concentric layers of protection for a seller. What a seller would most prefer, if something goes wrong with a product, is simply to repair or replace it, nothing more. This "repair or replacement" remedy is an outer wall, a first defense. If that wall is breached, because the limited remedy has failed of its essential purpose, the seller still would prefer at least not to be liable for potentially unlimited consequential damages, and so he builds a second inner rampart as a fallback position. That inner wall is higher, and more difficult to scale – it falls only if unconscionable.

The independent approach has not been immune to criticism, of course. The Eighth Circuit has rejected the independent approach under Minnesota law, based on the concern that "a buyer when entering into a contract does not anticipate that the sole remedy available will be rendered a nullity, thus causing additional damages." *Soo Line R.R. Co. v. Fruehauf Corp.,* 547 F.2d 1365, 1373 (8th Cir. 1977) (applying Minnesota law). Additionally, one commentator has chastised the independent approach for "rel[ying] on imprecise assumptions about the parties' intent and an unpersuasive interpretation of section 2-719." K. Murtagh, Note, *UCC Section 2-719: Limited Remedies and Consequential Damage Exclusions,* 74 CORNELL L. REV. 359, 362 (1989) (concluding that independent approach is "inherently weak"). This article suggests that by engaging in "literal construction of the parties' contract," the independent approach "encourages overly formalistic drafting," which "unfairly favors the party who can afford sophisticated bargaining techniques to ensure the use of his contract terms." 74 CORNELL L. REV. at 363. The article also contends that it is erroneous to conclude that the parties intend to shift the risk of consequential loss to the buyer, because "[t]he language structure itself does not indicate that the parties even considered the possibility of the ineffective limited remedy." 74 CORNELL L. REV. at 364. *Adams* and *Jones & McKnight,* two of the earliest cases adopting the dependent approach, implicitly concluded that the independent approach was simply unfair to the buyer. See *Adams,* 261 N.E.2d 1; *Jones & McKnight,* 320 F. Supp. at 43-44.

We recognize these objections to the independent approach, but do not find them compelling. The reasoning in *Adams* and *Jones & McKnight,* for example, is based on the seller's failure to perform being willful. This incorporates considerations of bad faith on the part of the seller. As we discuss below, the seller's bad faith is a possible basis for finding enforcement of a limitation of consequential damages to be unconscionable. However, the dependent approach strips away limitations of consequential damages whenever a limited remedy fails of its essential purpose, without regard to the good or bad faith of the seller, which we believe goes too far.

The objections to the independent approach in *Soo Line* and the law review article noted above are similarly unpersuasive. Both argue that the independent approach is unfair because the buyer may not intend to renounce consequential damages when the limited remedy has failed of its essential purpose. *Soo Line,* 547 F.2d at 1373; 74 CORNELL L. REV. at 364. But this seems to ignore the plain language of the contract in a fundamental way – for if the buyer does not intend to renounce consequential damages when the limited remedy has failed, in what context *could* the disclaimer of consequential damages operate? As noted above, we believe this is a fundamental defect in the dependent approach, that it renders the disclaimer of consequential damages an utter nullity. If a limited remedy has *not* failed of its essential purpose, that is of course the buyer's only remedy, by definition – this is what it means to have a limited remedy. So in this circumstance a disclaimer of limited damages would be of no effect because it would be redundant. If, as the above critics argue, the disclaimer of limited damages ought not to be enforced when the limited remedy *has* failed of its essential purpose, the language would never have any effect. Moreover, to the extent that the independent approach encourages parties to pay attention in the drafting process (see 74 Cornell L.Rev. at 363), we see this as a point in favor of the independent approach, rather than the contrary. . . .

Moreover, we disagree with the reasoning, although not necessarily the result, in *Adams.* There, in refusing to enforce the consequential damages limitation, our appellate court focused on the allegedly tortious nature of defendants' conduct which caused the limited remedy to fail of its essential purpose. The court concluded that defendants were entitled to none of the protections included in the contract because they had "repudiat[ed] . . . their obligations under the warranty." This implies that the sellers' alleged bad faith in repudiating their obligations under the warranty played a part in the analysis – but the dependent approach does not take the seller's good or bad faith into account. Under the dependent approach, the seller is stripped of the protection of a consequential damages disclaimer once a limited remedy has failed of its essential purpose, *regardless* of the seller's good or bad faith.

A seller's deliberate or negligent failure to supply a limited remedy can be taken into consideration in determining whether enforcement of a consequential damages waiver is unconscionable. The unconscionability determination is not restricted to the facts and circumstances in existence at the time the contract was entered into.

... Indeed, section 2-719(3) itself expressly provides that matters which become known only subsequent to the drafting of the contract – *i.e.,* the type of injuries suffered as a result of breach – are relevant to the unconscionability calculus. ... As many of the authorities favoring the dependent approach have noted, there is rarely any basis for concluding that when the parties entered into their contract, the buyer intended to assume the risk of the seller's willful or negligent default on his only obligation for breach of warranty. It may well be that in a case such as *Adams,* where the defendant is alleged to have acted in bad faith, the correct result would be to declare a consequential damages exclusion unenforceable. ... Accordingly, we believe that a plaintiff must be allowed to point to a defendant's conduct, or any other circumstance which he believes would make enforcement of a consequential damages exclusion unconscionable. But the plain language of the UCC indicates that this step, of evaluating whether the exclusion is unconscionable, must be taken before a contractual consequential damages exclusion may be done away with. ...

We conclude that the independent approach is the better-reasoned and more in accordance with the plain language of the UCC. This conclusion is buttressed by the fact that a majority of jurisdictions to consider the issue have adopted the independent approach. Illinois generally follows the majority interpretation of UCC provisions, in order to serve the underlying UCC policy of " 'mak[ing] uniform the law among the various jurisdictions.' " *Connick v. Suzuki Motor Co.,* 675 N.E.2d 584 (Ill. 1996), quoting [§ 1-102(2)(c)]. Contractual limitations or exclusions of consequential damages will be upheld unless to do so would be unconscionable, regardless of whether the contract also contains a limited remedy which fails of its essential purpose.

B. *Unconscionability*

Accordingly, the mere fact that the jury found the limited remedy to have failed of its essential purpose does not destroy the provision in the warranty excluding consequential damages. However, this does not mean that the exclusion of consequential damages will necessarily be upheld. Rather, that provision must be judged on its own merits to determine whether its enforcement would be unconscionable. ...

A determination of whether a contractual clause is unconscionable is a matter of law, to be decided by the court. ... Unconscionability can be either "procedural" or "substantive" or a combination of both. ... Procedural unconscionability refers to a situation where a term is so difficult to find, read, or understand that the plaintiff cannot fairly be said to have been aware he was agreeing to it, and also takes into account a lack of bargaining power. . . . Substantive unconscionability refers to those terms which are inordinately one-sided in one party's favor.

Hyundai argues that plaintiff introduced no evidence to support the trial court's determination that the consequential damages exclusion was unconscionable. We disagree. The record reveals a number of facts which tend to support a finding of unconscionability. The warranty was entirely preprinted. Plaintiff – a consumer – had no hand in its drafting, and no bargaining power at all with respect to its terms. Moreover, the clause in question is intended to limit the drafter's liability. Each of these facts leads this court to disfavor the clause. . . . However, we need not – and we do not – hold that these general circumstances alone or in combination render the clause unconscionable.

An additional fact particular to this case tips the balance in plaintiff's favor. That is the lack of evidence that the warranty, which contained the disclaimer of consequential damages, had been made available to the plaintiff at or before the time she signed the sale contract. The warranty and its consequential damages exclusion were contained in the owner's manual, which was placed in the glove compartment of the car, where it was unavailable to the consumer until after she took delivery. No portion of the sale contract contained in the record before us even mentions the warranty. Moreover, plaintiff testified without contradiction that she never saw any part of the written warranty, much less the disclaimer of consequential damages, until she looked in her owner's manual after she had signed the contract and driven the car off the lot. Thus, *on this record,* we must conclude that the warranty information, including the disclaimer of consequential damages, was not made available to the plaintiff at or before the time she signed the purchase contract.

In its petition for rehearing, Hyundai argues that the disclaimer is not procedurally unconscionable because it was written in capital letters in "plain, simple, understandable language, not legalese," that was "easy to see and easy to read." These aspects of the disclaimer are irrelevant, however, in the case of a limitation of liability withheld from the buyer until after the purchase contract has been signed. It simply does not matter how large the type was or how clearly the disclaimer was expressed if the consumer did not have the opportunity to *see* the language before entering into the contract to purchase the car. . . . As previously noted, procedural unconscionability refers to a situation where a term is so difficult to find, read, or understand that the plaintiff cannot fairly be said to have been aware he was agreeing to it. Surely, whatever other context there might be in which a contractual provision would be found to be procedurally unconscionable, that label must apply to a situation such as the case at bar where plaintiff has testified that she never saw the clause; nor is there any basis for concluding that plaintiff *could* have seen the clause, before entering into the sale contract. "[A] limitation of liability given to the buyer after he makes the contract is ineffective." *Frank's Maintenance,* 408 N.E.2d 403. . . .

II. Warranty Damages

. . . . Because the limited remedy failed of its essential purpose, plaintiff was entitled to pursue the other remedies afforded by the UCC. . . . Under the UCC, "The measure of damages for breach of warranty is the difference at the time and place of acceptance between the value of the goods accepted and the value they would have had if they had been as warranted, unless special circumstances show proximate damages of a different amount." [UCC § 2-714(2)] . . . . [The court remanded for a new trial on the damages question, as the trial court erred in excluding plaintiff's testimony regarding the car's value.–ed.]

CONCLUSION

For the reasons given above, the judgment of the appellate court is affirmed in part and reversed in part, and the judgment of the circuit court is also affirmed in part and reversed in part. We remand for a new trial on the issue of warranty damages. . . .

Justice McMORROW, dissenting from denial of rehearing

I initially joined the majority opinion in this case. I remain in agreement with the majority in its adoption of the independent approach in analyzing limitations of remedy and disclaimers of consequential damages. However, in light of arguments regarding unconscionability that were raised in Hyundai's petition for rehearing, as well as subsequent changes made by the court to its opinion, I believe that rehearing should be allowed. . . . [Discussion of the Magnuson Moss Act and regulations are omitted.]

I note, in addition, that there are difficulties with the majority's unconscionability holding even when considered solely as a matter of state contract law, without reference to the federal regulations. In finding Hyundai's consequential damages disclaimer unconscionable, the majority concludes that this exclusion is void and unenforceable as a matter of public policy. The clear implication of such a holding is that Hyundai did something wrong, such as hiding the exclusion "in a maze of fine print." *Frank's Maintenance & Engineering, Inc.*

v. C.A. Roberts Co., 408 N.E.2d 403 (Ill. Ct. App. 1980). However, in the case at bar Hyundai committed no such infraction. Instead, Hyundai's transgression was that it failed to make the warranty "available to the plaintiff at or before the time she signed the sale contract." 854 N.E.2d at 623. This raises the question of how Hyundai could have avoided this transgression and ensured that the warranty was conveyed to plaintiff. The majority insists that the inclusion of the warranty in the purchase contract is not the only way in which "plaintiff could . . . have received the warranty." There are other possibilities, the majority asserts, but these possibilities are not identified. 854 N.E.2d at 623–24.

If the warranty must be made available to the consumer at or before the time the purchase contract is signed, and if, as the majority concludes, the warrantor may not rely on the seller to meet this responsibility, then there is, in my view, only one possible way in which the warrantor could satisfy this obligation. The warrantor must have a representative physically present on the seller's premises to make sure that the warranty is conveyed to the consumer, thereby ensuring the warranty's enforceability. A moment's reflection reveals the unreasonableness of such a requirement. Under the majority's holding, which is not limited to automobile manufacturers, any manufacturer who warrants a product sold at a retail outlet would need to hire representatives for each of the many such outlets that sold the manufacturer's products. This is an impossible burden to place on the manufacturer. It is unreasonable for the majority to hold Hyundai responsible for failing to do something that cannot realistically be achieved.

There is another way in which the majority's decision here is objectionable. The majority reasons that, because Hyundai's consequential damages disclaimer was not provided to plaintiff at or before the time she signed the purchase contract, this exclusion was not part of the agreement and is void and unenforceable. However, according to the record evidence cited by the majority, it was the entire warranty, and not just the consequential damages exclusion, that was unavailable to plaintiff at the time she signed the contract. As the majority asserts:

> [P]laintiff testified without contradiction that she never saw any part of the written warranty, much less the disclaimer of consequential damages, until she looked in her owner's manual after she had signed the contract and driven the car off the lot. Thus, *on this record,* we must conclude that the warranty information, including the disclaimer of consequential damages, was not made available to the plaintiff at or before the time she signed the purchase contract. (Emphasis in original.)

854 N.E.2d at 623.

Under the majority's reasoning, if the consequential damages exclusion is void because it was not made available to plaintiff and was not part of the agreement entered into by plaintiff, the same is also true of the warranty as a whole. It follows that, if the warranty itself is void, *i.e.,* not part of the agreement, plaintiff should not be able to bring suit against Hyundai under the warranty. Nevertheless, in the case at bar, the majority holds, *sua sponte,* that Hyundai's exclusion is void because it was not conveyed to plaintiff. The majority does not, however, reach the same conclusion regarding the warranty as a whole. This is inconsistent.

The majority's holding regarding Hyundai's consequential damages disclaimer is objectionable for yet another reason. In my view, the majority's decision on this issue is detrimental to consumers. By holding that Hyundai's consequential damages exclusion is unenforceable because Hyundai failed to do something that it could not realistically accomplish, the majority is discouraging manufacturers from offering written warranties at all. While a manufacturer's decision to provide such warranties undoubtedly is influenced by competitive pressures, the benefits of offering a warranty will be considerably diminished if the manufacturer has no control over the scope of the warranty offered. Under the majority's holding, the ability of a manufacturer to control this scope through exclusions such as a disclaimer of consequential damages is severely constrained, if not eliminated. Faced with such a prospect, a manufacturer might very well conclude that it is no longer cost effective to offer a written warranty. Such a result would indeed be anticonsumer. . . .

Because of my disagreement with the majority on these points, I respectfully dissent from the modification of the opinion upon denial of rehearing. It is my belief that this court could benefit from briefing on these matters. I note, too, that this court allows successive petitions for rehearing where a majority opinion has been modified upon denial of rehearing. In light of the extensive modifications made by the majority here, I suggest the filing of such a petition. For the foregoing reasons, I vote to grant Hyundai's petition for rehearing.

Problem 5-9

Given the different standards applicable to liquidated damages clauses and limitations on remedy, it is important to distinguish between them. What is the difference, given that each may place a cap on damages?

CISG and UNIDROIT Principles. CISG Article 6 allows the parties to alter the effect of any of the CISG provisions. It does not specifically address limited remedies or liquidated damages terms. The UNIDROIT Principles allow for a specified sum of money as damages regardless of actual harm suffered. That agreed sum can be reduced if it is "grossly excessive" in relation to the harm suffered. UNIDROIT Art. 7.4.13. The Principles also allow for a limited remedy to be provided if such a remedy is not "grossly unfair" in light of the contract purposes. UNIDROIT Art. 7.1.6.

SECTION 2. PROVING THE TERMS OF THE CONTRACT: THE PAROL EVIDENCE RULE

Suppose the parties have reached an agreement that is enforceable as a contract under Article 2. Some or all of the terms of the agreement are contained in a writing that is signed by both parties. After performance commences, a dispute erupts over the obligations under the contract. The dispute may involve the meaning of the terms included in the writing. Alternatively, the dispute may involve a term that one party alleges that both sides had agreed to but which is not included in the writing. In either case, there is an honest disagreement. What evidence is admissible to determine meaning of terms in the writing? What evidence is admissible with respect to alleged terms that are not included in the writing? The place to start the analysis is with section 2-202, Article 2's version of the parol evidence rule.[7] Review as well the material in Chapter Three regarding usage of trade, course of dealing, and course of performance. UCC § 1-303.

The parol evidence rule operates as a gate keeper that determines what evidence the finder of fact may consider in deciding to what terms the parties have agreed. In general, it restricts the parties' ability to introduce evidence that would contradict a writing that memorializes their agreement. Do not confuse the parol evidence rule with the statute of frauds, which we studied in Chapter Two. Although both serve the same general goal (encouraging written terms) – the statute of frauds may require a writing for an agreement to be enforceable and the parol evidence rule

---

[7] Even though these materials will refer to a "writing," electronic records may also be the subject of a parol evidence rule dispute. *See* Electronic Signatures in Global and National Commerce Act (E-Sign), 15 U.S.C. § 7001; Uniform Electronic Transactions Act (UETA) § 7.

gives primacy to certain writings by not allowing the parties to contradict them – they have very different scopes. Indeed, it would be the extremely unusual case that presented problems under both rules. Statute of frauds problems tend to arise only when there is no signed writing; parol evidence rule questions arise only when there is a writing adopted by both parties. Moreover, the two rules have different effects. If the parties' agreement does not satisfy the statute of frauds, the agreement is unenforceable. If the parol evidence rule excludes evidence of some alleged terms, the remainder of the agreement is still enforceable, only the excluded terms are affected.

The first question to ask in any dispute about the parol evidence rule is whether the rule applies at all. Read section 2-202. For the rule to apply, the parties must have a writing "intended by the parties as a final expression of their agreement with respect to such terms as are included therein." This requirement of a final written expression is often phrased as a question whether the parties have intended to at least partially "integrate" their agreement into the writing. *Cf.* RESTATEMENT (SECOND) OF CONTRACTS § 210. Intent to partially integrate terms of the agreement into a writing means that the parties intended that, as to the terms discussed in the writing, the writing's terms are final. This partial integration should be distinguished from what is referred to as a "full integration." A full integration means that the parties intended not only that the writing be final as to what the writing addresses, but also that the writing is complete: that all the terms agreed to were expressed in the writing. Thus in a fully integrated writing, the terms stated in the writing are the final, complete, and exclusive statement of the terms in the record. Put another way, a fully integrated writing expresses the entire agreement.

Even when the parol evidence rule applies – either because a writing is a final written expression of the parties' agreement or because a writing purports to express the entire agreement – evidence of allegedly supplementary or contradictory terms might be excluded from the jury. However, whether proffered evidence will be excluded depends on several factors:

(i) whether the writing is a complete and exclusive statement of the parties' agreement (*i.e.,* the entire agreement or fully integrated) or merely a final written expression (*i.e.* partially integrated);

(ii) whether the proffered terms are oral, written or implicit terms based on course of performance, course of dealing, or usage of trade;

(iii) whether the proffered terms supplement or contradict the writing; and

(iv) whether the proffered terms (oral or written) arose prior to the writing or contemporaneously with it.

Problem 5-10

Complete the following chart by noting whether the evidence described would be admissible in the situation described. For example, is evidence of prior, oral supplementary terms admissible when there is a final, written expression of the parties' agreement, but that writing does not purport to contain the entire agreement? Is it admissible if the writing represents the parties' entire agreement (*i.e.*, if the writing is a complete and exclusive statement of the terms)?

Terms Sought to Be Admitted			Final Written Expression	Entire Agreement
Supplementary	Oral	Prior		
		Contemporaneous		
	Written	Prior		
		Contemporaneous		
	Usage of Trade, Course of Dealing & Performance			
Contradictory	Oral	Prior		
		Contemporaneous		
	Written	Prior		
		Contemporaneous		
	Usage of Trade, Course of Dealing & Performance			

As difficult as it may be to isolate and chart out the various rules in section 2-202, it is far more difficult to apply them. These difficulties usually fall into any of three recurring problems.

First, how is the court to distinguish among non-final writings, writings intended as a final expression of the parties' agreement, and writings intended as a complete and exclusive statement of the terms? If you think about it, how can any writing qualify as a complete and exclusive statement if there are indeed prior or contemporaneous agreements? The existence of parol evidence would seem to contradict the very idea that the writing contains the entire agreement of the parties.

Predictably there are differing views on how courts are to go about classifying the writing before them. One approach is to look at the "four corners" of the writing and from that writing and that writing alone determine whether the writing is complete. A merger clause – that is, a clause that expressly states that the parties' negotiations are merged into the writing and that the writing is a complete and exclusive statement of the parties' agreement – is highly probative, albeit not conclusive, on this point. Another approach is to consider the parol evidence itself to determine whether the writing is complete. One suspects that courts following the latter approach may reach a conclusion on the scope of the writing on whether they believe the parol evidence.

The second problem concerns how to distinguish parol evidence that supplements the writing from parol evidence that contradicts it.[8] Various tests have been proposed, including the following:

(i)   parol evidence is inconsistent if it directly contradicts or negates a term in the writing;

(ii) parol evidence is inconsistent if there is the absence of reasonable harmony between the proffered term and the term in the writing;

(iii) the parol evidence is inconsistent if the proffered term is one that the parties would certainly have included in the writing if they had in fact agreed to it; and

(iv) the parol evidence is supplementary if the proffered term is one that might have naturally been omitted from the writing.[9]

---

[8]   Indeed if there is a merger clause, would not all evidence of prior additional terms be contradictory?

[9]   The first two tests are articulated in *Alaska Northern Development, Inc. v. Alyeska Pipeline Service Co.*, 666 P.2d 33 (Alaska 1983), *cert. denied*, 464 U.S. 1041 (1984). The third test comes from the comment to section 2-202. The fourth test is from section 216 of the Restatement (Second) of Contracts.

The third problem concerns evidence offered to "explain" the terms expressed in the writing. *See* UCC § 2-202. Must the term in the writing be ambiguous in order for explanatory evidence to be admissible? The official comments reject a threshold requirement of ambiguity for the admission of evidence concerning course of performance, course of dealing, and usage of trade. *See* UCC § 2-202 cmt. 1(c). However, that comment does not speak to other types of explanatory evidence and whether it is admissible if the writing is not ambiguous. Here again, approaches differ. Some courts will admit the evidence only if they first conclude the writing is ambiguous. Others follow a more liberal approach and allow in any relevant evidence to explain terms in the writing, including evidence of prior negotiations and agreements. *See* RESTATEMENT (SECOND) OF CONTRACTS § 214.

There are four remaining things about the parol evidence rule to keep in mind. First, the parol evidence rule never bars evidence of subsequent terms. In other words, if one party alleges that the parties, after adopting a final written expression of their agreement, agreed to a new or different term, the parol evidence rule will never keep out evidence of that alleged agreement. However, we have already seen that the parties may, in their written agreement, require that future amendments be in writing. *See* UCC § 2-209(2).

Second, the parol evidence rule does not bar evidence of fraud or mistake, even if that evidence comes from the time period prior to execution of the record.[10]

Third, getting past the parol evidence rules does not mean that the allegedly supplementary or contradictory term will become part of the parties' contract. It merely means that the jury or other fact finder will receive the evidence. If the fact finder does not believe the evidence or is swayed by contrary evidence, the party offering the evidence may still ultimately fail in its efforts. In short, the parol evidence rule is merely a gatehouse to the fact finder, and getting past the gate does not prove the point, it merely enables arguments to be made.

Finally, assuming the evidence is admissible, how is it proven? Trade usage and other context evidence are facts to be established by the moving party. *See* UCC § 1-303. Because these facts are normally not presumed to exist, the moving party has the "burden of establishing" them, *i.e.*, that party must persuade the "trier of fact that the existence of the fact is more probable than its nonexistence." UCC

---

[10]   *See, e.g.,* David Frisch & John D. Wladis, *U.C.C. Survey: General Provisions, Sales, Bulk Transfers, and Documents of Title*, 47 BUS. LAW. 1517, 1520–21 (1992); RESTATEMENT (SECOND) OF CONTRACTS § 214.

§ 1-201(b)(8). The moving party, therefore, has both the burden of production and the burden of persuasion.

As you ponder the parol evidence rule and attempt to solve the problems below, consider what purposes the rule serves. Why should terms in a writing be accorded more respect than terms not in a writing? If you were drafting a written agreement for the parties to sign, what would you put in the document in order to exclude the types of evidence that may otherwise be used to explain, supplement, or contradict terms in that document?

Problem 5-11

Fiber Industries sold fiber to carpet manufacturers for use in making carpets. Salem Carpet bought trademark fiber from Fiber Industries on an order-by-order basis. There was no written documents other than the individual purchase orders and acknowledgment forms. Both Salem's purchase order form and Fiber Industries' acknowledgment form contained "merger" clauses, which provided that the form "contains all the terms and conditions of the purchase agreement and shall constitute the complete and exclusive agreement between Seller and Purchaser." In August, Fiber Industries announced that it was withdrawing from the carpet industry, but that it would supply all customers in an "orderly fashion" until the phase-out was complete. Salem accepted a final order of fiber at a contract price of $407,128.40, but refused to pay the full amount because of losses suffered as a result of Fiber Industries' withdrawal from the market. Salem claimed that there was a "customary practice" in the carpet industry obligating Fiber Industries to fill all orders made by Salem during the projected market life of any carpet style which utilized fiber manufactured by Fiber Industries. Salem was prepared to establish a usage that the "carpet manufacturer will continue to make its branded fiber available for the useful life of the carpet style or for sufficient time to allow the carpet manufacturer to produce and sell sufficient carpet to recoup the large start-up expenses incurred in introducing and marketing a new line of branded carpet."

A. Assume that both contract forms were silent on the issue. Assume, further, that the usage could be established. Should the court admit evidence of the usage?

B. Assume that instead of establishing that evidence under the rubric of "usage of trade," Salem wanted to introduce evidence to the same effect based upon the discussions of the parties that occurred before Salem ordered the fiber. Again assume that both contract forms were silent on the issue. Should that evidence be admitted?

C. Assume that Salem's purchase order provided that the seller of goods that are supplied pursuant to the purchase order promises to "support the integration of all materials supplied to the buyer into the carpet manufactured by the buyer." Assume that under the analysis pursuant to section 2-207, that term in the purchase order was part of the parties' agreement. Salem argues that the usage of trade evidence will demonstrate what was meant by that term.

1. Assuming the usage of trade is established, should evidence of that usage be admitted?

2. Assume that instead of establishing that evidence under the rubric of "usage of trade," Salem wanted to introduce evidence to the same effect based upon the discussions of the parties that occurred before Salem ordered the fiber. Should that evidence be admitted?

Problem 5-12

Lomborg, a boat dealer, advertised a 42 foot Pearson sailing sloop for sale. The boat was manufactured in 1960 and had a wooden hull. Fisk, an experienced sailor, had never purchased a sloop with a wooden hull. Without the assistance of a third party, Fisk examined the boat carefully and could find nothing wrong. Fisk questioned Lomborg who, at various times stated:

"This beauty was her owner's pride and joy";

"It's in great shape";

"The boat is sound";

"It rides the waves like a dream";

"The wood is solid throughout"; and

"We will replace any dry rot free of charge."

After hearing all of these statements, Fisk agreed to buy the sloop for $50,000. Fisk purchased the boat for personal use. At the time of contracting, Fisk signed a writing prepared by Lomborg which, on the front, provided in part as follows:

> WARRANTIES. Buyer is buying the goods AS IS WHERE IS and no representations or statements have been made by seller except as herein stated, so that no warranty, express or implied, arises apart from this writing.

Fisk took delivery of the boat, paid the purchase price and went for a long, wet sail. The boat appeared to leak at the stern. Fisk hired an expert to inspect the area and that expert found extensive dry rot, which had clearly been there at the time of the sale. The estimated cost to repair the boat was $15,000.

A. Fisk claimed damages for breach of warranty. Lomborg argued that all warranties, express or implied, had been disclaimed. Is Lomborg correct? Review section 2-316.

B. Should it matter when the disclaimers were delivered to Fisk? Suppose the writing with the disclaimers was delivered to Fisk after Fisk signed a purchase agreement to buy the boat?

CISG and UNIDROIT Principles. Article 11 of the CISG provides that no writing is required for an enforceable contract. Article 8 allows "all relevant circumstances" to be used to determine the intent of the parties. Article 9 allows for reliance on usage of trade and practices the parties have established between themselves. Thus, the CISG does not provide a screen for the admissibility of evidence that is comparable to the parol evidence rule. The UNIDROIT Principles are of similar effect, relying on interpretation based upon all relevant circumstances. UNIDROIT Arts. 4.1 through 4.7. However, if the document has a merger clause indicating that the document contains the complete agreement of the parties, the terms in that document cannot be contradicted or supplemented by evidence or prior statements or agreements. Those prior statements or agreements may, however, by used to explain the terms of the document. UNIDROIT Art. 2.1.17.

CHAPTER SIX

PERFORMANCE ISSUES

In this Chapter, we consider four matters relevant to the parties' obligations to perform: (i) assignment of contract rights and delegation of contract duties; (ii) a party's authority to terminate a contract for a reason other than breach; (iii) what recourse a party has when it becomes insecure about whether the other will perform and the effect of a repudiation; and (iv) excuse. There is no theme connecting these different concepts and rules, but all are worth studying before we move on to the next Chapter, where we begin in earnest to study breach and its effects.

SECTION 1.   ASSIGNMENT AND DELEGATION

Often one or both parties to a sales contract wish to transfer its contractual rights or obligations to someone else. When that is the case, any one or more of several questions may arise. For example, may the seller delegate its obligation to deliver conforming goods to another person? If the seller does delegate performance, must the buyer accept performance from that new person? May the seller assign to another person the seller's right to the payment due from the buyer? If so, does the buyer have to pay that other person? Similarly, may the buyer assign to another person the buyer's right to receive the goods, and if so, must the seller tender performance to that assignee? May the buyer delegate to someone else its obligation to pay for the goods, and if it does, will the seller have any recourse against the buyer if the delegatee does not pay?

The Article 2 provision on assignment and delegation, section 2-210, builds upon the common-law principles in this area. Unfortunately, in many first-year courses on contracts, assignment and delegation principles are not covered. Thus, for many students, this will be new material and for others it will be a summary review of these principles.

The first place to start is to get the terminology straight. Rights are *assigned*, duties are *delegated*. Thus, for example, the seller in an Article 2 contract has the obligation to deliver conforming goods in accordance with the contract terms and the right to receive payment in accordance with the contract terms. If the seller and a third person agree that the third person will tender the conforming goods to the buyer, the seller has *delegated* its obligation to perform. If, in contrast, the seller transfers the right to payment under the contract to a third person, the seller will have *assigned* its right. Similarly, a buyer may assign its right to receive goods or delegate its obligation to pay for them.

It is of course possible to assign rights and delegate duties to the same person, but that is not necessary. A buyer or seller may assign rights without delegating duties, or may delegate duties without assigning rights. Similarly, a buyer or seller may delegate duties to one person and assign rights to another.

How is an assignment of rights or a delegation of duties effectuated? Generally an assignment requires an agreement between the assignor and the assignee. Similarly, a delegation requires an agreement between the delegator and the delegatee. RESTATEMENT (SECOND) OF CONTRACTS §§ 327, 328.

The most interesting questions are: (i) whether the counter-party to the contract must agree to the other party's assignment or delegation to the third person, (ii) whether a contractual prohibition on assignment or delegation is effective; and (iii) what effect a delegation or assignment has on the parties to the contract.

Let's start with delegation. Read section 2-210(1), (6). It provides that parties are free – absent agreement to the contrary – to delegate their contractual duties. There is an exception, however, if the other party has a substantial interest in having the original promisor perform. Given the nature of the parties' primary duties – the seller to tender conforming goods and the buyer to pay for them – the buyer is far more likely than the seller to have a substantial interest in having its contracting party, rather than a delegatee, perform. Do you see why?

The rules regarding assignments are similar. Read section 2-210(2) and (3). Absent agreement to the contrary, each party is free to assign its right to receive performance from the other, and such an assignment does not generally require the consent of the person that is to render the performance. Thus, in a very typical case, the seller in an Article 2 transaction assigns to a third party its rights to receive payment from the buyer. The buyer in such a case generally has no ground for objection because the duty to pay is not affected much by the identity of the payee. In fact, many sellers regularly assign their rights to receive payment from buyers as a way of obtaining the funds needed to finance the seller's business.[1] Because of the need to permit such free transfers of payment rights, even if the agreement

---

[1]   This assignment is in fact an Article 9 transaction in which the assignment of the seller's right to receive payment (generally an account, in Article 9 terminology) is the creation of a security interest in that right to payment. The Article 9 rules on assignment of rights to payment are contained in sections 9-403 through 9-409 and generally have the same thrust as stated in section 2-210(3). The creation of a security interest in the right to payment that is generated out of an Article 2 sales contract is governed by Article 9.

between the buyer and seller purports to prohibit the seller from assigning its right to payment, the seller will nevertheless be permitted to do so, and making such an assignment will not constitute a breach of the contract with the buyer. *See* UCC §§ 2-210(3), 9-406(d).

Assignment is prohibited, even in the absence of a clause prohibiting assignment, if it would materially change the duty of the other party, materially change its duty, or materially increase the risk that it will not receive the return performance. UCC § 2-210(2). This limitation is most likely to apply to an effort of the buyer to assign its rights.

Problem 6-1

Fill out the chart below to show whether the assignment or delegation is allowed and, if permitted only in limited circumstances, what the applicable standard is.

	Assignment		Delegation	
	By Buyer	By Seller	By Buyer	By Seller
No Contractual Prohibition				
Contractual Prohibition				

In general, whenever one party assigns rights to a third party, the assignee steps into the shoes of the assignor and has the same rights as the assignor. To illustrate, assume a seller assigns its right to receive payment from the buyer. Once the buyer is notified of the assignment and instructed to pay the assignee, the buyer generally may discharge its obligation to pay only by rendering its performance (payment) to the assignee. RESTATEMENT (SECOND) OF CONTRACTS § 338; UCC § 9-406(a). However, absent an agreement by the buyer to the contrary, the buyer will retain the ability to assert against the assignee the same defenses to payment that the buyer could have asserted against the assignor/seller. *See* RESTATEMENT (SECOND) OF CONTRACTS §§ 336, 337; UCC §§ 9-403, 9-404.

The effect of a delegation is a bit different. A delegation of duties does impose the duty to perform on the delegatee. However, it does not normally relieve the delegating party of the obligation to perform. Thus, for example, if the seller delegates its duty to tender conforming goods to a third party, the third party becomes obligated to perform and seller remains responsible for any unexcused failure of that third party to perform.[2] Similarly, if the buyer delegates the duty to pay, and the delegatee does not pay in accordance with the contract terms, the seller will be permitted to seek relief against both the buyer and the delegatee (but will be limited to a single satisfaction).[3]

Problem 6-2

Seller agreed to sell specially manufactured goods to Buyer in return for a price. Seller and Buyer negotiated extensively over the specifications for the goods and one of the terms is that Buyer must approve the prototype that Seller will create before creating a full production run. Buyer is obligated to pay Seller for production of the prototype, if the prototype is satisfactory to Buyer.

A. Seller assigned the contract to Manufacturer, who accepted the assignment. Manufacturer has created the prototype. While there does not appear to be anything wrong with the prototype, Buyer does not want to deal with Manufacturer, preferring to deal with Seller. Does Buyer have to accept the prototype from Manufacturer? Does Buyer have to pay Manufacturer? How, if at all, would the analysis change if the contract between Seller and Buyer prohibited assignment?

B. Buyer assigned the contract to Best Company, which accepted the assignment. Seller created the prototype but does not want to deal with Best Company. What would you tell Seller? Would it matter if the contract between Seller and Buyer prohibited all contract assignments?

CISG and UNIDROIT Principles. The CISG does not address issues of assignment of rights and delegation of duties. Chapter 9 of the UNIDROIT

---

[2]   The seller would, however, be discharged of this responsibility if the buyer had agreed to a novation; that is, if the buyer had agreed to accept the third party's performance and to discharge the seller of the duty. *See* RESTATEMENT (SECOND) OF CONTRACTS § 318(3) & cmt. d.

[3]   For the relationship between delegation of duties and suretyship principles, *see* Gary L. Monserud, *The Privileges of Suretyship for Delegating Parties Under UCC Section 2-210 in Light of the New Restatement of Suretyship*, 37 WM. & MARY L. REV. 1307 (1996).

Principles contains numerous rules regarding assignment and delegation. These principles mirror the common-law approach described above with one notable exception. The baseline presumption is that the counter-party must consent to the assignment. UNIDROIT Art. 9.3.3. That basic presumption is subject to an exception if it is an assignment of the right to payment of a monetary obligation which may be assigned even though there is a term in the parties' agreement prohibiting assignment. UNIDROIT Art. 9.1.9. Such an assignment in contravention of an anti-assignment term is effective, although it is a breach of the contract between the assignor and the counter-party.

SECTION 2.   TERMINATION OF A CONTRACT

Article 2 uses two different terms to refer to the premature ending of a contract for the sale of goods: cancellation and termination. Cancellation is a right that an aggrieved buyer or seller has upon the other's breach. *See* UCC §§ 2-106(4), 2-703(f), 2-711(1). Termination, in contrast, refers to putting an end to a contract for a reason other than breach. Read section 2-106(3). The effect of termination is to discharge all executory (*i.e.* unperformed) obligations of the parties without further liability. However, rights and remedies are preserved to the extent they accrue from obligations due before the termination becomes effective. UCC § 2-106(3).

Typically, termination is something that occurs when the contract calls for the seller to provide goods to the buyer over an extended period of time. For example, the contract may call for the seller to provide either a stated quantity of goods each month or all of the buyer's requirements. The agreement may say nothing about termination, may identify a specific termination date, or may provide for termination upon the occurrence of a particular event or upon notification by either party of a decision to terminate.

If the agreement provides for termination upon a stated time or event, then that provision will govern termination, subject to the usual exceptions for lack of mutual assent, unconscionability, modification, and the like. If the agreement does not provide for termination upon an agreed time or event, then either party may terminate by giving reasonable notification to the other. *See* UCC § 2-309(2), (3). As to how far in advance a notification must be given to be "reasonable," consult section 1-205 on reasonable time. One test that courts have used is whether the notification was given in sufficient time for the recipient to obtain substitute arrangements or performance.[4]

The right to terminate is, of course, subject to the duty of good faith, UCC § 1-304, but that does not mean that the terminating party needs a good reason to terminate the contract. Consider the following discussion of good faith in *Santa Fe Custom Shutters & Doors, Inc. v. Home Depot U.S.A., Inc.*, 113 P.3d 347, 358–60 (N.M. Ct. App.), *cert. denied*, 113 P.3d 345 (N.M. 2005), in which a shutter manufacturer sued a retailer for terminating their contract after the manufacturer, in reliance on their contract, spent considerable sums to expand production:

> SFCS argues that notwithstanding the at-will nature of its business relationship with Home Depot, we should treat Home Depot's exercise of its right to terminate its relationship with SFCS as a breach of the duty of good faith. SFCS argues that unless we apply the duty of good faith to limit Home Depot's right to terminate,
>
> > [Home Depot] would be free to (a) entice, through misrepresentation, a company like [SFCS] to enter into a contractual relationship of indefinite duration requiring enormous up-front investments and debt, (b) promise a partnership likely to produce substantial profits, (c) fail to keep binding promises to professionally market the company's product, and (d) before the anticipated profits could be realized, terminate the arrangement in breach of any notion of good faith and fair dealing.
>
> We agree with SFCS that the implied duty of good faith applies in the context of a termination of a contract of indefinite duration. That does not mean, however, that the general duty of good faith overrides the right to terminate "at any time" specifically conferred by [UCC § 2-309(2)].
>
> > There can be no question that the broad terms of UCC § 1-203 [rev. UCC § 1-304] [recognizing an implied duty of good faith] mandate that the limitation of good faith apply to all actions taken under the authority of the Code. This, however, does not answer the question of what is meant by "good faith" in the context of a notice to terminate an indefinite duration contract. The very absence of any predicate that must be established as a condition precedent to terminating the contract emphasizes the absence of

---

[4]   *See Coburn Supply Co. v. Kohler Co.*, 342 F.3d 372 (5th Cir. 2003).

any significance to the good faith concept in this particular situation.

RONALD A. ANDERSON, ANDERSON ON THE UNIFORM COMMERCIAL CODE § 2-309:49 (3d ed. 1997 rev.). Other leading commentators agree: "We do not believe that ideas of good faith should be used to deprive a terminating party of the rights it would otherwise have under 2-309(2)." 1 JAMES J. WHITE & ROBERT S. SUMMERS, UNIFORM COMMERCIAL CODE 140 (4th ed. 1995). We agree with Home Depot that "[t]he essence of the at-will doctrine is the right of either party to cease doing business without liability for *future* profits the other party hopes it will earn if the relationship continues." (Emphasis added.)

The implied duty of good faith does not confer on a district court "a roving commission to do whatever its wishes in the name of fairness." *Cf. United Props. Ltd. v. Walgreen Props., Inc.,* 82 P.3d 535 (N.M. 2003) (discussing limitations on the authority of a district court exercising equity jurisdiction to relieve a party from the consequences of its failure to exercise an option in accordance with the terms of a lease). If SFCS desired the security of a contract binding Home Depot to a business relationship lasting a specific term of years, it was free to bargain for such a term. In the absence of such a term, Home Depot had the right to terminate its contractual relationship with SFCS "at any time," under [UCC § 309(2)], and this was so without regard to whether the contract had been in effect for a reasonable time when Home Depot terminated the contract. ANDERSON, *supra* at § 2-309:36. The district court concluded that SFCS was entitled to damages for lost profits calculated over a five-year period beginning January 1, 2000. In view of Home Depot's right to terminate its contracts with SFCS at any time, which there is no dispute Home Depot exercised on March 20, and July 17, 2000, the district court's use of the five-year period in calculating benefit-of-the-bargain damages was error.

Our decision does not inexorably lead to the hyperbolically dire consequences predicted by SFCS for several reasons. First, we see no reason for precluding a party who has been fraudulently induced to enter into a contract from electing to recover costs incurred in preparing to perform the contract as an alternative to seeking damages for the loss of the benefit of the bargain. *See* E. ALLAN FARNSWORTH, CONTRACTS § 12.16 (3d ed.1999) (discussing reliance interest as an alternative measure of damages for breach of contract); RESTATEMENT (SECOND) OF TORTS

§ 549(1)(b) (1977) (recognizing that victim of fraud may recover pecuniary loss suffered as the result of reliance upon the misrepresentation). SFCS could have sought recovery of damages measured by its "enormous" up-front investment; instead, SFCS elected to pursue damages measured by the benefit of the bargain. Second, if the breaching party's representations in fact are binding promises, those promises may be enforced under established principles of contract law. Under our holding, SFCS is entitled to damages based upon profits that would have accrued if Home Depot had professionally marketed SFCS's products and services over the period *prior to* termination. SFCS may also be entitled to *post*-termination damages if the district court determines on remand that Home Depot failed to provide reasonable notification of its decision to terminate its business relations with SFCS and SFCS suffered damages due to the lack of reasonable notification.

Based upon the reasoning of the New Mexico Court of Appeals, what does exercising the right in good faith to terminate a contract mean?

CISG and UNIDROIT Principles. CISG Article 29 provides that a contract may be terminated by agreement and if the contract provides that a termination must be in writing, such a term is enforceable unless a party has waived its right to insist on the writing and the other party has relied on that waiver. The CISG does not seem to address the same issue that section 2-309 addresses, that is the ability to give a notice of termination when the contract does not address the ability to terminate a contract of indefinite duration. The UNIDROIT Principles simply state that either party may end a contract of indefinite duration upon giving notice to the other party a "reasonable time in advance." UNIDROIT Art. 5.1.8.

SECTION 3.   INSECURITY AND REPUDIATION

A. INSECURITY AND ADEQUATE ASSURANCE

Once a buyer and seller enter into a contract for the sale of goods, either or both of the parties may become uneasy about the ability of the other party to perform. The reasons why a party may become worried that the other party may not perform are as varied as the types of goods and relationships that are the subject matter of "transactions in goods." For example, a defect in a specially manufactured prototype might lead the buyer to question the seller's ability to tender conforming goods. A shortage of needed raw materials may lead the buyer to question the seller's ability to tender any goods at all. A rail strike might imperil the seller's ability to deliver the goods on time. On the other side, news reports that the buyer is experiencing financial difficulty may give the seller concern about the buyer's ability to pay. A decision by the buyer to discontinue certain lines of business may cause the seller to question whether the buyer still wants and will accept the goods called for under the contract. Complaints by the buyer about minor problems with a prototype may give the seller reservations about whether the buyer is seeking an excuse to not perform.[5] What may a party do when it has grounds to question the other party's ability or willingness to perform?

Read section 2-609. It allows a party with reasonable grounds for insecurity to demand adequate assurance of future performance, and to suspend its own performance until it receives such assurances. The first question that must be considered is when does a party have reasonable grounds for insecurity? Notice that a party's reasons will be tested by an objective, not subjective, standard and if the transaction is between merchants, commercial standards apply to determine reasonable grounds for insecurity. UCC § 2-609(2).

Some circumstances are easy to deal with because Article 2 provides a statutory basis for finding the grounds for insecurity to be reasonable. For example, section 2-210(6) expressly provides that delegation of duties provides reasonable grounds for insecurity. In addition, if a seller discovers its buyer to be insolvent, the seller has the right to withhold delivery of the goods and insist on a cash payment. UCC § 2-702(1). In other circumstances, the reasonableness of any insecurity will be a question of fact, the resolution of which can be difficult to predict.

If a party has reasonable grounds for insecurity, it may make a written demand of the other for adequate assurance. The concerned party may then suspend its own performance while it awaits the reassurance. If the other party does not respond appropriately, the concerned party may treat that failure as a repudiation, cancel the contract, and pursue remedies for breach. *See* UCC §§ 2-610, 2-703(f), 2-711(1).

---

[5]   *See Brisbin v. Superior Valve Co.*, 398 F.3d 279 (3d Cir. 2005) (buyer's failure to respond timely to seller, not providing results of tests of prototypes, and engaging in "stalling" behavior gave seller reasonable grounds for insecurity regarding buyer's commitment to performing the contract); *Rad Concepts, Inc. v. Wilks Precision Instrument Co.*, 891 A.2d 1148 (Md. Ct. App. 2006) (buyer's failure to pay under one contract gave seller reasonable grounds for insecurity related to another contract).

The more difficult questions are: (i) for what should the concerned party ask? and (ii) what response would be adequate? Is the concerned party entitled to request that the other party agree to additional obligations that are not part of the contract? Is a response that simply acknowledges the contract and pledges future performance sufficient? There is much uncertainty in this process. That uncertainty is exacerbated by the fact that the concerned party may make a demand for assurance when it in fact does not have reasonable grounds for insecurity or may demand more assurance than it is entitled to receive. Such action in and of itself could give the other party reasonable grounds for insecurity or even constitute a repudiation of the concerned party's obligation under the contract.[6]

TOP OF IOWA COOPERATIVE V. SIME FARMS, INC.
608 N.W.2d 454 (Iowa 2000)

Ternus, Justice

The appellee, Top of Iowa Cooperative, sued the appellant, Sime Farms, Inc., for damages arising out of Sime Farms' failure to deliver corn under four hedge-to-arrive (HTA) contracts. Sime Farms claimed that the contracts were illegal and that, in any event, the Coop had repudiated the contract by making an unreasonable demand for assurances. A jury found in favor of the Coop and awarded damages against Sime Farms. We affirm.

I. *Background Facts and Proceedings*

A. *Hedge-to-arrive contracts.* Before we discuss the particular facts of this case, it is helpful to briefly review the nature of HTA contracts. "[I]n a basic HTA contract, a farmer and grain elevator enter into a contract that contemplates delivery of a specified quantity of grain at a fixed point in time in the future." *Andersons, Inc. v. Horton Farms, Inc.,* 166 F.3d 308, 319 (6th Cir.1998). In a typical HTA contract, the elevator sets the price it is willing to pay based on the open market

---

[6] For good background discussion, *see* Lawrence B. Wardrop, Jr., *Prospective Inability in the Law of Contracts,* 20 MINN. L. REV. 380 (1936); Alan G. Dowling, Note, *A Right to Adequate Assurance of Performance in All Transactions: UCC § 2-609 Beyond Sales of Goods,* 48 S. CAL. L. REV. 1358 (1975). *See also,* R. J. Robertson, Jr., *The Right to Demand Adequate Assurance of Due Performance: Uniform Commercial Code Section 2-609 and Restatement (Second) of Contracts Section 251,* 38 DRAKE L. REV. 305 (1988–89); Larry T. Garvin, *Adequate Assurance of Performance: Of Risk, Duress, and Cognition,* 69 U. COLO. L. REV. 71 (1998).

price on the Chicago Board of Trade (CBOT) for the delivery period, minus what is known as the basis.[7] (The basis is simply the elevator's cost of doing business, such as transportation costs, storage, labor, and utilities, plus a profit.) Upon entering into an HTA contract, the elevator hedges its purchase by simultaneously selling a futures contract on the CBOT, thereby protecting itself from any change in the cash price of corn at the date of delivery.

Although the transaction up to this point is relatively straightforward, there are several complicating factors. First, grain elevators must conduct their trading on the CBOT through licensed brokers. When the price of corn on the futures market rises, the contract with the broker typically requires the elevator to pay what is known as "margin money" – the difference between the original futures contract price and the current futures price – in order to maintain its futures position.[8] The elevator recovers the margin money when it sells the corn delivered by the farmer at a higher cash price.[9] Of course, if the farmer does not deliver, the elevator has

---

[7]   In the Midwest, the market price for grain such as corn is set on the open market established by the CBOT. During trading hours on the CBOT, contracts are bought and sold for the future delivery of corn in the months of December, March, May, July, and September. Contracts bought and sold on the CBOT are known as "futures contracts." The price established by the CBOT for the buying and selling of grain is widely disseminated to the public.

[8]   The requirement of margin payments arises from the nature of futures contracts. One court has explained these contracts in the following manner:

   Parties who enter futures contracts do not agree to pay the price that prevails when they buy the contracts; they agree to pay the price that prevails when the contracts expire (or the positions are closed by offsetting transactions). A contract for September corn, entered into in March, will fluctuate in price until September, when its final price is determined by the price of the cash commodity at the delivery point.

Nagel v. ADM Investor Servs., Inc., 65 F. Supp. 2d 740, 753 (N.D. Ill. 1999).

[9]   An example will illustrate how hedging works and how it protects the elevator from any price risk. We will make the following assumptions. The Coop contracts to purchase 20,000 bushels of corn from Sime Farms for a December 1995 delivery date. The CBOT price for December 1995 corn is $2.49 at the time of contracting, so Sime Farms is entitled to receive $2.49 minus the basis upon delivery. The Coop hedges this transaction by selling a futures contract on the CBOT at the same price of $2.49. In the months leading to December 1995, the price of December corn rises to $3.00. As the price rises, the broker requires the Coop to pay a total of $ .51 (margin money) to preserve its futures position. Sime Farms delivers the corn in December 1995, as agreed. The Coop pays Sime Farms $2.49 less the basis, which the Coop retains. As noted, the price of December corn is $3.00. The Coop then sells the delivered corn for $3.00, thereby netting $.51 and recovering its margin money. Thus,

no grain to sell, and it cannot recover its margin. Thus, the elevator's hedged position remains risk-free only so long as the farmer can be counted upon to deliver the grain specified under the contract.

In addition, HTA contracts prevalent in the 1990's had two features that distinguished them from traditional grain contracts where the parties agreed on a fixed price for a specified future delivery date. In HTA contracts, the basis was not set at the time of contracting. Rather, the farmer was allowed to choose when to set the basis, provided it was done within the time period specified in the contract. This contract term introduced an element of speculation into the contract, because an elevator's basis generally fluctuated. Consequently, a farmer who delayed setting the basis was open to the risk that the elevator's basis would increase, thereby lowering the price the farmer would receive for his grain.

The second element of risk in HTA contracts is introduced when the farmer is allowed to postpone delivery to a later date. This practice is known as rolling. When the price of grain rises by or near the time set for delivery, the farmer may prefer to sell his grain on the current cash market for a higher price rather than deliver the grain to the elevator for the contract price. Under these circumstances, the parties may agree to modify the contract by delaying, or rolling, the delivery date to a date in the future. To preserve its hedged position, the elevator buys back, at the current price, the futures contract it had previously sold on the CBOT and enters into another futures contract to sell grain on the new delivery date.

The complicating factor in rolling is that the price of corn for the new date of delivery generally is not the same as the current price for the old delivery date. This difference is called the spread. If the new price is higher, the spread is positive and will result in a gain or carry. If the new price is lower, however, it will result in a loss or inverse. This gain or loss is fixed at the time of the roll and is added to or deducted from the new contract price under the rolled HTA contract. Thus, when the farmer decides to roll, he can determine at that time whether he will incur a gain or loss. The problematic risk arises when the farmer rolls to a month when he will not have grain on hand to deliver. He has then exposed himself to an additional, unknown risk because he will have to roll again before he will be able to make the agreed-upon delivery. If the market deteriorates and the price of corn falls, the farmer may ultimately be required to deliver grain at a significant loss.

Unfortunately, this predicament is precisely the situation that faced Sime Farms in the summer of 1996, which brings us to the facts of this case. . . .

---

both parties end up with the proceeds they bargained for in the original contract.

B. *Factual background.*   Top of Iowa Cooperative is a farmer-owned cooperative that operates in several locations, including Lake Mills, Iowa. Prior to January 1995, the Lake Mills location was owned and operated as the Farmers Coop Elevator Company of Lake Mills. Sime Farms, Inc. is an Iowa corporation wholly owned by Mark Sime. As its name suggests, its business is farming. Sime Farms is a member of the Coop, and for many years prior to the time in question, did nearly all of its grain and agronomy business with the Coop's predecessor, Farmers Coop Elevator Company. (In the remainder of this opinion, we refer to both entities as the Coop.)

In the fall of 1994 and the spring of 1995, Sime Farms entered into three HTA contracts with the Coop. These contracts called for the delivery of a total of 40,000 bushels of corn in December 1995. This grain represented Sime Farms' entire annual corn production. One month before delivery was due under these contracts, Sime Farms contracted to sell an additional 20,000 bushels of corn for delivery in May 1996. The Coop hedged each contract by selling futures contracts on the CBOT for corresponding delivery dates.

In November 1995, Sime Farms rolled its December 1995 delivery dates to March 1996. Although the HTA contracts did not specifically address the ability of Sime Farms to roll, the contracts contemplated this possibility by providing for a fee of one cent per bushel for each roll. Handwritten modifications were made on the contracts indicating the new delivery dates. The contract price was also adjusted to reflect the spread between the current December 1995 futures price and the March 1996 futures price. This adjustment was a positive six cents, a seven-cent carry minus the one-cent roll fee. Sime Farms then sold its 1995 crop on the cash market at a price significantly higher than the December 1995 futures price it had contracted to receive under the original HTA contracts.

Although the roll to March 1996 resulted in a gain or carry, the parties were aware at the time of this roll that a roll to July 1996 or December 1996 would result in a significant inverse, or loss. The parties also knew that Sime Farms would have to roll again into at least December 1996 because it had no grain to deliver until it harvested its 1996 crop.

In February 1996, the contracts were rolled to May 1996. This roll resulted in a gain of slightly less than three cents per bushel, which was added to the contract price. In April 1996, all four contracts were rolled to July 1996. This roll resulted in a thirteen-cent-per-bushel loss or inverse, and so this amount was deducted from the price the Coop agreed to pay Sime Farms for July delivery. By late April 1996, the inverse between July 1996 and December 1996 was around $1.30 per bushel.

Because Sime Farms had no corn to deliver in July 1996, it was faced with the prospect of rolling into December 1996 at a significant loss, or breaching its contracts with the Coop. If Sime Farms breached the contracts, the Coop would have to repurchase the offsetting futures it held on the CBOT, resulting in a loss of the margin money it had paid.

By May 1996, the Coop was becoming increasingly concerned about farmers' abilities and willingness to perform on the outstanding HTA contracts. The Coop's manager, Paul Nesler, spoke with Mark Sime at least once in May regarding the inverse situation and the effect of rolling into December. Sime told Nesler that he would get back to the Coop about what he planned to do, but he never did. The Coop's concerns were heightened even further when, that same month, the Iowa Attorney General's office announced that some of the HTA contracts might be "illegal."

On June 6, 1996, the Coop sent a letter to Sime Farms and similarly-situated producers in which the Coop stated that "[i]n response to recent market and non-market developments," the Coop wanted to confirm that its customers holding HTA contracts were capable of and intended to perform. The Coop stated it would consider compliance with the following two conditions as adequate assurance of Sime Farms' ability and willingness to perform:

(1) payment in full of all commissions and margins previously paid by the Coop, or a binding letter of credit obligating an institutional lender to pay such commissions and margins; and

(2) the return of a signed copy of the Coop's letter agreeing to delivery of the agreed-upon quantity of grain on or before the delivery dates set forth in the contracts.

Finally, the Coop stated that a failure to provide the requested assurances would constitute a repudiation of the contract.

The next day Mark Sime came to the Coop to discuss the letter. Nesler informed Sime that Sime Farms could roll its contracts to December 1996 and would not be required to reimburse the Coop for the margin calls already paid. Nesler also told Sime that the Coop would consider a buy-out of the contracts by Sime Farms over a period of time at a low interest rate. Nesler called Sime a few days later to find out what Sime wanted to do. Sime told Nesler that the Coop would be receiving a letter from Sime Farms' lawyer.

The Coop did in fact receive a letter from Sime Farms' attorney later that day. In this letter Sime Farms took the position that the Coop's demand for assurances was an attempt to change the terms of the HTA contracts and that the Coop had no grounds to do so. Sime Farms also asserted the illegality of the contracts under the Commodity Exchange Act, 7 U.S.C. §§ 1-25. Sime Farms' attorney closed his letter by informing the Coop that Sime Farms did "not intend to deliver at a price which includes the losses your elevator agreed to assume in the contract relating to unfavorable margins." Upon receipt of this letter, the Coop terminated the futures positions it held in reliance on the Sime Farms HTA contracts. Sime Farms did not deliver grain under any of the contracts. This lawsuit followed.

C. *Course of the litigation.* The Coop claimed in this lawsuit that Sime Farms breached its contracts with the Coop by failing to give adequate assurances upon the Coop's reasonable demand for such assurances. *See* [§ 2-609] (providing that party's failure to provide adequate assurance after a justified demand is a repudiation of the contract). Sime Farms asserted several counterclaims, including a request for a declaratory judgment that the contracts were illegal and unenforceable under the Commodity Exchange Act. Sime Farms also claimed as an affirmative defense that the Coop breached the contracts by making an unwarranted and unreasonable demand for assurances. . . . [At trial, the trial court held the HTA contracts were not illegal and the jury found for the Coop on the breach of contract claim. – Eds.]

II. *Issues on Appeal*

Sime Farms . . . claims that the Coop, as a matter of law, did not have reasonable grounds to be insecure concerning Sime Farms' performance of the contracts . . . [and] that the Coop's demand for assurances amounted to a repudiation as a matter of law, thereby excusing Sime Farms from performing. . . .

IV. *Was The Trial Court Correct in Ruling That the Coop had Generated a Jury Question on the Issue of Whether the Coop had Reasonable Grounds for Insecurity?*

A. *Statement of issue.* One basis for the Coop's breach of contract claim was that Sime Farms failed to provide reasonable assurances upon the Coop's demand for such assurances. This claim arises from article 2 of the Iowa Uniform Commercial Code, which governs the sale of grain in Iowa. . . . Under the U.C.C., a party to a contract who has reasonable grounds to believe that the other party will be unwilling or unable to perform his contractual obligations may require the party to provide adequate assurances of performance.

Sime Farms sought a directed verdict on the basis that the Coop lacked reasonable grounds for insecurity as a matter of law and, therefore, had no right to make a demand for assurances. The trial court held that the Coop had generated a jury question on the issue of reasonable grounds for insecurity and, accordingly, denied Sime Farms' motion. This ruling is assigned as error on appeal. . . .

C. *Applicable legal principles.* Section [2-609] of the Iowa U.C.C. provides in relevant part:

1. A contract for sale imposes an obligation on each party that the other's expectation of receiving due performance will not be impaired. When reasonable grounds for insecurity arise with respect to the performance of either party the other may in writing demand adequate assurance of due performance and until that party receives such assurance may if commercially reasonable suspend any performance for which that party has not already received the agreed return.

2. Between merchants the reasonableness of grounds for insecurity and the adequacy of any assurance offered shall be determined according to commercial standards.

Because the reasonableness of a party's insecurity is determined by commercial standards, there must be an objective factual basis for the insecurity, rather than a purely subjective fear that the party will not perform. *See* R.J. Robertson, Jr., *The Right to Demand Adequate Assurance of Due Performance: Uniform Commercial Code Section 2-609 and Restatement (Second) of Contracts Section 251,* 38 DRAKE L. REV. 305, 322 (1988-89).

Generally, the existence of grounds for insecurity is a question of fact:
Whether a party has reasonable grounds for insecurity depends upon many factors including the [party's] exact words or actions, the course of dealing or performance between the particular parties and the nature of the industry. What constitutes reasonable grounds for insecurity in one case might not in another. Consequently, the trier of fact must normally answer whether grounds for insecurity exist.

1 JAMES J. WHITE & ROBERT S. SUMMERS, UNIFORM COMMERCIAL CODE § 6-2, at 286 (4th ed.1995) [hereinafter WHITE & SUMMERS] . . . . Nevertheless, occasions do arise where the undisputed facts establish that insecurity or the lack of insecurity existed as a matter of law. . . .

D. *Discussion.* The Coop's letter to Sime Farms reveals two grounds for insecurity: (1) the inverse in the market; and (2) statements in the press with respect to the unenforceability of HTA contracts. Because neither ground relates specifically to Sime Farms, Sime Farms asserts these facts do not provide reasonable grounds for the Coop to be concerned about Sime Farms' performance.

> "Clearly, the drafters of the Code did not intend that one party to a contract can go about demanding security for performance of the other whenever he gets nervous about a contract. Some reason for the demand for assurances must precede the demand."

Robertson, 38 DRAKE L.REV. at 323 (quoting *Cole v. Melvin*, 441 F. Supp. 193, 203 (D.S.D. 1977)). In many cases, the grounds for insecurity are specifically tied to the party or the contract. *See, e.g., AMF, Inc.,* 536 F.2d at 1170 (holding that where prototype had never performed satisfactorily and evidence existed that seller was not actively working on project, buyer had reasonable grounds for insecurity); *Scott v. Crown,* 765 P.2d 1043, 1046 (Colo. Ct. App. 1988) (finding fact that investigator told seller of active complaints against buyer and that buyer failed to make personal contact after seller refused to load wheat constituted grounds for insecurity). On the other hand, "[a] ground for insecurity need not arise from or be directly related to the contract in question." U.C.C. § 2-609 official cmt. 3.

> The grounds for insecurity need not arise from circumstances directly related to the parties or the contract itself. Thus, where the market price of a commodity is rising, the buyer may be justified in seeking assurances of performance from the seller *even though the seller did nothing to cause buyer's insecurity.*

WHITE & SUMMERS § 6-2, at 288 (emphasis added). Furthermore, in *Diskmakers, Inc. v. DeWitt Equipment Corp.,* 555 F.2d 1177 (3d Cir.1977), the Third Circuit Court of Appeals stated:

> "As between merchants, the test for determining when reasonable grounds for insecurity arise and what will constitute an adequate assurance of future performance is a commercial criterion. *Any facts which should indicate to a reasonable merchant that the promised performance might not be forthcoming when due should be considered reasonable grounds for insecurity . . . ."*

555 F.2d at 1180 (quoting N.J. Stat. Ann. § 12A:2-609 study cmt. 1 (1962)) (emphasis added).

We think the market conditions existing in June 1996, combined with the widely-publicized statements that HTA contracts were illegal and unenforceable, are facts that would support a jury finding that the Coop had a reasonable basis to be concerned that Sime Farms may not perform under its contracts. The inverse in the market unquestionably made delivery under the contracts an unprofitable venture for Sime Farms. Although the Coop agreed in the contracts to pay all margins and commissions, both parties understood that any inverse would be deducted from the contract price if Sime Farms chose to roll the contracts. Consequently, if a future roll became necessary, the ultimate risk of an inverse market rested with the producer, not the Coop. That was precisely the situation here; another roll was inevitable because Sime Farms had no grain to deliver under the July contracts. Consequently, it would eventually have to roll at least to December 1996, at which time the inverse would reduce its price per bushel to a level at which it would not even recover its costs of production. Clearly, a producer in these circumstances would have every incentive to claim that the contracts were illegal and unenforceable, as the Iowa Attorney General's office had opined.

In addition, the jury was entitled to consider the market factors in the context of the relationship between the Coop and Sime Farms. *See* WHITE & SUMMERS § 6-2, at 286 ("Whether a party has reasonable grounds for insecurity depends upon many factors including the [party's] exact words or actions, the course of dealing or performance between the particular parties and the nature of the industry."); *see also Johnson v. Land O'Lakes,* 181 F.R.D. 388, 395 (N.D. Iowa 1998) (stating that "evidence of the context in which the demand is made is certainly relevant and admissible"). The Coop's local manager, Paul Nesler, spoke with Mark Sime in May to determine what Sime Farms intended to do about its July contracts. Sime was clearly aware of the inverse in the market and his need to roll the contracts to December; yet he did not contact the Coop to take any steps to work out a plan.

Sime Farms places great reliance on the testimony of Nesler, who when asked, "Did you ever believe that he [Sime] wouldn't deliver before June 6, 1996?" responded, "No, I thought Mark would probably deliver." Sime Farms claims that this testimony establishes as a matter of law that the Coop was never insecure about Sime Farms' performance. Although Nesler signed the demand for assurances on behalf of the Coop, he testified he did not draft it. The jury could certainly have concluded that Nesler's personal feelings did not reflect the Coop's belief as to Sime Farms' likely performance. Moreover, Nesler stated several times in his testimony that he was concerned that Sime had not come to the Coop with a plan, especially in view of Nesler's request that he do so. The jury was entitled to consider Nesler's testimony in its entirety and, in doing so, could discount some testimony and give more credit to other testimony. The weight to be given Nesler's testimony was for the jury to determine.

We hold there was sufficient evidence to generate a jury question on whether the Coop had an objectively reasonable basis for insecurity. Therefore, the trial court did not err in refusing to grant Sime Farms' motion for directed verdict on this basis.

V. *Was the Coop's Demand for Assurances Unreasonable as a Matter of Law?*

A. *Issue and scope of review.* Sime Farms claimed at trial that the Coop's demand for assurances was unreasonable as a matter of law and, as a result, constituted a repudiation of the contract. It claims that the trial court erred in failing to grant its motion for directed verdict on this issue. We apply the same scope of review as set out in the preceding division of this opinion.

B. *Applicable law.* Sime Farms' repudiation argument rests on its contention that the Coop's demand for assurances imposed conditions that went beyond the contract and that the Coop's performance was contingent upon acquiescence to these conditions. Sime Farms contends such a demand constitutes an anticipatory repudiation.

We disagree with Sime Farms' contention. The mere fact that the assurances demanded by the Coop necessitated action beyond that required by the contract does not render the demand unreasonable as a matter of law. As noted by a leading treatise on the Uniform Commercial Code,

> [a]ll demands for adequate assurance call for more than was originally promised under the contract, and that is precisely what 2-609 authorizes. If, for example, it was appropriate to sell on open credit at the outset of a contract but subsequent events cause insecurity, 2-609 calls for modification of the contract to provide greater security to the seller than the seller could have demanded, absent such insecurity. Thus it is the very purpose of 2-609 to authorize one party to insist upon more than the contract gives.

WHITE & SUMMERS § 6-2, at 288; *see also* U.C.C. § 2-610 official cmt. 2 ("[A] demand by one or both parties for more than the contract calls for in the way of counter-performance is not in itself a repudiation."); Robertson, 38 DRAKE L.REV. at 341 (noting that an insecure promisee can demand assurance in the nature of additional performances not required by the underlying contract, provided there are reasonable grounds for insecurity). . . .

In summary, the mere fact that the Coop demanded performance beyond that required by the contract did not transform its demand into a repudiation as a matter of law. Therefore, the trial court did not err in submitting the question of the reasonableness of the Coop's demands to the jury. . . . Affirmed.

Compare the court's decision in *Top of Iowa Cooperative, supra,* with the following excerpt from a concurring opinion in *Pittsburgh-Des Moines Steel Co. v. Brookhaven Manor Water Co.,* 532 F.2d 572, 583–84 (7th Cir. 1976):

Although I agree with the result reached in the majority opinion, I differ with the reasoning. Reasonable men could certainly conclude that PDM had legitimate grounds to question Brookhaven's ability to pay for the water tank. When the contract was signed, the parties understood that Brookhaven would obtain a loan to help pay for the project. When the loan failed to materialize, a prudent businessman would have "reasonable grounds for insecurity." I disagree that there must be a fundamental change in the financial position of the buyer before the seller can invoke the protection of UCC § 2-609. Rather, I believe that the Section was designed to cover instances where an underlying condition of the contract, even if not expressly incorporated into the written document, fails to occur. *See* Comment 3 to UCC § 2-609. Whether, in a specific case, the breach of the condition gives a party "reasonable grounds for insecurity" is a question of fact for the jury.

UCC § 2-609, however, does not give the alarmed party a right to redraft the contract. Whether the party invoking that provision is merely requesting an assurance that performance will be forthcoming or whether he is attempting to alter the contract is a mixed question of law and fact, depending in part upon the court's interpretation of the obligations imposed on the parties. In this case, PDM would have been assured only if significant changes in the contract were made, either by receiving Betke's personal guarantee, by attaining escrow financing or by purchasing an interest in Brookhaven. The district court could probably conclude as a matter of law that these requests by PDM demanded more than a commercially "adequate assurance of due performance."

Problem 6-3

Seller agreed to manufacture special equipment for Buyer on credit. Delivery was to be in installments, with payment for each installment within 15 days of delivery. Seller commenced performance but, before any deliveries were made, Seller began to hear unfavorable comments about Buyer's credit. After a quick check, the following facts emerged: (1) Dun & Bradstreet had recently reduced Buyer's credit rating; (2) Buyer's working capital was fully stretched out and some suppliers were experiencing delays in payment; (3) Buyer had recently changed banks, and the "word" was out that Buyer's financial condition was "extended" and that care should be exercised before extending any credit; and (4) Buyer's overall financial condition had worsened since the date of the contract.

A. You represent Seller. On the day before the first delivery was due, Seller called you for a conference. With the credit information on the table, Seller stated that unless you could persuade it otherwise, it would refuse to deliver the goods unless Buyer paid cash. What would you recommend? *See* UCC §§ 1-201(b)(23), 2-702(1), 2-609. Does Seller have reasonable grounds to believe that Buyer is insolvent?

B. Assume you persuade Seller to exercise caution and talk to Buyer before taking action. Seller, therefore, gives Buyer a written demand for "adequate assurance" by asking for a letter of credit, and temporarily suspends the first delivery. UCC § 2-609(1). Buyer, in response, establishes solvency and claims that the current situation is "temporary" and refuses to provide a letter of credit as that was not the originally agreed payment mechanism. Buyer, however, states that long-term viability depends upon getting prompt delivery of the equipment, which is needed in the business, on credit. If there are delays, no assurances can be given. Has Seller demanded more than adequate assurance? Does Buyer's response constitute "adequate assurance" of due performance?

Problem 6-4

Seller agreed to manufacture special equipment for Buyer on credit. Delivery was to be in installments with payment for each installment 15 days after delivery. About one month before Seller was due to deliver the first installment, Buyer began to hear unfavorable things about Seller's financial condition: (1) Dun & Bradstreet had recently reduced Seller's credit rating; (2) Seller's working capital was fully stretched out and some suppliers were experiencing delays in payment; (3) Seller had recently changed banks, and the "word" was out that Seller's financial condition was "extended" and that care should be exercised before extending any credit; and (4) Seller's overall financial condition had worsened since the date of the contract.

Does Buyer have reasonable grounds for insecurity?   If so, what assurances would you suggest Buyer request?

Problem 6-5

Big Discount Corp. is a major retailer with stores throughout the United States. It is the largest retailer of discount consumer products and has such market power that it can command heavy discounts from its suppliers. Big Discount has a reputation for paying its suppliers late and for insisting they accept return of unsold merchandise. Most suppliers put up with this because they fear losing Big Discount as a customer, which would precipitate a significant decline in their sales volume. Big Discount requires all its suppliers to agree to a standard set of contract terms. As general counsel for Big Discount, you are considering adding the following two clauses to all future sales contracts:

> Under no circumstances shall Supplier be entitled to demand adequate assurance of future performance or to suspend its performance pending receipt from Big Discount of assurances of future performance.
>
> Big Discount may, whenever it desires, demand from Supplier adequate assurance of Supplier's future performance. Such a demand may include whatever assurances of Supplier's performance that Big Discount deems appropriate. Upon such a demand, Big Discount may suspend its own performance until it receives from Supplier the assurances demanded.

Would these clauses be enforceable?   Why or why not?

B. REPUDIATION

We now come to the concept of repudiation. Repudiation is not the failure to tender performance when due. Failing to perform a contract obligation by the required time is a breach of contract, but it is not a repudiation. A party repudiates a contract obligation when, *before* performance is due, that party signals to the other that it will not perform as required. That signaling may either be an outright statement such as "I will not perform" or it might be more implicit, such as by taking actions that indicate that the promised performance will not be forthcoming.

The materials above should make it clear that if a party reasonably demands assurances of future performance under section 2-609, it may treat the other party's refusal to adequately respond as a repudiation. Repudiation may also come from the demand for assurances itself, if that demand is unjustified or otherwise unreasonable.[10] Less clear is whether repudiation can arise from circumstances other than the conduct or communications of a party. For example, suppose the buyer learns that the seller's only manufacturing facility was destroyed in a storm. Would that constitute a repudiation by the seller? Read comment 1 to section 2-610.

When faced with a repudiation, what options does the other party to the contract have? The traditional answer was that the non-repudiating party had to continue its own performance because the repudiating party could always change its mind and tender performance when its performance was due. The more modern approach is contained in section 2-610. Under that approach, if there is a repudiation *and* the loss of the repudiated performance "substantially impairs" the value of the contract to the other party, the non-repudiating party may suspend its own performance and either await performance by the repudiating party or resort to remedies for breach. We will study those remedies in Chapters Seven and Nine. If the non-repudiating party chooses to wait, the repudiating party may retract its repudiation. *See* UCC §§ 2-610(a), 2-611.

Although these rules are relatively clear in the abstract, they are quite murky in their application. Consider the uncertainty attendant in the parties' interaction. If a party thinks the other side has repudiated, suspends its own performance, and resorts to remedies for breach, a court might later determine that the other party did not in fact repudiate. As a result, the party that suspended its performance may have itself, by that act, breached the contract. The whole process of demanding adequate assurances or declaring that the other side has repudiated is a bit like a game of chicken. Whoever blinks first loses. If you can bluff or bully the other side into accepting your position, then you win. But if you can't, you risk being declared in breach and incurring all the liabilities therefor. A lawyer faced with a call from a client in this situation is wise to be cautious. Consider the following problem. In doing so, note that the first step in determining whether there is reasonable grounds

---

[10]   *See, e.g., Carnes Co. v. Stone Creek Mechanical Inc.*, 412 F.3d 845 (7th Cir. 2005) (party refusing to perform until other party covered costs it was not obligated to absorb was a repudiation); *Thunder Basin Coal Co. v. Southwestern Public Service Co.*, 104 F.3d 1205 (10th Cir. 1997) (buyer repudiated when it stated it would perform only in accord with its own interpretation of the contract).

for insecurity or a repudiation, is to determine what each parties' contract obligations are.

Problem 6-6

Buyer contracted with the Ace Supply Co. for Ace to furnish at a fixed price a large quantity of specially tooled valves for use in an improved line of equipment. Ace agreed to deliver the valves in six equal installments at three month intervals. Buyer stated that the installments were geared to a long range production schedule and a projected increase in demand for the equipment. Buyer furnished design drawings to assist Ace in "tooling up," gave Ace six months of lead time, and advanced 25% of the contract price. Two weeks before the first installment was due, Buyer appeared in your office with the following email from Ace:

> As suggested in our telephone conversation of last week, our engineers have determined that the design drawings which you furnished us were incomplete to produce the valves that you need, based upon the prototype we have developed from the drawings. As determined in discussions between your engineers and ours, we have revised the drawings but now must retool our original model valve at considerable additional expense and some delay. Due to this delay, we will not be able to deliver the first installment as originally scheduled. We expect that you will cover the extra expenses we will incur. We anticipate catching up by the time the second installment is due.

Buyer disputes that its drawings were in error and wants to end the contract and recover the 25% advance. Upon close questioning, you discover the following: (1) the delay in delivery will "wreak havoc" with Buyer's production schedule and existing contractual commitments; (2) if the contract were canceled, Buyer would purchase half of the quantity of valves called for in the contract from another manufacturer who guaranteed full performance in four months; (3) Buyer's estimated demand for the valves was about 50% too high; and (4) in Buyer's judgment, Ace would "probably" meet the next installment and make up the late deliveries. What is your advice?

CISG and UNIDROIT Principles. Under the CISG Article 71, a party may suspend performance if it is apparent that the other party will not perform a substantial part of that party's contract obligation. That suspension includes withholding delivery of the goods. The party suspending performance must give notice that it is suspending performance and must continue performance if the other party provides adequate assurance of performance. This suspension with notice process does not apply if it appears that the other party will commit a "fundamental breach" of the contract. In that case, the aggrieved party may declare the contract avoided. CISG Art. 72. In that circumstance, if time permits and if the other party has not affirmatively declared it will not perform, the aggrieved party must give notice and allow the other party to provide adequate assurance of performance. A breach is fundamental when "it results in such detriment to the other party as substantially to deprive him of what he is entitled to expect under the contract, unless the party in breach did not foresee and a reasonable person of the same kind in the same circumstances would not have foreseen such a result." CISG Art. 25.

The UNIDROIT Principles are similar. If it is clear that there will be a "fundamental non-performance" the aggrieved party may put an end to the contract or may demand adequate assurance and withhold its own performance. Failure to provide adequate assurance also gives the aggrieved party the ability to put an end to the contract. UNIDROIT Arts. 7.3.3 and 7.3.4.

SECTION 4. EXCUSE FROM PERFORMANCE

As the time for the parties to perform their respective contract obligations draws nigh, one or both of them may encounter circumstances that make performance impracticable or more difficult than anticipated. When a party encounters difficulty in performance, it may seek a modification of its contractual obligation. If the parties agree to a modification, then the party that encountered difficulty will not be seeking an excuse from its contact obligations. But if there is no agreed modification, a party that encounters such a problem may seek to be excused from performing its contract obligation because of it. Article 2 has several provisions that address this situation: sections 2-613 through 2-616. Before analyzing those sections, however, one fundamental point needs to be made.

Contracts are risk allocation devices. The seller and buyer agree that the seller will provide goods pursuant to the contract requirements and the buyer agrees to accept and pay for those conforming goods. UCC § 2-301. By engaging in those mutual promises, the buyer has, to some degree, accepted the risk that it may not need or want the goods. The seller, in turn, has accepted the risk that it may not be able to provide the goods on time or at all. The parties may have contemplated some of the risks that might interfere with those respective performances and included a term in their agreement that excuses one or both parties from certain specified risks. For example, the parties may have agreed that either party may be excused if a fire, flood or war, prevents that party from performing. Such a term is commonly called a "force majeure" clause.

The most interesting and difficult issues arise when the parties did not include a force majeure clause in their agreement or the problem that developed is outside the scope of whatever such clause their agreement does contain. Might a party in such a case still be excused from performing? How is a court to determine whether excusing performance would be consistent with the allocation of risks in the contract or contrary to it?

To illustrate with a simple example, assume Seller has agreed to sell a car to Buyer for a set price. The day before the scheduled delivery date, and before the risk of loss has passed to the buyer,[11] the nearby river floods, the car is engulfed in water, it floats down the river, and is totally destroyed. Seller asks Buyer to forget the whole deal because Seller can no longer tender the car. Buyer refuses, arguing that Seller had the risk that the car would be damaged or destroyed prior to delivery and demands that Seller either provide a substantially similar car for the original contract price or pay Buyer damages for breach. If Seller is excused from performance, Seller will still suffer the loss of the value of the car (at least if it was not fully insured) but Buyer will not be entitled to recover damages for breach of contract. If Seller is not excused from performance, Seller will have to pay damages to Buyer in addition to suffering the loss of the value of the car. Such damages would typically be measured by the difference between the value of the car promised and the contract price. *See* UCC § 2-713(1). The excuse doctrine allocates the loss from the car's destruction to either Seller or Buyer, but does not prevent the destruction of the car.

With this background in mind, turn your attention to the relevant UCC provisions. The four sections deal with at least four different types of problems:

---

[11]　*See* section 2-509, discussed in Chapter Four.

Problem	UCC Section(s)
Destruction of identified goods	§ 2-613
Obstruction of delivery method	§ 2-614(1)
Obstruction of payment method	§ 2-614(2)
Damage to production facilities or other interference with tender	§ 2-615 (seller's rights) § 2-616 (buyer's rights)

Section 2-613 deals with the destruction of goods identified to the contract when it was made and is premised upon the common-law doctrine of impossibility of performance.[12] A classic example would be the car scenario discussed on the previous page: a used car dealer contracts to sell a particular car to a buyer and, before delivery, the car is destroyed through no fault of the seller.

Section 2-614 does two things. First, under certain circumstances it excuses one party from using the delivery or payment mechanisms called for in the contract. Second, it then requires that the excused party use and the counter-party accept commercially reasonable substitutes.

Section 2-615 is the most difficult of the excuse rules to understand and apply. It rests on a concept called "impracticability,"[13] and excuses performance when the impracticability results from the occurrence of a contingency "the non-occurrence of which was a basic assumption on which the contract was made." Not every difficulty that arises makes performance impractical. For example, events giving rise to excuse under section 2-613 (casualty to identified goods) are not covered by section 2-615. *See* UCC § 2-615 cmt. 1. In addition, the official comments attempt to distinguish between market events – such as increases in the cost of raw materials – which do not give rise to excuse, and capacity events – such as a shutdown of major sources of supply – which do. *See* UCC § 2-615 cmt. 4.

A seller asserting excuse under section 2-615 must seasonably notify the buyer, and if its capacity to perform has been diminished but not destroyed, allocate its ability to perform among its customers in a reasonable manner. UCC § 2-615(b), (c). The buyer generally has the option, however, to terminate the contract rather than to accept less than full performance. UCC § 2-616.

---

[12] *Cf.* RESTATEMENT (SECOND) OF CONTRACTS § 263. The Restatement uses the term "impracticability" rather than "impossibility." *See id.* at Ch. 11, Reporter's Note.

[13] *Cf.* RESTATEMENT (SECOND) OF CONTRACTS § 261.

One other point is worth noting. All of these provisions are subject to contrary agreement. In other words, the parties may, in their agreement, expressly provide either for no excuse under any circumstances or for excuse on a more lenient standard. Section 2-615 makes this point expressly but even the other provisions are subject to variation by agreement. *See* UCC § 1-302.

Before you tackle the problems that follow, consider the following explanation of the principles of excuse from *Speciality Tires of America, Inc. v. The CIT Group/Equipment Financing, Inc.*, 82 F. Supp. 2d 434, 437–40 (W.D. Pa. 2000).

> In the overwhelming majority of circumstances, contractual promises are to be performed, not avoided: *pacta sunt servanda*, or, as the Seventh Circuit loosely translated it, "a deal's a deal." *Waukesha Foundry, Inc. v. Industrial Engineering, Inc.*, 91 F.3d 1002, 1010 (7th Cir. 1996). This is an eminently sound doctrine, because typically
>
> > a court cannot improve matters by intervention after the fact. It can only destabilize the institution of contract, increase risk, and make parties worse off. . . . Parties to contracts are entitled to seek, and retain, personal advantage; striving for that advantage is the source of much economic progress. Contract law does not require parties to be fair, or kind, or reasonable, or to share gains or losses equally.
>
> *Industrial Representatives, Inc. v. CP Clare Corp.*, 74 F.3d 128, 131–32 (7th Cir. 1996). Promisors are free to assume risks, even huge ones, and promisees are entitled to rely on those voluntary assumptions. JOHN D. CALAMARI & JOSEPH M. PERILLO, THE LAW OF CONTRACTS§ 13.16, at 522 (4th ed. 1998). Futures contracts, as just one example, are so aleatory that risk-bearing is their sole purpose, yet they are fully enforceable.
>
> Even so, courts have recognized, in an evolving line of cases from the common law down to the present, that there are limited instances in which unexpectedly and radically changed conditions render the judicial enforcement of certain promises of little or no utility. This has come to be known, for our purposes, as the doctrines of impossibility and impracticability. Because of the unexpected nature of such occurrences, litigated cases usually involve, not interpretation of a contractual term, but the judicial filling of a lacuna in the parties agreement. Such "gap- filling," however, must be understood for what it is: a court-ordered, as opposed to bargained-for, allocation of risk between the parties. As such, it must be applied sparingly.

Traditionally, there were three kinds of supervening events that would provide a legally cognizable excuse for failing to perform: death of the promisor (if the performance was personal), illegality of the performance, and destruction of the subject matter; beyond that the doctrine has grown to recognize that

> relief is most justified if unexpected events inflict a loss on one party and provide a windfall gain for the other or where the excuse would save one party from an unexpected loss while leaving the other party in a position no worse than it would have without the contract.

CALAMARI & PERILLO, *supra* § 13.1, at 496. Thus, the Second Restatement of Contracts expresses the doctrine of impracticability this way:

> Where, after a contract is made, a party's performance is made impracticable without his fault by the occurrence of an event the non-occurrence of which was a basic assumption on which the contract was made, his duty to render that performance is discharged, unless the language or the circumstances indicate the contrary.

RESTATEMENT (SECOND) OF CONTRACTS § 261 (1981). Article 2 of the U.C.C., which applies to the sale of goods presented by the case *sub judice*, puts it similarly:

> Delay in delivery or non-delivery in whole or in part by a seller . . . is not a breach of his duty under a contract for sale if performance as agreed has been made impracticable by the occurrence of a contingency the non-occurrence of which was a basic assumption on which the contract was made. . . .

U.C.C. § 2-615(1).

The principal inquiry in an impracticability analysis, then, is whether there was a contingency the non-occurrence of which was a basic assumption underlying the contract. It is often said that this question turns on whether the contingency was "foreseeable," on the rationale that if it was, the promisor could have sought to negotiate explicit contractual protection. This, however, is an incomplete and sometimes misleading test. Anyone can foresee, in some general sense, a whole variety of potential calamities, but that does not mean that he or she will deem them worth bargaining over. *See* CALAMARI & PERILLO, *supra* § 13.18, at 526; JOHN E. MURRAY, MURRAY ON CONTRACTS, § 112, at 641 (3d ed. 1990) ("If 'foreseeable' is equated with 'conceivable', nothing is unforeseeable").

The risk may be too remote, the party may not have sufficient bargaining power, or neither party may have any superior ability to avoid the harm. As my late colleague Judge Teitelbaum recited two decades ago in a famous case of impracticability:

> Foreseeability or even recognition of a risk does not necessarily prove its allocation. Parties to a contract are not always able to provide for all the possibilities of which they are aware, sometimes because they cannot agree, often because they are too busy. Moreover, that some abnormal risk was contemplated is probative but does not necessarily establish an allocation of the risk of the contingency which actually occurs.

Aluminum Co. of Am. v. Essex Group, Inc., 499 F. Supp. 53, 76 (W.D. Pa. 1980) (applying Indiana law) (quoting *Transatlantic Financing Corp. v. United States,* 363 F.2d 312 (D.C. Cir. 1966)). So, while the risk of an unforeseeable event can safely be deemed not to have been assumed by the promisor, the converse is not necessarily true. *See* RESTATEMENT (SECOND) OF CONTRACTS § 261 cmt. c. Properly seen, then, foreseeability, while perhaps the most important factor,

> is at best one fact to be considered in resolving first how likely the occurrence of the event in question was and, second, whether its occurrence, based on past experience, was of such reasonable likelihood that the obligor should not merely foresee the risk but, because of the degree of its likelihood, the obligor should have guarded against it or provided for non-liability against the risk.

Wolf Trap, 817 F.2d at 1102–03.[14]

It is also commonly said that the standard of impossibility is objective rather than subjective – that the question is whether the thing can be done, not whether the promisor can do it. This too is more truism than test, although Pennsylvania courts have couched their decisions in this rhetoric. Indeed, the FIRST RESTATEMENT took such an approach, but the SECOND simply applies "the rationale . . . that a party generally assumes the risk of his own inability to perform his duty." . . . This holds particularly when

---

[14]　Another respected text defines the unforeseeable as "an event so unlikely to occur that reasonable parties see no need explicitly to allocate the risk of its occurrence, although the impact it might have would be of such magnitude that the parties would have negotiated over it, had the event been more likely." CALAMARI & PERILLO, *supra*, § 13.18, at 526.

the duty is merely to pay money . . . . It is therefore "preferable to say that such ['subjective'] risks as these are generally considered to be sufficiently within the control of one party that they are assumed by that party." 2 E. ALLAN FARNSWORTH, FARNSWORTH ON CONTRACTS § 9.6, at 619-20 (2d ed.1998). It is, of course, essential that the impossibility asserted by the promisor as a defense not have been caused by the promisor. *Id.* § 9.6, at 613–14.

Generally speaking, while loss, destruction or a major price increase of fungible goods will not excuse the seller's duty to perform, the rule is different when the goods are unique, have been identified to the contract or are to be produced from a specific, agreed-upon source. In such a case, the nonexistence or unavailability of a specific thing will establish a defense of impracticability. Thus, § 263 of the Second Restatement recites:

> If the existence of a specific thing is necessary for the performance of a duty, its failure to come into existence, destruction, or such deterioration as makes performance impracticable is an event the non-occurrence of which was a basic assumption on which the contract was made.

Problem 6-7

Seller, an art dealer, owned an etching by Picasso. Buyer, a collector, examined it at Seller's gallery and, after negotiations, Seller agreed to sell it to Buyer for $75,000. Under the written contract for sale, Buyer was to return with a cashier's check the next day and pick up the etching. Buyer returned check in hand but, alas, the Picasso was destroyed by fire during the night.

A. What are the rights and duties of the parties? *See* UCC §§ 2-613, 2-509. Would it matter what caused the fire? Suppose the fire was caused by a neglected coffee pot, a short in the wiring, or a lightening strike? *See* UCC § 2-613 & cmt. 1.

B. Suppose, instead, that the Picasso, unknown to Seller, had been stolen and was replevied from Seller by the true owner prior to Buyer's return rather than destroyed by fire? Any difference in analysis?

C. Assume that Seller had agreed to sell to Buyer print #10 from a series. After the agreement was made, print #10 was damaged by water. Seller has in its possession print #12, undamaged, from the same series. Is Seller excused from delivery?

D. In any case in which Seller would be able to be excused under section 2-613, what are Buyer's options?

Problem 6-8

Can UCC § 2-613 apply to fungible goods? If so, construct a scenario in which the seller of fungible goods would be excused from performance because of a casualty to the goods.

Problem 6-9

Supersonic Motors, Inc. manufactures rotor blades for jet engines. Its customers include several domestic defense contractors who manufacture aircraft for the U.S. military and several makers of civilian aircraft. On October 1, Supersonic agreed in writing to sell 60,000 rotor blades to Bingo Aircraft, a Seattle-based manufacturer of aircraft. The agreement calls for delivery of 5,000 rotor blades on the first day of each of the next twelve months.

A. In which, if any, of the following scenarios, would Supersonic be excused from performing in whole or in part?

1. Because of an economic boom in China and several developing countries, and the concomitant increase in the demand for industrial metals, the price of the aluminum and titanium that Supersonic needs to manufacture rotor blades has tripled since it entered into the agreement with Bingo. Performance under the contract with Bingo would now cause Supersonic to lose money.

2. Because of a strike by the Industrial Metal Workers of the World, Supersonic cannot get from any supplier the metal it needs to manufacture the rotor blades. No one knows how long the strike will last.

3. Because of a strike by Supersonic's employees, Supersonic cannot manufacture the rotor blades called for under the contract with Bingo. No one knows how long the strike will last.

4. Because of a strike by the nation's rail workers, Bingo cannot ship the rotor blades to Bingo by rail, as was anticipated. Shipment by truck would be possible but far more expensive and would significantly increase the chance of damage to the rotor blades during transit. No one knows how long the rail strike will last.

5. Because of a fire at Supersonic's only manufacturing plant, Supersonic cannot manufacture the rotor blades on time and it anticipates at least a four-month delay in its ability to deliver the goods.

B. On October 15, a freak meteor storm severely damages Supersonic's only manufacturing plant. It will take about ten months to repair the facility and resume normal production. Supersonic's warehouse of rotor blades was also damaged but 60,000 rotor blades of the type called for by the contract with Bingo were undamaged. Supersonic also has a contract to sell 120,000 rotor blades to BusAir. Supersonic now has to determine how to allocate the undamaged rotor blades between Bingo and BusAir?

1. Would it be permissible to sell all 60,000 to Bingo and none to BusAir, on the ground that this would at least make one customer happy?

2. Would it be permissible to sell all of the rotor blades to BusAir if BusAir is a regular customer and Bingo is not?

3. Would it be permissible to sell all of the rotor blades to whichever customer is willing to pay the most?

4. Would it be permissible to favor a customer that needs the rotor blades to manufacture military aircraft over a customer that needs the rotor blades to manufacture civilian aircraft?

Buyer's excuse. Neither section 2-613 nor 2-615 purport to excuse the buyer from performing; both provide relief only for sellers. Does that mean the buyer is never excused from performance based on unforeseen events? Consider Judge Posner's words:

Since impossibility and related doctrines are devices for shifting risk in accordance with the parties' presumed intentions, which are to minimize the costs of contract performance, one of which is the disutility created by risk, they have no place when the contract explicitly assigns a particular risk to one party or the other. As we have already noted, a fixed-price contract is an explicit assignment of the risk of market price increases to the seller and the risk of market price decreases to the buyer, and the assignment of the latter risk to the buyer is even clearer where, as in this case, the contract places a floor under price but allows for escalation. If, as is also the case here, the buyer forecasts the market incorrectly and therefore finds himself locked into a disadvantageous contract, he has only himself to blame and so cannot shift the risk back to the buyer by invoking impossibility or related doctrines. . . . Since "the very purpose of a fixed price agreement is to place the risk of increased costs on the promisor (and the risk of decreased costs on the promisee)," the fact that costs decrease steeply . . . cannot allow the buyer to walk away from the contract.[15]

Does Judge Posner's view hold force when the buyer is seeking to be excused because of a significant change in the market due to an event such as widespread flooding, acts of terrorism, war, or a change in government regulation? Suppose a new government regulation mandates that users of natural gas implement costly environmental controls and, because of that, the buyer cannot use as much natural gas as the contract calls for.[16] What if the buyer's whole purpose for the goods has been frustrated? Does the common-law doctrine of frustration of purpose remain available to help the buyer? See UCC §§ 1-103(b), 2-615 cmt. 9 ("the reason of the present section may well apply and entitle the buyer to the exemption").[17] Consider the following two problems.

Problem 6-10

Plumber and Supplier are both located in Microville, a small town that recently announced plans to build a sewer system to replace existing septic tanks. After Microville informed Plumber that Plumber was the low bidder on the sewer system installation contract, Plumber contracted to buy from Supplier 12,000 tube fittings. These fittings are used to connect residential plumbing to a central sewer system; they have no other use. Microville then decided that the sewer system was too expensive and would not be built.

A. Is Plumber entitled to any relief from the contract with Supplier?

B. The agreement between Plumber and Supplier provided that Plumber would pay for the tube fittings through a funds transfer from Plumber's

---

[15]   *Northern Indiana Public Service Co. v. Carbon County Coal Company*, 799 F.2d 265, 278 (7th Cir. 1986).

[16]   *See International Minerals & Chemical Corp. v. Llano, Inc.*, 770 F.2d 879 (10th Cir.), *cert. denied*, 475 U.S. 1015 (1986) (excusing the buyer from taking all the gas contracted for). *Compare* RESTATEMENT (SECOND) OF CONTRACTS § 264.

[17]   *Compare* RESTATEMENT (SECOND) OF CONTRACTS § 265.

bank, Great Northern Bank. Yesterday, Great Northern Bank was taken over by federal regulators and Plumber's deposit account was frozen. Supplier is ready to deliver the fittings and Plumber has asserted it is excused from performing the contract with Supplier. Is Plumber correct?

Problem 6-11

Trucking Services, Inc. has a fleet of semi-trailer trucks engaged in hauling goods across the country. In 2006, Trucking Services entered into a five-year contract with Oil Supply Co. for diesel fuel at a fixed price of $2.50 per gallon for the first year. The agreement calls for the price in subsequent years to be computed each December 1 based upon the wholesale price charged by Exxon Corp. at a refinery in Mississippi, plus 5 cents.

On December 1, 2006, the fuel for the second year was re-priced at $2.60 per gallon. On December 1, 2007, the fuel was re-priced for the third year at $3.40 per gallon. During the first six months of 2008, the wholesale price in the market went to $4.50 per gallon due to political unrest in the Middle East, insurgent activity in Africa, and storms in the Gulf of Mexico that reduced the production capacity of several hundred drilling platforms and oil refineries.

Exxon Corp. has refused to honor its long-term contract to sell diesel fuel to Oil Supply Co., which similarly called for a fixed price subject to annual re-pricing based on the wholesale price charged by Exxon Corp. at a refinery in Mississippi. As a result, instead of making 5¢ per gallon on its contract with Trucking Services, Oil Supply Co. is losing more than $1 per gallon (because it must buy at the wholesale market price and then sell at the substantially lower contract price), and is facing severe financial distress. Oil Supply Co. wants to renegotiate its deal with Trucking Services but Trucking Services has refused. You represent Oil Supply Co.

A. What advice would you give?
B. If you could redraft the agreement between Oil Supply Co. and Trucking Services, what would you provide in that agreement?
C. If you could redraft the agreement between Oil Supply Co. and Exxon, what would you provide in that agreement?

CISG and UNIDROIT Principles.[18] CISG Article 79 addresses excuse from performance. A party may be excused if it proves that the "failure was due to an impediment beyond his control and that he could not reasonably be expected to have taken the impediment into account" at the time the contract was formed, or that could not be avoided, or overcome. The party seeking excuse under this provision must give timely notice to the other party.

The UNIDROIT Principles have a provision that is very similar to CISG Art. 79. UNIDROIT Art. 7.1.7. In addition, the Principles address "hardship where the occurrence of events fundamentally alters the equilibrium of the contract either because the cost of a party's performance has increased or because the value of the performance a party receives has diminished" and those events were not reasonably foreseeable and were beyond the control of the parties. UNIDROIT Art. 6.2.2. In the case of hardship, a party may request renegotiation from the other party and if unable to reach agreement, may go to court for a readjustment of the benefits and burdens of the contract. UNIDROIT Art. 6.2.3.

---

[18]   For a discussion of excuse in the international arena, *see* Carla Spivack, *Of Shrinking Sweatsuits and Poison Vine Wax: A Comparison of Basis for Excuse Under U.C.C. § 2-615 and CISG Article 79*, 27 U. PA. J. INT'L ECON. L. 757 (2006); Francesco G. Mazzotta, *Why Do Some American Courts Fail to Get it Right?*, 3 LOY. U. CHI. INT'L L. REV. 85 (2005); Catherine Kessedjian, *Competing Approaches to Force Majeure and Hardship*, 25 INT'L REV. L. & ECON. 415 (2005).

CHAPTER SEVEN
BUYER'S REMEDIES FOR SELLER'S BREACH

SECTION 1. OVERVIEW

This Chapter addressed the various ways in which a seller may breach a contract for the sale of goods and the remedies the buyer has for that breach under Article 2. The next Chapter explores the buyer's rights and remedies under other law. Chapter Nine then considers the ways in which the buyer may breach and the seller's concomitant remedies for those breaches.

Determining breach. The place to start in determining whether the seller has breached is to identify the terms of the contract. In an Article 2 contract, the basic obligation of the seller is to deliver goods that conform to the contract requirements. UCC § 2-301. Obviously, everything that we have studied up to this point in time is important in determining whether the seller has complied with that obligation. The parties' agreement – including both express terms and terms implied through course of performance, course of dealing, and usage of trade – along with the Article 2 gap fillers, determine the seller's obligations on such matters as the type, quantity, and quality of the goods, the time for delivery, and the method of delivery. All of these items comprise the contract obligation.

Even after the terms are identified, it may not be entirely clear which party has breached. This is true for several reasons. First, many of the parties' obligations are couched in terms of reasonable behavior,[1] and parties may disagree over what is reasonable. Second, other obligations may be based on similarly vague or indefinite standards that are difficult to apply.[2] Third, the parties may slide into a

---

[1] *See, e.g.,* UCC §§ 2-306(1) (requiring that a quantity demanded in a requirements or output contract not be unreasonably disproportionate to a stated estimate or normal needs or output); 2-309(1) (requiring the seller to ship or deliver within a reasonable time); 2-503(1) (requiring that the seller's tender of the goods be at a reasonable hour, be held open for a reasonable time, and be accompanied by a notification reasonably necessary to enable the buyer to take delivery); 2-504(a) (requiring a seller to make a reasonable contract for the shipment of goods); 2-513(1) and 2-606(1)(b) (collectively giving the buyer a reasonable time to inspect the goods).

[2] *See, e.g.,* § 2-314(2) (requiring that goods, to be merchantable, pass without objection in the trade, be of fair average quality, be fit for their ordinary purpose, and be adequately contained, packaged, and labeled).

dispute in such a way that it is unclear who was the first to act improperly. For example, and as discussed in Chapter Six, consider a scenario in which a buyer asks for adequate assurances, the seller does not respond, and then the buyer refuses to go forward with the deal. The seller's failure to provide assurances might constitute a breach through repudiation. However, if the buyer was not entitled to request assurances, perhaps because the buyer had no reasonable grounds for insecurity, the seller's failure to respond would not be a repudiation and the buyer's later refusal to go forward would constitute a breach. Only after determining which party has breached the contract can one determine what remedies for that breach are available to the aggrieved party.

Finally, even if it is clear which party failed to perform, that failure may have been excused. For example, and as we also saw in Chapter Six, a seller who fails to tender the goods may be excused if the goods were destroyed through no fault of the seller. The buyer in that case will neither get the goods nor have a cause of action for breach.

It is also worth remembering that, even if you are certain that the seller breached, the parties may have limited the remedies available for that breach. As discussed in Chapter Five, the parties are generally free to limit or exclude the remedies normally available for breach through well-drafted disclaimers or liquidated damages clauses. So, in this Chapter, we will assume that the parties have an agreement that is enforceable (*i.e.,* a contract) under Article 2 (see Chapter Two), the seller has breached one or more obligations in the contract (see Chapters Three and Four), the buyer's remedies for breach have not been limited (see Chapter Five), and the seller's breach is not excused (see Chapter Six).

Typical seller's breaches and buyer's responses. There are several different ways in which a seller can breach a sales contract, and the remedies available to the buyer depend on the nature of the seller's breach. First, the seller may simply fail to tender any goods at all. This may occur if, prior to the time for tender, the seller repudiated the contract. Alternatively, the seller may fail to provide the goods without previously informing the buyer that no goods will be forthcoming. In each of these circumstances, the buyer has two basic remedy options: (i) seek specific performance – that is, use court processes to attempt to force the contracted goods out of the seller and recover damages from the seller for the delay; or (ii) cancel the contract and seek monetary damages from the seller measured either by the cost of a replacement transaction or by the market price of the goods. We will study these options in Section 2 of this Chapter.

Second, the seller may breach by making an improper tender. This could be as simple as tendering the goods after the time for doing so has expired or by tendering goods that are defective or otherwise fail to meet the contract requirements. In such cases, the buyer again has two basic choices: (i) reject the goods, cancel the contract with the seller, and seek monetary damages for the breach measured either by the cost of a replacement transaction or the market price of the goods; or (ii) accept the goods and seek damages measured by the reduction in value attributable to the nonconformity. Sometimes, the nonconformity is not apparent when the goods are tendered and the buyer accepts the goods unaware of the problem and therefore unaware of the right to reject them. For example, there might be microscopic cracks in metal girders that render them unfit for their ordinary purpose. Other goods may lack the tensile strength, elasticity, colorfastness, or viscosity specified in the contract. In some of these circumstances, the buyer who has accepted the goods may be able to revoke acceptance of the goods. That is, the buyer may be able to return the goods to the seller and seek damages as if the buyer had rejected the goods initially. We will study the buyer's rejection, acceptance, and revocation of acceptance remedies in Section 3 of this Chapter.

Finally, the seller may tender the goods and fail to perform installation services, or repair services as specified in the parties' agreement, or may perform those ancillary services in an unsatisfactory manner. The buyer's typical option in these cases is to recover damages for the harm caused by that breach. Article 2 does not contain any specific remedy provisions regarding remedies for breach of the seller's obligation to provide ancillary services, but does not preclude application of common-law concepts regarding damage remedies. UCC § 1-103.

All of the buyer's remedial options are grounded in the traditional principle of contract law of protecting the buyer's expectation interest. That is, all are designed to put the aggrieved buyer in the position it would have been in if the contract had been performed. UCC § 1-305. Given that perspective, and the common-law view that a contract breach is not a moral wrong, punitive damages are not generally available for breach of a sales contract. *See* UCC § 1-305 (prohibiting punitive damages except where specifically allowed).[3]

---

[3]   The common law of contracts does allow for punitive damages if there is an independent tort and some sort of wilfulness or malice. *See* RESTATEMENT (SECOND) OF CONTRACTS § 355; *McIntosh v. Magna Systems, Inc.*, 539 F. Supp. 1185 (N.D. Ill. 1982). Given that the usual breaches of sales contracts do not involve malice and the parties' obligation of "good faith" is not an independent obligation, UCC § 1-304, punitive damages are generally not available in Article 2 cases.

Although the buyer's remedies under Article 2 are designed to protect the buyer's expectancy, Article 2 does not simply codify that principle. Instead, it contains several specific rules, each applicable to one or more of the situations described above. The starting point for analyzing these statutory provisions is section 2-711, which provides an *incomplete* list of options. The other relevant provisions are sections 2-502, 2-712, 2-713, 2-714, 2-715, 2-716, and 2-717.

After discussing these remedies for the seller's breach, this Chapter then explores three additional topics. Section 4 addresses the effect of the seller's breach on the risk of loss for the goods. Section 5 address how the statute of limitations affects the buyer's ability to pursue remedies for the seller's breach. Section 6 then considers the buyer's remedies under Article 2 against a remote seller of the goods.

SECTION 2. SELLER'S REPUDIATION OR FAILURE TO TENDER GOODS

Assume the seller has repudiated its contract obligations or failed to tender the goods at the time required by the contract. Section 2-711 provides the buyer with two basic options: (i) attempt to recover the goods from the seller or (ii) cancel the contract with the seller and seek damages for the seller's breach. We first consider the ability of the buyer to obtain the goods from the seller and then consider the buyer's right to cancel the contract and sue the seller for damages.

A. BUYER'S ABILITY TO OBTAIN THE GOODS FROM THE SELLER

Article 2 gives an aggrieved buyer the right to force the seller to tender the goods in several limited circumstances. Read sections 2-716 and 2-502. These two sections cover three basic situations:

§ 2-716(1)	Specific Performance
§ 2-716(3)	Replevin of Identified Goods
§ 2-502	Recovery by a Pre-paying Buyer

To use one of these remedies, the buyer must obtain a court order. None of these remedies allows the buyer to engage in "self-help" behavior to get the goods from the seller.

First consider the remedy of specific performance. Under general contract law, specific performance – that is, a court order requiring the breaching party to perform its contract obligations – is not the usual remedy. The customary remedy is an award of monetary damages. An order for specific performance, which is a type of injunction, requires the requesting party to demonstrate that it is entitled to such equitable relief. That generally requires proof that an award of monetary damages would be inadequate, that the specific performance order would not be unduly difficult for the court to enforce or supervise, and that the order would not cause undue hardship or be unfair under the circumstances. The decision whether to award specific performance is within the discretion of the court.[4]

Article 2 builds upon this common-law foundation and slightly broadens the grounds for granting specific performance of a sales contract. Read section 2-716(1) and (2). There are two things worth noting about these provisions. First, subsection (1) provides that specific performance "may" be decreed. It does not purport to mandate specific performance in any instance.[5] Thus, the common-law limitations on specific performance presumably remain relevant.

Second, subsection (1) refers to two different circumstances when specific performance may be appropriate: (i) when the goods are unique; and (ii) other proper circumstances. The reason why specific performance may be available to contracts involving unique goods is easy to appreciate. In such cases, the buyer has no other source for the goods. Thus, if the Smithsonian were to contract to sell the Hope Diamond or the *Spirit of St. Louis* to another museum, that other museum would likely have a good claim to specific performance in the event the Smithsonian failed or refused to perform.[6]

---

[4]   *See* RESTATEMENT (SECOND) OF CONTRACTS §§ 357–69; Steven Shavell, *Specific Performance versus Damages for Breach of Contract; An Economic Analysis*, 84 TEX. L. REV. 831 (2006); Melvin A. Eisenberg, *Actual and Virtual Specific Performance, The Theory of Efficient Breach, and the Indifference Principle in Contract Law*, 93 CAL. L. REV. 975 (2005).

[5]   *See also* UCC § 2-716 cmt. 1 (similarly indicating that the remedy remains within "the court's sound discretion").

[6]   *See* RESTATEMENT (SECOND) OF CONTRACTS § 360, cmt. c.

Problem 7-1

Construct a scenario in which the goods contracted for are not unique but a decree of specific performance would nevertheless be appropriate.

Problem 7-2

You represent the buyer in a proposed sale of goods transaction. Although the goods involved are not unique, the buyer is adamant about avoiding the hassle, delay, and expense associated with finding another source of supply in the event the seller chooses not to perform. If you include a clause in the written agreement purporting to make an award of specific performance available in the event of the seller's breach, will such a clause be enforceable? Why or why not?

As an alternative to specific performance, the buyer could assert a right to replevy identified goods. Read section 2-716(3). Because replevin is a legal right, not an equitable remedy, it is not subject to judicial discretion or to the other limitations on the award of specific performance. A court will order replevin if the buyer proves that it has a right to possession of the goods that is superior to the rights of the seller.[7] Section 2-716(3) provides two grounds for assertion of that superior right to possession: (i) the buyer is unable to effect cover for goods – that is, the buyer cannot find substitute goods elsewhere; or (ii) the seller has shipped the goods under reservation, thereby in effect retaining a security interest in the goods to secure the buyer's obligation to pay the purchase price,[8] and the buyer has tendered the amount due. Both of these grounds require that the goods be identified to the contract.

Now read section 2-502, which allows a buyer who has prepaid in whole or part for the goods identified to the contract to assert a right to recover the goods. This right also applies to two different circumstances: (i) when the goods are purchased for personal, family, or household purposes; or (ii) when the seller becomes insolvent within ten days after receipt of the first payment.

---

[7]   State procedural statutes may have other requirements for ordering replevin such as posting a bond, if the replevin order is obtained before a final trial on the merits of the dispute between the buyer and the seller.

[8]   *See* UCC § 2-505.

Unlike the specific performance remedy, both the right of replevin in section 2-716(3) and the right to recover goods in section 2-502 require that the goods be identified to the contract for sale. Read section 2-501 on how the goods become identified to the contract for sale. Identification is the moment when the buyer begins to acquire property rights in specific goods (in addition to contract rights against the seller) and it typically occurs when the seller indicates which goods will be used to fulfill its obligations under this particular contract with this particular buyer.

It is important to emphasize, absent the buyer's successful exercise of a right to obtain the goods pursuant to sections 2-502 or 2-716, or the buyer obtaining an Article 9 security interest in the goods to secure the seller's obligation to deliver them to the buyer,[9] the buyer has no other right to force the goods out of the seller's hands. Thus, merely prepaying for the goods gives a buyer no right to extract the goods from the seller.

A buyer who obtains a court order requiring the seller to tender the goods is liable to pay the seller the unpaid portion of the contract price. That point is made expressly in section 2-502(1) but is no doubt also true with respect to situations covered by section 2-716. *See* UCC §§ 2-607, 2-709. Does such a buyer have a damage remedy for the harm caused by the delay in delivery? *See* UCC §§ 2-715, 1-103, 1-305. *Compare* UCC §§ 2-712(2), 2-713(1), 2-714(3).

Problem 7-3

A. Buyer contracted to purchase Seller's car for $5,000. At the time for delivery, Seller refused to deliver the car. In which of the scenarios depicted in the chart that follows, if any, will Buyer be able to obtain the car?

---

[9]   In that circumstance, Article 9 governs the buyer's right to recover the goods from the seller. *See generally* UCC § 9-609 (allowing self help repossession for the secured party (the buyer) in the event of the debtor's (the seller) default, as long as such repossession can be conducted without a breach of the peace); Thomas H. Jackson & Anthony T. Kronman, *A Plea for the Financing Buyer*, 85 YALE L.J. 1 (1975).

	Buyer made a $1,000 down payment	Buyer made no down payment
Buyer wants the car for family purposes		
Buyer wants the car for business purposes		

B. Seller contracted to manufacture and sell to Buyer award plaques for Buyer's top producing sales representatives. Buyer planned to present the plaques at a special ceremony at Buyer's annual shareholders meeting. One week before the delivery date under the contract, and before any plaques had been manufactured, Seller repudiated the contract.

1. Will Buyer be able to obtain the plaques from Seller?
2. How, if at all, would the analysis change if Seller had started to manufacture the plaques but repudiated the contract before it completed the manufacturing process?

C. On June 1, Steel Supplier contracted to sell to Builder 6,000 steel beams for use in one of Builder's construction projects. Although Builder did not know it, on that date Steel Supplier was insolvent. The contract called for Builder to make an initial $100,000 payment on June 15. The balance of the purchase price was due upon delivery, which was slated for July 1. Builder made the first payment on June 15. The following day, Steel Supplier segregated 6,000 steel beams from the remainder of its industry and marked them for shipment to Builder. Two days later, Steel Supplier informed Builder that it was insolvent and repudiated the contract. Is Builder entitled to recover the steel beams from Steel Supplier?

CISG and UNIDROIT Principles. CISG Article 46 allows a buyer to obtain specific performance of the seller's obligations unless the buyer has resorted to an inconsistent remedy. In some circumstances the buyer may be able to compel the seller to deliver substitute goods or to repair defective goods. CISG Article 28, however, allows a court to refuse to order specific performance, even if the buyer would be entitled to it under Article 46, if the domestic law of that court would not allow for specific performance in that circumstance.[10]

Under the UNIDROIT Principles, Article 7.2.2 allows for specific performance of non-monetary obligations subject to certain exceptions. Specific performance will not be required if performance is impossible, unduly burdensome, or uniquely personal. The requesting party may also not obtain specific performance if it could obtain substitute performance elsewhere or has unreasonably delayed the request for specific performance.

B. BUYER'S RIGHT TO CANCEL THE CONTRACT AND OBTAIN DAMAGES

If either the buyer is not entitled to get the goods from the seller who fails to deliver, or the buyer chooses not to try, the buyer may cancel the contract and seek monetary damages from the seller. UCC § 2-711(1).

Buyer's cancellation of the contract. When a buyer justifiably cancels a contract, the buyer's duty to perform under the contract is discharged but the buyer nevertheless retains its rights to obtain damages for the seller's breach. Cancellation in effect means that the buyer no longer expects the seller to perform and that the buyer will not be rendering any more performance. Read section 2-106(3) and (4). Article 2 does not prescribe any procedure for cancelling a contract and does not require that the buyer notify the seller that the contract has been cancelled. Indeed, the buyer should be careful in communicating with the seller; any notification of cancellation should not impair or discharge its right to obtain damages. *See* UCC § 1-306.

Damages. As noted above, the buyer's damage remedies are based upon the expectation principle; they seek to place the buyer in the position the buyer would have been in if the seller had fully performed. UCC § 1-305. When the seller has not delivered the goods, the buyer is entitled to a return of any price that has been paid. UCC § 2-711(1). In addition to recovering the price that has been pre-paid, the buyer has two different options for measuring its expectation interest. First, the

---

[10]   Harry M. Flechtner, *Buyers' Remedies in General and Buyers' Performance-Oriented Remedies*, 25 J.L. & COM. 339 (2005); Steven Walt, *For Specific Performance Under the United Nations Sales Convention*, 26 TEX. INT'L L.J. 211 (1991).

buyer may obtain substitute goods from someone else – that is, "cover" – and obtain damages from the seller measured by "the difference between the cost of cover and the contract price." UCC § 2-712(2). Let's pause for a moment. Consider which of the following two computations that phrase contemplates:

$$\text{damages} \;=\; \text{cost of cover} \;-\; \text{contract price}$$

$$\text{damages} \;=\; \text{contract price} \;-\; \text{cost of cover}$$

Even a moment's reflection should tell you that the buyer is damaged by the seller's non-delivery only if the cost of cover exceeds the contract price (so that the buyer paid more to acquire the goods from someone else than the buyer would have paid under the contract if the seller had performed). If the cost of cover was less than the contract price, the buyer is not damaged by – and in fact benefitted from – the seller's breach. Thus, the statutory formula is the first one listed above, not the second.

Alternatively, the aggrieved buyer may recover the difference between the market price and the contract price of the goods. UCC § 2-713. Consider which of the following is the proper expression of that formula:

$$\text{damages} \;=\; \text{market price} \;-\; \text{contract price}$$

$$\text{damages} \;=\; \text{contract price} \;-\; \text{market price}$$

In both cases – cover damages and market damages – the buyer may also recover incidental and consequential damages. UCC § 2-715. To illustrate the relationship between the specific damage remedies in Article 2 and the expectation principle, consider this example.

Example

State Street Motors contracts to sell a new car to Buyer for $40,000. Buyer pays $1,000 down and promises to pay the $39,000 balance upon delivery, which is slated to occur in two weeks (when State Street Motors expects to obtain the car from the manufacturer).

On the date for delivery, State Street Motors refuses to sell the car to Buyer. Perhaps State Street Motors was unable to obtain the car from the manufacturer, but the reason is not material. The point is, State Street Motors breaches by failing to tender performance. Buyer cancels the contract and State Street Motors becomes obligated to return the $1,000 down payment to Buyer. UCC § 2-711(1).

If, as is likely, the market price for such cars is fairly stable and, as is also likely, the $40,000 contract price was the car's fair market value – *i.e.*, was at the market price – Buyer is unlikely to have any damages. Buyer can probably find another seller willing to sell an identical car for $40,000. Whether Buyer chooses to purchase a car from another seller or not will make no difference. In either case, Buyer will have no other remedy (save perhaps a few incidental or consequential damages). The same would be true if the market price at the time for delivery were less than $40,000. Not only would Buyer have no additional damages, but Buyer would actually be better off because of the breach by State Street Motors: Buyer will have been excused from paying more for the car than it is worth.

If, on the other hand, the market price of the car at the time for delivery is $42,000 – which may be the case if the market price had risen after the original contract was formed or if the contract price had been below market at the time the parties reached their agreement – then Buyer will have two options. If Buyer purchases an identical car from another seller for $42,000, Buyer can recover the $2,000 difference between the original contract price and the cost of cover from State Street Motors. UCC § 2-712 (cover price minus contract price). After doing so, Buyer will be in the same economic situation as if the transaction with State Street Motors had been performed: Buyer will have a car and will have paid a net amount of $40,000 ($1,000 down payment + $42,000 cover price – return of $1,000 down payment – $2,000 in cover damages).

If Buyer does not purchase a substitute car, Buyer's expectation damages will be the same, but will be based on the market price of the car rather than the cost of cover. UCC § 2-713(1) (market price – contract price).

As you can see by this example, the remedial formulas are based upon the assumption that the cover price or the market price represents the value of the goods and that the aggrieved buyer has been damaged if it does not receive the full value of the goods to the extent that value exceeds the contract price for the goods.

Damages based on the cover price. An aggrieved buyer is not required to cover but often has both business and legal incentives to do so. From a business perspective, the buyer may need the goods for use in manufacturing or to otherwise maintain its operations. From a legal perspective, the buyer's ability to recover consequential damages depends upon whether the buyer has engaged in reasonable efforts to mitigate the harm caused by the breach. UCC § 2-715(2). For example, if failure to receive the goods will significantly disrupt the buyer's manufacturing or other operations such as by causing delay, obtaining substitute goods is often one relatively easy way to mitigate that type of consequential harm.[11]

In order to qualify as a cover transaction for purposes of section 2-712, the cover transaction must be made in good faith and without unreasonable delay. UCC § 2-712(1). These limitations are important to prevent the buyer from playing the market at the seller's expense. For example, if the market price for the goods fluctuates, the buyer – even one who needs the goods and knows it will eventually cover – might wait before entering into a cover transaction. If the market price goes down, the buyer pays less for the substitute goods and pockets the difference. If the market price rises, the buyer spends more but then seeks to treat the added cost as cover damages. The requirements that cover be effected in good faith and without unreasonable delay insulate the seller from this risk.

The good faith requirement may also help reduce the buyer's incentive to not seek the best price it could get for the cover transaction. Generally if someone else is paying the bill, there might be little incentive to obtain the goods at a reasonable price. The issue is whether the seller should be forced to pay a higher damage amount because the buyer did not take appropriate action under the circumstances to find the best price for the goods. While the price the buyer pays for the cover goods need not be the lowest possible price, the good faith limitation on recovering cover based damages helps to contain the buyer's discretion regarding the price it pays for the substitute goods.

Another limitation on cover damages is that the goods purchased must be a reasonable substitute for the goods due from the breaching seller. UCC § 2-712(1). This prevents the buyer from using the fortuity of the seller's breach to "upgrade" the quality of the goods. In other words, if the buyer purchases substitute goods that are of a higher quality than the goods contracted for, the buyer may not be entitled to cover damages.[12] While some difference in quality between the contracted for

---

[11]   Remember that if there is serious disruption to the buyer's operation, the buyer may want to consider making the case for specific performance or replevin under section 2-716.

[12]   *See TVI, Inc. v. Infosoft Technologies, Inc.*, 2008 WL 239784 (E.D. Mo. 2008); *Hessler v. Crystal Lake Chrysler-Plymouth, Inc.*, 788 N.E.2d 405 (Ill. Ct. App. 2003); *Ctkovic v.*

goods and the cover goods is tolerable, the seller should not have to pay for a significant upgrade in the quality.

Other issues occasionally arise in connection with cover. One such issue is whether the cover transaction can be with the breaching seller. For example, assume that the seller repudiates the contract but then offers to supply the same goods for a higher price. If the buyer accepts that substitute transaction, has the buyer covered so that the higher price sets its damages? If so, how is that situation to be distinguished from a mere modification to the original transaction? If the buyer refuses to buy the goods at the higher price, has the buyer acted unreasonably so that it has failed to mitigate its consequential damages?[13] Another recurring issue is whether the buyer "covers" by creating the goods internally instead of buying them from a third party. In that situation, how would the cost of cover be computed?[14]

Damages based on the market price. Compared to the many questions involved in determining if the cover price is appropriate to use in the buyer's damage calculation, the market price calculation seems relatively simple. If the buyer has not covered – and only if the buyer has not covered[15]– the buyer may seek damages based on the market price for the goods. That market price is based on the price at the time the buyer learned of the breach, UCC § 2-713(1), and at the place of tender, UCC § 2-713(2). Obviously, the place for tender will be determined from the agreement of the parties, as supplemented by the Code's gap fillers.

The time the buyer learned of the breach is somewhat more troublesome. Section 2-723 provides a special rule on the time for measuring market damages if trial on the issue occurs before the scheduled time for performance. This can occur if the contract for sale was a long-term supply contract. Outside the context of a long-term supply contract, however, the Code does not give much guidance on how

---

Boch, Inc., 2003 WL 139779 (Mass. App. Div. 2003).

[13]   *See Kelsey-Hayes Co. v. Galtaco Redlaw Castings Corp.*, 749 F. Supp. 794 (E.D. Mich. 1990).

[14]   *See Dura-Wood Treating Co. v. Century Forest Indus., Inc.*, 675 F.2d 745 (5th Cir.), *cert. denied*, 459 U.S. 865 (1982).

[15]   *See* UCC § 2-713 cmt. 5.

to determine when the buyer learned of the breach. A reccurring situation, giving rise to conflicting judicial decisions, involves a seller who has repudiated a contract. In such situations, the buyer has the right to wait a commercially reasonable time for the seller to perform or the buyer may immediately resort to remedies for breach. Review section 2-610. Should these options influence the determination of when the buyer learned of the breach?[16] If the market price fluctuates between the time the seller repudiates and a commercially reasonable time after repudiation, at which time should the market price be measured? Should the answer depend upon whether the buyer is actually awaiting the seller's performance? Another issue about when the buyer learned of the seller's breach can arise in a shipment contract. In some cases, the buyer may not learn of the breach until the goods fail to arrive at the destination, even though the seller breached days before by failing to tender the goods to the carrier. On which of those dates should the market price be measured?

How is market price proven? Read sections 2-723 and 2-724.

Expenses saved. The damage formulas based on the cover price and the market price both require that expenses saved as a consequence of the breach be deducted from the sum that the buyer is otherwise entitled to recover from the seller. This deduction is necessary to ensure that the damages awarded are limited to the amount necessary to protect the buyer's expectancy. To illustrate this principle, assume a seller agreed to sell equipment worth $100,000 to a buyer. The buyer expected to expend $1,000 to make modifications to its facilities to install the goods and, absent the sales contract, would have no need to make the modifications. The seller repudiates before the buyer makes any expenditures for the modifications. The buyer then decides either not to cover or to purchase substitute goods that do not necessitate the modifications. The buyer has saved $1,000 in expenses that should be deducted from the cover price-contract price or market price-contract price differential.

Buyer's incidental and consequential damages. Both section 2-712 (cover damages) and section 2-713 (market damages) also give the aggrieved buyer the

---

[16] *Compare Hess Energy, Inc. v. Lightning Oil Co.*, 338 F.3d 357 (4th Cir. 2003) (date of tender under the contract) *with Cosden Oil & Chemical Co. v. Karl O. Helm Aktiengesellschaft*, 736 F.2d 1064 (5th Cir. 1984) (commercially reasonable time after the repudiation).

right to recover incidental and consequential damages. Section 2-715 then defines what qualifies as incidental and consequential damages. Consequential losses are harms that the buyer suffers because the seller has not provided the goods. For example, assume the buyer has contracted to purchase a crank shaft to replace the broken one it uses in its mill. A failure to get the new crank shaft may result in a significant loss in business while the mill is shut down. Such lost profits may be recoverable. Under the common law, there are four principal limitations of the availability of an award for consequential damages:

(i)   the damages must actually be caused by the breach;
(ii) the consequential damages must arise from circumstances that the breaching party had reason to know about at the time the contract was formed;
(iii) the consequential damages must not have been readily avoidable by appropriate mitigating actions; and
(iv) the aggrieved party must prove the consequential damages with reasonable certainty.[17]

Section 2-715 expressly incorporates the first three of these limitations. No doubt the fourth also applies as a supplemental rule of law. *See* UCC §§ 1-103(b); 2-715 cmt. 4.

Incidental damages are a category of damages created by the drafters of Article 2. Under the common law, the types of damages comprising incidental damages would be subsumed within the category of consequential damages. Article 2 treats incidental damages separately because they are the sort of damages that arise naturally from the seller's breach and thus do not need to be subject to the common law's limiting principle of foreseeability. Rather, to recover incidental damages, the aggrieved party needs only to show that the incidental damages were caused by the breach and were reasonably incurred expenses. UCC § 2-715(1). Incidental damages that arise when the seller does not deliver the goods include the expenses associated with effecting cover, other than the cost of the cover goods. These may include, for example, the cost of long distance phone calls made to identify a willing seller of a suitable substitute goods.

Now use these principles to determine how buyer's damages should be measured in the following problems.

---

[17]   *See* RESTATEMENT (SECOND) OF CONTRACTS §§ 347, 350–352. *See also* George S. Geis, *Empirically Assessing Hadley v. Baxendale*, 32 FLA. ST. U. L. REV. 897 (2005).

Problem 7-4

State Street Motors contracts to sell a new car to Buyer for $40,000. The car is to have power windows, heated seats, and an enhanced stereo package. Buyer pays $1,000 down and promises to pay the $39,000 balance upon delivery, which is slated to occur in two weeks (when State Street Motors expects to obtain the car from the manufacturer).

On the date for delivery, State Street Motors refuses to sell the car to Buyer because State Street Motors was unable to obtain the car with the specified options from the manufacturer. Buyer cancels the contract and then purchases from a different seller a car of the same make and model. Buyer pays $42,000 for the substitute car, which also comes with a moon roof and air conditioning but lacks the enhanced stereo system. The enhanced stereo system is an option that retails for $500. What is the measure of Buyer's damages under section 2-712? What other facts might affect the analysis of this question?

Problem 7-5

On June 1, Blue Sky Airlines contracts to purchase 200,000 gallons of jet fuel from Supersonic Aviation at a price of $5 per gallon for delivery to Blue Sky's facilities in Chicago on July 1. On June 15, Supersonic Aviation repudiates the contract. Blue Sky Airlines makes the following purchases:

- 100,000 gallons of jet fuel on June 16 for $5.20 per gallon;
- 200,000 gallons of jet fuel on June 21 for $5.40 per gallon; and
- 200,000 gallons of jet fuel on June 28 for $5.60 per gallon.

A. If all of the June purchases are for delivery to Blue Sky's facilities in Chicago, what is the proper measure of Blue Sky's damages under section 2-712?

B. How, if at all, would that analysis change if the June 16th purchase called for delivery to Blue Sky's facilities in Atlanta?

Problem 7-6

Manufacturer, located in Phoenix, agreed to sell ten wooden desks to Buyer, located in Seattle. Each desk was a standard unit ordered from Manufacturer's catalog, priced at $500 per desk, for a total purchase price of $5,000. Buyer made a down payment of $100 and agreed to pay the rest

30 days after the Buyer received the desks in Seattle. The parties agreed to ship the goods F.O.B. Phoenix on June 1. The parties agreed that Manufacturer would use Excellent Cargo Haulers, Inc. to transport the goods. The cost of shipping the desks was approximately $50 per desk.

On May 20, Manufacturer notified Buyer that it would not be able to supply the desks ordered as it had discontinued its production of that model, and offered to sell a different model for $800 per desk. Buyer sent the following response:

> Due to your inability to supply the desks contracted for, please cancel our order and refund our down payment of $100 plus interest.

Buyer then purchased ten desks from Office Supply Co. located in Seattle for $6,000 with no charge for delivery to Buyer's office. The desks are bigger and contain more storage space than the desks Buyer had ordered from Manufacturer, but are made of metal instead of wood. Buyer spent approximately one week searching for desks that would work in its office space, and made numerous phone calls to find a supplier that could deliver the desks to Buyer on short notice. Even so, Office Supply was not able to deliver the desks to Buyer until June 15, delaying Buyer's office expansion by several weeks. Buyer estimates that it incurred losses as it had to pay employees who could not work and it lost sales due to the inability of its employees to do their jobs.

A. What are Buyer's remedies against Manufacturer?

B. What if Buyer was able to purchase ten desks from Office Supply Co. for $4,000? How does that change the analysis?

C. What if Buyer does not buy any desks at all and forgoes the planned office expansion due to a downturn in the economy? How does that change the analysis?

Problem 7-7

On April 1, Bride, who is planning a massive wedding reception on Long Island, contracts to purchase 5,000 lbs of live lobsters for $50,000 from Seafarer, a resident of Maine. The contract calls for delivery, F.O.B. Bar Harbor, Maine, on July 1. The cost of shipping the live lobsters from Bar Harbor to Long Island is $2,000. On June 1, Seafarer telephones Bride and repudiates the contract. Bride is unable to find sufficient lobsters elsewhere and ends up purchasing roast beef on June 15, which she then serves at the reception. If the market price of lobsters is as indicated on the following chart, what is the proper measure of Bride's damages? *See* UCC § 2-610.

	April 1	June 1	June 15	July 1
Bar Harbor	$10/lb.	$12/lb.	$13/lb.	$14/lb.
Long Island	$11/lb.	$13/lb.	$14/lb.	$15/lb.

Problem 7-8

Sand & Stone Supply Co. contracts to sell to Builder all the gravel Builder needs for road construction over a 10-year period. The price for the gravel is adjusted yearly based upon published averages. In the fifth year of performance, Sand & Stone repudiates the contract. Builder sues for damages a year later.

A. If the case comes up for trial the following year (*i.e.*, in year seven of the contract), what is the time for measuring market price?

B. If the case comes up for trial four years after the buyer filed the lawsuit (*i.e.*, after the contract would have expired on its own), what is the time for measuring market damages?

The damages formulas in sections 2-712 and 2-713 probably do a good job of protecting the aggrieved buyer's expectancy interests in most situations. However, it is impossible for one or two relatively simple statutory formulas to account for all the situations that may arise. As a result, the statutory formulas on occasion seem to yield a result inconsistent with the general rule of section 1-305(a) that the aggrieved party be put in the same position as if the contract had been fully performed.[18] What should happen then? Consider the following problems.

Problem 7-9

On March 1, Builder contracted to construct an office building for Developer. Under the terms of that contract, Builder is to acquire the necessary materials and Developer will recompense Builder at cost plus

---

[18]   Actually, the principle expressed in section 1-305(a) is that the aggrieved party be put in "as good a position" as if the contract had been performed.

10%. On April 1, Builder and Steel Supplier agree that Steel Supplier will sell Builder 500 steel girders of specified dimensions and hardness for a price of $70,000. Delivery is to occur by June 1. In May, Steel Supplier informs Builder that it will not be able to deliver the goods on time. Builder purchases the needed girders from a substitute seller who, because of the need for quick delivery, charges Builder $90,000. What is the proper measure of Builder's damages for Steel Supplier's breach? *See KGM Harvesting Co. v. Fresh Network*, 42 Cal. Rptr. 2d 286 (Cal. Ct. App. 1995).

Problem 7-10

Butane is in the business of buying and selling heating oil. Butane buys in bulk from large refineries in the Gulf Coast and sells quantities to distributors and retailers in the Midwest. On August 1, Butane contracts to purchase 100,000 gallons of heating oil from Supplier in New Orleans for $2.50 per gallon. The contract calls for delivery F.O.B. New Orleans on November 1. The cost of transporting the heating oil to Butane's facilities in St. Louis is expected to be $5,000.

On August 3, Butane contracts to sell 100,000 gallons to Customer. That contract states a price of $2.70 per gallon and calls for delivery on November 10, F.O.B. Butane's place of business in St. Louis. The cost of transporting the fuel to Customer is expected to be $500.

In October, the market price of heating oil skyrockets to $4.50 in New Orleans and $4.70 in St. Louis, and Supplier repudiates the contract with Butane. Butane is unable to procure heating oil from another source in time to make delivery to Customer, and so Butane reluctantly repudiates that contract.

A. Assuming Customer will hold Butane responsible for all of Customer's damages, what is the proper measure of Butane's damages against Supplier? *Compare H-W-H Cattle Co. v. Schroeder*, 767 F.2d 437 (8th Cir. 1985); *Allied Canners & Packing, Inc. v. Victor Packing Co.*, 209 Cal. Rptr. 60 (Cal. Ct. App. 1984), *with TexPar Energy, Inc. v. Murphy Oil USA, Inc.*, 45 F.3d 1111 (7th Cir. 1995); *Tongish v. Thomas*, 840 P.2d 471 (Kan. 1992).

B. Assuming Customer waives all its claims for breach against Butane, what is the proper measure of Butane's damages against Supplier?

C. How, if at all, would the analysis change if Butane planned to burn the
heating oil it purchased from Supplier for its own heating needs?

**Buyer's damages for seller's repudiation or nondelivery under CISG and
UNIDROIT Principles.** CISG Article 75 allows the buyer's damages to be
measured using the price of substitute goods and Article 76 allows the buyer's
damages to be measured using the "current" price of the goods, a reference to the
market price. The buyer's ability to use either provision to measure its damages
depends upon the buyer's ability to avoid the contract for fundamental breach. A
fundamental breach can occur when the seller repudiates its obligations under the
contract or when the seller fails to deliver any goods. CISG Arts. 25, 49, and 72.
To avoid the contract for fundamental breach, the buyer must give notice of that fact
to the seller. CISG Art. 26. The buyer may also be entitled to consequential
damages, CISG Art. 74, subject to reduction if the buyer fails to engage in
appropriate mitigation efforts, CISG Art. 77.

The UNIDROIT Principles are similar. An aggrieved party that has terminated
a contract may measure its damages using a replacement cost, UNIDROIT Art.
7.4.5, or by a current price, UNIDROIT Art. 7.4.6. The UNIDROIT Principles also
allow for recovery of consequential damages proven with sufficient certainty and
foreseeability and subject to a mitigation principle. UNIDROIT Principles Arts.
7.4.2 through 7.4.4 and 7.4.8.

SECTION 3.   SELLER'S TENDER FAILS TO CONFORM TO THE CONTRACT REQUIREMENTS

After any tender of goods by the seller, the buyer must either accept or reject
the goods. The buyer's decision to accept or reject the goods will significantly
affect each party's rights from that point forward. For example, if the buyer accepts
the goods, the buyer becomes obligated to pay the contract price. UCC § 2-607(1).
This is so even if the goods or the seller's tender did not conform to the contract
requirements. However, acceptance of the goods does not deprive the buyer of all
remedies for breach. The buyer may still maintain an action for damages for any
problem with the goods or the tender, UCC § 2-714, and may, in some situations,
even be entitled to revoke its acceptance, UCC § 2-608, and recover damages for
the seller's breach based upon a cover price or market price measurement, UCC
§§ 2-712, 2-713, 2-715.

In contrast, if the buyer rejects the goods after a nonconforming tender, the buyer generally does not become obligated to pay for the goods. In addition, the buyer has an action for breach of contract based upon the cover price or market price measurement. UCC §§ 2-712, 2-713, 2-715. However, in some circumstances, the seller may have a right to circumvent the buyer's cause of action by curing the problem with the goods or the tender. UCC § 2-508.

The remainder of this section discusses when the buyer has the right to reject, what the buyer must do to reject, the effect of rejection or acceptance, and how the decision to accept or reject the goods following a nonconforming tender determines the buyer's subsequent remedial options.[19] Before considering those questions, it is important to have a proper understanding of the meaning of rejection of the goods. Rejection of the goods is the buyer's determination to refuse the seller's tender of the goods. It is not a rescission or repudiation of the contract; it is merely a refusal of the seller's tender of performance.

A. ACCEPTANCE OR REJECTION OF THE GOODS

Analysis of the buyer's acceptance or rejection of the goods involves two separate inquiries: (i) does the buyer have the right to reject the goods; and (ii) has the buyer actually and effectively rejected the goods.

1. Buyer's Right to Reject

Analysis of the buyer's right to reject the goods begins with section 2-601, which states that the buyer may reject if "the goods or the tender of delivery fail in any respect to conform to the contract." Read the definition of "conforming" in section 2-106(2). This is known as the "perfect tender rule," and it places a rather high burden on the seller given that little in this world is perfect. However, the perfect tender rule is subject to two important limitations.

First, as expressly noted in section 2-601 and as discussed in Chapter Five, the parties may have agreed to limit the remedies available for a breach. *See* UCC

---

[19]   In Chapter Nine, we will discuss the buyer's breach by wrongfully rejecting the goods and what effect that the buyer's decision to reject or accept the goods has on the seller's remedies for the buyer's breach.

§§ 2-718, 2-719. For example, the parties' agreement may limit the buyer's right to reject the goods to situations involving major defects, rather than cosmetic problems. Alternatively, the agreement may provide that the buyer's exclusive remedy for a tender of nonconforming goods is recovery of liquidated damages. Such a provision would appear to preclude the buyer's ability to reject the goods for a nonconformity. On the other hand, the buyer's right to reject nonconforming goods is such an integral part of the structure of Article 2, courts may be reluctant to interpret such a clause as truly negating the buyer's right to reject and instead restrict the clause to accepted goods. More important, usage of trade, course of dealing, and course of performance – which are components of the parties' agreement – may circumscribe the buyer's right to reject goods for minor defects. Perhaps the general obligation of good faith imposed by section 1-304 does so as well.[20]

The second limitation on the buyer's right to reject arises in installment contracts. *Compare* UCC §§ 2-601 *with* 2-612. An installment contract is one which calls for delivery of the goods in separate lots, with acceptance after each delivery. UCC §§ 2-612(1), 2-307.[21] In such a contract, the buyer's remedies are limited in two ways. First, the buyer's right to reject an individual installment of goods is limited to instances in which the nonconformity of that installment substantially impairs the value of that installment and cannot be cured.[22] If the problem does not substantially impair the value of the installment to the buyer or if the seller gives adequate assurance that it plans to cure the nonconformity and the buyer is not entitled to cancel the entire contract, the buyer must accept that installment. UCC § 2-612(2). Second, the buyer is entitled to cancel an installment contract only if the nonconformity as to one or more installments substantially impairs the entire value of the entire contract. UCC § 2-612(3).

Nothing in the Code defines or explains "substantial impairment." Some courts have analogized the standard to the concept of "material breach" under the common

---

[20]   *See* William H. Lawrence, *Appropriate Standards for a Buyer's Refusal to Keep Goods Tendered by a Seller*, 35 WM. & MARY L. REV. 1635 (1994).

[21]   The mere fact that the buyer has agreed to *pay* in installments does not make the arrangement an installment contract.

[22]   If the nonconformity as to the installment is a defect in the required documents, the substantial impairment rule does not seem to apply. The buyer may reject the goods due to that nonconformity in the required documents.

law, which is similarly vague and often difficult to apply.[23] What is clear is that substantial impairment is to be judged not in the abstract, but in reference to the normal and specifically known purposes of the contract. UCC § 2-612 cmt. 4. Thus, a brief delay that would not normally provide grounds for rejecting an installment might nevertheless qualify as substantial impairment if the seller is aware that it will cause significant problems for the buyer.

One possible reason underlying this more restrictive rule on rejection of goods in installment contracts may be a desire to preserve the parties' relationship. The theory is that, unlike in a one-shot transaction, the parties in an installment contract have more at stake in continued cooperation and the law should recognize and respect this different. Do you agree? Is the underlying assumption correct?[24] Even if it is, might it not counsel in favor of expanding the seller's right to cure following rejection, rather than limiting the buyer's right to reject in the first instance?

In both installment contracts and non-installment contracts, a buyer who has the right to reject the goods need not choose the same action with respect to all the goods. Instead, the buyer may accept some of the goods and reject others, so long as the buyer accepts complete commercial units. *See* UCC § 2-601(c). Thus a buyer of three computers could accept two and reject one but a buyer of shoes could

---

[23] *E.g., Midwest Mobile Diagnostic Imaging, L.L.C. v. Dynamics Corp. of America*, 965 F. Supp. 1003 (W.D. Mich 1997), *aff'd*, 165 F.3d 27 (6th Cir. 1998). *See also* RESTATEMENT (SECOND) OF CONTRACTS § 241, indicating that the following factors are to be considered in determining whether a breach is material:

   (a) the extent to which the injured party will be deprived of the benefit which he reasonably expected;
   (b) the extent to which the injured party can be adequately compensated for the part of that benefit of which he will be deprived;
   (c) the extent to which the party failing to perform or to offer to perform will suffer forfeiture;
   (d) the likelihood that the party failing to perform or to offer to perform will cure his failure, taking account of all the circumstances including any reasonable assurances; [and]
   (e) the extent to which the behavior of the party failing to perform or to offer to perform comports with standards of good faith and fair dealing.

[24] "[T]ransactors do not necessarily want the relationship-preserving norms they follow in performing contracts and cooperatively resolving disputes among themselves to be used by third-party neutrals to decide cases when they are in an end-game situation." Lisa Bernstein, *Merchant Law in a Merchant Court: Rethinking the Code's Search for Immanent Business Norms*, 144 U. PA. L. REV. 1765, 1770 (1996).

not accept the left and reject the right and a car buyer could not accept the chassis and reject the motor. *See* UCC § 2-105(6) (defining "commercial unit").

Problem 7-11

Sterling, Inc. is a vegetable distributor and Bluto Foods Co. is a manufacturer of canned soups. On April 1, the parties entered into a written contract for the sale of 1,000 bushels of "Early Girl" tomatoes at $40.00 per bushel, to be shipped F.O.B. Sterling's place of business on or before July 15. The goods were to be delivered in a single lot and Bluto was to make payment 30 days after the goods were received. Nothing was said in the agreement about rejection.

A. Assuming there is no evidence regarding the impact upon the value of the bargain, in which of the following independent scenarios could Bluto properly reject all of the tomatoes?

1. A timely tender of 990 bushels of tomatoes.

2. A timely tender of 1,000 bushels of tomatoes, ten bushels of which contained a variety other than "Early Girl."

3. A tender of 1,000 bushels of "Early Girl" tomatoes that had been shipped on July 16.

4. A tender of 1,000 bushels of "Early Girl" tomatoes that were shipped on July 14 but, because of an erroneous delivery instruction by Sterling, transit took four more days than normal. UCC § 2-504.

B. Assume Sterling tendered 1,000 bushels but 50 of them were rotten.

1. May Bluto accept the 950 bushels of good tomatoes and reject the 50 bushels of rotten tomatoes?

2. May Bluto accept 500 bushels of the good tomatoes and reject the remainder?

C. Suppose Sterling agreed to ship 100 bushels by July 15, and 100 bushels each week for the next 9 weeks.

1. May Bluto reject the entire first shipment if it was ten bushels short? What if ten bushels had rotten tomatoes? What if the entire shipment were sent one day late?

2. Assume that in the first shipment, 10 bushels were missing. Sterling shipped the 10 bushels along with the second shipment, but the second shipment (110 bushels) had five bushels that were rotten. The third shipment arrived five days late and the fourth

shipment contained 200 bushels (which overwhelmed Bluto's capacity for properly dealing with the tomatoes). The fifth shipment contained 100 bushels and was on time, but 10 bushels contained a variety of tomatoes other than "Early Girl." May Bluto reject the fifth shipment and cancel the contract?

Problem 7-12

You represent Sterling, Inc., a vegetable distributor negotiating a contract to sell 1,000 bushels of "Early Girl" tomatoes to Bluto Foods Co., a manufacturer of canned soups. The contract will call for the tomatoes to be shipped in a single lot. What sort of clause would you draft to limit or eliminate the buyer's rejection right?

2.   Making the Rejection Effective

Acceptance and rejection of the goods are contrary actions. As noted in the discussion of the buyer's inspection rights in Chapter Four, the buyer cannot do both and the buyer cannot do neither. Perhaps because of that, Article 2 does not state what a buyer must do to reject the goods; it merely states what is not an effective rejection, *see* UCC § 2-602(1), and identifies the acts that qualify as acceptance. *See* UCC § 2-606. A buyer who wants to reject the goods must avoid doing anything that qualifies as an acceptance of them. Thus, for example, the buyer wishing to reject the goods must not inform the seller that the buyer will take or retain the goods despite their nonconformity, and must not do any act inconsistent with the seller's ownership of the goods. UCC § 2-606(1)(a), (c). Of course, merely taking possession of the goods does not, by itself, necessarily qualify as acceptance because that act is often merely a prelude to inspecting the goods.

However, doing nothing will not be effective as a rejection. A buyer who fails to make an effective rejection after the opportunity to inspect has expired is deemed to have accepted the goods and thus will be liable for the price of the goods, even though the buyer may also have a claim for breach of contract against the seller if the goods or tender were nonconforming to the contract requirements. UCC § 2-606(1)(b), 2-607(1), (2). Therefore, the buyer needs to reject within a reasonable time and must seasonably notify the seller of the rejection. UCC §§ 2-602(1), 1-205, 1-202. A failure to provide this notification in a timely manner renders the attempted rejection ineffective; that is the buyer will be deemed to have accepted the goods.

The timing of the buyer's notification to the seller of rejection is connected to the length of time that is necessary for a reasonable inspection of the goods as allowed under section 2-513. Under that section, the buyer has a reasonable time for inspection of the goods prior to acceptance. The amount of time that is reasonable will undoubtedly depend upon many factors, including the complexity of the goods.

Problem 7-13

A buyer can give or fail to give the section 2-602(1) notification in two different situations: when the buyer has a right to reject the goods and when the buyer does not have the right to reject the goods. As a result, there are four possible situations:

(i)   a right to reject coupled with a timely notification;
(ii) a right to reject coupled with an untimely notification;
(iii) no right to reject coupled with a timely notification; and
(iv) no right to reject coupled with an untimely notification.

Using the matrix below, and the Code sections cited above, determine for each of these situations: (i) whether the buyer has accepted the goods; and (ii) which party has breached the contract.

	Timely Notification of Rejection	Untimely Notification of Rejection
Right to Reject		
No Right to Reject		

Article 2 does not specify what the buyer's notification of rejection must include. No doubt the buyer must make clear in some manner that the buyer will not take or keep the goods. Therefore, the buyer need not specify the basis for rejection. In other words, the buyer need not – to have an effective rejection – detail the defects with the goods or nonconformity with the tender. Nevertheless, the buyer does have an incentive to include that information. Read section

2-605(1). This provision precludes the buyer from relying on an unstated defect to justify the buyer's rejection of the goods in certain circumstances. When this rule applies, the buyer's rejection of the goods will still be *effective*, but may no longer be *rightful*. If the buyer cannot rely on the unstated problem to justify the rejection, and if there are no other problems that justify the rejection, this section may make the rejection wrongful. Put simply, it can convert a breach by the seller (tendering nonconforming goods) into a breach by the buyer (failing to accept).

Problem 7-14

Review the matrix in problem 7-13. How, if at all, do the requirements placed on the buyer in section 2-605(1) affect the answer to the two questions posed? In other words, if the buyer fails to inform the seller of a problem with the goods in a situation in which the buyer had a right to reject and gave timely notification of rejection (the upper left box), what result will follow?

Problem 7-15

Your client is Bulk Movers, Inc., a commercial trucking company. It is negotiating to purchase five trucks from Semi-Tough Motors, Inc., a retailer, with one truck to be delivered on the first day of each of the next five months. When trucks are delivered, Bulk Movers wants to be able to drive the trucks and put them through a rigorous mechanical examination. Draft language to propose to Semi-Tough that would preserve Bulk Movers' right to reject any truck that does not conform to the contract requirements after the mechanical examination.

B. EFFECT OF REJECTION

Assume the buyer has rightfully and effectively notified the seller that it is rejecting the goods. The seller will typically respond in any one of three ways. First, the seller may want to try and fix the nonconformities and thus offer a cure to the buyer. Second, the seller may decide to simply take the goods back and refund whatever portion of the purchase price the buyer has already paid. Third, the seller may resist the buyer's efforts to reject and refuse to take the goods back. In each of these cases, the buyer may seek an award of damages based upon the seller's breach. In this section, we explore these three topics: the seller's right to cure, the buyer's actions with respect to the rejected goods, and the buyer's right to damages.

1. The Seller's Right to Cure

Upon learning of the buyer's rejection, the seller will often wish to cure the nonconformity. Sometimes the seller wants to do this for legal reasons: to avoid or reduce liability to the buyer for breach. More commonly, the seller wants to do this for business or ethical reasons: to salvage the transaction (and any profit associated with it), to have satisfied customers, and to fulfill its promises. Assuming the parties' agreement does not expand or limit the seller's right to cure,[25] section 2-508 governs the seller's ability to force a cure on the buyer. Notice, that nothing in that section requires the seller to cure the problem. Section 2-508 gives the seller a right but does not impose a duty. Notice also that nothing in that section, or Article 2, allows the buyer to require the seller to cure the breach.[26] Section 2-508 is a one-way provision, it gives the seller a right to cure if it chooses to do so, it does not give the buyer a right to force the seller to cure.

Problem 7-16

You represent the buyer who is negotiating the purchase of some custom-built manufacturing equipment. You are contemplating proposing a clause that would give the buyer the right to insist that the seller cure defects with the goods. What benefit, if any, would such a clause have?

Section 2-508 does not give the seller a right to cure all the time. Instead that right to cure is limited to two situations: (i) when the time for the seller's performance has not expired; and (ii) when the seller had reasonable grounds to believe that the goods would be acceptable. The first of these is fairly easy to understand, but also fairly limited. If the contract calls for delivery by June 1 and

---

[25]   *See Mercury Marine v. Clear River Constr. Co.*, 839 So. 2d 508 (Miss. 2003) (limitation of remedy clauses may preclude buyer's ability to reject the goods and require the buyer to accept the seller's proffered cure).

[26]   Although if the seller's breach consists of not repairing defective goods, the buyer may be able to get an award of specific performance. *See* UCC § 2-716.

the seller tenders nonconforming goods on May 17, the seller will have two weeks to cure the breach by tendering conforming goods. The second situation is less obvious.

Problem 7-17

Construct a scenario in which a seller who tendered nonconforming goods would have a right to cure because the seller had reasonable grounds for believing the tender would be acceptable. If possible, keep your scenario simple, one that involves a sale of household goods to a consumer.

Section 2-508 does not specify what qualifies as a cure. Presumably, it is something that negates the effect of the breach and puts the buyer in the position as if the seller had performed properly. What this means in any particular case will depend on the precise nature of the seller's breach.

For example, assume the seller has provided goods that fail to conform to the contract. To cure the breach, the seller will have to provide the buyer with conforming goods. In some circumstances that may mean that the seller can repair the goods; in other circumstances it may mean that the seller must provide replacement goods. If the repaired or replacement goods, as the case may be, do not then conform to the contract requirements, the seller will of course not have cured the breach.

But what if the seller's breach is a late delivery of conforming goods? Is it possible for the seller to cure that breach? Unless the seller can reverse time, the answer is no, that breach cannot be cured. Of course, even though late delivery may not be cured, the buyer may waive the breach or agree to some discount against the price or other compensation for the late delivery. While not a "cure" of the breach, the buyer's agreement to such compensation for the late delivery would constitute a settlement of the buyer's claim for breach of contract against the seller.

What is the consequence of the buyer refusing a cure that the seller has a right to provide and has attempted to provide? Has the buyer breached the contract?

Now try your hand at a few more problems.

Problem 7-18

Barbara purchased a car from State Street Motors. In each of the following independent scenarios, determine whether State Street Motors has offered to cure the breach.

A. While driving the car home from the showroom, the rear-view mirror fell off the windshield. State Street Motors offered to re-attach the mirror at no charge to Barbara.

B. The first time Barbara attempted to start the car after she got it home, the starter would not engage.

1. State Street Motors offered to replace the starter the next day with a new part provided by the manufacturer at no charge to Barbara.

2. State Street Motors offered to replace the starter with a new part provided by the manufacturer at no charge to Barbara. State Street Motors did not have a new starter on hand and it estimated that it would take three business days to receive one, unless Barbara were willing to pay the cost of express shipping. *See Travelers Indem. Co. v. Maho Machine Tool Corp.*, 952 F.2d 26 (2d Cir. 1991).

C. While driving the car home from the showroom, the entire exhaust system fell off. State Street Motors offered to replace the exhaust system with parts salvaged from other cars in its inventory. *Compare Bowen v. Foust*, 925 S.W.2d 211 (Mo. Ct. App. 1996); *Zabriskie Chevrolet, Inc. v. Smith*, 240 A.2d 195 (N.J. Super. Ct. 1968), *with Wilson v. Scampoli*, 228 A.2d 848 (D.C. 1967).

D. On the drive home from the showroom, the car stalled when Barbara stopped at a red light and would not restart. State Street Motors towed the car to its repair shop and replaced the battery. The car seemed to be running fine and Barbara drove it home. The next day, the car started but several electrical systems in the car went haywire; the horn would not stop sounding, the lights were blinking on and off, and the radio would not work. Barbara could not drive it given the problems the car was having. State Street Motors towed the car to the dealership and replaced several electrical components. Two days later, the check engine light on the dash board came on. Barbara brought the car back in, State Street Motors inspected it, and then assured her that the problems was due to an electrical malfunction in the dashboard (*i.e.*, there was nothing in fact wrong with the engine). State Street Motors offered to repair the car at no cost to Barbara. Barbara objected and told State Street Motors that she did not want the car any more. Instead, she wanted a new, trouble free car. State Street Motors refused to take the car back.

Problem 7-19

Buyer contracts to purchase bolts for its assembly process from Seller. Because there is limited storage space at Buyer's facility, and Buyer can store only a few days worth of bolts there, Seller has agreed to deliver the bolts "just in time" for use in the Buyer's process. Under the terms of the agreement, deliveries are scheduled for the beginning of the day every Tuesday and Friday for the next three months.

A. Due to a mix up at the Seller's shipping department, the bolts due to Buyer's plant on Friday were not delivered on Friday. Buyer called Seller and Seller promised that the bolts would be there no later than the following Monday afternoon. Buyer protests because, under current production rates, Buyer will not have enough bolts to get through the entire day on Monday. Seller says it will try and get the bolts there more quickly but cannot promise that the bolts will be there before the end of the day on Monday. What are Buyer's options at this point? What are the risks of each course of action? What should Buyer do to preserve the most flexibility in making arguments later on if Buyer sues Seller for breach of contract? Does section 2-508 apply to this situation?

B. Seller delivered a shipment of bolts to Buyer on Tuesday morning. Buyer tested a sampling of the bolts and notified Seller early that afternoon that Buyer was rejecting the bolts because they failed the testing process. Seller promises to send a new shipment of bolts that should arrive by Wednesday morning. Does Buyer have to accept that offer to cure? UCC §§ 2-508, 2-612.

C. Over the course of the first two months of the contract period, Seller's deliveries of bolts were often late and the bolts were of a poor (nonconforming) quality. Seller has consistently sent replacement bolts when Buyer has complained but Buyer's production process has been interrupted on several occasions. Buyer has called you because the bolts Seller delivered today were not of the required quality. When Buyer called Seller to reject the installment, Seller again promised to send new bolts by the next morning. Buyer is fed up and wants to find a new supplier. If Buyer refuses to allow Seller to send replacement bolts and cancels the contract, will Buyer have breached? UCC §§ 2-508, 2-612.

D. Buyer is negotiating with a new supplier for bolts. In light of the past experience with Seller, Buyer wants you to draft a clause that will allow the Buyer to demand a cure when it wants to, refuse a cure it does not want, and get out of the deal if it thinks the supplier is not performing adequately. Draft language to accomplish that goal.

2. *Care of the Rejected Goods*

In some cases, such as when the buyer is to pick up the goods at the seller's location, the buyer may reject the goods before any transfer of possession occurs. In such a case, the buyer will have no duty to care for the rejected goods. Similarly, if the seller is to deliver the goods to the buyer, on rare occasions it may be so obvious that the goods or tender are nonconforming that the buyer rejects the goods before they are offloaded and the buyer never takes possession of them. More commonly, though, the buyer takes delivery of the goods from the seller or a carrier before discovering the nonconformity and only later – after inspecting the goods – does the buyer reject them.

What does the buyer do with the rejected goods in its possession? The buyer is in essence a bailee, holding possession of goods that belong to another. *See* UCC § 2-401(4). Not surprisingly, Article 2 requires that a buyer in possession of the rejected goods take reasonable care of the goods for the time necessary to allow the seller to retrieve the goods. UCC § 2-602(2)(b). A merchant buyer may have further duties, including an obligation to comply with the seller's instructions regarding the goods and a duty to sell goods that are perishable or declining rapidly in value. UCC § 2-603.

The buyer may also have rights in the rejected goods. In particular, if the buyer has paid part of the price or has incurred expenses in dealing with the goods, the buyer will have a security interest – in other words, a lien – in the goods to secure those amounts. Read section 2-711(3). *See also* UCC § 9-110. The buyer may refuse to return the goods until the seller refunds the price paid and compensates the buyer for the expenses incurred. If the seller fails to do so, the buyer may sell the goods using the sale process found in section 2-706 (which will be discussed in Chapter Nine) and credit amounts received against the seller's obligations. In addition, if the seller fails instruct the buyer what to do with the goods, the buyer may sell the goods and remit the proceeds of the sale to the seller, minus the expenses of storage and conducting the sale. Read section 2-604.

A buyer who uses rejected goods, other than pursuant to its rights or duties outlined above, runs the risk that it will be deemed to have accepted the goods. *See* UCC § 2-606 cmt. 4. In other words, if the buyer's post-rejection use of the goods is inconsistent with the seller's ownership of the goods or otherwise wrongful as to the seller, the seller may treat the buyer's post-rejection actions as an acceptance of the goods (making the buyer liable for the price, UCC § 2-607(1)) or bring a claim for conversion (making the buyer liable for the value of the goods under tort law). *See* UCC § 2-602(2)(a).

One obvious implication of this rule is that the buyer should normally refrain from subjecting rejected goods to a manufacturing process. For example, a buyer of plastic resin that uses the resin to make injection moldings will likely be deemed to have accepted the resin despite any previous communications to the contrary.

Nevertheless, this rule can present a problem for the buyer. In some unusual situations, the buyer cannot realistically avoid using the goods despite having rejected them. Consider the case of a buyer who purchases new wall-to-wall carpeting, which the seller installs in the buyer's living room on a Friday afternoon. Within moments after the installer leaves, the buyer notices a noxious odor emanating from the carpet. The buyer calls the seller, unequivocally rejects the goods, and demands that they be removed. The seller promises to have the carpet taken out on Monday morning. Over the weekend, may the buyer walk on the carpet or must the buyer stay out of the living room to avoid accepting the goods?

There can be little doubt that this carpet purchaser will have a license to make limited use of the carpet over the weekend. But what if the buyer's use of the goods is avoidable but undertaken in an effort to minimize consequential damages? The paradigm case is a consumer who has purchased a car or mobile home, rightfully and effectively rejected that good, but needs to continue using it for transportation or living space because the seller refuses to allow the buyer to return the goods. The evolving majority view is that if the buyer's use is reasonable and necessary under the circumstances, that use is neither an acceptance nor a conversion of the rejected goods.[27] As one court noted:

---

[27] *Romy v. Picker Int'l, Inc.*, 1992 WL 70403 (E.D. Pa. 1992), *aff'd*, 986 F.2d 1409 (3d Cir. 1993) (use of MRI machine by doctor after revocation was reasonable and part of the duty to mitigate damages); *North River Homes, Inc. v. Bosarge*, 594 So. 2d 1153 (Miss. 1992) (use of mobile home for 12 months after revocation justified by seller's assurances of cure and buyer's financial inability to move); *Braden v. Stem*, 571 So. 2d 1116 (Ala. 1990) (buyer's use of used car for seven months after revocation justified because buyer needed the car to transport a child); *Cuesta v. Classic Wheels, Inc.*, 818 A.2d 448 (N.J. Super. Ct. App. Div. 2003) (use of the car for two years after attempted revocation could be reasonable,

The reasonableness of the buyer's use of a defective good is a question of fact for the jury that is to be based on the facts and circumstances of each case. Several factors that the jury may consider include the seller's instructions to the buyer after revocation of acceptance; the degree of economic and other hardship that the buyer would suffer if he discontinued using the defective good; the reasonableness of the buyer's use after revocation as a method of mitigating damages; the degree of prejudice to the seller; and whether the seller acted in bad faith.[28]

Problem 7-20

Bancroft purchased a new laptop computer over the internet from Silicon Systems, the manufacturer. Bancroft purchased the laptop for use on business when traveling and to replace an aging desktop computer that Bancroft used at home. When the laptop arrived, Bancroft noticed immediately that the screen was scratched. Nevertheless, Bancroft installed several software applications onto the laptop. Although the computer seemed to be operating properly, Bancroft called Silicon Systems to complain about the scratched screen and reject the computer. The customer service representative instructed Bancroft to return the laptop and promised to send a replacement after Silicon Systems received the damaged laptop. Bancroft objected to the delay, noting that this would take several days. Bancroft was scheduled to leave on a business trip in two days and needed a laptop to make a presentation. The customer service representative politely but firmly insisted that Silicon Systems would not send a replacement until it received the original back. The representative also indicated that if Bancroft used the original laptop on that trip or otherwise failed to send it back within 24 hours, Silicon Systems would have no way of knowing whether the laptop was damaged before or after Bancroft received it, and would therefore not take it back. Left with no alternative Bancroft took the laptop on the business trip and used it for the scheduled presentation. Has Bancroft accepted the laptop?

---

remanded for determination). *See* John R. Bates, *Continued Use of Goods After Rejection or Revocation of Acceptance: The UCC Rule Revealed, Reviewed, and Revised*, 25 RUTGERS L.J. 1 (1993).

[28]   *Johannsen v. Minnesota Valley Ford Tractor Co.*, 304 N.W.2d 654, 658 (Minn. 1981).

Notice that the captions of sections 2-602 and 2-603 refer to "rightfully rejected" goods and that section 2-711(3) applies only after a rightful rejection. Read section 1-107 regarding the effect of captions. Certainly, the buyer who has wrongfully but effectively rejected the goods should take reasonable care of the goods. After all, the buyer's effective rejection means that the buyer has not accepted the goods and the goods are thus the seller's property. *See* UCC § 2-401(4). However, that buyer is probably not protected by the provisions of sections 2-602, 2-603, 2-604 or 2-711. Therefore, if a buyer in that situation sells the goods, such action would probably be inconsistent with the seller's ownership interest and thus an acceptance. UCC § 2-606.

3. *Rejection and the Right to Damages*

If a seller makes a nonconforming tender, so that the buyer has a right to reject the goods, the seller will have breached the contract. The buyer's rejection of the goods effectively forces the seller to take the goods back. The buyer will then have a right to damages for the seller's breach and is in basically the same position as if the seller never delivered the goods. To the extent the buyer has paid any part of the price, the buyer is entitled to a return of the price paid, which the buyer may recover by foreclosing on its security interest in the rejected goods. The buyer is also entitled to an award of damages based either on a cover transaction or the market price. *See* UCC § 2-711. These cover or market price based damages are not part of the amount that can be collected by foreclosing on the security interest. *See* UCC § 2-711(3). In addition to cover or market price based damages, the buyer may also recover incidental and consequential damages. UCC § 2-715. Some of the likely incidental damages are included within the amount that is secured by the buyer's security interest in the goods. *Compare* UCC § 2-711(3) *with* § 2-715(1). The remaining incidental damages and the consequential damages are not recoverable through foreclosure of the security interest. The issues regarding proving cover or market price based damages, incidental, and consequential damages are the same as discussed previously.

C. ACCEPTANCE AND THE EFFECT OF ACCEPTANCE

As we have learned so far, the buyer accepts the goods by signifying to the seller that the buyer is accepting, by failing to effectively reject the goods after the time for inspection expires, or by dealing with the goods in a manner inconsistent with the seller's ownership. UCC § 2-606(1). Remember, it is not always clear when the time for inspection expires, so it is not always clear whether the buyer who has said nothing to the seller has in fact accepted the goods.

There are several important consequences to the buyer's acceptance of the goods:

(i)　the buyer is precluded from rejecting the goods, UCC § 2-607(2);

(ii)　the buyer becomes obligated to pay the contract price, UCC § 2-607(1), although if the seller's tender is in fact nonconforming, the buyer will still be entitled to various remedies, UCC §§ 2-714, 2-715;

(iii) the buyer must notify the seller of any breach within a reasonable time or will be barred from any remedy, UCC § 2-607(3)(a);

(iv) the buyer assumes the burden of proof on any claim of breach with respect to the accepted goods, UCC § 2-607(4);[29] and

(v)　in a non-installment contract, the buyer loses the right to cancel the contract, *compare* UCC § 2-711(1) *with* § 2-714, a point which can be important if the market price of the goods has declined since the contract was formed and the buyer would now like to put that loss on the seller.

1. Notice of Breach

The buyer's acceptance of the goods is ***not*** a waiver of its right to pursue claims for the seller's nonconforming performance. Instead, the buyer retains the right to

---

[29]　If the buyer rejects the goods, the burden of proof would rest on whoever becomes the plaintiff in the resulting lawsuit. If the buyer is the plaintiff, suing the seller for cover or for damages based on market price, the buyer would have the normal plaintiff's burden of proof to establish the elements of its case, one of which is that the seller breached the contract. If the seller is the plaintiff and is suing the buyer for breach of contract, alleging a wrongful rejection of the goods, the seller would have the burden of proof that the buyer breached the contract. That is, the seller would have to show that the goods were conforming and that the buyer therefore had no right to reject the goods.

sue for damages provided the buyer gives reasonable notification of the breach to the seller. UCC § 2-607(3)(a).

This notification requirement raises two issues. First, what is a "reasonable time" within which the buyer must notify the seller of the problem? *See* UCC §§ 1-205, 1-202. Second, what must the notification say? Read comment 4 to section 2-607.[30] Both of these issues are informed by the purpose of the notice requirement and by the harsh result of the buyer's failure to comply: the loss of all remedies.

What are the purposes of requiring the buyer to notify the seller of the breach with respect to accepted goods? A leading case has suggested that notification serves at least the following four purposes:

(1) to prevent surprise and allow the seller the opportunity to make recommendations on how to cure the nonconformance;

(2) to permit the seller the fair opportunity to investigate and prepare for litigation; . . .

(3) to open the way for normal settlement of claims through negotiation . . . [; and]

(4) to protect the seller from stale claims and provide certainty in contractual arrangements.[31]

Another reason is to permit the seller to preserve its rights against its own supplier, which might be particularly important if the statute of limitations were about to expire on the seller's claim against its supplier.[32]

Notice that the first reason identified above referred to giving the seller the opportunity to make recommendations on how to cure, not to facilitate the seller's right to cure. Other courts have expressly suggested that notification protects the

---

[30]   This rule should not be confused with section 2-605, which provides that the buyer's failure to particularize operates as a waiver of unstated defects. The rule of section 2-605 applies only to *rejected* goods; the notification requirement of section 2-607(3)(a) applies only to *accepted* goods.

[31]   *Aqualon Co. v. Mac Equipment, Inc.*, 149 F.3d 262, 269 (4th Cir. 1998)

[32]   *See Hebron v. American Isuzu Motors, Inc.*, 60 F.3d 1095, 1098–99 (4th Cir. 1995) (indicating that notification served the important function of "minimizing prejudice to the seller from the passage of time").

seller's right to cure,[33] but is that really correct? Review section 2-508 on when the seller has a right to cure.

Given the draconian effect of an untimely or inadequate notification, courts are fairly lenient. Nevertheless, most agree that some sort of pre-litigation notification is required. In other words, filing a complaint does not satisfy the requirement of section 2-607.

Problem 7-21

Baker makes bread for sale to markets and restaurants within a 30-mile radius. One April 1, one of Baker's automated baking machines broke down and Baker was unable to fix it. Before the end of the day, Baker ordered the necessary replacement parts from Supplier, explaining that they were needed to get the machine operating and that, without the machine, Baker had to reduce capacity and pay employees overtime wages to generate even that lower level of production. Supplier promised to deliver the replacement parts by April 4. It is now April 5 and Supplier has not yet delivered the goods. The delay is costing Baker substantial amounts of money. What notification of the breach, if any, must Baker provide to Supplier?

As with many of Article 2's rules on default, the parties may vary the effect of the notification requirement of section 2-607(3)(a) by specifying what would be a reasonable time. *See* UCC §§ 1-205(b), 1-302. Presumably, they could even dispense with the notification requirement entirely.

Problem 7-22

You are drafting a form that the seller of high-end kitchen appliances (*e.g.,* large stoves and sub-zero refrigerators) will use when it sells them to consumers and restaurants. The seller wants to make an express warranty that the goods are free from defects in materials and workmanship at the time of the sale. Draft a clause that details when the buyer must notify the seller of any breach with respect to any goods received. Do you need to worry about whether the clause you draft is unconscionable? *See* UCC §§ 2-302, 2-719. *Compare* UCC § 1-302(b).

---

[33]   *Id.* at 1099.

2. Damages

Assuming the buyer has given the seller adequate and timely notification of breach, the buyer will have a claim for damages against the seller for the nonconforming tender of goods that the buyer has accepted. Read sections 2-714 and 2-715. To understand those remedies, consider the situation the buyer is in.

The buyer has either accepted goods that fail to conform to the contract or has accepted conforming goods that were tendered in a nonconforming manner. As a result, the buyer is liable to the seller for the contract price of the accepted goods, even if those goods are defective or otherwise do not conform to the contract. UCC §§ 2-607(1), 2-709(1). The buyer, however, has not received the full benefit of the bargain it made with the seller. Section 2-714 is designed to compensate the buyer for its failure to receive the seller's promised performance. It does this by protecting the buyer's expectation interest in three distinct ways.

Subsection (1) covers a nonconforming tender. For example, it applies if a seller has delivered conforming goods late or has delivered less than the full quantity of goods called for in the contract. In such a case, the buyer is entitled to recover damages for the losses caused by the defect in the seller's performance. Subsection (2) applies to breach of warranty cases. It provides for damages based on the difference in value between the goods as delivered and the goods as promised. Subsection (3) authorizes the measures of recovery in subsections (1) and (2) to be supplemented by an award of incidental and consequential damages. *See* UCC § 2-715. If the buyer notifies the seller, the buyer may deduct its section 2-714 damages from any portion of the purchase price that the buyer still owes under the contract. UCC § 2-717.

Now try to apply these rules to a few problems. In doing so, remember the expectation principle discussed in connection with the buyer's other remedies. Consider whether the buyer's lost expectancy in a breach of warranty case is better measured by the cost of replacement or the cost of repair. Contemplate what might qualify as the "special circumstances" to which section 2-714(2) refers.

Problem 7-23

Blaisdell Soup, Inc. contracted on May 1 to purchase 10,000 bushels of # 1 grade tomatoes for $10 per bushel from Sun Farms, Inc. The market price at the time the contract was entered into was $8 per bushel.

A. On August 10, the time for delivery, Sun Farms tendered 10,000 bushels of # 2 grade tomatoes. Caught at the end of the season and unable to get the higher grade of tomatoes elsewhere, Blaisdell Soup accepted the tomatoes. Grade #2 tomatoes at that time had a market price at $7 per bushel. The market price of # 1 grade tomatoes was $9 per bushel. Sun Farms claims the contract price of $100,000. What damages may Blaisdell Soup deduct from the price under section 2-714(2)?

B. How, if at all, would the answer to Part A change if, at the time of acceptance, the market price of # 1 tomatoes had risen in value to $12 per bushel and # 2 tomatoes were worth $9 per bushel?

C. On August 10, the time for delivery, Sun Farms tendered 10,000 bushels of what appeared to be # 1 grade tomatoes, which Blaisdell Soup accepted. Upon unpacking the crates, however, Blaisdell Soup discovered that the entire lot was decaying. Blaisdell Soup salvaged the lot for $1,000 and purchased replacement tomatoes from another grower for $13 per bushel. What is the proper measure of Blaisdell Soup's damages?

D. On August 10, the time for delivery, Sun Farms tendered 6,000 bushels of #2 tomatoes instead of the 10,000 #1 grade tomatoes contracted for. Blaisdell Soup accepted the tomatoes and resold them for $7 per bushel. Blaisdell Soup then purchased 10,000 bushels of #1 tomatoes from another supplier for $11 per bushel. How should damages be measured?

E. How, if at all, would the answer to Part D change if Blaisdell Soup did not purchase any replacement tomatoes?

Problem 7-24

Seller agreed to manufacture, sell, and deliver 500 railroad cars to Railroad for the approximate price of $10 million ($20,000 per car). After delivery and acceptance of the goods, Railroad discovered cracks in the structure and weld of many cars. Seller refused to repair, claiming it had no responsibility for the alleged defects, and Railroad implemented its own program of repair at a total cost of $5 million ($10,000 per car). Railroad brought suit under section 2-714(2) and alleged: (1) the value of each car as warranted was $20,000; (2) the cost to repair each car was $10,000; and (3) the value of the car as repaired was $19,000. Therefore, the "difference in value" under section 2-714(2) is $11,000 per car, the cost to repair plus the difference in value between the car as warranted and the car as repaired.

A. Is Railroad correct? What arguments should Seller make in defense? Does it make any difference if the cars were worth $15,000 as delivered?

B. Suppose Railroad spent $10,000 per car to repair and the value of each car as repaired was $22,000. How much should Railroad recover?

As in the case of non-delivery, the buyer's right to an award of consequential damages is limited in four ways. The buyer must prove that the breach actually caused the loss, the loss was foreseeable, the loss could not have been reasonably prevented, and the type and amount of the loss is reasonably certain. Even with these limitations, a buyer's incidental and consequential damages can far exceed the contract price.

Problem 7-25

Silicon Solutions, Inc., which manufactures circuit boards for use in personal computers, contracted to sell 10,000 circuit boards to Baseline Computers Corp. over the course of one year for $50 per board. The circuit boards were to be manufactured according to specifications that Silicon Solutions and Baseline Computers agreed to at the beginning of the contract period. After Silicon Solutions had supplied 4,000 circuit boards to Baseline, and Baseline had installed those boards into computers that had been sold to customers, Baseline started to receive numerous customer complaints regarding the performance of the computers with the Silicon Solutions circuit boards. After a month-long investigation, and after Baseline had received and installed another 1,000 Silicon Solutions circuit boards, Baseline determined that Silicon Solutions had not manufactured the boards according to the required specifications.

Baseline stopped accepting Silicon Solutions circuit boards and cancelled the contract. Baseline then purchased 5,000 replacement boards from Awesome Manufacturers, Inc. for $60 per board. Baseline installed replacement boards in the 1,000 computers with Silicon Solutions boards that it still owned. It also has pledged to repair at no charge to its customers the 4,000 computers that it sold with Silicon Solutions boards. To date, 1,000 computers have been returned for repair and the average cost of shipping – which Baseline has paid – has been $25 per computer. Each computer takes two hours to repair and reprogram. Baseline Computers bills its technician's time at $50 per hour. Silicon Solutions does not want its defective circuit boards back and it costs Baseline Computers 20 cents per board to dispose of them in an environmentally safe manner.

A. If Baseline has already paid for the 5,000 boards received from Silicon Solutions and given proper notification of the breach, how much in damages is Baseline entitled to recover from Silicon Solutions?

B. Because of these events, Silicon Solutions is considering including in its future agreements with its customers and Baseline is considering including in its future agreements with its suppliers a clause that clearly allocates the risk of defective component parts.

1. If your last name begins with a letter from A to M, draft such a clause on behalf of Silicon Solutions.

2. If your last name begins with a letter from N to Z, draft such a clause on behalf of Baseline.

D. REVOCATION OF ACCEPTANCE OF THE GOODS

A buyer who accepts goods may no longer reject the goods. UCC § 2-607(2). However, under section 2-608, a buyer is entitled to revoke acceptance in the following, limited circumstances:

(A) a nonconformity "substantially impairs" the value of the goods to the buyer;

(B) there has been no substantial change in the condition of the goods other than one caused by the nonconformity; and

(C) at least one of the following:

(i) the buyer had a reasonable assumption that the nonconformity would be cured but it has not been cured;

(ii) the nonconformity was difficult to discover and that difficulty induced the buyer to accept the goods; or

(iii) the seller assured the buyer that the goods were conforming and those assurances induced the buyer to accept the goods without discovery of the nonconformity.

Right to revoke acceptance. As you can see, this right to revoke acceptance is a fairly restricted one. Whereas a buyer may generally reject goods for any nonconformity, a buyer may revoke acceptance of the goods only if their nonconformity substantially impairs their value. We have encountered a "substantial impairment" standard before, when we considered rejection of goods in installment contracts. However, the language of the two provisions is slightly different. The standard for revocation of acceptance requires that the nonconformity substantially impair the value of the goods "to him," meaning to the buyer. UCC § 2-608(1). Those words are noticeably absent from the rule on rejection of goods in an installment contract. *Cf.* UCC § 2-612(2), (3). Query if this difference in language has any impact on how the standard is to be applied.

Notice of revocation. As we saw with rejection, the buyer must notify the seller of the intention to revoke acceptance within a reasonable time after the ground for revocation was or should have been discovered. A revocation is not effective until such notification is sent. UCC §§ 2-608(2), 1-202(d). However, the time period for giving notice of revocation of acceptance is apparently longer than the period for giving notification of rejection. *See* UCC § 2-608 cmt. 4. Moreover, no specific content of the notification is required. *See* UCC § 2-608 cmt. 5. In other words, the standards applicable to notification following an initial rejection do not apply. *Cf.* UCC §§ 2-605, 2-607(3)(a).

Suppose the buyer has no right to revoke acceptance under the standard in section 2-608 but nonetheless gives a timely notification of revocation that contains all the required content. Is this treated as a wrongful but effective revocation, with the same consequences as a wrongful but effective rejection? No. There is no such thing as a wrongful but effective revocation. A buyer can successfully revoke acceptance of the goods only when the buyer both has the right to revoke and gives effective notification of revocation. If the attempted revocation is either not justifiable or is justifiable but the buyer fails to give an effective notification, the buyer will not have undone the acceptance of the goods. *See* UCC § 2-709 cmt. 5.

Effect of a justifiable and effective revocation. Revocation of acceptance of the goods is not a cancellation or termination of the contract or rescission of the contract. UCC § 2-608 cmt. 1. It is merely undoing the acceptance of the goods that have been tendered. The buyer will still be entitled to expectation-based damages using either the cover price or market price measurement, plus incidental and consequential damages.

Care of goods after revocation. A buyer who justifiably and effectively revokes acceptance of the goods is treated exactly as if the buyer had rejected the goods. Thus, the buyer is not liable for the purchase price, may cancel the contract, and may seek damages measured in the same way as if the seller had repudiated or not delivered. UCC § 2-711(1). The buyer also has all the rights and duties with respect to goods in its possession as a buyer who rejects, including the right to a security interest in the goods to cover the price paid and any incidental damages incurred. UCC §§ 2-711(3), 2-602(2), 2-603, 2-604.

Revocation and the right to cure. One issue of some controversy is whether the seller has a right to cure following revocation.[34] A simple syllogism suggests that the seller does: (i) the buyer has the same rights and duties regarding the goods as if the buyer had rejected them, UCC § 2-608(3); (ii) the seller often has a right to cure after rejection, *see* UCC § 2-508, and thus (iii) the seller may have a right to cure following revocation. However, to the extent that the buyer revokes under section 2-608(1)(a) – having accepted on the reasonable belief the cure would be forthcoming and after waiting a reasonable time, the nonconformity remains uncured – it makes no sense to give the seller yet more time to cure. A revocation of acceptance under section 2-608(1)(b) may, however, give rise to a right to cure.[35]

Problem 7-26

In which, if any, of the following scenarios will the buyer have a right to revoke acceptance of the goods? Assume in each case that the seller has made an implied warranty of merchantability that has not been disclaimed.

A. Armani purchased 100 bolts of Egyptian cotton fabric to make shirts. After using about 45 bolts to make shirts, Armani discovered that the shirts permanently discolored when pressed, making the shirts unfit for sale and the remaining fabric unsuitable for use.

B. Biker purchased a new motorcycle for personal use. Two weeks after accepting the motorcycle, a crack in the fuel line caused gasoline to escape and ignite. The entire bike was engulfed in flames. The bike was destroyed and Biker was seriously injured.

C. Cantankerous purchased a new mobile home for personal use. Several weeks after accepting delivery, and after the first hard rain,

---

[34] *See* Howard Foss, *The Seller's Right to Cure When the Buyer Revokes Acceptance: Erase the Line in the Sand*, 16 S. ILL. U. L.J. 1 (1991).

[35] *Cf. Lile v. Kiesel*, 871 N.E.2d 995 (Ind. Ct. App. 2007) (no right to cure following revocation).

Cantankerous noticed a leak in the roof. The seller promptly repaired the leak but a few weeks later a new leak developed in a different location.

1. Although the seller attempted to repair the second leak, it reappeared after the next rain.

2. After again attempting to repair the second leak, it reappeared for the third time following another rain.

3. The seller concludes that the only way to permanently repair the leak is to remove the roof (a process that involves sawing it off), install new flashing, and then reattach the roof. Seller is willing to do this at no charge but Cantankerous does not want a mobile home with a roof that has been sawn off and reattached.

D. Dartmouth ordered 500 green 3-ring binders from an office supply store. Dartmouth planned to distribute the binders at a conference it was putting on for potential customers. When the binders arrived, Dartmouth inspected them and noticed that they were assorted colors, not all green. This rendered the binders unsuitable for Dartmouth's purpose, so Dartmouth contacted the supply store, which promised to send replacements immediately. No replacements ever arrived.

Problem 7-27

On February 1, Sterling Inc. contracted to manufacture and sell to Ballistics, Inc. a new machine capable of manufacturing 50 bullets per minute. The price was $500,000, of which 25% was to be paid at the time of contracting with the balance due 30 days after delivery. Ballistics made the down payment. Under the agreement, Sterling was to deliver, install, and test the machine by June 1.

On June 1, Sterling delivered and installed the machine and gave it a two-hour test run. Ballistics' purchasing officer, who was present, was impressed and saw no apparent problems, but said that she would like "a little more time to see how it works." By June 14, Ballistics' personnel had noticed a problem in production rate and by June 21 it was clear that the machine, even though operating smoothly, was producing only 40 bullets per minute. Ballistics' engineers searched for the problem but could not find it. Ballistics continued to use the machine throughout this period, but the purchasing officer was already looking for a different manufacturer.

On July 1, Sterling telephoned to inquire how things were going and to request payment of the balance of the price. Ballistics, for the first time, informed Sterling that the machine was not producing bullets at the required rate. The same day, Ballistics faxed a notice to Sterling stating, in essence, that: (1) the machine's production did not conform to the contract; (2) Ballistics would not pay the price; and (3) Sterling should pick up the machine immediately.

On July 5, Sterling's engineers appeared at Ballistics' plant and asked to inspect the machine. By July 7, Sterling's engineers conceded that there was a problem with the machine that existed at the time it was installed. Sterling offered to repair the machine at its cost and stated that when repaired the machine would be "good as new." Ballistics declined the offer, stating that Sterling had no right to "cure" the defect and that Ballistics would not pay the balance of the price unless Sterling delivered a new machine. Sterling refused, stating that repair was its best offer.

On July 10, Ballistics contracted with Epoch Manufacturing for a similar machine. The price was $750,000 and delivery was promised for September 1. Ballistics continued to use Sterling's machine until September 1, when Epoch's machine was delivered and installed. Epoch's machine works perfectly. Sterling refused to pick up its machine or to give directions to Ballistics for disposition. The machine is now stored in a separate building on Ballistics' property.

Sterling is threatening to sue Ballistics for the price of the machine. Ballistics, in turn, wants its down payment back along with cover damages. How should a court resolve this situation?

Problem 7-28

You are a district court judge. The following case has just been tried in a bench trial. The following are the facts you have heard.

Standard Plywood, Inc., a lumber wholesaler located in Billings, Montana, and Bargain Village, Inc., a lumber yard located in Minneapolis, Minnesota, signed a written document that provided as follows:

> Standard Plywood will deliver to Bargain Village, Inc., FOB Billings, 50 pallets of plywood sheets 50" by 65" on November 1. Price is $100 per pallet. Shipment will be by rail or truck at discretion of seller.

On October 30, Standard Plywood delivered to Burlington Northern Railyard in Billings, 45 pallets of plywood sheets measuring 50" by 65" for shipment to Bargain Village in Minneapolis. Standard Plywood obtained a non-negotiable bill of lading from Burlington Northern naming itself as consignee and sent the document to Bargain Village by Federal Express on November 1. Bargain Village received the non-negotiable bill of lading on November 2.

On November 5, Burlington Northern notified Bargain Village that 45 pallets were available for pickup. Bargain Village went to the railyard and wanted to inspect the plywood before loading it on its trucks. Burlington Northern called Standard Plywood to see if inspection should be allowed. Standard Plywood replied that Bargain Village was not entitled to inspect the goods as it had not paid for them. Bargain Village argued with Standard Plywood but to no avail. Bargain Village then loaded the 45 pallets unopened and transported them to its place of business.

Upon opening the pallets on November 6, Bargain Village discovered the pallets contained 90 sheets of plywood per pallet. Bargain Village telephoned Standard Plywood to complain that the shipment did not contain 50 pallets and that each of the 45 pallets delivered was short 10 sheets. Standard Plywood replied that, as far as it knew, in the wholesale trade each pallet always has 90 sheets, not 100. Bargain Village maintained at trial that it had never heard of such a thing, each pallet it had purchased from other wholesalers always contained 100 sheets.

On November 30, Bargain Village sent Standard Plywood a fax stating that it rejected the plywood "due to the shortage in delivery" and requested that Standard Plywood send instructions as to what to do with the plywood. Standard Plywood faxed a reply stating that Bargain Village had no right to reject or revoke, that it would not take the plywood back, and demanded the price for 45 pallets of plywood. Bargain Village stored the plywood from the 45 pallets in its warehouse for a month and then sold the plywood for $80 per pallet in December. Standard Plywood sued Bargain Village for the price of the plywood (45 pallets times $100 per pallet). Bargain Village denied liability for the price and counterclaimed for damages for breach of contract.

Write the opinion deciding the case.

E. NONCONFORMING TENDER UNDER THE CISG AND UNIDROIT

CISG. The buyer's remedies for the seller's breach of a contract governed by the CISG are somewhat different than those of a buyer under an Article 2 contract. The seller has the general duty to deliver the goods required by the contract. Art. 30. That duty includes the obligation to provide goods that conform to the contract requirements. Art. 36. Once the goods are tendered, the buyer has the obligation – not merely a right, but an obligation – to examine them. Art. 38. If the seller delivers nonconforming goods, the buyer must give notice of the nature of the nonconformity within a reasonable time after the buyer discovered or should have discovered the nonconformity, as long as that time period is not longer than two years (or the time period of an explicit guarantee). Art. 39. Failure to give notice as required precludes the buyer from being able to rely on the nonconformity to show a breach by the seller. However, this bar on remedies is subject to two exceptions: (i) if the seller was aware or should have been aware of the lack of conformity and failed to tell the buyer, Art. 40; or (ii) if the buyer had a reasonable excuse for failing to give notice, Art. 44.

The buyer has several remedial options when the seller delivers nonconforming goods. First, the buyer may require the seller to tender a conforming performance, if that is reasonable under the circumstances. That conforming performance may be by either substitute goods or repair. The buyer is entitled to request substitute goods only if the original tender was a fundamental breach, Art. 46, and only if the buyer can return the originally delivered goods, Art. 82. The buyer may allow the seller additional time for tendering that conforming performance and, unless the seller notifies the buyer that it will not perform within that time period, the buyer may not exercise any other remedies for breach while awaiting performance. The buyer, however, does not waive its rights to damages for delay. Art. 47. The seller may also insist on providing a cure, and if reasonable under the circumstances, the buyer will be required to accept that cure. Art. 48.

Second, if the seller does not cure, then the buyer may reduce the price owed for the goods based upon the value of the goods actually delivered. Art. 50. If the buyer refuses a cure that the seller is entitled to make under Article 48, the buyer cannot reduce the price owed.

Third, the buyer may be able to declare the contract avoided if the seller has either committed a fundamental breach (Art. 25) or failed to deliver the goods and refuses or fails to deliver the goods within a further set time period. Arts. 49, 51(2). The buyer has to act within a reasonable time to declare the contract avoided. Art.

49. In an installment contract, the buyer may declare the contract avoided if the failure of the seller to perform is a fundamental breach of the entire contract. Art. 73. If the contract is avoided, the buyer may recover damages based upon a reasonable replacement transaction, Art. 75, or based upon the market price, Art. 76. Damages include liability for consequential losses, Art. 74, unless the buyer failed to give reasonable notice of the nonconformity. Art. 44. The buyer has to take reasonable action to mitigate damages. Art. 77.

Avoidance of the contract releases the parties from future obligations but preserves the aggrieved party's right for damages. Avoidance of the contract also entitles each party to restitution of the benefit transferred to the other side. Art. 81. Subject to some specific exceptions, a buyer may not declare the contract avoided if it is unable to make restitution of any goods delivered. Art. 82. The buyer who has declared the contract avoided must preserve the goods delivered. Art. 86. The buyer may store them and recover the expense of doing so, Art. 87, and in some circumstances sell the goods for the benefit of the seller. Art. 88.

Thus the ability of the buyer to force the goods back onto the seller is determined by whether the buyer may avoid the contract for fundamental breach. Fundamental breach is most closely related to the concept of substantial impairment, not perfect tender. Art. 25.

UNIDROIT Principles. As discussed earlier, the UNIDROIT Principles were drafted for use in many different types of international contracts, not just contracts for the sale of goods. Thus there are no specific provisions on rejection, acceptance, or revocation of acceptance of the goods. The focus is more broadly on an aggrieved party's rights when the other side tenders a nonconforming performance. Having said that, the concepts in the UNIDROIT Principles are similar to the concepts in the CISG.

The aggrieved party may require the nonperforming party's performance in some circumstances, Art. 7.2.2, including the right to require repair or replacement of the defective performance, Art. 7.2.3. The nonperforming party may, in some circumstances, insist on curing the initially tendered nonconforming performance. Art. 7.1.4. The aggrieved party may also be entitled to terminate the contract if the nonperforming party's failure to perform is a fundamental non-performance, Art. 7.3.1, as long as the aggrieved party gives timely notice of that termination. Art. 7.3.2. Termination relieves both parties of future obligations to perform but preserves the aggrieved party's right to remedies for the other side's nonperformance. Art. 7.3.5. Upon termination, each side must make restitution of the performance received. Art. 7.3.6. In this circumstance, the aggrieved party would then be able to seek damages for the failure to obtain the contracted for performance based either on a replacement transaction or on proof of the current price for the performance, Art. 7.4.5, Art. 7.4.6, as well as damages for further harm. All damages must be certain, foreseeable, and appropriately mitigated. Art. 7.4.1 through Art. 7.4.4, Art. 7.4.8. If the aggrieved party does not terminate the contract, then it would be able to recover for the harm caused by the failure to receive a fully conforming performance, as long as those damages are certain, foreseeable, and appropriately mitigated. Art. 7.4.1 through Art. 7.4.4, Art. 7.4.8. The aggrieved party would be able to set off those damages against any amounts owed under the contract to the other party. Art. 8.1.

SECTION 4.   SELLER'S BREACH AND THE RISK OF LOSS FOR THE GOODS

As we learned in Chapter Four, until the seller tenders or delivers the goods, the seller generally has the risk of loss for those goods. Section 2-509 provides the point at which the risk of loss passes to the buyer when the goods and the tender are conforming to the contract. However, if the goods or the tender do not conform to the contract such that the buyer has a right to reject the goods, section 2-510(1) provides that the risk of loss remains with the seller.

Problem 7-29

Sterling, Inc. is a vegetable distributor and Bluto Foods Co. is a manufacturer of canned soups. On April 1, the parties entered into a written contract for the sale of 1,000 bushels of "Early Girl" tomatoes at $40.00 per bushel, to be shipped F.O.B. Sterling's place of business on or before July 15 and delivered in "green" condition, a term having definite meaning in the trade. The goods were to be delivered in a single lot and Bluto was to make payment 30 days after the goods were received. Nothing was said in the agreement about rejection.

Sterling arranged for Carrier to transport the tomatoes from the fields where they were grown to Bluto's manufacturing facility. However, Sterling neglected to arrange for transport in refrigerated cars, so by the time the tomatoes arrived at Bluto's facility, the tomatoes were overripe, rotting, and definitely not in "green" condition.

A. If the tomatoes were in "green" condition when delivered to Carrier, who would have the risk of loss for these tomatoes? UCC §§ 2-601, 2-503, 2-504, 2-509, 2-510. Advise Bluto about what to do now.

B. If the tomatoes were not in "green" condition when delivered to Carrier, who would have the risk of loss for these tomatoes?

C. How, if at all, would the analysis change if the contract between Sterling and Bluto stated that shipment was "F.O.B. Bluto's facility"?

D. Assume that Sterling arranged for Carrier to refrigerate the tomatoes during transport, but Sterling did not give notice to Bluto that the tomatoes had been shipped. Carrier's boxcar containing the tomatoes had an equipment failure and the tomatoes were not refrigerated during the entire time of transport. The tomatoes arrived in rotten condition. Who has the risk of loss for the tomatoes? Who has an action against Carrier for the damage to the tomatoes? UCC §§ 7-309, 2-722.

Even if the goods or the tender are nonconforming, and the buyer has the right to reject the goods, if the buyer nevertheless accepts the goods, the buyer will have thereby assumed the risk of loss for the goods. UCC § 2-510(1).

If the buyer rightfully revokes acceptance of the goods, often the buyer will still have possession of the goods even though title to the goods re-vests in the seller. UCC § 2-401(4). Nothing in Article 2 explicitly provides whether the risk of loss remains with the buyer or passes back to the seller. However, section 2-510(2) does indicate that the buyer may treat the risk of loss as having remained with the seller from the beginning "to the extent of any deficiency in [the buyer's] effective insurance coverage." Thus, apparently, the risk of loss remains with the revoking buyer who has insurance but passes back to the seller to the extent the buyer is uninsured or underinsured. Whether the buyer's insurance covers the goods in the buyer's possession after revocation of acceptance is a matter left to the insurance contract and insurance law; Article 2 does not speak to it. The revoking buyer does have an insurable interest in the goods, UCC § 2-501, but that does not mean the buyer's insurance policy will in fact cover those goods.

What if the revoking buyer fails to take reasonable care of the goods and that failure is the cause of the loss that ensues? Although the seller might have the risk of loss to the extent of any deficiency in the buyer's insurance coverage, the buyer would have a duty to care for the goods, UCC §§ 2-603, 2-608(3), and thus should be accountable for damages stemming from the buyer's failure to take reasonable care of the goods.

CISG and UNIDROIT Principles. Under the CISG, the risk of loss for the goods passes to the buyer when the goods are given to the first carrier unless the parties agree that the risk will pass to a particular carrier at a particular place. In order for that main rule to operate, the goods must be identified to the contract with the buyer. Art. 67. If the goods are already in transit when the contract is formed, the risk passes to the buyer at the time the contract is formed unless the seller knows at that time that the goods have already been lost or damaged. Art. 68. If the goods are not being shipped, then the risk passes to the buyer when the goods are tendered to the buyer for delivery. Art. 69. If the goods are lost or damaged after the risk has passed to the buyer, the buyer is obligated to pay for the goods, unless the loss or damage is due to the seller's actions or omissions. Art. 66. If the seller commits a fundamental breach of contract, the passage of the risk of loss is unaffected, but the buyer has all of its remedies for breach of contract. Art. 70. The buyer will be excused from making restitution of the goods, if the contract is avoided for fundamental breach, if the loss or damage to the goods was not the buyer's fault. Art. 82. The UNIDROIT Principles do not address risk of loss.

SECTION 5.   STATUTE OF LIMITATIONS

A buyer seeking to recover damages from a seller for breach of contract must bring its cause of action within the time period prescribed by the applicable statute of limitations. The statute of limitations for claims under Article 2 is four years, although the parties are free to reduce that time to one year. UCC § 2-725(1).

Even with a clear limitations period, there are two recurring issues under most statutes of limitations. First, when does the cause of action accrue? Second, is there anything that might stop or toll the running of the limitations period? Read section 2-725. As you can see, section 2-725(2) provides that a claim for breach of warranty normally accrues when the seller tenders delivery. This is true even if the buyer is then unaware of the problem. However, there is an exception if the warranty "explicitly extends to future performance of the goods" and "discovery of the breach must await the time of such performance," in which case the cause of action accrues when the buyer discovers or should have discovered the breach with respect to the future performance.

Thus, for example, a seller who simply warrants that the goods are merchantable will not have to deal with a suit commenced more than four years after the goods are tendered. Any breach of that warranty occurs upon tender. But what if the seller warrants that "the goods will function properly for one year"? Is that a promise of future performance such that a cause of action breach might not accrue until some time later? How should a seller's unfulfilled promise to repair or replace defective goods be treated? Is it even a breach of warranty claim at all? These are, by far, the most commonly litigated issues under section 2-725.[36] Consider the following recent case.

MYDLACH V. DAIMLERCHRYSLER CORP.
875 N.E.2d 1047 (Ill. 2007)

Justice Fitzgerald delivered the judgment of the court, with opinion:

Plaintiff, Lucy Mydlach, filed a three-count complaint in the circuit court of Cook County against defendant, DaimlerChrysler Corporation, alleging claims under the Magnuson-Moss Warranty-Federal Trade Commission Improvement Act (Magnuson-Moss Act or Act) (15 U.S.C. § 2301 *et seq.* (1994)). The circuit court granted defendant's motion for summary judgment, holding that the claims were time-barred under the four-year statute of limitations contained in section 2-725 of the Uniform Commercial Code. The appellate court affirmed in part and reversed in part. For the reasons discussed below, we affirm in part and reverse in part the judgment of the appellate court and remand the matter to the circuit court for further proceedings.

BACKGROUND

On June 20, 1998, plaintiff purchased a used 1996 Dodge Neon, manufactured by defendant, from McGrath Buick-Nissan (McGrath) in Elgin, Illinois. The vehicle was originally put into service on June 24, 1996, with a three-year/36,000-mile limited warranty. The warranty provided, in relevant part, as follows:

The "**Basic Warranty**" begins on your vehicle's **Warranty Start Date** which is the **earlier** of (1) the date you take delivery of your new vehicle, **OR** (2) the date the vehicle was first put into service * * *.

The "Basic Warranty" covers the cost of all parts and labor needed to repair any item on your vehicle (except as noted below) that's defective in material, workmanship, or factory preparation. You pay nothing for these repairs.

---

[36] Larry T. Garvin, *Uncertainty and Error in the Law of Sales: The Article Two Statute of Limitations*, 83 B.U. L. REV. 345 (2003).

The "**Basic Warranty**" covers every Chrysler supplied part of your vehicle, **EXCEPT** its tires and cellular telephone. * * *

* * *

These warranty repairs or adjustments (parts and labor) will be made by your dealer at no charge using new or remanufactured parts.

* * *

The "**Basic Warranty**" lasts for 36 months from the vehicle's Warranty Start Date **OR** for 36,000 miles on the odometer, whichever occurs first.

(Emphasis in original.)

At the time of plaintiff's purchase in 1998, the car's mileage was 26,296. Thus, the warranty had approximately one year or 10,000 miles remaining.

Beginning July 7, 1998, plaintiff brought the car to McGrath and another authorized dealership several times for a variety of problems, including a recurring fluid leak. Plaintiff claimed that the dealerships' repair attempts were unsuccessful and, as a result, she could not use the vehicle as intended. Plaintiff ultimately filed suit against defendant on May 16, 2001, seeking legal and equitable relief, as well as attorney fees and costs, under the Magnuson-Moss Act. Plaintiff alleged breach of written warranty (count I), breach of the implied warranty of merchantability (count II), and revocation of acceptance (count III).

The case initially proceeded to arbitration, where a decision was entered in favor of defendant. Plaintiff rejected the arbitrators' decision and the case was returned to the trial court. After further discovery, defendant filed a motion for summary judgment. Defendant argued that counts I and II of plaintiff's complaint were subject to the four-year statute of limitations found in section 2-725 of the UCC and that, as provided by section 2-725(2), the statute of limitations commenced upon "tender of delivery" of the vehicle to its original purchaser in June 1996. Thus, according to defendant, plaintiff's suit, filed in May 2001, was outside the four-year limitations period. With respect to count III, defendant argued that plaintiff was not entitled to seek revocation of acceptance because no privity existed between plaintiff and defendant, and because plaintiff could not prove the underlying breach of implied warranty claim.

Plaintiff responded that her claims were not time-barred because the "tender of delivery" referenced in the UCC was the tender of delivery to her, and not to the original purchaser. Plaintiff also argued that a lack of privity is not a bar to a claim for revocation of acceptance against a manufacturer who is also a warrantor.

Relying on *Nowalski v. Ford Motor Co.*, 781 N.E.2d 578 (Ill. Ct. App. 2002), the trial court agreed with defendant that plaintiff's claims were time-barred and granted defendant's motion for summary judgment on all three counts. The trial court denied plaintiff's motion for reconsideration, and plaintiff appealed.

The appellate court reversed the trial court's grant of summary judgment on counts I and III, and affirmed the grant of summary judgment on count II. As to the limitations issue, the appellate court followed *Cosman v. Ford Motor Co.,* 674 N.E.2d 61 (Ill. Ct. App. 1996), rather than *Nowalski,* and held that:

> plaintiff's right to bring a breach of written warranty action based on the promise to repair accrued when defendant allegedly failed to successfully repair her car after a reasonable number of attempts and that the four-year statute of limitations did not begin to run until that time.

The appellate court also held that plaintiff could properly pursue revocation of acceptance as an equitable remedy under the Magnuson-Moss Act if her breach of warranty claim was successful.

We allowed defendant's petition for leave to appeal. Because plaintiff does not seek cross-relief as to count II of her complaint, the only counts before this court are counts I and III.

ANALYSIS

[The Court's discussion of the Magnuson-Moss Act is omitted. The Court found that the manufacturer's warranty was a Magnuson-Moss warranty and concluded that the statute of limitations in Article 2 should apply to the Magnuson-Moss warranty claim. We will consider the Magnuson-Moss Act in Chapter Eight. – Eds.].

Preliminarily, we note that the future-performance exception to the four-year limitations period, set forth in [UCC § 2-725(2)], is not at issue in this case. As will be discussed in greater detail below, a repair or replacement warranty like the one issued by defendant here "has nothing to do with the inherent quality of the goods or their future performance." *Cosman,* 674 N.E.2d at 68. *See also* C. Reitz, *Manufacturers' Warranties of Consumer Goods,* 75 WASH. U. L.Q. 357, 364 n. 24 (1997) ("Promises to repair or replace refer to future performance of sellers, not to future performance of goods"); L. Lawrence, *Lawrence's Anderson on the Uniform Commercial Code* § 2-625:129, at 332 (3d ed.2001) (discussing difference between a warranty of future performance and a covenant to repair or replace). Accordingly, we turn our attention to the balance of the statute and the parties' arguments relative thereto.

Defendant argues that section 2-725 should be applied as written. Thus, because the statute provides that a "breach of warranty occurs when tender of delivery is made," and tender of delivery of the Dodge Neon was first made in June

1996, plaintiff's suit, filed in May 2001, was untimely. *See Nowalski,* 781 N.E.2d at 584 (holding that cause of action for breach of three-year/36,000-mile limited warranty accrued when the vehicle was delivered and not when defendant failed to successfully repair the vehicle). Plaintiff argues that a repair warranty cannot be breached until the manufacturer fails to repair the vehicle after a reasonable opportunity to do so, and that the appellate court did not err in finding her complaint was timely filed. *See Cosman,* 674 N.E.2d at 68 (holding that breach of six-year/60,000-mile limited power-train warranty "cannot occur until Ford refuses or fails to repair the powertrain if and when it breaks").[37]

We begin our analysis by turning to the language of article 2 of the UCC. Section 2-725(2) plainly states that "[a] breach of warranty occurs when tender of delivery is made." The *Nowalski* opinion, on which defendant relies, concluded that once article 2 of the UCC is chosen as the analogous state statute from which to borrow the statute of limitations, the analysis begins and ends with the "tender of delivery" language quoted above. *Nowalski,* 781 N.E.2d at 584. We disagree. . . .

Although the parties agree that defendant's warranty is a "written warranty" under the Magnuson-Moss Act, they disagree as to whether the warranty is an "express warranty" under the UCC. Defendant argues that the repair warranty qualifies as an express warranty and that plaintiff's claim is therefore governed by the tender-of-delivery rule in section 2-725(2). Plaintiff argues that it does not qualify as an express warranty and that her claim is not subject to the tender-of-delivery rule.

Section 2-313 of the UCC explains how express warranties are created. . . . The UCC makes plain that an express warranty is related to the quality or description of the goods. . . .

In other words, an express warranty, for purposes of the UCC, obligates the seller to deliver goods that conform to the affirmation, promise, description, sample or model. If a seller delivers conforming goods, the warranty is satisfied. If the seller delivers nonconforming goods, the warranty is breached at that time. Even if the buyer is unaware that the goods, as delivered, do not conform to the seller's affirmation, promise, description, sample or model, the warranty has been breached. Under this scenario, the statutory pronouncement that "[a] breach of warranty

---

[37]   The same divergence of opinion on the limitations issue that is exemplified by *Nowalski* and *Cosman* exists among our sister states. *See generally* L. Garvin, *Uncertainty and Error in the Law of Sales: The Article Two Statute of Limitations,* 83 B.U.L. REV. 345, 377–81 (2003) (discussing the split among state courts in their approach to repair or replacement promises).

occurs when tender of delivery is made" makes perfect sense, and the four-year limitations period commences at that time. . . .

The warranty in the present case, however, is not related to the quality or description of the goods at tender. It does not warrant that the vehicle will conform to some affirmation, promise, description, sample or model. Rather, the warranty promises only that the manufacturer will repair or replace defective parts during the warranty period. As defendant made clear in its brief before this court:

> DaimlerChrysler's limited warranty was not a promise that the vehicle would be defect free and in the event of a breach of warranty, Plaintiff would be limited to repair or replacement of the vehicle. Rather, DaimlerChrysler's limited warranty promised to cover the cost to repair or replace defective parts in the automobile for the time period covering 36 months or 36 thousand miles.

Although defendant's warranty qualifies as a "written warranty" under the [Magnuson-Moss] Act, it is not an "express warranty" under the UCC, and is thus not the type of warranty that can be breached on "tender of delivery". . . . Accordingly, we reject defendant's argument that the four-year limitations period for breach of the repair warranty commenced upon delivery of the Dodge Neon in 1996, and we overrule the *Nowalski* opinion on which defendant relies.

Our conclusion that the repair warranty is not a UCC express warranty, and thus not subject to the tender-of-delivery rule set forth in the second sentence of section 2-725(2), does not render section 2-725(2) irrelevant for purposes of determining when the limitations period began on plaintiff's claim under the Magnuson-Moss Act. The first sentence of section 2-725(2) remains applicable. The first sentence states: "[a] cause of action accrues *when the breach occurs,* regardless of the aggrieved party's lack of knowledge of the breach." (Emphasis added.) . . . . Although the UCC does not expressly state when the breach of a repair promise occurs, we may refer to the law that exists outside of the UCC. *See* [UCC § 1-103] ("Unless displaced by the particular provisions of this Act, the principles of law and equity shall supplement its provisions").

Generally, "[w]hen performance of a duty under a contract is due any non-performance is a breach." RESTATEMENT (SECOND) OF CONTRACTS § 235, at 211 (1979). Performance under a vehicle manufacturer's promise to repair or replace defective parts is due not at tender of delivery, but only when, and if, a covered defect arises and repairs are required. In that event, if the promised repairs are refused or unsuccessful, the repair warranty is breached and the cause of action accrues, triggering the four-year limitations period. . . . This is the approach advocated by some commentators. For example, in his discussion of the appropriate treatment of a manufacturer's express warranty to repair or replace defective parts, Professor Lawrence states:

> The sounder approach is to recognize that the failure to repair or replace is merely a breach of contract and not a breach of warranty, and therefore no cause of action arises until the seller has refused to repair or replace the goods. This is because until the seller has failed or refused to make the repairs or provide a replacement, the buyer, not being entitled to such a remedy, has no right to commence an action for damages. As a result, the action is timely if brought within four years of the seller's failure or refusal.

L. LAWRENCE, LAWRENCE'S ANDERSON ON THE UNIFORM COMMERCIAL CODE § 2-725:101, at 303 (3d ed.2001).

The correctness of this approach is manifest when we consider consumer claims for breach of repair warranties that run for periods longer than the three years/36,000 miles at issue here. For example, consider the case of a consumer who purchases a vehicle carrying a five-year/50,000-mile repair warranty. If the four-year limitations period commences at "tender of delivery," the limitations period for a breach of the repair promise occurring in year five will expire before the breach even occurs, thus rendering the repair warranty unenforceable during its final year. Statutes of limitations, however, are intended "to prevent stale claims, not to preclude claims before they are ripe for adjudication." *Guzman v. C.R. Epperson Construction, Inc.,* 752 N.E.2d 1069 (2001). Even a four-year warranty could be rendered unenforceable if breach of the repair promise occurred near the end of the warranty period. In that case, the buyer would have only the briefest of periods in which to file suit.

Defendant argues that concerns about the enforceability of longer-term repair warranties are inapplicable to the facts of this case and without merit. We disagree. Although the repair warranty at issue here ran for three years, our holding in this case will apply equally to longer-term warranties. Such warranties are common in the automobile industry. Adoption of defendant's position would be an invitation to manufacturers and sellers of automobiles, as well as other goods, to engage in misleading marketing. That is, a manufacturer or seller could use the marketing advantage of a longer repair warranty, yet escape the accompanying obligations of that warranty by pleading the statute of limitations in defense. Such a result is contrary to the very purpose of the Magnuson-Moss Act: "to improve the adequacy of information available to consumers" and "prevent deception." 15 U.S.C. § 2302(a) (1994).

Defendant also argues that unless the tender-of-delivery rule in section 2-725 is given effect, the limitations period for breach of limited warranty actions will be "limitless" and "uncertain." This argument is without merit. Because the promise to repair or replace defective parts is only good during the warranty period, the latest a breach of warranty can occur is at the very end of that period. Accordingly, the statute of limitations will expire, at the latest, four years after the warranty period has run. If breach of a repair warranty occurs earlier in the warranty period, the limitations period for that breach will expire sooner, but in no event will the warrantor's exposure extend beyond the warranty period, plus four years. Thus, contrary to defendant's argument, commencing the four-year limitations period from the date the warrantor fails or refuses to repair the vehicle does not result in a limitless limitations period.

We recognize, of course, that a fact question may arise as to the date on which a repair warranty was breached which, in turn, would create some uncertainty as to when the four-year limitations period should commence. Fact questions of this nature, however, frequently arise in cases where the statute of limitations has been pled in defense. Resolution of this type of uncertainty is a classic function of the trier of fact. . . . We therefore reject defendant's argument that commencing the limitations period when the warrantor fails or refuses to repair the defect – rather than at tender of delivery – will create unacceptable uncertainty in the limitations period.

Turning to the facts of this case, the record indicates that plaintiff brought her vehicle to McGrath and another authorized dealer on several occasions beginning in July 1998. At that point, assuming the alleged defects were covered defects, defendant was obligated (through its authorized dealer) to make good on its repair promise. Plaintiff's lawsuit, filed in May 2001, is therefore timely. Accordingly, we affirm that portion of the judgment of the appellate court which reversed the grant of summary judgment in favor of defendant as to count I of the complaint. . . .

[The court's discussion concerning the ability to revoke acceptance against a remote seller is omitted. The Court held that such revocation is not permitted. – Eds.]

CONCLUSION

For the reasons discussed above, we affirm the judgment of the appellate court reversing the trial court's grant of summary judgment in favor of defendant as to count I of the complaint, and reverse the judgment of the appellate court reversing the trial court's grant of summary judgment in favor of defendant as to count III of the complaint. We remand this matter to the trial court for further proceedings.

Problem 7-30

On June 1, 2006, Bristol Manufacturers contracted to purchase factory equipment from Sunshine Fabricators for delivery and installation no later than June 25. Sunshine warranted that the goods were free from defects and would function according to promised specifications for a period of one year from the date of delivery. The equipment was delivered on June 25, but the installation was not completed until July 1. On April 1, 2007, Bristol notified Sunshine that the machine had stopped working. Several days later, Sunshine technicians arrived at Bristol's plant and attempted to fix the problem. After three weeks of effort, the equipment still did not work. The technicians left the premises on April 26, 2007 insisting that they would return to repair the machine. They never did and in August 2007, Bristol notified Sunshine that it considered Sunshine to have breached the contract. In an effort to keep its business functioning, Bristol removed the equipment from the floor, put it in storage, and then installed replacement equipment acquired from a different seller. In October 2010, Bristol consults you, its attorney, about the matter. Does Bristol have a valid claim for breach of contract? If so, has the statute of limitations run on Bristol's claims for breach of contract? Why or why not?

CISG and UNIDROIT Principles. The CISG does not have any limitations period, but the United States has ratified the Convention on the Limitations Period in the International Sale of Goods. In general, the limitations period is four years from accrual of the cause of action, with the cause of action accruing when the breach occurred, subject to several specific rules on when the breach occurs. Arts. 8 through 12. For example, a claim for nonconformity of the goods accrues when the goods are handed over to the buyer unless the seller has made a specific undertaking regarding the goods for a period of time. Arts. 10 and 11. There are also several provisions on "tolling" the limitations period. Arts. 12 through 21.

The UNIDROIT Principles contain several provisions addressing limitations on bringing the action with a general three year time period from the time the obligee knows of the facts giving rise to the claim. Art. 10.2. The Principles also contain several tolling rules. Arts. 10.4 through 10.8.

SECTION 6.   PRIVITY ISSUES

The discussion of buyer's remedies has addressed what the buyer may do when it is faced with a breach by its seller. In many cases, however, the buyer is not pursuing a remedy against its seller, rather, the buyer is pursuing a remedy against a remote seller, such as a manufacturer. To facilitate a discussion of the Article 2 remedies that a buyer may have against a remote seller, consider the following scenario:

Manufacturer
 | – April 1
Distributer
 | – June 1
Retailer
 | – August 1
Buyer

Buyer purchased a new microwave oven from Retailer on August 1.   The microwave was made by Manufacturer, who had sold it to Distributor, who in turn had sold it to Retailer. When Buyer first plugs the microwave into an electrical outlet and attempts to use it to cook some food, the microwave turns on (*i.e.*, the interior lights go on and the plate in the center rotates) but the food does not cook. Retailer has gone out of business and Buyer has no information about or ability to identify Distributor. So, Buyer seeks recourse against Manufacturer.

Buyer's rights against Manufacturer are complicated by a series of issues and questions. These include:

1.   Did Manufacturer make any warranties or promises to Buyer about the goods? In dealing with this question, consider what evidence might be used to show that Manufacturer made an express warranty under section 2-313.[38] Consider also whether section 2-314 creates an implied warranty from Manufacturer to Buyer that the goods will be merchantable.[39]

---

[38]   *See In re McDonalds French Fries Litigation*, 503 F. Supp. 2d 953 (N.D. Ill. 2007).

[39]   *See Curl v. Volkswagen of Am. Inc.*, 871 N.E.2d 1141 (Ohio 2007).

2. Did Manufacturer make any express or implied warranties to Distributor or Retailer that may be extended to Buyer for harm of this type? Read section 2-318. Section 2-318 is based upon the concept of third-party beneficiary rights under a contract.

3. Assuming a source of warranty liability does exist, so that Buyer has a viable cause of action against Manufacturer, to what remedies is Buyer entitled? For example, may Buyer reject or revoke acceptance of the microwave and obtain from Manufacturer a refund of the price?[40] UCC §§ 2-601, 2-608, 2-711. If so, would the refund amount be the price that Buyer paid to Retailer or the presumably lower price that Distributor paid to Manufacturer? If Buyer does return the microwave to Manufacturer, may Buyer also obtain market damages under section 2-713 or cover damages under section 2-712? If Buyer does not return the microwave, may Buyer obtain an award of damages against Manufacturer under section 2-714? If so, must Buyer give notification of the breach to Manufacturer or would notification to Retailer satisfy the obligation under section 2-607?[41] By when must such notification be given? Would Buyer be entitled to an award of incidental and consequential damages against Manufacturer? UCC § 2-715. If so, must the consequential harm have been foreseeable by Manufacturer or would be it sufficient if Retailer has reason to know of the harm at the time of the sale to Buyer?

4. When does the statute of limitations period start to run on the breach of warranty claim against Manufacturer, when Manufacturer tendered delivery to Distributor or when Retailer tendered delivery to Buyer?[42]

These questions should illustrate the difficulty of applying a statutory regime based upon privity considerations to a non-privity relationship.

Now consider the following case, which deals primarily with whether the implied warranty of merchantability extends to a remote buyer down the chain of title.

---

[40]   *See Mydlach v. DaimlerChrysler Corp., supra.*

[41]   *See In re Bausch & Lomb Inc. Contact Lens Solutions Products Liability Litigation,* 2008 WL 2308759 (D.S.C. 2008).

[42]   *See Mydlach v. DaimlerChrysler Corp., supra.*

HYUNDAI MOTOR AMERICA, INC. V. GOODIN
822 N.E.2d 947 (Ind. 2005)

Boehm, Justice

We hold that a consumer may sue a manufacturer for economic loss based on breach of the implied warranty of merchantability even if the consumer purchased the product from an intermediary in the distribution chain. There is no requirement of "vertical" privity for such a claim.

Facts and Procedural Background

On November 18, 2000, Sandra Goodin test drove a Hyundai Sonata at AutoChoice Hyundai in Evansville, Indiana. The car was represented as new and showed nineteen miles on the odometer. Goodin testified that when she applied the brakes in the course of the test drive she experienced a "shimmy, shake, pulsating type feel." The AutoChoice salesperson told her that this was caused by flat spots on the tires from extended inactivity and offered to have the tires rotated and inspected. After this explanation, Goodin purchased the Sonata for $22,710.00.

The manufacturer, Hyundai, provided three limited warranties: 1 year/12,000 miles on "wear items;" 5 years/60,000 miles "bumper to bumper;" and 10 years/100,000 miles on the powertrain. Hyundai concedes that brake rotors, brake calipers, and brake caliper slides were subject to the 5 year/60,000 mile warranty covering "[r]epair or replacement of any component originally manufactured or installed by [Hyundai] that is found to be defective in material or workmanship under normal use and maintenance." To claim under this warranty, a vehicle must be serviced by an authorized Hyundai dealer who is then reimbursed by Hyundai for any necessary parts or labor.

Three days after the car was purchased, Goodin's husband, Steven Hicks, took it back to AutoChoice for the promised tire work. Goodin testified that she continued to feel the shimmy but did nothing further for a month. On December 22, she took the car to a different Hyundai dealer, Bales Auto Mall, in Jeffersonville, Indiana, for an unrelated problem and also made an appointment six days later for Bales to inspect the brakes. Bales serviced the brake rotors for warping, but on May 1, 2001, Goodin returned to Bales complaining that the vehicle continued to vibrate when the brakes were applied. Bales found the rotors to be out of tolerance and machined them. Eighteen days later Goodin again returned to Bales, reporting that she still felt vibrations and for the first time also heard a "popping" noise. Goodin told the service advisor at Bales that she thought there may be a problem with the suspension, and Bales changed and lubed the strut assembly. Eleven days later Goodin once more brought the car to Bales reporting continued shimmy and also a "bed spring type" noise originating from the brakes. The Bales mechanic was unable to duplicate the brake problem, but balanced and rotated the tires as Goodin had requested. One week later Goodin returned to Bales where she and Jerry Hawes, Bales's Service Manager, test drove the Sonata. The brake problem did not occur during the test drive, but Hawes identified a noise from the direction of the left front tire and repaired the rubber mounting bracket.

Goodin told Hawes that the brake problem had occurred about seventy percent of the time. The problem was worse when it was wet or cool, was consistently occurring when she drove down a steep hill near her home, and was less frequent when a passenger's weight was added. Goodin made arrangements to leave the car with Hawes at Bales, but, according to Hawes, over a several day period he could not duplicate the symptoms Goodin reported.

On August 24, 2001, Goodin took her car back to her original dealer, AutoChoice, reporting that the brakes "squeak and grind when applied." Goodin left the car with AutoChoice where the left front rotor was machined and loose bolts on the front upper control arm were tightened. Goodin testified that after this five-day procedure the brakes began to make the same noises and vibrations even before she arrived home.

In October 2001 Goodin hired an attorney who faxed a letter to Hyundai Motor America giving notice of her complaint and requesting a refund of the purchase price. On November 13, 2001, Goodin filed a complaint against Hyundai Motor America, Inc. alleging claims under the Magnuson-Moss Warranty Act, 15 U.S.C. §§ 2301-2312, for breach of express warranty, breach of implied warranty, and revocation of acceptance. On April 23, 2002, in anticipation of litigation, Goodin hired William Jones to inspect her car. Jones noted that the odometer read 57,918 miles and the car was still under warranty. Jones drove the car approximately five miles and found "severe brake pulsation on normal stops" which "was worse on high speed stops." Although he did not remove the tires to inspect the brake rotors, Jones opined that the rotors were warped and defective or there was "a root cause that has not been discovered and corrected by the repair facilities." His ultimate conclusion was that the "vehicle was defective and unmerchantable at the time of manufacture and unfit for operation on public roadways." Three weeks later, after the 5 year/60,000 mile warranty had expired, Goodin's husband, Hicks, replaced the rotors with new rotors from a NAPA distributor. After this repair, according to Hicks, the pulsation went from "very bad" to "mild" and "less frequent."

Steven Heiss, District Parts and Service Manager for Hyundai Motor America served as the liaison between Hyundai and the dealers and provided warranty training. If a dealer is not performing repairs correctly, Hyundai, through its liaisons, addresses the problem. Heiss inspected Goodin's Sonata on October 21, 2002. At that point the Sonata had been driven 77,600 miles. He testified that during his twenty-three mile test drive he neither heard the noise described by Goodin nor felt any vibration from the brakes. However, Heiss did hear a "droning noise" which he later concluded was due to a failed left rear wheel bearing. He regarded this as a serious problem and not one caused by abuse or misuse of the vehicle. The wheel bearing would have been covered by the 5 year/60,000 mile warranty. Before his inspection, Heiss had been told that the rotors had been changed by Hicks five months earlier, and when Heiss measured the rotors he found that they were out of standard. Heiss testified a miscast from the factory was one of a number of possible reasons for damaged rotors.

At the conclusion of a two day trial, the jury was instructed on all claims. Over defendants' objection, the instructions on implied warranties made no reference to a privity requirement. The jury returned a verdict for Hyundai on Goodin's breach of express warranty claim, but found in favor of Goodin on her claim for breach of implied warranty of merchantability. Damages of $3,000.00 were assessed . . . .

Hyundai orally moved to set aside the verdict as contrary to law on the ground that Goodin purchased the car from AutoChoice and therefore did not enjoy vertical privity with Hyundai. The court initially denied that motion, but the following day set aside the verdict, holding lack of privity between Goodin and Hyundai precluded a cause of action for breach of implied warranty. Goodin then moved to reinstate the verdict, and, after briefing and oral argument, the trial court granted that motion on the ground that Hyundai was estopped from asserting lack of privity.

Hyundai appealed, asserting: (1) it was not estopped from asserting a defense of lack of privity; and (2) lack of vertical privity barred Goodin's recovery for breach of implied warranty of merchantability. The Court of Appeals agreed on both points, holding that Hyundai was not estopped from asserting that privity was an element of Goodin's prima facia case, and, because privity was lacking, Goodin did not prove her case. . . . The Court of Appeals was "not unsympathetic" to Goodin's claims but regarded itself as bound by a footnote in *Martin Rispens & Son v. Hall Farms, Inc.,* 621 N.E.2d 1078, 1084 n.2 (Ind.1993), where this Court stated: "In Indiana, privity between the seller and the buyer is required to maintain a cause of action on the implied warranties of merchantability." *Id.* at 784. We granted transfer.

Vertical Privity

. . .

C. *Origins of Privity*

Indiana has adopted the Uniform Commercial Code, notably its provision that: "A warranty that the goods shall be merchantable is implied in a contract for their sale if the seller is a merchant with respect to goods of that kind." Ind. Code § 26-1-2-314(1) (2004). Hyundai asserts, and the Court of Appeals found, Indiana law requires vertical privity between manufacturer and consumer when economic damages are sought. Goodin argues that traditional privity of contract between the consumer and manufacturer is not required for a claim against a manufacturer for breach of the implied warranty of merchantability. . . .

Privity originated as a doctrine limiting tort relief for breach of warranties. The lack of privity defense was first recognized in *Winterbottom v. Wright*, 152 Eng. Rep. 402 (Ex. 1842). In that case, the court sustained a demurrer to a suit by an injured coachman for breach of warranty by a third party who contracted with the owner to maintain the coach. In this century, however, *MacPherson v. Buick Motor Co.*, 111 N.E. 1050 (N.Y. 1916), and *Henningsen v. Bloomfield Motors, Inc.*, 161 A.2d 69 (N.J. 1960), established that lack of privity between an automobile manufacturer and a consumer would not preclude the consumer's action for personal injuries and property damage caused by the negligent manufacture of an automobile. "Vertical" privity typically becomes an issue when a purchaser files a breach of warranty action against a vendor in the purchaser's distribution chain who is not the purchaser's immediate seller. Simply put, vertical privity exists only between immediate links in a distribution chain. *Rheem Mfg. Co. v. Phelps Heating & Air Conditioning, Inc.*, 714 N.E.2d 1218, 1228 n.8 (Ind. Ct. App. 1999). A buyer in the same chain who did not purchase directly from a seller is "remote" as to that seller. *Id.* "Horizontal" privity, in contrast, refers to claims by nonpurchasers, typically someone who did not purchase the product but who was injured while using it. Goodin purchased her car from a dealership and is thus remote from the manufacturer and lacks "vertical" privity with Hyundai.

"Although warranty liability originated as a tort doctrine, it was assimilated by the law of contracts and ultimately became part of the law of sales." 2 Hawkland, UCC Series, § 2-318:1 at 771 (2001). But "privity is more than an accident of history. It permitted manufacturers and distributors to control in some measure their risks of doing business." Richard W. Duesenberg, *The Manufacturer's Last Stand: The Disclaimer*, 20 Bus. Law 159, 161 (1964). Because vertical privity involves a claim by a purchaser who voluntarily acquired the goods, it enjoys a stronger claim to justification on the basis of freedom of contract or consensual relationship. It nevertheless has come under criticism in recent years, and this is the first opportunity for this Court to give full consideration to this issue.

D. *Indiana Case Law*

Although this Court did not address the issue, even before the Products Liability Act, both the Court of Appeals and federal courts applying Indiana law held that a claimant was not required to prove privity to succeed in a personal injury action in tort based on breach of implied warranties. Three federal court decisions drew on these decisions to conclude that privity of contract is not required in Indiana to maintain a cause of action for personal injury based on breach of an implied warranty.

However, several Court of Appeals decisions subsequently held that recovery of economic loss for alleged failure of the expected benefit of the bargain based on breach of implied warranty under the UCC required a buyer to be in privity of contract with the seller.

This Court has mentioned the common law privity requirement in the context of actions sounding in contract only once, and that in a footnote. *Martin Rispens & Son v. Hall Farms, Inc.,* 621 N.E.2d 1078 (Ind.1993), addressed negligence and express and implied warranty claims by a farmer against both the direct seller and the grower of seed that allegedly damaged the farmer's crops. The footnote cited to the UCC and two Court of Appeals decisions and other courts have taken the footnote as settled Indiana law on this issue. As the Court of Appeals put it in its decision in this case:

> [T]he [footnote] indicates our supreme court's unequivocal acceptance that privity between a consumer and a manufacturer is required in order to maintain a cause of action for breach of an implied warranty of merchantability. . . . Any change in the law removing the privity requirement in implied warranty actions should be left to that court. . . . To the extent Goodin argues that this result is inequitable, we are not entirely unsympathetic. Whether the cons of the vertical privity rule outweigh the pros is something for either our supreme court or the General Assembly to address.

In *Martin Rispens,* the implied warranty claims were rejected based on an effective disclaimer of implied warranty, under Indiana Code section 26-1-2-316(2) which permits parties to agree to exclude or modify implied warranties if done in a particular manner. The farmer did not present privity as an issue on transfer to this

Court and neither party briefed it.   It was not necessary to the decision. Accordingly, the language in *Martin Rispens,* though often cited, is dicta and we accept the invitation from the Court of Appeal to reconsider it.

Indiana law, as developed in the Court of Appeals, has already eroded the privity requirement to some degree. In *Thompson Farms, Inc. v. Corno Feed Products, Inc.,* 366 N.E.2d 3 (Ind. App. 1977), the Court of Appeals permitted the plaintiff to recover on an implied warranty where it was shown that the contractual arrangements between the manufacturer and the dealer who sold to the plaintiff created an agency relationship;   and the manufacturer's agents participated significantly in the sale both through advertising and personal contact with the buyer. Under those circumstances the Court of Appeals held that the manufacturer was a "seller" within the meaning of Indiana Code section 26-1-2-314. *Richards v. Goerg Boat & Motors, Inc.,* 384 N.E.2d 1084 (Ind. App. 1979), involved a defective boat sold by a dealer where the manufacturer's agents also engaged in personal contact with the buyer by giving demonstrations and attempting to adjust the loss after the sale. The Court of Appeals then, following *Thompson Farms, Inc.,* held that the participation in the sale by the manufacturer was sufficient to bring it into the transaction as a seller within the requirements of Indiana Code section 26-1-2-314. However, if the plaintiff could not show perfect vertical privity or an exception to the rule, then the plaintiff could not prove the claim. *Candlelight Homes, Inc. v. Zornes,* 414 N.E.2d 980, 982 (Ind. Ct. App. 1981).

E. *Statutory Developments in Indiana*

The Product Liability Act, Indiana Code § 34-20-2-1 *et seq.* (1999), does not require a personal injury plaintiff to prove vertical privity in order to assert a products liability claim against the manufacturer. Even before the Product Liability Act in 1978, the requirement of privity of contract in warranty actions in Indiana began to erode in 1963 with the passage of the Uniform Commercial Code under section 2-318:

> A seller's warranty whether express or implied extends to any natural person who is in the family or household of his buyer or who is a guest in his home if it is reasonable to expect that such person may use, consume or be affected by the goods and who is injured in person by breach of the warranty. A seller may not exclude or limit the operation of this section.

I.C. § 26-1-2-318. Section 2-318 was taken verbatim from the UCC as originally prepared by the Uniform Code Committee Draftsmen in 1952. It eliminated "horizontal" privity as a requirement for warranty actions. However, that version of 2-318 took no position on the requirement of vertical privity.

The purpose of the original version of section 2-318, which remains unchanged in Indiana today, was to give standing to certain non-privity plaintiffs to sue as third-party beneficiaries of the warranties that a buyer received under a sales contract. That version of section 2-318 provided only that the benefit of a warranty automatically extended to the buyer's family, household, and houseguests. It was intended to, and did, accomplish its goal of "freeing any such beneficiaries from any technical rules as to [horizontal] privity." U.C.C. § 2-318 cmt. 2. Some states refused to enact this version of section 2-318, and others adopted nonuniform versions of the statute. In 1966, in response to this proliferation of deviant versions of a purportedly uniform code, the drafters proposed three alternative versions of section 2-318. Only California, Louisiana, and Texas have failed to adopt one of these three versions of section 2-318.

The majority of states, including Indiana, retained or adopted the 1952 version of section 2-318, which now appears in the Uniform Commercial Code as "Alternative A." Alternative B provides that "any natural person who may reasonably be expected to use, consume or be affected by the goods and who is injured in person by breach of warranty" may institute a breach of warranty action against the seller. U.C.C. § 2-318 cmt. 3. Alternative B expands the class of potential plaintiffs beyond family, household, and guests, and also implicitly abolishes the requirement of vertical privity because the seller's warranty is not limited to "his buyer" and persons closely associated with that buyer. Alternative B is applicable only to claims for personal injury.

> Because Alternatives A and B of 2-318 are limited to cases where the plaintiff is "injured in person," they do not *authorize* recovery for such loss. But neither do they *bar* a non-privity plaintiff from recovery against such a remote manufacturer for direct economic loss. Thus, Alternatives A and B of 2-318 do not prevent a court from abolishing the *vertical* privity requirement even when a non-privity buyer seeks recovery for direct economic loss.

1 James J. White & Robert S. Summers, Uniform Commercial Code 593 (4th ed. 1995) (emphasis in original).

Alternative C is the most expansive in eliminating the lack-of-privity defense. It provides that: "A seller's warranty whether express or implied extends to any person who may reasonably be expected to use, consume or be affected by the goods and who is injured by breach of the warranty." Alternative C expands the class of plaintiffs to include other nonpurchasers such as the buyer's employees and invitees, and bystanders. Alternative C also eliminates the vertical privity requirement, but is not restricted to "personal" injury. Because Alternative C refers simply to "injury," plaintiffs sustaining only property damage or economic loss in some states have been held to have standing to sue under this language. This is consistent with the stated objective of the drafters that the third alternative follow "the trend of modern decisions as indicated by Restatement of Torts 2d § 402A (Tentative Draft No. 10, 1965) in extending the rule beyond injuries to the person." *Hawkland, supra,* at 770.

The commentaries to the UCC were careful to explain that these alternatives were not to be taken as excluding the development of the common law on the issue of vertical privity:

> [Alternative A] expressly includes as beneficiaries within its provisions the family, household and guests of the purchaser. Beyond this, the section in this form is neutral and is not intended to enlarge or restrict the developing case law on whether the seller's warranties, given to his buyer who resells, extend to other persons in the distributive chain.

U.C.C. § 2-318, cmt. n. 3.

F. *Privity as an Obsolete Requirement as Applied to Consumer Goods*

There is a split of authority in other jurisdictions with similar or identical versions of section 2-318 on the availability of implied warranty claims by remote purchasers, particularly if only economic loss is claimed, as in the present case. Courts of other jurisdictions that have retained or adopted Alternative A note that the statute speaks only to horizontal privity, and is silent as to vertical privity. *See, e.g., Morrow v. New Moon Homes, Inc.,* 548 P.2d 279, 287 (Alaska 1976); *Kassab v. Central Soya,* 432 Pa. 217, 246 A.2d 848, 855 (1968), *overruled on other grounds, AM/PM Franchise Ass'n v. Atlantic Richfield Co.,* 526 Pa. 110, 584 A.2d 915, 926 (1990). As the Pennsylvania Supreme Court put it: "Merely to *read* the language [of § 2-318] is to demonstrate that the code simply fails to treat this problem.... There thus is nothing to prevent this court from joining in the growing number of jurisdictions which, although bound by the code, have nevertheless abolished vertical privity in breach of warranty cases." *Kassab v. Central Soya,* 246 A.2d 848, 856 (Pa. 1968) (emphasis in original), *overruled on other grounds, AM/PM Franchise Ass'n v. Atlantic Richfield Co.,* 584 A.2d 915, 926 (Pa. 1990). Indiana has not legislated on this issue since 1966 when the UCC adopted these three alternatives. More recently, the "Buyback Vehicle Disclosure" statute eliminated the lack-of-privity defense for actions under that section. *See* I.C. § 24-5-13.5-13(c) (1995). In short, the General Assembly in keeping Alternative A left to this Court the issue of to what extent vertical privity of contract will be required.[43]

Courts that have abolished vertical privity have cited a variety of reasons. Principal among these is the view that, in today's economy, manufactured products typically reach the consuming public through one or more intermediaries. As a result, any loss from an unmerchantable product is likely to be identified only after the product is attempted to be used or consumed. Others have cited the concern that privity encourages thinly capitalized manufacturers by insulating them from responsibility for inferior products. Yet others have focused on the point that if implied warranties are effective against remote sellers it produces a chain of lawsuits or crossclaims against those up the distribution chain. And some focus on the reality in today's world that manufacturers focus on the consumer in communications promoting the product.

Finally, some jurisdictions have abolished privity in warranty actions where only economic losses were sought based on the notion that there is "no reason to distinguish between recovery for personal and property injury, on the one hand, and economic loss on the other." *Hiles Co. v. Johnston Pump Co.,* 560 P.2d 154, 157

---

[43]   Several jurisdictions that have adopted Alternative A have abolished privity. *See Morrow v. New Moon Homes,* 548 P.2d 279, 291–92 (Alaska 1976); *Manheim v. Ford Motor Co.,* 201 So. 2d 440 (Fla.1967); *Groppel Co., Inc. v. U.S. Gypsum Co.,* 616 S.W.2d 49, 58 (Mo. Ct. App.1981) (abolishing vertical privity and extending implied warranty to remote purchasers even when only economic loss is claimed); *Peterson v. N. Am. Plant Breeders,* 354 N.W.2d 625, 631 (Neb. 1984); *Hiles Co. v. Johnston Pump Co.,* 560 P.2d 154, 157 (Nev. 1977); *Spring Motors Distrib., Inc. v. Ford Motor Co.,* 489 A.2d 660, 676 (N.J. 1985); *Old Albany Estates Ltd. v. Highland Carpet Mills, Inc.,* 604 P.2d 849, 852 (Okla.1979); *Spagnol Enters., Inc. v. Digital Equipment Corp.,* 568 A.2d 948, 952 (Pa. Super. 1989); *Dawson v. Canteen Corp.,* 212 S.E.2d 82, 82–83 (W. Va. 1975).

Others have retained the common law privity rule. *See Flory v. Silvercrest Indus.,* 633 P.2d 383, 388 (Ariz. 1981); *Ramerth v. Hart,* 983 P.2d 848, 852 (Idaho 1999) (upheld vertical privity requirement but left open the possibility of a different conclusion if the combination of the privity requirement and the economic loss rule proved unjust); *Presnell Constr. Managers, Inc. v. EH Constr., LLC,* 134 S.W.3d 575, 579 (Ky. 2004); *Energy Investors Fund, L.P. v. Metric Constructors, Inc.,* 525 S.E.2d 441, 446 (N.C. 2000); *Hupp Corp. v. Metered Washer Serv.,* 472 P.2d 816 (Or. 1970); *Messer Griesheim Indus. v. Cryotech of Kingsport, Inc.,* 131 S.W.3d 457, 463 (Tenn. Ct. App. 2003); *City of La Crosse v. Schubert, Schroeder & Associates, Inc.,* 240 N.W.2d 124, 126 (Wis. 1976), *overruled on other grounds, Daanen & Janssen v. Cedarapids, Inc.,* N.W.2d 842 (Wis. 1998).

(Nev. 1977). A variance on this theme is the view that abolishing privity "simply recognizes that economic loss is potentially devastating to the buyer of an unmerchantable product and that it is unjust to preclude any recovery from the manufacturer for such loss because of a lack of privity, when the slightest physical injury can give rise to strict liability under the same circumstances." *Groppel Co., Inc. v. U.S. Gypsum Co.*, 616 S.W.2d 49, 59 (Mo. Ct. App. 1981). One court preserving the privity requirement expressed the view that "there may be cases where the plaintiff may be unfairly prejudiced by the operation of the economic loss rule in combination with the privity requirement." *Ramerth v. Hart,* 983 P.2d 848, 852 (Idaho 1999).

In Indiana, the economic loss rule applies to bar recovery in tort "where a negligence claim is based upon the failure of a product to perform as expected and the plaintiff suffers only economic damages." *Martin Rispens,* 621 N.E.2d at 1089. Possibly because of the economic loss rule, Goodin did not raise a negligence claim here. Furthermore, at oral argument Goodin's attorney pointed to the warranty disclaimer in the Buyer's Order as a bar to Goodin's ability to sue her direct seller, AutoChoice, which could then have sued Hyundai for reimbursement. This disclaimer, Goodin contends, precluded a chain of claims ultimately reaching the manufacturer. Therefore, Goodin claims that if this Court does not abolish the vertical privity requirement she will be left without a remedy for Hyundai's breach of its implied warranty of merchantability, and Hyundai's implied warranty becomes nonexistent in practical terms.

The basis for the privity requirement in a contract claim is essentially the idea that the parties to a sale of goods are free to bargain for themselves and thus allocation of risk of failure of a product is best left to the private sector. Otherwise stated, the law should not impose a contract the parties do not wish to make. The Court of Appeals summarized this view well:

> Generally privity extends to the parties to the contract of sale. It relates to the bargained for expectations of the buyer and seller. Accordingly, when the cause of action arises out of economic loss related to the loss of the bargain or profits and consequential damages related thereto, the bargained for expectations of buyer and seller are relevant and privity between them is still required.
>
> Implied warranties of merchantability and fitness for a particular use, as they relate to economic loss from the bargain, cannot then ordinarily be sustained between the buyer and a remote manufacturer.

Richards, 384 N.E.2d at 1092. We think that this rationale has eroded to the point of invisibility as applied to many types of consumer goods in today's economy. The UCC recognizes an implied warranty of merchantability if "goods" are sold to "consumers" by one who ordinarily deals in this product. Warranties are often explicitly promoted as marketing tools, as was true in this case of the Hyundai warranties. Consumer expectations are framed by these legal developments to the point where technically advanced consumer goods are virtually always sold under express warranties, which, as a matter of federal law run to the consumer without regard to privity. 15 U.S.C. § 2310. . . . Given this framework, we think ordinary consumers are entitled to, and do, expect that a consumer product sold under a warranty is merchantable, at least at the modest level of merchantability set by UCC section 2-314, where hazards common to the type of product do not render the product unfit for normal use.

Even if one party to the contract – the manufacturer – intends to extend an implied warranty only to the immediate purchaser, in a consumer setting, doing away with the privity requirement for a product subject to the Magnuson-Moss Warranty Act, rather than rewriting the deal, simply gives the consumer the contract the consumer expected. The manufacturer, on the other hand is encouraged to build quality into its products. To the extent there is a cost of adding uniform or standard quality in all products, the risk of a lemon is passed to all buyers in the form of pricing and not randomly distributed among those unfortunate enough to have acquired one of the lemons. Moreover, elimination of privity requirement gives consumers such as Goodin the value of their expected bargain, but will rarely do more than duplicate the Products Liability Act as to other consequential damages. The remedy for breach of implied warranty of merchantability is in most cases, including this one, the difference between "the value of the goods accepted and the value they would have had if they had been as warranted." I.C. § 26-1-2-714(2). This gives the buyer the benefit of the bargain. In most cases, however, if any additional damages are available under the UCC as the result of abolishing privity, Indiana law would award the same damages under the Products Liability Act as personal injury or damage to "other property" from a "defective" product. *Gunkel v. Renovations, Inc.,* 822 N.E.2d 150 (Ind. 2005).

For the reasons given above we conclude that Indiana law does not require vertical privity between a consumer and a manufacturer as a condition to a claim by the consumer against the manufacturer for breach of the manufacturer's implied warranty of merchantability.

———————

We will return to privity issues when we consider the liability of a seller under other law in the next Chapter. For now, try your hand at the following problems.

Problem 7-31

Manufacturer makes photocopiers for business use. Manufacturer is very proud of its products and expressly warrants on its order acknowledgment forms that the copiers will not break down for three years from the date of purchase. Manufacturer sold a copier to Distributor on June 1, 2008.

Distributor sells business machines made by several different companies, including Manufacturer. Because Distributor does not make anything on its own, and therefore has no control over the quality of the products it sells, Distributor expressly and effectively disclaims all express and implied warranties in its sales agreements. Distributor advises its customers to seek recourse against the maker of any malfunctioning product Distributor has sold. Among other things, this protects Distributor if one of its suppliers makes a defective product and then goes out of business, leaving Distributor on the hook for any warranty liability. On December 1, 2008, Distributor sold the copier it purchased from Manufacturer to Retailer.

Retailer sells business machines, including photocopiers, in a single metropolitan area. Retailer expressly warrants that all products it sells will not break down for one year from the date of purchase. Retailer sold the copier it obtained from Distributor to Buyer on April 1, 2009.

A. Against whom, if anyone, will Buyer have a cause of action if the jurisdiction in which all the sales occurred has abolished the need for vertical privity and the copier malfunctions on:
1. November 1, 2009?
2. November 1, 2010?
3. November 1, 2011?
B. How, if at all, would the analysis of Part A change if the jurisdiction in which all the sales occurred has not abolished the need for vertical privity?
C. Buyer is a corporation and uses the machine to set up a home office for a senior vice president. It put the copier in the vice president's home. The copier malfunctioned on November 1, 2009 by short circuiting in a manner that started a fire and destroyed the vice president's home.

Fortunately, no one was injured. If the jurisdiction in which all the parties are located has abolished the need for vertical privity and has enacted one of the standard alternatives in section 2-318, against whom, if anyone, does the vice president have a cause of action? Give a separate analysis for each of the alternatives A through C in section 2-318.

CISG and UNIDROIT Principles. The CISG and the UNIDROIT Principles do not address remedies for entities that are not in privity of contract.

CHAPTER EIGHT

BUYER'S REMEDIES UNDER OTHER LAW

SECTION 1.   OVERVIEW

Modern contract law – including Article 2 of the Uniform Commercial Code – is grounded in the principle of freedom of contract. In that sense, it is premised on a centuries-old model of contracting in which the parties are located near each other and freely negotiate the terms of every deal. Under that premise, everyone is free to contract or to refrain from contracting except on the terms they desire. Although modern law in some ways has recognized how antiquated these premises are,[1] freedom of contract remains a fundamental underlying premise.

In the modern age, most contracting is done through the use of standardized forms in either print or electronic format. As a result, many buyers – most notably consumers – are unable to effectuate any changes to the standard terms presented by prospective sellers. Rather the seller presents terms on a take-it-or-leave-it basis. In addition, many sellers of similar types of products have similar terms, so that the ability of a buyer to shop for more favorable terms is non-existent. Even if sellers of a product do offer different terms, most buyers lack the time, incentive, and awareness to shop around for the best terms. They tend to focus on price, convenience, and the business reputation of the seller, not on the terms of the sale.

In this environment, sellers have every economic incentive to attempt to limit liability to the lowest level possible in the event the goods fail to function properly, even if the seller otherwise offers good customer service. In other words, the seller may choose to do more than its contracts require, but would prefer to have the option to base its decision on business considerations, not on legal requirements.

To illustrate this point, consider this scenario. Buyer purchases a computer to use in its business. Because of a defect in the computer's hard drive, Buyer loses all of its customer data and eventually Buyer's business fails. The computer seller may not have warranted the hard drive against defects because it adequately disclaimed all warranties under Article 2. Perhaps more likely, it warranted the hard drive against defects but limited remedies to a refund or replacement of the hard drive, and adequately excluded liability for all consequential losses. The seller may, either as a matter of customer service or pursuant to its warranty, replace Buyer's hard drive. But in no event will the seller be liable for the damages caused

---

[1]   *See, e.g.*, UCC § 2-207.

by the loss of the customer data and the eventual failure of Buyer's business. That is the point of the seller either disclaiming all warranties or excluding liability for consequential harm. If Buyer attempts to recover that type of loss from the seller, the seller will pull out the documentation in which the warranty disclaimer or the limitation on recovery of consequential damage is maintained, and inform Buyer that the seller is not liable for that type of harm.

We have already seen three ways in which Article 2 provides some modicum of protection for buyers:

(i)   limitations on the process a seller may use to disclaim the implied warranty of merchantability, UCC § 2-316;

(ii) restoration of Article 2's default rules on remedies if a limited remedy fails of its essential purpose, UCC § 2-719(2); and

(iii) an invitation to courts to police bargains they find to be unconscionable, UCC §§ 2-302, 2-719(3).

Whether these protections are adequate for buyers is highly questionable. The broadest of the three – unconscionability – typically requires both procedural and substantive problems with the bargain before relief will be available, and therefore requires an individualized determination of the facts of the case. The other protections require litigation to determine if the seller has properly disclaimed the warranty or provided an adequate limited remedy. Litigation is an expensive proposition.

Another possible way to protect buyers would be to mandate a certain set of minimum terms or ban certain abusive terms. The European Union has decided to use this method to protect buyers.[2] That approach would be problematic in the United States, however, because it directly contradicts the deeply ingrained freedom of contract principle. Moreover, there would be great difficulty in getting the relevant players to agree on the terms that should be mandated or prohibited.

---

[2] *See* European Union, Council Directive 93/13/EEC of 5 April 1993 on unfair terms in consumer contracts; Jennifer S. Martin, *An Emerging Worldwide Standard for Protections of Consumers in the Sale of Goods: Did We Miss an Opportunity with Revised UCC Article 2?*, 41 TEX. INT'L L.J. 223 (2006); Larry Bates, *Administrative Regulation of Terms in Form Contracts: a Comparative Analysis of Consumer Protection*, 16 EMORY INT'L L. REV. 1 (2002); Linda J. Rusch, *The Relevance of Evolving Domestic and International Law on Contracts in the Classroom: Assumptions About Assent*, 72 TUL. L. REV. 2043, 2073–75 (1998).

Nevertheless, a hodgepodge of federal and state statutes, along with some common-law tort developments, provide some protections to buyers in particular circumstances. In this Chapter, we examine a sampling of these additional buyer protections, with the caveat that any particular state may have different protections for buyers and careful research is required whenever one is trying to determine if the buyer has any remedies in addition to those available under UCC Article 2.[3]

SECTION 2.   MAGNUSON-MOSS WARRANTY ACT

The Magnuson-Moss Warranty Act (MMWA)[4] is a federal law adopted in 1975 that governs written warranties of consumer products. It was enacted to make such warranties more understandable and to ensure that they provide certain minimum rights. It is essentially a kind of truth-in-labeling law for written warranties of consumer products. All such warranties must be clearly designated as either a "full warranty" or a "limited warranty" and must clearly identify how long they last (*e.g.*, three months; lifetime). MMWA § 103. There are important rules on both types of warranty. Some of these rules are in the Act itself, *see* MMWA §§ 104, 108, others are contained in regulations promulgated by the Federal Trade Commission.[5] You should be sure to consult both the Act itself and the regulations issued under it when presented with any issue or problem to which the Act might apply.

The Magnuson-Moss Act does not require sellers or manufacturers of goods to make a warranty. It merely regulates the warranties they do make. Moreover, the Act does not displace what we have learned about warranties under UCC Article 2.

---

[3]   Congress has regulated a variety of specific products, such as cigarettes and medical devices. When Congress regulates a product, and that product causes harm, courts must confront the degree to which the federal scheme preempts state law, such as Article 2 or common-law tort actions. Because each federal scheme is different, the degree of preemption, if any, may be different. *See Altria Group, Inc. v. Good*, 129 S. Ct. 538 (U.S. 2008) (fraud claim under Maine Unfair Trade Practices Act not preempted by the Federal Cigarette Labeling and Advertising Act).

[4]   It is codified in the United States Code at 15 U.S.C. §§ 2301–12. The text references the provisions by the section numbers in the bill, instead of the United States Code section numbers.

[5]   The Federal Trade Commission Rules are in 16 C.F.R. pts. 700–03.

Instead, the Act gives additional rights to a buyer whenever the Act applies.[6] *See* MMWA § 111(b). Indeed, anyone who makes a warranty governed by the Act is prohibited from disclaiming any implied warranty that would arise under Article 2. *See* MMWA §§ 104(a)(2), 108.

The key benefit of the Act is that if a warrantor violates its obligations under the Act, the injured "consumer" is entitled to recover the reasonable attorney's fees incurred in any successful enforcement action. MMWA § 110(d). This effectively allows buyers – when the Act applies – to convert state-law implied warranty claims into federal claims which give rise to recovery of attorney's fees. This right is critical because it gives injured consumers the ability to prosecute a claim that would otherwise be too small to justify the expense involved. Accordingly, this right to attorney's fees is liberally enforced, even when the amount at stake is small in comparison:

> In rendering its opinion, the district court commented favorably on the professional standing of plaintiff's trial counsel and found the skill, time, and labor involved reasonable. The court further stated that the fee of $125 an hour requested by plaintiff's counsel was reasonable. Thus, the only justifications for limiting plaintiff's fees to approximately fifteen percent of the amount requested are the result obtained and the low value of the case. We conclude that the district court abused its discretion in failing to consider the remedial nature of the acts involved.
>
> In consumer protection as this, the monetary value of the case is typically low. If courts focus only on the dollar value and the result of the case when awarding attorney fees, the remedial purposes of the statutes in question will be thwarted. Simply put, if attorney fee awards in these cases do not provide a reasonable return, it will be economically impossible for attorneys to represent their clients. Thus, practically speaking, the door to the courtroom will be closed to all but those with either potentially substantial damages, or those with sufficient economic resources to afford the litigation expenses involved. Such a situation would indeed be ironic: it is but precisely those with ordinary consumer complaints and those who

---

[6]   If there is a direct conflict between the requirements of the federal act and applicable state law, then the federal act would control pursuant to the federal supremacy clause in the Constitution. *See* U.S. Const. Art. IV.

cannot afford their attorney fees for whom these remedial acts are intended.[7]

A more detailed exploration of the Magnuson-Moss Act must begin with its scope. Unfortunately, the Act does not have a single provision that identifies the situations to which it applies. Therefore, one must peruse the operative sections of the act, identify the key words, and then review the statutory definitions of those terms to ascertain the scope of the Act.

Problem 8-1

A. Make a list of the terms you think are important in defining the scope of the Magnuson-Moss Act and read the definitions of those terms in MMWA § 101. Draft a succinct and accurate statement of the scope of the Magnuson-Moss Act.

B. To which, if any, of the following transactions might the Magnuson-Moss Act apply? What additional facts do you need to know to determine whether the Act in fact applies to these transactions?
  1. The purchase of a motor home for use by an individual as a recreational vehicle.
  2. The purchase of a motor home by ABX News for use by one of its crews to travel from place to place in gathering news stories.
  3. The lease of a motor home by an individual to use on a month-long vacation touring the southwest.[8]

Once you decide that the Magnuson-Moss Act applies to a transaction, the next step is to determine what impact, if any, it has.[9] The key to this is the distinction

---

[7]   *Jordan v. Transnational Motors, Inc.*, 537 N.W.2d 471, 473–74 (Mich. Ct. App. 1995).

[8]   *Compare Parrot v. DaimlerChrysler Corp.*, 130 P.3d 530 (Ariz. 2006) (lessee is not a "consumer" under the Magnuson-Moss Act); *DiCintio v. DaimlerChrysler Corp.*, 768 N.E.2d 1121 (N.Y. 2002) (same), *with American Honda Motor Co. v. Cerasani*, 955 So. 2d 543 (Fla. 2007) (lessee is a "consumer" under the Magnuson-Moss Act); *Peterson v. Volkswagen of Am., Inc.*, 697 N.W.2d 61 (Wis. 2005) (same).

[9]   The Magnuson-Moss Act is a consumer protection law and thus, as with most laws of that type, disclosure of information is important. Section 102 of the Act requires the "warrantor" to make the "written warranty" available in readily understandable language. When must that disclosure be made? *See* 16 C.F.R. pt. 702. In your shopping for consumer

between a full warranty and a limited warranty. Read MMWA §§ 104, 108. Notice
that a warranty designated as a "full warranty" will be deemed to meet the standards
applicable to such warranties even if the text of the writing does not purport to do
so. MMWA § 104(e).

Most warrantors, if they make a written warranty under the Act, do not make
a full warranty. Rather, they make a limited warranty. Do you see why?

Problem 8-2

A. Find a written warranty provided to you in connection with the
    purchase of a consumer good. Is it designated a "full" or a "limited"
    warranty? Does it comply with the Magnuson-Moss Act requirements?
B. List all of the differences between a "written warranty" under the
    Magnuson-Moss Act and an "express warranty" under UCC section
    2-313.
C. Identify how, if at all, the implied warranty of merchantability may be
    disclaimed or limited by:
    1. A supplier making a Magnuson-Moss Act full warranty.
    2. A supplier making a Magnuson-Moss Act limited warranty.
D. Identify how, if at all, a clause excluding the buyer's ability to recover
    consequential damages is affected if the supplier makes a full or
    limited warranty under the Magnuson-Moss Act.

One of the key benefits of the Magnuson-Moss Act is that it eliminates the need
for vertical privity with respect to a claim under a written warranty. It does this in
two ways. First, the "warrantor" under the Act need not be the seller; it could be
the manufacturer. *See* MMWA § 101(4), (5). Second, the "consumer" entitled to
enforce the written warranty includes "any person to whom such product is
transferred." MMWA § 101(3). This ensures, among other things, that someone
who receives a warranted consumer product as a gift can benefit from the written
warranties that accompany the product.[10] Note, if "transferred" refers not only to
transfers of ownership but also to transfers of possession, then this rule might also
solve many horizontal privity problems as well.

---

products, have you ever seen the MMWA disclosure of a "written warranty" as contemplated
in the FTC regulation?

[10]   These principles also apply to service contracts covered by the Act.

Less clear is whether the Act abrogates the privity requirement for actions based on the implied warranty of merchantability or the implied warranty of fitness for particular purpose. Courts are divided on whether a manufacturer who makes a written warranty covered by the Act can be directly liable to the consumer on an implied warranty if the applicable state law requires vertical privity.[11] Similarly, it remains unclear whether a consumer enforcing remedies under the Magnuson-Moss Act are entitled to revoke acceptance against a remote seller even if that remedy is not available under Article 2.[12]

Problem 8-3

A. A trucking company occasionally sells its used trucks to independent buyers when it buys new trucks to replace its aging fleet. In making these sales, the trucking company gives a 30-day limited warranty against defects in the engine. It also disclaims all implied warranties in a manner that satisfies the tests of UCC section 2-316. A buyer of one of the used trucks complained that the truck it bought was not merchantable because the chassis had cracks in it. Assuming the truck sold was indeed not merchantable, is the trucking company liable for that breach of warranty?

B. Manufacturer sold a new truck to Truck Dealer. In that transaction, Manufacturer disclaimed all implied warranties pursuant to the rules in UCC section 2-316. Manufacturer did, however, provide a written limited warranty, to be given to any buyer of the vehicle from Truck Dealer. That warranty promised to repair any defects in material or workmanship in the truck's engine appearing during the first 100,000 miles or three years, whichever came first. When Buyer purchased the vehicle from Truck Dealer, Truck Dealer provided the written warranty

---

[11]   *Compare Voelker v. Porsche Cars N. Am., Inc.*, 353 F.3d 516 (7th Cir. 2003) (state law privity rules still apply for actions on implied warranties); *Rentas v. DaimlerChrysler Corp.*, 936 So. 2d 747 (Fla. Ct. App. 2006) (privity required to bring action for breach of implied warranty), *with Rothe v. Maloney Cadillac, Inc.*, 518 N.E.2d 1028 (Ill. 1988) (privity not required to assert implied warranty of merchantability claim against remote seller who had made a written warranty).

[12]   *See Mydlach v. DaimlerChrysler Corp.*, 875 N.E.2d 1047 (Ill. 2007) (revocation of acceptance not available against remote seller); *Gochey v. Bomardier, Inc.*, 572 A.2d 921 (Vt. 1990) (revocation of acceptance allowed against manufacturer).

to Buyer. Does Buyer get an implied warranty of merchantability from the manufacturer?

Another possible benefit of the Magnuson-Moss Act – one that has engendered considerable debate – may be a prohibition on subjecting warranty claims to binding arbitration. The Magnuson-Moss Act expressly permits a consumer's claim to be subject to informal settlement procedures. *See* MMWA § 110(a)(3). Submission to these procedures can be a *precondition* to bringing suit in court, but courts disagree on whether the procedures can serve as a *substitute for* judicial action.[13]

Problem 8-4

Standard Luxury Vehicles, Inc., an authorized dealer of Wanderer Motor Homes, sold a Wanderer Luxury II motor home to Bridget for $80,000. In the discussion prior to the sale, Standard's owner told Bridget that the motor home was an energy efficient model and should get at least 15 miles per gallon in a normal mix of city and highway driving. Bridget was intending to take the motor home across the United States, stopping to golf at every public course Bridget could find as research for a book on public golf courses. Standard knew what Bridget intended since she told Standard's owner in the course of looking at various models of motor homes. The document that Bridget signed when she agreed to buy the motor home provided the following:

---

[13] Amy J. Schmitz, *Curing Consumer Warranty Woes Through Regulated Arbitration*, 23 OHIO ST. J. ON DISP. RESOL. 627 (2008); *Koons Ford of Baltimore, Inc. v. Lobach*, 919 A.2d 722 (Md. 2007) (arbitration clause in warranty is not enforceable); *Davis v. Southern Energy Homes, Inc.*, 305 F.3d 1268 (11th Cir. 2002), *cert. denied*, 538 U.S. 945 (2003) (arbitration clause in warranty is enforceable).

Even if the Magnuson-Moss Act renders the arbitration clause unenforceable, that effect may be limited to claims arising under the written warranty. Plaintiffs who are suing solely on implied warranties and using the Magnuson-Moss Act as a vehicle for attorney's fees may still be bound to arbitrate.

> The Wanderer Luxury II motor home is warranted by the manufacturer to be free of defects in materials or workmanship at the time of delivery. Buyer's sole remedy is that an authorized dealer will repair or replace any defective parts for 1 year from the date of delivery. DEALER AND MANUFACTURER MAKE NO OTHER WARRANTIES, EXPRESS OR IMPLIED, INCLUDING THE WARRANTY OF MERCHANTABILITY AND FITNESS FOR A PARTICULAR PURPOSE. Dealer or Manufacturer are not liable for any consequential or incidental damages. This writing is the complete, exclusive and final statement of all terms of the sale.

Bridget took delivery of the motor home on March 1, 2007. On March 5, 2007, Bridget returned the motor home to the dealership due to whistling sounds in the windows. Standard resealed the windows and Bridget took the motor home back on March 10, 2007. From April through November, Bridget returned the motor home to Standard four separate times to fix various items such as a leak in the roof, a malfunctioning refrigerator, a cracked sewage hose, and an overheating engine. Bridget's trouble with the motor home continued throughout the winter (December through February) including a propane leak in the stove resulting in a short hospital stay for Bridget and her spouse due to gas inhalation and a leaky shower stall resulting in ruined carpeting. Each time Bridget took the motor home to Standard, the problem was successfully repaired. However, each time, Bridget had to drive from wherever she was on her golf odyssey to Standard's dealership. As a result, Bridget only got to play about half of the golf courses she had planned on, resulting in a delay in her book project.

On March 1, 2008, Bridget drove the motor home to Standard's location and told Standard that she was returning the motor home due to the many problems that she had experienced, including the fact that, over the course of the year, the motor home averaged only 10 miles per gallon. Bridget demanded return of her purchase price. Standard refused to take the motor home back and told Bridget the one-year warranty period was up and she was on her own with the motor home. The manufacturer did not respond to Bridget's complaint. Advise Bridget. Include in your analysis all parties' likely arguments.

SECTION 3.   UNFAIR AND DECEPTIVE PRACTICES

Federal law prohibits unfair and deceptive acts and practices in commercial activity. The relevant statutory provisions are amazing for their brevity:

15 U.S.C. § 45(a)

Declaration of unlawfulness; power to prohibit unfair practices . . .

(1) Unfair methods of competition in or affecting commerce, and unfair or deceptive acts or practices in or affecting commerce, are hereby declared unlawful.

(2) The [Federal Trade] Commission is hereby empowered and directed to prevent persons, partnerships, or corporations, . . . from using unfair methods of competition in or affecting commerce and unfair or deceptive acts or practices in or affecting commerce.

The Federal Trade Commission has issued a variety of regulations pursuant to the authority granted to it in the act. Three of these regulations merit our attention.

First, the FTC has a rule regarding a "cooling off" period for sales made at a location other than the seller's place of business. 16 C.F.R. pt. 429. The basic import of this regulation is that it is an unfair and deceptive practice to use high pressure sales tactics in the buyer's home. To guard against that practice, in certain defined situations, the buyer is given a three-day right to cancel the sale and the seller is required to inform the buyer of that right. 16 C.F.R. § 429.1. Although the transactions to which the regulation applies are often referred to as in-home sales, they need not actually occur in the buyer's home. The regulation also applies to sales made in temporary locations, such as convention centers and fairgrounds. 16 C.F.R. § 429.0.

Second, the FTC has issued a rule that in a mail order or telephone sale, the seller must be able to ship the merchandise to the buyer within the time the seller represents, or the buyer is entitled to cancel the order. 16 C.F.R. pt. 435. This guards against an unfair trade practice of getting advance payment for an item and then delaying fulfilment of the order unreasonably. Third, the FTC has issued a regulation regarding accurate disclosure of any warranty offered in the sale of a used vehicle and accurate representation of the mechanical condition of the used vehicle. 16 C.F.R. pt. 455. This rule guards against the unfair trade practice of misrepresenting the warranties offered and the state of the used vehicle. These are just three examples of the types of actions that the FTC has determined to be unfair and deceptive trade practices.

The FTC enforces the act and the regulations issued under it by bringing enforcement actions against sellers.[14] Most courts hold that the buyer does not have a private right of action under the act and regulations. However, many states have similar statutes prohibiting unfair and deceptive trade practices. While these statutes often empower a state official, such as the attorney general, to enforce the law, many also provide for a private cause of action. *See, e.g.,* Wash. Rev. Code ch. 19.86. These state acts can reach a substantial amount of unscrupulous behavior, including bait-and-switch tactics, advertising great deals and then not having a reasonable number of the goods on hand for sale, and all the conduct prohibited by the FTC regulations. The buyer's ability to recover against the seller for unfair and deceptive trade practices is thus usually under the state analogs to the federal act and regulations.[15]

The FTC has engaged in enforcement action regarding other aspects of seller behavior, including protecting the customers' data from piracy, and prohibiting false and misleading information to consumers regarding the advertising for products.[16] A seller engaging in selling goods needs to be thoroughly aware of the prohibitions regarding unfair and deceptive trade practices that operate at both the state and federal level. Conversely, a buyer who is stuck with a malfunctioning or disappointing product should determine whether there is a means of recovery using the prohibitions on unfair and deceptive trade practices.

SECTION 4.   LEMON-LAWS

Most states have enacted laws that protect consumer buyers of new vehicles. The basic approach of these laws is to give the dealer or manufacturer a specified

---

[14]   For an interesting decision in which the FTC found violations of the Magnuson-Moss Act to be an unfair trade practice, *see In the Matter of Gateway 2000, Inc.*, 126 F.T.C. 888 (1998).

[15]   Mark E. Budnitz, *The Federalization and Privatization of Public Consumer Protection Law in the United States: Their Effect on Litigation and Enforcement*, 24 GA. ST. U. L. REV. 663 (2008).

[16]   *See, e.g.,* Stephen F. Ambrose, Jr., *et al., Survey of Significant Consumer Privacy Litigation in the United States in 2007*, 63 BUS. LAW. 653 (2008); Jean Noonan and Michael Goodman, *Third-Party Liability for Federal Law Violations in Direct-to-Consumer Marketing: Telemarketing, Fax, and E-mail*, 63 BUS. LAW. 585 (2008).

time in which to repair defects or nonconformities covered by a warranty. If the vehicle is not repaired within that time or after a certain number of attempts, the buyer is entitled to a replacement vehicle or a refund of the purchase price. That is the general approach, but of course the laws vary in the details. For example, some may apply only to sales of vehicles while others also cover extended leases. Some may protect only consumer buyers while others protect all buyers. Some may impose liability on the seller, some on the manufacturer, and some on both. And some may give relief only if the problems substantially impair the value of the vehicle while others are not so limited.

Moreover, the time for repair will vary from state to state, as will the process the buyer must follow to seek redress under the act and the applicable limitations period. Other variations involve the remedies available, in particular whether the buyer is entitled to incidental, consequential, or punitive damages and whether the seller is entitled to any offset for the buyer's use of the vehicle.[17] Note also, if the buyer traded in a used vehicle, the seller may have already resold it before the buyer seeks to rescind purchase of the new, defective vehicle. In such a case, it will be impossible to return the used car to the buyer. Accordingly, even though the parties may have negotiated a net deal, the price stated for each vehicle in the contract will be very important in determining the amount of restitution to which the buyer is entitled.

Consider the following case exploring the application of Oregon's lemon law.

LILES V. DAMON CORP.,
345 Or. 420 (2008)

Durham, J.

Plaintiffs brought this action under ORS 646A.400 to ORS 646A.418, commonly known as Oregon's Lemon Law, seeking replacement of a motor home that they had purchased. The issue on review concerns the proper interpretation of ORS 646A.402, which we quote below in full. Under that statute, a statutory remedy is "available to a consumer" if, among other things, the manufacturer of a

---

[17]   *See* Annotation, *Validity, Construction and Effect of State Motor Vehicle Warranty Legislation (Lemon Laws)*, 88 A.L.R. 5th 301 (2001); Phillip R. Nowicki, *State Lemon Law Coverage Terms: Dissecting the Differences*, 11 LOY. CONSUMER L. REP. 39 (1999); Joan Vogel, *Squeezing Consumers: Lemon Laws, Consumer Warranties, and a Proposal for Reform*, 1985 ARIZ. ST. L. J. 589.

motor vehicle has received "direct written notification" from the consumer and "has had an opportunity to correct the alleged defect." ORS 646A.402(3).

After a trial, the trial court found that plaintiffs had satisfied the statutory requirements and granted relief. Specifically, the court rejected defendant's contention that ORS 646A.402(3) obligated plaintiffs to afford defendant the opportunity to correct the alleged defect *after* sending written notification to defendant and *before filing* their action. In its judgment, the court made the following finding of fact:

> The Court finds that the manufacturer did receive adequate written
> notification of these defects from the Plaintiffs and that the manufacturer
> also had ample opportunity to correct the defects.

On appeal, the Court of Appeals reversed. The Court of Appeals concluded that the conditions in the statute applied in sequence: that is, the delivery of the consumer's "direct written notification" of the defect must occur before the manufacturer has any "opportunity to correct" the defect under the statute. Moreover, the court determined that each statutory condition "must be met before seeking a remedy under the Lemon Law[,]" meaning that plaintiffs had to satisfy each condition *before filing* their action. According to the Court of Appeals, plaintiffs had satisfied the written notice requirement but, after doing so, had not provided defendant an opportunity to correct the alleged defect before filing their action. This court granted review to determine whether the Court of Appeals had correctly construed the requirements in Oregon's Lemon Law.

We view the evidence in the light most favorable to plaintiffs, who prevailed at trial. On December 30, 2002, plaintiffs purchased a motor home from a dealer in Sandy, Oregon. Defendant manufactured the motor home. According to the trial court's finding, plaintiffs

> began contacting the factory representatives by phone in April of 2003
> regarding the water leak problems they were experiencing with the unit.
> They contacted the factory representative about the many problems with the
> motor home numerous times between April 2003 and December 2003. The
> Plaintiffs also presented numerous times between April 2003 and
> December 2003. The Plaintiffs also presented numerous repair orders from
> the selling dealer representing many unsuccessful attempts to repair the
> water leaks in this unit during that same period [of] time.

The vehicle dealer performed most of the unsuccessful attempts to repair the leaks. However, the trial court found that, on one occasion, defendant directed plaintiffs to submit the vehicle for repair at a different repair shop. That attempted repair occurred on December 9, 2003, but it, too, was unsuccessful. According to the trial court, that attempted repair "was specifically authorized by the manufacturer as their attempt to cure the defect[ ]" and "was an opportunity to correct the defect before the lawsuit was filed even though written notice wasn't given."

On December 23, 2003, an attorney representing plaintiffs sent a letter to defendant under Oregon's Lemon Law. The letter described the water leak problems and plaintiffs' unsuccessful efforts to resolve them through multiple repair efforts and through several discussions with defendant's representatives, including its president and "the field person for Damon in charge of repairs." The letter requested the replacement remedy under the Lemon Law, ORS 646A.404(1)(a), which we quote below. . . . Defendant received the letter described above on December 29, 2003. Plaintiffs filed their action the next day, December 30, 2003. In January 2004, plaintiffs informed defendant that it could have access to the vehicle, but defendant took no further action to assess or repair the rainwater leaks. The case was tried to the court sitting without a jury on February 24, 2005, and the court entered judgment for plaintiffs on June 7, 2005. As noted, the Court of Appeals reversed, and we allowed plaintiffs' petition for review.

This case requires the interpretation of several statutory provisions in Oregon's Lemon Law. We begin with the text and context of the statutes and endeavor to give meaning to all parts of those statutes.

ORS 646A.402 provides:

The remedy under the provisions of ORS 646A.400 to 646A.418 is available to a consumer if:

> (1) A new motor vehicle does not conform to applicable manufacturer's express warranties;
>
> (2) The consumer reports each nonconformity to the manufacturer, its agent or its authorized dealer, for the purpose of repair or correction, during the period of one year following the date of original delivery of the motor vehicle to the consumer or during the period ending on the date on which the mileage on the motor vehicle reaches 12,000 miles, whichever period ends earlier; and
>
> (3) The manufacturer has received direct written notification from or on behalf of the consumer and has had an opportunity to correct the alleged defect. "Notification" under this subsection includes, but is not limited to, a request by the consumer for an informal dispute settlement procedure under ORS 646A.408.

ORS 646A.404(1) describes the remedy that is available to a consumer:

If the manufacturer or its agents or authorized dealers are unable to conform the motor vehicle to any applicable manufacturer's express warranty by repairing or correcting any defect or condition that substantially impairs the use, market value or safety of the motor vehicle to the consumer after a reasonable number of attempts, the manufacturer shall:

> (a) Replace the motor vehicle with a new motor vehicle; or
>
> (b) Accept return of the vehicle from the consumer and refund to the consumer the full purchase or lease price paid, including taxes, license and registration fees and any similar collateral charges excluding interest, less a reasonable allowance for the consumer's use of the vehicle.

ORS 646A.406 creates a presumption, potentially usable during litigation, about whether the vehicle manufacturer or dealer has undertaken a "reasonable number of attempts" to conform the vehicle to applicable manufacturer's express warranties. That statute provides, in part:

> (1) It shall be presumed that a reasonable number of attempts have been undertaken to conform a motor vehicle to the applicable manufacturer's express warranties if, during the period of one year following the date of original delivery of the motor vehicle to a consumer or during the period ending on the date on which the mileage on the motor vehicle reaches 12,000 miles, whichever period ends earlier:
>
> > (a) The same nonconformity has been subject to repair or correction four or more times by the manufacturer or its agent or authorized dealer, but such nonconformity continues to exist; or
> >
> > (b) The vehicle is out of service by reason of repair or correction for a cumulative total of 30 or more business days.
>
> (2) A repair or correction for purposes of subsection (1) of this section includes a repair that must take place after the expiration of the earlier of either period.
>
> . . .
>
> (4) In no event shall the presumption described in subsection (1) of this section apply against a manufacturer unless the manufacturer has received prior direct written notification from or on behalf of the consumer and has had an opportunity to cure the defect alleged.

ORS 646A.412(1) describes additional remedies available to a consumer in a successful action under the statute "against a manufacturer . . . ." ORS 646A.414(1) confirms that the statute does not create an action against a vehicle dealer.

Several features of the statutory text are noteworthy. The statutory remedy is "available to a consumer" under ORS 646.402 only if the consumer communicates certain information to others. First, under ORS 646A.402(2), the consumer must "report[ ]" the defects to "the manufacturer, its agent or its authorized dealer, for the purpose of repair or correction" within the timeframe that the subsection describes. The statute does not require that communication to be in writing. Second, the consumer or someone acting on the consumer's behalf must give the manufacturer "direct written notification." The statute does not describe the information that the consumer's written notice must contain beyond confirming that a consumer's request for an informal dispute settlement procedure under ORS 646A.408 constitutes notification. There is no dispute here that plaintiffs satisfied both of the statutory notice requirements described above.

The issue presented is whether defendant "has had an opportunity to correct the alleged defect" under ORS 646A.402(3). As noted, defendant contends that the opportunity for correction must occur *after* it receives the consumer's written notification under ORS 646A.402(3) but also *before* the consumer files an action. Defendant asserts that plaintiffs afforded it no opportunity to correct the defect under the statute because only one day elapsed between its receipt of plaintiffs' attorney's letter on December 29, 2003, and the filing of the action on December 30, 2003.

Defendant's contention that a single day did not afford a reasonable opportunity to correct the vehicle's defects fails because it proceeds from an erroneous construction of ORS 646A.402(3). Notably, the statute does not state that the consumer's written notification and the manufacturer's opportunity for correction are *prefiling* requirements – that is, required procedural steps that must occur before the filing of the action. Rather, ORS 646A.402 states that those requirements are conditions that must exist if the statutory remedy is to be "available to a consumer[.]"

That distinctive terminology refers to conditions that the court must assess when it exercises its authority to grant or deny the requested remedy; it does not create a prefiling requirement. When the legislature has created prefiling procedural requirements in other contexts, it has used terms that unmistakably convey that intent. . . . ORS 646A.402(3) lacks any counterpart to the substantive terms of those prefiling requirements. . . .

The "opportunity to correct" requirement in ORS 646.402(3) assures the manufacturer that it will have a chance to repair or correct the nonconformity of which the consumer complains before the court determines the availability of the statutory remedies to the consumer. The statute affords at least two opportunities to the consumer to identify the nonconformity for that purpose: (1) the report to the manufacturer, its agent or its authorized dealer under ORS 646A.402(2), and (2) the written notification under ORS 646.402(3). As noted, the first of those methods may be accomplished orally, in writing, or a combination of both.

It is significant that ORS 646A.402(3) does not require the consumer's "direct written notification" to include any specific contents, such as a particular description of the vehicle's defects. The written notification under subsection (3) may consist of as simple a message as a request for an informal dispute settlement procedure that might not include any "allegations" of a vehicle's defects.

The terms of ORS 646A.402, viewed in their entirety, indicate that, when the court determines whether a statutory remedy is available to the consumer, the consumer must have (1) reported the vehicle's defect to the manufacturer, its agent, or authorized dealer in a timely manner; and (2) given a direct written notification to the manufacturer. In addition, the manufacturer must have had an opportunity to correct *that* defect, not some different defect. The ordinary meaning of the word "alleged" in ORS 646A.402(3) does not confine the manufacturer's opportunity to repair solely to a defect that the consumer has described in the written notification.

Finally, the legislature's intent becomes clear when we contrast the wording of ORS 646A.402(3) with that of ORS 646A.406(4), quoted above. In the latter statute, the legislature has assured manufacturers that the described presumption in favor of the consumer will not apply against them "unless the manufacturer has received *prior* direct written notification from or on behalf of the consumer and has had an opportunity to cure the defect alleged." (Emphasis added.) The term "prior" in that context confirms that, for purposes of applying the presumption, the consumer notification must precede the manufacturer's opportunity to cure the defect.

The legislature did not include the word "prior" in ORS 646A.402(3) and, if possible, we must accord legal meaning to that omission. That task is not difficult in this case. In ORS 646A.406(4), the legislature determined that a manufacturer should be protected from the operation of the evidentiary presumption unless it had engaged in specific conduct: failing to use an opportunity to cure the vehicle defect *after* receiving direct written notification from the consumer. By contrast, under ORS 646A.402(3), the written notification is a condition regarding the availability of the statutory remedy and it serves to ensure that the manufacturer is aware of the consumer's dispute, but it need not necessarily precede the manufacturer's opportunity to correct in order for the statutory remedy to be available.

We can discern the legislature's intent from an examination of the statutory text in context. In doing so, we have given effect to every part of the pertinent statutes, including the legislature's omission of the word "prior" in ORS 646A.402(3), as noted above. Because the legislature's intent is clear from our inquiry into text and context, further inquiry is unnecessary.

In this case, before the trial court adjudicated the availability of the statutory remedy to plaintiffs under ORS 646A.402, defendant had an opportunity to correct the defect that was the subject of plaintiffs' action. On December 9, 2003, plaintiffs, acting on defendant's instructions, submitted their vehicle for repair at a facility selected by defendant. That attempted repair was unavailing. A separate opportunity to repair occurred when plaintiffs made the vehicle available to defendant in January 2004, after plaintiffs filed this action. Defendant took no action in response to that opportunity to repair the vehicle. The filing of the action did not cut off defendant's opportunity to correct the defects in plaintiffs' vehicle. We are satisfied that defendant had an ample opportunity to cure the vehicle's alleged defects before the trial court determined that the statutory remedy was available to plaintiffs under ORS 646.402.

The decision of the Court of Appeals is reversed. The judgment of the circuit court is affirmed.

SECTION 5.   LIABILITY USING TORT LAW PRINCIPLES

As we learned in studying warranties under UCC Article 2, the implied warranty of merchantability requires that the goods sold be, among other things, fit for their ordinary purpose. UCC § 2-314(2)(c). This protects the buyer's likely expectations in the bargain and was an erosion of the doctrine of *caveat emptor*.[18]

---

[18]   Warranty disputes involving claims protecting this economic bargain arose between sellers and buyers who were in privity of contract. In the early Seventeenth Century, however, these claims were asserted in tort as an action on the case. The buyer had to establish the elements of deceit, *i.e.*, that the seller made an express representation about the nature of the goods knowing it to be false. By 1790, the action of deceit, with its requirements of scienter by the representor and reliance by the representee, had developed

However, the implied warranty of merchantability is not made by all sellers. Non-merchants and merchants not in the business of selling goods of that kind do not make the warranty. Moreover, because the warranty is a creature of contract, even merchants who normally would make the warranty may disclaim it pursuant to the rules of section 2-316. Indeed, merchants can disclaim all warranty liability.

So, consider the case of a merchant seller who has not made a written warranty covered by the Magnuson-Moss Act, not made any express warranties under section 2-313, and has properly disclaimed all implied warranties under section 2-316. Yet the goods sold malfunction and cause harm. Is there any basis for holding the seller liable for that harm? This is where tort law comes into play, in particular, the law of products liability.

Section 402A of the Restatement (Second) of Torts, which was intended to summarize the developing case law in this area, establishes the standard for imposing strict liability – as opposed to liability arising from negligence – of a merchant seller.[19] It provides:

---

into a separate writ or action. At about the same time, the English courts first permitted an express warranty claim to be brought in assumpsit, the action in which most contract claims were pursued. By 1802, scienter was no longer a requirement in assumpsit for breach of an express warranty, but other limiting formalities, *i.e.*, that the representation must be an express term of the contract and intended by the seller to be a warranty, still remained. This early interaction between representations of quality made in exchange transactions and the tort forms of action led Dean Prosser to conclude that warranty was a "freak hybrid born of the illicit intercourse of tort and contract." William L. Prosser, *The Assault Upon the Citadel (Strict Liability to the Consumer),* 69 YALE L.J. 1099, 1126 (1960). During the Nineteenth Century, warranty theory developed into the tripartite form which we know today: an express warranty, an implied warranty of fitness for particular purpose, and an implied warranty of merchantability (fitness for "ordinary" purposes).

[19]   For a discussion of the principles of tort products liability and the history of its evolution *see* David G. Owen, *The Evolution of Products Liability Law,* 26 REV. LITIG. 955 (2007); Linda J. Rusch, *Products Liability Trapped By History: Our Choice of Rules Rules Our Choices,* 76 TEMPLE L. REV. 739 (2003); Marshall S. Shapo, *Products at the Millennium: Traversing a Transverse Section,* 53 S.C. L. REV. 1031 (2002); James J. White, *Reverberations from the Collision of Tort and Warranty,* 53 S.C. L. REV. 1067 (2002); Frances E. Zollers, *et al., Looking Backward, Looking Forward: Reflections on Twenty Years of Product Liability Reform,* 50 SYRACUSE L. REV. 1019 (2000); William K. Jones, *Product Defects Causing Commercial Loss: The Ascendancy of Contract over Tort,* 44 U. MIAMI L. REV. 731 (1990); Richard E. Speidel, *Warranty Theory, Economic Loss, and the Privity Requirement: Once More Into the Void,* 67 B.U. L. REV. 9 (1987); David A. Rice, *Product Quality Laws and the Economics of Federalism,* 65 B.U. L. REV. 1 (1985); Ingrid M. Hillinger, *The Merchant of Section 2-314: Who Needs Him?,* 34 HASTINGS L.J. 747

(1) One who sells any product in a defective condition unreasonably dangerous to
     the user or consumer or to his property is subject to liability for physical harm
     thereby caused to the ultimate user or consumer, or to his property, if
          (a) the seller is engaged in the business of selling such a product, and
          (b) it is expected to and does reach the user or consumer without
          substantial change in the condition in which it is sold.
(2) The rule stated in Subsection (1) applies although
          (a) the seller has exercised all possible care in the preparation and sale of
          his product, and
          (b) the user or consumer has not bought the product from or entered into
          any contractual relation with the seller.

Note that section 402A deals only with personal injury and damage to property
other than the goods sold. It does not apply if the only harm is to the defective
goods themselves.

Section 402A and the cases under it raise a number of interesting issues that are
typically explored in law school courses on torts or products liability. We
concentrate on only two of them. First, whether there is any meaningful difference
between whether a product is defective under section 402A and whether it is
unmerchantable under UCC section 2-314. Second, whether and to what extent the
damages available in a strict products liability action differ from those available for
breach of the implied warranty of merchantability.

Apart from strict liability under section 402A, many states recognize a tort
cause of action for misrepresentation.[20] This cause of action generally requires a
material misrepresentation of fact on which the plaintiff justifiably and
detrimentally relies. Such claims often bear a striking similarity to claims from
breach of an express warranty, and we explore the relationship between
misrepresentation and express warranty in the last part of this section.

(1983); Herbert D. Titus, *Restatement (Second) of Torts Section 402A and the Uniform
Commercial Code,* 22 STAN. L. REV. 713 (1970); William L. Prosser, *The Implied Warranty
of Merchantable Quality,* 27 MINN. L. REV. 117 (1943); Karl N. Llewellyn, *On Warranty of
Quality and Society,* 36 COLUM. L. REV. 699 (1936); Walton H. Hamilton, *The Ancient
Maxim Caveat Emptor,* 40 YALE L.J. 1133 (1931); Samuel Williston, *Representation and
Warranty in Sales–Heilbut v. Buckleton,* 27 HARV. L. REV. 1 (1913); Emlin McClain,
Implied Warranties in Sales, 7 HARV. L. REV. 213 (1903).

[20]   *See* RESTATEMENT (SECOND) OF TORTS § 525 (fraudulent misrepresentation causing
pecuniary loss); § 552 (negligent misrepresentation causing pecuniary loss); RESTATEMENT
(THIRD) OF TORTS § 9 (liability for misrepresentation causing harm to person or property).

A. PRODUCT DEFECT DEFINED

The key requirement of the implied warranty of merchantability is that the goods sold be fit for their ordinary purpose. Accordingly, any good that is not fit for its ordinary purpose will breach that warranty – in other words, it will be defective. A slightly different standard applies to determine whether a product is defective for the purpose of strict liability in tort. Consider the following case.

CASTRO V. QVC NETWORK, INC.
139 F.3d 114 (2d Cir. 1998)

Calabresi, Circuit Judge

In this diversity products liability action, plaintiffs-appellants alleged, in separate causes of action for strict liability and for breach of warranty, that defendants-appellees manufactured and sold a defective roasting pan that injured one of the appellants. The United States District Court for the Eastern District of New York (Leonard D. Wexler, *Judge*) rejected appellants' request to charge the jury separately on each cause of action and, instead, instructed the jury only on the strict liability charge. The jury found for appellees and the court denied appellants' motion for a new trial. This appeal followed. We hold that, under New York law, the jury should have been instructed separately on each charge, and, accordingly, reverse and remand for a new trial on the breach of warranty claim.

I. BACKGROUND

In early November 1993, appellee QVC Network, Inc. ("QVC"), operator of a cable television home-shopping channel, advertised, as part of a one-day Thanksgiving promotion, the "T-Fal Jumbo Resistal Roaster." The roaster, manufactured by U.S.A. T-Fal Corp. ("T-Fal"), was described as suitable for, among other things, cooking a twenty-five pound turkey.[21] Appellant Loyda Castro bought the roasting pan by mail and used it to prepare a twenty-pound turkey on Thanksgiving Day, 1993.

---

[21] At the time that QVC and T-Fal agreed to conduct the Thanksgiving promotion, T-Fal did not have in its product line a pan large enough to roast a turkey. T-Fal therefore asked its parent company, located in France, to provide a suitable roasting pan as soon as possible. The parent provided a pan (designed originally without handles and for other purposes). To this pan two small handles were added so that it could be used to roast a turkey. T-Fal shipped the pan to QVC in time for the early November campaign.

Mrs. Castro was injured when she attempted to remove the turkey and roasting pan from the oven. Using insulated mittens, she gripped the pan's handles with the first two fingers on each hand (the maximum grip allowed by the small size of the handles) and took the pan out of the oven. As the turkey tipped toward her, she lost control of the pan, spilling the hot drippings and fat that had accumulated in it during the cooking and basting process. As a result, she suffered second and third degree burns to her foot and ankle, which, over time, has led to scarring, intermittent paresthesia, and ankle swelling.

It is uncontested that in their complaint appellants alleged that the pan was defective and that its defects gave rise to separate causes of action for strict liability and for breach of warranty. Moreover, in the pre-charge conference, appellants' counsel repeatedly requested separate jury charges on strict liability and for breach of warranty. The district court, nevertheless, denied the request for a separate charge on breach of warranty. Judge Wexler stated that "you can't collect twice for the same thing," and deemed the warranty charge unnecessary and "duplicative." The court, therefore, only gave the jury the New York pattern strict products liability charge.

The jury returned a verdict for appellees QVC and T-Fal. . . . Appellants subsequently moved, pursuant to Federal Rule of Civil Procedure 59, that the jury verdict be set aside and a new trial be ordered for various reasons including that the court had failed to charge the jury on appellants' claim for breach of warranty. . . . [T]he district court denied appellants' Rule 59 motion, reasoning that the breach of warranty and strict products liability claims were "virtually the same." This appeal followed.

II. DISCUSSION

. . .

A. Two Definitions of "Defective" Product Design

Products liability law has long been bedeviled by the search for an appropriate definition of "defective" product design.[22] Over the years, both in the cases and in the literature, two approaches have come to predominate. The first is the risk/utility theory, which focuses on whether the benefits of a product outweigh the dangers of

---

[22] *See generally* W. Page Keeton, *The Meaning of Defect in Products Liability Law,* 45 MO. L.REV. 579 (1980); W. Page Keeton, *Product Liability and the Meaning of Defect,* 5 ST. MARY'S L.J. 30 (1973); Guido Calabresi & Jon T. Hirschoff, *Toward a Test for Strict Liability in Torts,* 81 YALE L.J. 1055 (1972).

its design.[23] The second is the consumer expectations theory, which focuses on what a buyer/user of a product would properly expect that the product would be suited for.[24]

Not all states accept both of these approaches. Some define design defect only according to the risk/utility approach. . . . Others define design defect solely in terms of the consumer expectations theory. . . . [25]

One of the first states to accept both approaches was California, which in *Barker v. Lull Engineering Co.,* 573 P.2d 443 (Cal. 1978), held that "a product may be found defective in design, so as to subject a manufacturer to strict liability for resulting injuries, under either of two alternative tests" – consumer expectations and risk/utility. *Id.* at 455.[26] Several states have followed suit and have adopted both theories.

---

[23] According to the New York Court of Appeals, the risk/utility calculus, which requires "a weighing of the product's benefits against its risks," *Denny v. Ford Motor Co.,* 662 N.E.2d 730, 735 (N.Y. 1995), is " 'functionally synonymous'" with traditional negligence analysis, *id.* Despite the fact that there are some significant differences, the risk/utility calculus is in many ways similar to the Learned Hand negligence test.

[24] The New York Court of Appeals explains that "the UCC's concept of a 'defective' product requires an inquiry only into whether the product in question was 'fit for the ordinary purposes for which such goods are used.' " *Denny,* 662 N.E.2d at 736 (quoting U.C.C. § 2-314(2)(c)). Thus, the breach of warranty cause of action "is one involving true 'strict' liability, since recovery may be had upon a showing that the product was not minimally safe for its expected purpose." *Id.* Some scholars have characterized this inquiry as centering on whether the manufacturer or the user is in a better position to decide about safety. *See* Calabresi & Hirschoff, *supra* note [19], at 1060.

[25] Still others apply a "modified consumer expectations test" that incorporates risk/utility factors into the consumer expectations analysis. . . .

[26] The court stated:
First, a product may be found defective in design if the plaintiff establishes that the product failed to perform as safely as an ordinary customer would expect when used in an intended or reasonably foreseeable manner. Second, a product may alternatively be found defective in design if the plaintiff demonstrates that the product's design proximately caused his injury and the defendant fails to establish, in light of the relevant factors, that, on balance, the benefits of the challenged design outweigh the risk of danger inherent in such design.
Barker, 573 P.2d at 455–56. Placement of the burden of proving the product's risks and utility on the manufacturer is not, however, a necessary part of the risk/utility test. . . .

. . . . Prior to the recent case of *Denny v. Ford Motor Co.,* 662 N.E.2d 730 (N.Y. 1995), it was not clear whether New York recognized both tests. In *Denny,* the plaintiff was injured when her Ford Bronco II sports utility vehicle rolled over when she slammed on the brakes to avoid hitting a deer in the vehicle's path. The plaintiff asserted claims for strict products liability and for breach of implied warranty, and the district judge – over the objection of defendant Ford – submitted both causes of action to the jury. The jury ruled in favor of Ford on the strict liability claim, but found for the plaintiff on the implied warranty claim. On appeal, Ford argued that the jury's verdicts on the strict products liability claim and the breach of warranty claim were inconsistent because the causes of action were identical.

This court certified the *Denny* case to the New York Court of Appeals to answer the following questions: (1) "whether, under New York law, the strict products liability and implied warranty claims are identical"; and (2) "whether, if the claims are different, the strict products liability claim is broader than the implied warranty claim and encompasses the latter."

In response to the certified questions, the Court of Appeals held that in a products liability case a cause of action for strict liability is not identical to a claim for breach of warranty. . . . Moreover, the court held that a strict liability claim is not per se broader than a breach of warranty claim such that the former encompasses the latter. . . . Thus, while claims of strict products liability and breach of warranty are often used interchangeably, under New York law the two causes of action are definitively different. The imposition of strict liability for an alleged design "defect" is determined by a risk-utility standard, ... The notion of "defect" in a U.C.C.-based breach of warranty claim focuses, instead, on consumer expectations. . . .

B. When Should a Jury be Charged on Both Strict Liability and Warranty Causes of Action?

Since *Denny,* then, it has been settled that the risk/utility and consumer expectations theories of design defect can, in New York, be the bases of distinct causes of action: one for strict products liability and one for breach of warranty. This fact, however, does not settle the question of when a jury must be charged separately on each cause of action and when, instead, the two causes are, on the facts of the specific case, sufficiently similar to each other so that one charge to the jury is enough.

While eminent jurists have at times been troubled by this issue,[27] the New York Court of Appeals in *Denny* was quite clear on when the two causes of action might meld and when, instead, they are to be treated as separate. It did this by adding its own twist to the distinction – namely, what can aptly be called the "dual purpose" requirement. . . . Thus in *Denny,* the Court of Appeals pointed out that the fact that a product's overall benefits might outweigh its overall risks does not preclude the possibility that consumers may have been misled into using the product in a context in which it was dangerously unsafe. . . . And this, the New York court emphasized, could be so even though the benefits in other uses might make the product sufficiently reasonable so that it passed the risk/utility test.

In *Denny,* the Ford Bronco II was not designed as a conventional passenger automobile. Instead, it was designed as an off-road, dual purpose vehicle.[28] But in its marketing of the Bronco II, Ford stressed its suitability for commuting and for suburban and city driving. . . . Under the circumstances, the Court of Appeals explained that a rational factfinder could conclude that the Bronco's utility as an off-road vehicle outweighed the risk of injury resulting from roll-over accidents (thus passing the risk/utility test), but at the same time find that the vehicle was not safe for the "ordinary purpose" of daily driving for which it was also marketed and sold (thus flunking the consumer expectations test). . . .

That is precisely the situation before us. The jury had before it evidence that the product was designed, marketed, and sold as a multiple-use product. The pan

---

[27]   Thus Justice Traynor in the early and seminal California strict products liability case, *Greenman v. Yuba Power Products,* 377 P.2d 897 (Cal. 1963), did not make a clear distinction between them. *See id.* at 901 ("[I]t should not be controlling [for purposes of establishing a manufacturer's liability] whether plaintiff selected the [product] because of the statements in the brochure, or because of the [product's] own appearance of excellence that belied the defect lurking beneath the surface, or because he merely assumed that it would safely do the jobs it was built to do."). And likewise, Judge Eschbach in *Sills v. Massey-Ferguson, Inc.,* 296 F. Supp. 776 (N.D. Ind. 1969), stated that although they represented different causes of action, in the case before him, he could not distinguish between them, and then added that "[w]hile this court is unwilling to hold that there is *never* a significant difference between the two theories, it is plain that the outcome of the vast majority of cases is not affected by this fine legal distinction." *Id.* at 779.

[28]   Indeed, as Ford argued, the design features that appellant complained of – high center of gravity, narrow track width, short wheel base, and a specially tailored suspension system--were important to preserve the vehicle's utility for off-road use. . . . But, it was these same design features that made the vehicle susceptible to rollover accidents during evasive maneuvers on paved roads. . . .

was originally manufactured and sold in France as an all-purpose cooking dish without handles. And at trial, the jury saw a videotape of a QVC representative demonstrating to the television audience that the pan, in addition to serving as a suitable roaster for a twenty-five pound turkey, could also be used to cook casseroles, cutlets, cookies, and other low-volume foods.[29] The court charged the jury that "[a] product is defective if it is not reasonably safe[,] [t]hat is, if the product is so likely to be harmful to persons that a reasonable person who had actual knowledge of its potential for producing injury would conclude that it should not have been marketed in that condition." And, so instructed, the jury presumably found that the pan, because it had many advantages in a variety of uses, did not fail the risk/utility test.

But it was also the case that the pan was advertised as suitable for a particular use – cooking a twenty-five pound turkey. Indeed, T-Fal added handles to the pan in order to fill QVC's request for a roasting pan that it could use in its Thanksgiving promotion. The product was, therefore, sold as appropriately used for roasting a twenty-five pound turkey. And it was in that use that allegedly the product failed and injured the appellant.

In such circumstances, New York law is clear that a general charge on strict products liability based on the risk/utility approach does not suffice. The jury could have found that the roasting pan's overall utility for cooking low-volume foods outweighed the risk of injury when cooking heavier foods, but that the product was nonetheless unsafe for the purpose for which it was marketed and sold – roasting a twenty-five pound turkey – and, as such, was defective under the consumer expectations test. That being so, the appellants were entitled to a separate breach of warranty charge.[30]

---

[29] Appellants also introduced into evidence a "sell sheet" prepared by T-Fal, which described for the QVC salespersons the uses and characteristics of the product, including not only cooking a twenty-five pound turkey, but also an extensive list of several low-volume foods, such as cake, lasagna, and stuffed potatoes. While the "sell-sheet" was an internal document, and therefore, could not have influenced consumer expectations, it does shed light on the meaning of the videotaped commercial.

[30] Appellees argue that "[t]he roaster had only a single purpose which was to be a vessel for cooking." But that misses the point of the dual purpose test. Indeed, the same argument could have been made in the *Denny* case: that the Ford Bronco II had a single purpose, namely driving. What characterizes both of these cases, however, is that there was evidence before the jury of the "dual purposes" to which the products could be put. As the Court of Appeals stated in *Denny,* it is "the nature of the proof and the way in which the fact issues

III. CONCLUSION

In light of the evidence presented by appellants of the multi-purpose nature of the product at issue, the district court, applying New York law, should have granted appellants' request for a separate jury charge on the breach of warranty claim in addition to the charge on the strict liability claim. Accordingly, we reverse the order of the district court denying the motion for a new trial, and remand the case for a new trial on the breach of warranty claim, consistent with this opinion.

Section 2 of the Restatement (Third) of Torts defines a product defect as follows:

> A product is defective when, at the time of sale or distribution, it contains a manufacturing defect, is defective in design, or is defective because of inadequate instructions or warnings. A product:
>
> (a) contains a manufacturing defect when the product departs from its intended design even though all possible care was exercised in the preparation and marketing of the product;
>
> (b) is defective in design when the foreseeable risks of harm posed by the product could have been reduced or avoided by the adoption of a reasonable alternative design by the seller or other distributor, or a predecessor in the commercial chain of distribution, and the omission of the alternative design renders the product not reasonably safe;
>
> (c) is defective because of inadequate instructions or warnings when the foreseeable risks of harm posed by the product could have been reduced or avoided by the provision of reasonable instructions or warnings by the seller or other distributor, or a predecessor in the commercial chain of distribution, and the omission of the instructions or warnings renders the product not reasonably safe.

This definition was very controversial in the development of the Restatement (Third) of Torts.[31] It also presents an obvious potential overlap with the failure of

---

[are] litigated [that] demonstrate[ ] how the two causes of action can diverge." . . . In the instant case, given the evidence before the jury of the pan's dual purposes, the failure to charge the jury on breach of warranty could not be harmless error.

[31] *See e.g.,* James A. Henderson, Jr. & Aaron D. Twerski, *Achieving Consensus on Defective Product Design*, 83 CORNELL L. REV. 867 (1998); John F. Vargo, *The Emperor's New Clothes: The American Law Institute Adorns a "New Cloth" for Section 402A Products Liability Design Defects - A Survey of the States Reveals a Different Weave*, 26 U. MEM. L. REV. 493 (1996); Marshall S. Shapo, *In Search of the Law of Products Liability: The ALI*

goods to be fit for their ordinary purpose.[32] Do you agree with how the court in *Castro* dealt with that potential overlap? Should there be different tests for a design defect under tort law and unmerchantable goods under contract law?[33]

Problem 8-5

The New York Court of Appeals in *Denny v. Ford Motor Co.*, 662 N.E.2d 730 (N.Y. 1995) ruled that: (1) a cause of action for strict liability is not identical to a claim for breach of warranty; and (2) a strict liability claim is not necessarily broader than a breach of warranty claim such that the former encompasses the latter. Relying on that, the Second Circuit in *Castro* ruled that a claim for breach of the implied warranty of merchantability might exist even though the jury had concluded that there was no viable strict products liability claim. However, is the inverse situation possible? Can a strict products liability claim exist even though there is no actionable claim for breach of the implied warranty of

---

Restatement Project, 48 VAND. L. REV. 631 (1995); Thomas C. Galligan, *Contortions Along the Boundary Between Contracts and Torts*, 69 TUL. L. REV. 457 (1994). For a brief historical view by the co-reporters of the development of the new Restatement, *see* James A. Henderson, Jr. & Aaron D. Twerski, *What Europe, Japan and Other Countries, Jr. Can Learn from the New American Restatement of Products Liability*, 34 TEX. INT'L L.J. 1 (1999).

[32]   *See* Aaron D. Twerski, *Chasing the Illusory Pot of Gold at the End of the Rainbow: Negligence and Strict Liability in Design Defect Litigation*, 90 MARQ. L. REV. 7 (2006) (discussion of the Restatement Third as in essence a negligence standard); Ellen Wertheimer, *The Biter Bit Unknowable Dangers, The Third Restatement, and the Reinstatement of Liability Without Fault*, 70 BROOK. L. REV. 889 (2005) (discussing evolution of the design defect concept); James A Henderson, Jr. & Aaron D. Twerski, *A Fictional Tale of Unintended Consequences: A Response to Professor Wertheimer*, 70 BROOK. L. REV. 939 (2005).

[33]   The Restatement (Third) approach in comment n to § 2 provides:
This Restatement contemplates that a well coordinated body of law governing liability for harm to persons or property arising out of the sale of defective products requires a consistent definition of defect, and that the definition properly should come from tort law, whether the claim carries a tort label or one of implied warranty of merchantability.
See also David G. Owen, *Proof of Product Defect*, 93 KY. L. J. 1 (2004–05) (discussing the factors and evidence relevant to proving product defect).

merchantability?   Construct a scenario in which the warranty of merchantability is made but not breached and yet a strict liability claim would exist under the standard set forth in section 402A of the Restatement (Second) of Torts.

B. THE ECONOMIC LOSS RULE AS A LIMIT ON TORT LIABILITY

Suppose a seller sells an unmerchantable generator to a homeowner. The generator explodes, destroying itself, causing personal injury to the homeowner, and burning down the homeowner's garage where the generator was installed. The homeowner has suffered harm due to the loss of value of the generator itself, recoverable under UCC section 2-714 and consequential losses due to the personal injury and damage to other property, recoverable under UCC section 2-715. Suppose, further, that the homeowner would be foreclosed from recovery by one or more limitations upon warranty liability found in the UCC, *e.g.*, failure to give notice of the breach, lack of contractual privity, an enforceable consequential damage exclusion, a disclaimer of warranty liability, or expiration of the statute of limitations. If the homeowner pursues a claim in strict products liability in tort, most courts would apply some version of the economic loss rule to limit the damages available. Reread Restatement (Second) of Torts section 402A. Under this rule, a tort recovery would be restricted to the damages for personal injury and the damages for losses to property other than the generator that was the subject of the sales contract.[34] Consider the following discussion of the economic loss rule and its rationale.[35]

---

[34]   Ralph C. Anzivino, *The Economic Loss Doctrine: Distinguishing Economic Loss From Non-Economic Loss*, 91 MARQ. L. REV. 1081 (2008); David Gruning, *Pure Economic Loss in American Tort Law: An Unstable Consensus*, 54 AM. J. COMP. L. 187 (2006); Anita Bernstein, *Keep It Simple: An Explanation of the Rule of No Recovery for Pure Economic Loss*, 48 ARIZ. L. REV. 773 (2006); Linda J. Rusch, *Products Liability Trapped by History: Our Choice of Rules Rules Our Choices*, 76 TEMP. L. REV. 739 (2003); Eileen Silverstein, *On Recovery in Tort for Pure Economic Loss*, 32 U. MICH. J. L. REFORM 403 (1999); Richard C. Ausness, *Replacing Strict Liability with a Contract-Based Products Liability Regime*, 71 TEMP. L. REV. 171 (1998).

[35]   Should the rationale of this case apply to contracts that are not governed by Article 2? *See Paramount Aviation Corp. v. Agusta*, 288 F.3d 67 (3d Cir. 2002) (holding that in a contract for services, the economic loss rule does not apply); *Quest Diagnostics, Inc. v. MCI*

LOCKHEED MARTIN CORP. v. RFI SUPPLY, INC.
440 F.3d 549 (1st Cir. 2006)

Torruella, Circuit Judge

This case involves three parties: Plaintiff Lockheed Martin Corporation ("Lockheed"), Defendant Rantec Power Systems, Inc. ("Rantec"), and Third-Party Defendants Factory Mutual Research Corporation ("FMRC") and Factory Mutual Insurance Corporation (collectively, the "FM Entities"). Lockheed appeals the district court's grant of Rantec's motion for summary judgment against Lockheed. . . . We affirm . . . .

I. *Factual Background and Procedural History*
   A. Lockheed and Rantec

Lockheed is an advanced technology company incorporated in Maryland that also has its principal place of business in Maryland. Rantec is a Delaware corporation with its principal place of business in Missouri. Rantec designs and constructs anechoic chambers.[36] On April 15, 1992, Lockheed and Rantec entered into a written contract in which Rantec agreed to design and construct an anechoic chamber at a Lockheed facility in Merrimack, New Hampshire. As part of the contract, Rantec was required to "design, fabricate, and install a fire detection and sprinkler system" in the chamber. The contract contained a warranty clause providing that "[a]ll equipment and workmanship shall be guaranteed to be free from defects by [Rantec] for a period of one (1) year after final acceptance, unless a different warranty is specified." Rantec completed construction of the chamber in late 1992, and final acceptance occurred in 1993.

The fire detection system consisted of, *inter alia,* smoke detectors, fire alarms, valves, telescoping sprinkler assemblies ("TSAs"), and sprinkler heads. The TSAs were retracted above and outside the chamber and were designed to extend into the chamber when the detection system identified smoke or fire but not immediately release water. Once the temperature exceeded a certain level, a fusible link

---

Worldcom, Inc., 656 N.W.2d 858 (Mich. Ct. App.), *appeal denied,* 671 N.W.2d 886 (Mich. 2003) (economic loss doctrine does not bar recovery when person suffers economic harm and not in a contractual relationship with the plaintiff).

[36]   An anechoic chamber is a steel shielded room padded with foam material to absorb light and sound. These chambers are used by Lockheed to test antenna signals for aerospace and military applications.

incorporated in the sprinkler head would melt and water would be released into the chamber.

The present case stems from two incidents involving flooding of Lockheed anechoic chambers. In December 1996, an anechoic chamber at a Lockheed facility in California suffered water damage when three of the TSAs broke and water flooded the chamber. On March 27, 1997, the sprinkler system at the anechoic chamber in New Hampshire malfunctioned. The fire suppression system activated due to a defect in an electronic panel sold and installed by another contractor not party to this suit. The TSAs extended and some of the sprinkler heads broke and released a large amount of water into the chamber. The foam and sub-flooring of the chamber suffered $400,000 of damage. According to Lockheed, also damaged by the flood were a pedestal and positioning system costing over $160,000. These items were not provided under the contract with Rantec. Lockheed did not include these items in its complaint and did not amend its complaint to add these items.

On December 20, 1999, Lockheed brought suit against Rantec . . . alleging claims stemming from the incidents in California and New Hampshire. . . . Lockheed raised the following claims regarding the New Hampshire events: (1) negligence, (2) strict liability, and (3) implied warranties.

B. Rantec and the FM Entities

FMRC performs testing, issues product standards, and publishes a directory of "FM Approved" products for use in fire suppression systems. Rantec's claims against the FM Entities stemmed from FMRC's approval of Rantec's TSAs on the condition that they be equipped with certain sprinkler heads-the sprinkler heads that broke when the TSAs extended into Lockheed's anechoic chamber. After Lockheed sued Rantec, Rantec moved to add the FM Entities as Third-Party Defendants. . . .

C. Proceedings Below

. . . [T]he district court granted Rantec's motion for summary judgment against Lockheed . . .[and] found that the economic loss doctrine barred Lockheed's tort claims and that the implied warranties' claims were barred by the statute of limitations. . . .

II. *Discussion*

. . .

B. Lockheed's Tort Claims

The parties agree that New Hampshire law governs this case. The district court found that, under New Hampshire law, Lockheed's tort claims were barred by what is known as the economic loss rule. Under the economic loss rule, a party generally may not recover in tort for "economic loss." We begin by discussing how the New Hampshire courts have defined "economic loss" and applied the economic loss rule.

The New Hampshire Supreme Court has defined "economic loss" as "the diminution in the value of a product because it is inferior in quality," *Ellis v. Robert C. Morris, Inc.,* 513 A.2d 951, 954 (N.H. 1986), *overruled on other grounds by Lempke v. Dagenais,* 547 A.2d 290, 297–98 (N.H. 1988), and "that loss resulting from the failure of the product to perform to the level expected by the buyer[, which] is commonly measured by the cost of repairing or replacing the product," *Lempke,* 547 A.2d at 296. The New Hampshire Supreme Court has also stated that "[w]hen a defective product accidentally causes harm to persons or property, the resulting harm is treated as personal injury or property damage. But when damage occurs to the inferior product itself . . . the harm is characterized as economic loss." *Ellis,* 513 A.2d at 954. The New Hampshire Supreme Court has also noted that "[i]t is clear that the majority of courts do not allow economic loss recovery in tort, but that economic loss is recoverable in contract," *Lempke,* 547 A.2d at 296, and that a party usually may not recover damages for economic loss via a tort claim. . . . . The district court found that the flooding was caused by a malfunction of the anechoic chamber and that the only thing damaged was the chamber itself. The district court therefore concluded that Lockheed suffered only economic loss and could not recover on its negligence or strict liability claims.

Lockheed argues that, under New Hampshire law, the economic loss rule does not bar tort actions where a defect "actually poses an affirmative risk of harm to persons or property." Lockheed would have us look to how the damage occurred and, if we find that the defect or accident posed an affirmative risk to persons or property, find that its tort claims are not barred by the economic loss rule.[37]

---

[37]   In making this argument, Lockheed states that its view is consistent with "that of the overwhelming majority of courts around the country." We disagree. As the United States Supreme Court noted in *East River Steamship Corp. v. Transamerica Delaval, Inc.,* 476 U.S. 858 (1986), the majority of courts have held that a party may not recover in tort when a product's malfunction damages only the product itself, regardless of the manner in which the damage occurred or the risk posed by the defect.

However, we see nothing in the New Hampshire cases dealing with economic loss indicating that, when determining whether or not loss is economic, the New Hampshire courts would inquire into the risk posed by an accident or defect in a product. Instead, the New Hampshire cases are clear that when a product harms only itself, the loss is economic and may not be recovered in tort. For example, in a recent New Hampshire Supreme Court case, the court stated that "[w]hen a defective product accidentally causes harm to persons or property [*other than the defective product itself*], the resulting harm is treated as personal injury or property damage." *Kelleher v. Lumber,* 891 A.2d 477, 494 (2005) (quoting *Ellis,* 513 A.2d at 954) (alteration in original) (emphasis added). The court went out of its way to add the phrase "other than the defective product itself," which was not present in *Ellis.* The implication of this statement is that, when a defective product accidentally causes harm to itself, that harm is *not* treated as personal injury or property damage but is instead treated as economic loss, which is not recoverable in tort. The New Hampshire Supreme Court has therefore clearly rejected the logic behind Lockheed's argument.

We also think that this approach comports with the policies behind several fundamental tenets of contract and tort law. Lockheed argues that the purpose of the economic loss doctrine is to distinguish between a product that fails to perform as promised and a product whose defect poses an actual risk of injury or damage, and that the dividing line between tort and contract should not hinge on the fortuity of what happened to be damaged. To our knowledge, the New Hampshire courts have not explicitly addressed these arguments. However, the United States Supreme Court has done so in *East River S.S. Corp. v. Transamerica Delaval, Inc.,* 476 U.S. 858 (1986). In *East River,* an admiralty case, the Court discussed the merits of the majority view of the economic loss doctrine – that damage to a product caused by that product is economic loss and not recoverable in tort – as well as the view argued by Lockheed-that the economic loss doctrine should turn on the affirmative risk posed by the defective product. In rejecting the position advocated by Lockheed, the Court stated that such a position, "which essentially turn[s] on the degree of risk, [is] too indeterminate to enable manufacturers easily to structure their business behavior." *Id.* at 870. The Court also stated that

> [t]he distinction that the law has drawn between tort recovery for physical injuries and warranty recovery for economic loss is not arbitrary and does not rest on the "luck" of one plaintiff in having an accident causing physical injury. The distinction rests, rather, on an understanding of the nature of the responsibility a manufacturer must undertake in distributing

his products. When a product injures only itself the reasons for imposing
tort duty are weak and those for leaving the party to its contractual
remedies are strong.

Id. at 871. As the Court noted, "[e]ven when the harm to the product itself occurs
through an abrupt, accident-like event, the resulting loss due to repair costs,
decreased value, and lost profits is essentially the failure of the purchaser to receive
the benefit of its bargain-traditionally the core concern of contract law."[38] *Id.* at
870.

Further, Lockheed's position would eviscerate the line between tort and
contract and would allow tort, in many ways, to swallow up contract law. As the
Supreme Court noted in East River, "[p]roducts liability grew out of a public policy
judgment that people need more protection from dangerous products than is
afforded by the law of warranty. It is clear, however, that if this development were
allowed to progress too far, contract law would drown in a sea of tort." *Id.* at 866.
Lockheed's view would lead to just that result. It would allow any party who
suffered damage as a result of a product's malfunction to bring a tort claim by
asserting that the malfunction occurred in a way that might have harmed another
person or property, regardless of whether any other person or property was actually
harmed. We think the better approach is to look at what in fact happened, not what
could have happened.

In sum, it is clear from the New Hampshire cases, especially *Kelleher,* the New
Hampshire Supreme Court's most recent case regarding the economic loss rule, that
New Hampshire has adopted the majority view of the economic loss rule which the

---

[38]   Lockheed admits that if there had been a fire in the chamber but the sprinkler system
failed to extinguish it, or if the sprinkler system had interfered with the chamber's ability to
send or receive signals, then it would likely be barred by the economic loss doctrine because
these situations would have involved a failure of the chamber to perform. Lockheed attempts
to distinguish these situations from the flooding of the chamber, arguing that the flooding had
nothing to do with the chamber's ability to perform. However, we see no difference between
the situations. Part of the chamber's ability to perform was the fire suppression system's
ability to extend the TSAs into the chamber if there was a fire but not release water until a
certain temperature was reached. Here, there were two failures to perform: (1) the sprinklers
descended into the chamber when there was not a fire, and (2) the sprinklers released water
into the chamber even though there was no fire. This latter occurrence was, in many ways,
a failure of the sprinkler system to perform one of its most basic functions-to not release
water into the chamber simply because the TSAs had been deployed. We therefore reject
Lockheed's attempts to distinguish the present situation from other situations where it admits
that there would be a failure of performance.

Supreme Court discussed in *East River.* Therefore, if the flooding caused by the allegedly defective sprinkler systems damaged only the product itself, then the economic loss rule prohibits Lockheed from recovery on its tort claims.

We turn now to address whether the flooding damaged only the product itself. Lockheed makes two arguments regarding this issue. First, it argues that the fire suppression system and the anechoic chamber were different products, and that the defect in the fire suppression therefore damaged another product – the anechoic chamber. However, as Rantec points out, the parties' contract for the anechoic chamber included the fire suppression system as a component part of the chamber, not a separate product. As part of the contract, the parties included a document entitled "Tapered Anechoic Chamber, Compact Range Chamber Technical Specification." Paragraph 1.0 of this document, entitled "Introduction," stated that "[t]his document provides specification information for a tapered anechoic chamber. . . ." Paragraph 2.0, entitled "Tapered Anechoic Chamber and Control Room," stated that "[t]he specification is for a tapered anechoic chamber to be used as a general purpose facility for RCS test and antenna pattern measurements. . . . The contractor will design, fabricate, and test the chamber, including all HVAC, fire detection and suppression" utilities. From these provisions, it is clear that the fire suppression system was a component part of the anechoic chamber according to the technical specifications for the chamber agreed upon by the parties. The anechoic chamber and fire suppression system are therefore properly regarded as a single unit. As the Supreme Court noted in *East River,* "[s]ince all but the very simplest of machines have component parts, [a contrary] holding would require a finding of property damage in virtually every case where a product damages itself." 476 U.S. at 867.

Lockheed's second argument is that there were in fact other items in the chamber when it was flooded: a pedestal and positioning system. However, as Rantec points out, Lockheed never mentioned these items in its complaint and never amended its complaint to include these items. Lockheed attempts to get around this issue by arguing that, under the Federal Rules of Civil Procedure's notice pleading standard, it was not required to itemize its damages in the complaint. Lockheed also argues that the complaint, fairly read, gave notice to Rantec that these other items were in the chamber. We disagree for several reasons. First, while the Federal Rules of Civil Procedure require only notice pleading, there is nothing in the complaint that would put Rantec on notice that Lockheed was claiming anything other than damage to the chamber itself. A review of the complaint reveals no mention of other items in the chamber. Instead, the complaint repeats several times that "plaintiff's anechoic chambers were doused with water and severely damaged."

Lockheed also specified that the "anechoic foam and sub-flooring in the chamber" was damaged. Nothing in the complaint provides the slightest indication that there were other items in the chamber or that Lockheed suffered damage to anything other than the chamber itself. We see no reason to allow Lockheed to claim damage to other items when it never bothered to mention or even hint toward damage to anything beyond the anechoic chamber itself in the complaint. . . . Because Lockheed failed to give any indication in its complaint that it was alleging damage to anything other than the anechoic chamber, we will not consider alleged damage to the pedestal and positioning system in this appeal.

C. Lockheed's Implied Warranties Claims

Lockheed also brought claims for breach of implied warranties under New Hampshire's Uniform Commercial Code ("UCC").[39] The district court assumed, *arguendo,* that the contract was governed by the UCC. The court then found that the UCC's statute of limitations – codified as N.H. Rev. Stat. § 382-A:2-725 ("Section 2-725") – applied to Lockheed's claims. Section 2-725 provides for a four-year statute of limitations commencing at the time the cause of action accrues. . . . The district court found that Lockheed accepted the chamber in 1993 and did not file its complaint until 1999. The court therefore found that Lockheed's claims were barred by the statute of limitations. The court, moreover, found no reason for equitable tolling.

On appeal, Lockheed makes two arguments. First, it argues that the statute of limitations in Section 2-725 does not apply to its case. Alternatively, it argues that equitable tolling applies. . . . This is a case of a party who received a product that malfunctioned several years after purchase. Such cases occur all the time, and we see no reason to apply the rarely used doctrine of equitable tolling to Lockheed's case. We therefore find that Lockheed's implied warranties' claims are barred by the four-year statute of limitations period in Section 2-725.

III. *Conclusion*

For the foregoing reasons, we affirm the district court's grant of summary judgment in favor of Rantec as to Lockheed's claims. . . .

––––––––––––

----

[39]   Lockheed could not bring any express warranty claims because the warranty in the contract was for one year and had long expired.

In *Jimenez v. The Superior Court of San Diego County*, 58 P.3d 450 (Cal. 2002) the defendants manufactured windows which were installed by others in mass-produced homes. The defendants did not own or control the homes under construction. The windows were defective with the result that physical damage to other parts of the homes occurred. The court in a long opinion with a strong dissent held: (i) the manufacturer was strictly liable in tort to the purchaser of the homes for harm resulting from the defects; and (ii) strict liability extended to physical damage to other parts of the houses in which the windows were installed. In rejecting an argument that recovery was barred by the economic loss rule, the court held that the "economic loss rule allows a plaintiff to recover in strict products liability in tort when a product defect causes damage to 'other property' that is property other than the product itself," *id.* at 483, and that the damaged homes were property other than the defective windows.

In concurring, Judge Kennard suggested that the economic loss doctrine would bar recovery in tort for damage to property in which a defective product was installed only if the installed component had lost its separate identity (the component became part of the whole). According to Judge Kennard, the windows were "not so integrated into houses as to lose their separate identity." *Id.* at 487. Thus, damage to other parts of the house was not damage to the product itself.

In dissent, Judge Brown argued that the economic loss doctrine should apply under what he called a "product sold" test:

> Here plaintiff bought their homes as single integrated products complete with windows and other constituent parts one would expect in a home. They allege the windows were defective and caused damage to the other parts of their homes, but plaintiffs suffered no personal injury from these defects, nor was any property, other than the homes themselves, damaged. In other words, the product they bought – their homes – did not meet the quality standard they expected at the time of purchase. In those circumstances, the economic loss rule limits their recovery to the bargain. If for some reason, such as a limited warranty, they find their contractual remedies inadequate, that fact is a function of their bargain with the other; it is not a loss the general public should have to subsidize.

Id. at 496. Which is the better view and why?

CISG. Article 5 provides that the Convention "does not apply to the liability of the seller for death or personal injury caused by the goods to any person." Thus, the classic personal injury products liability case – whether brought against the seller or anyone else – would be governed by other law. Property damage, including economic loss to the goods sold, are recoverable under Article 74, which states that damages for "breach of contract by one party consist of a sum equal to the loss, including loss of profit, suffered by the other party as a consequence of the breach." But even if there is a breach of contract through the tender of non-conforming goods under Article 35, the CISG appears to be limited to direct contractual relations between the seller and the buyer. *See* CISG Art. 1(1), which states that the CISG "applies to contract of sale of goods between parties whose places of business are in different states" and Article 35(1) which states that the seller must deliver goods that are of the quality and description "required by the contract." The CISG is silent on whether parties other than the buyer's immediate seller may be liable for damages resulting from their manufacture or sale of defective products.

UNIDROIT Principles. The Principles have no specific provisions regarding liability for personal injury. The aggrieved party is entitled to full compensation for harm suffered as a result of breach of contract, including physical suffering. UNIDROIT Art. 7.4.2. The Principles apply to the parties to the contract and to intended beneficiaries of the contract, UNIDROIT Art. 5.2.1 through 5.2.6, but do not speak to the issues of liability to other persons who may not fall into that category.

C. MISREPRESENTATION

As noted at the beginning of this section, the relationship between the tort of misrepresentation and the law of express warranty is an uncertain one. The question is basically whether the buyer may recover in tort against a seller for misrepresentation when the buyer may not be able to recover against the seller for breach of an express warranty, typically because the warranty action is barred by the statute of limitations, UCC § 2-725, or the requirement of timely notice of breach of warranty in the case of accepted goods, UCC § 2-607. The buyer may also be seeking tort recovery because the seller has adequately disclaimed liability for consequential damages in the sales contract. UCC § 2-719.

A cause of action for misrepresentation generally requires a material misrepresentation of fact on which the plaintiff justifiably and detrimentally relies.

The evidence needed to prove such reliance is often the same evidence that would be necessary to show that a statement was part of the basis of the parties' bargain, and thus qualifies as an express warranty. Accordingly, there would appear to be substantial overlap between a claim for misrepresentation and a claim for breach of an express warranty.

On the other hand, while an action for breach of an express warranty requires no showing of evil intent, an action for misrepresentation typically requires negligence, recklessness, or actual fraud by the seller who made the misrepresentation. Moreover, a successful plaintiff on a misrepresentation cause of action is generally entitled to reliance damages, as opposed to compensation based on lost expectancy.

Given these similarities and differences, one question courts must often confront is whether the cause of action for misrepresentation is barred if the buyer seeks to recover only for the economic losses it has suffered due to the misrepresentation.[40] In other words, if the buyer is not seeking damages for personal injury or for losses to other property, but is instead seeking to recover only for the loss in the value of the sold item and consequential harm (including reliance costs and lost profits), the claim is arguably one which should be subject to the terms of their negotiated relationship – *i.e.*, to their contract – and not left to the law of tort. On the other hand, at a certain level, a seller should not be able to engage in knowing fraudulent misrepresentations and then be able to disclaim its liability for the resulting harm. Consider the discussion of these issues in the following case.

CERABIO LLC V. WRIGHT MEDICAL TECHNOLOGY, INC.
410 F.3d 981 (7th Cir. 2005)

Rovner, Circuit Judge

In this contract dispute, CERAbio, LLC and its sole member, Phillips Plastics Corporation (collectively "CERAbio"), claims that it delivered all of the assets of the corporation, including its technological know-how, to Wright Medical Technology, Inc. (Wright), but that Wright failed to pay the remaining half of the agreed-upon sales price. Wright countered that not only was the technological

---

[40]   Steven C. Tourek, *et al.*, *Bucking the "Trend": The Uniform Commercial Code, The Economic Loss Doctrine, and Common Law Causes of Action for Fraud and Misrepresentation*, 84 IOWA L. REV. 875 (1999).

knowledge provided by CERAbio worthless and that it therefore had not performed its end of the deal, but that CERAbio had also committed fraud and had been negligent both in the formation and performance of the contract. Upon CERAbio's motion, the district court granted summary judgment on Wright's tort counter claims. At trial, the jury ruled in favor of CERAbio on the contract claims. On appeal, Wright challenges the district court's ruling on summary judgment . . . .

I.

Wright designs, manufactures, and sells medical devices and products, including bone replacement products known as biologics, frequently used during implantation surgery to replace lost bone and provide a framework for new bone growth. In the late 1990's, CERAbio developed a bone replacement product made from tricalcium phosphate ("TCP"). The Food and Drug Administration approved the new product, Apatight, for use in humans as a bone void filler. CERAbio obtained patents for the Apatight production process and material.

In early 2001, Wright representatives learned about Apatight at a trade conference. CERAbio was strictly a research and development company which did not manufacture or sell Apatight or other products commercially. Wright markets and sells biologics worldwide and was looking to expand its product offerings in the bone replacement market, so a match seemed ideal. CERAbio negotiated with Wright to provide Apatight to Wright which Wright would then market and sell. Eventually, the negotiations evolved and Wright decided to purchase substantially all of CERAbio's assets, including all patents and know-how.

Prior to entering into the Agreement, CERAbio informed Wright that it had an established and repeatable process for producing Apatight and that all of the raw materials necessary were commercially available. Under the terms of the August 5, 2002 Agreement between the parties ("Agreement"), Wright agreed to pay $3 million for the CERAbio assets with $1.5 million payable upon closing and a second installment of $1.5 million due no later than three days after Wright verified that it was able to produce Apatight ("Verification"). The contract defined the parameters of Verification and required that CERAbio transfer assets to Wright, that it train Wright's employees, and that Wright produce three test lots of Apatight using the specific work instructions supplied by CERAbio. Wright had sixty days to attempt to produce the three test lots of Apatight in its Memphis facility using commercially reasonable efforts. If it failed to do so, under the Agreement, CERAbio would have the opportunity to access Wright's manufacturing equipment and cooperate with Wright to produce the three Apatight test lots again, using commercially reasonable efforts.

After the closing, Wright attempted to buy TCP powder, one of the key raw materials needed to manufacture Apatight, but found that it was no longer available. Plasma Biotal, the manufacturer of the necessary TCP powder, had started making a new TCP powder with a different particle size – one that would not work properly utilizing the Apatight manufacturing instructions. Plasma Biotal still had a limited supply of the original powder, but it had become contaminated. Wright and CERAbio dispute when CERAbio became aware that the powder was unavailable and the role that the unavailability of the powder played in the ability to seal the deal. From this point forward, the statements of facts in the two briefs begin to read like two unrelated novels. When the facts are digested, however, it appears that the parties do not wholly dispute the course of events, but instead dispute where the blame lies.

According to the appellant Wright, CERAbio knew prior to closing on the Agreement that the TCP powder was unavailable, but nevertheless represented to Wright that all of the materials necessary to produce Apatight were generally commercially available. To support this claim, Wright points to the deposition of CERAbio's senior product development engineer, Dr. Ying Ko, who testified that CERAbio knew prior to closing that the TCP powder was no longer available. CERAbio does not necessarily disagree that it knew of the availability problem, it focuses instead on the fact that it was possible to work around the problem and to produce Apatight without the original TCP powder. And so while it may have known that one form of the powder was unavailable, CERAbio says, it thought that other powders were available and acceptable alternatives. It thus counters Dr. Ko's testimony by pointing to evidence that Plasma Biotal had assured Dr. Ko that it could produce an "original style" powder. It further implies also that even if CERAbio did know that the powder was unavailable, the Agreement between the two parties put the onus on Wright to engage in due diligence in order to verify the availability of all necessary materials. Finally, it claims that Wright itself was aware of the powder unavailability problem prior to the closing. CERAbio's spin, in a nutshell, is that the unavailability of the TCP powder was not CERAbio's fault and that with some revisions to the work instructions Apatight could be produced using the new powder, but that Wright never gave CERAbio the chance. It also argues that Wright eventually found a manufacturer who could make a "look-alike" powder but decided instead to shut CERAbio out of the process, produce the virtually identical ceramic bone replacement, Cellplex, on its own, and claim it as its own new creation to avoid paying the remainder of the $1.5 million fee and royalties.[41]

Wright, of course, has a different story to tell. Shortly after closing, CERAbio informed Wright that the instructions had to be changed due to the unavailability of the TCP powder – a problem that CERAbio claimed not to have known about prior to closing on the Agreement. Wright claims that, based on these representations, it consented to oral modifications of the Agreement – permitting CERAbio to make changes to the work instructions and to attempt twelve "pre-verification" production runs over the course of several months. Wright points to evidence that CERAbio did, in fact, know about the availability problem prior to closing and argues that had it known that CERAbio had hidden its knowledge of the unavailability, it never would have agreed to the modification.

In the meantime, in light of the powder unavailability, efforts to resolve the problem proceeded on two fronts. Plasma Biotal tried to replicate the old powder it had been producing originally, and CERAbio employees were working at Wright from late August 2002, to early November 2002, to see if they could alter the work instructions to come up with a process for manufacturing Apatight using the new powder. These attempts were called "pre-verification" efforts since the formal Verification process described in the Agreement could not begin without the old powder or an appropriate substitute. Both parties agree that no successful test lots were produced during this time. CERAbio claims that Verification failed because Wright threw CERAbio's scientists out just as they were on the cusp of success. It did so, says CERAbio, because Wright had independently learned that Plasma Biotal had developed a new "look-a-like" powder that would work in the process and it wanted to proceed to develop the TCP bone replacement product on its own to avoid paying royalties. CERAbio claims that had it known about the existence of the new powder, it could have completed the Verification process in two or three weeks.

Wright, on the other hand, claims that after two or three months of unsuccessful tries (the exact amount of time is the subject of some debate, but not relevant for these purposes), it became clear to Wright that the effort was fruitless. On November 8, 2002, Wright notified CERAbio that it considered CERAbio to be in

---

[41]   Under the Agreement Wright was to pay 7.5% royalties on products primarily derived from CERAbio technology and 3% on products incorporating the transferred technology in part.

breach of the Agreement, and proceeded with its own efforts to produce a bone replacement product.

Both parties agree that Wright eventually succeeded in creating a marketable bone replacement product called Cellplex. Wright, of course, argues that it created Cellplex using a completely different process than the one invented by CERAbio. CERAbio claims that the process for manufacturing Cellplex differs only slightly from the process CERAbio developed to manufacture Apatight and then sold to Wright, and that the two end products are virtually identical.

CERAbio sued Wright for the second $1.5 million installment it believes Wright owes under the Agreement. Wright countered with its own contract claim alleging that CERAbio failed to provide its end of the bargain under the terms of the Agreement and therefore was not entitled to the final payment. In addition, Wright claimed that CERAbio's misrepresentations caused Wright to incur unplanned expenses in excess of $500,000, direct damages of over $880,000, and lost profits as of the time of trial of over $6.7 million.

Wright also counter-sued claiming fraudulent inducement of the contract, fraud in the performance of the contract, pre-contract negligent representation, and negligent misrepresentation in the performance of the contract. The district court judge granted summary judgment for CERAbio on all of Wright's tort claims. . . .

On appeal, Wright challenges the district court's [summary judgment on the tort claims]. . . .

II.

. . . . CERAbio moved the district court for summary judgment on all of the defendant's counter claims other than its claim for breach of contract, namely Wright's counterclaims for pre-contract fraudulent inducement and negligent misrepresentation, and post-contract fraudulent and negligent misrepresentation in the performance of the contract. [The court determined that Wisconsin law applied to this issue. –ed.]

. . . . The district court concluded that each of Wright's four tort-based counterclaims was barred by the economic loss doctrine. The economic loss doctrine seeks to preserve the distinction between contract and tort law and to prevent parties from eschewing agreed-upon contract remedies and seeking broader remedies under tort theory than the contract would have permitted. *Ins. Co. of N. Am. v. Cease Elec. Inc.*, 688 N.W.2d 462, 467 (Wis. 2004). "Economic loss" for purposes of the doctrine is "the loss in a product's value which occurs because the product is inferior in quality and does not work for the purposes for which it was manufactured and sold." *Id.* The economic loss doctrine "forbids commercial contracting parties (as distinct from consumers, and other individuals not engaged in business) to escalate their contract dispute into a charge of tortious misrepresentation if they could easily have protected themselves from the misrepresentation of which they now complain." *All-Tech Telecom, Inc. v. Amway Corp.*, 174 F.3d 862, 866 (7th Cir. 1999) (applying Wisconsin law). In short, parties cannot use tort principles to circumvent the terms of an agreement. . . . doctrine's purpose is to "maintain the fundamental distinction between tort law and contract law; protect commercial parties' freedom to allocate economic risk by contract; and encourage the party best situated to assess the risk of economic loss, the commercial purchaser, to assume, allocate, or insure against that risk." *Digicorp, Inc. v. Ameritech Corp.*, 662 N.W.2d 652, 659 (Wis. 2003).

Recently (since the parties briefed the issue on appeal), the Wisconsin Supreme Court has held that the economic loss doctrine does not apply to claims for the negligent provision of services. *Cease Elec.*, 688 N.W.2d at 472. Wright claims that the contract between itself and CERAbio centered on the provision of services, that is, the installation of equipment, training, and achievement of Verification. CERAbio, on the other hand, maintains that the Asset Purchase Agreement is a contract for the sale of all assets of a business, not a service contract like the one in *Cease Electric.* We agree with CERAbio that the service contract exception should not apply. Our review of the Asset Purchase Agreement confirms that it was indeed a contract for the sale of all of the assets of CERAbio. The fact that some of the assets included technological knowledge and skills that had to be transferred from CERAbio's employees to Wright's employees does not alter the fundamental nature of the contract as one for the sale of goods. Moreover, the policy considerations that prompted the Wisconsin Supreme Court to exempt service contracts from the economic loss doctrine are simply not at play here. Most service contracts, the Wisconsin Supreme Court reasoned (like those to mow the lawn or unclog a drain), are oral and informal and parties rarely hire attorneys to allocate risks and limit remedies. *Cease Elec.*, 688 N.W.2d at 470–71. In many service contracts, furthermore, the information disparities between the parties make it unlikely that each party can negotiate the terms with the same level of bargaining power. *Id.* at 471. None of these policy considerations apply in this case. Wright and CERAbio, both well-represented, sophisticated business parties, drafted complex, detailed agreements which could and indeed did allocate risks and assign remedies. We conclude, therefore, that the economic loss doctrine applies.

The question then becomes whether there are any exceptions to the economic loss doctrine that might keep Wright's tort claims alive. The district court correctly discerned that Wisconsin recognizes a fraud in the inducement exception to the economic loss doctrine. The court below, however, incorrectly stated that the Wisconsin Supreme Court had expressly adopted a narrow exception akin to the one announced in a Michigan case – *Huron Tool and Eng'g Co. v. Precision Consulting Servs., Inc.,* 532 N.W.2d 541 (Mich. Ct. App. 1995). That very narrow exception limits fraud in the inducement claims to situations where the claimed fraud is extraneous to, rather than interwoven with the contract, that is, where the fraud concerns those matters that were not expressly or impliedly addressed in the contract. *Digicorp,* 662 N.W.2d at 662. *Digicorp,* however, did not so hold. Although four justices of the five-member court recognized some form of a fraud in the inducement exception to the economic loss doctrine, only two justices announced their recognition of a narrow *Huron-Tool*-like exception. *Id.* at 662. Two justices dissented announcing that they would have upheld the previous broad exception set forth in *Douglas-Hanson Co. v. BF Goodrich Co.,* 598 N.W.2d 262 (Wis. Ct. App. 1999), *aff'd,* 607 N.W.2d 621 (Wis. 2000), allowing a plaintiff to make a claim for intentional misrepresentation when the misrepresentation fraudulently induces a plaintiff to enter into a contract. *Digicorp,* 662 N.W.2d at 670. A third justice concluded in a dissent that any fraud in the inducement exception was unnecessary. *Id.* at 667. In short, a majority (three) of the justices overruled the broad exception announced in *Douglas-Hanson,* but a separate, but different three-member majority rejected the narrow *Huron Tool* exception. *See Tietsworth v. Harley Davidson, Inc.,* 677 N.W.2d 233, 243–44 (Wis. 2004). The most we can discern from *Digicorp,* therefore, is that the fraud in the inducement exception to the economic loss doctrine is more narrow than that announced in *Douglas-Hanson* and that it does not apply when the fraud pertains to the character and quality of the goods that are the subject matter of the contract. *Id.* at 244.[42]

---

[42]   Like Wisconsin, Delaware and Tennessee also limit the fraud in the inducement exception to matters not expressly addressed in the contract. *See Trinity Indus., Inc. v. McKinnon Bridge Co., Inc.,* 77 S.W.3d 159, 172 (Tenn. Ct. App. 2001) ("Courts should be particularly skeptical of business plaintiffs who-having negotiated an elaborate contract or having signed a form when they wish they had not-claim to have a right in tort whether the tort theory is negligent misrepresentation, strict tort, or negligence."); *Christiana Marine Serv. Corp. v. Texaco Fuel and Marine Mktg., Inc.,* 2002 WL 1335360, *5 (Del. Super. Ct. 2002) ("The economic loss doctrine . . . forbids plaintiffs from recovering in tort for losses suffered that are solely economic in nature . . . . While initially a doctrine related to product

This is enough information, however, for us to conclude that the fraud in the inducement exception should not apply to the specific facts of this case. Recall that the purpose of the fraud in the inducement exception is to address the "special situation where parties to a contract appear to negotiate freely – which normally would constitute grounds for invoking the economic loss doctrine – but where in fact the ability of one party to negotiate fair terms and make an informed decision is undermined by the other party's fraudulent behavior." *Digicorp*, 662 N.W.2d at 662 (quoting *Huron Tool*, 532 N.W.2d at 545). It does not address the situation where "the only misrepresentation by the dishonest party concerns the quality or character of the goods sold, [as] the other party is still free to negotiate warranty and other terms to account for possible defects in the goods." *Id.* Tort remedies are inappropriate where commercial contracting parties could have easily protected themselves from the misrepresentation of which they now complain. *All-Tech Telecom*, 174 F.3d at 866. In this case, the parties to the contract were two sophisticated and well-represented business entities. The crux of their agreement centered around the sale and purchase of the assets of CERAbio's business – primarily a process for producing Apatight. Wright's primary concern should have been, and indeed was, whether it was purchasing a process that could be replicated by Wright. Of course, if it could not, Wright would be paying $3 million dollars for a product with no value to it. Wright was free to, and in fact did, negotiate warranty and other terms to account for the possibility that the process could not be replicated. Wright's remedies, therefore must be limited to contract claims.

As we have cautioned before, we do not mean to imply that the tort of misrepresentation is abolished in all cases in which the plaintiff and defendant are commercial entities with a pre-existing contractual relationship. *Id.* at 866. The fraud in the inducement exception to the economic loss doctrine, however, does not apply in this particular case where two sophisticated commercial entities created contractual remedies to address the concern that the product Wright was purchasing from CERAbio might not result in the desired outcome either because the process was not repeatable or because the starting materials were not available. The alleged fraud in this case pertains to the character and quality of the product that is the subject matter of the contract. *See Tietsworth*, 677 N.W.2d at 244. "Misrepresentations such as these, that ultimately concern the quality of the product

---

liability actions, the courts have expanded the doctrine's application beyond its original scope to any kind of dispute arising from a commercial transaction where the alleged damages do no harm to a person or to property other than the bargained for item."). . . .

sold, are properly remedied through claims for breach of warranty." *Cooper Power Sys., Inc. v. Union Carbide Chems. & Plastics Co., Inc.,* 123 F.3d 675, 682 (7th Cir. 1997).

Whether or not the process was repeatable was addressed contractually by the complex process set forth in the contract for Verification. The agreement between the parties was contingent upon Wright producing three test lots meeting the specifications outlined in the Agreement. Of course, if the starting materials were not available, Verification could not be achieved. The Agreement addressed the availability of starting materials in another manner as well. The disclaimer of warranty provision contained in the Non-Disclosure Agreement specified that CERAbio provided all information to Wright on an "as is" basis and that CERAbio:

> makes no warranty, either express or implied, concerning the Information, including, without limitation, its accuracy, completeness, or to the non-infringement of intellectual property rights or other rights of third persons or Discloser. Recipient assumes all risk in, and Discloser will not be liable for any damages arising out of, use of information including, without limitation, business decisions made or inferences drawn by Recipient in reliance on the Information or the fact of the disclosure of the Information.

. . . This type of disclaimer is referred to as a non-reliance clause. Furthermore, the integration clause in the asset purchase agreement incorporates this non-disclosure agreement and likewise allocates to Wright the risk that the information provided by CERAbio might be incomplete or incorrect. This clause states:

> This Agreement, including schedules and exhibits referred to herein, and the NDA [Non-Disclosure Agreement] embody the entire agreement and understanding of the parties hereto . . . . There are no restrictions, promises, representations, warranties, covenants or undertakings of Seller contained in any material made available to Buyer pursuant to the terms of the NDA, or the correspondence between Seller and Buyer.

. . . . These provisions allocated to Wright the risk that the information provided by CERAbio might be incomplete or incorrect. Wright assured CERAbio in writing that it would not rely on information provided by CERAbio. Not only does this non-reliance clause verify that the alleged fraud was interwoven with the parties' contractual agreement, and thus barred by the economic loss doctrine, it also confirms the district court's finding that Wright could not have reasonably relied on CERAbio's oral representation as to the viability of the process or the availability of starting materials.

Wright challenges the proposition that commercial parties can never demonstrate reasonable reliance on misrepresentation in the face of a non-reliance clause. For this portion of the dispute, we must consider the force and effect of a clause in the contract – the non-reliance clause – which the parties agreed to construe in accordance with Delaware law. Although the Delaware Supreme Court has offered no definitive conclusion, recent opinions of the Delaware chancery courts have repeatedly concluded that "sophisticated parties to negotiated commercial contracts may not reasonably rely on information that they contractually agreed did not form a part of the basis for their decision to contract." *H-M Wexford LLC v. Encorp, Inc.,* 832 A.2d 129, 142 (Del. Ch. 2003). . . .

Wright lashes at this windmill of Delaware authority by arguing that none of the cases established a *per se* rule that commercial parties can never demonstrate reasonable reliance on misrepresentations in the face of a purported non-reliance clause. Wright claims instead that those courts made fact-specific determinations about whether plaintiffs could have reasonably relied upon the defendants' misrepresentations. This may, in fact, be the case, but it does not get Wright anywhere. The relevant facts in *Great Lakes* have a familiar ring. The case involved "two highly sophisticated parties, assisted by industry consultants and experienced legal counsel, [who] entered into carefully negotiated disclaimer language after months of extensive due diligence . . . [and who] explicitly allocated their risks and obligations in the Purchase Agreement." *Id.* at 555. Noting the carefully negotiated and crafted nature of the agreements, the *Great Lakes* court concluded that "to allow [the buyer] to assert, under the rubric of, claims that are explicitly precluded by contract, would defeat the reasonable commercial expectations of the contracting parties and eviscerate the utility of written contractual agreements." *Id.* at 556. The same is true here.

This philosophy is not unique to the Delaware courts. This court and others have held that a written anti-reliance clause in a stock purchase agreement precludes any claim of deceit by prior representations. *Rissman v. Rissman,* 213 F.3d 381, 383 (7th Cir. 2000). In *Rissman* we pointed out that a non-reliance clause is part of the negotiated bargain. *Id.* at 384. CERAbio could have assumed the risk of claims based on oral statements it made, but it likely would have increased the purchase price accordingly. *Rissman,* 213 F.3d at 388. . . . Even were we to take a less absolute, case-by-case assessment of the validity of the non-reliance clause (as urged by the concurrence in *Rissman*), our conclusion would not differ. In this case the parties were sophisticated commercial entities assisted by counsel and the facts surrounding the materiality and intentionality of the misrepresentation are highly contested. *See Rissman,* 213 F.3d at 388 (Rovner, J., concurring) (considering factors that might be relevant in determining whether an investor's reliance on prior statements was reasonable despite the existence of a non-reliance clause). We are not unsympathetic to the notion that Wright was purchasing a secret process and therefore in all likelihood it could not investigate independently whether the starting materials were commercially available, but "[c]ontractual language serves its function only if enforced consistently," *id.* at 385, and parties to contracts are best served by rulings enforcing the express terms of agreements into which they enter.

Wright and CERAbio bargained for the allocation of risks contained in the Agreement and Wright accepted the risk that it might receive faulty oral information from CERAbio. The district court correctly concluded, therefore, that Wright's counterclaim for fraudulent inducement could not stand.

Wright's other counterclaims allege negligent misrepresentation in the formation of the contract, negligent misrepresentation in the performance of the contract, and fraud in the performance. Any economic loss caused by these acts, however, is best addressed through the contractual remedies to which the parties agreed.

For example, Wright claims that CERAbio negligently misrepresented information that induced Wright to enter into the Agreement. Although the Wisconsin Supreme Court has not yet specifically addressed the economic loss doctrine in this context, the appellate courts have laid the ground work. . . . It is no stretch to assume that the Wisconsin Supreme Court would follow suit. In describing the policy reasons surrounding the economic loss doctrine, that court has followed a path that protects commercial parties' freedom to allocate economic risk and encourages the party best situated to assess the risk of economic loss, and to assume, allocate, or insure against that risk. . . . For the same reasons, we conclude that the district court was correct in determining that the economic loss doctrine would preclude Wright's claims that CERAbio negligently or fraudulently misrepresented information during the performance of the contract to convince the defendant that verification had occurred. These are simple contract claims disguised in tort claim clothing. If CERAbio breached its duties to perform its tasks during Verification, Wright's remedy lies in contract.

Wright argues that Tennessee law applies to its post-contract fraud claims. But under Tennessee law, like Wisconsin law, we see no support for allowing Wright to wrap its contract claims in tort language. In *Ritter v. Custom Chemicides, Inc.,* 912 S.W.2d 128, 133 (Tenn. 1996), the Tennessee Supreme Court made clear that it was joining the economic loss doctrine bandwagon noting that negligence theory was an inappropriate method to resolve injuries causing economic loss (in the *Ritter* case, from product liability). *Id.* "When a product does not perform as expected," the *Ritter* court went on to explain, "the buyer's remedy should be governed by the rules of contract, which traditionally protect expectation interests." *Id.* This conclusion followed logically from a much earlier Tennessee Supreme Court decision ruling that a cause of action for breach of contract – even negligent or fraudulent – remains in contract rather than tort. *Mid-South Milling Co. v. Loret Farms, Inc.,* 521 S.W.2d 586, 588 (Tenn. 1975). The Tennessee appellate court has applied *Ritter* and *Mid-South Milling* to a contract for the sale of goods, holding that "[i]n a contract for the sale of goods where the only damages alleged come under the heading of economic losses, the rights and obligations of the buyer and seller are governed exclusively by contract." *Trinity Indus., Inc. v. McKinnon Bridge Co., Inc.,* 77 S.W.3d 159, 171 (Tenn. Ct. App.2001). The *Trinity Indus.* court noted the breadth of the economic loss doctrine in Tennessee stating, "[c]ourts should be particularly skeptical of business plaintiffs who-having negotiated an elaborate contract . . . claim to have a right in tort whether the tort theory is negligent misrepresentation, strict tort, or negligence." *Id.* at 172.

For these reasons we uphold the district court's ruling granting summary judgment to CERAbio on Wright's counter claims sounding in tort. . . .

———————

Now read UCC section 2-721 and the following provisions of the Restatement (Second) of Torts.

Section 525

One who fraudulently makes a misrepresentation of fact, opinion, intention or law for the purpose of inducing another to act or to refrain from action in reliance upon it, is subject to liability to the other in deceit for pecuniary loss caused to him by his justifiable reliance upon the misrepresentation.

Section 552

(1) One who, in the course of his business, profession or employment, or in any other transaction in which he has a pecuniary interest, supplies false information for the guidance of others in their business transactions, is subject to liability for pecuniary loss caused to them by their justifiable reliance upon the information, if he fails to exercise reasonable care or competence in obtaining or communicating the information.

(2) Except as stated in Subsection (3), the liability stated in Subsection (1) is limited to loss suffered

(a) by the person or one of a limited group of persons for whose benefit and guidance he intends to supply the information or knows that the recipient intends to supply it; and

(b) through reliance upon it in a transaction that he intends the information to influence or knows that the recipient so intends or in a substantially similar transaction.

(3) The liability of one who is under a public duty to give the information extends to loss suffered by any of the class of persons for whose benefit the duty is created, in any of the transactions in which it is intended to protect them.

How should the idea of misrepresentation in tort be reconciled with the idea of breach of express warranty in contract?

Problem 8-6

Return to Problem 8-4. Assume that Standard intentionally misled Bridget regarding the mileage that the motor home would obtain. Should Bridget have any tort remedy for that misrepresentation?

CHAPTER NINE

SELLER'S REMEDIES FOR BUYER'S BREACH

SECTION 1. OVERVIEW

This Chapter addresses the various ways in which a buyer may breach a contract for the sale of goods and the remedies available to the seller for the buyer's breach.

Determining breach. In an Article 2 contract, the basic obligation of the buyer is to accept and pay for goods that conform to the contract requirements. UCC § 2-301. Much of what we studied in Chapters Two through Six regarding the terms of the contract is relevant in determining whether a breach has occurred and, if so, by whom. For example, if the seller tendered the goods, a review of the contract terms is necessary to determine whether the goods are in fact conforming. If the goods do conform to the contract requirements, the buyer will have an obligation to accept and pay for them and the buyer will be in breach by refusing to accept or failing to pay. If the goods tendered are nonconforming, it will be the seller who is in breach.

Similarly, if the seller refused to tender the goods, it will be necessary to determine whether that refusal was justified, perhaps because the seller reasonably demanded assurances of future performance and the buyer did not respond. If the seller's refusal to tender performance was not justified, the seller will be in breach. If it was justified, the buyer will have breached and the seller will be entitled to seek redress. In short, just as we saw in the discussion of buyer's remedies, it is critical to evaluate the parties' behavior in sequence and in reference to the terms of the contract.

Entitlement to remedies. Even if the buyer has breached the contract, that breach may in some rare circumstances be excused (Chapter Four), with the effect that the seller will not be entitled to pursue remedies for breach. Even if the buyer's breach is not excused, the contract may restrict the seller's remedies for breach pursuant to a liquidated damages clause or some other limitation (Chapter Three). For purposes of this Chapter, we will assume that the parties have an enforceable Article 2 contract, that the buyer has breached one or more contract obligations, that breach is not excused, and that the seller's remedies have not been limited.

Typical breaches and remedies. The remedies available to an aggrieved seller are catalogued, albeit incompletely, in section 2-703. Read that provision. Did you notice what is conspicuously missing? If you did not, read it again. There is no conjunction connecting the various subsections; there is neither an "and" nor an "or." Thus, the section lists the various remedies but does not indicate which may be used together and which are mutually exclusive alternatives. *See* UCC § 2-703 cmt. 1.

The answer to that problem lies in part in section 1-305, which as we learned in Chapter Seven states that UCC remedies should put the non-breaching party in a position as if the contract had been fully performed. In short, the UCC adopts the traditional, common-law principle that the aggrieved party is entitled to expectation damages. Of course, that principle by itself does not say much about when each of the listed remedies is available and when it is not. We need something more.

We also learned in Chapter Seven that the remedies available to the buyer for the seller's breach depend on two principal things: (i) the nature of the breach; and (ii) who has the goods. Those the two factors are also critical in determining the remedies available to the seller following the buyer's breach.

Let us start by considering what happens if the buyer has accepted the goods, that is, the buyer has the goods and breached the contract by failing to pay the price when due. This is probably the most common way buyers breach contracts for the sale of goods. In such a case, the buyer is liable for the price, plus incidental damages. The result of that remedy is the buyer ends up with the goods and the seller ends up with the contract price. The parties' expectations are therefore realized, assuming the buyer in fact pays the judgment. In some limited cases the seller may be entitled instead to reclaim the goods from the buyer. This remedy restores the parties to their pre-contract position, and is thus a restitutionary remedy, not an expectancy measure of recovery. Both of these remedies are discussed in Section 2 of this Chapter.

The buyer may also breach by: (i) repudiating its obligation to pay for or accept the goods, (ii) failing to make a payment when due (even if it does not repudiate its obligations), (iii) wrongfully but effectively rejecting the goods, (iv) wrongfully refusing to allow the seller to cure when the seller has a right to cure, or (v) wrongfully attempting to revoke acceptance of the goods. If the seller still has the goods or they are in transit, the seller may be allowed to withhold or stop delivery of the goods and to recover damages for the buyer's breach of contract. If the goods have been delivered to the buyer, the buyer's wrongful refusal to keep them may mean that the goods end up back in the seller's possession. In either case, when the seller has the goods, the seller's damages will be measured in one of three alternative ways: (i) the difference between the contract price and the resale price of the goods; (ii) the difference between the contract price and the market price of the goods; or (iii) the lost profit on the breached transaction. In addition to recovery based upon one of these measurements, the seller is also entitled to incidental, but not consequential, damages. All of these measures are designed to give the seller the benefit of the bargain. The seller may also be entitled to cancel the contract. In some extremely limited circumstances, the seller may be entitled to the price of the goods even though the buyer has not accepted or kept the goods. These remedies will be discussed in Section 3 of this Chapter.

After discussing the seller's remedies for the buyer's breach, this Chapter focuses on two related matters. Section 4 discusses the effect of the buyer's breach on the risk of loss and Section 5 discusses the effect of the statute of limitations on the seller's remedies.

SECTION 2.   SELLER'S REMEDIES WHEN THE BUYER HAS THE GOODS

A buyer who has accepted the goods becomes obligated to pay the purchase price. *See* UCC § 2-301. Accordingly, Article 2 has a very clear remedy for a seller when the buyer has accepted the goods but has breached by refusing to pay: the seller is entitled to recover the contract price of the goods plus incidental damages. Read UCC § 2-709. This measure of damages protects the seller's expectancy. Of course, as we have already seen, the buyer may still be entitled to an offset to the extent that the accepted goods are nonconforming, and the seller has therefore breached an express or implied warranty. UCC §§ 2-714, 2-717.

Example

Bacchanalian Catering, Inc. contracted to purchase from Specialty Displays a large, custom-manufactured sign depicting the company's logo: the Roman god Bacchus. Under the terms of the contract, the purchase price was $6,400, the seller was to deliver by July 1, and the buyer was to pay within 30 days after delivery. Specialty Displays delivered the sign on June 30. Bacchanalian Catering accepted the sign before noticing that the logo was not colored precisely as the contract required. When Specialty Displays refused to cure the defects, Bacchanalian Catering spent $1,300 changing the company's logo on brochures and stationery to match the logo on the sign. Despite the nonconformity of the sign's color, Bacchanalian Catering is liable for the $6,400 price. However, that obligation may be offset by the damages caused by the breach, measured by any difference in value between the goods as promised and the goods as delivered, together with incidental and consequential damages. UCC § 2-714. Assuming the sign is worth $6,400 despite the improper coloration, Bacchanalian Catering would still be permitted to deduct the $1,300 spent on new brochures and stationery, provided those expenses are recoverable consequential damages under section 2-715. UCC § 2-717.

The seller's right to the price when the buyer accepts the goods is a useful remedy only if the buyer has the ability to pay. In many cases, a more effective remedy – albeit one that does not protect the seller's expectancy – would be to get the goods back. Most laypersons and some merchant sellers are surprised to learn, however, that an unpaid seller does not normally have the right to return of the goods. There are, however, two main exceptions to this general rule.

First, the seller may have a *contractual* right to get the goods. Such a right is created when the buyer grants a security interest in the purchased goods to secure the buyer's obligation to pay the purchase price. A security interest is a consensual lien on personal property – the analog to a mortgage on real property – and is governed by UCC Article 9. Any seller with concern about the buyer's ability to pay the purchase price should take a security interest in the goods to secure that payment obligation. If the buyer then fails to make payment when due, the seller would be entitled either to peaceably repossess the goods or to obtain a writ of replevin instructing the sheriff to seize the goods and return them to the seller. *See* UCC § 9-609. The necessary language in the parties' agreement for the seller to have a security interest can be very short and simple. A single sentence "seller retains a security interest in the goods sold to secure the buyer's obligations under this agreement" would suffice. So too would a phrase that the seller "retains title" to the goods sold, because the UCC treats such a clause as one that merely creates a security interest. That language does not actually prevent title from passing to the buyer once the goods have been delivered to the buyer. UCC §§ 1-201(b)(35), 2-401(1).

The second way in which the seller may be able to recover the goods is through a *legal* right called "reclamation."[1] Reclamation is available in two very limited circumstances. In the first situation, the buyer has tendered payment, but the payment mechanism has failed. The classic example of this occurs when the buyer tenders a check that is later dishonored when the seller submits it for collection. Section 2-507 gives the seller the right to reclaim the goods within a reasonable time after the payment mechanism fails, provided the sale was a "cash sale," that is, provided the buyer was supposed to make payment on delivery. If the buyer purchased on credit (delivery now, payment later) and the buyer's subsequent check for the purchase price bounces, the seller does not have a right to reclaim under section 2-507.

The other situation giving rise to a right of reclamation occurs when the seller has agreed to sell the goods on credit and shortly after delivery discovers that the buyer is insolvent. UCC § 2-702(2). *See also* UCC § 1-201(b)(23) (defining "insolvency"). The seller may reclaim the goods by making a demand on the buyer within ten days of the buyer's receipt of the goods. The ten-day time period does not apply if the buyer has made a "misrepresentation of solvency" in writing within three months before the goods were delivered.[2]

A seller who successfully reclaims the goods from the buyer under section 2-702(2) is precluded from all other remedies, including apparently incidental damages. UCC § 2-702(3). There is no similar limitation following reclamation under section 2-507. Is this distinction justifiable? Why should the seller who reclaims under section 2-702 not be entitled to expectation damages? Perhaps the principle underlying section 2-702(2) is that the buyer has engaged in fraudulent behavior by taking the goods when it is insolvent and thus the seller is entitled to rescind the contract for sale as a remedy for that fraud. With a rescission of the contract and recovery of the goods, the seller is no longer entitled to expectation-

---

[1]   Even though the right of reclamation is not expressly limited to the situation where the buyer has accepted the goods, in practical effect, that is the only time that it matters. If the buyer has effectively rejected the goods, the seller has a right to take the goods back because of the rejection, not based upon any right of reclamation. If the buyer has not effectively rejected the goods, the buyer will have accepted the goods. UCC § 2-606.

[2]   The additional time to reclaim if the buyer has made a written misrepresentation of solvency may be limited if the buyer seeks bankruptcy protection. *See* 11 U.S.C. § 546(c).

Both of these reclamation rights operate only against the buyer. In Chapter Ten, we will consider whether those rights are effective against creditors of the breaching buyer or people who purchase the goods from the breaching buyer.

based damages for breach of the contract.[3] Perhaps another point worth noting is that if the buyer truly is insolvent, the buyer's unsecured creditors (those without any liens to secure the obligation that buyer owes them) are unlikely to be fully paid the debts due them. By allowing the seller to reclaim the goods, the seller is to some extent already being made whole, and thereby favored over those other creditors of the buyer. To entitle the seller to more would be unfair to those other creditors.

Because the sellers' reclamation rights are quite limited, sellers – particularly those who sell on credit – should consider taking a security interest in the goods sold to better protect their right to payment.

CISG and UNIDROIT Principles. Neither the CISG nor the UNIDROIT Principles use the acceptance or rejection concept to control the remedies that the aggrieved seller may recover. Under the CISG, the aggrieved seller has two basic options if the buyer has the goods. First, Article 62 allows the aggrieved seller to require the buyer to pay the price. Alternatively, Article 81 entitles the seller to avoid the contract, recover the goods from the buyer (the seller must also make restitution to the buyer), and seek damages. Both remedies are subject to the limitation in Article 28 that allows a court to refuse to order a remedy if the court's local law would permit such a refusal.

The UNIDROIT Principles are similar. The aggrieved seller may require the buyer to pay the price. Art. 7.2.1. Alternatively, the aggrieved seller could terminate the contract for fundamental nonperformance, Art. 7.3.1, which allows each party to make a claim for restitution of what they have provided under the contract. Art. 7.3.6. The aggrieved seller would still be able to recover damages for the buyer's breach. Arts. 7.3.5, 7.4.1. through 7.4.8.

SECTION 3.   SELLER'S REMEDIES WHEN THE SELLER HAS THE GOODS

There are several ways in which a seller may end up with the goods after the buyer breaches. For example, a buyer may breach by repudiating its obligation to perform or by failing to make a required payment before tender of delivery. In such

---

[3]   *See* Larry T. Garvin, *Credit, Information, and Trust in the Law of Sales: The Credit Seller's Right of Reclamation*, 44 UCLA L. REV. 247 (1996).

cases, the seller's first remedial option is to withhold or stop delivery of the goods to the buyer. UCC § 2-703(a), (b). Alternatively, a buyer may refuse to accept goods that conform to the contract or unjustifiably attempt to revoke acceptance, thereby leaving the goods with or returning the goods to the seller. Whatever the nature of the buyer's breach, the seller who has the goods may also wish to recover damages. This section first addresses the seller's ability to withhold or stop delivery of the goods and then discusses the seller's four alternative measures of damages.

A. SELLER'S ABILITY TO WITHHOLD OR STOP DELIVERY

The provisions allowing the seller to withhold or stop delivery are found in UCC §§ 2-703(a), (b), 2-702(1) and 2-705.[4] Collectively, these provisions allow the seller to keep the goods from the buyer if the buyer has repudiated, failed to make payment, or is insolvent.[5] However, the seller's authority is limited in several ways. To understand the limits it is important first to understand the terminology used in these provisions. Withholding delivery refers to situations in which the seller has the goods. Stopping delivery refers to situations in which a carrier or other bailee has the goods. The second important thing to understand is the scope of these different provisions, which is illustrated by the following chart:

	Withhold Delivery	Stop Delivery
For Buyer's Breach	§ 2-703(a)	§§ 2-703(b), 2-705
For Buyer's Insolvency	§ 2-702(1)	§§ 2-702(1), 2-705

---

[4]   A related right is found in section 2-505 regarding the seller's ability to ship under reservation, which in essence allows the seller to claim a security interest in the goods and withhold the goods from the buyer until the buyer pays the price. Review the material in Chapter Four on shipment under reservation.

      The seller may have rights to withhold or stop delivery under other law, such as UCC Article 9, if the seller has taken a security interest in the goods and the buyer's actions are a default under the security agreement. The rights of a seller as a secured party under Article 9 are beyond the scope of these materials.

[5]   Determining insolvency is not an easy matter. Read section 1-201(b)(23).

By and large, the seller's right to withhold delivery after the buyer's repudiation or breach is unlimited. However, the seller's right to stop delivery is more restricted. That is because of the burden it imposes on carriers. *See* UCC § 2-705 cmt. 1. Moreover, even if the seller has a right to stop delivery to the buyer, that does not mean that a carrier must follow the seller's instructions. *See* § 2-705(3). Thus, when goods are with a carrier, the first question to consider is whether the seller has a right as against the buyer to stop delivery. The second question is whether the seller may require the carrier to stop delivery and return the goods. The third question is what liability will the seller have to the carrier or the carrier have to the buyer if the carrier follows the seller's instructions and stops delivery of the goods. Read UCC §§ 2-703(a), (b), and 2-705 and try the following problem.

Problem 9-1

Seattle Gems, Inc., a gem wholesaler, contracted to sell diamonds to Bellevue Jewelry, Inc., F.O.B. Seattle Gems' place of business. Upon notification of shipment, Bellevue Jewelry was to make a funds transfer to Seattle Gems' bank account. Seattle Gems shipped the diamonds to Bellevue Jewelry using Federated Carriers. Federated issued a negotiable bill of lading naming Seattle Gems as consignee. Bellevue Jewelry failed to make the funds transfer after Seattle Gems notified Bellevue Jewelry the goods had been shipped. Seattle Gems contacted Federated and instructed Federated not to deliver the package to Bellevue Jewelry, but to hold it until Seattle Gems otherwise notified Federated.

A. Did Seattle Gems act rightfully in ordering Federated to hold the package? What difference, if any, would it make if Seattle Gems had reliable information that Bellevue Jewelry had defaulted on its obligations to its primary lender?

B. Does Federated have to obey Seattle Gems' instructions? What risk is Federated taking if it delivers the goods contrary to Seattle Gems' instruction?

C. How does your analysis change if Federated issued a nonnegotiable bill of lading?

CISG and UNIDROIT Principles. Under the CISG, the seller may prevent delivery of the goods to the buyer if it becomes clear that the buyer will not substantially perform its obligations because of a deficiency in the buyer's ability to perform, the buyer's conduct in performing or preparing to perform, or creditworthiness. That right to withhold delivery applies even if the seller has already placed the goods in transit. The seller must notify the buyer so as to give the buyer an opportunity to provide adequate assurance that the buyer will perform. Art. 71. If the buyer has repudiated or failed to render pre-delivery performance such that the buyer has committed a fundamental breach, the seller may declare the contract avoided and thus would not be obligated to deliver the goods. Arts. 72, 81.

The UNIDROIT Principles allow the seller to withhold its performance if the buyer has not performed as required by the contract. Art. 7.1.3.

B. SELLER'S RIGHT TO CANCEL THE CONTRACT

In a non-installment contract, whenever the buyer breaches a contract for the sale of goods, the seller may cancel the contract and seek damages for the buyer's breach. UCC § 2-703(f). Review section 2-106(3) and (4) on the distinction between termination and cancellation. As we have already seen, cancellation allows the aggrieved party – in this case, the seller – to end the contract as a remedy for the buyer's breach. No notification is required and it means that the seller neither expects the buyer to perform in the future nor plans to tender performance of its own remaining contract obligations. Cancellation does not waive the seller's right to seek damages for breach from the buyer, either as to the buyer's past performance or as to the buyer's future performance.

The seller's right to cancel is limited in installment contracts. *See* UCC §§ 2-612(3), 2-703. The buyer's breach with respect to one or more installments gives the seller the right to cancel the whole contract – and thereby terminate the obligation to tender further installments – only if that breach is a "substantial impair[ment] of the value of the whole contract." Of course, even if the buyer's breach does not impair the value of the whole contract for the seller, it nevertheless gives the seller a right to demand adequate assurance of future performance, UCC § 2-612 cmt. 6, and to suspend its own performance until the buyer provides such assurances. UCC § 2-609(1).

Problem 9-2

Burgess Heating, Inc. agreed to buy 500 stoves from Sizzle Stoves for $200 per stove. The parties agreed that Sizzle would deliver the stoves in two installments (approximately 15 days apart), with 20% paid upon delivery of the first installment and the remaining amount paid in 30 days.

Sizzle delivered 250 stoves to Burgess. Burgess gave Sizzle a check for $20,000. That check was dishonored. Burgess has accepted the delivered stoves and is expecting delivery of the remaining stoves. The remaining 250 stoves are sitting in Sizzle's warehouse. Sizzle has consulted you regarding its options against Burgess. Advise Sizzle.

CISG. If a buyer commits a fundamental breach, *see* Art. 25, the seller may avoid the contract. If the seller elects to avoid the contract, the seller generally must notify the buyer unless the breach is the buyer's repudiation of its obligation. Art. 72. In an installment contract, if it appears that the buyer has breached its obligations as to one or more installments such that the seller has grounds to conclude that the buyer's performance as to the future installments would be a fundamental breach, the seller may avoid the contract. Art. 73. The effect of the avoidance is to effectively cancel the contract leaving the seller's ability to pursue damages intact. Art. 81.

UNIDROIT Principles. The seller may terminate the contract if the buyer's failure to perform is a fundamental non-performance. Arts. 7.3.1, 7.3.3. The seller must give notice of the termination to the buyer. Art. 7.3.2. Termination does not affect the seller's rights to damages for the buyer's breach. Art. 7.3.5.

C. SELLER'S DAMAGES

The seller has the following four, general options for computing damages when the buyer breaches by refusing to accept (*i.e.,* wrongfully rejecting) or to keep possession (*i.e.*, wrongfully attempting to revoke acceptance) of the goods:

(i)   Resell the goods and recover the difference between the market price of the goods and the contract price, UCC § 2-706;

(ii) Recover the difference between the market price of the goods and the contract price, UCC § 2-708(1);

(iii) If the previous two measures would be inadequate, recover the lost profit on the transaction, UCC § 2-708(2); and

(iv) If the goods are not readily marketable to anyone else, recover the contract price, UCC § 2-709.

All four measures expressly authorize the seller to also recover incidental damages. They also have something else in common: all are designed to protect the seller's expectancy in one way or another. They are all therefore consistent with the principle, expressed in section 1-305, of putting the aggrieved seller in the position as if the breaching buyer had fully performed its contractual obligations. To demonstrate this point, and the relationship among the four alternatives, consider the following example:

Example

Dealer contracts to sell a lithograph to Buyer for $10,000. Buyer is required to pay $2,000 one week before delivery and the remaining $8,000 at delivery. If all goes according to plan, on the date of delivery, Dealer will have $10,000 and Buyer will have the lithograph. Of course, the lithograph may be worth more or less than $10,000 at the time of contracting, and may be worth the same or a different amount at the time of delivery.

Now assume that Buyer fails to pay the $2,000 down payment and therefore has breached the contract. Dealer cancels the contract and refuses to deliver the lithograph to Buyer. Thus Dealer has the lithograph instead of the $10,000 that Buyer promised to pay.

If the lithograph were really worth only $9,000, Dealer could presumably sell it for that amount and then recover the $1,000 difference between the contract price and the resale price from Buyer under section 2-706. That would leave Dealer with $10,000 ($9,000 from the resale purchaser and $1,000 in damages from Buyer) and no lithograph, which is exactly what Dealer expected to have. Alternatively, Dealer could keep the lithograph and recover the $1,000 (the contract price minus the lithograph's market price value) from Buyer under section 2-708(1). Dealer would therefore have a $9,000 lithograph and a $1,000 recovery, and thus a total equal to what Dealer expected to have.[6] As this scenario suggests, normally there should not be much difference between the market

---

[6]   Although resale damages may seem like a more pure measure of lost expectancy than market damages do (because the seller expected to part with the goods and does indeed part with them following a resale but may still have them when using market damages), it is worth noting that market damages are the more traditional remedy. Moreover, market damages can be analogized to the seller reselling to itself at the market price.

price and the resale price of the goods, and thus not much difference between recovery under section 2-706 and section 2-708(1).[7]

If the lithograph were worth $11,000, neither section 2-706 nor 2-708(1) would yield any recovery from Buyer. That is because Dealer has *apparently* not been harmed by Buyer's breach. Quite the opposite, Buyer's breach appears to have left Dealer with a lithograph worth $11,000 instead of the $10,000 Dealer expected to have. However, sometimes Dealer's true injury is not apparent.

Consider what happens if Dealer resells the lithograph to another buyer for $10,000. Dealer now has the money and not the lithograph. This appears to be what Dealer expected to have if Buyer had performed. Do not overlook the significance of this. If the original contract price was for the fair market value of the goods, which is most often the case, and the market price has not changed from the time the contract was formed to the time the seller was supposed to tender the goods, which is also likely, a seller is likely to have little or no damages if the buyer reneges on the deal. But what if there were many copies of the lithograph, and Dealer could have sold one to Buyer, one to the resale purchaser, and still fill all the other orders that might come in? On such facts, Buyer's breach will have caused Dealer to lose volume. Put another way, the resale was not really enabled by or in substitution for Buyer's breach. Dealer would have made two sales had Buyer not breached, but because Buyer breached Dealer made only one; Dealer has lost a sale. On these facts, Dealer may be entitled to recover the profit Dealer failed to realize on the sale to Buyer. UCC § 2-708(2). This lost-profit measure of recovery compensates Dealer's expectation interest on the breached contract.

Now consider what happens if Dealer is unable to resell the lithograph at all because there is no market for it (perhaps it is a portrait of Buyer that no one else would want). In that circumstance, Dealer is stuck with goods worth $0 instead of the $10,000 Dealer expected to have. Dealer will therefore be entitled to recover the contract price from Buyer. UCC § 2-709. Of course, to prevent overcompensation, if Dealer gets the price from Buyer, Dealer will have to hold the lithograph for Buyer.

---

[7]   What situation would likely lead to a significant difference between the resale price of the goods and the market price of the goods?

With this simple example in mind, we now examine each of these remedial formulas in more detail.   We will first study the three alternative damage measurements – damages based upon resale price, market price, or lost profit – followed by a brief look at the seller's ability to recover the price. We will then examine the seller's claim for incidental damages. Finally, we will examine how these remedies work when the buyer has prepaid in whole or part for the goods.

1.   Damages Based upon Resale of the Goods

No seller is required to resell the goods in order to set its damages. However, there are often both legal and business reasons for the seller to do so. The legal reason is that market damages may be difficult to prove, particularly if the goods are unusual or unique. As a result, the resale price may be easier to determine than the market price. The business reason is that sellers typically do not want to keep the goods. If the seller is a merchant engaged in the business of selling goods of that kind, the seller will want to get rid of this excess inventory. Even if the seller was making an isolated sale, say perhaps of used equipment, the seller may want to get rid of the goods to free up space for something else. Put simply, sellers generally do not want to retain goods they have already contracted to sell. However, reselling the goods does not automatically mean that the resale price will be used to calculate the seller's damages. For the seller to be able to recover resale damages, the resale must satisfy several requirements. Read section 2-706.

For a resale to be proper under section 2-706, "every aspect of the sale . . . must be commercially reasonable." UCC § 2-706(2). In addition, if the resale will be a public sale – that is, an auction – the seller must generally provide the breaching buyer with reasonable notification of the time and place of the resale and make the goods available for reasonable inspection by prospective bidders.   UCC § 2-706(4)(b), (c). If, as is more common, the resale will be a private sale – that is, anything other than an auction – the seller must normally give the breaching buyer reasonable notification of its intention to resell. UCC § 2-706(3). As you can see, the reference to reasonableness makes each of these requirements somewhat vague, with the result that the seller can rarely be certain that a planned resale will in fact be proper.[8]

---

[8]   Article 9 of the UCC imposes many of the same standards on a secured party who wants to dispose of the collateral. *See* UCC §§ 9-610, 9-611. Thus, judicial decisions under

Assuming that the seller's resale does satisfy with the requirements of section 2-706, the measure of the seller's damages are:

$$
\begin{array}{r}
\text{Contract price} \\
-\text{ Resale price} \\
+\text{ Incidental damages} \\
-\text{ Expenses saved} \\
\hline
=\text{ Damages}
\end{array}
$$

Problem 9-3

A. You represent a merchant that buys, repairs, and sells used photocopy machines. The merchant wants to know what it must do when reselling goods following a buyer's breach of a sales contract to preserve its ability to use the resale price as the basis for computing its damages against the breaching buyer. Write a manual for the seller explaining what the seller should and should not do when reselling goods after a contract is breached.

B. Supersonic Aviation, located in Cincinnati, Ohio, agreed to sell Blue Sky Airlines, located in Florida, 100,000 gallons of jet fuel at $5.00 per gallon. The contract provided for shipment of the fuel to Blue Sky, F.O.B. Miami, FL. The cost of shipping the fuel would have been 10¢ per gallon. After the market price for jet fuel fell, Blue Sky repudiated the deal. Supersonic Aviation then resold the fuel in a transaction complying with section 2-706 to Federated Shipping, located in Cleveland, for $4.50 per gallon, F.O.B. Cincinnati. The cost of shipping the fuel to Cleveland was 2¢ per gallon. What are Supersonic Aviation's damages?

Sometimes, particularly if the contract calls for the sale of fungible goods, the goods will not be identified at the time the contract is made. They may even not be identified at the time the buyer breaches if the breach is by repudiation. In such cases, the seller may use section 2-704 in conjunction with section 2-706. Read

---

Article 9 may be useful in analyzing whether a seller has complied with the requirements of section 2-706. Since 2001, Article 9 has contained some statutory safe harbors for the application of its analogous rules. *See* UCC §§ 9-612, 9-613, 9-614. It is less clear whether these safe harbor rules would be relevant to an Article 2 resale.

section 2-704. Section 2-704(1) allows the seller to identify goods to the breached contract. The seller can then resell these goods pursuant to section 2-706.

Sometimes, the seller has begun, but not completed, manufacturing the goods when the buyer breaches. Section 2-704 gives the seller two options in such cases: (i) resell the goods in their unfinished state and recover damages based upon that resale; or (ii) resell the goods after finishing them. However, the seller must exercise reasonable commercial judgment to mitigate damages in deciding which option to follow.

Problem 9-4

Bacchanalian Catering, Inc. contracted to purchase from Specialty Displays a large, custom-manufactured sign depicting the company's logo: the Roman god Bacchus. Under the terms of the contract, the purchase price was $6,400, the seller was to deliver by July 1, and the buyer was to pay within 30 days after delivery. In mid-June, after concluding that its logo was alienating some potential customers, Bacchanalian Catering decided it no longer wanted the sign and so informed Specialty Displays.

At that point, Specialty Displays had expended about $4,000 of the $4,800 it had expected to incur in performing under the contract and had nearly completed manufacturing the sign. The sign was not readily marketable to anyone else in its unfinished state. However, it could be disassembled and some of its parts salvaged for other uses. The salvage value would be about $100 more than the cost of disassembly. Alternatively, Specialty Displays could spend another $2,000 to modify the sign so that it might appeal to other buyers. The president of Specialty Displays estimates that there is a 50% chance that it could sell the modified sign to another buyer for $5,000. What should Specialty Displays do?

2. Damages Based upon Market Price of the Goods

Just as an aggrieved buyer is permitted to use the market price of the goods to set its damages against a breaching seller, an aggrieved seller may use the market price of the goods to set its damages against a breaching buyer. Read section 2-708(1). The formula for measuring market damages is much the same as the formula for computing resale damages:

Unpaid contract price
  − Market price
+ Incidental damages
  − Expenses saved

= Damages

Notice that, unlike in the measure of resale damages in section 2-706, the word "unpaid" modifies the phrase "contract price" in the first line. Later in this section, we will consider whether a buyer who has pre-paid in whole or part gets a credit for the price paid against the damages owed. For now, you should ignore the word "unpaid." If that causes you concern, if you are reticent to disregard the clear text of the Code, bear in mind that it is very difficult to draft a statutory measure of damages that works for all situations, and thus it is advisable to view all the formulas in the damages rules of Article 2 more as strongly worded suggestions than as statutory mandates. The goal, as expressed in section 1-305, is to provide the aggrieved party with a recovery based on its lost expectancy. If a damage formula fails to do that in some cases, it is generally a good idea to stick with the guiding principle and depart from the formula. We will see this again when we cover the measure of damages for lost profits. Thus, the general measure of the seller's market damages is really:

Contract price
  − Market price
+ Incidental damages
  − Expenses saved

= Damages

Notice that the market price is to be determined at the time and place the seller was to tender the goods. As discussed in Chapter Four, the time and place for tender must be determined from the parties' contract: that is, from the parties' agreement as supplemented, to the extent necessary, by Article 2's gap fillers.

Query, though, whether it makes sense to calculate market damages based on the market price at the time the goods were to be tendered if the buyer repudiated before then. Recall that under section 2-610 the seller as the aggrieved party may either await performance for a commercially reasonable time or immediately resort to remedies for breach. If the seller elects to treat the buyer's repudiation as an immediate breach, why should the computation of the damage amount have to wait for some later time?

One of the difficulties in applying section 2-708(1) is the difficulty in proving what the market price is at the relevant time and place. Sections 2-723 and 2-724 provide some guidance on this point, and the latter is particularly helpful if the goods are fungible commodities subject to widely distributed price quotations. However, proving the market price of unique goods can be very difficult. Even for goods such as used cars and rare coins, which may be the subject of standard price quotations, value may vary significantly with condition.

Another issue lurking in section 2-708(1) is whether market damages are or should be available if the seller has resold the goods. Certainly the aggrieved seller cannot obtain damages under both section 2-706 and 2-708(1). Even though the roadmap of damages in section 2-703 does not expressly preclude the use of both provisions simultaneously, using them together would clearly overcompensate the seller and violate the principle of section 1-305. However, may the seller resell and still collect market damages under section 2-708(1)? Read section 2-706 cmt. 2.[9] Would the resale price that the seller obtained be good evidence of the market price for the goods?

Remembering the expectation principle for damages, consider why there might be a difference between the resale price and the market price. If the cause of the difference is market fluctuation based upon the difference in time between when the goods were sold and when the market price is measured, who should bear the risk of that market fluctuation? If the cause of the difference is the seller's negotiating skill in making the deal with the second buyer, does that help you decide which measurement is the better measure of the seller's expectancy interest? What if the seller obtains recovery from the buyer based upon market damages, and then subsequently resells the goods for a price that is higher than the market price that was the basis of the damages against the buyer? Should the seller have to reduce the judgment amount by the amount of the difference between the resale price and the market price? Should the timing of the resale transaction matter to the way in which the seller's expectancy interest is measured?

Problem 9-5

Supersonic Aviation, located in Cincinnati, Ohio, agreed to sell Blue Sky Airlines, located in Florida, 100,000 gallons of jet fuel at $5.00 per

---

[9]   Remember, as discussed in Chapter Seven, if the buyer engages in a cover transaction within the meaning of section 2-712, the buyer is precluded from recovering damages based upon the market price.

gallon. The contract provided for shipment of the fuel to Blue Sky, F.O.B. Miami, FL, with shipment to be made no later than February 25, and delivery at the destination by March 1. The cost of shipping the fuel would have been 10¢ per gallon. Blue Sky repudiated the deal on February 15, after the market price for jet fuel fell to $4.00 per gallon. Thereafter, the market price started to rise again. On February 25, the market price of jet fuel was $4.25 per gallon; on March 1, the market price of jet fuel was $4.50 per gallon. On March 7, Supersonic Aviation resold the fuel to Federated Shipping, located in Cleveland, for $4.75 per gallon, F.O.B. Cincinnati. Supersonic Aviation's cost of storing the fuel from February 25 to March 7 was $1,000.

A. If Supersonic Aviation notified Blue Sky on February 17 of its intent to resell the fuel, what are Supersonic Aviation's damages?

B. If Supersonic Aviation never notified Blue Sky of its intent to resell the fuel, what are Supersonic Aviation's damages?

There is one exception to the rule that the market price is measured at the time of the tender of the goods. Section 2-723 provides that if the buyer has repudiated and the case comes to trial before the time for performance (the seller's tender of the goods) was due, the time for measuring the market price is when the seller learned of the buyer's repudiation.

Problem 9-6

Supersonic Aviation, located in Cincinnati, Ohio, agreed to sell Blue Sky Airlines, located in Florida, 10,000 gallons of jet fuel at $5.00 per gallon for 10 years. The contract provided for shipment of the fuel to Blue Sky, FOB Miami, FL, with shipment to be no later than February 25 of each year, and delivery at the destination by March 1. The cost of shipping the fuel was 10¢ per gallon. Blue Sky repudiated the deal in the sixth year, when similar jet fuel was selling for $4.00 per gallon. Blue Sky does not take delivery in years seven, eight, or nine of the contract. The case comes up for trial in August of the ninth year of the contract. Supersonic Aviation submits proof that the market price of jet fuel is currently $4.50 per gallon. It also submits evidence that the market price was $4.10 in year seven, $4.20 in year eight, and $4.40 in year nine.

A. What amount or amounts should be used to compute market damages?

B. What amount or amounts should be used to compute market damages
    if the case came to trial in year eleven (that is, after the ten-year term
    of the contract would have run) and the market price in year ten was
    $5.50 per gallon?

3. The Lost Profit Measurement

The lost profit measurement appears to be a remedy of last resort. Section
2-708(2) provides that the lost profit measurement is available only if market
damages are "inadequate to put the seller in as good a position as performance
would have done." While the section does not explicitly provide that lost profits
are available if resale damages under section 2-706 would also be inadequate, that
is probably an implicit requirement.

Neither section 2-708 nor the comments to it identify the circumstances when
damages measured by the market price (or resale price) would be inadequate to
protect the seller's expectation interest. The one generally accepted circumstance
– but perhaps not the only one – is when the seller is a "lost volume" seller. But it
is not enough that the seller merely have lost volume by the buyer's breach.
Consider one court's description of when a seller is a lost volume seller:

> We agree . . . that, under some circumstances, the measure of damages
> provided under 2-708(1) will not put a reselling seller in as good a position
> as it would have been in had the buyer performed because the breach
> resulted in the seller losing sales volume. However, we disagree with the
> definition of "lost volume seller" adopted by other courts. Courts awarding
> lost profits to a lost volume seller have focused on whether the seller had
> the capacity to supply the breached units in addition to what it actually
> sold. In reality, however, the relevant questions include, not only whether
> the seller could have produced the breached units in addition to its actual
> volume, but also whether it would have been profitable for the seller to
> produce both units. As one commentator has noted, under
>> the economic law of diminishing returns or increasing marginal
>> costs[,] . . . as a seller's volume increases, then a point will
>> inevitably be reached where the cost of selling each additional item
>> diminishes the incremental return to the seller and eventually
>> makes it entirely unprofitable to conclude the next sale. . . .

Thus, under some conditions, awarding a lost volume seller its presumed lost profit will result in overcompensating the seller, and 2-708(2) would not take effect because the damage formula provided in 2-708(1) does place the seller in as good a position as if the buyer had performed.[10]

Another situation in which the seller may seek its lost profit is when it is a jobber. A jobber functions as a middleman, buying goods and reselling them, making a profit on the spread between the buy price and the resale price. In many situations, the jobber is in the same position as a lost volume seller, because the jobber may have as many buyers as it can possible resell the goods to and is able to obtain an unlimited supply of goods for resale.

After determining that a seller is entitled to recover under section 2-708(2), the next task is to calculate the lost profit.[11] Typically, a seller's profit on a transaction would be computed as follows:

$$\text{lost profit} = \text{sale price} - \text{cost of production}$$

Costs of production come in two basic varieties: (i) fixed costs (also known as "overhead") that do not vary with the number of items produced or purchased; and (ii) variable costs that increase as the number of items produced or purchased increases.

$$\text{lost profit} = \text{sale price} - (\text{fixed costs} + \text{variable costs})$$
$$\text{or}$$
$$\text{lost profit} = \text{sale price} - \text{fixed costs} - \text{variable costs}$$

Examples of fixed costs include the rent the seller pays on its manufacturing plant and the annual salary of its chief executive officer. A typical variable cost would be the costs of raw materials used to manufacture the finished goods.

Determining what portion of the seller's fixed costs (overhead) should be allocated to the breached contract can be very difficult. For example, how much of the chief executive officer's annual salary should be allocated to the breached contract? Does the amount of time the officer spent negotiating the deal matter? What portion of the seller's annual insurance premiums and advertising costs should

---

[10]   *R.E. Davis Chemical Corp. v. Diasonics, Inc.*, 826 F.2d 678, 683–84 (7th Cir. 1987).

[11]   *See* John M. Breen, *The Lost Volume Seller and Lost Profits Under UCC § 2-708(2): A Conceptual and Linguistic Critique*, 50 U. MIAMI L. REV. 779 (1996).

be counted? Fortunately, we need not answer these questions because the damages formula in section 2-708(2) specifically authorizes recovery for these costs by indicating in the parenthetical that the seller is also entitled to reasonable overhead. Read section 2-708(2). Thus, the statutory computation is:

recovery = sale price − fixed costs − variable costs + fixed costs

The two entries for fixed costs cancel each other out and we end up with:

recovery = sale price − variable costs

In essence, this formula calculates lost profit using the marginal cost of production. Unfortunately, by taking fixed costs (overhead) out of the calculation and leaving variable costs in, it becomes necessary to determine which of the seller's costs fall into which classification. While some costs – such as those for the chief executive officer's annual salary on one hand, and the cost of raw materials on the other – are easy to classify, other costs are not. Many expenses, such as employee wages and electricity might fall under either category, depending on the situation. For example, if the lost sale was minor in relation to the seller's normal output, the seller may have incurred no extra labor or utility costs to produce the goods that were supposed to go to the breaching buyer. However, if manufacturing the goods for the lost sale would have required the seller to pay overtime and run equipment for longer hours, such expenses would be better viewed as variable costs. One thing is clear, though: how a seller treats expenses for income tax purposes will have little or no bearing on whether they qualify as fixed costs or variable costs for the purpose of measuring damages.[12]

If you have read section 2-708(2) carefully, you may have noticed that the formula also calls for incidental damages and "due allowance for costs reasonably incurred and due credit for payments or proceeds of resale." "Due allowance for costs reasonably incurred" is a reference to reliance costs that the seller has actually expended and would normally recoup if it was getting the sale price. However, because the seller is not getting the sale price but only its profit margin, it is not able to recoup those actual reliance expenditures without adding them on to the lost profit measure. The last part of the quoted phrase, "due credit for . . . proceeds of resale" is clearly a mistake and courts properly ignore it. The reason it is a mistake is that, if followed literally, a lost profit seller would have no recovery. Because the

---

[12]   *See, e.g., Sure-Trip, Inc. v. Westinghouse Engineering*, 47 F.3d 526 (2d Cir. 1995).

gross proceeds of a resale almost always exceed the seller's expected profit, subtracting those proceeds from the lost profit measure would almost always leave the seller with nothing. That does not comport with either the principle of section 1-305 or the purpose of section 2-708(2).

Keeping all this in mind, try your hand at the following problem.

Problem 9-7

On July 1, Best Woodworking Inc. contracted to purchase an industrial lathe for $90,000 from Sawtooth Supply Company, a distributor of machinery manufactured by Mammoth Machines. Delivery was to occur on October 1. Sawtooth Supply then placed an order for the lathe with Mammoth Machines for $80,000, with delivery by September 15. On August 15, and without justification, Best Woodworking repudiated the contract with Sawtooth Supply. Sawtooth Supply then promptly canceled its order with Mammoth Machines, which charged Sawtooth Supply its customary cancellation charge of $1,000.

Sawtooth Supply comes to you for advice. The market price of the equipment at the "time and place for tender," October 1, was estimated to be $90,000. Sawtooth Supply has incurred $2,000 to purchase parts that it expected to use to modify the lathe before delivering it to Best Woodworking. Sawtooth Supply expected to – but did not – spend an additional $1,500 to inspect, prepare, and install the lathe if Best Woodworking had not repudiated. Sawtooth Supply also estimates that approximately $500 of its annual overhead is allocable to each machine that it sells.

A. What is Sawtooth Supply's lost profit on this contract?

B. What damages should Sawtooth Supply recover?

What if the seller would not have made any profit on the contract that the buyer breached? Should the buyer be able to use that fact to argue that the seller is overcompensated if the seller attempts to recover damages based upon the market price or the resale price of the goods? The leading case indicates no, the lost profit measurement should not be used to limit the other measurements of the seller's expectation interest because section 2-708(2) authorizes using the seller's lost profit only if the other remedy measurements are inadequate, not if the lost profit measurement results in the least amount of damages.[13]

4. Recovering the Price

Normally when the buyer has breached by repudiating the contract or by refusing to accept the goods, the seller still has the goods and, if it chooses to seek an award of damages, uses one of the three formulas previously discussed: resale damages, market damages, or lost profits. Occasionally, however, the seller is able to recover the full contract price. We have already seen that section 2-709 authorizes the seller to recover the price when the buyer has accepted the goods. It also authorizes the seller to recover the price in two circumstances where the buyer has not accepted the goods. One of these circumstances is when the goods have suffered a casualty after the risk of loss has passed to the buyer. Issues relating to risk of loss are discussed in section 4 of this Chapter. The other circumstance is where the seller is unable to resell the goods. Re-read UCC § 2-709.

If the seller is unable to resell the goods, using the resale price of the goods is unlikely to be a reliable way to measure the seller's expectation interest. Using the market price to compute damages could work reasonably well, *provided* the seller's inability to sell implied that the market price of the goods was $0. However, the seller's inability to sell could be attributable to reasons other than a lack of buyers and, in any event, the goods may have some value even though proving what that is may be difficult. Using the lost profit measurement to calculate damages would be undesirable for the seller because it compensates the seller only for the difference between the contract price and the cost of production. If the seller is left with goods that it cannot sell, the seller would be left without any way to recoup those costs of production.

For these reasons, section 2-709 allows the seller to recover the contract price for the goods it cannot sell. Of course, if the seller obtains a judgment for the price, the seller must hold the goods for the buyer or credit against the judgment any resale price obtained for the goods if a resale becomes viable. This is consistent with the focus on the expectation interest of the seller and ensuring that the seller is not overcompensated.

---

[13]   *Trans World Metals, Inc. v. Southwire Co.*, 769 F.2d 902 (7th Cir. 1985).

The major challenge in applying this section is determining when the goods are not readily resalable. Consider one court's view:

> The evidence at trial clearly established that all of Foxco's goods were specially manufactured for the customer who ordered them and that it was difficult for Foxco to resell fabric manufactured for one purchaser to another buyer. Further, it was normally very difficult to sell Foxco's spring fabric after the spring buying season had ended; the precipitous decline of the knitted fabric market presented an additional barrier to resale. It was not until the next spring buying season returned that Foxco, in September 1975, finally sold a portion of the goods identified to Fabric World's October 1974 order.
>
> Fabric World argues that Foxco made no effort whatsoever to resell the goods during the months that intervened (between the contract breach and Foxco's eventual disposition of the fabric in September 1975) despite the presence of some market for the goods in that interim period. Thus Fabric World concludes, the requisites of § 2-709(1)(b) were not satisfied. Under § 2-709(1)(b), however, Foxco was required only to use *reasonable* efforts to resell its goods at a *reasonable* price. From the time of Fabric World's breach to September 1975 there was a 50% decline in the market price of this material. We cannot say that the jury was precluded from finding that Foxco acted reasonably under the circumstances or that there was no reasonable price at which Foxco could sell these goods. Fabric World breached its contract with Foxco, and the jury was entitled to a charge which gave Foxco the full benefit of its original bargain.[14]

Problem 9-8

Standard Shipping, Inc. contracted to sell a customized shipping container to Blaster Electronics, Inc., for use in shipping sensitive electronic cargo. The contract price was $3,000. Just as Standard Shipping was about to deliver the container, Blaster Electronics repudiated. The container cost $1,800 to build. Non-customized containers generally sell for $2,000 each.

A. Standard Shipping is unable to find a buyer willing to pay $3,000 for the customized container but has an offer to buy for $1,500. Is

---

[14] *Foxco Indus., Ltd. v. Fabric World, Inc.*, 595 F.2d 976, 984 (5th Cir. 1979).

Standard Shipping entitled to recover the contract price from Blaster Electronics?

B. No one is willing to buy the customized container but Standard Shipping could sell the container for scrap for $500. Is Standard Shipping entitled to recover the contract price from Blaster Electronics?

Problem 9-9

Review Problem 9-4 and section 2-704. May Specialty Displays recover the price from Bacchanalian Catering?

5. *Incidental Damages*

All four formulas used to measure the seller's damages – resale, market, lost profit, and price – expressly allow the seller to recover incidental damages in addition to the amount otherwise computed from the applicable formula. *See* UCC §§ 2-706(1), 2-708(1), (2), 2-709(1). Read section 2-710, which identifies some of the incidental damages that an aggrieved seller might suffer. Unlike the buyer's remedies, however, none of these provisions purports to authorize the seller to recover consequential damages for the buyer's breach. Because section 1-305(a) indicates that consequential damages are unavailable unless specifically provided for in the UCC or in other law, most courts have held that an Article 2 seller is not entitled to consequential damages.[15] Thus one of the challenges is to separate incidental (recoverable) damages from consequential (nonrecoverable) damages. Note, for this purpose it is the nature of the damages, not their amount, that matters. Incidental damages can in fact be quite large.[16]

---

[15]   *See, e.g., Nina Industries, Ltd. v. Target Corp.*, 2005 WL 323745 (S.D.N.Y. 2005); *cf.* Roy Ryden Anderson, *In Support of Consequential Damages for Sellers*, 11 J.L. & COM. 123 (1992). *Compare* RESTATEMENT (SECOND) OF CONTRACTS § 351, cmt. e.

[16]   *See Commonwealth Edison Co. v. Allied Chemical Nuclear Products, Inc.*, 684 F. Supp. 1429 (N.D. Ill. 1988) ($293 million in incidental damages – consisting of storage costs – when nuclear fuel re-processor which was supposed to take spent nuclear fuel in trade for equivalent fissile material failed to do so).

Problem 9-10

Buyer has defaulted by failing to pay when due the price of a piece of equipment that Seller was to manufacture. Seller has begun, but not completed, manufacturing the goods. Which, if any, of the following types of harm qualify as incidental, and thus are recoverable as damages?

A. Interest on a loan Seller obtained before Buyer's breach to finance the operation of Seller's business and to purchase equipment.

B. Interest on a loan Seller obtained before Buyer's breach to finance Seller's performance on the contract with Buyer.

C. Interest on a loan Seller obtained after the breach to make a profitable investment that Seller had planned to finance with the price paid by Buyer.

D. Interest on a loan Seller obtained after the breach to finish work on the goods and to obtain a commercially reasonable resale.

6.   Restitution to a Breaching Buyer

If the buyer has prepaid in whole or part for the goods before repudiating or otherwise breaching the contract, an issue arises as to whether the buyer is entitled to receive back all of its payment. One possible approach, consistent with the principle expressed in section 1-305(a), would be to say that the buyer is entitled to full restitution, but the seller may offset the damages under whichever of the damages measures applies. Another approach would be to regard the requirement of a down payment or prepayment as a sort of liquidated damages clause – that the seller is entitled to retain the payment received, provided it passes the test in section 2-718(1).

Article 2 does neither of these. Instead, in some rather complicated provisions, it does something close to the first approach but also allows the seller to retain the lesser of $500 or 20% of the contract price. This formula functions as a type of statutory liquidated damages. Read section 2-718(2)– (4). Now try the following problem.

Problem 9-11

On July 1, Best Woodworking Inc. contracted to purchase an industrial lathe for $90,000 from Sawtooth Supply Company, distributor of machinery manufactured by Mammoth Machines. The contract called for delivery September 1. Pursuant to the contract, Best Woodworking made a down payment of $20,000. Sawtooth Supply then placed an order for the lathe with Mammoth Machines for $80,000, with delivery to be made directly to Best Woodworking. On August 1 and without justification, Best Woodworking repudiated the contract with Sawtooth Supply. Sawtooth Supply then promptly canceled its order with Mammoth Machines, which charged Sawtooth Supply its customary cancellation charge of $1,000.

At the time of the repudiation, the market price of the lathe was $85,000. Because the economy was in a mild recession, the market price declined to $80,000 on September 1.

A. If Sawtooth Supply's agreement with Best Woodworking provides Sawtooth Supply is entitled to $10,000 as liquidated damages in the event Best Woodworking repudiates, how much of the $20,000 down payment is Best Woodworking entitled to receive back?

B. If Sawtooth Supply's agreement with Best Woodworking has no liquidated damages clause, how much are Sawtooth Supply's damages and how much of the $20,000 down payment is Best Woodworking entitled to receive back? *See Neri v. Retail Marine Corp.*, 285 N.E.2d 311 (N.Y. 1972).

Problem 9-12

On March 1, Superior Equipment, Inc., located in Chicago, contracted to manufacture custom lathes for Bristol Woodworking, Inc., located in Phoenix, for $80,000, delivery F.O.B. Chicago no later than November 1. Cost of shipping was estimated at $2,000. At the time that Bristol and Superior entered into the contract, Bristol made a down payment of $20,000. Superior delivered the lathes on time. Bristol accepted the lathes but one week later demanded that Superior take the lathes back and return its down payment. Bristol's demands were unjustified because both the lathes and Superior's tender had conformed to the contract requirements. Nevertheless, Superior took the lathes back.

Superior estimated its costs of producing the lathes was $70,000. On November 1, the market price of the lathes in Chicago was $60,000. The market price in Phoenix was $55,000. Superior was looking for a buyer for the lathes in Phoenix in order to avoid having to ship the lathes again, and was expending $100 per day for storage of the lathes in Phoenix.

Two months after taking the lathes back, Superior sold the lathes in Denver for $50,000, F.O.B. Denver, and incurred $1,500 in shipping costs to send them from Phoenix to Denver. Calculate Superior's damages.

7. CISG and UNIDROIT Principles

The CISG allows an aggrieved seller to recover damages based upon the either difference between the contract price and a resale price, Art. 75, or the difference between the contract price and the market price, Art. 76. Both damage remedies require that the seller has avoided the contract for fundamental breach. To avoid a contract, the buyer's breach must be fundamental, Arts. 25, 64, and the seller must notify the buyer, Art. 26. If the buyer has already paid the price for the goods, the seller's ability to avoid the contract is limited. Art. 64. In addition to the damages measured by those formulas, the seller is entitled to recover consequential damages that were foreseeable at the time the contract was made. Art. 74. Such consequential damages can include lost profits, *id.*, but are subject to a generalized obligation to take reasonable actions to mitigate loss. Art. 77. If the aggrieved seller does not or cannot avoid the contract, the seller is entitled to recover the price. Art. 62. However, a court may refuse to award that remedy if the court's local law would not permit that remedy. Art. 28.

The UNIDROIT Principles allow the seller to recover the price. Art. 7.2.1. Alternatively, an aggrieved seller may recover damages from the breaching buyer based upon what is required to "fully compensate" the seller. Art. 7.4.2. The seller's damages may be measured based upon the difference between the contract price and the resale price, Art. 7.4.5, or the difference between the contract price and the market price, Art. 7.4.6. The seller can also recover consequential damages that are reasonably certain and foreseeable. Arts. 7.4.3, 7.4.4. The seller is not able to recover damages for harm that it could have avoided. Art. 7.4.8.

SECTION 4. SELLER'S REMEDIES FOLLOWING A CASUALTY TO THE GOODS

In Chapter Four, we learned that three principles underlie the rules on when the risk of loss passes. First, the party who controls the goods, and is thus in the best position to avoid the loss, should bear the risk. *See* UCC § 2-509 cmt. 3. Second, the party most likely to have insurance protection under the circumstances should bear the risk. *Id.* Third, the party in breach should bear the risk of loss. *Compare* UCC § 2-509 *with* § 2-510. We then saw that, absent breach, the risk of loss generally passes to the buyer when the seller makes a conforming tender of delivery, if the seller is a merchant, or upon the buyer's receipt of the goods, if the seller is a non-merchant. UCC § 2-509(3). Slightly different rules apply if the tender is to occur through a carrier or a bailee. UCC § 2-509(1), (2).

A principal corollary to the risk of loss rules studied in Chapter Four is that if the risk of loss has passed to the buyer, and within a reasonable time thereafter the goods are lost or damaged, the buyer is liable to the seller for the price of the goods. UCC § 2-709(1)(a). This situation is usually encountered in a shipment contract (where the risk of loss passes to the buyer when the seller tenders conforming goods to the carrier) and the goods are lost or damaged in transit.

We now explore how the buyer's breach affect the risk of loss. Read section 2-510(3). If the buyer unjustifiably repudiates or breaches after conforming goods have been identified to the contract but before the risk of loss would have passed to the buyer under section 2-509, the buyer will bear the risk of loss for goods lost or damaged within a reasonable time after that breach, if the seller has a deficiency in its insurance coverage. Remember that if the goods are identified to the contract, but have not yet been tendered to the buyer, both the buyer and the seller will have an insurable interest in the goods. UCC § 2-501. Whether one or both have insurance coverage for those goods depends upon construction of the insurance policies.[17]

Problem 9-13

Sterling Corp. and Bryce Industries agreed that Bryce would purchase ten standard lathes for $1,000 per lathe, FOB point of shipment, delivery November 1. On October 25, Sterling rigged the lathes for shipment to Bryce.

---

[17] Nothing in Article 2 explicitly addresses whether the risk passes back to the seller if, after accepting the goods, the buyer attempts an unjustified revocation and the seller takes the goods back. Presumably, once the seller takes the goods back, the seller should have the risk of loss for the goods. Prior to the seller taking the goods back, the breaching buyer should probably have the obligation to at least take reasonable care of the goods, although Article 2 does not address this situation. *See* UCC § 2-602.

A. Bryce notified Sterling on October 28 that it would not take any of the lathes due to a downturn in Bryce's business. That night, the warehouse where Sterling had stored all of its lathes was destroyed by a fire caused by lightening. What are Sterling's remedies against Bryce?

B. Sterling properly contracted with Federated Carriers to deliver the lathes. Sterling made proper arrangements with Federated for shipment, and duly notified Bryce when the lathes were delivered to Federated. When the lathes were delivered two days later to Bryce, three of them were noticeably damaged beyond repair. Bryce rejected the three damaged lathes by timely notification to Sterling and accepted the other seven. Upon using the seven lathes, Bryce discovered that those seven had also been damaged in transit. Bryce notified Sterling that it was revoking acceptance of those seven lathes. Sterling has sued Bryce for the full contract price. Is Sterling entitled to the price?

CISG and UNIDROIT Principles. Under the CISG, the risk of loss principles in Articles 66 through 70 do not appear to affect the seller's remedies for the buyer's breach. The UNIDROIT Principles do not address risk of loss issues.

SECTION 5.   THE STATUTE OF LIMITATIONS

As we learned in Chapter Seven, section 2-725 provides a four-year limitations period after a cause of action for breach accrues. The cause of action accrues when the breach occurs. When the seller is the aggrieved party, the seller's cause of action will often arise when the buyer fails to pay or otherwise render its required performance, wrongfully rejects the goods, or wrongfully attempts to revoke acceptance. It is a little less clear when the seller's cause of action accrues when the buyer repudiates. Recall that the seller is entitled either to treat the buyer's repudiation as a breach or to await performance for a commercially reasonable time. UCC § 2-610. Because there will usually be uncertainty as to when that commercially reasonable time expires, a cautious seller should commence any action within four years of the repudiation.

While the seller may have a breach of warranty claim if the buyer made a warranty of noninfringement when the buyer supplied specifications for the goods, review UCC § 2-312, there is very little litigation on the issue of the statute of limitations when the seller is the aggrieved party. One reoccurring issue is what statute of limitations governs when the seller has also taken a security interest in the goods and is seeking to exercise its security interest, or collect a deficiency judgment. Some courts hold that a statute of limitations other than section 2-725 applies, such as the general statute of limitations that applies to breach of contract actions,[18] whereas other courts hold that section 2-725 applies to that situation.[19]

CISG and UNIDROIT Principles. The statute of limitations issues when the seller is the aggrieved party are the same as previously discussed when the buyer is the aggrieved party. Review the material from Chapter Seven.

---

[18]   *See, e.g., Orix Financial Services, Inc. v. Holmes*, 2007 WL 3143707 (S.D.N.Y. 2007).

[19]   *See, e.g., D.A.N. Joint Venture III, L.P. v. Armstrong*, 2007 WL 634457 (Ohio Ct. App. 2007).

Chapter Ten

Third Party Claims to the Goods

SECTION 1. PROPERTY CONCEPTS

It is no doubt obvious that a contract for the sale of goods transfers ownership of the goods. Indeed, that is the essence of a "sale" transaction. Article 2 recognizes this effect on ownership by defining a sale as "the passing of title from the seller to the buyer for a price." UCC § 2-106(1). "Title" is an undefined term but it is useful to think of it as a shorthand for ownership, or at least nominal ownership (ownership in name).

Even though transferring title (ownership) to the goods is the purpose of an Article 2 sales transaction, the drafters attempted to reduce reliance on title concepts to determine the buyer's and seller's rights against each other in the performance of the sales contract. *See* UCC § 2-101 cmt. Thus, title issues are not generally relevant to such issues as who breached the contract, the seller's right to reclaim the goods from the buyer, or the buyer's right to specific performance. Even risk of loss analysis has been divorced from ownership concepts and instead relies largely on whether the seller has fulfilled its tender obligation. In short, Article 2 is primarily about the parties' *contract* rights, not their *property* rights.

In some circumstances, however, who has an ownership interest in the goods is very important. For those circumstances, section 2-401 provides for when title passes from the seller to the buyer. Courts use this provision to determine who has title when dealing with such issues as whether the goods are covered under an insurance policy,[1] whether the goods are part of the seller's or buyer's bankruptcy estate,[2] or who has liability for sales tax.[3]

Title and ownership concepts are also important when dealing with *property* claims to the goods.[4] As much as the Article 2 drafters tried to make title issues

---

[1]   *See, e.g., Collins v. Mountjoy,* 2008 WL 746979 (Ohio Ct. App. 2008); *Concord General Mut. Ins. Co. v. Sumner,* 762 A.2d 849 (Vt. 2000).

[2]   *See, e.g., In re Alofs Mfg. Co.,* 209 B.R. 83 (Bankr. W.D. Mich. 1997).

[3]   *See, e.g., In re Valley Media, Inc.* 226 Fed. Appx. 120 (3d Cir. 2007).

[4]   *See* Linda J. Rusch, *Property Concepts in the Revised U.C.C. Articles 2 and 9 Are Alive and Well,* 54 SMU L. Rev. 947 (2001); Jeanne L. Schroeder, *Death and Transfiguration: The Myth That The U.C.C. Killed "Property",* 69 Temp. L. Rev. 1281 (1996); William L.

irrelevant to the rights of the buyer and seller as against each other, title concepts are vital when dealing with property-based claims to the goods by persons other than the buyer or seller. This Chapter addresses these third-party, property-based claims to the goods and the buyer's and seller's rights when faced with those claims. To give some context to this point, consider the following simple hypothetical which illustrates some of the circumstances where these property claims may be asserted.

Illustration

Seller, an equipment dealer, and Buyer enter into a contract in which Buyer agrees to buy a lawn tractor for use at the golf course that Buyer runs. Assume that the lawn tractor is identified to the contract for sale. Seller is in possession of the lawn tractor. Buyer wants to get possession of the tractor but it turns out that Seller has actually sold the tractor twice and the other buyer is contending it has a superior claim to the tractor. Who has a superior claim to possession of the tractor as between the two buyers? What if instead of selling the tractor twice, Seller allowed one of its principal lenders to take a security interest in the tractor to secure a debt that Seller owes that lender? What if one of Seller's judgment creditors, in an attempt to collect on the judgment, levied on the lawn tractor, thereby obtaining an execution lien on it? Does Buyer have a property claim to the tractor that is superior to the interests of these creditors?

Now assume Seller has delivered the lawn tractor to Buyer. Does Buyer take the lawn tractor free of any pre-existing property claims asserted by Seller's creditors? Does Seller have any property claim to the tractor to the extent that Buyer has not paid for the tractor? If Seller has a property claim to the tractor, is that claim superior to the property-based claims of Buyer's creditors, such as a creditor to whom Buyer has granted a security interest? Would Seller's property-based claim, if it exists, be superior to the claim of someone who purchased the tractor from Buyer?

These questions are just some of the many issues that may arise regarding the resolution of competing property-based claims to goods that are the subject matter of the sales contract. When two or more people assert property-based claims to the

---

Tabac, *The Unbearable Lightness of Title Under the Uniform Commercial Code*, 50 MD. L. REV. 408 (1991).

same goods, it sets up a classic priority issue, posing the question of which person's claim to the goods has priority over the other.

It is important when working through these issues to have a clear understanding of the basis of each person's property claim. This is because the resolution of the priority question often hinges on how each claimant acquired its property interest. The rights of unpaid transferors, pre-paying transferees, donees, secured creditors, and lien creditors are all different. Thus, to continue the illustration above, the priority of Buyer's claim to the tractor against the claim of Seller's secured party may be resolved differently from the competing claims of the two persons who each purportedly purchased the tractor from Seller.

Most, if not all, property-based claims to the goods arise because of some interaction a third party has with either the buyer or the seller. These relationships between the parties can be diagramed as follows:

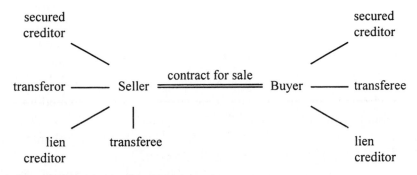

We will revisit this diagram throughout the remainder of this Chapter, as we discuss the rights of the various parties it identifies.

Once you have identified the nature of the property-based claims to the goods, the next step is to ascertain when each claim arose. A fundamental tenet of property law is that a transferor of a property right may transfer only the rights that the transferor has, or has been given power to transfer by some rule of law.[5] Like many fundamental legal principles, it is often expressed in Latin: *nemo dat qui non habet* (one cannot give what one does not have). Section 2-403 codifies this basic

---

[5]   We have already looked at that concept when we examined the warranty of title in Chapter Three.

principle.[6] Although some competing property-based claims may be resolved in ways that are inconsistent with this principle, for the most part sequence matters.

Finally, the last step in the analysis is to identify the appropriate priority rule that resolves a contest between two competing property claims to the same goods. The applicable rule may be found in the UCC, in other state statutes, or in the common law. If there are three or more competing property claims, more than one priority rule may apply. For example, assume that parties A, B and C each assert a property-based claim to the same goods. To properly analyze the situation, you may need to consult three different priority rules, one for each of the following contests: (i) A v. B; (ii) A v. C; and (iii) B v. C.

Before digging into the details of property-based claims to the goods, it is important to understand when title normally passes to the buyer. Read section 2-401.

Problem 10-1

In the absence of the parties' agreement otherwise, when does title to the goods pass from the seller to the buyer in a sales transaction under section 2-401? Compare these default rules on title passage to the default rules on tender of delivery in section 2-503 and passage of the risk of loss in section 2-509. How are the tender of delivery rules and risk of loss rules similar to and different from the title passage rules?

CISG and UNIDROIT Principles. The CISG provides that "except as otherwise expressly provided in this Convention, it is not concerned with: . . .the effect which the contract may have on the property in the goods sold." CISG Art. 4. In short, the CISG does not purport to resolve any third-party's claim to the goods. As a result, courts in the United States may use Article 2 principles to

---

[6]   Subsection (1) provides that a person may only transfer the rights it had and provides two circumstances in which the transferor has the power to transfer greater rights than the transferor had. In subsection (1), the transferor has power to transfer greater rights than it has if it took possession of the goods in a transaction for purchase in which the transferor obtained voidable title, and then delivered the goods to a good faith purchaser for value. In subsection (2), a merchant-seller has the power to transfer to a buyer in ordinary course of business the rights of the person who entrusted the goods to the merchant.

determine who has title, to the extent that is relevant in a contract otherwise covered by the CISG.[7] The UNIDROIT Principles do not deal with title issues.

SECTION 2.   BUYER'S RIGHTS AGAINST PERSONS WHO CLAIM AN INTEREST IN THE GOODS THROUGH THE SELLER

When goods subject to a sales contract are in the seller's possession, the seller will usually still have an ownership claim to the goods. That is because title to the goods does not usually pass to the buyer until the seller completes its tender obligation. UCC § 2-401. However, the buyer too will have property rights in the goods, even while they remain in the seller's possession, if the goods are identified to the contract. UCC § 2-501. Thus, it will often be the case that both the buyer and the seller have property rights in the goods at the same time. This should not be surprising. As you no doubt learned in property class, ownership of property can be broken out into different interests, and all of the individual property interests need not be held by the same person.

The buyer's property rights, standing alone, do not entitle the buyer to force the seller to turn over the goods. Instead, as discussed in Chapter Seven, the buyer will have the right to compel the seller to transfer possession of the goods to the buyer only if the buyer can satisfy the conditions stated in section 2-502 (pre-paying buyer) or section 2-716 (specific performance or replevin). Thus a property-rights analysis does not help us determine whether the seller or the buyer has the superior right to possession of the goods as against each other.[8]

Property rights are important, however, in resolving the claims of third parties. Given that the seller and buyer may both have property rights in the goods at the same time, and the fact that each party's rights are normally transferrable, it is fairly easy for third-party claims to the goods to exist.

In this section, we consider two basic types of property-based claims to the goods arising from interactions with the seller by people other than the buyer. In one type of property-based claim, a person is asserting rights in the goods as an owner. In the other type of property-based claim, the person is asserting a property

---

[7]   *Usinor Industeel v. Leeco Steel Products Inc.*, 209 F. Supp. 2d 880 (N.D. Ill 2002).

[8]   However, a pre-paying buyer could obtain a security interest in the goods to secure the seller's obligation to deliver the goods. Security interests are discussed *infra.*

interest in the goods to secure an obligation, that is, a lien. We explore how both types of claims fare against the buyer's property rights to the goods.

How could multiple ownership claims arise in the goods? The seller could have sold the goods to multiple buyers. Alternatively, the person who transferred the goods to the seller could be claiming an ownership interest in those goods because something went wrong in the transaction in which the seller acquired the goods. Part A below addresses the buyer's rights against both such claimants – people who assert an ownership interest in the goods based upon interaction with the seller. Part B then addresses the buyer's rights against creditors who assert a lien or security interest in the goods pursuant to an interaction with the seller. In each part, we identify when each property-based claim arose and the applicable priority rule used to resolve the dispute.

One last preliminary point is worth making. You may be tempted to think that the relative rights of the buyer and the seller – whether grounded in property or in contract – should be determinative of the relative rights of the buyer and a third-party claiming through the seller. In other words, you might assume that if the buyer's rights are better than the seller's, then the buyer's rights will be better than the third party's rights derived from its interaction with the seller, and that if the buyer's rights are inferior to the seller's, then the buyer's rights will be inferior to the rights of the third party derived from its interaction with the seller. Alas, it is not that simple. There is no substitute for the methodical process of identifying the basis of each party's claim to the goods, determining when that claim arose, and then isolating and applying the correct priority rule to the dispute.

A. BUYER'S RIGHT AGAINST PERSONS ASSERTING OWNERSHIP INTERESTS

In this section, we consider two typical priority disputes based upon competing ownership type property claims.[9] Revisiting the diagram at the beginning of this Chapter, this section is concerned with the parties that are highlighted in bold in the version below.

---

[9]   To the extent there is a claim of a third party to the goods, the Buyer has a possible cause of action against the Seller for breach of a warranty of title as explored in Chapter Three. But that breach of contract right as against the Seller does not answer the question as to the priority of the potential ownership claims in the goods as between the Buyer and another person.

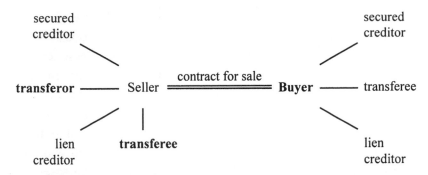

Let's start with the transferor's possible property claims. The transferor could be an owner from whom the Seller stole or borrowed the goods. In that situation, the Seller would not have any property rights in the goods, rather all the property rights still reside in the transferor/owner. In that circumstance, the Seller would have no rights at all to transfer to the Buyer and the Buyer should lose in a priority contest with the transferor. Review UCC § 2-403(1).

Alternatively, the transferor could have sold the goods to the Seller. Prior to delivery, the transferor would still have property rights in the goods because title would not normally have passed to the Seller. *See* UCC § 2-401. Of course, once the goods are identified to the contract, the Seller, who is buying the goods from the transferor, would have property rights under section 2-501, but would have the ability to compel delivery of the goods only to the extent so provided in section 2-502 or 2-716. Moreover, as we studied in Chapter Nine, the Seller may also be subject to the transferor's right to stop delivery under section 2-705. Even after delivery, the transferor may have the right to reclaim the goods from the Seller. UCC §§ 2-507, 2-702(2).

How do these rights of the transferor fare against the rights of the Buyer? That depends upon what rights the Buyer has. Remember, under Article 2, the earliest point in time that the Buyer could have any property right at all is when the goods are identified to the contract between the Seller and Buyer. UCC § 2-501. Until that point, the Buyer has no property-based claim whatsoever to assert against the transferor in a priority contest over the goods, and would therefore lose.

After identification, the result can differ. How soon can identification occur? Specifically, can the goods be identified to the contract between the Seller and the Buyer if the Seller does not yet have possession? Probably. Consider specially ordered goods. The Seller could be a distributor of goods who took the Buyer's order, and then placed an order for the goods from the manufacturer (*i.e.*, the transferor in the diagram) tailored to the Buyer's specifications. Once the manufacturer starts to create the goods that are designated for Buyer's order, the goods would be identified to the contract between the Seller and the manufacturer, and arguably identified to the contract between the Seller and the Buyer.

Assuming the Buyer has property rights created by identification, then we need to consult section 2-403. Subsection (1) states the basic property concept that the Seller may transfer to the Buyer only the rights the Seller has or has power to transfer. Thus, the argument is that if the rights of the transferor are superior to the rights of the Seller, and the Buyer's rights are derived from the Seller, the Buyer's rights are inferior to the rights of the transferor. However, as you may remember from our brief study in Chapter Three, section 2-403 provides for two situations when the Seller has the power to transfer greater rights than the Seller actually has. Subsection (1) deals with transferring greater rights to a good faith purchaser for value and subsection (2) allows some sellers to transfer greater rights to a buyer in ordinary course of business. Review the relevant definitions for "good faith," "purchaser" and "buyer in ordinary course of business" in section 1-201. Notice that to qualify as a buyer in the ordinary course of business (but not as a good faith purchaser for value), the buyer has to either take possession or have a right to possession under Article 2. Whether the Buyer in our situation has the right to possession (against the Seller) will depend upon application of sections 2-502 or 2-716. Alternatively, if the Buyer qualifies as a good faith purchaser for value and the Seller did what was required under section 2-403(1), the Buyer's property claim will have priority over the transferor's property claim. Similarly, if the transferor entrusted the goods to a merchant seller, and the Buyer qualified as a buyer in ordinary course of business, the Buyer would have priority over the transferor's claim.

Now try your hand at the following problem. It may help you to place each person in their relative position on the diagram, identify the type of property interest each person has, and draw a time line to reflect when each person's property interest arose. The key to analysis here is painstaking and careful attention to the details.

Problem 10-2

A. Seller, who had stolen a diamond necklace from Owner, sold it to Buyer who knew nothing of the theft. As between Owner and Buyer, who is entitled to the necklace?

B. Seller purchased a used diamond necklace from Transferor, and a few days later sold and delivered the necklace to Buyer. Shortly thereafter,

Seller and Buyer learn that Transferor had stolen the necklace from Owner. As between Owner and Buyer, who is entitled to the necklace?

C. Seller, who had acquired a diamond necklace from Transferor by paying for it with a check that was later dishonored, sold and delivered the necklace to Buyer.

    1. As between Transferor and Buyer, who is entitled to the necklace?

    2. How, if at all, would the analysis change if Buyer had paid for the necklace but had not yet taken possession of it?

D. Transferor sold a diamond necklace to Seller, promising to deliver it the next week. Seller then made an agreement to sell the necklace to Buyer and Buyer paid 25% of the purchase price to Seller.

    1. Seller was to make a funds transfer by Friday to Transferor. Seller did not make the funds transfer and Transferor refused to deliver the necklace to Seller. As between Transferor and Buyer, who is entitled to the necklace?

    2. Transferor and Seller had agreed that Seller would pay 50% at time of delivery and the balance in two days. Transferor delivered the necklace to Seller when Seller paid 50% of the price, but Seller did not pay the balance. Seller, in the meantime, delivered the necklace to Buyer. As between Transferor and Buyer, who is entitled to the necklace?

E. Seller, who had borrowed a diamond necklace from Friend to wear at a party, sold and delivered the necklace to Buyer. As between Friend and Buyer, who is entitled to the necklace?

F. Seller, a jeweler who had received a diamond necklace from Owner to repair and clean it, sold and delivered the necklace to Buyer.

    1. As between Owner and Buyer, who is entitled to the necklace?

    2. How, if at all, would the analysis change if Buyer had paid for the necklace but had not yet taken possession of it?

Let us now discuss the rights of a transferee. Just as the rules in section 2-403 can be useful in resolving a priority contest between the Buyer and a transferor, they can also help resolve a battle between the Buyer and a transferee. Consider the following problem. In doing so, determine whether and how section 2-403 applies to each transaction.

Problem 10-3

A. Seller, a jeweler, contracted to sell a diamond necklace to Buyer, who paid in full but asked to be allowed to pick it up the following week. Seller agreed. Two days later, Seller sold and delivered the same necklace to Transferee.

1. As between Buyer and Transferee, who is entitled to the necklace?

2. How, if at all, would the analysis change if Seller were not a merchant?

B. Seller, a jeweler, contracted to sell a diamond necklace to Buyer, who made a down payment and promised to pay the remainder of the purchase price the following day. Buyer agreed to allow Seller to retain possession until Buyer paid the price in full. Later that day, Seller sold the same necklace to Transferee, who paid the price in full but allowed Seller to maintain possession until Purchaser could come back to pick it up, sometime the following afternoon. Before Transferee came back to pick up the necklace, Buyer returned, paid the rest of the purchase price and took delivery of the necklace. As between Buyer and Transferee, who is entitled to the necklace?

As you may remember from our study of rejection and revocation of acceptance in Chapter Seven, the buyer may have a security interest in the goods to secure repayment of any part of the price that has been paid and some of the incidental expenses connected with the rejected goods or effecting cover. UCC § 2-711(3). In order for the buyer to claim the security interest, the buyer must be in possession of the goods and it will lose its security interest if it gives up possession of the goods to its seller.[10] The buyer may sell the goods pursuant to the sale process in section 2-706 as a method of enforcing its security interest.

If the buyer has such a security interest, what is the priority of that interest as against the potential interest of a transferor (who sold the goods to the buyer's seller)[11] or a transferee (who purchased the goods from the seller but has not taken delivery)? As we learned in completing Problem 10-2, the transferor who sold the

---

[10]   Even though the buyer has a security interest, title to the goods will revert to the seller. UCC § 2-401(4).

[11]   If the buyer's seller had no rights in the goods (for example if the seller stole the goods from the transferor), the buyer's security interest would not be effective, as seller would have not had any rights in the goods that would have transferred to the buyer in the first instance.

goods to the Seller has only one Article 2 right in this circumstance, that is, the right to reclaim the goods. Both the cash and credit reclamation rights are subject to the rights of a good faith purchaser from the seller under section 2-403. UCC §§ 2-702(3), 2-507 cmt. 3. Thus in our diagram, if Buyer was asserting its Article 2 security interest against a transferor asserting a right to reclaim the goods, the Buyer would be a good faith purchaser, and the Buyer's right to enforce its security interest should be superior to the transferor's right to assert its reclamation claim.

Article 2 is less clear on the relative rights of a buyer with a security interest in the goods and a transferee with a right to specific performance or replevin under section 2-716, or the right to obtain the goods under section 2-502. However, Article 9 provides the answer. If the transferee qualifies as a buyer in ordinary course of business, *see* UCC § 1-201(b)(9), then the transferee will take free of the Buyer's security interest. UCC § 9-320(a).

B. BUYER'S RIGHT AGAINST SELLER'S CREDITORS

Now we will consider the property-based claims to the goods of the seller's creditors. The parties we are concerned with in this section are in bold on the diagram below.

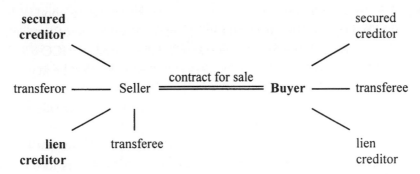

There are two general types of property-based claims to the goods made by creditors of the Seller: (i) those that arise when the creditor uses judicial process to collect a debt; and (ii) those that arise by agreement between the Seller and the creditor. The creditor that obtains a property interest in the Seller's goods using judicial process to collect on a judgment is call a lien creditor. The claim itself is variously called a judicial lien, an execution lien, or an attachment lien. The rules for determining priority between a lien creditor and the Buyer are found in the laws governing collection and in UCC Article 2.

A creditor whose property rights in the goods is based upon an agreement with the Seller is called the secured creditor. The claim itself is called a security interest. The rules for determining priority between the Buyer and a secured creditor of the Seller are found in UCC Article 9.

We explore the lien creditor versus Buyer contest first.

1. Buyer Against Seller's Lien Creditor

Under general principles of debtor and creditor law, a creditor who has a claim against a person – whether based in contract, tort, restitution, or some other principle of law – does not generally have any property rights in the personal property of the debtor. Even if the claim is reduced to judgment, the judgment creditor typically has no property rights in the judgment debtor's goods or other personal property. Rather, under most states' law, the creditor must take additional action to obtain a lien – an interest in property that secures payment of a judgment – on the debtor's personal property. In most states, that additional step is to levy on the debtor's personal property pursuant to a legal process generally called "execution on judgments" (states may have different names for their processes, but the essential concepts have a surprising degree of uniformity). Levy generally occurs when the relevant executive authority, such as the county sheriff or U.S. marshal, acting pursuant to a judicial order,[12] takes either actual or constructive possession of the goods. Under most states' law, the creditor obtains a lien on the goods once the levy takes place, and at that point in time becomes a lien creditor. Thus in the diagram above, the lien creditor would not have a property interest in the goods that are the subject of the sales contract between the Buyer and Seller unless and until it had levied on the goods. In a few states, a judgment creditor can acquire a lien on the judgment debtor's personal property by filing a notice of the lien in a particular state office. In either case, before the lien creditor has a property interest in the goods, the lien creditor would have no basis for using property law to trump the Buyer's property rights in the goods.

Under the law of most states, a lien creditor's lien attaches only to the property rights the seller had at the time that the levy takes place. Unless some statute

---

[12]   If the order is entered before judgment is entered against the debtor, it is typically called a "writ of attachment"; if it is issued after judgment is entered, it is typically called a "writ of execution."

provides to the contrary, the lien creditor's property rights (the lien) in the goods levied upon are no greater than the rights of the debtor (the Seller in our example) in that property. This is a reflection of the fundamental property-law principle discussed earlier: a person may transfer only the rights the person has.

Now read section 2-402(1). Although the rule of this provision does not, on its face, apply to lien creditors, it does mean that a creditor's status as creditor will not be enough to defeat the property rights of the Buyer. Once we add to this rule the general principle that a lien creditors' rights are typically no greater than the rights of the judgment debtor (the Seller in our hypothetical), we see that the lien creditor is subject to whatever rights the Buyer could assert against the Seller to get the goods, provided the Buyer had those rights at the time the lien creditor levied on the goods. Thus the time when the lien creditor's lien attached to the goods will often be critical to who wins the priority battle.

Problem 10-4

Buyer, a consumer, made a $300 down payment on a new stereo at Dealer's store. Buyer and Dealer agreed that Buyer could take possession of the stereo upon payment of the remainder of the $800 purchase price. Dealer marked the stereo with Buyer's name and stored the stereo in Dealer's warehouse. Creditor, who had a judgment against Dealer, had the sheriff levy on Dealer's inventory, including the stereo that was marked for Buyer. Creditor thereby acquired a judicial lien on the stereo. Buyer returned to the store with the $500 remaining purchase price and wanted the stereo. Dealer was unable to deliver the stereo because of the levy.

A. As between Creditor and Buyer, who has the superior right to possession of the stereo? *See* UCC §§ 2-402(1), 1-201(b)(13).

B. How, if at all, would the analysis in Part A change if Creditor acquired its judicial lien on the stereo – before Dealer contracted to sell the stereo to Buyer – by properly filing a notice of the judgment in the state's secretary of state's office?

C. How, if at all, would the analysis in Part B change if Buyer took delivery of the stereo before Creditor filed a notice of the judgment in the state's secretary of state's office?

Occasionally, a lien creditor can use fraudulent transfer law to nullify the Buyer's property rights and thereby claim priority in the goods. In particular, in some states, a Seller who retains possession of goods sold can be deemed to be engaged in a fraudulent attempt to mislead the Seller's creditors into believing that those goods would be available to the seller's creditors for payment in the event of a levy.[13] In short, retaining possession of goods already sold might make it appear to the Seller's creditors that the seller owns more assets – the goods – than the Seller really owns. As a result, those states effectively nullify the sale and allow the Seller's creditors to levy on the goods, and thereby permit the creditors to obtain rights to the goods superior to the Buyer who left the goods with the Seller.

Read section 2-402(2), which is a partial response to those decisions. The first clause acknowledges that there may be a rule of applicable state law that allows a creditor of the seller to treat the seller's retention of goods sold as fraudulent, and thus to invalidate the sale. The real import of subsection (2), however, is in the final clause. It creates an exception for a merchant seller's possession of goods sold for a commercially reasonable time and in good faith. Such conduct is deemed not fraudulent as against the Seller's creditors even if the state follows the general principle that treats retention of possession as fraudulent. Applying this exception would in effect make rights of a Buyer who left the goods with the Seller superior to the lien of the Seller's lien creditor if the Buyer had the right to obtain possession of the goods from the Seller.

Now consider a different type of property right of the Buyer: the Buyer's security interest arising under section 2-711(3). The Buyer's security interest will arise upon the Buyer's rightful and effective rejection or justifiable and effective revocation of acceptance. In considering how this security interest affects the Buyer's right to the goods, bear in mind that the lien creditor's lien could arise at any of the following distinct times: (i) before identification of the goods to the contract; (ii) after identification of the goods to the contract but before delivery of the goods to the Buyer; (iii) after delivery of the goods to the Buyer.

Assume the lien creditor acquired its lien before the goods were identified to the contract for sale. At the time the judicial lien arose, the buyer would have no property interest in the goods and thus under first-in-time principles, the lien creditor's rights should be superior to the buyer's rights even if the seller subsequently delivered the goods to the buyer and the buyer is asserting a security interest in the goods under section 2-711(3). Of course, this sequence of facts is unlikely to arise if the judicial lien was created by levy because in that case the seller would not generally be able to subsequently deliver the goods to the buyer.

---

[13]   *See, e.g.,* Cal. Civ. Code § 3440(a).

Now assume the lien creditor acquired its lien after the goods were identified to the contract for sale but before the seller delivered the goods to the buyer. Section 2-402(1) teaches that if the buyer had the right to force the seller to deliver the goods under section 2-502 or section 2-716, the lien creditor's rights would be subordinate to the buyer's rights. Thus, if the buyer was later asserting its security interest, that security interest should also be superior to the lien creditor's rights, although nothing in Article 2 specifically answers this question. If the buyer did not have the ability to force the seller to deliver the goods under section 2-502 or 2-716, then section 2-402(1) would not apply, and under basic first-in-time principles, the lien creditor's lien would be superior to the buyer's later arising security interest.

Now assume the seller delivers the goods and the lien creditor tries to levy on the goods in the buyer's possession. Here, the buyer's argument is that the seller no longer has a property right in the goods as title has transferred to the buyer under section 2-401 and thus there are no seller's rights to which the lien creditor can attach its property interest. Thus when the buyer asserts its security interest in the goods, there is no priority contest because the lien creditor has no property interest in the goods.

2. Buyer Against Seller's Secured Creditors

We now consider what happens if the Seller in our diagram has granted a security interest in the goods to a secured creditor. To be clear, the Seller has an agreement with the secured creditor that gives the secured creditor a security interest in the same goods that the Buyer has contracted to buy. In a dispute between the Buyer and the Seller's secured creditor over the goods, the priority of the parties' respective property rights in the goods will be determined not by Article 2, but by Article 9. Under Article 9, the default rule is that the secured creditor wins. *See* UCC § 9-201. There are, however, several exceptions that may come to the aid of the Buyer. Understanding those exceptions requires some knowledge of Article 9. Accordingly, what follows is a very distilled version of Article 9's basic principles. A more complete exploration of these principles must await a course on secured transactions.[14]

---

[14]   As we have seen many times in this course, Article 2 is merely one source of commercial law. Other Articles of the UCC, along with principles and rules of general contract law and the law governing debtor-creditor relations, are some of the other components of commercial law that can be relevant to a sales transaction.

First, remember that merely because the Seller owes money to a creditor does not mean that the creditor has a property interest in any of the Seller's assets. To obtain a property interest in the Seller's assets – in our example, the Seller's goods – the Seller and the secured creditor must have entered into an agreement that grants the creditor a property interest in the goods to secure an obligation that the Seller owes to the creditor. The process of creating this property interest (referred to as a "security interest") is called "attachment." *See* UCC § 9-203. The intricacies of attachment are left to a secured transactions course. For our purposes, the important point is that attachment of the security interest requires the agreement of the Seller.

Second, the priority of the creditor's security interest in the goods depends on several factors, the most important of which is whether the secured creditor has "perfected" its interest. Perfection is a term of art under Article 9. Generally, when the Seller has possession of the goods subject to the security interest, the secured creditor will perfect its security interest by filing a document called a "financing statement." To be perfected, the secured creditor's financing statement must contain certain specified information and be filed in the correct public office. The details behind that summary are quite complex and also are relegated to a course on secured transactions. For the purpose of studying sales, we will simply designate whether the secured creditor has or has not made a filing sufficient to perfect its security interest.

With this basic understanding, let's explore the two priority rules most likely to allow the Buyer to take the goods free of the Seller's creditor's security interest. The first is section 9-317(b), which deals with a secured creditor who has not made a filing sufficient to perfect its security interest. Read UCC § 9-317(b). This rule is in large measure a timing rule: it protects the Buyer if the goods are delivered to the Buyer before the secured creditor perfects its security interest, although other requirements must also be satisfied for the Buyer to prevail.[15]

Section 9-317(b) will not help the Buyer if the secured creditor has perfected its interest at the time the Buyer has taken delivery. However, the Buyer may nevertheless prevail under section 9-320(a). Read that provision. This priority rule protects a buyer in ordinary course of business from a security interest created by that buyer's seller, even if the security interest is perfected. We encountered buyers

---

[15]   Section 9-317(e) is an exception to the priority rule stated in subsection (b). Exploration of that exception would require much more than a dip into the Article 9 scheme and thus is not covered in this course.

in ordinary course of business when we explored the entrustment rule in section 2-403(2). Reread the definition of buyer in ordinary course of business in section 1-201(b)(9) and review the materials covered previously as to when the Buyer becomes a buyer in ordinary course of business. Now try the following problem.

Problem 10-5

Sublime Diversions manufactures and sells gaming tables (tables with inlaid chess boards, built-in holders for poker chips, *etc.*). To finance its operations, Sublime borrowed money from First Bank and granted the bank a security interest in all its inventory (the gaming tables) and equipment (*e.g.,* manufacturing machines, computers, office furniture). Busted contracted to purchase some goods from Sublime and paid half the purchase price. Using the matrix below, determine in which of the open boxes, if any, Busted will take free of First Bank's security interest in the goods sold and identify the provision that allows Busted to do so.

		First Bank's security interest is perfected	First Bank's security interest is unperfected
Busted contracted to buy a used band saw	Busted has received the goods from Sublime		
	Busted has a right to compel delivery under § 2-502 or § 2-716		
	Busted has neither received the goods nor has the right to compel delivery		
Busted contracted to buy a gaming table	Busted has received the goods from Sublime		
	Busted has a right to compel delivery under § 2-502 or § 2-716		
	Busted has neither received the goods nor has the right to compel delivery		

One more wrinkle to be added to this priority contest is the situation where the Buyer has a security interest in the goods pursuant to section 2-711(3). If the Buyer has taken free of the security interest of the Seller's creditor, then there is no priority contest. The secured creditor simply has no property interest at all.[16] If the Buyer has not taken the goods free from the creditor's security interest, then relative priority of the security interest of the Buyer and the Sellers' creditor is governed by section 9-110. Under that section, the Buyer's security interest will have priority over the creditor's security interest even though the creditor's security interest was attached and perfected before the Buyer's security interest arose, as long as the Seller (the debtor) does not get possession of the goods.

So far we have assumed that the Seller has granted a security interest to a financing creditor, someone who has loaned the Seller funds and secured the obligation to repay with a security interest in the Seller's property pursuant to a security agreement with the Seller. But, that is not the only way that a security interest in the goods may arise through an interaction with the Seller. Article 2 provides for two circumstances in which security interests arise as a result of a sales contract.

First, a seller of goods may, pursuant to the terms of the sales contract, purport to "retain title" to the goods despite making delivery to the buyer. This is normally done if the buyer has not yet fully paid for the goods. However, such a clause in the sales agreement does not actually prevent title from passing to the buyer. Instead, section 2-401 provides that the seller has merely retained a security interest in the buyer's goods. *See also* UCC § 1-201(b)(35). The sales contract therefore doubles as a security agreement. The second circumstance occurs when the seller ships the goods under reservation pursuant to section 2-505. That action is also sufficient to create a security interest in the goods. Thus to return to our diagram, the transferor to the Seller may create a security interest in the goods under Article 2 by either "retaining title" or shipping under reservation.

Even though these security interests arise under Article 2, their priority is governed by Article 9. Thus sections 9-317(b) and 9-320(a) will determine whether

---

[16]   This analysis may change if the security interest of the Seller's secured creditor reattaches to the goods. The Buyer's effective and rightful rejection of the goods or justified and effective revocation of acceptance cause title to the goods to revest in the Seller. UCC § 2-401(4). The secured creditor's security interest may reattach to the goods pursuant to the terms of the security agreement with the Seller. In such a case, the Buyer's security interest would have priority over the secured creditor's interest under section 9-110.

the Buyer takes free of these security interests in the same way as if the security interest had arisen under Article 9.[17]

SECTION 3.   SELLER'S RIGHTS AGAINST PERSONS WHO CLAIM AN INTEREST IN THE GOODS THROUGH THE BUYER

We now switch to the other side of the diagram and consider how the Seller's rights to the goods fare against those who may claim a property interest in the goods based upon some interaction with the Buyer. The usual competitors with the Seller are the Buyer's transferee, secured creditor, or lien creditor. Thus the parties we are concerned with in this section are in bold in the diagram below.

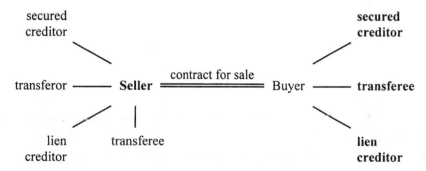

The reason such contests can arise is that a Seller, who has contracted to sell goods to the Buyer, remains the owner of the goods. As we have already seen, merely entering into the contract for sale does not divest the Seller of its ownership interest. This is true even if the Buyer has obtained property rights in the goods through identification, and then transferred those rights to someone else. Moreover, as we have previously discussed, the Seller also may have a right to stop delivery of the goods, and, if the goods have already been delivered, may have a right to reclaim them. UCC §§ 2-705, 2-702, 2-507.

The priority of the Seller's claim to the goods varies with the nature of the competing claimant's property interest in the goods. Thus, for example, the Seller's rights against the Buyer's transferee are different from the Seller's rights against the Buyer's secured creditor. We therefore discuss these three priority contests in turn:

---

[17]   In applying these priority rules, one must take into account the effect of section 9-110 which governs security interests arising under section 2-401 or 2-505.

(i) Seller vs. Buyer's transferee; (ii) Seller vs. Buyer's lien creditor; and (iii) Seller vs. Buyer's secured creditor.

The Seller's rights also depend on whether the Seller is asserting merely its rights under Article 2 or whether the Seller can also claim a security interest granted by the Buyer. Often times, a buyer who has not paid the seller in full for the goods will grant the seller a security interest in the goods to secure payment of the remainder of the price. However, the priority of such a security interest is largely independent of the seller's role in the transaction as seller and in any event is likely to be fully explored in a course on secured transactions.[18] Therefore, we concern ourselves here with the Seller's rights under Article 2.

A. SELLER AGAINST BUYER'S TRANSFEREE

We first consider the Seller's rights against a non-creditor transferee from the Buyer.

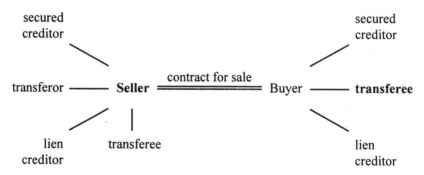

The transferee is most commonly a subsequent buyer, but could also be a donee or an entity that succeeds to the Buyer's property rights by operation of law.[19] The good news is that we have effectively already covered this priority battle when we covered the Seller's transferor's rights against the Buyer. A transferor's rights against the Buyer are the same as the Seller's rights against a transferee. There is no difference in the analysis.

---

[18]   For those who are curious, the relevant Article 9 sections are:
     Seller as secured party vs. Buyer's transferee   UCC §§ 9-317(b), 9-320;
     Seller as secured party vs. Buyer's lien creditor   UCC § 9-317(a), (e); and
     Seller as secured party vs. Buyer's secured creditor   UCC §§ 9-322(a), 9-324.

[19]   For example, the transferee could be the estate of a deceased Buyer.

If the Seller still has possession of the goods or the goods have been stopped in transit, the Buyer's transferee will not be able to force the Seller to deliver the goods to it unless the Buyer could force the Seller to deliver possession to the Buyer. UCC § 2-403(1) (the Buyer can only transfer the rights it has or has power to transfer). Once the Seller delivers the goods to Buyer, the transferee could have rights superior to the Seller by virtue of one of the two exceptions to section 2-403 that protect good faith purchasers for value and buyers in ordinary course of business. Similarly, if the Seller tried to exercise its reclamation rights under either section 2-507 or 2-702(2), the Seller would lose if the transferee qualified as a good faith purchaser for value of the goods or a buyer in ordinary course of business. Finally, if the transferee has a security interest under section 2-711(3), the transferee's status as a good faith purchaser for value or buyer in ordinary course of business should protect its security interest from the Seller's right to reclaim. We explored all of these rules in Problem 10-2 and the accompanying text.

B. SELLER AGAINST BUYER'S LIEN CREDITOR

A lien creditor of the Buyer acquires its lien – its property interest in the goods – through judicial process. Remember, in most states, that occurs when the creditor causes the sheriff or marshal to levy on the goods pursuant to a writ. In a few states, the lien can be created by filing a notice of the judgment in a public office. In either case, the lien attaches to only those rights in the goods that the Buyer has.

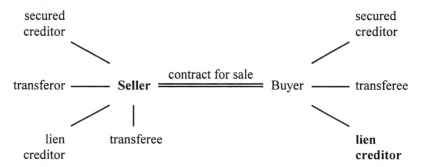

Based on these principles, the earliest point in time that a lien creditor could acquire a lien on goods that are subject to a contract for sale between the Seller and the Buyer is when the goods are identified to that contract. That is because identification is the point in time when the Buyer first obtains a property interest in the goods which could be captured by a judicial lien. While the Seller still has possession of those goods, however, the lien creditor would be able to gain priority over the Seller's property interest – that is, compel the Seller to transfer the goods – only if the Buyer would be able to so compel the Seller. Thus, a lien creditor's right to goods that are still in the Seller's possession will depend upon the Buyer's rights under section 2-502 or 2-716 to compel the Seller to deliver the goods to the Buyer. Because the Buyer must pay the Seller for the goods to exercise these rights, the lien creditor must do so as well, if the Buyer has not already paid.[20]

Much the same analysis applies if the goods are in transit. Because the lien creditor's rights are no greater than the Buyer's rights, if the Seller is entitled to stop the goods in transit as against the Buyer, the lien creditor's rights in the goods are subject to that right as well. *See* UCC §§ 2-705, 9-110, cmt. 5.

After the Buyer obtains possession of the goods, the Seller may have a right to reclaim the goods under section 2-507 or 2-702(2). Those sections do not address the priority of the Seller's reclamation right as against the Buyer's lien creditor. At common law, the reclaiming Seller prevailed over the Buyer's lien creditor, regardless of the timing of the lien creditor's levy as against the Seller making the reclamation demand. Without any contrary rule in Article 2, the common law rule may be appropriate to apply. *See* UCC § 1-103. *Cf.* UCC § 2-702(3).

Problem 10-6

Sterling Manufacturing agreed to sell specially manufactured equipment to Bristol for $100,000. Sterling was to deliver on August 1. Bristol was to pay half the purchase price upon delivery and pay the balance ten days later. Sterling identified the equipment to the contract on July 1. Under the relevant state law, a creditor with a judgment may acquire a judicial lien on goods of the judgment debtor merely by filing a notice in a designated office of the county in which the debtor is located.

---

[20]   The Seller's priority over a lien creditor would be further assured if the Seller had a security interest in the goods under section 2-401 or 2-505. In such a case, as long as the Buyer does not obtain possession of the goods, the Seller's security interest would be governed by section 9-110 which provides that the Seller's security interest has priority over the claims of other secured creditors. That section does not mention what the Seller's priority is over a lien creditor. However, another priority rule in Article 9 provides that the Seller's security interest in these circumstances would have priority over the lien creditor's lien because the Seller's security interest is deemed perfected. *See* UCC § 9-317(a), (e).

A. On July 15, Lacy, a creditor with a judgment against Bristol, acquired a judicial lien on Bristol's goods by filing a notice in the public records in the county where Bristol is located. On August 1, Sterling tendered delivery but Bristol did not tender the payment due upon delivery. Sterling refused to allow Bristol to take the equipment. As between Lacy and Sterling, who has superior rights to the equipment?

B. On July 15, Lacy, a creditor with a judgment against Bristol, acquired a judicial lien on Bristol's goods by filing a notice in the public records in the county where Bristol is located. On August 1, Sterling repudiated its obligation to deliver the equipment. Bristol desperately needs the equipment and cannot get any other replacement equipment, given the specially manufactured nature of this equipment. As between Lacy and Sterling, who has superior rights to the equipment?

C. On August 1, Sterling tendered delivery of the equipment, Bristol made the required payment with a check, and Bristol took possession of the equipment. On August 5, Sterling learned that the check had been dishonored by Bristol's bank. On August 6, Lacy, a creditor with a judgment against Bristol, acquired a judicial lien on Bristol's goods by filing a notice in the public records in the county where Bristol is located. Sterling demanded that Bristol return the goods. As between Sterling and Lacy, who has superior rights to the equipment?

C. SELLER AGAINST BUYER'S SECURED CREDITOR

One of the requirements for a security interest to attach is that the debtor have rights in the collateral. Thus, unless the Buyer has a property interest in the goods, the Buyer will not be able to grant an effective security interest in the goods to its secured creditor. Therefore, until the goods are identified to the contract of sale between the Buyer and Seller, a secured creditor of the Buyer could not have a security interest in the goods. In short, prior to identification, there can be no priority contest at all. Seller has the only property interest.

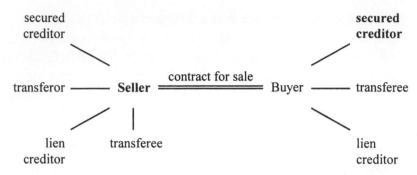

After identification of the goods to the contract, the Buyer can transfer a security interest in the goods, even if the goods remain in the possession of the Seller. Nevertheless, until the Seller delivers them, the Seller will remain the principal owner of the goods. UCC § 2-401. In such situations, the Seller's rights have priority over the rights of the Buyer's secured creditor under the derivation principle embodied in section 2-403(1): the Buyer may transfer to the secured creditor only those rights the Buyer has. Because the Buyer is subject to the Seller's rights to keep possession or stop delivery, the Buyer's secured party is subject to those rights as well. *See* UCC § 9-110, cmt. 5.

The results are substantially different if the Seller has delivered the goods to the Buyer and is seeking to reclaim them under section 2-507 or 2-702(2). Those rights of the Seller are subject to the rights of a good faith purchaser for value. *See* UCC §§ 2-403(1), 2-702(3). Because the Buyer's secured creditor – unlike a lien creditor – qualifies as a "purchaser" of the goods under section 1-201(b)(29) and (30) and because the Buyer's debt to the secured creditor constitutes value given, *see* section 1-204(2), the secured creditor will defeat the Seller's reclamation rights as long as the secured creditor has acted in good faith.

What if the Seller claims a security interest in the delivered goods under section 2-401 (retention of title) or 2-505 (shipment under reservation)? As long as the Buyer does not obtain possession of the goods, the Seller will win over Buyer's secured creditor. UCC § 9-110. After the Buyer gains possession of the goods, the relative priority of the security interests of the Seller and the Buyer's secured creditor is a matter governed by Article 9, not by Article 2. There are things the Seller may be able to do to attain priority. However, that discussion is very complex and beyond the scope of this course. Full exploration awaits you in a course on secured transactions.

Problem 10-7

Sterling Manufacturing agreed to sell specially manufactured equipment to Bristol for $100,000. Sterling was to deliver on August 1. Bristol was to pay half the purchase price upon delivery and pay the balance ten days later. Sterling identified the equipment to the contract on July 1. Bristol granted SP a security interest in all of its equipment to secure a loan that SP made to Bristol.

A. On July 2, as between SP and Sterling, who has superior rights to the equipment?

B. Sterling tendered delivery on August 1 and Bristol paid the required payment with a check. Bristol then took possession of the equipment. On August 5, Sterling found out the check had been dishonored by Bristol's bank. As between SP and Sterling, who has superior rights to the equipment?

CHAPTER ELEVEN

LEASES

SECTION 1. SCOPE

A. OVERVIEW

We now turn our attention to another important type of commercial transaction: leases of goods. Article 2A of the Uniform Commercial Code, as enacted by the states, governs leases of goods. It is of comparatively recent vintage (1989) compared to other articles of the UCC and is modeled on Article 2 (thus it is inserted between Articles 2 and 3). While many of the provisions in Article 2A are similar or identical to the analogous rules of Article 2, there are also many that are different. In addition, several provisions in each article have no analog in the other. The differences between the two articles are designed to account for the differences between lease and sale transactions and the business practices associated with them. Because there is so much similarity between Articles 2 and 2A, it would be overly time consuming and somewhat repetitive to now study all of Article 2A. Instead, this Chapter focuses on the differences between them.

The place to start the discussion is with the distinction between a lease and a sale. Recall that a sale is defined as the passing of title to the goods from the seller to the buyer for a price. UCC § 2-106(1). Now read the definition of a lease in section 2A-103(1)(j). Notice that instead of passing title, a lease is the transfer of more limited property rights, the right to possess or use the goods[1] for a term. The critical distinction is that in a lease transaction, the lessor has the right to get the goods back at the end of the lease term. This fundamental difference underlies all the differences in the law governing the two transactions, particularly in the parties' remedies for breach and their rights against third parties' property-based claims to the goods.

B. DISTINGUISHING A LEASE FROM A SALE

Unfortunately, the distinction between a lease and a sale is often much easier to state than to apply. Consider a transaction in which a merchant leases a new

---

[1] Compare the definition of goods in section 2-105(1) with the definition of goods in section 2A-103(1)(h). Can you explain the reasons for the differences?

laptop computer to a customer for 99 years. The transaction *purports* to be a lease. The merchant has the *right* to get the computer back at the end of the lease term. But what are the economic realities? Putting aside the fact that both parties will likely have passed away long before the lease term ends, the reality is that the computer too will have died. Personal computers simply do not have a useful life anywhere near that long. Even if the computer still functions, it will no doubt be hopelessly antiquated due to technological advancements in the interim. We may not know now what those advancements will be, but we can predict with reasonable certainty that the computer will have minimal or no value after 99 years. Indeed, it may have negative value due to the cost of disposal. So, is the transaction a lease or really a sale?

Before trying to answer that question, it is important to understand that the consequences of the distinction are legion. First, if it is a sale, then Article 2 applies. If it is a lease, then Article 2A applies. Given the similarity between those two articles, that distinction will often not matter much. However, the following other consequences, which are noted on the chart below, may matter greatly.

First, there are significant tax and accounting consequences to the distinction. For example, if the transaction is a true lease, then the lessor is the tax owner and may claim any depreciation deduction. Moreover, the rent would be income to the lessor and potentially a deductible expense for the lessee. On the other hand, if the transaction is a sale, the putative lessee – who is really a buyer – would be the tax owner of the goods and may claim any available depreciation allowance. The rental payments would not be deductible by the lessee or income to the lessor. Instead, the lessor – as a seller – may have recognizable gain or loss on the sale.

Second, if the lessee seeks bankruptcy protection, the characterization of the transaction will greatly affect what happens to the goods. If the transaction is a lease, the goods may be retained by the lessee only if the lease contract is performed according to its terms. If the transaction is a sale, it may be possible for the lessee/buyer to keep the goods while paying the lessor/seller over time either the amounts due under the lease or the value of the goods, whichever is less.

Third, and perhaps most important, if the transaction is really a sale, then not only will Article 2 govern, but so too will Article 9. That is because of the rule of section 2-401(1). As we have already seen, reservation of title by a seller of goods is limited in effect to the retention of a security interest. In a transaction structured as a lease, the lessor retains title. If the economic realities are such that the putative lease is really a sale, then the seller's/lessor's retention of title (by structuring the transaction as a lease) is limited to a security interest.

The potential application of Article 9 to the transaction is very important, particularly to the putative lessor. That is because a true lessor need not provide public notice of its property rights in the goods to be protected against the rights of the lessee's creditors. However, if the transaction is a sale, and putative lessor is therefore really a seller and a secured party, it must perfect its security interest, typically by filing a financing statement in the designated state office.[2]

THE SIGNIFICANCE OF THE SALE/LEASE DISTINCTION

	Sale & Security Interest (structured as a lease)	True Lease
Governing Law	Articles 2 & 9	Article 2A
Tax/Accounting Depreciation Allowance	Buyer/Lessee	Lessor
Tax/Accounting Payments	No effect.	Income to Lessor and deduction to Lessee.
Rights of Creditors of Buyer/Lessee	Can potentially get goods if Lessor/Seller did not perfect a security interest.	Cannot get goods, may be able to attach rights to lessee's leasehold interest.
Effect of Bankruptcy by Buyer/Lessee	If Lessor/Seller perfected its security interest, its property rights are protected but can be modified. Lessor/Seller entitled to lesser of debt or value of goods.	Lessor entitled to have all lease obligations performed or the goods returned.

The law could have allowed the parties' designation of their transaction to control. It could have provided that a transaction structured as a lease will be treated as a lease and a transaction structured as a sale will be treated as a sale. It could have, but it did not. *See* UCC §§ 2A-102, 9-109(a)(1) (both indicating that

---

[2]   Article 9 allows a lessor/seller to file a financing statement in order to protect itself in the event the transaction is determined to be a sale with a security interest. The filing itself cannot be used as evidence that the transaction is in fact a sale. UCC § 9-505.

the form of a transaction is not determinative of whether the Article applies). Instead, section 1-203 contains some rather complicated rules to determine whether a transaction is a sale or a lease for the purposes of Articles 2, 2A and 9.[3] These rules are based on the economic substance of the transaction. Neither form nor intent controls.

Read section 1-203. Subsection (a) informs us that the determination is a factual one. What it fails to do is actually state what the test is. Nevertheless, based on the remainder of the section and the comments, it is clear that the key issue here is whether there is a reasonable chance that the lessor will get the goods back when the goods still have meaningful economic value.[4] If the answer is yes, then the leasing structure of the transaction will be respected and the deal will be treated as a lease. If the answer is no, either because it is very unlikely that the lessor will ever get the goods back or because the goods will have no significant value when the lessor does get them, then the transaction will be treated as a sale with a retained security interest. The rules of subsection (c), (d), and (e) occasionally provide some help in making this assessment.

Subsection (b) provides a test, that if met, means that the transaction is a sale with a retained security interest. It is a sort of safe harbor rule. If the test is not met, then the analysis reverts to the factual test in subsection (a).

Problem 11-1

Consider the following transactions in which an equipment dealer "leases" a new $200,000 skid loader to a construction company. The construction company is responsible for all maintenance and insurance on the skid loader. The construction company is obligated to pay the entire $200,000 price even if it returns the skid loader to the dealer before the end of the "lease" term. In which of these scenarios, if any, is the transaction really a sale?

    A. A 5-year lease at $3,900 per month (paying $3,900/month for five years amortizes, *i.e.*, pays off, a $200,000 debt with 6% interest.)

---

[3] The distinction between a sale and a lease for tax purposes will be governed by tax law.

[4] *See* Edwin E. Huddleson, III, *Old Wine in New Bottles: UCC Article 2A-Leases*, 39 ALA. L. REV. 615, 625 (1988).

      1. The dealer gets the skid loader at the end of the "lease" term.

      2. The construction company has an option to buy for $5,000 at the end of the "lease" term.

      3. The construction company has an option to buy for $100 at the end of the "lease" term.

B. A 25-year lease at $2,000 per month. The dealer gets the skid loader at the end of the 25 years.

C. How, if at all, does the analysis change in any of the scenarios if the construction company may return the skid loader to the equipment dealer before the end of the lease term without any further obligation to make any remaining monthly payments?

C. FINANCE LEASES

A transaction that is a true lease may also be used as a financing mechanism when it is a "finance lease." While the definition in section 2A-103(1)(g) is very long, the basic concept of a finance lease is very simple. The lessee picks out the goods from a supplier based upon the lessee's specifications. The finance lessor (typically a bank or other entity that has agreed to finance the transaction) buys the goods from the supplier. That transaction is governed by Article 2 as a sale of goods. The finance lessor then leases the goods to the finance lessee pursuant to a finance lease.[5]

Perhaps an illustration may help. In a traditional lease, the lessee deals directly with the lessor. In doing so, the lessee may obtain needed financing from a lender and may grant the lender a security interest in the leased goods to secure that loan:

---

[5]   The lease between the finance lessor and the finance lessee must qualify as a "true" lease under section 1-203, or it will be treated as a sale and secured transaction.

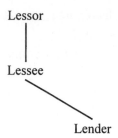

In a finance lease, the lender assumes the role of lessor, by purchasing or leasing the goods from the supplier and then leasing them to the lessee. The form of the transaction is depicted on the left below, but its substance more closely resembles the structure on the right.

Finance Lease

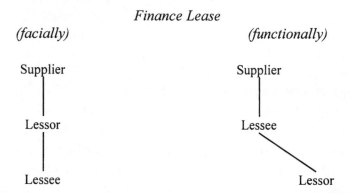

The lessor in a finance lease does not want to accept any responsibility for the quality of the goods. The lessor's role is really just to provide financing to the lessee.[6] Rather, it is the supplier to whom the lessee expects to look for the warranties and other quality assurances regarding the functioning of the goods. Article 2A accommodates this economic reality by having special rules applicable to finance leases. As a result, throughout Article 2A, some provisions apply to all leases and some provisions apply only to finance leases.

---

[6]   Although the finance lessor is in essence providing financing to enable the lessee to obtain the goods, the transaction between the lessor and lessee must be a true lease under the test in section 1-203 in order to qualify as a finance lease, that is the finance lessor must have a meaningful residual economic interest in the goods. Because the finance lessor will have that residual interest, but does not actually want the goods back, the finance lease generally provides that the lessee may purchase the lessor's interest at the end of the lease term for a fair market value price.

D. INTERSECTION WITH OTHER LAWS

A lease of goods often involves motor vehicles that are subject to a certificate of title law. Article 2A generally defers to the provisions of that other law. See UCC §§ 2A-104, 2A-105. Transactions subject to Article 2A may also be covered by consumer protection law. Again, Article 2A generally defers to that other law. UCC § 2A-104.

However, it is worth noting that many of the laws we considered in Chapter Eight, such as the Magnuson-Moss Warranty Act and state lemon laws, may not apply to leases. Moreover, even if a transaction in the form of a lease would be re-characterized as a sale for the purposes of Articles 2, 2A, and 9, other law may not abide by that re-characterization and may still regard the transaction as a lease and outside the other law's scope. This is yet another reason why sellers may choose to structure their transactions as leases: to avoid application of some laws, particularly consumer protection laws. Accordingly, lawyers need to thoroughly understand whether and how other laws in their jurisdiction apply to leases or to sales structured as leases.

Until recently, leases of goods have been fairly localized transactions. Perhaps because of that, neither the CISG, which governs many international sales of goods, nor any other international convention governs leases of goods. To the extent the parties wanted to adopt the UNIDROIT Principles of International Commercial Contracts, they could do so in a lease transaction.[7]

---

[7]   UNIDROIT has sponsored a project to develop a Draft Model Law on Leasing. *See* www.unidroit.org.

SECTION 2.   LEASE FORMATION

A. Basic Formation Principles

Analogous Provisions	
Article 2	Article 2A
§ 1-201(b)(3)	§ 2A-103(1)(k)
§ 1-201(b)(12)	§ 2A-103(1)(*l*)
§ 2-204	§ 2A-204
§ 2-205	§ 2A-205
§ 2-206	§ 2A-206
§ 2-207	n/a

Article 2A contains provisions on contract formation that are very similar to the Article 2 provisions on that subject. First, the definitions of "lease agreement" and "lease contract" in section 2A-103(1)(k) and (*l*) largely mirror the definitions of "agreement" and "contract" in section 1-201. Second, the rules in sections 2-204 through 2-206 are largely replicated in sections 2A-204 through 2A-206, with one exception. Section 2A-206 does not contain an equivalent to section 2-206(1)(b) on formation following an order for prompt or current shipment. This reflects the differences between how sales agreements are formed and how leases are entered into. Rarely do prospective lessees submit orders to lease goods. Even more rare would be for a lessor to respond to such an order by simply shipping the goods. Instead, lease transactions usually involve greater interaction and negotiation between the lessor and the lessee. In particular, they need to determine the length of the lease term, which party will be responsible for maintenance and insurance, and various other terms. It is this difference in the practices surrounding formation that explains why Article 2A also has no analog to the battle-of-the-forms rules in section 2-207. Leases are usually the product of negotiation, not an exchange of standard forms.

That is not to say that a lease transaction cannot be entered into through electronic interaction. As we learned in covering Article 2, the provisions of the Uniform Electronic Transactions Act (if enacted in the relevant state) and the federal E-Sign statute (15 U.S.C. § 7001) permit parties to use electronic communications and E-Sign provides some consumer protections to ensure the consumer has assented to electronic communication. These provisions apply to transactions governed by Article 2A just as they applied to transactions governed by Article 2.[8]

With these exceptions – no equivalent to section 2-106(1)(b), section 2-207, or the CISG – all we have learned about the formation of sales contracts is relevant to the formation of a lease contract under Article 2A. Article 2A does not add any additional rules on contract formation that are unique to the lease transaction.

B. STATUTE OF FRAUDS

Analogous Provisions	
Article 2	Article 2A
§ 2-201	§ 2A-201

As we learned in Chapter Two, Article 2 requires some agreements for the sale of goods (those for more than $500) to satisfy the statute of frauds in order to be enforceable. UCC § 2-201. Article 2A has a statute of frauds that is modeled on the one in Article 2, but has some significant differences. Read section 2A-201.

Problem 11-2

Identify all the differences between the statute of frauds section 2-201 and section 2A-201 other than one governs a sale transaction and the other governs a lease transaction.

---

[8]   UETA § 3; E-Sign, 15 U.S.C. § 7003(a).

C. UNCONSCIONABILITY

Analogous Provisions	
Article 2	Article 2A
§ 2-302	§ 2A-108(1), (3)
n/a	§ 2A-108(2), (4)

The concept of unconscionability is an important control on overreaching by a contracting party. The basic principle, articulated in section 2-302, that courts need not enforce unconscionable agreements or terms, is repeated in section 2A-108(1) and (3). Article 2A adds to this basic rule some additional protections for "consumer leases," a term defined in section 2A-103(1)(e). Read that definition. The additional protections, which are found in section 2A-108(2) and (4) focus on "procedural" unconscionability and provide relief if unconscionable conduct induced the contract or occurred in collecting on a claim arising from the lease contract. In those situations, there is no requirement that the consumer lease agreement be substantively unconscionable for relief to be available. Article 2A also differs from Article 2 by expressly providing for a consumer lessee who prevails on a claim of unconscionability to recover reasonable attorney's fees. *See* UCC § 2A-108(4).

SECTION 3.   LEASE TERMS

A. AGREEMENT AND CONTRACT

Article 2A is based upon the same fundamental concepts of "agreement" and "contract" that underlie Article 2. Thus, the bargain in fact of the parties, as augmented by the Article 2A gap fillers, will comprise the lease contract. Review the definitions of "lease agreement" and "lease contract" in section 2A-103. The concepts of usage of trade, course of dealing and course of performance are just as relevant to an Article 2A transaction as they are to an Article 2 transaction. *See* UCC §§ 1-303 and 2A-207. Similarly, every Article 2A transaction is subject to the good faith obligation stated in section 1-304.

Unlike Article 2, however, Article 2A has relatively few gap-filler provisions. Notably absent are any provisions that are comparable to the following sections of Article 2:

§ 2-304 (how price payable);

§ 2-305 (open price term);

§ 2-306 (output and requirements contracts);

§ 2-307 (delivery in single lot);

§ 2-308 (place of delivery);

§ 2-309 (time for performance);

§ 2-310 (time for payment);

§ 2-311 (cooperation respecting performance);

§ 2-503 and § 2-504 (tender of delivery); and

§ 2-505 (shipment under reservation).

Most of these omissions can be explained by the fact that lease agreements tend to be more complete than sales agreements. The parties do not generally, as a matter of practice, rely on gap fillers when entering into a lease. Instead, the parties tend to have express terms addressing the numerous items that may be addressed by the Article 2 gap fillers. Another reason why Article 2A lacks gap fillers on these subjects is that lease agreements have no nearly universal way of dealing with many of them, and thus there is no obvious choice for what the gap filler rule would be. In particular it may not make sense to apply the gap-filler provisions in Article 2 to the different rights and obligations of the parties in a lease transaction.

Remember, however, that a lease transaction is based upon contract principles, just as a sale transaction is. To the extent that Article 2A does not explicitly displace the common-law principles of contract law, those principles may help fill in the gaps in Article 2A. UCC § 1-103.

In addition to the protection for consumer lessees in section 2A-108 regarding unconscionability, Article 2A contains a restriction on two typical contract clauses: choice of law and choice of forum. Read UCC § 2A-106. This restriction is applicable to consumer leases, UCC § 2A-103(1)(e). As stated in the comment, however, this section does not restrict the parties' ability to choose a nonjudicial forum such as arbitration. Thus clauses providing that the parties have agreed to arbitrate all disputes would be enforceable, if enforceable under otherwise applicable contract law.

B. WARRANTIES

Analogous Provisions	
Article 2	Article 2A
n/a	§ 2A-209
§ 2-312	§ 2A-211
§ 2-313	§ 2A-210
§ 2-314	§ 2A-212
§ 2-315	§ 2A-213
§ 2-316	§ 2A-214(1)–(3)
n/a	§ 2A-214(4)
§ 2-317	§ 2A-215
§ 2-318	§ 2A-216

Article 2A contains the same three warranties of quality that are found in Article 2: express warranty, section 2A-210; implied warranty of merchantability, section 2A-212; and the implied warranty of fitness for a particular purpose, section 2A-313. There are no material differences between the express warranty provisions in section 2A-210 and section 2-313. The substance of the implied merchantability warranty and the implied warranty of fitness for a particular purpose in Article 2A are also the same as the comparable provisions in Article 2, with one exception.

In a finance lease, the finance lessor does not make either implied warranty. *See* UCC §§ 2A-212(1), 2A-213. A finance lessor could make an express warranty, including an *express* warranty of merchantability or fitness for a particular purpose, but that would be unusual. The reason that a finance lessor does not make either of the *implied* warranties, and does not normally make express warranties, is that the finance lessor is really just a lender: someone providing the funds necessary to purchase or obtain the goods from the supplier and then is charging the finance lessee for the use and possession of those goods. Instead, the finance lessee typically looks to the supplier of the goods (the party that provided the goods to the finance lessor) for its remedies. Section 2A-209 therefore provides that the implied warranties that would normally accompany the supplier's transaction with the finance lessor – whether under Article 2 or Article 2A – flow directly to the finance lessee. Review the definition of "finance lease" in section 2A-103(1)(g), read section 2A-209, and then try the following problem.

Problem 11-3

Sensational Electronics manufactures computer servers for use in networks. Lasting Data operates a data storage business that relies heavily on computer servers. Three months ago, Lasting Data began negotiating with Sensational Electronics to acquire 30 new servers. The parties had a draft agreement that included several express warranties and disclaimed any implied warranty of fitness for particular purpose. When it became clear that the cost of the servers was more than Lasting Data could afford out of its operating funds and existing bank line of credit, Lasting Data approached Boston Finance for assistance. Boston Finance agreed to purchase the servers from Sensational Electronics and then lease the servers to Lasting Data. Boston Finance reviewed the draft agreement between Sensational Electronics and Lasting Data, made a few changes to the risk of loss provisions, and then Boston Finance and Sensational Electronics executed the agreement. On the same day, Boston Finance and Lasting Data executed an agreement by which Lasting Data leased the servers from Boston Finance. After the servers were delivered and installed at Lasting Data's facility, several of the servers malfunctioned.

A. Which warranties, if any, did Sensational Finance make to Lasting Data regarding the servers?

B. Which warranties, if any, did Boston Finance make to Lasting Data regarding the servers?

C. How, if at all, would the analysis of Parts A and B change if the agreement between Sensational Electronics and Boston Finance was a lease agreement rather than a sale?

D. How, if at all, would the analysis of Parts A and B change if the agreement between Boston Finance and Lasting Data obligated Lasting Data to purchase the servers at the end of the lease term?

Just as a seller of goods may disclaim all implied warranties of quality, if it follows the requirements of section 2-316, so too may a lessor disclaim all of the implied warranties of quality in the lease transaction. To do so, the lessor must comply with section 2A-214. The first three subsections of section 2A-214 follow fairly closely the requirements found in section 2-316.

Article 2A also follows the Article 2 model on extending warranties to persons lacking privity with the lessor. *Compare* UCC § 2-318 *with* UCC § 2A-216.[9] Under section 2A-216, if the lessee is a beneficiary of a warranty, that section determines whether someone other than the lessee has the benefit of the warranty.

A lessor in a lease transaction makes a warranty of non-infringement that is substantially similar to the warranty of non-infringement in a sale of goods. *Compare* UCC § 2A-211(2), (3) *with* UCC § 2-312(3). In addition, under section 2A-211, the lessor makes a transfer warranty that is analogous to a seller's warranty of title. Of course, because a lease transaction is not a transfer of all of the property rights in the goods, merely the right to use and possess the goods, the lessor warrants merely that no one has a claim arising from an interaction with the lessor that will interfere with the lessee's rights under the lease. Finally, unlike Article 2, Article 2A contains an explicit provision on how to disclaim the warranty of non-interference and the warranty of non-infringement. UCC § 2A-214(4).

C. FINANCE LEASES AND THE OBLIGATION TO PAY

We have already seen that warranties flow somewhat differently in a finance lease than in an ordinary lease or in a sale transaction. The other important difference between an ordinary lease and a finance lease concerns the lessee's payment obligation. This difference reflects the fact that the finance lessor is really only a lender, providing the financing necessary for the lessee to acquire the use and possession of the goods from the supplier. Accordingly, unless the finance lessor makes an express warranty concerning the goods – which would be uncommon – the finance lessor has no responsibility for the functioning of the goods. A corollary to this is that the finance lessor wants to be paid by the lessee regardless of whether the goods are satisfactory or defective. The finance lessor expects the lessee to look to the supplier if there are any problems with the goods, but expects the lessee to pay regardless. Read section 2A-407. The import of that section is that, once the lessee accepts the goods, the lessee's promise to pay becomes irrevocable and independent of the promises of the supplier and the lessor regarding the functioning of the goods or of the lessor's performance obligations. This

---

[9]   This extension of warranty protection to persons other than the lessee is different from and in addition to the rules in section 2A-209, which extend a supplier's warranties to the finance lessee in finance lessee.

obligation to pay is called a "hell or high water" term, because the lessee has promised to pay come "hell or high water" (in other words, without exception or excuse). Section 2A-407 makes this a presumed term (a gap filler) in a finance lease that is not a consumer lease.[10] In a consumer lease, the parties may contract for a similar term unless precluded by some law other than Article 2A.

Problem 11-4

Return to Problem 11-3.

A. How does section 2A-407 affect Lasting Data's obligations under the lease with Boston Finance?

B. You represent Boston Finance and are drafting the lease agreement for the transaction with Lasting Data. Is there anything you should put in the lease agreement to supplement the rules in section 2A-407? If so, what should you put in and why? *See Wells Fargo Bank Minnesota, N.A. v. B.C.B.U.,* 49 Cal. Rptr. 3d 324 (Cal. Ct. App. 2006).

D. REMEDY LIMITATIONS

Analogous Provisions	
Article 2	Article 2A
§ 2-718	§ 2A-504
§ 2-719	§ 2A-503

A lease agreement may limit the remedies normally available for breach. The rules in Article 2A regarding remedy limitations are very similar to the analogous rules in Article 2, but there are a few notable differences. First, section 2A-503(2) provides that if a remedy limitation is unconscionable, then the limitation is not enforceable. This result is implicit in Article 2, but not stated expressly. *See* UCC § 2A-503 cmt. 2. Second, section 2A-503(3) expressly provides that consequential

---

[10] Because the UCC does not displace many common-law doctrines, *see* UCC § 1-103(b), a lessee may be able to prevent enforcement of a hell-or-high-water clause in the agreement and prevent application of the rules of section 2A-407. *See Faust Printing, Inc. v. MAN Capital Corp.,* 2007 WL 4442325 (N.D. Ill. 2007) (fraudulent inducement claim may be basis to avoid liability under a "hell or high water" clause of a finance lease).

damages may be either liquidated pursuant to section 2A-504 or limited pursuant to section 2A-503. In contrast, section 2-719(3) expressly provides that consequential damages may be limited but does not expressly state that they may be liquidated, although that right is probably available under section 2-718(1).

Third, and far more significant, is that the standard for the enforceability of a liquidated damages clause is different. Section 2A-504 requires that liquidated damages be reasonable in light of anticipated harm, whereas section 2-718 allows the parties to liquidate damages as long as the measure is reasonable in light of either anticipated or actual harm and the difficulty of obtaining an otherwise adequate remedy.

E. PAROL EVIDENCE

Analogous Provisions	
Article 2	**Article 2A**
§ 2-202	§ 2A-202

As we learned in Chapter Five, the parol evidence rule in section 2-202 helps ensure the primacy of writings by limiting the evidence that a party to a sales contract may submit to supplement or contradict a writing that at least partially integrates the parties' agreement. Article 2A has an almost identical parol evidence rule. *Compare* UCC § 2A-202 *with* § 2-202.

F. MODIFICATION

Analogous Provisions	
Article 2	**Article 2A**
§ 2-209	§ 2A-208

In Chapter Three, we examined the several principles on modification contained in section 2-209. A modification needs no consideration to be binding, the parties may have an effective no-oral-modification clause (a clause that prevents subsequent modification except through a signed writing), an ineffective attempt to modify may operate as a waiver, and in certain circumstances a waiver may be retracted. *See* UCC § 2-209. Section 2A-208 contains each of these rules. The only difference between section 2A-208 and section 2-209 is that the former has no analog to section 2-209(3) on the relationship between the modification and the statute of frauds. The comment to section 2A-208 notes that the courts should resolve on a case-by-case basis the impact of an oral modification on a lease that otherwise satisfies the statute of frauds, noting that enforcing the modification might sometimes be inappropriate but that enforcing the lease as it was prior to the modification might occasionally be even worse.

SECTION 4.   PERFORMANCE ISSUES

A. INSECURITY AND REPUDIATION

Analogous Provisions	
Article 2	Article 2A
§ 2-609	§ 2A-401
§ 2-610	§ 2A-402
§ 2-611	§ 2A-403

Article 2A approaches reasonable grounds for insecurity and the ability to request adequate assurance in the same manner as Article 2. *Compare* UCC § 2-609 *with* § 2A-401. The aggrieved party's ability to deal with a repudiation in a lease contract is the same as an aggrieved party's ability to deal with a repudiation in a sales contract. *Compare* UCC §§ 2-610, 2-611 *with* § 2A-402, 2A-403. Thus the concepts discussed in Chapter Six regarding insecurity, adequate assurance, and repudiation are equally relevant to the lease transaction.

B. RISK OF LOSS AND INSURANCE ABSENT BREACH

Analogous Provisions	
Article 2	Article 2A
§ 2-501	§ 2A-218
§ 2-509	§ 2A-219

The risk of loss rules for leases of goods are substantially different from the risk of loss rules for sales. This difference is probably attributable to the different types of property interests at stake. In a sales contract, the property rights to the goods pass from the seller to the buyer. While there may be a period of time when both parties have property rights in the goods, that period is likely to be relatively short (at least in relationship to the useful life of the goods). Thus, the purpose of rules on risk of loss is to determine when the risk of loss passes from the original holder of all the property rights (the seller) to the new holder of the property rights (the buyer). In lease contracts, however, both parties will have property rights in the goods for the entire lease period. So, risk of loss rules are less concerned with when risk of loss passes from one party to the other and more concerned with how to allocate the risk of loss between the parties during the term of the lease.

You might think that the logical way to handle this would be for the risk of loss to be shared between the parties, with the lessor bearing the risk to the extent of its residual interest in the goods and the lessee bearing the risk to the extent of its leasehold interest in the goods. However, that is not the approach the drafters took. You might then think that the lessee should have the entire risk of loss because the lessee is the one with custody of the goods. That might make sense, but it too is not what Article 2A provides. Instead, for leases other than finance leases, the lessor retains the risk of loss. UCC § 2A-219(1). Bear in mind, however, that the parties are free by agreement to alter this rule, *see* UCC § 1-302, and they frequently do. Many lease agreements place the risk of loss on the lessee during the lease term.

In a finance lease, however, the default rule is that the risk of loss does pass to the lessee. If neither party is in default, the risk of loss will pass to the finance lessee at one of the times stated in section 2A-219(2). These times for passage of the risk of loss are largely the same as those in section 2-509, with a couple of minor differences. First, it contains only one time for the risk of loss to pass when the goods are held by a bailee and to be delivered without being moved. *Compare* UCC § 2-509(2) *with* § 2A-219(2)(b). This may be because documents of title are not usually used in delivering goods to the lessee in a lease transaction. Second, in a finance lease, the risk of loss passes when the lessee receives the goods if the *supplier*, not the *lessor*, is a merchant. This mirrors the rule from Article 2 which focuses on the merchant status of the seller, but takes into account the supplier's role in the transaction. *Compare* UCC § 2-509(3) *with* § 2A-219(2)(c).

Irrespective of the risk of loss, the lessee acquires an insurable interest in the goods once the goods are identified to the lease contract. UCC §§ 2A-218(1), (2), 2A-217. Because the lessor retains property rights in the goods, the lessor also retains an insurable interest in the goods even if the lessee has acquired possession of them. UCC § 2A-218(3). The lessor loses its insurable interest in the goods if and when the lessee exercises an option to buy the goods. UCC § 2A-218(3). The parties may agree which party must insure the goods and who has a right to proceeds of that insurance. UCC § 2A-218(5).

C. EXCUSE

Analogous Provisions	
Article 2	**Article 2A**
§ 2-613	§ 2A-221
§ 2-614	§ 2A-404
§ 2-615	§ 2A-405
§ 2-616	§ 2A-406

In Chapter Six, we considered the ability of the seller or the buyer in a sales transaction to be excused from its contract obligations. Article 2A follows the Article 2 model with few changes. Section 2A-221, the lease analog to section 2-613, deals with the lessor's excuse when the lease contract requires the particular goods that are identified to the contract when the contract is made. The Article 2A rule appears to operate the same as the Article 2 rule except that if the lease is a finance lease that is not a consumer lease, the lessee, if it chooses to take the goods, does not get an allowance for the damage to the goods to offset against the rent due. In other words, in that situation, the finance lessee who accepts the goods is going to have to pay full rent. This result is consistent with the hell-or-high-water rule in section 2A-407.

Section 2A-404 follows the model from section 2-614 regarding shipping and payment substitutions without substantive change. Sections 2A-405 and 2A-406 follow the same principles as sections 2-615 and 2-616 in allowing a lessor, or a supplier in a finance lease transaction, to seek excuse based upon commercial impracticability. Again, the one difference in treatment between the sale transaction and the lease transaction is that in a finance lease that is not a consumer lease, the finance lessee who accepts part of the quota allocated to it is still obligated to pay the entire amount of the lease payments, instead of only an allocable share.

D. ASSIGNMENT AND DELEGATION

Analogous Provisions	
Article 2	Article 2A
§ 2-210	§ 2A-303

The lessor has two basic rights under a lease contract: the right to the residual interest in the goods and the right to the rental payments. If the lessor assigns the right to payment (with or without the residual interest in the goods), that assignment is a secured transaction subject to Article 9. *See* UCC § 9-109. Generally, clauses in the lease agreement that purport to prohibit the lessor from assigning its rights under the lease are not effective to prevent the transfer from taking effect or to create an event of default that would give the lessee remedies for the lessor's breach. UCC §§ 2A-303(2), 9-406(d), 9-407.

The lessee has the right to possession of the goods that are the subject of the lease. If the lease contract makes transfer of that right a default under the lease, but the lessee transfers that right anyway, then the lessor may exercise its remedies against the lessee. UCC § 2A-303(4)(a). If the lease contract does not make such a transfer a default, but merely prohibits it (a very unlikely circumstance), the transfer is effective unless a damage award against the lessee would not be adequate, in which case the lessor can obtain a court order disallowing the transfer. UCC § 2A-303(4)(b). The lessee of course also has the duty to pay rent. Even if the lessee effectively delegates this duty to someone else, the lessee is not released from the obligation. UCC § 2A-303(6). This is the same rule that appears in section 2-210(1).

SECTION 5.   LESSOR'S DEFAULT AND LESSEE'S REMEDIES

A. OVERVIEW

Analogous Provisions	
Article 2	Article 2A
n/a	§ 2A-502
§ 2-711	§ 2A-508

The lessee's right to exercise remedies is keyed to the lessor's default under the lease contract as determined by the parties' agreement and Article 2A. UCC § 2A-501. The lessor's typical defaults are a repudiation of a lease contract, a failure to deliver the goods, or delivery of goods that do not conform to the contract. *See* UCC § 2A-508. The lessee has no general obligation to notify the lessor of the default, but this rule is subject to several exceptions and can be modified by the terms of the agreement. UCC § 2A-502. The lessee's remedies are catalogued in section 2A-508. The lessee may also have additional remedies pursuant to the lease agreement. As is true in Article 2, the focus in Article 2A is on putting the aggrieved lessee in the same position it would have been in if the lessor had fully performed. UCC § 1-305.

B. LESSOR'S FAILURE TO DELIVER

Analogous Provisions	
Article 2	Article 2A
§ 2-502	§ 2A-522
§ 2-612	§ 2A-510
§ 2-712	§ 2A-518
§ 2-713	§ 2A-519
§ 2-715	§ 2A-520
§ 2-716	§ 2A-521
§ 2-723	§ 2A-507(1)–(3)
§ 2-724	§ 2A-507(4)

When the lessor fails to deliver the goods or repudiates the lease contract before the delivery date, the lessee has to choose whether to attempt to obtain the goods from the lessor or cancel the contract and seek damages. If the lessee wants to obtain the goods from the lessor, the lessee may do so through specific performance or replevin, just as a buyer in a sales contract may seek specific performance or replevin from the seller. The standard for granting such relief is largely the same. *Compare* UCC § 2-716 *with* § 2A-521. A pre-paying lessee has the right to recover identified goods if the lessor became insolvent within ten days after the lessee has made the first payment. UCC § 2A-522. This rule mirrors the rule in section

2-502(1)(b) for pre-paying buyers. However, the protection for a pre-paying consumer buyer contained in section 2-502(1)(a) has no analog in section 2A-522.

If the lease is *not* an installment lease contract, the lessee may respond to the lessor's failure to deliver by canceling the contract. UCC § 2A-508(1)(a), 2A-505. In contrast, if the lease is an installment lease contract – that is, a lease that calls for delivery in separate lots, UCC § 2A-103(1)(i) – the lessee may cancel the contract only if the lessor's default substantially impairs of the value of the entire contract. *See* UCC § 2A-510(2).

The lessee may, of course, also seek damages for the lessor's failure to deliver the goods. These remedies are very similar to a buyer's remedies for nondelivery. First, the lessee may recover the rent that has been paid. UCC § 2A-508(1)(b). In addition, the lessee may cover and obtain damages based upon the cover price, UCC § 2A-518, or may seek damages based upon a market price measurement, UCC § 2A-519. On top of this, the lessee is entitled to incidental and consequential damages. UCC § 2A-520.

Computation of the lessee's cover damages is complicated because the lessee is authorized to cover either by entering into a substitute lease or by purchasing goods similar to those called for by the breached lease. If the lessee enters into a substitute lease that is substantially equivalent to the breached lease, the damages are calculated as the present value of all the rent due under the new lease (for the period that is comparable to the breached lease) minus the present value of all the rent due under the breached lease. UCC § 2A-518(2). Added to this amount are any incidental and consequential damages. Subtracted from this amount are expenses saved as a result of the lessor's breach. If the lessee covers either by entering into a lease that is not substantially similar to the breached contract or by purchasing replacement goods, the lessee's damages are calculated, not based on the cover transaction, but using a market rent formula. UCC § 2A-518(3). Under this market rent formula, the lessee is entitled to the difference between the present value of the market rent minus the present value of the rent under the breached lease, plus incidental and consequential damages, minus expenses saved as a result of the lessor's breach. UCC § 2A-519(1). Market rent is determined at the time of default. UCC § 2A-519(1). Section 2A-507 provides guidance on how to determine the market rent.

C. LESSOR'S NONCONFORMING TENDER OF THE GOODS

Analogous Provisions	
Article 2	Article 2A
§ 2-508	§ 2A-513
§ 2-513	n/a
§ 2-601	§ 2A-509(1)
§ 2-602(1)	§ 2A-509(2)
§ 2-602(2)(b), (c)	§ 2A-512(1)(a), (c)
§ 2-603	§ 2A-511(1)–(3)
§ 2-604	§ 2A-512(1)(b), (2)
§ 2-605	§ 2A-514
§ 2-606	§ 2A-515
§ 2-607	§ 2A-516
§ 2-608	§ 2A-517
§ 2-706(5)	§ 2A-511(4)

Article 2A uses the same rejection, acceptance, cure, and revocation of acceptance model as does Article 2. If the lessor tenders goods that fail to conform to the contract, the lessee has a right to reject them. UCC § 2A-509. For non-installment contracts, Article 2A follows the perfect tender rule. UCC § 2A-509(1). In installment lease contracts, the lessee may reject the goods only if the nonconformity in the installment substantially impairs the value of that installment and cannot be cured or the lessor fails to give adequate assurance of a cure. UCC § 2A-510. Rejection of the goods must occur within a reasonable time and is ineffective unless the lessee seasonably notifies the lessor. UCC § 2A-509(2). Just as we saw in Chapter Seven when discussing the rights and duties of a rejecting buyer, a lessee who rejects the goods may in some circumstances have to state all ascertainable defects that justify rejection or the lessee will be deemed to have waived them. UCC § 2A-514. The lessee's ability to reject is countered somewhat by the lessor's right to cure. That right to cure is the same as the seller's right to cure under Article 2. *Compare* UCC § 2A-513 *with* § 2-508.

After rejecting the goods, the lessee has an obligation to hold the goods with reasonable care. UCC § 2A-512(1)(a). A merchant lessee has the obligation to follow reasonable instructions from the lessor as to dealing with the goods. UCC § 2A-511. In some circumstances, the lessee may sell the goods or otherwise dispose of them without liability to the lessor. UCC §§ 2A-511(2), 2A-512(1)(b). The lessee has a security interest in the goods to secure any prepayments made and may enforce that security interest by disposing of the goods. UCC § 2A-508(5). The purchaser or transferee from these sales will take the goods free of any claim of the lessor or supplier as the case may be. UCC §§ 2A-511, 2A-512. These sections parallel the rules in Article 2.

After a timely and rightful rejection of the goods, the lessor has the same right to cure that a seller has. *Compare* UCC § 2A-513 *with* § 2-508. Absent cure, the lessee will be entitled to recover damages based either upon the cost of cover or the market rent, plus incidental and consequential damages, minus expenses saved as a consequence of the breach. UCC §§ 2A-518, 2A-519, 2A-520.

A lessee has the right to inspect the goods (although there is no section in Article 2A that parallels section 2-513) and will have accepted them if after that time, it fails to timely reject the goods, or it signifies to the lessor or the supplier that the goods are conforming or it will take them in spite of a nonconformity. UCC § 2A-515. Upon acceptance of the goods, the lessee is obligated to pay the rent and may no longer reject the goods. UCC §§ 2A-516(1), (2), 2A-529(1)(a). A lessee who has accepted the goods despite a nonconformity in the goods or tender has a damage remedy for the breach, provided the lessee notifies the lessor (and in a finance lease, the supplier) of breach in a timely manner. UCC 2A-516(3). The damage remedy focuses on the diminishment in the present value of the use of the goods, because that is the loss the lessee has suffered. UCC § 2A-519(3), (4). *Cf.* UCC § 2-714. In addition, the lessee is entitled to recover incidental and consequential damages. In a lease other than a finance lease subject to section 2A-407, the lessee may deduct the damages from the rent owed. UCC § 2A-508(6). *Cf.* UCC § 2-717.

For leases that are not finance leases, the lessee has the same right to revoke acceptance of the goods that a buyer has in a sales transaction. *Compare* UCC § 2A-517 *with* § 2-608. That is, the lessee may revoke acceptance of the goods if the nonconformity substantially impairs the value of the goods and the lessee accepted the goods either on the assumption the nonconformity would be cured or without having discovered the nonconformity due to the lessor's assurances or the difficulty in discovering the problem. The lessee may also revoke acceptance of goods if the lessor defaults (*i.e.*, breaches the lease in a manner that is not related to conformity of the goods) under the lease contract and that default substantially impairs the value of the goods. UCC § 2A-517(2). Of course, the parties are free to expand or contract the lessee's right to revoke. *See* UCC § 2A-517(3).

In a commercial finance lease, the only statutory basis for revocation of acceptance is that the nonconformity substantially impairs the value of the goods and the lessee accepted the goods without discovery of the nonconformity due to the lessor's assurances. UCC §§ 2A-517, 2A-516(2). This restriction on the ability of a finance lessee to revoke acceptance is necessary in order to give effect to the hell-or-high-water rule contained in section 2A-407. In a consumer finance lease, the lessee may also revoke acceptance of goods if the lessor defaults in a way that substantially impairs the value of the goods. UCC § 2A-517(2). This right is particularly important for the consumer lessee because it avoids the obligation to pay all the rent despite the nonconformity.

A justified revocation of acceptance must take place within a reasonable time after the basis for the revocation is or should have been discovered and is effective when the lessee notifies the lessor. Revocation is not allowed if there is a substantial change in the condition of the goods that is not caused by the nonconformity that justifies revocation. A revoking lessee has the same obligation to take care of the goods as if the lessee had rejected the goods. UCC § 2A-517(4), (5).

If a lessee justifiably and effectively revokes acceptance of the goods, then the lessee has the right to recover damages based either on a cover transaction or on market rent for the goods, plus incidental or consequential damages, minus expenses saved as a consequence of the lessor's breach. UCC §§ 2A-518, 2A-519, 2A-520.

Problem 11-5

Sensational Electronics manufactures computer servers for use in networks. Lasting Data operates a data storage business that relies heavily on computer servers. Several months ago, Lasting Data began negotiating with Sensational Electronics to acquire 30 new servers, with financing from Boston Finance. Last month, Boston Finance purchased the servers from Sensational Electronics and then leased the servers to Lasting Data. Before doing so, Boston Finance sent the purchase agreement to Lasting Data for approval.

After 20 servers were installed in Lasting Data's facility, five of the servers malfunctioned. Sensational Electronics failed to deliver the remaining ten servers after Lasting Data complained about the five that had malfunctioned.

Lasting Data may be able to obtain replacement servers from another manufacturer but is not sure that it will be able to do so for the same price as Sensational Electronics offered. In any event, while it decides what to do and until it can bring its server capacity up to the desired amount, it is experiencing difficulty in servicing all of its customers on a timely basis. What are Lasting Data's remedies, if any, against both Sensational Electronics and Boston Finance?

D. RISK OF LOSS FOLLOWING THE LESSOR'S BREACH

Analogous Provisions	
Article 2	Article 2A
§ 2-510	§ 2A-220

Section 2A-220 parallels section 2-510 on the effect of breach on the risk of loss. If the lessee has the right to reject the goods because of a nonconformity in the goods or the tender, the risk of loss remains on the lessor or the supplier until cure of the nonconformity or acceptance of the goods. If the lessee rightfully and effectively revokes acceptance, and the lessee has a deficiency in its insurance coverage for the goods, the risk of loss is treated as resting on the lessor to the extent of the deficiency. Given the very limited circumstances in which the lessee in a finance lease may be able to revoke acceptance of the goods, the comment to section 2A-220 indicates that the risk of loss in that situation should rest on the lessor, not the supplier, to the extent the lessee's insurance coverage is insufficient.

E. STATUTE OF LIMITATIONS

Analogous Provisions	
Article 2	Article 2A
§ 2-725	§ 2A-506

Article 2A contains a four-year statute of limitations period for actions for breach of a lease contract. UCC § 2A-506(1). The four year period runs from when the cause of action accrues. So, far, this is the same as the rules applicable to sales contracts. However, whereas a cause of action for breach of a sales contract accrues in most circumstances when the breach occurs, regardless of when it is or should be discovered,[11] *see* UCC § 2-725(2), a cause of action for breach of a lease agreement accrues under a more liberal standard: when the breach takes place or when the breach is or should be discovered, whichever is later. UCC § 2A-506(2). Other law determines whether there are circumstances in which the running of the limitations period is tolled. UCC § 2A-506(4).

SECTION 6.   LESSEE'S DEFAULT AND LESSOR'S REMEDIES

A. OVERVIEW

Analogous Provisions	
Article 2	Article 2A
§ 2-703	§ 2A-523

When a lessee defaults in its obligations under the lease, the lessor's main objective is usually to recover the goods and then obtain damages for the breach. Unlike in a sales transaction, the lessor has a strong claim to the return of the goods because of the lessor's residual reversionary interest in them. However, the lessor does not have to attempt to recover the goods. The lessor has several remedial choices and those choices are catalogued in section 2A-523. The lessor may also have additional remedies pursuant to the lease agreement. As was true in Article 2, the focus in Article 2A is on putting the aggrieved lessor in the same position it would have occupied if the lessee had fully performed. UCC § 1-305.

---

[11]   As you recall, Article 2 provides that a cause of action accrues when the breach is or should have been discovered when a warranty "explicitly extends to future performance of the goods and discovery of the breach must await the time of such performance." UCC § 2-725(2).

B. LESSEE'S REPUDIATION OR BREACH PRIOR TO DELIVERY

Analogous Provisions	
Article 2	Article 2A
§ 2-704	§ 2A-524
n/a	§ 2A-525
§ 2-705	§ 2A-526
§ 2-706	§ 2A-527
§ 2-707	n/a
§ 2-708	§ 2A-528
§ 2-709	§ 2A-529
§ 2-710	§ 2A-530
n/a	§ 2A-532

If the lessee repudiates or has defaulted in its obligations under the lease prior to delivery, the lessor may withhold delivery of the goods. UCC §§ 2A-523(1)(c), 2A-525. The lessor also has that right if the lessee is discovered to be insolvent, even if that event is not technically a default under the lease. UCC § 2A-525(1). If the goods are in transit, the lessor has the right to stop the delivery as determined under section 2A-526. These sections parallel in significant part sections 2-702(1) and 2-705.

In addition to keeping the goods from the lessee, the lessor may cancel the lease contract, although in an installment lease contract, the right to cancel requires a substantial impairment of the value of the whole contract. UCC §§ 2A-523(1), 2A-510(2). *Cf.* UCC §§ 2-703, 2-612(3). In an installment lease contract, the lessor might well seek to cancel to avoid having to deliver future installments to the lessee.

A lessor who, because of the lessee's breach, has rightfully withheld or stopped delivery of the goods is entitled to recover damages from the lessee for the breach. Those damages are usually measured in one of three ways:

(i) by reference to a substitute lease transaction, UCC § 2A-527;

(ii) by reference to market rent, UCC § 2A-528(1); or

(iii) by reference to the lessor's lost profit, UCC § 2A-528(2).

In a rare case, where the lessor is unable to dispose of the goods on a reasonable basis, the lessor may be entitled to the rent due under the lease. UCC § 2A-529.

These remedies thus parallel the seller's remedies in sections 2-706, 2-708, and 2-709. These remedies are alternative ways in which to measure the lessor's expectancy.

Even though these remedies are modeled on the similar Article 2 provisions, the calculation of damages is somewhat different. That is because the lease is designed to compensate the lessor for the right to use or possess the goods merely for a period of time, not for the full value or useful life of the goods. If the lessor enters into a substitute lease transaction that is substantially similar to the breached lease, the lessor is entitled to recover any unpaid rent under the breached lease that has accrued up to the time the substitute lease agreement was entered into plus the difference between the present value of the remaining payments under the breached lease and the present value of the payments under the substitute lease that will be due during the remaining term of the breached lease. UCC § 2A-527(2). To this amount incidental damages are added and expenses saved as a result of the lessee's breach are subtracted. Article 2A follows Article 2 in not providing for the lessor to recover consequential damages.

If the lessor does not enter into a substantially similar lease transaction – either because the lessor does not enter into a substitute lease at all, the substitute lease is not substantially similar, or the lessor sells the goods – then the lessor is entitled to recover damages under section 2A-528(1). Those damages are the accrued unpaid rent under the breached lease as of the date of the lessee's default plus the difference between the present value of the rental payments remaining under the breached lease term minus the present value of the market rent for the goods for the same term. Again, incidental damages are added and expenses saved as a consequence of the lessee's breach are subtracted.

If these market rent-based damages are inadequate to protect the lessor's expectancy interest, the lessor is entitled to recover the present value of the profit it would have realized on the breached lease, plus a reasonable overhead amount and incidental damages. The lessor is also allowed to recover unpaid reliance costs, but the damages must be reduced by the proceeds of a disposition, taking into account the fact that the lessor is entitled to retain the residual value of the goods. UCC § 2A-528(2).

Finally, if the lessor is unable after reasonable effort to dispose of the goods, the lessor may recover the unpaid rent that has accrued by the date of the judgment, plus the present value of the rent for any remaining term of the breached lease. Incidental damages are added to this amount and expenses saved in consequence of the breach are subtracted. UCC § 2A-529(1)(b).

If the leased goods are not yet finished, or have not yet been identified to the contract, the lessor may finish the goods, dispose of them in the unfinished state, or identify them to the contract in an effort to minimize loss. UCC § 2A-524. This is the analog to section 2-704 for an aggrieved seller.

A breaching lessee who has prepaid part or all of the rent from whom the lessor has withheld the goods or stopped delivery of the goods is entitled to at least partial restitution of that amount, after accounting for any enforceable amount of liquidated damages, or if no agreement to liquidated damages, to deduction of the lessor's damages as calculated under Article 2A. If there is no enforceable liquidated damages clause in the lease agreement, the lessor is entitled to deduct 20% of the present value of the rent the lessee was obligated to pay. That amount is capped in a consumer lease at $500. UCC § 2A-504(3), (4). These rules are very similar to the rules in section 2-718(2).

C. LESSEE'S WRONGFUL REFUSAL TO KEEP THE GOODS

If the lessee wrongfully rejects the goods,[12] the lessor is entitled to recover damages to the same extent as if the lessee had wrongfully repudiated prior to delivery. Thus, the lessor may recover damages based on a substitute lease transaction, market rent, lost profit, or the rent under the breached lease if the goods cannot be reasonably disposed of.

Problem 11-6

On March 1, Superior Equipment, Inc., located in Chicago, contracted to lease custom lathes to Bristol Woodworking, Inc., located in Phoenix, for $80,000 for a three-year term, delivery F.O.B. Chicago no later than November 1. Cost of shipping was estimated at $2,000. At the time that Bristol and Superior entered into the contract, Bristol made a down payment of $20,000. Superior delivered the lathes on time. Bristol accepted the lathes but one week later demanded that Superior take the lathes back and return its down payment. Bristol's demands were unjustified because both the lathes and Superior's tender had conformed to

---

[12]   Or if the lessee wrongfully attempts to revoke acceptance of the goods and the lessor voluntarily takes the goods back.

the contract requirements. Nevertheless, Superior took the lathes back and stored them in Phoenix at a cost of $100 per day.

On November 8, the market rent for a three-year term for the lathes was $60,000 in Chicago, and $55,000 in Phoenix. Two months after taking the lathes back, Superior leased the lathes in Denver for $50,000 for a two-year term, F.O.B. Denver, and incurred $1,500 in shipping costs to send them from Phoenix to Denver. Calculate Superior's damages.

D. LESSEE'S DEFAULT WHILE IN POSSESSION OF THE GOODS

Now assume that the lessee has defaulted while it has possession of the goods. If the lessee has accepted the goods, the lessor has the option to pursue an action for the entire rent that is due under the lease. The lessor is entitled to the accrued and unpaid rent as of the time of the judgment, plus the present value of the remaining rent due under the breached lease, plus incidental damages, minus expenses saved as a consequence of the breach. UCC § 2A-529(1)(a).

Instead of pursuing a judgment for the rent, the lessor may seek to recover the goods coupled with damages for the lessee's breach. Because this is a lease transaction, and the lessor has a residual interest in the goods, the lessor always has a right to regain possession of the goods when the lessee has defaulted. UCC § 2A-525(2). The lessor is authorized to use self-help – that is, to take the goods without judicial process – provided the lessor can do so without breach of the peace. UCC § 2A-525(3). This "breach of the peace" standard is borrowed from Article 9 and there is a wealth of case law interpreting what it means in the context of a secured party repossessing goods after a debtor's default. It is essentially a fact intensive inquiry, but there are a few basic points on which there is general agreement. The lessor may not engage in conduct that threatens or creates a substantial risk of violence or injury. The lessor may engage in a trespass but may not break and enter, particularly into residential property. If the lessor is unable to repossess the goods without a breach of the peace, the lessor may seek a court order to get the goods from the lessee. UCC § 2A-525(3).

E. RISK OF LOSS FOLLOWING THE LESSEE'S BREACH

The lessee is liable for the rent if conforming goods are delivered, the risk of loss has passed to the lessee, and the goods are lost or damaged within a reasonable time after that risk of loss has passed to the lessee. UCC § 2A-529(1)(a). Because the risk of loss does not usually pass to the lessee in a non-finance lease, UCC § 2A-219, this provision will have effect only in a finance lease or if the parties have made an agreement for the risk of loss to pass to the lessee in a non-finance lease.

If the lessee repudiates or defaults, regardless of whether it has the risk of loss, the lessee is treated as having the risk of loss for a commercially reasonable time after the repudiation or default to the extent the lessor's insurance coverage, or in a finance lease, the supplier's insurance coverage, is insufficient. UCC § 2A-220(2).

F. STATUTE OF LIMITATIONS

Article 2A has a limitations period of four years from when the cause of action accrues. UCC § 2A-506(1). Article 2A contains different rules than Article 2 on when the cause of action accrues by providing for a discovery rule instead of a rule that focuses only on when the breach occurs. A cause of action for breach of the lease agreement accrues when the breach takes place or when the breach should be or is discovered, whichever is later. UCC § 2A-506(2). Other law determines whether there are circumstances in which the running of the limitations period is tolled. UCC § 2A-506(4).

SECTION 7.   PROPERTY RIGHTS IN THE LEASED GOODS

A. OVERVIEW

As we know, both the lessor and the lessee have property rights in the leased goods. The lessee has the right to possession and use of the goods during the leased term and the lessor has the residual property interest in the leased goods. For the most part, both the lessor and the lessee are free to transfer their respective interests to someone else. *Cf.* UCC § 2A-303. What we analyze here are the circumstances in which one of them can transfer some or all of the rights of the other. Put another way, this section addresses the ability of third parties to claim rights in the goods that would have priority over either the lessor's residual interest or the lessee's right to use and possess the goods.[13]

The discussion that follows is, by necessity, brief. The goal is not so much to fully explore each of the relevant rules, but to explain their different scope, so that you can later isolate the rule that would apply to a situation that may arise.

B.   LESSOR'S ABILITY TO TRANSFER GOODS FREE OF LESSEE'S RIGHTS

Analogous Provisions	
Article 2	**Article 2A**
§ 2-403	§ 2A-304 § 2A-307(2)

In Chapter Ten, we saw that section 2-403 contains two rules that create an exception to the general principal of property law that one cannot give what one does not have. First, section 2-403(1) allows a buyer with voidable title to transfer good title to a good faith purchaser for value. These situations could be diagramed as follows (the buyer is depicted in bold italics because the buyer is the transferor in the transactions to which the provision is speaking).

---

[13]   For purposes of this discussion of property rights, we are ignoring the intersection of Article 2A and certificate of title laws. For the most part, Article 2A defers to the rules found in certificate of title statutes. *See* UCC §§ 2A-104, 2A-105. The property rights provisions in Article 2A continue this deference by providing that a third party who is asserting property based rights in the leased goods subject to a certificate of title statute gets no greater rights than that provided by Article 2A and the certificate of title statute. UCC §§ 2A-304(3), 2A-305(3).

We also do not cover third party claims to the leased goods when the goods are fixtures or accessions. Article 2A provides special rules for those types of goods to accommodate the varied interests that may arise. *See* UCC §§ 2A-309, 2A-310. These situations are too complex to explore in this course.

§ 2-403(1)

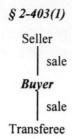

Seller

| sale

Buyer

| sale

Transferee

Second, section 2-403(2) empowers a seller to transfer the rights of an owner of goods to a buyer in ordinary course of business if the seller is a merchant who deals in goods of that kind and the owner has entrusted the goods to the seller. The following diagram illustrates this scenario (this time the seller is depicted in bold italics because the seller is the transferor in the transactions to which the provision is speaking).

§ 2-403(2)

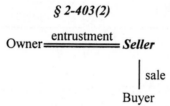

Owner ══entrustment══ **Seller**

| sale

Buyer

Article 2A has analogous rules that apply to transfers by the lessor. Section 2A-304 deals with situations in which a person with voidable title leases the goods to a good faith lessee for value:[14]

§ 2A-304(1)

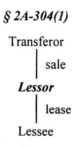

Transferor

| sale

Lessor

| lease

Lessee

---

[14]   Because section 2-403(1) applies to all purchasers for value, and a lessee qualifies as a "purchaser" under section 1-201(b)(29), (30), section 2-403(1) may already protect good faith lessees for value. Nevertheless, the drafters protected them in section 2A-304(1) to remove any doubt on this point.

The same provision also purports to cover another situation: when a lessor first leases the goods to one person and then leases them again – for either the same or at least an overlapping lease term – to someone else:

§ 2A-304(1)

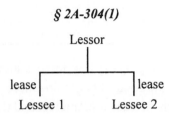

In general, the subsequent lessee takes subject to the original lease. There are, however, two major exceptions to this rule. First, if the lessor is disposing of the leased goods as a method of setting damages pursuant to a breach of the lease contract, the buyer or lessee from the lessor takes free of the existing breached lease contract. UCC § 2A-527(4). Second, if the lessee has entrusted the goods back to the lessor, the subsequent lessee takes the goods free of the original lessee's rights under section 2A-304(2) if the subsequent lessee is a lessee in ordinary course of business.

Another entrustment rule is apparently implicit in section 2A-307(2). Although that provision does not on its face appear to be referring to entrustment situations, comment 3 to section 2A-304 indicates that section 2A-307(2) does indeed protect a lessee in ordinary course of business in the following situation :

§ 2A-307(2)

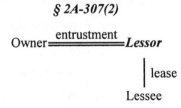

Taking the comment as true, section 2A-307(2) is closely analogous to the rule of section 2-403(2), from which it was derived. The major difference is that in the lease context the owner is not deprived of all rights to the goods, the owner simply takes subject to the lease (*i.e.,* loses the goods for the leasehold term).

C. LESSEE'S ABILITY TO TRANSFER GOODS FREE OF LESSOR'S RIGHTS

Analogous Provisions	
Article 2	Article 2A
§ 2-403	§ 2A-305

Under normal principles of property law, lessees should be able to transfer their limited leasehold interest in the goods, but nothing more. If the law were otherwise, if a lessee could transfer both its leasehold interest and the lessor's residual interest in the goods, few owners would be willing to lease their goods to anyone other than the most saintly of lessees. The risk would simply be too great. Accordingly, a lessee should not – and generally does not – have the power to transfer rights in the goods free of the lessor's residual interest.

However, section 2A-305 provides for two situations in which the lessee may transfer greater rights than it has. The first is subsection (1), which is another analog to section 2-403(1). It allows a lessee with a voidable leasehold to transfer a good leasehold interest to a good faith sublessee or buyer. This provision does not allow the subsequent transferee to override the lessor's residual interest in the goods, it merely allows the lessee to transfer a better leasehold than what the lessee had.

§ 2A-305(1)

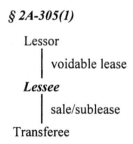

Second, subsection (2) is another entrustment rule. It applies if the lessee is a merchant who deals in goods of the kind leased and allows that lessee to transfer the goods free of the lessor's rights to a buyer or lessee in ordinary course of business. Thus, this rule gives the lessee the ability to eliminate the lessor's residual interest in the goods.

§ 2A-305(2)

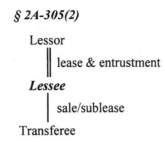

A final rule that allows a lessee to transfer more rights in the goods than the lessee itself has is section 2A-511(4). It provides that if a lessee is disposing of the goods after the lessor's breach, the purchaser takes the goods free of the lessor's interest under the lease contract. This rule too operates to eliminate the lessor's residual interest in the goods.

D. LESSEE'S RIGHTS AGAINST LESSOR'S CREDITORS

A lessor's creditors may be interested in attaining an interest in the leased goods to satisfy obligations the lessor owes to those creditors. Is the lessee's interest in the goods subject to the claims of the lessor's creditors? The answer to that question depends upon what type of creditor is making the claim to the leased goods.

If the creditor is someone who has furnished services or materials to the leased goods and has a lien under other law for the value of those services or materials as long as those goods are in the creditor's possession, then the lessee's rights under the lease contract is subject to that lien, regardless of when the lien arose.[15] UCC § 2A-306.

If the creditor's lien on the goods arose prior to the lease contract being entered into, the lessee will be subject to that lien, unless the lien is an Article 9 security interest and the provisions of Article 9 allow the lessee to take free of the security interest in the goods. UCC § 2A-307(2), (3). A lessee will take free of an Article 9 security interest in the leased goods created by the lessor if the lessee qualifies as a lessee in ordinary course of business, UCC § 9-321(c), or if the lessee gives value and takes possession of the goods without knowledge of the security interest and at

---

[15] If the other law creating the statutory lien provides a different priority rule, that priority rule will govern.

a time when the security interest is not perfected, UCC § 9-317(c). This protection for a lessee from a security interest created by the lessor parallels the protection for a buyer of the goods from a security interest created by the seller. UCC §§ 9-320, 9-317(b).

If the creditor's lien on the goods arose subsequent to the lease contract being entered into, the creditor of the lessor is generally subject to the lessee's rights under the lease contract. This rule is subject to two exceptions. The first exception is for the statutory lien creditor as discussed above. The second exception is found in section 2A-308. If the creditor of the lessor is entitled to treat the lease contract with the lessee as a fraudulent transfer (as determined under other law), the lessee would be subject to the creditor's claim. *Compare* UCC § 2-402.

E. LESSOR'S RIGHTS AGAINST LESSEE'S CREDITORS

The lessee's creditors generally do not have rights to the leased goods that are superior to the lessor's property rights in the goods. UCC § 2A-307(1). There is only one exception to this rule. If the creditor is someone who has furnished services or materials to the leased goods and has a lien under other law for the value of those services or materials as long as those goods are in the creditor's possession, then the lessor's rights under the lease contract are subject to that lien, regardless of when the lien arose.[16] UCC § 2A-306.

---

[16]   If the other law creating the statutory lien provides a different priority rule, that priority rule will govern.